The McGraw·Hill Companies

NATION OF NATIONS: A NARRATIVE HISTORY OF THE AMERICAN REPUBLIC, VOLUME I: TO 1877

Published by McGraw-Hill, a business unit of The McGraw-Hill Companies, Inc., 1221 Avenue of the Americas, New York, NY 10020.

1 2 3 4 5 6 7 8 9 0 DOW/DOW 0 9 8 7 6 5 4

ISBN 0–07–287099–0

Vice president and editor-in-chief: *Emily Barrosse*
Publisher: *Lyn Uhl*
Sponsoring editor: *Steven Drummond*
Development editor: *Kristen Mellitt*
Marketing manager: *Katherine Bates*
Senior Media Producer: *Sean Crowley*
Production editor: *Holly Paulsen*
Manuscript editor: *Joan Pendleton*
Art director: *Jeanne M. Schreiber*

Design manager: *Gino Cieslik*
Cover designer: *Gino Cieslik*
Interior designer: *Maureen McCutcheon*
Art manager: *Robin Mouat*
Art editors: *Cristin Yancy and Emma Ghiselli*
Photo research coordinator: *Nora Agbayani*
Photo researcher: *Deborah Bull and Deborah Anderson, PhotoSearch, Inc.*
Illustrators: *Patty Isaacs*
Production supervisor: *Rich Devitto*

The text was set in 10/12 Berkeley Medium by The GTS Companies, York, PA Campus, and printed on acid-free 45# Publisher's Matte Thin Bulk by R.R. Donnelley, Willard.

Cover images: (clockwise from upper left) Library of Congress, Prints & Photographs Division [reproduction number LC-USZC4-4586]; (Detail) *The Battle of Princeton* by William Mercer, Courtesy of The Historical Society of Pennsylvania Collection, Atwater Kent Museum of Philadelphia; © Gianni Dagli Orti/Corbis; © The Corcoran Gallery of Art/Corbis; © Bettmann/Corbis; Library of Congress, Prints & Photographs Division, Civil War Photographs [reproduction number LC-USZC4-7983]; Dolly Madison (1768–1849), c. 1817 (oil on canvas), Otis, Bass (1784–1861)/© New-York Historical Society, New York, USA/www.bridgeman.co.uk; Library of Congress, Prints & Photographs Division, Civil War Photographs [reproduction number LC-USZC4-7947]; *Declaration of Independence* (detail), U.S. Capitol Art Collection/Courtesy, Architect of the Capitol; © Burstein Collection/Corbis; © Corbis; Library of Congress, Prints & Photographs Division [reproduction number LC-USZC4-4075]; Theodor de Bry, Plate 8 (16.1 × 19.6), from Part IV(g) first published in 1594.

The credits for this book begin on page C-1, a continuation of the copyright page.

Text Permissions:
Page 268 From Charles A. Johnson, *Frontier Camp Meeting*, copyright 1955, 1985 SMU Press. Reprinted with permission.

Library of Congress has cataloged the combined version as follows:

Nation of nations : a narrative history of the American republic / James West Davidson ...
[et al.]. — 5th ed.
    p. cm.
  Includes bibliographical references (p.) and index.
  ISBN 0–07–287098–2 — ISBN 0–07–287099–0 (v. 1 : pbk : acid-free paper) — ISBN
0–07–287100–8 (v. 2 : pbk : acid-free paper)
  1. United States—History—Textbooks. I. Davidson, James West.
78.1.N346 2004
—dc22
                                                    2004052436

.mhhe.com

Volume I: To 1877
Chapters 1–17

Nation of Nations

A Narrative History of the American Republic

Fifth Edition

James West Davidson

William E. Gienapp
Harvard University

Christine Leigh Heyrman
University of Delaware

Mark H. Lytle
Bard College

Michael B. Stoff
University of Texas, Austin

*Here is not merely a nation but
a teeming nation of nations*

Walt Whitman

Boston   Burr Ridge, IL   Dubuque, IA   Madison, WI   New York   San Francisco   St. Louis
Bangkok   Bogotá   Caracas   Kuala Lumpur   Lisbon   London   Madrid   Mexico City
Milan   Montreal   New Delhi   Santiago   Seoul   Singapore   Sydney   Taipei   Toronto

William E. Gienapp

1944–2003

Inevitably, contingency brings grief as well as joy. We are saddened to report the passing of our dear friend and co-author, William E. Gienapp. It would be hard to imagine a colleague with greater dedication to his work, nor one who cared more about conveying both the excitement and the rigor of history to those who were not professional historians—as has been attested by so many of his students at the University of Wyoming and at Harvard. Bill had a quiet manner, which sometimes hid (though not for long) his puckish sense of humor and an unstinting generosity. When news of his death was reported, the *Harvard Crimson,* a student newspaper known more for its skepticism than its sentimentality, led with the front-page headline: "Beloved History Professor Gienapp Dies." Bill went the extra mile, whether in searching out primary sources enabling us to assemble a map on the environmental effects of the Lowell Mills, combing innumerable manuscript troves in the preparation of his masterful *Origins of the Republican Party,* or collecting vintage baseball caps from the nineteenth and twentieth centuries to wear (in proper chronological sequence, no less) to his popular course on the social history of baseball. When an illness no one could have predicted struck him down, the profession lost one of its shining examples. His fellow authors miss him dearly.

brief contents

contents

AFTER THE FACT
Historians Reconstruct the Past:
Tracking the First Americans 16

Chapter 6

The American People and the American Revolution (1775–1783)   170

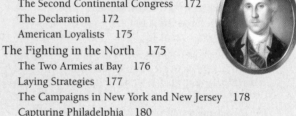

Chapter 7

Crisis and Constitution (1776–1789)   196

Part Three

The Republic Transformed and Tested   293

Chapter 10

The Opening of America (1815–1850)   298

Chapter 11

The Rise of Democracy (1824–1840)   330

Chapter 12

The Fires of Perfection (1820–1850)   362

Chapter 13

The Old South (1820–1860)   392

Chapter 14

Chapter 15

Chapter 16

AFTER THE FACT
Historians Reconstruct the Past:
What Caused the New York Draft Riots?   525

Chapter 17

Reconstructing the Union (1865–1877)   530

list of maps & charts

preface
to the fifth edition

All good history begins with a good story: that has been the touchstone of *Nation of Nations*. Narrative is embedded in the way we understand the past; hence it will not do simply to compile an encyclopedia of American history and pass it off as a survey.

Yet the narrative keeps changing. A world that has become suddenly and dangerously smaller requires, more than ever, a history that is broader. That conviction has driven our revision for the fifth edition of *Nation of Nations*.

The events following on the heels of September 11, 2001, have underlined the call historians have made over the past decade to view American history within a global context. From its first edition, published in 1990, *Nation of Nations* has taken such an approach, with global essays opening each of the book's six parts to establish an international framework and a global timeline correlating events nationally and worldwide. In the fourth edition, we added global focus sections within chapter narratives and a final chapter ("Nation of Nations in a Global Community") highlighting the ties of the United States to the rest of the world.

Changes to the Fifth Edition

The fifth edition expands on the global coverage that has been so important to our text by adding new narratives that place American history in an international perspective. These narratives are not separate special features. Sometimes only a paragraph in length, sometimes an entire section, they are designed to be an integral part of the text. New material includes

- A section on the Barbary pirates and cultural identities in Chapter 9

- Information comparing debt peonage in the New South with similar circumstances in India, Egypt, and Brazil in Chapter 18
- A section on worldwide recovery from the Great Depression in Chapter 25
- A map on the spread of the influenza pandemic in autumn 1918 in Chapter 23
- More on a global labor migrations in Chapter 26
- A section about Vatican II and American Catholics in Chapter 29

Other important content and pedagogical changes include

- Two new After the Fact essays exploring cultural history topics that have received recent scholarly attention. The new essay in Part Two focuses on Sally Hemings and Thomas Jefferson, and the new essay in Part Four, "Engendering the Spanish-American War," looks at contemporary constructions of gender as the United States went to war with Spain in 1898.
- Updates to Chapter 33, including a new section and map on the election of 2000 and material on recent court cases regarding affirmative action.
- To conclude the book, a new epilogue, "Fighting Terrorism in a Global Age," which includes a chart showing terrorist incidents by region and a map on the war on terror in Afghanistan and Iraq.
- The addition of date ranges to chapter titles, to provide students with more guidance as to the chronology of events.
- An "Interactive Learning" section at the end of every chapter, directing students to relevant materials on the Primary Source Investigator CD-ROM.

- In addition to the Additional Readings feature at the end of each chapter, a full bibliography for the book can be found at www.mhhe.com/davidsonnation5.

Information about Supplements

The supplements listed here accompany *Nation of Nations: A Narrative History of the American Republic*, Fifth Edition. Please contact your local McGraw-Hill representative for details concerning policies, prices, and availability, as some restrictions may apply.

For the Student

- Packaged free with every copy of the book, **Primary Source Investigator CD-ROM** (007295700X) includes hundreds of documents to explore, short documentary movies, interactive maps, and more. Find more information about the CD-ROM where it is packaged in your book.
- Located on the book's Web site (www.mhhe.com/davidsonnation5), the **Student Online Learning Center** offers interactive maps with exercises, extensive Web links, quizzes, counterpoint essays with exercises, a bibliography, and more.

For the Instructor

- A set of **Overhead Transparencies** (0072956976) includes maps and images from the textbook.
- An **Instructor's Resource CD-ROM** (0072456992) provides materials for instructors to use in the classroom, including PowerPoint presentations and electronic versions of the maps in the textbook. An instructor's manual and computerized test bank are also included.
- Located on the book's Web site (www.mhhe.com/davidsonnation5), the **Instructor Online Learning Center** offers PowerPoint presentations, an image bank, an instructor's manual, a bibliography, and more.

Acknowledgments

Wayne Ackerson
Salisbury State University

Robert Alderson
Georgia Perimeter College

Jay Antle
Johnson County Community College

Alan C. Atchison
Southwest Texas State

Eirlys M. Barker
Thomas Nelson Community College

Vince Clark
Johnson County Community College

P. Scott Corbett
Oxnard College

Mary Paige Cubbison
Miami Dade Community College

George Gerdow
Northeastern Illinois University

Ronald Goldberg
Thomas Nelson Community College

Michael Hamilton
Seattle Pacific University

Reid Holland
Midland Technical College

Lisa Hollander
Jefferson College

Carol Keller
San Antonio College

Lawrence Kohl
University of Alabama

Janice M. Leone
Middle Tennessee State University

Daniel Littlefield
University of South Carolina

Susan Matt
Weber State University

Randy D. McBee
Texas Tech University

Robert M. S. McDonald
United States Military Academy

Paul C. Milazzo
Ohio University

Roberto M. Salmón
University of Texas, Pan American

Richard Straw
Radford University

William Woodward
Seattle Pacific University

In addition, friends and colleagues contributed their advice and constructive criticism in ways both small and large. We owe a debt to Myra Armstead, Lawrence A. Cardoso, Dinah Chenven, Christopher Collier, James E. Crisp, R. David Edmunds, George Forgie, Erica Gienapp, Richard John, Virginia Joyner, Philip Kuhn, Stephen E. Maizlish, Drew McCoy, James McPherson, Walter Nugent, Vicki L. Ruiz, Jim Sidbury, David J. Weber, Devra Weber, and John Womack.

The division of labor for this book was determined by our respective fields of scholarship: Christine Heyrman, the colonial era, in which Europeans, Africans, and Indians participated in the making of both a new America and a new republic; William Gienapp, the 90 years in which the young nation first flourished, then foundered on the issues of section and slavery; Michael Stoff, the post–Civil War era, in which industrialization and urbanization brought the nation more centrally into an international system regularly disrupted by depression and war; and Mark Lytle, the modern era, in which Americans finally faced the reality that even the boldest dreams of national greatness are bounded by the finite nature of power and resources both natural and human. Finally, because the need to specialize inevitably imposes limits on any project as broad as this one, our fifth author, James Davidson, served as a general editor and writer, with the intent of fitting individual parts to the whole as well as providing a measure of continuity, style, and overarching purpose. In producing this collaborative effort, all of us have shared the conviction that the best history speaks to a larger audience.

James West Davidson
William E. Gienapp
Christine Leigh Heyrman
Mark H. Lytle
Michael B. Stoff

Global Essay

Each of the book's six parts begins with an essay that sets American events into a global context.

Global Timeline

Each global essay includes a time line comparing political and social events in the United States with developments elsewhere.

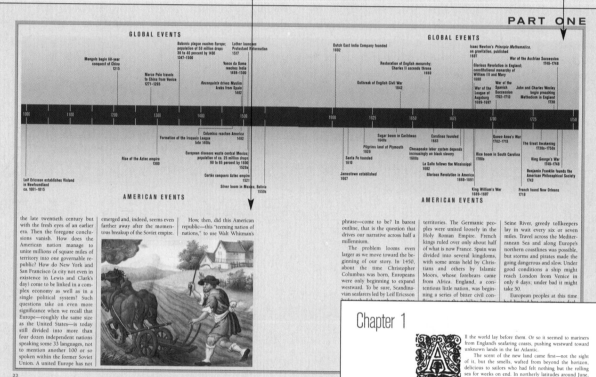

PART ONE

GLOBAL EVENTS

Mongols begin 60-year conquest of China
1215

Marco Polo travels to China from Venice
1271–1295

Bubonic plague reaches Europe; population of 50 million drops 30 to 40 percent by 1400
1347–1500

Luther launches Protestant Reformation
1517

Vasco da Gama reaches India
1498–1500

Reconquista drives Muslim Arabs from Spain
1492

Dutch East India Company founded
1602

Outbreak of English Civil War
1642

Restoration of English monarchy; Charles II ascends throne
1660

Isaac Newton's *Principia Mathematica,* on gravitation, published
1687

Glorious Revolution in England; constitutional monarchy of William III and Mary
1688

War of the League of Augsburg
1689–1697

War of the Spanish Succession
1702–1713

War of the Austrian Succession
1740–1748

John and Charles Wesley begin preaching Methodism in England
1738

1000 1100 1200 1300 1400 1500 1600 1625 1650 1675 1700 1725 1750

Leif Ericsson establishes Vinland in Newfoundland
ca. 1001–1015

Rise of the Aztec empire
1300

Formation of the Iroquois League
late 1400s

Columbus reaches America
1492

European diseases waste central Mexico; population of ca. 25 million drops; 90 to 95 percent by 1600
1520s

Cortés conquers Aztec empire
1521

Silver boom in Mexico, Bolivia
1550s

Santa Fe founded
1610

Jamestown established
1607

Pilgrims land at Plymouth
1620

Sugar boom in Caribbean
1640s

Carolinas founded
1663

Chesapeake labor system depends increasingly on black slavery
1680s

La Salle follows the Mississippi
1682

Glorious Revolution in America
1688–1691

King William's War
1689–1697

Queen Anne's War
1702–1713

Rice boom in South Carolina
1700s

Benjamin Franklin founds the American Philosophical Society
1743

French found New Orleans
1718

The Great Awakening
1730s–1750s

King George's War
1740–1748

AMERICAN EVENTS

the late twentieth century but with the fresh eyes of an earlier era. Then the foregone conclusions vanish. How does the American nation manage to unite millions of square miles of territory into one governable republic? How do New York and San Francisco (a city not even in existence in Lewis and Clark's day) come to be linked in a complex economy as well as in a single political system? Such questions take on even more significance when we recall that Europe—roughly the same size as the United States—is today still divided into more than four dozen independent nations speaking some 33 languages, not to mention another 100 or so spoken within the former Soviet Union. A united Europe has not

22

emerged and, indeed, seems even farther away after the momentous breakup of the Soviet empire.

How, then, did this American republic—this "teeming nation of nations," to use Walt Whitman's

phrase—come to be? In barest outline, that is the question that drives our narrative across half a millennium.

The problem looms even larger as we move toward the beginning of our story. In 1450, about the time Christopher Columbus was born, Europeans were only beginning to expand westward. To be sure, Scandinavian seafarers led by Leif Ericsson

territories. The Germanic peoples were united loosely in the Holy Roman Empire. French kings ruled over only about half of what is now France. Spain was divided into several kingdoms, with some areas held by Christians and others by Islamic Moors, whose forebears came from Africa. England, a contentious little nation, was beginning a series of bitter civil con-

Seine River, greedy tollkeepers lay in wait every six or seven miles. Travel across the Mediterranean Sea and along Europe's northern coastlines was possible, but storms and pirates made the going dangerous and slow. Under good conditions a ship might reach London from Venice in only 9 days; under bad it might take 50.

European peoples at this time

Preview

A preview introduces each chapter's main themes.

Chapter 1

All the world lay before them. Or so it seemed to mariners from England's seafaring coasts, pushing westward toward unknown lands in the far Atlantic.

The scent of the new land came first—not the sight of it, but the smells, wafted from beyond the horizon, delicious to sailors who had felt nothing but the rolling sea for weeks on end. In northerly latitudes around June, it would be the scent of fir trees or the sight of shore birds wheeling about the masts. Straightaway the captain would call for a lead to be thrown overboard to sound the depths. At its end was a hollowed-out socket with a bit of tallow in it, so some of the sea bottom would stick when the lead was hauled up. Even out of sight of land, a good sailing master could tell where he was by what came up—"oosy sand" or perhaps "soft worms" or "popplestones as big as beans." If the ship was approaching unknown shores, the captain would hope to sight land early in the day, allowing time to work cautiously toward an untried harbor on uncharted tides.

Old World, New Worlds

1400–1600

preview • In the century after 1492, Europeans expanded boldly and often ruthlessly into the Americas, thanks to a combination of technological advances in sailing and firearms, the rise of new trading networks, and stronger, more centralized governments. Spain established a vast and profitable empire but at fearful human cost. A diverse Mesoamerican population of some 20 million was reduced to only 2 million through warfare, European diseases, and exploitation.

Since the time of King Arthur, the English living along the rugged southwestern coasts of Devon and Cornwall had followed the sea. From the wharves of England's West Country seaports like Bristol, ships headed west and north to Ireland, bringing back animal hides as well as timber for houses and barrels. Or they turned south, fetching wines from France and olive oil or figs and raisins from the Spanish and Portuguese coasts. In return, West Country ports offered woven woolen cloth and codfish, caught wherever the best prospects beckoned.

Through much of the fifteenth century the search for cod drew West Country sailors north and west, toward Iceland. In the 1480s and 1490s, however, a few English tried their luck farther west. Old maps, after all, claimed that the bountiful *Hy-Brasil*—Gaelic for "Isle of the Blessed"—lay somewhere west of Ireland. These western ventures returned with little to show for their daring until the coming of an Italian named Giovanni Caboto, called John Cabot by the English. Cabot, who hailed from Venice, obtained the blessing of King Henry VII to hunt for unknown lands. From the port of Bristol his lone ship set out to the west in the spring of 1497.

Cabot discovers Newfoundland

This time the return voyage brought news of a "new-found" island where the trees were tall enough to make fine masts and the codfish were plentiful. After returning to Bristol, Cabot marched off to London to inform His Majesty, received 10 pounds as his reward, and with the proceeds dressed himself in dashing silks. The multitudes of London flocked after him, wondering over "the Admiral"; then Cabot returned triumphantly to Bristol to undertake a more ambitious search for a northwest passage to Asia. He set sail with five ships in 1498 and was never heard from again.

26

XX

AFTER THE FACT
Historians Reconstruct the Past

Sally Hemings and Thomas Jefferson

The rumors began in Albemarle County, Virginia, more than two hundred years ago; they came to the notice of a journalist by the name of James Callender. A writer for hire, Callender had once lent his pen to the Republicans, but turned from friend into foe when the party failed to reward him with a political appointment. When his story splashed onto the pages of the *Recorder*, a Richmond newspaper, the trickle of rumor turned into a torrent of scandal. Callender alleged that Thomas Jefferson, during his years in Paris as the American minister, had contracted a liaison with one of his own slaves. The woman was the president's mistress even now, he insisted, in 1802. She was kept at Monticello, and Jefferson had fathered children with her. Her name was Sally Hemings.

Solid information about Sally Hemings is scarce. She was one of six children, we know, born to Betty Hemings and her white master, John Wayles, a Virginia planter whose white daughter, Martha Wayles Skelton, married Jefferson in 1772. We know that Betty Hemings was the child of an African woman and an English sailor, which means Betty's children with Wayles, Sally among them, were quadroons—light-skinned men and women whose ancestry was one-quarter African. We know that Sally accompanied one of Jefferson's daughters to Paris as her maid in 1787 and that, upon returning to Virginia a few years later, she performed domestic work at Monticello. We know that she had six children and that the four who survived to adulthood escaped from slavery into freedom: Jefferson assisted his two eldest children, Beverly and Harriet, in leaving Monticello in 1822, and her two younger children, Madison and Eston, were freed by Jefferson's will in 1827. We know that shortly after Jefferson's death, his daughter, Martha Jefferson Randolph, freed Sally Hemings and that she lived with her two younger sons in Charlottesville until her own death in 1835.

We know, too, that Jefferson's white descendants stoutly denied (and, to this day, some still deny) any familial connection with the descendants of Sally Hemings. Even though Callender's scandal quickly subsided, doing Jefferson no lasting political damage, his white grandchildren were still explaining away the accusations half a century later. In the 1850s, Jefferson's granddaughter, Ellen Coolidge Randolph, claimed that her brother, Thomas Jefferson Randolph, had told her that one of Jefferson's nephews, Samuel Carr, fathered Hemings's children. In the 1860s, Henry Randall, an early biographer of Jefferson, recalled a conversation with Thomas Jefferson Randolph in the 1850s in which he attributed paternity to another nephew, Samuel's brother Peter Carr.

Until the end of the twentieth century, most scholars resolved the discrepancy of this dual claim by suggesting that one of the Carr nephews had fathered Sally Hemings's children. And all of Jefferson's most eminent twentieth-century biographers—Douglass Adair, Dumas Malone, John Chester Miller, and Joseph J. Ellis—contended that a man of Jefferson's character and convictions could not have engaged in a liaison with a slave woman. After all, Jefferson was a Virginia gentleman and an American philosophe who believed that reason should rule over passion; he was also an eloquent apostle of equality and democracy and an outspoken critic of the tyrannical power of masters over slaves. And despite his opposition to slavery, Jefferson argued in his *Notes on the State of Virginia* (1785) for the likelihood that peoples of African descent were inferior intellectually and artistically to those of European descent. Because of that conviction, he warned of the dire consequences that would attend the mixing of the races.

The official version of events did not go unchallenged. Madison Hemings, a skilled carpenter who, a year after his mother's death, moved from Virginia to southern Ohio, publicly related an oral tradition repeated among his family. When interviewed by a Pike County, Ohio, newspaper in 1873, Madison reported that his mother had been Thomas Jefferson's "concubine" and that Jefferson had fathered all of her children. Even so, nearly a century passed before Madison Hemings's claims won wider attention. In 1968, the historian Winthrop Jordan noted that Sally Hemings's pregnancies coincided with Jefferson's stays at Monticello. In 1975, Fawn Brodie's best-selling "intimate history" of Jefferson portrayed his relationship with Sally Hemings as an enduring love affair; four years later, the African American novelist Barbara Chase-Riboud set Brodie's findings to fiction.

This view of Monticello was painted shortly after Jefferson's death. It portrays his white descendants surrounded by a serene landscape.

Jefferson owned 5000 acres of land in Albemarle County, Virginia, his "home farm" of Monticello and three "quarter farms"—Lego, Tufton, and Shadwell. Sally Hemings and her children lived at the Monticello plantation.

288

289

After the Fact: Historians Reconstruct the Past

The book includes eight essays that demonstrate the methods used by historians to analyze a variety of sources, ranging from typescript drafts of presidential memoirs or handwritten notations in church records to military casualty estimates, public monuments, and even climate data derived from the analysis of tree rings.

Global Coverage

A section of the narrative in each chapter discusses American history from a global perspective, showing that the United States did not develop in a geographic or cultural vacuum and that the broad forces shaping it also influenced other nations.

---

34   Part One   The Creation of a New America

keep pace with the "Price Revolution," landlords raised rents, adding to the burden of the peasantry.

To Europe's hopeful and desperate alike, this climate of disorder and uncertainty led to dreams that the New World would provide an opportunity to renew the Old. As Columbus wrote eagerly of Hispaniola: "This island and all others are very fertile to a limitless degree. . . . There are very large tracts of cultivated land. . . . In the interior there are mines and metals." Columbus and many other Europeans expected that the Americas would provide land for the landless, work for the unemployed, and wealth beyond the wildest dreams of the daring.

The Conditions of Colonization

Sixteenth-century Europeans sought to colonize the Americas, not merely to escape from scarcity and disruption at home. They were also propelled across the Atlantic by dynamic changes in their society. Revolutions in technology, economics, and politics made overseas settlement practical and attractive to seekers of profit and power.

Expansion of trade and capital

The improvements in navigation and sailing also fostered an expansion of trade. By the late fifteenth century Europe's merchants and bankers had devised more efficient ways of transferring money and establishing credit in order to support commerce across longer distances. And although rising prices and rents pinched Europe's peasantry, that same inflation enriched those who had goods to sell, money to lend, and land to rent. Wealth flowed into the coffers of sixteenth-century traders, financiers, and landlords, creating a pool of capital that those investors could plow into colonial development. Both the commercial networks and the private fortunes needed to sustain overseas trade and settlement were in place by the time of Columbus's discovery.

Political centralization

The direction of Europe's political development also paved the path for American colonization. After 1450 strong monarchs in Europe steadily enlarged the sphere of royal power at the expense of warrior lords. Henry VII, the founder of England's Tudor dynasty, Francis I of France, and Ferdinand and Isabella of Spain began the trend, forging modern nation-states by extending their political control over more territory, people, and resources. Those larger, more centrally organized states were able to marshal the resources necessary to support colonial outposts abroad and to sustain the professional armies and navies capable of protecting empires abroad.

Europeans, Chinese, and Aztecs on the Eve of Contact

It was the growing power of monarchs as well as commercial and technological development that allowed early modern Europeans to establish permanent settlements—even empires—in another world lying an ocean away. But that conclusion raises an intriguing question: why didn't China, the most advanced civilization of the early modern world, engage in expansion and colonization? Or for that matter, if events had fallen out a little differently, why didn't the Aztecs discover and colonize Europe?

The Chinese undoubtedly possessed the capability to navigate the world's oceans and to establish overseas settlements. A succession of Ming dynasty emperors and their efficient bureaucrats marshaled China's resources to develop a thriving shipbuilding industry and trade with ports throughout southeast Asia and India. By the opening of the fifteenth century, the Chinese seemed poised for even greater maritime exploits. Seven times between 1405 and 1433, China's "treasure

Daily Lives

POPULAR ENTERTAINMENT
Exploring the Wondrous World

In 1786 Charles Willson Peale, painter and jack-of-all-trades, opened a museum of natural history in his home on Lombard Street in Philadelphia. Americans had always been fascinated by freaks of nature and "remarkable providences" (see Daily Lives, "A World of Wonders and Witchcraft," on pages 94–95). But unlike seventeenth-century colonials, Peale was not searching for signs of the supernatural in everyday life. A student of the Enlightenment, Peale intended his museum to be "a school of useful knowledge" that would attract men and women of all ages and social ranks. By studying natural history, Peale believed, citizens would gain an understanding of themselves, their country, and the world and thereby help sustain civilization in the United States. The sign over the door read, "Whoso would learn wisdom, let him enter here!"

Inside, the visitor found a wide assortment of items from around the world. Peale displayed nearly a hundred paintings he had completed of leading Americans, stuffed birds and animals, busts of famous scientists, cases of minerals, and wax figures representing the races of the world. Among the technological innovations that were showcased, a machine called a *physiognotrace* produced precise silhouettes. Moses Williams, a former slave, operated the machine and did a thriving business, selling 8880 profiles in the first year. Peale's backyard soon contained a zoo with a bewildering assortment of animals, including two grizzly bear cubs, an eagle, numerous snakes, monkeys, and a hyena. Prominent acquaintances such as Benjamin Franklin, George Washington, and Thomas Jefferson sent specimens, and the collection eventually totaled some 100,000 items.

Peale's most famous exhibit was a skeleton of a mastodon (he misnamed it a mammoth, thereby adding a synonym for *huge* to the American vocabulary). Assembled from several digs he had conducted with great publicity in upstate New York, it stood 11 feet high at the shoulder and was the first complete mastodon skeleton ever mounted. Billed "the ninth wonder of the world," it was

housed in a special "Mammoth Room" that required a separate admission fee.

In gathering and mounting his specimens, Peale sought "to bring into one view a world in miniature." He carefully labeled plants, animals, insects, and birds and

In this self-portrait, Charles Willson Peale lifts a curtain to reveal the famous Long Room of his museum. Partially visible on the right behind Peale is the great mastodon skeleton, at which a woman gazes in awe, while in the rear a father instructs his son on the wonders of nature.

arranged them according to accepted scientific classifications. He also pioneered the grouping of animals in their natural habitat. Stuffed tigers and deer stood on a plaster mountainside, while below, a glass pond was filled with fish, reptiles, and birds. For the safety of visitors who could not resist handling the exhibits, the birds, whose feathers were covered with arsenic, were eventually put in glass-fronted cases with painted habitats behind them.

Peale refused to indulge the popular taste for spectacles and freaks. He hesitated before accepting a five-legged cow with two tails, fearing it would lower the institution's dignity and compromise its serious purpose. He declined to display a blue sash belonging to George Washington because it had no educational value, and only after Peale's death was it exhibited. He put curiosities away in cabinets and showed them only on request.

Peale's museum was an expression of its founder's republican ideals of order, stability, and harmony. It was, in his mind, an institute of eternal laws, laid bare for the masses to see and understand. Peale hoped the museum would instill civic responsibility in its patrons, and he often told the

story of how two hostile Indian chiefs, meeting by accident in the museum, were so impressed with its harmony that they agreed to sign a peace treaty.

The museum attracted thousands of curious customers and prospered in its early years. It was one of the major attractions in Philadelphia and became famous throughout the nation. Yet Peale's vast collection soon overwhelmed his scientific classification scheme, and his grandiose plans always outran his funds and soon his space as well. Refusing to slow his collection efforts, Peale moved his museum in 1794 to Philosophical Hall, and then in 1802 he took over the second floor of Independence Hall.

Before he retired in 1810, Peale tried vainly to interest the national government in acquiring his collection and creating a national museum. Under the direction of his son, the museum struggled on, but it was unable to satisfy the growing popular appetite for showmanship rather than education. The museum finally closed its doors in 1850, but during the Republic's formative years it offered thousands of Americans a unique opportunity, as the ticket of admission promised, to "explore the wondrous world."

limits and threatened the liberties of citizens, states had the right to interpose their authority.

But Jefferson and Madison were not ready to rend a union that had so recently been forged. The two men intended for the Virginia and Kentucky resolutions only to rally public opinion to the Republican cause. They opposed any effort to resist federal authority by force. Furthermore, other states openly rejected the doctrine of "interposition." During the last year of the Adams administration, the Alien and Sedition Acts quietly expired. Once in power, the Republicans repealed the Naturalization Act.

250

The Election of 1800

With a naval war raging on the high seas and the Alien and Sedition Acts sparking debate at home, Adams suddenly shocked his party by negotiating a peace treaty with France. It was a courageous act, for Adams not only split his party in two but also ruined his own chances for reelection by driving Hamilton's pro-British wing of the party into open opposition. The nation benefited, however, for France signed a peace treaty ending its undeclared war. Adams, who bristled with pride and independence, termed this act "the most disinterested, the most determined and the most successful of my whole life."

251

Daily Lives

Every chapter contains an essay focusing on one of five themes that give insight into the lives of ordinary Americans: clothing and fashion; time and travel; food, drink, and drugs; public space/private space; and popular entertainment.

Marginal Headings

Succinct notes in the margins highlight key terms and concepts.

542 Part Three The Republic Transformed and Tested

From the beginning of Reconstruction, African Americans demanded the right to vote as free citizens. The Fifteenth Amendment, ratified in 1870, secured that right for black males. In New York, black citizens paraded in support of Ulysses Grant for president. Parades played a central role in campaigning: this parade exhibits the usual banners, flags, costumes, and a band. Blacks in both the North and the South voted solidly for the Republican party as the party of Lincoln and emancipation, although white violence in the South increasingly reduced black turnout.

The New State Governments

New state constitutions The new southern state constitutions enacted several significant reforms. They put in place fairer systems of legislative representation, allowed voters to elect many officials who before had been appointed, and abolished property requirements for officeholding. In South Carolina, for the first time, voters were allowed to vote for the president, governor, and other state officers.* The Radical state governments also assumed some responsibility for social welfare and established the first statewide systems of public schools in the South. Although the Fourteenth Amendment prevented high Confederate officials from holding office, only Alabama and Arkansas temporarily forbade some ex-Confederates to vote.

Race and social equality All the new constitutions proclaimed the principle of equality and granted black adult males the right to vote. On social relations they were much more cautious. No state outlawed segregation, and South Carolina and Louisiana were the only states that required integration in public schools (a mandate that was almost universally ignored). Sensitive to status, mulattoes pushed for prohibition of social discrimination, but white Republicans refused to adopt such a radical policy.

Economic Issues and Corruption

The war left the southern economy in ruins, and problems of economic reconstruction were as difficult as those of politics. The new Republican governments encouraged industrial development by providing subsidies, loans, and even

*Previously, presidential electors as well as the governor had been chosen by the South Carolina legislature.

Summary

A bulleted summary reinforces each chapter's main points.

Interactive Learning

Lists at the end of every chapter direct students to relevant interactive maps, short documentary movies, and primary source materials located on the Primary Source Investigator CD-ROM.

Additional Reading

Annotated references to both classic studies and recent scholarship encourage further pursuit of the topics and events covered in the chapter.

Significant Events

A chronology at the end of each chapter shows the temporal relationship among important events.

before them) turned for labor to the African slave trade. Only after slavery became firmly established as a social and legal institution did England's southern colonies begin to settle down and grow: during the late seventeenth century for the Chesapeake region and the early eighteenth for the Carolinas. That stubborn reality would haunt Americans of all colors who continued to dream of freedom and independence.

chapter summary

During the seventeenth century, plantation economies based on slavery gradually developed throughout the American South.

- Native peoples everywhere in the American South resisted white settlement, but their populations were drastically reduced by warfare, disease, and enslavement.
- Thriving monocultures were established throughout the region—tobacco in the Chesapeake, rice in the Carolinas, and sugar in the Caribbean.
- African slavery emerged as the dominant labor system in all the southern colonies.
- Instability and conflict characterized the southern colonies for most of the first century of their existence.
- As the English colonies took shape, the Spanish extended their empire in Florida and New Mexico, establishing military garrisons, missions, and cattle ranches.

interactive learning

The Primary Source Investigator CD-ROM offers the following materials related to this chapter:

- Interactive maps: **The Atlantic World, 1400–1850** (M2) and **Growth of the Colonies, 1610–1690** (M3)
- A collection of primary sources on the English colonization of North America, such as an engraving that

illustrates the dress and customs of Native Americans living near Jamestown, letters and documents about the peace resulting from the marriage of Pocahontas and John Rolfe, and the terrible collapse of that peace captured in a contemporary engraving of the Indian massacre of Jamestown settlers. Also included are several sources on the origins of slavery in America: a document that presents one of the earliest restrictive slave codes in the British colonies, images of Portuguese slave trading forts on the coast of West Africa, and a sobering diagram of the human cargo holds of that era's slave-trading ships.

additional reading

The best treatment of early Virginia is Edmund S. Morgan, *American Slavery, American Freedom* (1975). A more intimate portrait of an early Virginia community can be found in Darrett and Anita Rutman's study of Middlesex County, *A Place in Time* (1984). Karen Kupperman offers an excellent overview of relations between whites and Indians not only in the early South but throughout North America in *Settling with the Indians* (1980), while James Merrell sensitively explores the impact of white contact on a single southern tribe in *The Indians' New World* (1989). Two other notable treatments of slavery

and race relations in Britain's southern colonies are Richard Dunn's study of the Caribbean, *Sugar and Slaves* (1972), and Peter Wood's work on South Carolina, *Black Majority* (1974). And for the Spanish borderlands, see David J. Weber, *The Spanish Frontier in North America* (1992).

The Chesapeake has always drawn more notice from early American historians than South Carolina has, but in recent years some important studies have redressed that neglect. The best overview of that colony's development remains Robert Weir, *Colonial South Carolina* (1982); for fine explorations of more specialized topics, see Daniel C. Littlefield, *Rice and Slaves* (1981); Peter Coclanis, *The Shadow of a Dream* (1989); and Timothy Silver, *A New Face on the Countryside* (1990). For a fuller list of readings, see the Bibliography at www.mhhe.com/davidsonnation5.

significant events

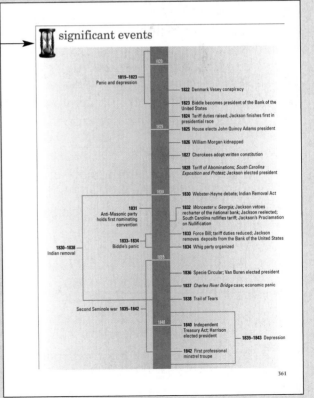

1819–1823 Panic and depression

1822 Denmark Vesey conspiracy

1823 Biddle becomes president of the Bank of the United States

1824 Tariff duties raised; Jackson finishes first in presidential race

1825 House elects John Quincy Adams president

1826 William Morgan kidnapped

1827 Cherokees adopt written constitution

1828 Tariff of Abominations; *South Carolina Exposition and Protest*; Jackson elected president

1830 Webster-Hayne debate; Indian Removal Act

1831 Anti-Masonic party holds first nominating convention

1832 *Worcester v. Georgia*; Jackson vetoes recharter of the national bank; Jackson reelected; South Carolina nullifies tariff; Jackson's Proclamation on Nullification

1833 Force Bill; tariff duties reduced; Jackson removes deposits from the Bank of the United States

1833–1834 Biddle's panic

1834 Whig party organized

1830–1838 Indian removal

1836 Specie Circular; Van Buren elected president

1837 *Charles River Bridge* case; economic panic

1838 Trail of Tears

Second Seminole war **1835–1842**

1840 Independent Treasury Act; Harrison elected president

1839–1843 Depression

1842 First professional minstrel troupe

361

Printer Ornaments and Initial Blocks

History records change over time in countless ways. The flow of history is reflected not only in the narrative of this text but in the decorative types used in its design.

  Over the years printers have used ornamental designs to enliven their texts. Each chapter of *Nation of Nations* incorporates an ornament created during the period being written about. Often these ornaments are from printers' specimen books, produced by type manufacturers so printers could buy such designs. In other chapters the ornaments are taken from printed material of the era.

The initial blocks—the large decorative initials beginning the first word of every chapter—are drawn from type styles popular during the era covered by each of the book's six parts.

 Part 1 uses hand-engraved initials of the sort imported from England and Europe by colonial printers in the seventeenth and eighteenth centuries.

 Part 2 displays mortised initial blocks. These ornaments had holes cut in the middle of the design so a printer could insert the initial of choice. These holes provided greater flexibility when the supply of ornaments was limited.

Part 3 features initial blocks cut from wood, an approach common in the early and middle nineteenth century. This design, Roman X Condensed, allowed more letters to be squeezed into a limited space.

Part 4 makes use of a more ornamental initial block common in the late nineteenth and early twentieth centuries. Some Victorian designs became quite ornate. This font, a style that is relatively reserved, is Latin Condensed.

Part 5 illustrates an initial block whose clean lines reflect the Art Deco movement of the 1920s and 1930s. Printers of the New Era turned away from the often-flowery nineteenth-century styles. This font is Beverly Hills.

Part 6 features an informal style, Brush Script Regular. First introduced during World War II, this typeface reflects the more casual culture that blossomed during the postwar era.

about the authors

James West Davidson received his Ph.D. from Yale University. A historian who has pursued a full-time writing career, he is the author of numerous books, among them *After the Fact: The Art of Historical Detection* (with Mark H. Lytle), *The Logic of Millennial Thought: Eighteenth-Century New England,* and *Great Heart: The History of a Labrador Adventure* (with John Rugge). He is coeditor, with Michael Stoff, of the *Oxford New Narratives in American History* and is at work on a study of Ida B. Wells for the series.

William E. Gienapp has a Ph.D. from the University of California, Berkeley and taught at the University of Wyoming before going to Harvard University, where he was Professor of History until his death in 2003. In 1988 he received the Avery O. Craven Award for his book *The Origins of the Republican Party, 1852–1856.* He edited *The Civil War and Reconstruction: A Documentary Collection* and most recently published *Abraham Lincoln and Civil War America* and a companion volume, *This Fiery Trial: The Speeches and Writings of Abraham Lincoln.*

Christine Leigh Heyrman is Professor of History at the University of Delaware. She received a Ph.D. in American Studies from Yale University and is the author of *Commerce and Culture: The Maritime Communities of Colonial Massachusetts, 1690–1750.* Her book *Southern Cross: The Beginnings of the Bible Belt* was awarded the Bancroft Prize in 1998.

Mark H. Lytle, who received a Ph.D. from Yale University, is Professor of History and Environmental Studies and Chair of the History Program at Bard College. He was recently reappointed Mary Ball Washington Professor of History at University College, Dublin, in Ireland. His publications include *The Origins of the Iranian-American Alliance, 1941–1953, After the Fact: The Art of Historical Detection* (with James West Davidson), and "An Environmental Approach to American Diplomatic History" in *Diplomatic History.* His most recent book, *The Uncivil War: America in the Vietnam Era,* will be published in 2005, and he is completing a biography of Rachel Carson.

Michael B. Stoff is Associate Professor of History at the University of Texas at Austin. The recipient of a Ph.D. from Yale University, he has received many teaching awards, most recently the Friars' Centennial Teaching Excellence Award. He is the author of *Oil, War, and American Security: The Search for a National Policy on Foreign Oil, 1941–1947* and coeditor (with Jonathan Fanton and R. Hal Williams) of *The Manhattan Project: A Documentary Introduction to the Atomic Age.* He is currently working on a brief narrative of the bombing of Nagasaki.

introduction

*H*istory is both a discipline of rigor, bound by rules and scholarly methods, and something more: the unique, compelling, even strange way in which we humans define ourselves. We are all the sum of the tales of thousands of people, great and small, whose actions have etched their lines upon us. History supplies our very identity—a sense of the social groups to which we belong, whether family, ethnic group, race, class, or gender. It reveals to us the foundations of our deepest religious beliefs and traces the roots of our economic and political systems. It explores how we celebrate and grieve, how we sing the songs we sing, how we weather the illnesses to which time and chance subject us. It commands our attention for all these good reasons and for no good reason at all, other than a fascination with the way the myriad tales play out. Strange that we should come to care about a host of men and women so many centuries gone, some with names eminent and familiar, others unknown but for a chance scrap of information left behind in an obscure letter.

Yet we do care. We care about Sir Humphrey Gilbert, "devoured and swallowed up of the Sea" one black Atlantic night in 1583; we care about George Washington at Kips Bay, red with fury as he takes a riding crop to his retreating soldiers. We care about Octave Johnson, a slave fleeing through Louisiana swamps trying to decide whether to stand and fight the approaching hounds or take his chances with the bayou alligators; we care about Clara Barton, her nurse's skirts so heavy with blood from the wounded, that she must wring them out before tending to the next soldier. We are drawn to the fate of Chinese laborers, chipping away at the Sierras' looming granite; of a Georgian named Tom Watson seeking to forge a colorblind political alliance; and of desperate immigrant mothers, kerosene lamps in hand, storming Brooklyn butcher shops that had again raised prices. We follow, with a mix of awe and amusement, the fortunes of the quirky Henry Ford ("Everybody wants to be somewhere he ain't"), turning out identical automobiles, insisting his factory workers wear identical expressions ("Fordization of the Face").

We trace the career of young Thurgood Marshall, crisscrossing the South in his own "little old beat-up '29 Ford," typing legal briefs in the back seat, trying to get black teachers to sue for equal pay, hoping to get his people somewhere they weren't. The list could go on and on, spilling out as it did in Walt Whitman's *Leaves of Grass:* "A southerner soon as a northerner, a planter nonchalant and hospitable, / A Yankee bound my own way . . . a Hoosier, a Badger, a Buckeye, a Louisianian or Georgian. . . ." Whitman embraced and celebrated them all, inseparable strands of what made him an American and what made him human:

> In all people I see myself, none more and not one
> a barleycorn less; And the good or bad I say of
> myself, I say of them.

To encompass so expansive an America, Whitman turned to poetry; historians have traditionally chosen *narrative* as their means of giving life to the past. That mode of explanation permits them to interweave the strands of economic, political, and social history in a coherent chronological framework. By choosing narrative, historians affirm the multicausal nature of historical explanation—the insistence that events be portrayed in context. By choosing narrative, they are also acknowledging that, although long-term economic and social trends shape societies in significant ways, events often take on a logic (or an illogic) of their own, jostling one another, being deflected by unpredictable personal decisions, sudden deaths, natural catastrophes, and chance. There are literary reasons, too, for preferring a narrative approach, because it supplies a dramatic force usually missing from more structural analyses of the past.

In some ways, surveys such as this text are the natural antithesis of narrative history. They strive, by definition, to be comprehensive: to furnish a broad, orderly exposition of their chosen field. Yet to cover so much ground in so limited a space necessarily deprives readers of the context of more detailed accounts. Then, too, the resurgence of social history—with its concern for class and race, patterns of rural and urban life, the spread of market and industrial economies—lends itself to more analytic, less chronological treatments. The challenge facing historians is to incorporate these areas of research without losing the story's narrative drive or the chronological flow that orients readers to the more familiar events of our past.

With the cold war of the past half-century at an end, there has been increased attention to the worldwide breakdown of so many nonmarket economies and, by inference, to the greater success of the market societies of the United States and other capitalist nations. As our own narrative makes clear, American society and politics have indeed come together centrally in the marketplace. What Americans produce, how and where they produce it, and the desire to buy cheap and sell dear have been defining elements in every era. That market orientation has created unparalleled abundance and reinforced striking inequalities, not the least a society in which, for two centuries, human beings themselves were bought and sold. It has made Americans powerfully provincial in protecting local interests and internationally adventurous in seeking to expand wealth and opportunity.

It goes without saying that Americans have not always produced wisely or well. The insistent drive toward material plenty has levied a heavy tax on the global environment. Too often quantity has substituted for quality, whether we talk of cars, education, or culture. When markets flourish, the nation abounds with confidence that any problem, no matter how intractable, can be solved. When markets fail, however, the fault lines of our political and social systems become all too evident.

In the end, then, it is impossible to separate the marketplace of boom and bust and the world of ordinary Americans from the corridors of political maneuvering or the ceremonial pomp of an inauguration. To treat political and social history as distinct spheres is counterproductive. The primary question of this narrative—how the fledgling, often tumultuous confederation of "these United States" managed to transform itself into an enduring republic—is not only political but necessarily social. In order to survive, a republic must resolve conflicts between citizens of different geographic regions and economic classes, of diverse racial and ethnic origins, of competing religions and ideologies. The resolution of these conflicts has produced tragic consequences, perhaps, as often as noble ones. But tragic or noble, the destiny of these states cannot be understood without comprehending both the social and the political dimensions of the story.

160°W 140°W 120°W 100°W 80°W 60°W 40°W 20°W

80°N

KALAALLIT NUNAAT
(DEN.)

ICELAND

ALASKA
(U.S.)

60°N

CANADA

UNITED
(KING
IRELAND

40°N

UNITED STATES

ATLANTIC

AZORES
(PORT.)

PORTUGAL

SI

Tropic of Cancer

MADEIRA IS.
(PORT.)

CANARY IS.
(SP)

MOROCC

WESTERN
SAHARA
(MOR.)

20°N

HAWAII (U.S.)

MEXICO

BAHAMAS

CUBA

DOMINICAN
REPUBLIC   27

HAITI

MAURITANIA

BELIZE
HONDURAS

JAMAICA

29
30   31
32
33
34

28

CAPE
VERDE   SENEGAL

GAMBIA
GUINEA BISSAU   GUINEA

BL

GUATEMALA
EL SALVADOR

NICARAGUA

GRENADA

PACIFIC

COSTA RICA

PANAMA

VENEZUELA

GUYANA

SURINAME

FRENCH GUIANA (FR.)

SIERRA
LEONE

LIBERIA

CÔTE   EC
D'IVOIRE

COLOMBIA

S

GALÁPAGOS IS.
(EC.)

ECUADOR

OCEAN

EQUATOR

KIRIBATI

OCEAN

SAMOA

AMERICAN
SAMOA (U.S.)

FRENCH POLYNESIA
(FR.)

PERU

BRAZIL

TONGA

20°S

BOLIVIA

Tropic of Capricorn

CHILE

PARAGUAY

40°S

ARGENTINA   URUGUAY

FALKLAND IS. (U.K.)

60°S

80°S

0	1000	2000 Miles
0	1000	2000 Kilometers

1. NETHERLANDS
2. BELGIUM
3. LUXEMBOURG
4. ESTONIA
5. LATVIA
6. LITHUANIA
7. CZECH REPUBLIC
8. SLOVAKIA
9. SWITZERLAND
10. AUSTRIA
11. HUNGARY
12. SLOVENIA
13. CROATIA
14. BOSNIA AND HERCEGOVINA
15. SERBIA AND MONTENEGRO
16. MACEDONIA
17. ALBANIA
18. MOLDOVA
19. GEORGIA
20. ARMENIA
21. AZERBAIJAN
22. LEBANON
23. ISRAEL
24. LAOS
25. THAILAND
26. CAMBODIA
27. PUERTO RICO (U.S.)
28. ST. KITTS AND NEVIS
29. ANTIGUA AND BARBUDA
30. DOMINICA
31. ST. LUCIA
32. ST. VINCENT AND THE GRENADINES
33. BARBADOS
34. TRINIDAD AND TOBAGO

primary source investigator CD-ROM

*H*istory comes alive through narrative; but the building blocks of that narrative are primary sources. McGraw-Hill's Primary Source Investigator (PSI) CD-ROM provides instant access to hundreds of the most important and interesting documents, images, artifacts, audio recordings, and videos from our past. You can browse the collection across time, source types, subjects, historical questions, textbook chapters, or your own custom search terms. Clicking on a source opens it in our Source Window, packed with annotations, investigative tools, transcripts, and interactive questions for deeper analysis.

As close companions to the primary sources, original secondary sources are also included on the PSI: 5- to 8-minute documentaries and interactive maps complete with underlying statistical data. Together these features weave a rich historical narrative or argument on topics that are difficult to fully grasp from primary sources alone. Each secondary source also provides links back to related primary sources, enabling you to test a secondary source's argument against the historical record.

While examining any of these sources you can use our notebook feature to take notes, bookmark key sources, and save or print copies of all the sources for use outside the archive. After researching a particular theme or time period, you can use our argument-outlining tool to walk you through the steps of composing a historical essay or presentation.

Through its browsing and inspection tools, Primary Source Investigator helps you practice the art of historical detection using a real archive of historical sources. This process of historical investigation follows three basic steps:

- *Ask*   Use our browsing panels to search and filter the sources.
- *Research*   Use the Source Window to examine sources in detail and the Notebook to record your insights.
- *Argue*   Practice outlining historical arguments based on archival sources.

Nation of Nations

Prologue

The land that they made their own became the hearth of civilization in the Americas. It was a fitting tribute to their ancestors who, thousands of years earlier, had discovered and colonized a truly new world, one in which no human beings had ever lived. No less bold, their descendants created cultures that rank among the most brilliant in all the ancient world. They invented farming, built the first cities, and developed complex ways of organizing society, government, and religious worship. They devised precise calendars and elegant hieroglyphic systems of writing. They crafted useful tools and fashioned beautiful works of art.

These were the peoples of ancient Mesoamerica during the first millennium C.E.*—some living on the Yucatán Peninsula, some along the gulf coast of Mexico, others in the highlands of central Mexico, and still others on the narrow strip of land from Guatemala to Panama. What the Greeks and Romans of antiquity were to Europe, the earliest settlers of Mesoamerica were to their side of the Atlantic—the founders of classical civilizations, empires whose cultural influence left a profound impression on other peoples, including those living hundreds of miles to the north.

Settling and Civilizing the Americas

preview • The civilizations that arose in the Americas during the first millennium C.E. rivaled the classical civilizations of the ancient world. Mesoamerica was the hearth of these vibrant cultures—cultures whose influence reached far into North America. Yet just as Greek and Roman civilizations declined, so did many Mesoamerican cultures—until the Aztecs of the fifteenth century flourished, seemingly on the brink of projecting their power and influence over even vaster distances.

Peopling the Continents

Hunters cross the Bering Strait

Like all of the Western Hemisphere's first human inhabitants, the ancestors of these ancient Mesoamericans came from northeastern Asia. At least 15,000 years ago during the most recent Ice Age, they crossed the Bering Strait, then a narrow bridge of land connecting Siberia to Alaska. Gradually these Stone Age wanderers filtered southward, some following the Pacific coastline in small boats, but most making their way down a narrow, glacier-free corridor along the eastern base of the Rocky Mountains and onto the northern Great Plains. There they found a bountiful supply of big-game animals, including their quarry of choice—enormous woolly mammoths and mastodons whose carcasses supplied their bands not only with meat but also with skins for clothing, tusks and bones for fashioning spear points, and oil for light. With the passage of generations, some of the nomads pressed farther south and east, and within a few thousand years, the descendants of these Stone Age Siberians, people whom Columbus would wishfully dub "Indians," had spread throughout the length and breadth of the Americas.

*Common Era, equivalent to the Christian Era or A.D.; B.C.E. is Before the Common Era, equivalent to B.C.

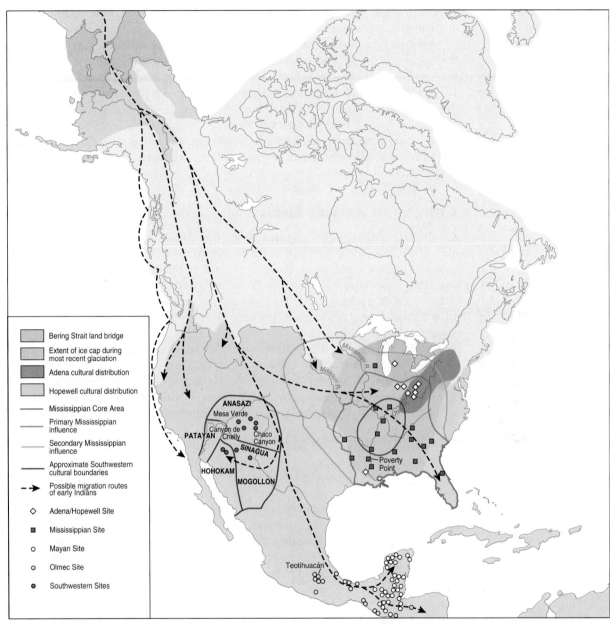

Early Peoples of North America
Migration routes across the Bering Strait from Asia were taken by peoples whose descendants created the major civilizations of ancient Americans. The influence of Mesoamerica is most striking among the cultures of the Southwest and the Mississippians.

As the new world of the Americas was settled, it was also changing dramatically. The last Ice Age literally melted away as warmer global temperatures freed the great reservoirs of water once locked in glaciers. A rise in sea levels inundated the Bering Strait, cutting off migration over the land bridge, and as meltwater flooded the land, new lakes filled and new rivers flowed. The emergence of new climates, waterways, environments, and ecosystems made for an ever greater diversity among the human beings who ranged across those increasingly varied landscapes. The first human inhabitants of the Americas had fed, clothed, warmed, and armed themselves by hunting mammoths and mastodons, animals that did not

Diversified societies

survive the end of the Ice Age. As the glaciers receded, later generations adapted to changing conditions.

So it was that distinctive regional cultures developed among the peoples in different parts of the Americas—sometime between 10,000 and 2500 years ago. Those who remained in the Great Plains turned to hunting herds of bison; those in the deserts of the Great Basin foraged seeds and edible plants; those in the Pacific Northwest relied mainly on fishing; and those east of the Mississippi, besides fishing and gathering, tracked deer and bear and trapped smaller game animals and birds. Over these same centuries, each tribe developed its own language, social organization, government, and religious beliefs and practices. Cultural unity gave way to cultural variety.

Cultures of Ancient Mexico

Of all these early regional cultures, those that proved most crucial to the evolution of ancient North America lay to the south, within the slim crescent of land connecting North and South America. It was in Mesoamerica, about 9000 years ago, that agriculture began in the Western Hemisphere. Here farmers first tilled American soil, growing maize (Indian corn, its ears originally only about the size of a human finger) and slowly learning to cultivate other crops such as beans, squashes, tomatoes, and chilis.

Olmec city-building

About 1500 B.C.E., the peoples who had been working the soil many thousands of years began to turn their once-tiny farming villages into larger societies, into richer and more advanced cultures. As the abundant food supply steadily expanded their populations, new groups emerged who specialized in certain kinds of work. While some people continued to labor on the land, others became craftworkers and merchants, architects and artists, warriors and priests. Their built environment reflected that social change as humble villages expanded into skillfully planned urban sites that were centers of trade, government, artistic display, and religious ceremony. Their inhabitants constructed large plazas and pyramidal structures, erected stone-carved altars and enormous heads chiseled from basalt. That was the singular achievement of the ancient people known as the Olmecs, the first city-builders in the Americas.

The Olmec cultural influence gradually spread throughout Mesoamerica, perhaps as a result of their trade with neighboring peoples. By about 100 B.C.E., the Olmecs' example had inspired the flowering of Teotihuacán from a small town in central Mexico into a metropolis of towering pyramids, bustling marketplaces, palaces decorated with mural paintings that housed an elite of warriors and priests, schools for their children, and sprawling suburbs where the commoners lived. At its height, around 650 C.E., Teotihuacán spanned 15 square miles and its population was larger than that of ancient Rome.

Mayan civilization

More impressive still was the achievement of the Mayas, who benefited from their contacts with both the Olmecs and Teotihuacán. In the lowland jungles of Mesoamerica they built cities filled with palaces, bridges, aqueducts, baths, astronomical observatories, and pyramids topped with temples. Their priests developed a written language, their mathematicians discovered the zero, and their astronomers devised a calendar more accurate than any then existing. In its glory, between the third and ninth century C.E., the Mayan empire boasted some 50 urban centers scattered throughout the Yucatán Peninsula, Belize, Guatemala, and Honduras.

But neither the earliest urban centers of the Olmecs, nor the glittering city-state of Teotihuacán, nor even the fabulous kingdom of the Mayas survived. Like the ancient civilizations of Greece and Rome, they thrived for many centuries and then fell. The reasons for their collapse remain one of the past's mysteries. Military attack may have brought about their ruin, or perhaps the pressure of their large population on the resources of surrounding fields and forests caused drastic changes in the ecology and environment. Whatever catastrophes caused their downfall, which occurred between about 650 and 950 C.E., those who survived fled the ruins. Some migrated elsewhere in Mesoamerica or to South America or even to the islands of the Caribbean. But others—possibly many others—moved north into the Southwest and Southeast of the present-day United States. After all, Mesoamerican merchants had been exchanging ideas as well as goods with the peoples living in those regions for many centuries.

The clay figure of an ancient Mayan ballplayer doubles as a whistle. The popularity of ball games spread from Mesoamerica into the southwestern regions of the present-day United States.

Cultures of the Southwest

By whatever means it was transmitted, Mesoamerican influence powerfully affected those tribes who had settled in the sagebrush deserts beneath the Southwest's vast canopy of sky. Farming had spread to this northernmost frontier of Mesoamerica by about 1000 B.C.E., and its most successful ancient practitioners in the region were the Mogollon and Hohokam peoples, two cultures that flourished in southern Arizona and New Mexico during the first millennium C.E. Both clustered their subterranean, dirt-roofed dwellings known as pit houses near streams, which allowed them to adopt the systems of irrigation as well as the maize cultivation of central Mexico. The Hohokam, who had originally emigrated from the south, even modeled their platform mounds and ball-playing courts on those of Mexico.

Mogollon and Hohokam peoples

Their neighbors to the north, in what is now known as the Four Corners of Arizona, Colorado, New Mexico, and Utah, were the Anasazi, a name given them by later tribes in the region that means "the ancient ones." The Anasazi devised an even more productive agriculture, and this prosperity allowed the growing number of their people to turn their energies toward more than mere survival. Their most stunning achievements were villages of cliff dwellings—apartment-like structures up to four stories high and containing hundreds of rooms, carved out of the rock at places like Mesa Verde (Colorado) and Canyon de Chelly (Arizona). More than 100 towns in Chaco Canyon (New Mexico), the largest center of Anasazi settlement, were linked by miles of wide, straight roads.

The Anasazi

Besides their impressive dwellings, the Anasazi filled their towns with religious shrines, astronomical observatories, and stations for sending signals to other villages. Their craftworkers fashioned exquisitely woven baskets and pottery painted with black and white geometric designs as well as turquoise jewelry that they traded to central Mexico. For more than a thousand years, Anasazi civilization prospered, reaching its zenith between about 900 and 1100 C.E. During those three centuries, the population grew to approximately 30,000 spread over 50,000 square miles, a total area larger than present-day California.

This artist's depiction of Pueblo Bonita, one of the nine Great House complexes of Chaco Canyon, suggests the sophistication of Anasazi architecture. By the end of the eleventh century, Pueblo Bonita stood four stories high at the rear and contained 800 rooms as well as many towers and terraces and a large central plaza.

Cultures of the Eastern Woodlands

Mesoamerican influence spread less evenly among the peoples who ranged across the Eastern Woodlands of North America, the region lying east of the Mississippi and south of the Subarctic belt of lower Canada. The environments that became most densely settled were its major river valleys (of the Mississippi, Ohio, Tennessee, and Cumberland), the shores of the Great Lakes, and the coast of the Atlantic. Everywhere the earliest inhabitants depended on a combination of fishing, gathering, and hunting—mainly deer, but also bear, raccoon, and a variety of birds. Around 2000 B.C.E., some groups in the temperate, fertile Southeast began growing the gourds and pumpkins first cultivated by Mesoamerican farmers, and later they also adopted the cultivation of maize. But unlike the ancient peoples of the Southwest, most Eastern Woodland tribes continued to rely for their subsistence primarily on animals, fish, and nuts, all of which were abundant enough to meet their needs and even to expand their numbers.

Indeed, some of the most striking cultural achievements of the ancient Eastern Woodlands were the work of peoples who did not practice agriculture but instead depended exclusively on hunting and gathering. About 1000 B.C.E., those who lived in a place now known as Poverty Point in northeastern Louisiana fashioned spectacular earthworks—six semicircular rings that rose nine feet in height and covered more than half a mile in diameter. While these structures might have been sites for studying the planets and stars, other mounds—hundreds built about

Adena and
Hopewell cultures

2000 years ago by the Adena and Hopewell cultures of the Ohio and Mississippi valleys—served as the burial places of their leading men and women. Alongside the corpses mourners heaped their richest goods—headdresses of antlers, necklaces of copper, troves of shells and pearls—rare and precious items imported from as far north as Canada, as far west as Wyoming, and as far east as Florida. All these mounds attest powerfully not only to the skill and sheer numbers of their builders, but also to the complexity of these ancient societies, their elaborate religious practices, and the wide scope of their trading networks.

Mississippian culture

Even so, the most magnificent culture of the ancient Eastern Woodlands, the Mississippian, owed much of its prominence to farming. By the twelfth century C.E.,

An artist's reconstruction of the city of Cahokia, c. 1100 C.E., the hearth of Mississippian culture. Note how tiny the human figures are compared to the massive proportions of the temples.

these peoples had emerged as the premier city-builders of North America, and their towns radiated for hundreds of miles in every direction from the hub of their trading network at Cahokia, a port city of more than 20,000 located directly across from present-day St. Louis at the confluence of the Missouri and the Mississippi rivers. Cahokia's many broad plazas swarmed with farmers hawking their corn, squash, and beans and with craftworkers and merchants displaying their wares. But what commanded every eye were the structures surrounding the plazas—more than 100 flat-topped pyramidal mounds crowned by religious temples and the palaces of rulers. This shape distinguished Mississippian mounds from earlier ones in North America, which were circular or elliptical, but it made the mounds remarkably similar to those in ancient Mesoamerica. It is highly likely, then, that either by traders or emigrants, Mesoamerican influences were carried far into this interior region of North America, shaping these peoples' agriculture, architecture, social structure, and religious ceremonies.

The maize cultivation pioneered in Mexico made its earliest and deepest ## Beyond the Mesoamerican Sphere

impression on the ancient societies of southwestern and southeastern North America. Most other groups on the continent, farther from the sphere of Mesoamerican influence, remained hunters and gatherers, following the ancestral ways of many generations.

Cultures of the Great Plains

The sole exception could be found in the farming villages of the Great Plains, a sweeping swath of rich prairie drained by the Missouri River and situated between the Eastern Woodlands and the Great Basin. Tribes like the Hidatsa, the Mandan, and the Pawnee finally settled along the tree-lined rivers and streams of this region and cultivated corn, beans, squash, and sunflowers, a food supply that they supplemented by hunting.

Migratory peoples

But the other peoples of the Plains—Teton Sioux, Blackfeet, Comanche, Cheyenne, and Crow in the North and Apache in the South—migrated with the seasons and relied for their survival almost entirely on hunting buffalo. Like all Plains tribes, they pursued game on foot, for the horses that had once roamed the Americas became extinct after the last Ice Age. Usually, large groups of men worked together to drive the buffalos over cliffs or to trap them in corrals. The only major change in that Plains culture took place around 550 C.E., when the bow and arrow replaced the spear, which had been the hunters' favored weapon for some 10,000 years.

Cultures of the Great Basin

Some peoples west of the Great Plains also kept to older ways of subsistence. Among them were the Utes, Shoshones, and Paiutes of the Great Basin, which includes present-day Nevada and Utah, eastern California, and western Wyoming and Colorado. These tribes scoured their stark, arid landscape for the limited supplies of food it yielded, moving with each passing season to make the most of their environment. Men tracked elk and antelope and trapped smaller animals, birds, even toads, rattlesnakes, and insects. But the staples of their diet were edible seeds, nuts, and plants, which women gathered and stored in woven baskets to consume in times of scarcity. Families occasionally hunted together or wintered in common quarters, but because the desert heat and soil defied farming, these bands usually numbered no more than about 50 people.

This ornately carved and painted house post once supported the main beams of a dwelling belonging to a Kwakiutl whaler in the Pacific Northwest. A man of wealth and high rank, he has a whale painted on his chest and copper ornaments on his arms. Two smaller figures, in shadow by the whaler's knees, each support one end of a plank seat. These were his household slaves, most likely children captured in an attack on rival tribes.

Cultures of the Subarctic and Arctic

Most of present-day Canada and Alaska were equally inhospitable to agriculture. In the farthest northern reaches—a treeless belt of Arctic tundra—temperatures fell below freezing for eight or nine months of the year; likewise, immediately to the south the Subarctic, although densely forested, had only about 100 frost-free days each year. As a result, the peoples of both regions survived by fishing and hunting. The Inuits, or Eskimos, of northern Alaska harvested whales from their umiaks, boats that could bear more than a ton and that were made by stretching walrus skin over a driftwood frame. In the central Arctic, they tracked seals. The inhabitants of the Subarctic, both Algonquian-speaking peoples in the East and the Athapaskan speakers of the West, moved from their summer fishing camps to berry patches in the fall to moose and caribou hunting grounds in the winter.

Whether on the Great Plains, in the Great Basin, or in the Arctic, most societies of hunters and gatherers were smaller than those that relied entirely or in part on agriculture. These nomadic groups also tended to be simpler in their social structure, their political organization, and their modes of religious worship. Typically, families were roughly equal in wealth and prestige, and governing authority lay with either the male family head or the most expert hunter of a small band. Shamans—any person claiming special spiritual powers—enlisted the supernatural to assist individuals. But there are important exceptions to that pattern—not only the Adena and Hopewell cultures of the ancient Eastern Woodlands but, even more dramatically, the seafaring cultures of the Pacific Northwest.

Cultures of the Pacific Northwest

The rugged stretch of coast from the southern banks of present-day British Columbia to northern California has always been an extraordinarily rich natural environment. Its mild climate and abundant rainfall yield forests lush with plants and game; its bays and rivers teem with salmon and halibut, its oceans with whales and porpoises, and its rocky beaches with seals, otters, abalone, mussels, and clams. To survive, even to prosper, in such a place, there was no need to till the soil, only to reap the foods nature provided. In that work, the peoples of the Pacific Northwest excelled—the Nootkan and the Makah, the Tlingit, Tshimshian, and Kwakiutls. From their villages on the banks of rivers, the shores of bays, and the beaches of low-lying offshore islands, they speared or netted salmon, trapped sea mammals, gathered shellfish, and launched canoes. The largest of these craft, from which they harpooned whales, measured 45 feet bow to stern and nearly 6 feet wide.

By the fifteenth century these fecund lands supported a population of perhaps 130,000. They also permitted a culture with the leisure time needed to create works of art as well as an elaborate social and ceremonial life. The peoples of the Northwest built houses and canoes from red cedar; carved bowls and dishes from red alder; crafted paddles and harpoon shafts, bows, and clubs from Pacific yew; wove baskets from bark and blankets from mountain goat wool. They evolved a society of sharp distinctions between nobles, commoners, and slaves, the latter being mainly women and children captured in raids on other villages. Those who were free devoted their lives to accumulating and then distributing their wealth among other villagers in elaborate potlatch ceremonies in order to confirm or enhance their social prestige.

Social and ceremonial distinctions

North America and the Caribbean on the Eve of European Invasion

Over many generations, cultural patterns changed little for those peoples who learned to adapt to whatever their environments granted or withheld in the Pacific Northwest, Arctic and Subarctic, Great Basin, and Great Plains. And little would change until they encountered Europeans.

But for many others who lived elsewhere in North America, the centuries immediately preceding the arrival of Columbus marked a period of cataclysmic decline. During those centuries, the continent's most impressive civilizations collapsed as suddenly and mysteriously as had the Olmecs and Mayas of Mesoamerica. In the Southwest, the Mogollon culture went into eclipse around the twelfth century, the Hohokam and the Anasazi by about the fourteenth century. In the Eastern Woodlands, the story was strikingly similar: the Adena and Hopewell cultures as well as that of the Mississippians had faded by the fourteenth century.

Sudden declines

There is no shortage of speculation about what brought down North America's most impressive ancient civilizations—drought, warfare, and epidemic disease head the list of possible causes. But as yet, there is no way of knowing why so many cultures that had attained such heights declined and fell—and did so in rapid succession within the span of a few centuries. Nor is there any way of knowing at present why many other North American cultures, some built on the ruins of these earlier civilizations, endured and even flourished, up to and beyond their first encounters with the invading Europeans.

Enduring Cultures

Pueblos

Among the survivors were the Pueblos, the heirs of the artistic and architectural traditions of the Anasazi and their predecessors in the Southwest. The Pueblos were sedentary farmers who lived in permanent villages, growing crops of corn, beans, squash, and cotton. Like most agricultural peoples, they called on their gods to bring rain and good harvests, ceremonies that the Pueblos conducted in kivas, underground circular dwellings that resemble the pit houses of the earlier Mogollons and Hohokams. And to ensure their safety, the Pueblos situated their villages atop high, steep mesas. That was their best defense against attacks by Athapaskan-speaking tribes, mainly the Apache and the Navajo, hunters and gatherers from western Canada and Alaska who entered the Southwest around 1300 C.E.

Muskogean peoples

In the Eastern Woodlands, the Mississippian heritage passed to various Muskogean tribes, the dominant group in the Southeast by the fifteenth century. That legacy was preserved best by the Natchez of the lower Mississippi valley, who adopted both the temple mound–building tradition and the rigid social distinctions of that earlier civilization. Below the chief, or "Great Sun," of the Natchez stood a hereditary nobility of lesser "Suns" who demanded respect from the lowly "Stinkards," the common people.

Iroquois

By the fifteenth century, agriculture had come to figure prominently not only among the Muskogean peoples but also among the Iroquois, the second major tribal group of the Eastern Woodlands. They were concentrated in present-day upstate New York and Pennsylvania as well as in the hill country of the Carolinas and Georgia. Like the Muskogean tribes, the Iroquois lived in permanent villages. The distinctive feature of their architecture was not the temple mound but rather the longhouse (some stretching up to 100 feet in length) that might shelter as many as 10 families.

An artist traveling with the English explorer Francis Drake (probably in the 1590s) painted this Indian tending a tropical Caribbean garden. Maize corn flourishes (right) as well as beans on two poles, while a papaya tree can be seen (upper left) as well as a manioc shrub (middle left) and gourds (lower left). Many of these crops—corn and manioc especially—eventually became important staples in diets around the globe.

Indians of North and Central America circa 1500

The Algonquins were the third major group of Eastern Woodlands people. **Algonquins**
They lived along the Atlantic seaboard and the Great Lakes in bands smaller than
those of either the Muskogeans or the Iroquois. By the fifteenth century, the coastal
tribes from southern New England to Virginia had adopted agriculture to
supplement their diets, but those in the colder northern climates with shorter
growing seasons depended entirely on hunting, fishing, and gathering plants like
wild rice.

Cultures of equal and even greater resources persisted and flourished during **Caribbean cultures**
the fifteenth century in the Caribbean, particularly on the Greater Antilles—the

islands of present-day Cuba, Haiti, Jamaica, and Puerto Rico. Although the earliest inhabitants of the ancient Caribbean, the Ciboneys, probably came from the Florida peninsula, it was the Arawaks, later emigrants from northern South America, who expanded throughout the Greater Antilles and the Bahamas. Through a canoe-borne commerce dating at least from the time of the Mayan empire, the Arawaks established close ties with Mesoamerica. They modeled not only their agriculture but also their society and government on the example of Central America's most glittering civilizations. Arawak chiefs known as caciques, along with a small number of noble families, ruled island tribes, controlling the production and distribution of food and tools and exacting tribute from the great mass of commoners, farmers, and fisherfolk. Attending to these elites were the poorest Arawak peoples—servants who bedecked their masters and mistresses in brilliant diadems of feathers, fine woven textiles, and gold nose and ear pieces and then shouldered the litters from which the rulers paraded their finery.

Cultural diversity of North America

Thus, by the end of the fifteenth century, tremendous cultural diversity characterized North America. Its peoples numbered about 4.5 million—with another 4 million living on the islands of the Caribbean—and they were spread among more than 350 societies speaking nearly as many distinct languages. (The total precontact population for all of the Americas is estimated at between 57 and 112 million.) Some relied entirely on farming; others on hunting, fishing, and gathering; still others on a combination of the two. Some, like the Natchez and the Iroquois, practiced matrilineal forms of kinship, in which women owned land, tools, and even children. Among others, like the Algonquins, patrilineal kinship prevailed, and all property and prestige descended in the male line. Some societies, like those of the Great Plains and the Great Basin in the West, the Inuit in the Arctic, and the Iroquois and Algonquins in the East, were roughly egalitarian, while others, like many in the Caribbean and the Pacific Northwest, were rigidly divided into nobles and commoners and servants or slaves. Some, like the Natchez and the Arawaks, were ruled by powerful chiefs; others, like the Algonquins and the Pueblos, by councils of village elders or heads of family clans; still others in the Great Basin, the Great Plains, and the far North, by the most skillful hunter or the most powerful shaman in their band. Those people who relied on hunting practiced religions that celebrated their kinship with animals and solicited their aid as guardian spirits, while predominantly agricultural peoples sought the assistance of their gods to make the rain fall and the crops ripen.

The Rise of the Aztec Empire

Already rich in a long history of human achievement, of which its diversity stood as one legacy, late-fifteenth-century North America might also have been a world poised on the brink of a cultural renaissance. For even as many of its people were rebuilding on the ruins of earlier civilizations, a new empire to the south, one more stunning in its sheer scope and magnificence than any of its predecessors in Mesoamerica, was taking shape.

In the middle of the thirteenth century, the Aztecs, a people who originally lived on Mesoamerica's northern frontiers, swept into central Mexico. By the end of the fifteenth century, they ruled over a vast empire from their capital at Tenochtitlán, an island metropolis of at least a quarter of a million people. At its center lay a large

Aztec merchants, or pochtecas, spoke many languages and traveled on foot great distances throughout Mesoamerica and parts of North America. The one shown (above, left) carries a cane and bears a sack of trade goods (topped off by a parrot). The pochtecas' patron god, Yacatecuhtli, is often portrayed with a long nose and most likely is the same deity depicted by the shell and copper masks (inset) found at many sites of ancient Mississippian culture.

plaza bordered by sumptuous palaces and the Great Temple of the Sun. Beyond stood three broad causeways connecting the island to the mainland, many other tall temples adorned with brightly painted carved images of the gods, zoological and botanical gardens, and well-stocked marketplaces. Through Tenochtitlán's canals flowed gold, silver, exotic feathers and jewels, cocoa, and millions of pounds of maize—all trade goods and tribute from the several million other Mexican peoples subjugated by the Aztecs.

Unsurpassed in power and wealth, technological and artistic attainments, theirs was also a highly stratified society. The Aztec ruler, or Chief Speaker, shared governing power with the aristocrats who monopolized all positions of religious, military, and political leadership, while the commoners—merchants, farmers, and craftworkers—performed all manual labor. There were slaves as well, some captives taken in war, others from the ranks of commoners forced by poverty to sell themselves or their children.

It is tantalizing to imagine what might have happened. What if Aztec civilization had continued to flourish and expand, to export its influence by trade or migration into the sixteenth century and beyond? Would the Aztecs have emerged as the Olmecs and Mayas of a later age—an empire that projected its power and influence over vast distances and millions of people? Would their civilization have become a new cultural hearth, one that shaped, once again, the destiny of North America?

There is no way of knowing, because the grandeur of the Aztecs did not outlast the opening of the sixteenth century. Instead, a reversal of historical fortunes took place, one as sudden as it was startling. The Aztecs, themselves unexpected invaders from the north who fashioned Mesoamerica's most glorious civilization, were conquered by yet another group of invaders, still more unexpected, from the west.

prologue summary

During the thousands of years after bands of Siberian nomads migrated across the Bering Strait to Alaska, their descendants spread throughout the Americas, creating civilizations that rivaled those of ancient Europe, Asia, and Africa.

- Around 1500 B.C.E. Mesoamerica emerged as the hearth of classical civilization in the Western Hemisphere, a process started by the Olmecs and brought to its height by the Mayans.

  - These Central American peoples devised complex ways of organizing society, government, and religious worship and built cities remarkable for their art, architecture, and trade.

  - Both commerce and migration spread cultural influences throughout the hemisphere, notably to the islands of the Caribbean basin and to North America, an influence that endured long after these empires declined.

- Mesoamerican cultures influenced the Mogollons, the Hohokams, and the Anasazi of the Southwest as well as the Mississippians and other peoples living in the southern portion of the Eastern Woodlands.

  - Such influences included not only the practice of agriculture but also elements of Mesoamerican architecture, social structure, and religious worship.

- Inhabitants of the Great Plains, the Great Basin, the Arctic, and the Subarctic evolved their own diverse cultures distinct from the Mesoamerican, relying for subsistence on fishing, hunting, and gathering.

- Peoples of the Pacific Northwest boasted large populations and prosperous economies as well as an elaborate social, ceremonial, and artistic life.

- By the end of the fifteenth century, many of North America's most impressive early civilizations had collapsed.

  - Yet these cultures influenced those that succeeded them, including the Pueblos of the Southwest; the Muskogean, Iroquois, and Algonquin tribes of the Eastern Woodlands; and the Arawaks of the Caribbean basin.

- The worlds of these diverse peoples may have been poised on the brink of a cultural renaissance, because the Aztec civilization began growing rapidly beginning in the fourteenth century.

additional reading

The best descriptions of ancient American civilizations are offered by Brian M. Fagan, *Kingdoms of Gold, Kingdoms of Jade: The Americas before Columbus* (1991); and Jesse D. Jennings, ed., *Ancient North America* (1983). Francis Jennings, *The Founders of America* (1993), provides provocative coverage of the same topic, while Roger G. Kennedy, *Hidden Cities: The Discovery and Loss of Ancient North American Civilization* (1994), gives a fascinating account of how white Americans responded to encountering the ruins of ancient American cultures.

For native civilizations throughout the Americas in the fifteenth century, the best brief treatment is Alvin M. Josephy, ed., *America in 1492* (1992); On the Aztec empire specifically see Inga Clendinnen, *Aztecs: An Interpretation* (1991); and Brian M. Fagan, *The Aztecs* (1984). For exhaustive surveys of all regional cultures in North America, consult Alice B. Kehoe, *North American Indians* (1992); and William C. Sturtevant, general editor, *Handbook of North American Indians,* 20 volumes projected (1978–); Carl Waldman, *Atlas of the North American Indian* (1985), is also an excellent source of information, offering much more than good maps.

significant events

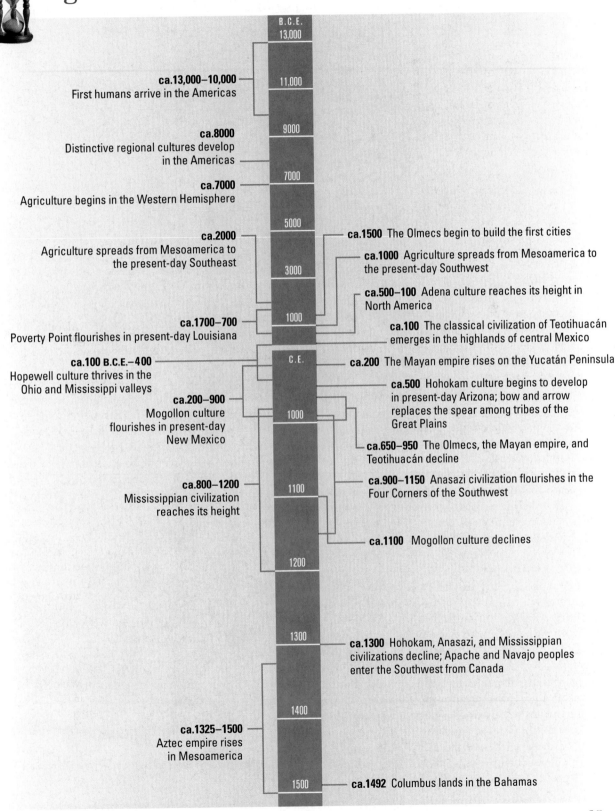

B.C.E.
13,000

11,000

ca.13,000–10,000
First humans arrive in the Americas

9000

ca.8000
Distinctive regional cultures develop
in the Americas

7000

ca.7000
Agriculture begins in the Western Hemisphere

5000

ca.1500 The Olmecs begin to build the first cities

ca.2000
Agriculture spreads from Mesoamerica to
the present-day Southeast

ca.1000 Agriculture spreads from Mesoamerica to
the present-day Southwest

3000

ca.500–100 Adena culture reaches its height in
North America

1000

ca.1700–700
Poverty Point flourishes in present-day Louisiana

ca.100 The classical civilization of Teotihuacán
emerges in the highlands of central Mexico

C.E.

ca.100 B.C.E.–400
Hopewell culture thrives in the
Ohio and Mississippi valleys

ca.200 The Mayan empire rises on the Yucatán Peninsula

ca.200–900
Mogollon culture
flourishes in present-day
New Mexico

ca.500 Hohokam culture begins to develop
in present-day Arizona; bow and arrow
replaces the spear among tribes of the
Great Plains

1000

ca.650–950 The Olmecs, the Mayan empire, and
Teotihuacán decline

ca.900–1150 Anasazi civilization flourishes in the
Four Corners of the Southwest

ca.800–1200
Mississippian civilization
reaches its height

1100

ca.1100 Mogollon culture declines

1200

1300

ca.1300 Hohokam, Anasazi, and Mississippian
civilizations decline; Apache and Navajo peoples
enter the Southwest from Canada

1400

ca.1325–1500
Aztec empire rises
in Mesoamerica

1500

ca.1492 Columbus lands in the Bahamas

Tracking the First Americans

Sometimes the most ordinary circumstances end in the most extraordinary discoveries. One of those times was a morning in 1908 when George McJunkin, an African American cowboy scanning the range near Folsom, New Mexico, for stray cattle dropped his gaze into a dry gully and spotted some large bones poking through the soil. Intrigued, he began digging and found a stone spear point lodged in the skeleton. He carried the lot back to his ranch, where they remained for the next seventeen years. Then McJunkin's curiosities somehow came to the attention of archaeologists, who identified the bones as those of a long-extinct form of bison that had ranged throughout the Southwest at least ten thousand years earlier. They realized, too, that only a spear-wielding human could have killed the bison.

That discovery rocked the scientific community, which for the previous century had confidently declared that Indians had first arrived in the Americas only about 4000 years ago. Shortly thereafter, in 1932, another shock wave followed when some amateur collectors digging at Clovis, New Mexico, unearthed bones and spearheads suspected to be even older. Finally, in 1949, scientists established the great antiquity of both finds by using "radiocarbon dating," a method for measuring decay rates of the radioactive isotope of carbon, which exists in organic matter like bone and starts to break down immediately after an organism dies. Tests revealed that the Indians whose hunting grounds were now called Folsom and Clovis had been turning bison into bones between 10,800 and 11,500 years ago.

Those conclusions pointedly raised the question of exactly how much earlier the first American an-cestors of such hunters had come to the New World. This tantalizing mystery puzzles (and divides) archaeologists and anthropologists, geologists and historians, right down to the present. Such men and women devote their lives to the hard work of digging in remote sites or exploring the ocean's floor, to the harder work of analyzing their finds in laboratories, and to the hardest work of all—trying to make sense of what it all means. Their efforts have yielded much new evidence and increasingly sophisticated techniques for understanding its significance, but many important questions still remain unanswered.

Even so, almost all of them agree on a number of points. First, whoever the first inhabitants of the New World were, they came, originally, from the

Arrowheads known as Clovis points found with the skeleton of a mammoth.

whose more limited skills had restricted their settlements to the tropical and temperate parts of the world.

The new species multiplied rapidly, and the pressure of its growing population pushed many into settling in less hospitable regions—including the Arctic frontier of Siberia in northeastern Asia. Indeed, a third point of general agreement among scholars is that the descendants of these migrants to Siberia continued the wandering ways of their ancestors and somehow, at some time, wandered into North America by way of Alaska. The research of physical anthropologists documents key biological similarities between Siberians and American Indians. Both groups share not only certain genetic variants that suggest their descent from common ancient ancestors but also distinctive formations of the roots and crowns of their teeth known as sinodonty.

But how did Asians get to Alaska—a region now separated from Siberia by fifty miles of ocean known as the Bering Strait? It is not impossible that they sailed across, for some *Homo sapiens sapiens* could build boats sturdy enough to navigate short stretches of open ocean. Archaeologists have discovered that Southeast Asians floated across 55 miles of ocean on rafts to reach Australia some

Old World: scientists have found no fossil remains to support the view that human beings evolved into modern men and women in the Americas. Second, these first Americans were almost certainly fully evolved human beings, known as *Homo sapiens sapiens*—not their less-developed forerunners, the Neanderthals, or even earlier ancestors. These *Homo sapiens sapiens* excelled at surviving anywhere, armed as they were with the intellectual ability to plan and project and the technology to sew warm clothing and to store food. About 35,000 years ago, these resourceful adapters came to predominate, edging out the Neanderthals,

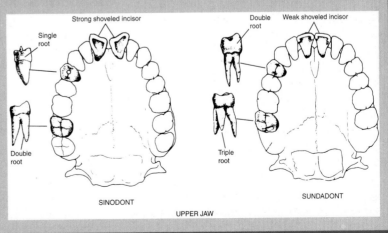

Strong shoveled incisor

Single root

Double root

SINODONT

Double root

Weak shoveled incisor

Triple root

SUNDADONT

UPPER JAW

35,000 years ago. Could their contemporaries in northeast Asia, using bark canoes, have made a voyage of similar length over the Bering Strait? Not impossible, scientists conclude, but not likely either, if only because navigating calm, tropical waters of the southern Pacific is far less difficult than mastering the Bering Strait, which even in summer is choked with ice floes. Such an undertaking would have been even more daunting to the earliest Siberians, who, as anthropologists have discovered, were land-based hunters, not seafaring folk.

So most scientists now believe that Siberians did not sail to the New World: instead, they walked. They were able to do that because the Bering Strait is not a timeless feature of Arctic geography. On the contrary, geologists have discovered, submerged far below the Bering Strait lie traces of a landmass that once connected Siberia to Alaska. Even in the late nineteenth century, some naturalists suspected that such a land bridge had once existed after noting that the vegetation and wildlife of Siberia were nearly identical to those in Alaska. By the 1930s, scientists had enough information to speculate that what turned a waterway into an exposed, inhabitable lowland plain was the coldest phase of the last Ice Age, which began about 30,000 years earlier when plunging temperatures caused the world's oceans to drop in depth by freezing great expanses of seawater into sheets of ice. Those climatic changes formed "Beringia," a land bridge between Siberia and Alaska that existed from about 25,000 B.P. (before the present) until about 15,000 B.P. During those millennia, most scientists now believe, Siberians gradually settled the

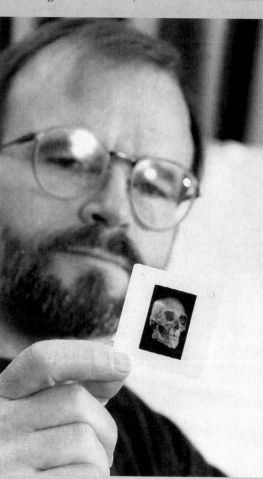

Indians of North America, ca. 1490 Dr. James Chatters, an anthropologist, found a skull approximately 9300 years old along the Columbia River in 1996. The skull's Eurasian features suggest that at least some migrants over the Bering Strait may also have been of European stock.

length of this link to the Americas. Thereafter, when temperatures began to warm again and the seas rose and closed over Beringia, some of its inhabitants strayed into Alaska.

But even today, some scientists doubt this account. True, no one has yet discovered an archaeological site in Alaska—or anywhere else in the Americas—that can be positively dated to earlier than about 15,000 B.P. Yet a few archaeologists working mainly in South America claim to have found artifacts in rock shelters dating to 30,000 B.P. Many others argue that such "finds" are the result of not human manufacture but natural processes like erosion. Then, too, those scientists who take the position that the first Americans arrived 30,000 years ago or even earlier—before the existence of the Beringia land bridge—must prove the improbable: that Siberians crossed into Alaska by sailing across the Bering Strait.

A recent discovery in the state of Washington is also prompting scientists to wonder whether the first inhabitants of the Americas might have included peoples other than Asians. In 1996, the sheriff of a small desert town, puzzled by a half-buried human skeleton found along the shores of the Columbia River, showed the bones to an anthropologist, James Chatters. Like McJunkin's find of almost a century earlier, this skeleton encased a stone spear point, and radiocarbon dating revealed it to be nearly as old (9300 years) as the Folsom bones. Also like McJunkin's specimen, this one has sparked debate within the scientific community. Chatters and others who measured the skull discovered that it was far narrower than any Indian skull of similar antiquity. They concluded—astonishingly—that the Kennewick Man, as he came to be known, was Caucasoid in appearance. Within the past thirty years, other ancient skull remains with Caucasian features have been found, but none so well preserved as the Columbia River specimen, which even has some teeth intact. It appeared to be the strongest evidence that in addition to the Siberian migrations, some people of European stock may have somehow crossed to the Americas.

But more recent comparisons of the skull with all other known ethnic groups led a panel of scientists to conclude that the Kennewick Man is not a distant relative either of present-day Indians or of Caucasians. The closest resemblance is to the Ainu people of Japan's Sakhalin Islands and to Polynesians of the South Pacific. If such a link were established, it would strengthen the hypothesis that some of the earliest Americans reached the continent by boat, either hopscotching along the Bering Strait or even sailing across the Pacific. Both the Ainu and the Polynesians were maritime peoples.

For their part, many Indians still living along the Columbia River reject all scientific explanations of their origins in favor of religious accounts—tribal creation myths which proclaim that their people have always lived in the Americas. Angered by the conduct of earlier anthropologists, who freely dug up Indian grave sites, they have demanded the right to rebury the skeleton under the terms of the Native American Graves Protection and Repatriation Act of 1990.

So the debates about America's first colonizers continue, and if recent history is any guide, so too will the discoveries. This part of the past, like every other, holds in store many surprises for those in the present determined to probe its secrets.

BIBLIOGRAPHY Keeping up with recent discoveries in this field poses many challenges. New discoveries turn up frequently, and most reports of those findings are written in a highly technical language. Fortunately, a few well-written books provide a guide to both the early Asian migration to and throughout the Americas and the evolution of scholarly debate. Brian M. Fagan, *The Great Journey* (London, 1987), is lucid, and the same author has more recently written a more detailed textbook on both ancient Native American archaeology and history, *Ancient North America* (1991). A less comprehensive but elegantly written treatment of these topics is William MacLeish's *The Day before America* (1994). Students seeking more advanced and specialized information should consult Stuart J. Fiedel, *Prehistory of the Americas* (2d ed., Cambridge, 1992). Bear in mind, too, that the science section of each Tuesday's *New York Times* regularly features articles on the ongoing research of archaeologists, anthropologists, and geologists. For the report on the Columbia River skeleton, see *The New York Times* for September 30, 1996, A12, and October 16, 1999, A12.

THE CREATION OF A NEW AMERICA

After 1492 the first Americans were no longer alone. In that year—a full 500 years ago—the civilizations of Europe and Africa first made sustained contact with those of North America. The transformations arising out of that event have been astonishing. To gain a rough sense of the scale involved, in both time and space, it is worth looking briefly not at the moment of first contact but at a vista to be glimpsed nearer the midpoint of our story: with Meriwether Lewis and William Clark in August 1805, atop the continental divide. The two men, on orders from President Thomas Jefferson, had been sent on the first American exploratory mission to report on the lands west of the Mississippi. From Lewis and Clark's vantage point, high in the Rocky Mountains, what can we see?

At first glance we see largely what we expect: a seemingly endless land stretching from sea to sea. But living as we do in the twenty-first century, we tend to take for granted that the country spread before us will be united under a single national government. Only hindsight makes this proposition seem natural. In 1800 the sheer size of the land made the notion of political unity difficult to grasp, for the United States themselves remained a group of colonies only recently unified. And the lands west of the Mississippi were still controlled primarily by scores of independent Indian nations.

The methods that Lewis and Clark used to communicate underscore the wide variety of North American cultures that we have already surveyed. With no common language spanning the territory, speech making for the voyagers became a series of translations that reflected the route over which the party had traveled. In present-day Idaho, Clark addressed the Tushepaw tribe in English. His speech was translated into French by a trapper in the party; then a second trapper translated into Minataree, a language that his Indian wife, Sacajawea, understood. Sacajawea, the only female member of the party, had grown up farther west with the Shoshone, so she in turn translated the Minataree into Shoshone, which a boy from the Tushepaw nation understood. He translated the Shoshone into his own people's tongue.

If the territory that Lewis and Clark crossed seemed a patchwork of governments and cultures, the young "United States" appeared nearly as heterogeneous. Dutch-speaking patroons could be found along New York's Hudson River, Welsh and German farmers along Pennsylvania's Lancaster Pike, Swedes in Delaware, Gaelic-speaking Scots scattered through the Appalachian backcountry, African Americans speaking the Gullah dialect along the Carolina coast. In 1800 many of these settlers knew more about their homelands in Europe or Africa than they did about other regions of North America.

Thus our first task in studying the American past becomes one of translation. We must view events not with the jaded eyes of

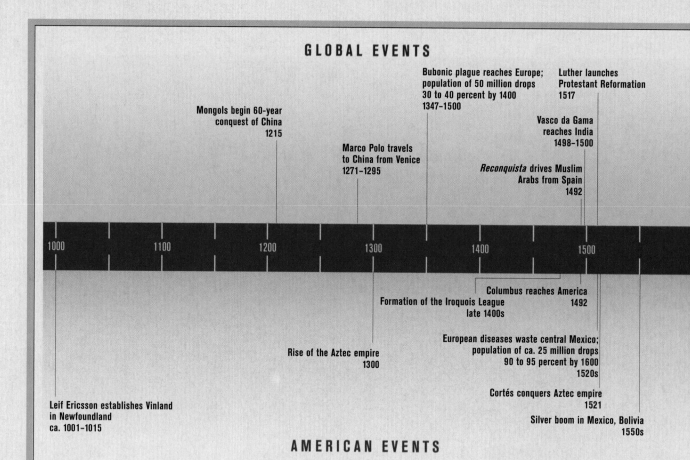

GLOBAL EVENTS

- Mongols begin 60-year conquest of China 1215
- Marco Polo travels to China from Venice 1271–1295
- Bubonic plague reaches Europe; population of 50 million drops 30 to 40 percent by 1400 1347–1500
- *Reconquista* drives Muslim Arabs from Spain 1492
- Vasco da Gama reaches India 1498–1500
- Luther launches Protestant Reformation 1517

1000   1100   1200   1300   1400   1500

- Leif Ericsson establishes Vinland in Newfoundland ca. 1001–1015
- Rise of the Aztec empire 1300
- Formation of the Iroquois League late 1400s
- Columbus reaches America 1492
- European diseases waste central Mexico; population of ca. 25 million drops 90 to 95 percent by 1600 1520s
- Cortés conquers Aztec empire 1521
- Silver boom in Mexico, Bolivia 1550s

AMERICAN EVENTS

the late twentieth century but with the fresh eyes of an earlier era. Then the foregone conclusions vanish. How does the American nation manage to unite millions of square miles of territory into one governable republic? How do New York and San Francisco (a city not even in existence in Lewis and Clark's day) come to be linked in a complex economy as well as in a single political system? Such questions take on even more significance when we recall that Europe—roughly the same size as the United States—is today still divided into more than four dozen independent nations speaking some 33 languages, not to mention another 100 or so spoken within the former Soviet Union. A united Europe has not

emerged and, indeed, seems even farther away after the momentous breakup of the Soviet empire.

How, then, did this American republic—this "teeming nation of nations," to use Walt Whitman's

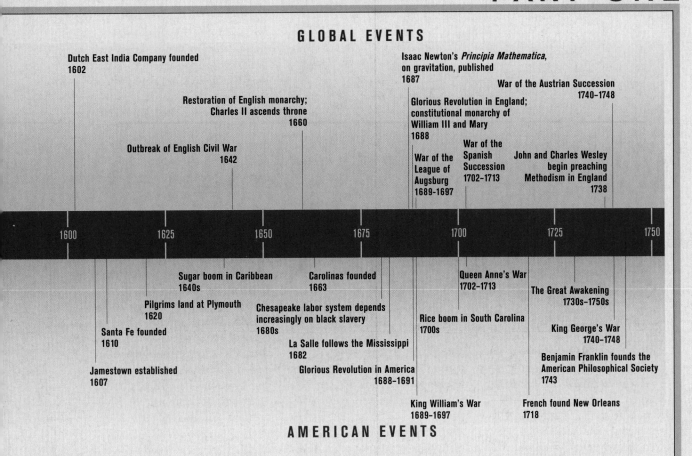

GLOBAL EVENTS

Dutch East India Company founded
1602

Isaac Newton's *Principia Mathematica*,
on gravitation, published
1687

War of the Austrian Succession
1740–1748

Restoration of English monarchy;
Charles II ascends throne
1660

Glorious Revolution in England;
constitutional monarchy of
William III and Mary
1688

Outbreak of English Civil War
1642

War of the
League of
Augsburg
1689–1697

War of the
Spanish
Succession
1702–1713

John and Charles Wesley
begin preaching
Methodism in England
1738

| 1600 | 1625 | 1650 | 1675 | 1700 | 1725 | 1750 |

Sugar boom in Caribbean
1640s

Carolinas founded
1663

Queen Anne's War
1702–1713

The Great Awakening
1730s–1750s

Pilgrims land at Plymouth
1620

Chesapeake labor system depends
increasingly on black slavery
1680s

Rice boom in South Carolina
1700s

King George's War
1740–1748

Santa Fe founded
1610

La Salle follows the Mississippi
1682

Benjamin Franklin founds the
American Philosophical Society
1743

Jamestown established
1607

Glorious Revolution in America
1688–1691

King William's War
1689–1697

French found New Orleans
1718

AMERICAN EVENTS

phrase—come to be? In barest outline, that is the question that drives our narrative across half a millennium.

The problem looms even larger as we move toward the beginning of our story. In 1450, about the time Christopher Columbus was born, Europeans were only beginning to expand westward. To be sure, Scandinavian seafarers led by Leif Ericsson had reached the northern reaches of the Americas, planting a settlement in Newfoundland around 1000 C.E. But news of Vinland, as Leif called his colony, never reached most of Europe. The site was soon abandoned and forgotten. In Columbus's day localism still held sway. Italy was divided into five major states and an equal number of smaller

territories. The Germanic peoples were united loosely in the Holy Roman Empire. French kings ruled over only about half of what is now France. Spain was divided into several kingdoms, with some areas held by Christians and others by Islamic Moors, whose forebears came from Africa. England, a contentious little nation, was beginning a series of bitter civil conflicts among the nobility, known eventually as the Wars of the Roses.

Localism was also evident in the patterns of European trade. Goods moving overland were usually carried by wheeled carts or pack animals over rutted paths. Along rivers and canals, lords repeatedly taxed boats that crossed their territories. On the

Seine River, greedy tollkeepers lay in wait every six or seven miles. Travel across the Mediterranean Sea and along Europe's northern coastlines was possible, but storms and pirates made the going dangerous and slow. Under good conditions a ship might reach London from Venice in only 9 days; under bad it might take 50.

European peoples at this time had limited but continuous dealings with Africa, mostly along the Mediterranean Sea. There, North African culture had been shaped since the seventh century by the religion of Islam, whose influence spread as well into Spain. Below the Sahara desert the Bantu, an agricultural people, had migrated over the course of 2000 years from their West African homeland to

PART ONE

establish societies throughout the continent. The tempo of these migrations increased as the Bantu learned to produce iron and—equally important—introduced bananas into their diet after the plants were imported to Africa and Asia around 300 to 500 C.E. As a result, the sub-Saharan African population rose sharply from around 11 million at the beginning of the first millennium C.E. to more than 22 million at the end of it.

Traditionally, Bantu agricultural societies governed themselves through family and kinship groups, clustered in villages of around a hundred people and linked with nearby villages in a district. But larger political states developed in response to the arrival of Muslim trading caravans penetrating the Sahara desert beginning around 800 C.E. The first was Ghana, a kingdom that flourished in the eleventh and twelfth centuries. It was followed in the thirteenth century by the even larger Mali empire. Mali's princes controlled almost all the considerable trade in gold, ivory, and slaves, sending and receiving desert caravans that boasted as many as 25,000 camels. Yet Mali too was split by factions from within and military challenges from without. By the 1490s the Songhai empire had replaced Mali as the most important centralized kingdom in West Africa.

In 1490 these three worlds—Europe, Africa, the Americas—remained largely separate from one another. Europe's fleeting encounter with North America had long been forgotten; the empires of interior Africa remained unvisited by Europeans and largely unknown. Only Portugal had begun to explore the West African coast by sea. Yet currents of change would soon bring these three worlds together in vibrant and creative as well as violent and chaotic ways. What social and economic forces spurred so many Europeans—desperate and opportunistic, high-minded and idealistic—to turn west to the Americas in pursuit of their dreams? How did the civilizations of North and South America react to the European invaders? And not least, how did the mix of cultures from Africa, Europe, and North America come together to create what was truly a new America, in which some of the most independent-minded individuals prospered in provinces that exhibited some of the harshest examples of human slavery? These are among the questions we seek to answer as our narrative unfolds.

Chapter 1

A ll the world lay before them. Or so it seemed to mariners from England's seafaring coasts, pushing westward toward unknown lands in the far Atlantic.

The scent of the new land came first—not the sight of it, but the smells, wafted from beyond the horizon, delicious to sailors who had felt nothing but the rolling sea for weeks on end. In northerly latitudes around June, it would be the scent of fir trees or the sight of shore birds wheeling about the masts. Straightaway the captain would call for a lead to be thrown overboard to sound the depths. At its end was a hollowed-out socket with a bit of tallow in it, so some of the sea bottom would stick when the lead was hauled up. Even out of sight of land, a good sailing master could tell where he was by what came up—"oosy sand" or perhaps "soft worms" or "popplestones as big as beans." If the ship was approaching unknown shores, the captain would hope to sight land early in the day, allowing time to work cautiously toward an untried harbor on uncharted tides.

Since the time of King Arthur, the English living along the rugged southwestern coasts of Devon and Cornwall had followed the sea. From the wharves of England's West Country seaports like Bristol, ships headed west and north to Ireland, bringing back animal hides as well as timber for houses and barrels. Or they turned south, fetching wines from France and olive oil or figs and raisins from the Spanish and Portuguese coasts. In return, West Country ports offered woven woolen cloth and codfish, caught wherever the best prospects beckoned.

Through much of the fifteenth century the search for cod drew West Country sailors north and west, toward Iceland. In the 1480s and 1490s, however, a few English tried their luck farther west. Old maps, after all, claimed that the bountiful *Hy-Brasil*—Gaelic for "Isle of the Blessed"—lay somewhere west of Ireland. These western ventures returned with little to show for their daring until the coming of an Italian named Giovanni Caboto, called John Cabot by the English. Cabot, who hailed from Venice, obtained the blessing of King Henry VII to hunt for unknown lands. From the port of Bristol his lone ship set out to the west in the spring of 1497.

This time the return voyage brought news of a "new-found" island where the trees were tall enough to make fine masts and the codfish were plentiful. After returning to Bristol, Cabot marched off to London to inform His Majesty, received 10 pounds as his reward, and with the proceeds dressed himself in dashing silks. The multitudes of London flocked after him, wondering over "the Admiral"; then Cabot returned triumphantly to Bristol to undertake a more ambitious search for a northwest passage to Asia. He set sail with five ships in 1498 and was never heard from again.

Old World, New Worlds

1400–1600

preview • In the century after 1492, Europeans expanded boldly and often ruthlessly into the Americas, thanks to a combination of technological advances in sailing and firearms, the rise of new trading networks, and stronger, more centralized governments. Spain established a vast and profitable empire but at fearful human cost. A diverse Mesoamerican population of some 20 million was reduced to only 2 million through warfare, European diseases, and exploitation.

Cabot discovers
Newfoundland

During the sixteenth century, West Country fisherfolk from England sailed from harbors like Plymouth, shown here. Such seaports were small; the fortifications dotting the coastline and a wall around the town itself were used to defend against invaders.

By the 1550s Cabot's island, now known as Newfoundland, attracted 400 vessels annually, fishermen not only from England but also from France, Portugal, and Spain. The trip was not easy. Individual merchants or a few partners outfitted small ships with provisions, fishing boats, and guns to ward off sea-roving pirates. As early in the season as they dared, crews of 10 or 20 would catch the spring easterlies, watching as familiar roofs and primitive lighthouses burning smoky coal sank beneath the horizon.

The fishing season

Weeks after setting sail the sailors sighted Newfoundland's fog-shrouded beaches. Seals and walruses played along the rocks offshore, and the encircling sea teemed with cod and flounder, salmon and herring. Throughout the summer men launched little boats from each harbor and fished offshore all day and into the night. With lines and nets and baskets weighted with stones, they scooped fish from the sea and then dried and salted the catch on the beach. In odd hours, sailors traded with the native Indians, who shared their summer fishing grounds and the skins of fox and deer.

The harbor of present-day St. John's, Newfoundland, served as the informal hub of the North Atlantic fishery. Portuguese, English, and French vessels all dropped anchor there, either to take on supplies in the spring or to prepare for the homeward voyage in autumn. Besides trading, there was much talking, for these seafarers knew as much as anyone about the new world of wonders that was opening to Europeans. They were acquainted with names like Cristoforo Colombo, the Italian from Genoa whom Cabot might have known as a boy. They listened to Portuguese tales of sailing around the Horn of Africa in pursuit of spices and to stories of Indian empires to the south, rich in gold and silver that Spanish treasure ships were bringing home.

Indeed, Newfoundland was one of the few places in the world where so many ordinary folk of different nations could gather and talk, crammed aboard dank

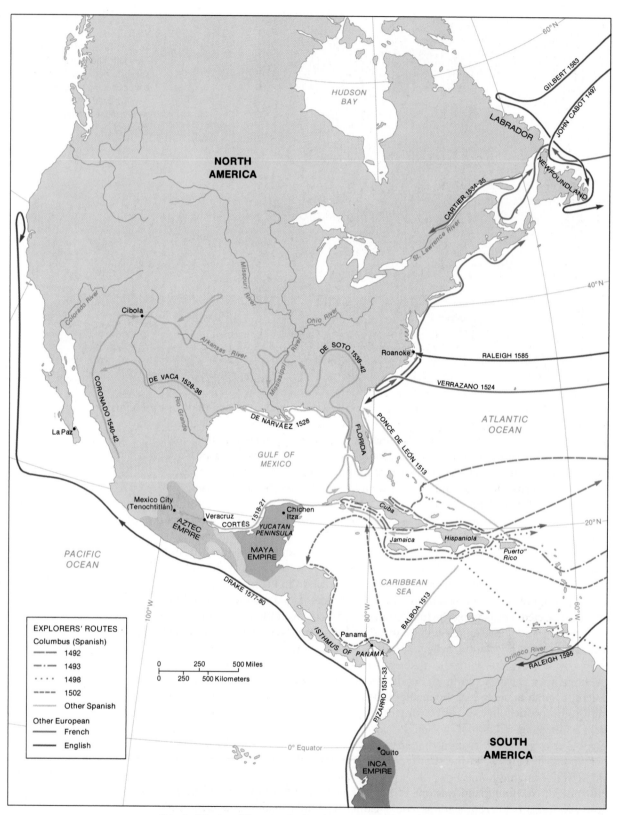

EXPLORERS' ROUTES
Columbus (Spanish)
- – – – 1492
- –·– ·– 1493
- ········ 1498
- – – – – 1502
- ———— Other Spanish

Other European
- ———— French
- ———— English

0   250   500 Miles
0   250   500 Kilometers

Principal Routes of European Exploration

ships moored in St. John's harbor, huddled before blazing fires on its beaches, or crowded into smoky makeshift taverns. When the ships sailed home in autumn, the tales went with them, repeated in the tiniest coastal villages by those pleased to have cheated death and the sea one more time. Eager to fish, talk, trade, and take profits, West Country mariners were almost giddy at the prospect of Europe's expanding horizons.

The Meeting of Europe, Africa, and America

Most seafarers who fished the waters of Newfoundland's Grand Banks remain unknown today. Yet it is well to begin with these ordinary fisherfolk, for the European discovery of the Americas cannot be looked upon simply as the voyages of a few bold explorers. Adventurers like Christopher Columbus and John Cabot were only the most visible representatives of a much larger expansion of European peoples and culture that began in the 1450s. That expansion arose out of a series of gradual but telling changes in the fabric of European society—changes that were reflected in the lives of ordinary seafarers as much as in the careers of explorers decked out in flaming silks.

Some of these changes were technological, arising out of advances in the arts of navigating and shipbuilding and the use of gunpowder. Some were economic, involving the development of trade networks like those linking Bristol with ports in Iceland and Spain. Some were demographic, bringing about a rise in Europe's population after a devastating century of plague. Other changes were religious, adding a dimension of devout belief to the political rivalries that fueled discoveries in the Americas. Yet others were political, making it possible for kingdoms to centralize and extend their influence across the ocean. Portugal, Spain, France, and England—all possessing coasts along the Atlantic—led the way in exploration, spurred on by Italian "admirals" like Caboto and Colombo, Spanish "conquistadors" like Hernando Cortés and Francisco Pizarro, and English sea dogs like Humphrey Gilbert and Walter Raleigh. Ordinary folk rode these currents too. The great and the small alike were propelled by forces that were remolding the face of Europe.

Changes in European society

The Portuguese Wave

In 1450 all the world known to western Europeans was Asia and Africa. Most sailors traveled only along the coast of western Europe, following the shores between Norway and the southern tip of Spain, seldom daring to lose sight of land. Beginning in the fifteenth century, bolder seafarers groped down the coast of western Africa, half expecting to be boiled alive in the Atlantic as they approached the equator. Europeans had traded with Asia through the Muslims of the eastern Mediterranean and across an overland route called the "Silk Road." But they had only vague notions about "the Indies"—China and Japan, the Spice Islands, and the lands lying between Thailand and India. What little they knew, they had learned mainly from Marco Polo, whose account of his travels in the East was not published until 1477, more than 150 years after his death.

But a revolution in European geography began in the middle decades of the fifteenth century, as widening networks of travel and trade connected Europeans to civilizations beyond western Europe. The Portuguese took the lead, encouraged by Prince Henry, known as the Navigator. The devout Henry, a member of

Revolution in geography

Portugal's royal family, had heard tales of Prester John, a Catholic priest rumored to rule a Christian kingdom somewhere beyond the Muslim kingdoms of Africa and Asia. Henry dreamed of joining forces with Prester John and trapping the Muslims in a vise. To that end, he helped finance a series of expeditions down the coast of West Africa. He founded an informal school of navigation on the Portuguese coast, supplying shipmasters with information about wind and currents, as well as navigational charts.

Portuguese merchants, who may or may not have believed in Prester John, never doubted that there was money to be made in Africa. They invested in Prince Henry's voyages in return for trading monopolies of ivory and slaves, grain and gold. A few may have hoped that the voyages down the coast of West Africa would lead to a direct sea route to the Orient. By discovering such a route, Portugal would be able to cut out the Muslim merchants who funneled all the Asian trade in silks, spices, dyes, drugs, and perfumes through Mediterranean ports.

The Portuguese focus on Africa and Asia

While Portugal's merchants were establishing trading posts along the west coast of Africa, its mariners were discovering islands in the Atlantic: the Canaries, Madeira, and the Azores. Settlers planted sugarcane and imported slaves from Africa to work their fields. The Portuguese might have pressed even farther west but for the daring of Bartholomeu Dias. In 1488 Dias rounded the Cape of Good Hope on the southern tip of Africa, sailing far enough up that continent's eastern coast to claim discovery of a sea route to India. Ten years later Vasco da Gama reached India itself, and Portuguese interests ultimately extended to Indochina and China. With the trade of Africa and Asia to occupy them, they showed less interest in exploring the Atlantic.

This stately ivory mask made by an African artist in the early sixteenth century for the Court of Benin (present-day Nigeria) is adorned with 10 bearded heads of white men, representing Portuguese explorers and traders who had first arrived in Benin in 1472.

By 1500, all of seafaring Europe sought the services of Portuguese pilots, prizing their superior maps and skills with the quadrant. That instrument made it possible to determine latitude fairly accurately, allowing ships to plot their position after months out of the sight of land. The Portuguese had also pioneered the caravel, a lighter, more maneuverable ship that could sail better against contrary winds and in rough seas. More seaworthy than the lumbering galleys of the Middle Ages, caravels combined longer, narrower hulls—a shape built for speed—with triangular lateen sails, which allowed for more flexible steering.

Despite its focus on the Indies, Portugal continued to dominate trade along Africa's west coast. And the farther south the Portuguese extended their influence along the Atlantic rim of sub-Saharan Africa, the more likely they were to meet with native peoples who had had no earlier encounters with Europeans and, indeed, had no knowledge of the existence of other continents. On catching their first sight of a Portuguese expedition in 1455, the inhabitants of one village on the Senegal River marveled at the strangers' clothing and their white skin. As an Italian member of that expedition recounted, some Africans "rubbed me with their spittle to discover whether my whiteness was dye or flesh." Equally astonishing were the Portuguese ships and weapons, especially their deadly cannon and muskets. While some Africans concluded that these white newcomers must surely be either wizards or cannibals, dangerous men who should be either shunned or killed, others eagerly enlisted Europeans as military allies and trading partners, hoping to gain both power and practical knowledge.

This African fortune-teller reads the palm of her white client in this seventeenth-century painting by a Franco-Flemish artist, Nicolas Regnier. In early modern Europe, class and religion were more important in defining social divisions than color and ethnicity. Slaves, servants, and free workers of all races often worked and socialized together.

The debate among West Africans about whether to resist or accommodate the new European presence grew sharper as the interest of Portuguese traders in purchasing slaves increased. Before the end of the fifteenth century, most slaves in Europe were white, but among slaves of color, whether black or of mixed race (mulattoes), most were Muslims of North African ancestry and their numbers were concentrated in the Mediterranean. After the 1480s, however, darker-skinned, non-Muslim men and women from all along the west coast of Africa began to appear in greater numbers among the ranks of slaves and servants, as well as among craft-workers and musicians everywhere in western Europe, even as far north as the Netherlands and England. Their presence was most pronounced in Portugal and Spain: by the middle of the sixteenth century, people of African descent accounted for 10 percent of the population of Lisbon, Portugal's capital city.

Even so, the slave trade to the Atlantic islands and western Europe opened by the Portuguese at the end of the fifteenth century was small in scale compared with what was to come. The Atlantic slave trade did not take its full toll on Africa until Spain had made a much greater mark on the Americas.

The Spanish and Columbus

From among the international community of seafarers and pilots, it was a sailor from Genoa, Cristoforo Colombo, who led the Spanish to the Americas. Columbus (the Latinized version of his name survives) had knocked about in a number of harbors, picking up valuable navigation skills by sailing Portugal's merchant ships to Madeira, West Africa, and the North Atlantic. In the Irish port of Galway, Columbus saw two boats drift into the harbor, bearing the dead bodies of "a man and a woman of extraordinary appearance." Most likely they were Lapps or Finns, the victims of a shipwreck. But everyone in Galway, including Columbus, assumed that they were Chinese, "blown across" the Atlantic.

His experiences convinced Columbus that the quickest route to the Indies lay west, across the Atlantic—and that his destiny was to prove it. Perhaps a mere 4500 miles, he reckoned, separated Europe from Japan. His wishful estimate raised eyebrows whenever Columbus asked European monarchs for the money to meet his destiny. Most educated Europeans agreed that the world was round, but they also believed that the Atlantic barrier between themselves and Asia was far wider than Columbus allowed and that it was impossible to navigate. The kings of England, France, and Portugal dismissed him as a crackpot.

The *reconquista*

Almost a decade of rejection had grayed Columbus's red hair when Spain's monarchs, Ferdinand and Isabella, finally agreed to subsidize his expedition in 1492. For the past 20 years they had worked to drive the Muslims out of their last stronghold on the Iberian peninsula, the Moorish kingdom of Granada. In 1492 they completed this *reconquista,* or battle of reconquest, expelling many Jews as well. Yet the Portuguese, by breaking the Muslim stranglehold on trade with Asia, had taken the lead in the competition to smite the Islamic powers. Ferdinand and Isabella were so desperate to even the score with Portugal that jealousy overcame common sense: they agreed to take a risk on Columbus.

Columbus's first voyage across the Atlantic could only have confirmed his conviction that he was destiny's darling. His three ships, no bigger than fishing vessels that sailed to Newfoundland, plied their course over placid seas, south from Seville to the Canary Islands and then due west. A little more than two months after leaving Spain, on October 11, branches, leaves, and flowers floated by their hulls, signals that land lay near. Just after midnight, a sailor spied cliffs shining white in the moonlight. On the morning of October 12, the *Niña,* the *Pinta,* and the *Santa Maria* set anchor in a shallow sapphire bay, and their crews knelt on the white coral beach. Columbus christened the place San Salvador (Holy Savior).

Like many men of destiny, Columbus did not recognize his true destination. At first he confused his actual location, the Bahamas, with an island off the coast of Japan. He coasted along Cuba and Hispaniola (Haiti), expecting at any moment to catch sight of gold-roofed Japanese temples or to happen upon a fleet of Chinese junks. He encountered instead a gentle, generous people who knew nothing of the Great Khan but who showed him their islands. Columbus's journals note that they wore little clothing (see Daily Lives: "Barbaric" Dress—Indian and European, pages 46–47), but they did wear jewelry—tiny pendants of gold suspended from the nose. He dubbed the Arawak people "Indians"—inhabitants of the Indies.

The four voyages of Columbus

Columbus crossed the Atlantic three more times between 1493 and 1504. On his second voyage he established a permanent colony at Hispaniola and explored other Caribbean islands. On his third voyage he reached Venezuela on the continent of South America, and on his last sailing he made landfalls throughout Central America. Everywhere he looked for proof that these lands formed part of Asia.

Columbus died rich in titles, treasure, and tales—everything but recognition. During the last decade of his life, most Spaniards no longer believed that Columbus had discovered the Indies or anyplace else of significance. And shortly after his death in 1506, another Italian stamped his own name on the New World. Amerigo Vespucci, a Florentine banker with a flair for self-promotion, cruised the coast of Brazil in 1501 and again in 1503. His sensational report of his travels misled a German mapmaker into crediting Vespucci with discovering the barrier between Europe and Asia, and so naming it "America."

Europe in the age of discovery was a world graced by the courage of explorers like Columbus and the genius of

The European Background of American Colonization

artists like Michelangelo. It was also a world riddled with war, disease, and uncertainty. In 1450 the continent was still recovering from the ravages of the Black Death, an epidemic of the bubonic plague. Under such vibrant, often chaotic conditions, a sense of crisis was mixed with a sense of possibility. Indeed, it was this blend of desperation and ambition that made the newly discovered Americas so attractive to Europeans. Here were strange and distant lands like the island paradises spoken of in legends, like that of the fabled kingdom of Atlantis. Here were opportunities and riches for the daring to grasp. Here were salvation and security for those escaping a world full of violence and sin or oppressed by disease and poverty.

Life and Death in Early Modern Europe

During the fourteenth and the fifteenth centuries 90 percent of Europe's people, widely dispersed in small villages, made their living from the land. But warfare, poor transportation, and low grain yields all created food shortages, and undernourishment produced a population prone to disease. Under these circumstances life was nasty, brutish, and usually short. One-quarter of all children died in the first year of life. People who reached the ripe age of 40 counted themselves fortunate.

It was also a world of sharp inequalities, where nobles and aristocrats enjoyed several hundred times the income of peasants or craftworkers. It was a world with no strong, centralized political authority, where kings were weak and warrior lords held sway over small towns and tiny fiefdoms. It was a world of hierarchy and dependence, where the upper classes provided land and protection for the lower orders. It was a world of violence and sudden death, where homicide, robbery, and rape occurred with brutal frequency. It was a world where security and order of any kind seemed so fragile that most people clung to tradition and feared change.

Into that world in 1347 came the Black Death. In only four years that plague swept away one-third of Europe's population, disrupting both agriculture and commerce. For the next century, recurring outbreaks created additional social disruption and economic depression. Yet the sudden drop in population restored the balance between people and resources. Survivors of the Black Death found that the relative scarcity of workers and consumers made for better wages, lower prices, and more land.

But by the time Columbus reached America, nearly 150 years after the outbreak of the Black Death, Europe again confronted its old problem. Too many people were again competing for a limited supply of food and land. Throughout the sixteenth century diets became poorer, land and work less available, crime and beggary more common. Inflation compounded these problems when prices doubled at the end of the fifteenth century and then quadrupled between 1520 and 1590. To

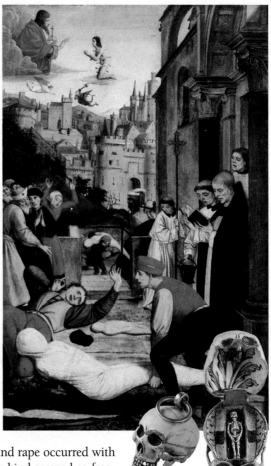

St. Sebastian Interceding for the Plague-Stricken City captures the desperation of Europeans during an outbreak of the Black Death. At the top, St. Sebastian, a Christian martyr, intercedes with God to end the suffering. This skull pendant, dating from the 1600s, opens to reveal a skeleton in a coffin. The popularity of this jewelry points up how deeply early modern Europeans were preoccupied with death.

keep pace with the "Price Revolution," landlords raised rents, adding to the burden of the peasantry.

To Europe's hopeful and desperate alike, this climate of disorder and uncertainty led to dreams that the New World would provide an opportunity to renew the Old. As Columbus wrote eagerly of Hispaniola: "This island and all others are very fertile to a limitless degree. . . . There are very large tracts of cultivated land. . . . In the interior there are mines and metals." Columbus and many other Europeans expected that the Americas would provide land for the landless, work for the unemployed, and wealth beyond the wildest dreams of the daring.

The Conditions of Colonization

Sixteenth-century Europeans sought to colonize the Americas, not merely to escape from scarcity and disruption at home. They were also propelled across the Atlantic by dynamic changes in their society. Revolutions in technology, economics, and politics made overseas settlement practical and attractive to seekers of profit and power.

Expansion of trade and capital

The improvements in navigation and sailing also fostered an expansion of trade. By the late fifteenth century Europe's merchants and bankers had devised more efficient ways of transferring money and establishing credit in order to support commerce across longer distances. And although rising prices and rents pinched Europe's peasantry, that same inflation enriched those who had goods to sell, money to lend, and land to rent. Wealth flowed into the coffers of sixteenth-century traders, financiers, and landlords, creating a pool of capital that those investors could plow into colonial development. Both the commercial networks and the private fortunes needed to sustain overseas trade and settlement were in place by the time of Columbus's discovery.

Political centralization

The direction of Europe's political development also paved the path for American colonization. After 1450 strong monarchs in Europe steadily enlarged the sphere of royal power at the expense of warrior lords. Henry VII, the founder of England's Tudor dynasty, Francis I of France, and Ferdinand and Isabella of Spain began the trend, forging modern nation-states by extending their political control over more territory, people, and resources. Those larger, more centrally organized states were able to marshal the resources necessary to support colonial outposts and to sustain the professional armies and navies capable of protecting empires abroad.

Europeans, Chinese, and Aztecs on the Eve of Contact

It was the growing power of monarchs as well as commercial and technological development that allowed early modern Europeans to establish permanent settlements—even empires—in another world lying an ocean away. But that conclusion raises an intriguing question: why didn't China, the most advanced civilization of the early modern world, engage in expansion and colonization? Or for that matter, if events had fallen out a little differently, why didn't the Aztecs discover and colonize Europe?

The Chinese undoubtedly possessed the capability to navigate the world's oceans and to establish overseas settlements. A succession of Ming dynasty emperors and their efficient bureaucrats marshaled China's resources to develop a thriving shipbuilding industry and trade with ports throughout southeast Asia and India. By the opening of the fifteenth century, the Chinese seemed poised for even greater maritime exploits. Seven times between 1405 and 1433, China's "treasure fleet"—300 ships manned by 28,000 sailors and commanded by Zheng He (pro-nounced "Jung Huh")—unfurled their red silk sails off the south China coast and sailed as far as the kingdoms of eastern Africa. The treasure fleet's largest craft were nine-masted junks measuring 400 feet long that boasted multiple decks and lux-ury cabins with balconies. In contrast, when Columbus's three ships set sail to find the Indies, the biggest was a mere 85 feet long, and the crew aboard all three totaled just 90 men.

Zheng He could have been another Columbus, given the resources available to him. But the Chinese had little incentive either to seek out the world's trade or to conquer and colonize new territories. Unlike western Europeans, they faced no shortages of land or food, and they led the world in producing luxury goods. On the other hand, China faced the threat of attack from the Mongols on its north-western border—a threat so pressing that in 1433 the Ming emperor mobilized all the country's wealth and warriors to fend it off. Thus ended the great era of Chinese maritime expansion. All foreign trade was suspended, and Zheng He's treasure fleet, which would remain the world's most impressive navy until the beginning of the twentieth century, rotted away in the ports of southern China.

Why China did not explore farther

As for the Aztecs, their cultural development paralleled that of early modern Europe in many ways. Both societies were predominantly rural, with most inhab-itants living in small villages and engaging in agriculture. In both places, merchants and specialized craftworkers clustered in cities, organized themselves into guilds, and clamored for protection from the government. Aztec noble and priestly classes, like those in Europe, took the lead in politics and religion, demanding tribute from the common people. Finally, both societies were robustly expansionist, bent on bringing new lands and peoples under their control.

Yet despite their formidable talents, the Aztecs lacked the knowledge of ocean navigation. Equally important, Aztec rulers had not established their sovereign authority over powerful nobles. The absence of a strong, centralized power made it impossible for the Aztecs to launch a more ambitious expansion. Although their armies put down disturbances in conquered territories and protected trade routes, the Aztecs had not developed the resources to impose their way of life on other places. Instead, conquered city-states within the Aztec empire retained their dis-tinctive languages and customs—and bitterly resented Aztec rule. The result was an empire vulnerable to division from within and to attack from abroad.

Barriers to Aztec colonization

By the reckoning of the Aztecs it was the year 12-House—a time, they believed,

Spain's Empire in the New World

when the fate of the whole world hung by a thread. According to their calendar, a 52-year cycle had come to an end. Now the gods might extinguish the sun with a flood or a great wind. The end of this particular cycle had been marked with a chilling omen. In one of the canals, fishermen caught a bird "the color of ashes" with a strange mirror in the crown of its head. They brought the creature to their ruler, Moctezuma II, who looked in the mirror and saw ranks of men mounted on animals resembling deer and moving across a plain.

Two years later, the Aztecs' worst fears were fulfilled. Dust rose in whirlwinds on the roads from the hooves of horses and the boots of men in battle array. "It was as if the earth trembled beneath them, or as if the world were spinning . . . as it spins during a fit of vertigo," one Aztec scribe recorded. This was no image in a magic mirror: Hernando Cortés and his army of Spaniards were marching on Tenochtitlán. By Cortés's calculations, it was A.D. 1519.

Spanish Conquest

Balboa and Magellan

To Cortés and the other Spanish explorers who had followed Columbus across the Atlantic, a new and remarkable world was opening. By 1513 the Spanish had explored and mastered the Caribbean basin. Also in 1513, Vasco Núñez de Balboa crossed the Isthmus of Panama and glimpsed the Pacific Ocean. North and South America were revealed as continents of vast size, separated from Asia by another ocean. And Ferdinand Magellan finally did reach the Orient by sailing west across the immense Pacific. After his death in the Philippines in 1521, Magellan's shipmates completed the first circumnavigation of the globe.

From their bases in the islands of the Caribbean, the Spanish pressed outward. To the north they met mostly with disappointment. Juan Ponce de León vainly scoured the shores of the Florida peninsula for the fabled "Fountain of Youth" as well as Indian populations he might enslave to work the gold mines of the Caribbean. Several decades later, Hernando de Soto plundered his way through Florida and into the southeastern interior as far west as the Mississippi River. Between 1540 and 1542 Francisco Vásquez de Coronado moved through Arizona, New Mexico, Texas, Oklahoma, and Kansas. But reports of fantastic cities of gold proved to be merely the stuff of dreams.

Cortés conquers the Aztecs

During these same decades, however, the Spanish found golden opportunities elsewhere. Those who had first rushed to Hispaniola immediately started scouring the island for gold—and enslaving Indians to work the mines. As for Cortés, when Moctezuma's ambassadors met him on the road to Tenochtitlán in 1519 and attempted to appease him with gold ornaments and other gifts, an Indian witness recorded, "the Spaniards . . . picked up the gold and fingered it like monkeys. . . . Their bodies swelled with greed." For nearly half a year Cortés dominated the indecisive Moctezuma by imprisoning him in his own capital. The Aztecs drove the Spanish out after Moctezuma's death, but Cortés returned with reinforcements, set siege to Tenochtitlán, and in 1521 conquered it. The Aztec empire lay in ruins.

Role of the Conquistadors

To the conquistadors—a motley lot of minor nobles, landless gentlemen, and professional soldiers—the newfound land seemed more than a golden opportunity. They resented the Spanish monarchy's growing strength at home and aimed to re-create in the New World a much older world of their own dreaming. Like medieval knights, Cortés and other conquistadors hoped to establish themselves as a powerful nobility that would enjoy virtual independence from the Spanish Crown an ocean away.

For a time the conquistadors succeeded. By the 1540s Cortés and just 1500 men had taken all of Mexico and the southwestern portion of North America. During the 1530s the ruthless Pizarro brothers and an even smaller band of conquistadors sailed along South America's Pacific coast and overthrew the Incas in Peru, an Andean civilization as impressive as that of the Aztecs. They also laid claim to Ecuador, Chile, Argentina, and Bolivia.

Reasons for Spain's success

How did a handful of gentlemen heading a rabble of soldiers, seamen, and criminals bring down sophisticated Indian empires in the span of a generation? To begin with, the Spanish enjoyed the edge of surprise and technological superiority. The sight of ships and the explosion of guns at first terrified the Indians, as did men on horseback whom some Indians, at first, took to be single creatures.

Both the Aztecs and the Spanish tried to understand the new in terms of the familiar. Hence an Aztec artist portrayed Cortés as an Indian with strange clothes and stranger beard (left), while a European artist depicted Moctezuma in the style of a Greco-Roman warrior (right).

The only domesticated animals known to the Aztecs were small dogs; the Spanish provided them with their first glimpse of horses and, later, cattle, sheep, oxen, pigs, goats, donkeys, mules, and chickens.

What delivered a more lasting shock to Indian civilizations was exposure to European infections. Smallpox, influenza, typhus, and measles, disease strains against which the Indians had developed no biological resistance, ravaged entire villages and tribes. Tenochtitlán surrendered to Cortés after a siege of 85 days, during which many died from starvation but many more died of smallpox contracted from the Spanish. When the Spanish finally entered the conquered city, "the streets, squares, houses, and courts were filled with bodies, so that it was almost impossible to pass. Even Cortés was sick from the stench in his nostrils."

An equally important factor in the swift conquest was the political disunity within Indian empires. The Aztecs and Incas had subdued the native Indian populations of Mexico and Peru only 100 years before the Spanish invasion. Resentment at Aztec and Inca rule brought the conquistadors eager allies among the subject Indian tribes. But by aiding the Spanish overthrow of the Aztecs and the Incas, the native Indians only substituted one set of overlords for another.

Spanish Colonization

The conquistadors did not long enjoy their mastery in the Americas. The Spanish monarchs, who had just tamed an aristocracy at home, were not about to allow a colonial nobility to arise across the Atlantic. The Crown bribed the conquistadors into retirement—or was saved the expense when men like the Pizarro brothers were assassinated by their own followers. The task of governing Spain's new

Royal control replaces the conquistadors

colonies passed from the conquistadors to a small army of officials, soldiers, lawyers, and Catholic bishops, all appointed by the Crown, reporting to the Crown, and loyal to the Crown. Headquartered in urban centers like Mexico City (formerly Tenochtitlán), an elaborate, centralized bureaucracy administered the Spanish empire, regulating nearly every aspect of economic and social life.

Few Spaniards besides imperial officials settled in the Americas. By 1600 only about 5 percent of the colonial population was of Spanish descent, the other 95 percent being either Indian or African. Even by 1800 only 300,000 Spanish immigrants had come to Central and South America. Indians remained on the lands that they had farmed under the Aztecs and the Incas, now paying Spanish overlords their taxes and producing livestock for export. The Indians were not enslaved outright, but the Spanish compelled them to provide yearly tributes of food and other goods, a system known as *encomienda*. The Spanish also established sugar plantations in the West Indies; these were worked by black slaves who were being imported from Africa in large numbers by 1520.

Discovery of silver

Spain's colonies returned even more spectacular profits to the mother country after 1540, when silver deposits were discovered in both Mexico and Peru. Silver mining developed into a large-scale capitalist enterprise requiring substantial investment. European investors and Spanish immigrants who had profited from cattle raising and sugar planting poured their capital into equipment that would

Spanish America, ca. 1600 By 1600, Spain was extracting large amounts of gold and silver from Central and South America, as well as profits from sugar plantations in the Caribbean. Each year Spanish treasure ships ferried bullion from mines such as the one at Potosí to the Isthmus of Panama, where it was transported by land to the Caribbean coast, and from there to Spain. An expedition from Acapulco sailed annually to the Philippines as well, returning with Asian spices and other trade goods.

mine the silver deposits more efficiently: stamp mills, water-powered crushing equipment, and pumps. To provide workers, the Spanish government introduced another form of forced labor, known as *repartimiento*. Whole villages of Indians were pressed into service in the mines, joining black slaves and free white workers employed there.

In the last decades of the sixteenth century the economies of Mexico and Peru revolved solely around the mines. By 1570 the town of Potosí, the site of a veritable mountain of silver, had become larger than any city in either Spain or its American empire, with a population of 120,000. Local farmers who supplied mining centers with food and Spanish merchants in Seville who exported European goods to Potosí profited handsomely. So, too, did the Spanish Crown, which claimed one-fifth of the silver extracted. All told, between 1500 and 1600 some 16,000 tons were exported from Spanish America to Europe.

The Effects of Colonial Growth

Its American riches made Spain the dominant power in Europe. But that dominance was purchased at a fearful human cost. Devastated by warfare, disease, and exploitation, the Indians of the Caribbean were virtually wiped out within a century. In Mesoamerica, a native population of 20 million was reduced to 2 million.

Only a few of the Spanish spoke out against the exploitation of the natives. Among them was Bartolomé de Las Casas, a Spanish priest who became a bishop in southern Mexico. His writings, reprinted in many translations and illustrated with gruesome drawings, circulated throughout Europe, becoming the basis of the "Black Legend" of Spanish oppression in the Americas.

Most Spaniards did not share Las Casas's scruples. They justified their conquest by claiming that they had "delivered" the Indians from Aztec and Inca tyranny and replaced native "barbarism" and "paganism" with European civilization and Christianity. The sheer size of the Spanish conquest fostered a heady sense of superiority. By the beginning of the seventeenth century Spain's dominions in the Americas spanned 8000 miles, stretching from Baja California to the Straits of Magellan at South America's southern tip. The prevailing mood was captured by the portrait of a Spanish soldier that adorns the frontispiece of his book about the West Indies. He stands with one hand on his sword and the other holding a pair of compasses on top of a globe. Beneath is inscribed the motto "By compasses and the sword / More and more and more and more."

The Reformation in Europe

For most of the sixteenth century, Spain met with little interference in the Americas from rival European nations. One reason was religious upheaval in Europe. During the second decade of the sixteenth century—the same decade in which Cortés laid siege to Tenochtitlán—religious changes of enormous significance began in Europe. That revolution in Christianity, known as the Protestant Reformation, would figure as a crucial force in shaping the later history of the Americas.

Backdrop to Reform

During the Middle Ages, the Roman Catholic church defined what it meant to be a Christian in western Europe. Like other institutions of medieval society the

Catholic church was a hierarchy. At the top was the pope in Rome, and under him were the descending ranks of other church officials—cardinals, archbishops, bishops. At the bottom of the Catholic hierarchy were parish priests, each serving his own village, as well as monks and nuns living in monasteries and convents. But medieval popes were weak, and their power was felt little in the lives of most Europeans. Like political units of the era, religious institutions of the Middle Ages were local and decentralized.

Rise of the papacy

Between about 1100 and 1500, as the monarchs of Europe were growing more powerful, so too were the popes. As the papacy grew in wealth and power, a larger bureaucracy of church officials emerged. The Catholic church acquired land throughout Europe and added to its income through tithing (collecting taxes from church members) and by collecting fees from those appointed to church offices. In the thirteenth century, church officials also began to sell "indulgences." For ordinary believers who expected to spend time after death purging their sins in purgatory, the purchase of an indulgence promised to shorten that punishment by drawing on a "treasury of merit" amassed by the good works of Christ and the saints.

By the fifteenth century the Catholic church and the papacy had become enormously powerful but increasingly indifferent to popular religious concerns. Church officials meddled in secular politics. Popes and bishops flaunted their wealth, while poorly educated parish priests neglected their pastoral duties. At the same time, popular demands for religious assurance grew increasingly intense. The concern for salvation swelled in response to the disorienting changes sweeping the continent during the fifteenth and sixteenth centuries—the widening gulf between rich and poor, the rise in prices, and the discovery of America.

The Teachings of Martin Luther

Into this climate of heightened spirituality stepped Martin Luther, who abandoned studying the law to enter a monastery. Like many of his contemporaries, Luther was consumed by fears over his eternal fate. He was convinced that he was damned, and he could not find any consolation in the Catholic church. Catholic doctrine taught that a person could be saved by faith in God and by his or her own good works—by leading a virtuous life, observing the sacraments (such as baptism, the Mass, and penance), making pilgrimages to holy places, and praying to Christ and the saints. Because Luther believed that human nature was innately evil, he despaired of being able to lead a life that "merited" salvation. If men and women are so bad, he reasoned, how could they ever win their way to heaven with good works?

Justification by faith alone

Luther finally broke through his despair by reading the Bible. It convinced him that God did not require fallen humankind to earn salvation. Salvation, he concluded, came by faith alone, the "free gift" of God to undeserving sinners. The ability to live a good life could not be the *cause* of salvation but its *consequence:* once men and women believed that they had saving faith, moral behavior was possible. Luther elaborated that idea, known as "justification by faith alone," between 1513 and 1517.

Luther was ordained a priest and then assigned to teach at a university in Wittenberg, Germany. Still, he became increasingly critical of the Catholic church as an institution. In 1517 he posted on the door of a local church 95 theses attacking the Catholic hierarchy for selling salvation in the form of indulgences.

In early modern Europe, the uncertainties of religious war and economic upheaval created a pervasive social and spiritual unease, reflected in both these engravings. A contemporary of Martin Luther portrayed St. Anthony (left) being tormented by a host of demons. Their bizarre and twisted shapes bear a notable resemblance to the sea monsters (right) menacing the oceans leading to the newly discovered worlds of Asia and the Americas.

The novelty of this attack was not Luther's open break with Catholic teaching. Challenges to the church had cropped up throughout the Middle Ages. What was new was the passion and force behind Luther's attacks. Using the blunt, earthy Germanic tongue, he expressed the anxieties of many devout laypeople and their outrage at the church hierarchy's neglect. The "gross, ignorant asses and knaves at Rome," he warned, should keep their distance from Germany, or else "jump into the Rhine or the nearest river, and take . . . a cold bath."

The pope and his representatives in Germany at first tried to silence Martin Luther, then excommunicated him. But opposition only pushed Luther toward more radical positions. He asserted that the church and its officials were not infallible; only the Scriptures were without error. Every person, he said, should read and interpret the Bible for himself or herself. In an even more direct assault on church authority, he advanced an idea known as "the priesthood of all believers." Catholic doctrine held that salvation came only through the church and its clergy, a privileged group that possessed special access to God. Luther asserted that every person had the power claimed by priests.

Although Luther had not intended to start a schism within Catholicism, independent Lutheran churches were forming in Germany by the 1520s. And during the 1530s, Luther's ideas spread throughout Europe, where they were eagerly taken up by other reformers.

The Contribution of John Calvin

The most influential of Luther's successors was John Calvin, a French lawyer turned theologian. Calvin agreed with Luther that men and women could not merit their salvation. But while Luther's God was a loving deity who extended his mercy

John Calvin promoted an activist theology.

to sinful humankind, Calvin conceived of God as an awesome sovereign, all-knowing and all-powerful, the controlling force in human history who would ultimately triumph over Satan. To bring about that final victory, Calvin believed, God had selected certain people as his agents for ushering in his heavenly kingdom. These people—"the saints," or "the elect"—had been "predestined" by God for eternal salvation in heaven.

The elect

Calvin's emphasis on predestination led him to another distinctively Protestant notion—the doctrine of calling. How could a person learn whether he or she belonged to the elect who were saved? Calvin answered: strive to behave like a saint. God expected his elect to serve the good of society by unrelenting work in a "calling," or occupation, in the world. In place of the Catholic belief in the importance of good works, Calvin emphasized the goodness of work itself. Success in attaining discipline and self-control, in bringing order into one's own life and the entire society, revealed that a person might be among the elect.

Calvin fashioned a religion to change the world. Whereas Luther believed that Christians should accept the existing social order, Calvin called on Christians to become activists, reshaping society and government to conform with God's laws laid down in the Bible. He wanted all of Europe to become like Geneva, the Swiss city that he had converted into a holy commonwealth in which the elect regulated the behavior and morals of everyone else. And unlike Luther, who wrote primarily for a German audience, Calvin addressed his most important book, *The Institutes of the Christian Religion* (1536), to Christians throughout Europe. Reformers from every country flocked to Geneva to learn more about Calvin's ideas.

The English Reformation

While the Reformation went forward in Europe, King Henry VIII of England was striving for a goal more modest than those of Luther and Calvin. He wanted only to produce a male heir to carry on the Tudor dynasty. When his wife, Catherine of Aragon, gave birth to a daughter, Mary, Henry decided to do something less modest. He set out to get his marriage to Catherine annulled by the pope. This move angered Catherine's nephew, the king of Spain, who persuaded the pope to refuse. Defiantly, Henry went ahead with the divorce and married his mistress, Anne Boleyn.

Henry VIII breaks with Rome

Henry then widened this breach with Rome by making himself, and not the pope, the head of the Church of England. In 1534 Parliament formalized the relationship with the Act of Supremacy. But Henry, who fancied himself a theologian, had no fondness for Protestant doctrine. Under his leadership the Church of England remained essentially Catholic in its teachings and rituals.

England's Protestants gained ground during the six-year reign of Edward VI but then found themselves persecuted when his Catholic half sister, Mary, became queen in 1553. Five years later the situation turned again, when Elizabeth (Anne Boleyn's daughter) took the throne, proclaiming herself the defender of Protestantism.

Still, Elizabeth was no radical Calvinist. A vocal minority of her subjects were reformers of that stripe, calling for the English church to purge itself of bishops, elaborate ceremonies, and other Catholic "impurities." Because of the austerity and zeal of such Calvinist radicals, their opponents proclaimed them "Puritans."

English Puritans

The Protestant Reformation shattered the unity of Christendom in western Europe. Spain, Ireland, and Italy remained firmly Catholic. England, France, Scotland, the Netherlands, and Switzerland developed either dominant or substantial Calvinist constituencies. Much of Germany and Scandinavia opted for Lutheranism. As these religious groups competed for political power and the loyalties of believers, brutal wars racked sixteenth-century Europe. Protestants and Catholics slaughtered each other in the name of Christianity.

England's Entry into America

In 1562 Queen Elizabeth gave her blessing to an English army that set sail for France to aid Calvinists there being suppressed by the government. Perhaps the most dashing of the army's captains was a red-faced and robust West Country gentleman, Sir Humphrey Gilbert. "There is not a valliant er man that liveth," the Earl of Warwick assured the queen.

Like so many West Country boys in search of honor and fortune, Gilbert was eager to seize the main chance. In the early 1560s, that chance seemed to be fighting for the Protestant cause in France. Gilbert's stepfather, the seafarer Walter Raleigh, had done a good deal of his own seizing, mostly from Spanish silver ships along the South American coast. Like the conquistadors, Raleigh wanted more. He merely decided he could get more a bit more easily if he let Spain dig and refine the silver first.

If France had not beckoned, Humphrey Gilbert would surely have been happy to harass the Spanish too, along with his stepbrother, the young Walter Raleigh (named after his plundering father). But as Gilbert and young Raleigh came of age, they began to consider more ambitious schemes than the mere plundering of treasure. They looked to conquer Spain's empire—or, at least, to carve out for England a rival empire of its own. During the late 1570s and 1580s, when Queen Elizabeth felt confident enough to challenge Spain in the Americas, Gilbert and Raleigh were ready to lead the way.

Ambitious West Country gentlemen

The English Colonization of Ireland

During the 1560s, however, England was too deeply distracted by religious and political turmoil to pursue dreams of glory across the Atlantic. For Elizabeth, privateers like the senior Walter Raleigh stirred up more trouble than they were worth. Spain, after all, was England's ally against a common rival, France. And the Netherlands, which was then controlled by Spain, imported a good deal of English cloth. Elizabeth had good reason to pursue a policy that would soothe Spain, not offend it.

Reasons for England to soothe Spain

The queen also worried about Catholic Ireland to the west. She feared that the French or the Spanish might use the island as a base for invading England. Beginning in 1565 Elizabeth encouraged a number of her subjects, mainly gentlemen and aristocrats from the West Country, to sponsor private ventures for subduing the native Irish and settling English families on Irish land. Among the gentlemen eager to win fame and fortune were Humphrey Gilbert and Walter Raleigh.

The English invaders of Ireland, almost all ardent Protestants, regarded the native Catholic inhabitants as superstitious, pagan savages. "They blaspheme, they murder, commit whoredome," complained one Englishman, "hold no wedlocke, ravish, steal and commit all abomination without scruple." Thus the English found it easy enough to justify their conquest. They proclaimed it their duty to teach the Irish the discipline of hard work, the rule of law, and the truth of Christianity. And

English repression of the Irish

Martin Frobisher, his face frozen
in a glare and a horse pistol
fixed in his fist, exemplified the
ruthless ambition of England's
West Country adventurers.

Joint stock companies

while the Irish were learning civilized ways, they would not be allowed
to buy land or hold office or serve on juries or give testimony in courts
or learn a trade or bear arms.

When the Irish rebelled at that program of "liberation," the English
ruthlessly repressed native resistance, slaughtering not only combatants
but civilians as well. Most English in Ireland, like most Spaniards in
America, believed that native peoples who resisted civilization and Christianity should be subdued at any cost. No scruples stopped Humphrey
Gilbert, in an insurgent country, from planting the path to his camp with
the severed heads of Irish rebels.

England's efforts to settle and subdue Ireland would serve as a rough
model for later efforts at colonization. The approach was essentially military, like that of the conquistadors. More ominously, it sanctioned the
savage repression of any "inferior race." Not only Gilbert but also Raleigh
and many other West Country gentry soon turned their attention toward
North America. "Neither reputation, or profytt is to be wonne" in Ireland,
concluded Gilbert. They wanted more.

Renewed Interest in the Americas

After hard service in France and Ireland, Gilbert and Raleigh returned to
England. Elizabeth's court buzzed with gossip of their boasting and pride,
"which exceedeth [that] of all men alive." Her cautious bureaucrats, who
had been enlarging royal power, considered the two swaggering gentlemen insufferable if not downright dangerous, much as the Spanish officials distrusted their conquistadors. Still, England was becoming more
receptive to the schemes of such hotheaded warrior lords for challenging Spain overseas. English Protestantism, English nationalism, and
English economic interests all came together to increase support for English exploration and colonization.

The turning point for the English came during the 1570s when Calvinist
Dutch in the Netherlands rebelled against their rule by Catholic Spain. The
Spanish retaliated savagely by sacking the city of Antwerp, which was England's
major European market for cloth. Forced to look elsewhere for markets and
investment opportunities, merchants combined in joint stock companies to
develop a trade with Africa, Russia, the East Indies, and the Mediterranean. These
private corporations, in which many shareholders pooled small amounts of capital, also began to plow money into Atlantic privateering voyages. They pressed
Elizabeth to unleash England's sea rovers on Spain's silver ships.

Joining English merchants in the new interest in overseas exploration were
gentry families. The high birthrate among England's upper classes throughout
the sixteenth century had produced a surplus of younger sons, who stood to
inherit no share of family estates. The shortage of land for their sons at home
stirred up support among the gentry for England to claim territory across the
Atlantic.

With the backing of England's leading merchants and gentry, Elizabeth now
needed little encouragement to adopt a more belligerent stance toward Spain. But
she got more encouragement from Spain itself, which made no secret of wanting
to restore England to Catholicism, by armed invasion if necessary. Elizabeth was
not yet prepared to provoke open warfare with Spain, but she watched with interest
the exploits of a new generation of English explorers in North America.

The Failures of Frobisher and Gilbert

The adventurer who first caught the queen's eye was Martin Frobisher, the veteran of slaving voyages to West Africa, privateering raids in the Atlantic, fighting in Ireland, and other unsavory enterprises. In 1576 he sailed on another search for a Northwest Passage to Asia.

After sailing north of Labrador, Frobisher returned to England with an Eskimo (plucked, kayak and all, from the Atlantic) and a shiny black stone that seemed to be gold ore. With royal backing, Frobisher made two more voyages to his "New Peru" in 1577 and 1578, hauling back nearly 2000 tons of black rock. Closer inspection revealed all the rock to be fool's gold, and Frobisher's reputation fell under a cloud.

Because Humphrey Gilbert had refused to invest in this fiasco, Frobisher's disgrace became Gilbert's opportunity. In 1578 Elizabeth granted Gilbert a vague patent—the first English colonial charter—to explore, occupy, and govern any territory in America "not actually possessed of any Christian prince or people." That charter, ignoring the Indian possession of North America, made Gilbert lord and proprietor of all the land lying between Florida and Labrador.

Gilbert pictured himself and his heirs as manorial lords of a colony filled with loyal tenant farmers paying rents in return for protection. In a sense his dreams resembled those of Spain's conquistadors: to re-create an older, nearly feudal world that would remain largely free of royal control. Yet Gilbert's vision also looked forward to a utopian society. He planned to encourage England's poor to emigrate by providing them free land and a government "to be chosen by consent of the people." *Gilbert's colonial plans*

In the end, the dreams foundered in a stormy present. Gilbert set sail in June 1583, but a late start forced him to turn back before he could scout the North American coast. Then his two ships met with foul weather. Gilbert, with characteristic bravado, sat on the deck of the smaller *Squirrel,* reading a book. "We are as neere to Heaven by sea as by land," he shouted across the heaving swells. The men aboard the *Golden Hind* recognized the words of Thomas More, whose *Utopia*—a dialogue about an ideal society in the New World—Gilbert held in his hand. Gilbert was nearer to heaven than he hoped. Around midnight, the crew of the *Golden Hind* saw the lights of the *Squirrel* extinguished and the ship "devoured and swallowed up by the sea."

Raleigh's Roanoke Venture

Raleigh had been eager to accompany his stepbrother's ill-fated expedition, but Elizabeth's many favors made it hard for him to leave. He was dining on food from palace kitchens, sleeping in a bed adorned with green velvet and spangled plumes of white feathers. Still, Raleigh was restless—and envious when another West Country adventurer, Sir Francis Drake, returned from circumnavigating the globe in 1580, his ships heavy with Spanish plunder.

Raleigh's ambitions led him to Richard Hakluyt, a clergyman with a passion for spreading knowledge of overseas discoveries. At Raleigh's request, Hakluyt wrote an eloquent plea to Elizabeth for the English settlement of America, titled *A Discourse Concerning Westerne Planting.* The temperate and fertile lands of North America, Hakluyt argued, would provide a perfect base from which to harry the Spanish, search for a Northwest Passage, and extend the influence of Protestantism. He also stressed the advantages of colonies as sources of new commodities, as markets for English goods, and as havens for the poor and unemployed. *Hakluyt publicizes America*

Daily Lives

CLOTHING AND FASHION

"Barbaric" Dress—Indian and European

It was remarkable to sixteenth-century Europeans how many things seemed to be missing from Indian culture. Even more remarkable, the Indians themselves did not seem to notice. Michel de Montaigne, a French philosopher who had never been to America but liked to talk with explorers and read their accounts, managed to compile quite a list. According to Montaigne, Indians had "no kind of traffic [trade], no knowledge of letters, no intelligence of numbers, no name of magistrate, nor of politics, no use of service [servants], of riches, or of poverty, no contracts, no successions, no partitions, no occupation but idle, no apparel but natural. . . ." When other Europeans, with and without experience in America, made similar lists, they never failed to mention that last crucial item missing in Indian culture—clothing. Even Europeans who never traveled beyond their villages associated America's inhabitants with nakedness, for woodcuts, engravings, and paintings showed native peoples either entirely nude or clad in skimpy loincloths or grass skirts.

Europeans interpreted the simplicity of Indian dress in two different ways. Some saw the lack of clothing as evidence of "barbarism." André Thevet, a shocked French visitor to Brazil in 1557, voiced this point of view when he attributed nakedness to simple lust. If the Indians could weave hammocks, he sniffed, why not shirts? But other Europeans viewed unashamed nakedness as the Indians' badge of innocence. As remnants of a bygone "golden age," they believed, Indians needed clothing no more than government, laws, regular employment, or other corruptions of civilization.

In fact, Indians were no more "naked" than they were without trade, politics, employment, or religion. While the simplest tribes of the Caribbean and Brazil wore little, the members of more advanced Indian cultures in Central and North America clothed themselves with animal pelts sewn into mantles and robes, breechclouts, leggings, and moccasins. They wrought bird feathers into headdresses and ear decorations and fashioned reptile skins into belts and pouches. Even more formidably clad were the Eskimos of the far North, who dressed head to foot in sealskin suits with waterproofed seams, turning the furry side inward for warmth in the winter and outward in the summer.

By the late sixteenth century, Europeans, and especially the English, were paying more heed

Columbus meeting the natives on Hispaniola

Raleigh's chance to settle American lands finally came in 1584, when Elizabeth granted him a patent nearly identical to that of Gilbert. By the summer Raleigh had sent Philip Amadas and Arthur Barlowe across the Atlantic, their two small ships coasting the Outer Banks of present-day North Carolina. Amadas and Barlowe established cordial relations with the Roanoke tribe, ruled by a "werowance," or chief, named Wingina. The enthusiastic Hakluyt promptly envisioned a colony that would become the Mexico of England, full of plantations producing sugar and silk and mountains yielding gold. Elizabeth knighted Raleigh and allowed him to name the new land "Virginia," after his virgin queen. The following summer a full-scale expedition returned to Roanoke Island.

to what the Indians wore, hoping to assure prospective colonists that the natives would not affront European standards of modesty. Captain John Smith, for example, left descriptions of the attire of Virginia's tribes, noting in a telling comparison that "the better sort use large mantels of deare skins not much differing in fashion from the Irish mantels." Even more reassuringly, Smith added, "The women are alwaies covered about their midles with a skin and very shamefast [ashamed] to be seen bare."

If natives struck whites as starkly underdressed, Europeans seemed, by the Indians' standards, grotesquely overdressed. Indeed, European fashion was ill suited to the environment between the Chesapeake and the Caribbean. Elizabethan gentlemen strutted in silk stockings attached with garters to padded, puffed knee breeches, topped by long-sleeved shirts and tight quilted jackets called "doublets." Men of lesser status wore coarse woolen hose, canvas breeches, shirts, and fitted vests known as "jerkins"; when at work, they donned aprons of dressed leather. Women wore gowns with long, full skirts, low-cut bodices, aprons, and hosiery held up by garters. Ladies went about in silk and wore hoods and mantles to ward off the sun, while the rest dressed in flannels or canvas and covered their heads with linen caps or coifs. Both sexes favored long hair, and men sported mustaches and beards.

Such fashions complicated life in the American environment, especially since heavy clothing and even shoes rotted rapidly from sweat and humidity. The pungent aroma of Europeans also compounded the discomfort of natives who came in contact with them. For despite sweltering heat, the whites who swaddled themselves in woolens and brocades also disdained regular bathing and regarded Indian devotion to daily washing as another uncivilized oddity.

It would have been natural for Indians to wonder why the barbaric newcomers did not adapt their dress to a new setting. The answer may be that for Europeans—entering an alien environment inhabited by peoples whom they identified as "naked savages"—the psychological risk of shedding familiar apparel was simply too great. However inappropriate or even unhealthy, heavy, elaborate dress afforded the comfort of familiarity and distinguished "civilized" newcomer from "savage" native in America.

Raleigh apparently aimed to establish on Roanoke a mining camp and a military garrison modeled on Frobisher's venture of the 1570s. In a stroke of genius, he included in the company of 108 men a scientist, Thomas Hariot, to study the country's natural resources and an artist, John White, to make drawings of the Virginia Indians. *A Briefe and True Reporte of the New Found Land of Virginia* (1588), written by Hariot and illustrated by White, served as one of the principal sources about North America and its Indian inhabitants for more than a century. Far less inspired was Raleigh's choice to lead the expedition—two veterans of the Irish campaigns, Sir Richard Grenville and Ralph Lane. Even his fellow conquistadors in Ireland considered Lane proud and greedy. As for Grenville, he was given to

The first colony
at Roanoke

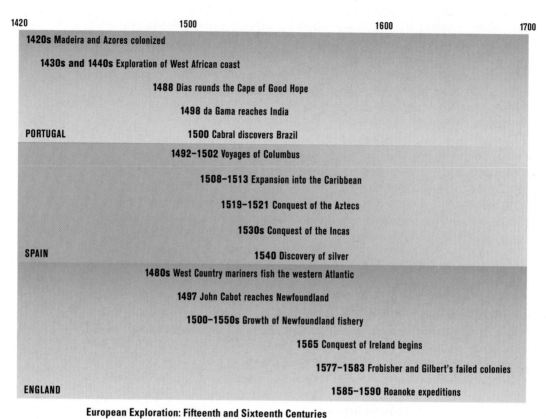

1420		1500		1600	1700

1420s Madeira and Azores colonized

1430s and 1440s Exploration of West African coast

1488 Dias rounds the Cape of Good Hope

1498 da Gama reaches India

PORTUGAL   **1500** Cabral discovers Brazil

1492–1502 Voyages of Columbus

1508–1513 Expansion into the Caribbean

1519–1521 Conquest of the Aztecs

1530s Conquest of the Incas

SPAIN   **1540** Discovery of silver

1480s West Country mariners fish the western Atlantic

1497 John Cabot reaches Newfoundland

1500–1550s Growth of Newfoundland fishery

1565 Conquest of Ireland begins

1577–1583 Frobisher and Gilbert's failed colonies

ENGLAND   **1585–1590** Roanoke expeditions

European Exploration: Fifteenth and Sixteenth Centuries

breaking wineglasses between his teeth and then swallowing the shards to show that he could stand the sight of blood, even his own.

The bullying ways of both men quickly alienated the natives of Roanoke. After a year, in response to rumors of an imminent Indian attack, Lane and his men attacked Wingina's main village and killed him. All that averted an Indian counterattack was the arrival of Drake and Frobisher, fresh from freebooting up and down the Caribbean. The settlement's 102 survivors piled onto the pirate ships and put an ocean between themselves and the avenging Roanokes.

A Second Attempt

Undaunted, Raleigh organized a second expedition to plant a colony farther north, in the Chesapeake Bay. He now projected an agricultural community modeled on Humphrey Gilbert's manorial dreams. He recruited 119 men, women, and children, members of the English middle class, and granted each person an estate of 500 acres. He also appointed as governor the artist John White, who brought along a suit of armor for ceremonial occasions.

From the moment of first landfall in July 1587, everything went wrong. The expedition's pilot, Simon Ferdinando, insisted on putting off the colonists at Roanoke Island rather than the Chesapeake. Even before Ferdinando weighed anchor, the settlers were skirmishing with the local Indians. Sensing that the situation on Roanoke could quickly become desperate, White sailed back with Ferdinando, hoping to bring reinforcements.

But White returned home in 1588 just as the massive Spanish navy, the Armada, was marshaling for an assault on England. Elizabeth was enlisting every seaworthy ship and able-bodied sailor in her realm to stave off invasion. Spain's Armada was defeated, but Raleigh left the Roanoke colonists to shift for themselves. When White finally returned to Roanoke Island in 1590, he found only an empty fort and a few cottages in a clearing. The sole clue to the colony's fate was carved on a post: CROATOAN. It was the name of a nearby island off Cape Hatteras.

Had the Roanoke colonists fled to Croatoan for safety? Had they moved to the mainland and joined Indian tribes in the interior? Had they been killed by Wingina's people? The fate of the "lost colony" remains a mystery. White sailed back to England, leaving behind the little cluster of cottages, which would soon be overgrown with vines, and his suit of armor, which was already "almost eaten through with rust."

All the world lay before them. Or so it had seemed to the young men from England's West Country who dreamed of gold and glory, conquest and colonization. Portugal had sent slave and gold traders to Africa, as well as merchants to trade with the rich civilizations of the Indies. Spanish conquerors like Cortés had toppled Indian empires and brought home silver. But England's would-be conquistadors had met only with frustration. In 1600, more than a century after Columbus's first crossing, not a single English settlement existed anywhere in the Americas. The Atlantic had swallowed up Gilbert and his hopes for a manorial utopia; Roanoke lay in ruins.

What was left of the freebooting world of West Country adventurers? Raleigh, his ambition unquenchable, sailed to South America in quest of a rich city named El Dorado. In 1603, however, Elizabeth's death brought to the English throne her cousin James I, the founder of the Stuart dynasty. The new king arrested the old queen's favorite for treason and left him to languish 15 years in the Tower of London. Set free in 1618 at the age of 64, Raleigh returned to South America, his lust for El Dorado undiminished. Along the way he plundered some Spanish silver ships, defying James's orders. It was a fatal mistake, for England had made peace with Spain. Raleigh lost his head.

James I did not want to harry the king of Spain; he wanted to imitate him. The Stuarts were even more determined than the Tudors to enlarge the sphere of royal power. There would be no room in America for a warrior nobility of conquistadors, no room for a feudal fiefdom ruled by the likes of Raleigh or Gilbert. Instead, there would be English colonies in America like the new outpost of Jamestown, planted on the Chesapeake Bay in Virginia in 1607. There would be profitable plantations and other bold enterprises, enriching English royalty and managed by loyal, efficient bureaucrats. Settling America would strengthen English monarchs, paving their path to greater power, just as the dominions of Mexico and Peru had enlarged the authority of the Spanish Crown. America would be the making of kings and queens.

Or would it? For some Europeans, weary of freebooting conquistadors and sea rovers, the order and security that Crown rule and centralized states promoted in western Europe would be enough. But others, the desperate and idealistic men and women who sailed to the world that lay before them, would want more.

chapter summary

During the late fifteenth century, Europeans made their first contact with North and South America, where native cultures were numerous and diverse.

- A combination of technological advances, the rise of new trade networks and techniques, and increased political centralization made Europe's expansion overseas possible.

- The pressure of Europe's growing population on its limited resources of land and food made expansion overseas essential.

- Spain took the lead in exploring and colonizing the Americas, consolidating a vast and profitable empire of its own in the place of Aztec and Inca civilizations.

- Both divisions within Indian empires and the devastating effects of European diseases made Spanish conquest possible.

- England, fearful of Spain's power, did not turn its attention to exploration and colonization until the 1570s and 1580s.

- England's merchants and gentry in search of new markets and land lent support to colonizing ventures, although early efforts, such as those at Roanoke, failed.

interactive learning

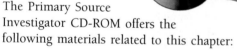

The Primary Source Investigator CD-ROM offers the following materials related to this chapter:

- Interactive maps: **Early Native Peoples in the Era of European Contact (M1)** and **The Atlantic World, 1400–1850 (M2)**

- A collection of primary sources, including several that allow investigation of Native American cultures before the arrival of Columbus: an Iroquois creation story that describes the origins of the world, an engraving that depicts an Indian marketplace circa 1500, and early paintings of Native American fishing techniques made by explorers traveling along the eastern coast of North America. Others provide insight into the mind-set of medieval Europeans on the eve of their great expansion into the Atlantic World: a medieval world map, a strikingly more modern Portuguese map showing a water route to Asia around Africa, and several of the key inventions that made trans-Atlantic navigation possible.

additional reading

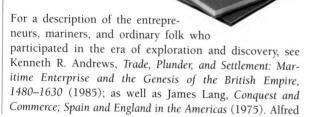

For a description of the entrepreneurs, mariners, and ordinary folk who participated in the era of exploration and discovery, see Kenneth R. Andrews, *Trade, Plunder, and Settlement: Maritime Enterprise and the Genesis of the British Empire, 1480–1630* (1985); as well as James Lang, *Conquest and Commerce; Spain and England in the Americas* (1975). Alfred Crosby Jr. provides a fascinating account of the biological and ecological effects of contact between Native Americans and Europeans in *The Columbian Exchange* (1972). M. Leon Portilla's *The Broken Spears* (1962) is a vivid account of Cortés's conquest seen through Aztec eyes, while the Spanish perspective is supplied by Bernal Diaz, *The Conquest of New Spain*, trans. J. M. Cohen (1963). The best scholarly overviews of the Spanish invasion and its American empire are Hugh Thomas, *Conquest: Montezuma, Cortes, and the Fall of Old Mexico* (1993); and James Lockhart, *The Nahuas after Conquest: A Social and Cultural History of the Indians of Central Mexico, Sixteenth through Eighteenth Centuries* (1992).

For a good introduction to the Reformation, see Owen Chadwick, *The Reformation* (1964). For early English attempts at colonization, in both Ireland and the Americas, consult the works of Nicholas Canny in the Bibliography. David Beers Quinn, *Set Fair for Roanoke* (1985), contains tantalizing speculation about what happened to the lost colony at Roanoke, and the best overview of English society in this period remains Wallace Notestein, *The English People on the Eve of Colonization, 1603–1630* (1954).

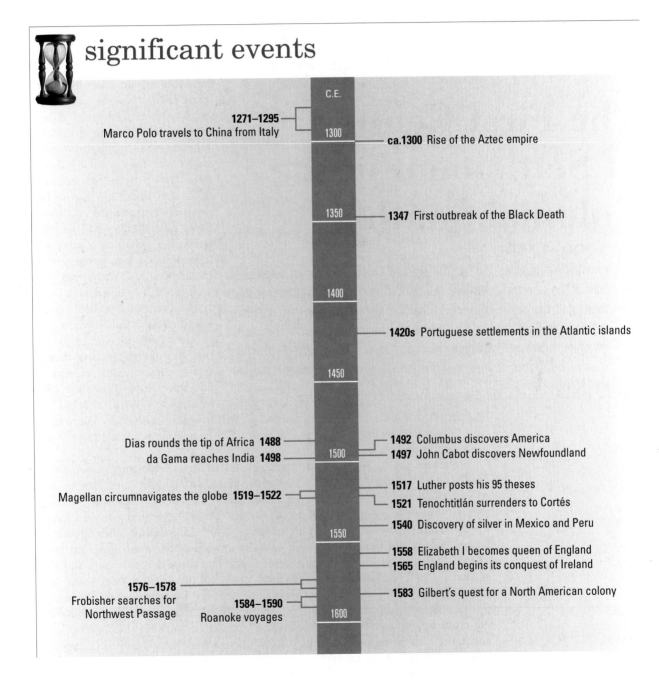

significant events

C.E.

1271–1295 Marco Polo travels to China from Italy

1300   — **ca.1300** Rise of the Aztec empire

1350   — **1347** First outbreak of the Black Death

1400

— **1420s** Portuguese settlements in the Atlantic islands

1450

Dias rounds the tip of Africa **1488** — — **1492** Columbus discovers America
da Gama reaches India **1498** — 1500 — **1497** John Cabot discovers Newfoundland

— **1517** Luther posts his 95 theses
Magellan circumnavigates the globe **1519–1522** — — **1521** Tenochtitlán surrenders to Cortés

— **1540** Discovery of silver in Mexico and Peru

1550

— **1558** Elizabeth I becomes queen of England
— **1565** England begins its conquest of Ireland

1576–1578
Frobisher searches for
Northwest Passage   **1584–1590**   — **1583** Gilbert's quest for a North American colony
                                    Roanoke voyages
                                                    1600

Chapter 2

I n the year 1617, as Europeans counted time, on a bay they called the Chesapeake, in a land they named Virginia, an old Indian chief surveyed his domain. It had all worked according to plan, and Powhatan, leader of the Pamunkeys, had laid his plans carefully. While in his prime, the tall, robust man had drawn some 30 smaller tribes along the Virginia coast into a powerful confederacy. As tribute for his protection and leadership, Powhatan collected food, furs, and skins. He installed his relatives as these tribes' new leaders and as his new vassals.

By 1607 Powhatan's confederacy numbered nearly 9000, a political alliance that had overcome formidable obstacles. The natives of Virginia, like the peoples who inhabited the length of eastern North America, were seminomadic. They lived for most of the year in small villages and ranged over tribal hunting and fishing grounds, following the game from one season to the next. Rivalries over trade, territorial boundaries, and leadership had often erupted into armed conflict. Some coastal tribes had fiercely resisted Powhatan's efforts to incorporate them; some tribes to the west still threatened the security of his confederacy.

After 1607 Powhatan was forced to take into account yet another tribe. The English, as this new people called themselves, came by sea, crammed into three ships. They were 100 men and 4 boys, all clad in heavy, outlandish clothing, many dressed in gaudy colors. The ships followed a river deep into Powhatan's territory and built a fort on a swampy, mosquito-infested site that they called Jamestown.

The First Century of Settlement in the Colonial South

1600–1750

preview • Instability and conflict wracked England's southern colonies for most of the seventeenth century. But by 1720, one-crop plantation economies dominated the region—tobacco in the Chesapeake, rice in the Carolinas, sugar in the Caribbean. In the process, the original system of labor, based on white indentured servitude, gave way to the slave labor fueled by a massive importation of Africans. Spain too extended its empire in Florida and New Mexico.

Powhatan was not frightened. The English had larger boats and louder, more deadly weapons than his people did. But the Indians quickly learned how to use guns, and they vastly outnumbered the English, an inferior race who seemed unlikely to live long and prosper in Powhatan's land. They could not even manage to feed themselves from the rich resources of the Chesapeake. With bows and arrows, spears and nets, Indian men brought in an abundance of meat and fish. The fields tended by Indian women yielded generous crops of corn, beans, squash, and melon, and edible nuts and fruits grew wild. Still the English starved, and not just during the first few months of their settlement but for several years afterward.

Powhatan could understand why the English refused to grow food. Cultivating crops was women's work—like building houses; or making clothing, pottery, and baskets; or caring for children. And the English settlement included no women until two arrived in the fall of 1608. Yet even after more women came, the English still starved, and they expected—no, they demanded—that the Indians supply them with food.

Most incredible to Powhatan was that the inferior English considered themselves a superior people. They boasted constantly about the power of their god—they had only one—and denounced the Indians' "devil-worship" of "false gods." The English also boasted without end about the power of their king, James I, who expected Powhatan to become his vassal. The English had even planned a "coronation" to crown Powhatan as a "subject king." He had not been impressed. "If your king has sent me presents," he responded, "I also am a king, and this is my land. . . . Your father is to come to me, not I to him." In the end the English did come to Powhatan, only to find what "a fowle trouble there was to make him kneele to receave his crowne. . . . [he] indured so many perswasions, examples and instructions as tired them all. At last by leaning hard on his shoulders, he a little stooped, and . . . put the Crowne on his head."

It was inconceivable to Powhatan that he should willingly bow before this King James, the ruler of so savage a race. When the Indians made war, they killed the male warriors of rival tribes but adopted their women and children. But when Powhatan's people withheld food or defended their land from these invaders, the English retaliated by murdering Indian women and children. To make matters worse, the English could not even keep order within their own tribe. Too many of them wanted to be chiefs, and they squabbled constantly among themselves.

Captain John Smith

Only one man, a brash fellow called Captain John Smith, had briefly been able to bring order to the English settlement. Powhatan granted him a grudging respect, though he boasted so much that even other English seemed modest by comparison. Smith bragged endlessly of his earlier exploits across the ocean, where he had fought as a soldier of fortune. He told wonderful tales of his irresistible appeal to beautiful women who had rescued him from harrowing perils. A rough man, he bullied the Indians for food and would have enslaved them if it had been in his power. Even so, Smith took a genuine interest in Indian ways.

But Smith returned to England in 1609 after being injured when some of the white people's gunpowder blew up by mistake. Thereafter the English returned to squabbling and starving. Small wonder that some English had deserted their settlement to live among Powhatan's people. Anyone could see the superiority of Indian culture to English ways.

Powhatan's strategy

The temptation to wipe out the helpless, troublesome, arrogant tribe of English—or simply to let them starve to death—had been almost overwhelming. But Powhatan allowed the English to survive because he had decided that even these barbaric people had their uses. English labor, English trading goods, and, most important, English guns would help him quell resistance within his confederacy and subdue his Indian rivals to the west. In 1614 Powhatan cemented his claim

When the English attempted to crown Powhatan as a subject king, he may have sent King James I this cloak as a reciprocal present. Made from four tanned deerskins, the mantle is decorated with many small marine shells sewn into designs. In addition to human and animal figures, the cloak has 34 roundlets that may represent the Indian districts under Powhatan's control.

No stranger to self-promotion, Captain John Smith included this portrait of himself and verses celebrating his ennobling exploits at the beginning of his *Description of New England* (1616). As the military armor and knightly bearing suggest (note Smith on horseback, lower right), the outspoken captain stood in the tradition of West Country adventurers and Spanish conquistadors.

on the English and their weapons with the marriage between his favorite child, Pocahontas, and a white settler, John Rolfe.

By 1617 events had vindicated Powhatan's strategy of tolerating the English. His empire flourished, ready to be passed on to his brother, Opechancanough. Powhatan's people still outnumbered the English, who seldom starved outright now but continued to fight among themselves and sicken and die. Only one thing had changed in the Chesapeake by 1617: the English were clearing woodland along the rivers and planting tobacco.

That was the doing of Powhatan's son-in-law, Rolfe, a man as strange as the rest of his tribe, all of them eager to store up wealth and worldly goods. Rolfe had been obsessed with finding a crop that could be grown in Virginia and then sold for gain across the sea. When he succeeded by growing tobacco, other English followed his lead. Odder still, not women but men tended the tobacco fields. Here was more evidence of English inferiority. Men wasted long hours laboring when they might supply their needs with far less effort.

In 1617 Powhatan, ruler of the Pamunkeys, surveyed his empire, and sometime in that year, he looked no longer. He had lived long enough to see the tobacco fields lining the riverbanks, straddling the charred stumps of felled trees. But he died believing that he had bent the English to his purposes—died before those stinking tobacco weeds spread over the length of his land and sent his hard-won empire up in smoke.

English Society on the Chesapeake

While the chief of the Chesapeake was expanding his dominions and consolidating his power, the king of England was doing the same. Just as Spain had begun to profit from the riches of silver mines and sugar plantations, James I of England hoped that the wealth and power of his kingdom would grow as English colonists settled the American coasts north of Spain's empire. The first newcomers clustered along the many bays of the Chesapeake, as well as in a few island outposts of the Caribbean. A generation later, during the 1670s and 1680s, colonists from the Caribbean hopscotched to the mainland to found colonies along the Carolina coast. As the English struggled to put down roots, the ambitions of merchants and planters and kings clashed with the conflicting goals of Indian leaders like Powhatan.

Instability of the southern colonies

The result was a chaotic and deadly landscape. During much of the seventeenth century, ambitious colonists scrambled to control the land and the labor needed to secure profits from tobacco, sugar, and rice. Only after decades of uncertainty, violence, and high mortality did the colonies along the southern Atlantic crescent begin to prosper. Even then, stability was bought at a high price. In order to supply the workers so desperately sought by plantation owners, English colonists introduced the institution of slavery.

The Mercantilist Impulse

As European powers began establishing permanent colonies in America, they were putting into practice a theory about how best to attain national wealth and influence. That idea, which guided Europe's commercial expansion for 200 years, was named "mercantilism" by the eighteenth-century economist Adam Smith. Mercantilists called for the state to regulate and protect industry and commerce. Their primary objective was to enrich the nation by fostering a favorable balance of trade. Once the value of exports exceeded the cost of imports, they theorized, gold and silver would flow into home ports.

Mercantilism

If a nation could make do without any imports from other countries, so much the better, and it was here that the idea of colonies entered the mercantilist scheme. Colonial producers would supply raw materials that the mother country could not produce, while colonial consumers swelled demand for the finished goods and financial services that the mother country could provide. Convinced that colonies would enhance national self-sufficiency, mercantilists urged states to sponsor overseas settlements.

Mercantilist notions appealed to Europe's monarchs. A thriving trade meant that more taxes and customs duties would fill royal coffers, increasing royal power. That logic led James I to lend his approval to the private venture that brought the first white settlers to the Chesapeake.

The Virginia Company

In 1606 the king granted a charter to a number of English merchants, gentlemen, and aristocrats, incorporating them as the Virginia Company of London. The members of the new joint stock company sold stock in their venture to English investors, as well as awarding a share to those willing to settle in Virginia at their own expense. With the proceeds from the sale of stock, the company planned to send to Virginia hundreds of poor and unemployed people as well as scores of skilled craftworkers. These laborers were to serve the company for seven years in return for their passage, pooling their efforts to produce any commodities that would return a profit to stockholders. If gold mines like Spain's could not be found, perhaps North America would yield other valuable commodities—furs, pitch, tar, or lumber. In the spring of 1607 the first expedition dispatched by the Virginia Company, 104 men and boys, founded Jamestown.

Making the first of many mistakes, Jamestown's settlers pitched their fort on an inland peninsula in order to prevent a surprise attack from the Spanish. Unfortunately, the marshy, thickly wooded site served as an ideal breeding ground for malaria. The Virginia Company settlers, weakened by bouts of malaria and then beset by dysentery, typhoid, and yellow fever, died by the scores.

Jamestown's problems

Even before sickness took its toll, many of Jamestown's first settlers had little taste for labor. The gentlemen of the expedition expected to lead rather than to work, while most other members of the early colonizing parties were gentlemen's servants and craftworkers who knew nothing about growing crops. The settlers resorted to bullying Powhatan's people for food. Many colonists suffered from malnutrition, which heightened their susceptibility to disease. Only 60 of Jamestown's 500 inhabitants lived through the winter of 1609–1610, known as the "starving time." Some desperate colonists unearthed and ate corpses; one settler even butchered his wife.

In Jamestown's early years its military orientation was clear. The fort's heavy palisades and its strategic location upriver and some distance inland underscore the colonists' concern for defense—as does the imposing figure of Powhatan seated at the right.

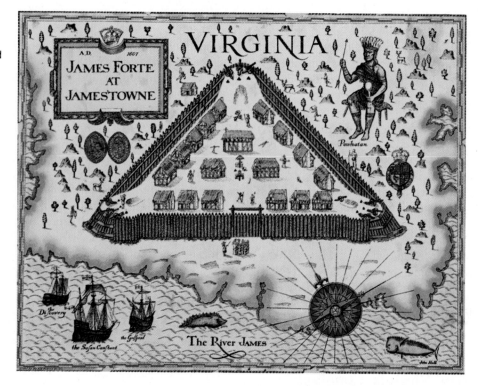

Reports of starvation and staggering death rates stiffened the Virginia Company's resolve: in 1611 it imposed on the colonists what amounted to martial law. Company officials in Virginia organized the settlers into work gangs and severely punished the lazy and the disorderly. Still the company failed to turn a profit. And after 1617, skirmishes with the Indians became more brutal and frequent as rows of tobacco plants steadily invaded tribal lands.

Reform and a Boom in Tobacco

Key reforms

Desperate to salvage their investment, Virginia Company managers in 1618 set in place sweeping reforms. To attract more capital and colonists, the company established a "headright" system for granting land to individuals. Those already settled in the colony received 100 acres apiece. New settlers each received 50 acres, and anyone who paid the passage of other immigrants to Virginia—either family members or servants—received 50 acres per "head." The company also abolished martial law, allowing the planters to elect a representative assembly. Along with a governor and an advisory council appointed by the company, the House of Burgesses had the authority to make laws for the colony. It met for the first time in 1619, beginning what would become a strong tradition of representative government in the English colonies.

The new measures met with immediate success. The free and unfree laborers who poured into Virginia during the 1620s made up the first wave of an English migration to the Chesapeake that numbered between 130,000 and 150,000 over the seventeenth century. Drawn from the ranks of ordinary English working people, the

The Smokers (left), painted by Adriaen Brouwer, a seventeenth-century Dutch artist, suggests that the use of tobacco was both popular and disreputable. Native American peoples such as the Mayan (right) had been cultivating and smoking tobacco long before the arrival of Europeans.

immigrants were largely men, outnumbering women by six to one. Most were young, ranging in age from 15 to 24. Because of their youth, most lacked skills or wealth.

Some of those who came to the Chesapeake as free immigrants prospered, lured by the chance to make a fortune in tobacco. During the 1620s Virginia's tobacco economy took off. As demand soared and prices peaked in European markets, colonists with an eye for profit planted every inch of their farms in tobacco and reaped windfalls. But for the vast majority of settlers—and, specifically, the three-quarters of all immigrants who arrived in the Chesapeake as indentured servants—the future was far grimmer.

For most of the new servants, the crossing to Virginia was simply the last of many moves made in the hope of finding work. Although England's population had been rising since the middle of the fifteenth century, the demand for farm laborers was falling because many landowners were converting croplands into pastures for sheep. The search for work pushed young men and women out of their villages, sending them through the countryside and then into the cities. Down and out in London, Bristol, or Liverpool, some decided to make their next move across the Atlantic and signed indentures. Pamphlets promoting immigration promised abundant land and quick riches once servants had finished their terms of four to seven years.

Even the most skeptical immigrants were shocked at what they found. The death rate in Virginia during the 1620s was higher than that of England during times of epidemic disease. The life expectancy for Chesapeake men who reached the age of 20 was a mere 48 years; for women it was lower still. Servants fared worst of all, because malnutrition, overwork, and abuse made them vulnerable to disease. As masters scrambled to make quick profits, they extracted the maximum amount of work before death carried off their laborers. An estimated 40 percent of servants did not survive to the end of their indentured terms.

Indentured servants

The expanding cultivation of tobacco also claimed many lives by putting unbearable pressure on Indian land. After Powhatan's death in 1617, leadership of the confederacy passed to Opechancanough, who watched, year after year, as the tobacco mania grew. In March 1622 he coordinated a sweeping attack on white settlements that killed about one-fifth of Virginia's white population. Swift English retaliation wiped out whole tribes and cut down an entire generation of young Indian men.

News of the Indian war jolted English investors into determining the true state of their Virginia venture. It came to light that, despite the tobacco boom, the Virginia Company was plunging toward bankruptcy. Nor was that the worst news. Stockholders discovered that more than 3000 immigrants had not survived the brutal conditions of Chesapeake life. An investigation by James I brought out the grisly truth, causing the king to dissolve the Virginia Company and take control of the colony himself in 1624. Henceforth Virginia would be governed as a royal colony.

Settling Down in the Chesapeake

During the 1630s and 1640s the fever of the tobacco boom broke, and a more settled social and political life emerged in Virginia. The settlers who had become wealthy by exploiting servant labor now began to acquire political power. They established local bases of influence in Virginia's counties, serving as justices of the peace and sheriffs, maintaining roads and bridges, collecting taxes, and supervising local elections. They organized all able-bodied adult males into militias for local defense and sat on vestries, the governing bodies of local Anglican parishes, hiring the handful of clergy who came to Virginia and providing for the neighborhood poor.

The biggest tobacco planters of each county also dominated colony politics. Even though King James had replaced the Virginia Company's government with his own royal administration, the colony's elected assembly continued making laws for the colony. Along with the council (the upper house of the legislature), the assembly resisted interference in Virginia's affairs from the royal governor, the king's representative.

The colony's growing stability was reflected in improved conditions for less powerful Virginians. Although servants still streamed into the colony, the price of tobacco leveled off. That meant planters were less likely to drive their servants to death in search of overnight fortunes. As tobacco became less profitable, planters raised more corn and cattle, and mortality rates declined as food supplies rose. Freed servants who survived their indentures usually worked a few more years as hired hands or tenant farmers. In doing so, most managed to save enough money to buy their own land and become independent planters. For women who survived servitude, prospects were even better. With wives at a premium, single women stood a good chance of improving their status by marriage. Even so, high mortality rates still fractured families: one out of every four children born in the Chesapeake did not survive to maturity, and among those children who reached their eighteenth birthday, one-third had lost both parents to death.

By 1650 Virginia could boast about 15,000 inhabitants, although much of that increase resulted from servants and free immigrants arriving in the colony every year. But Virginians looking to expand into more northerly bays of the Chesapeake found their way blocked by a newer English colony.

The Founding of Maryland and the Renewal of Indian Wars

Unlike Virginia, which was first settled by a private corporation and later converted into a royal colony, Maryland was founded by a single aristocratic family, the Calverts. Indeed, it was the first of several such "proprietary" colonies given by English monarchs to loyal followers. Thus in 1632, Maryland became the private preserve of the Calverts. They held absolute authority to dispose of 10 million acres of land, administer justice, and establish a civil government. All these powers they exercised, granting estates, or "manors," to their friends and dividing other holdings into smaller farms for ordinary immigrants. From all these "tenants"—that is, every settler in the colony—the Calverts collected "quitrents" every year, fees for use of the land. The Calverts appointed a governor and a council to oversee their own interests while allowing the largest landowners to dispense local justice in manorial courts and make laws for the entire colony in a representative assembly.

Proprietary colonies

Virginians liked nothing at all about Maryland. To begin with, the Calvert family was Catholic and had extended complete religious freedom to all Christians, making Maryland a haven for Catholics. Worse than that, the Marylanders were a source of economic competition. Two thousand inhabitants had settled on Calvert holdings by 1640, virtually all of them planting tobacco on land coveted by the Virginians.

Another obstacle to Virginia's expansion was the remnant of the Powhatan confederacy, still determined to repel white invaders. Opechancanough led a new generation of Indians into battle in 1644 against the encroaching Virginia planters. The hostilities inflicted as many casualties on both sides as the fighting did in 1622.

Changes in English Policy in the Chesapeake

Throughout the 1630s and 1640s colonial affairs drew little concern from royal officials. England itself had become engulfed first by a political crisis and then by a civil war.

The conflict grew out of efforts by both James I and Charles I (who succeeded his father in 1625) to expand their royal power and rule the nation without the nuisance of having to consult Parliament. When Parliament condemned Charles for usurping its power to raise money, he simply dissolved that body in 1629. But when the Scots invaded England in 1639, Charles found he could raise funds to pay for an army only by calling Parliament back into session. By then, many of the merchants and landed gentlemen who were members were beginning to believe that the Stuart kings might be more trouble than they were worth. In 1642 Parliament and its Puritan allies squared off against Charles I and his royalist supporters, defeating them in battle; and in 1649 they beheaded the king. England became a republic ruled by Oliver Cromwell, the man who had led Parliament's army.

The English Civil War

In truth, Cromwell's "republic" more accurately resembled a military dictatorship. After his death, most English were happy to see their throne restored in 1660 to Charles II, the son of the beheaded king. And the new king was determined to ensure that not only his subjects at home but also his American colonies abroad contributed to England's prosperity. His colonial policy was reflected in a series of regulations known as the Navigation Acts.

The first, passed by Parliament in 1660, gave England and English colonial merchants a monopoly on the shipping and marketing of all colonial goods. It also ordered that the colonies could export certain "enumerated commodities" only to

Oliver Cromwell

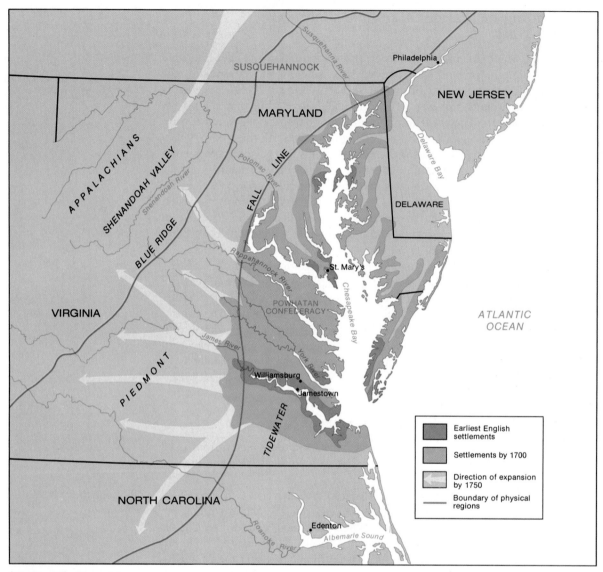

Colonies of the Chesapeake
Settlements in Virginia and Maryland spread out along the many bays of the Chesapeake, where tobacco could easily be loaded from plantation wharves. The "fall line" on rivers, dividing Tidewater and Piedmont regions, determined the extent of commercial agriculture, since ships could not pick up exports beyond that point.

England or other British ports. These goods included sugar, tobacco, cotton, ginger, and indigo (a blue dye). In 1663 Parliament added another regulation, giving British merchants a virtual monopoly on the sale of European manufactured goods to Americans by requiring that most imports going to the colonies pass through England. In 1673 a third Navigation Act placed duties on the coastal trade of the American colonies and provided for customs officials to collect tariffs and enforce commercial regulations.

Parliament later made minor modifications in the Navigation Acts, adding other exports such as rice to the category of enumerated commodities, prohibiting the colonies from exporting certain textiles or hats, and offering incentives to encourage colonists to produce indigo and iron. All these regulations were mercantilistic. That is, they were designed to ensure that England—and no foreign nations or their merchants—would profit from colonial production and trade.

The regulations of trade put in place by Restoration kings Charles II and James

Chesapeake Society in Crisis

II and their Parliaments had a decisive impact on colonials. Chesapeake planters chafed under the Navigation Acts. They were accustomed to conducting their affairs as they pleased—and they were often pleased to trade with the Dutch. What was worse, the new restrictions came at the same time as a downturn in tobacco prices. In the effort to consolidate its empire, England unintentionally worsened the economic and social difficulties of Chesapeake society.

The Conditions of Unrest

The Chesapeake colonies were heading for trouble partly because of their success. As inhabitants had started to live longer, more servants survived their terms of service. Once free, they set up as independent tobacco planters. More planters meant more production, and overproduction sent the price of tobacco plummeting, especially between 1660 and 1680. To maintain their advantage, the biggest planters bought up all the prime property along the coast, forcing newly freed servants to become tenants or to settle on unclaimed land in the interior. Either way, poorer men lost. Depending on bigger planters for land and credit made the small farmers vulnerable to debt. Moving to the frontier made them vulnerable to Indian attack.

Diminishing opportunities

The slim resources of small planters were stretched even thinner, not only from county taxes but also from export duties on tobacco paid under the Navigation Acts. During the hard times after 1660, many small planters fell deeply into debt, and some were forced back into servitude. By 1676 one-quarter of Virginia's free white men were landless. Many former servants were unable to gain a foothold even as tenants.

Diminishing opportunity in the 1660s and 1670s provided the tinder for unrest in Virginia. As the discontent of poor men mounted, so did the worries of big planters. The assembly of the colony lengthened terms of servitude, hoping to limit the number of servants entering the free population. It curbed the political rights of landless men, hoping to stifle opposition by depriving them of the vote. But these measures only set off a spate of mutinies among servants and protests over rising taxes among small planters.

Bacon's Rebellion and Coode's Rebellion

Those tensions came to a head in 1676 when civil war erupted. The immediate catalyst of the rebellion was renewed skirmishing between whites expanding westward and Indians. Virginia's royal governor, William Berkeley, favored building forts to contain the Indian threat, but frontier farmers opposed his plan as an expensive and ineffective way to defend their scattered plantations. As they clamored for an expedition to punish the Indians, Nathaniel Bacon stepped forward to lead it.

Wealthy and well connected, Bacon had arrived recently from England, expecting to receive every favor from the governor—including permission to trade with the Indians from his frontier plantation. But Berkeley and a few select friends already held a monopoly on the Indian trade. When they declined to include Bacon, he took up the cause of his poorer frontier neighbors against their common enemy, the governor. Other recent, well-to-do immigrants who resented being excluded from Berkeley's circle of power and patronage also joined Bacon.

Nathaniel Bacon

In the summer of 1676 Bacon marched into Jamestown with a body of armed men and bullied the assembly into approving his expedition to kill Indians. While

Bacon carried out that grisly business, slaughtering friendly as well as hostile tribes, Berkeley rallied his supporters and declared Bacon a rebel. Bacon retaliated by turning his forces against those led by the governor. Both sides sought allies by offering freedom to servants and slaves willing to join their ranks. Many were willing: for months the followers of Bacon and Berkeley plundered one another's plantations. In September 1676 Bacon reduced Jamestown itself to a mound of ashes. It was only his death from dysentery a month later that snuffed out the rebellion.

Political upheaval also shook Maryland, where colonists had long resented the sway of the Calvert family. As proprietors, the Calverts and their favorites monopolized political offices, just as Berkeley's circle had in Virginia. Well-to-do planters wanted a share of the Calverts' power. Smaller farmers, like those in Virginia, wanted a less expensive and more representative government. Compounding the tensions were religious differences: the Calverts and their friends were Catholic, but other colonists, including Maryland's most successful planters, were Protestant.

The unrest among Maryland's discontented planters peaked in July 1689. A former member of the assembly, John Coode, gathered an army, captured the proprietary governor, and then took grievances to authorities in England. There Coode received a sympathetic hearing. The Calverts' charter was revoked and not restored until 1715, by which time the family had become Protestant.

Growing stability

After 1690 rich planters in both Chesapeake colonies fought among themselves less and cooperated more. In Virginia older leaders and newer arrivals divided the spoils of political office. In Maryland Protestants and Catholics shared power and privilege. Those arrangements ensured that no future Bacon or Coode would mobilize restless gentlemen against the government. By acting together in legislative assemblies, the planter elite managed to curb the power of royal and proprietary governors for decades.

But the greater unity among the Chesapeake's leading families did little to ease that region's most fundamental problem. That was the sharp inequality of white society. The gulf between rich and poor planters, which had been etched ever more deeply by the troubled tobacco economy, persisted long after the rebellions of Bacon and Coode. All that saved white society in the Chesapeake from renewed crisis and conflict was the growth of black slavery.

From Servitude to Slavery

Like the tobacco plants that spread across Powhatan's land, a labor system based on slavery had not figured in the first plans for the Chesapeake. Both early promoters and planters preferred buying English servants to importing alien African slaves. Black slaves, because they served for life, were more expensive than white workers, who served only for several years. Because neither white nor black emigrants lived long, cheaper servant labor was the logical choice. The black population of the Chesapeake remained small for most of the seventeenth century, comprising just 5 percent of all inhabitants in 1675.

The lives of servants and slaves

Africans had arrived in Virginia by 1619, most likely brought by the Dutch, who dominated the slave trade until the middle of the eighteenth century. The lives of those newcomers resembled the lot of white servants, with whom they shared harsh work routines and living conditions. White and black bound laborers socialized with each other and formed sexual liaisons. They conspired to steal from their masters and ran away together; if caught, they endured similar punishments. There was more common ground: many of the first black settlers did not arrive directly from Africa but came from the Caribbean, where some had learned English and had adopted Christian beliefs. And not all were slaves: some were indentured servants, and a handful were free.

A number of changes after 1680 caused planters to invest more heavily in slaves than in servants. First, declining mortality rates in the Chesapeake made slaves the more profitable investment. Although slaves were more expensive than servants, planters could now expect to get many years of work from their bondspeople. Equally important, masters would have title to the children that slaves would now live long enough to have. At the same time, the influx of white servants was falling off just as the pool of available black labor was expanding. When the Royal African Company lost its monopoly on the English slave trade in 1698, other merchants entered the market. The number of Africans sold by British dealers swelled to 20,000 annually.

Africa and the Atlantic Slave Trade

But rising demand from the Chesapeake for slaves—and later, from all the colonies of mainland North America—played only a part in spurring growth of the Atlantic slave trade. Rather, it was the spread of plantation economies in the Caribbean and South America that created and sustained the traffic in human beings. Between the mid–fifteenth and the late nineteenth centuries, perhaps as many as 13 million men, women, and children crossed the Atlantic as slaves—a number not equaled by voluntary European migrants to the Americas until as late as the 1880s. For a century after Columbus's arrival, the traffic in slaves to the Americas had numbered a few thousand annually. But as sugar cultivation steadily prospered after 1600, slave imports rose to 19,000 a year during the seventeenth century and mushroomed to 60,000 a year in the eighteenth century. All told, as many as 21 million people were captured in West Africa between 1700 and 1850: some 9 million among them entered the Americas as slaves, but millions died before or during the Atlantic crossing, and as many as 7 million remained slaves in Africa.

The rapid growth of the Atlantic slave trade transformed not only the Americas but also Africa. Slavery became more widespread within West African society, and slave trading more central to its domestic and international commerce. Most important, the African merchants and political leaders most deeply invested in the slave trade used their profits for political advantage—to build new chiefdoms and states. Their ambitions and the greed of European slave dealers drew an increasingly large number of Africans, particularly people living in the interior, into slavery's web. By the late seventeenth century, Africans being sold into slavery were no longer only those who had put themselves at risk by committing crimes, running into debt, or voicing unpopular political and religious views. The larger number were instead captives taken by soldiers or kidnappers in raids launched specifically to acquire prisoners for the slave trade. During the decades after 1680, captives coming directly from Africa made up more than 80 percent of all new slaves entering the Chesapeake and the rest of mainland North America. Many were shipped from the coast of Africa that Portuguese explorers had first probed, between the Senegal and Niger rivers, and most of the rest from Angola, farther south.

Seized by other Africans, captives were yoked together at the neck and marched hundreds of miles through the interior to coastal forts or other outposts along the Atlantic. There, they were penned in hundreds of prisons, in lots of anywhere from twenty or thirty to more than a thousand. They might be forced to wait for slaving vessels in French *captiveries* below the fine houses of traders on the island of Goree, or herded into "outfactories" on the Banana Islands upstream

Effect of the slave trade on Africa

African Transatlantic Slave Trade, 1450–1760 Toward the end of the seventeenth century, Chesapeake and Carolina planters began importing increasing numbers of slaves. In Africa, the center of that trade lay along a mountainous region known as the Gold Coast, where more than a hundred European trading posts and forts funneled the trade. Unlike most of the rest of West Africa's shoreline, the Gold Coast had very little dense rain forest. Despite the heavy trade, only about 4 percent of the total transatlantic slave trade went to North America.

NORTH
AMERICA

ATLANTIC
OCEAN

BRITISH COLONIES

WEST INDIES

4%

FRENCH 17%

BRITISH 24%

THE
MIDDLE
PASSAGE

SPANISH 13%

CENTRAL
AMERICA

GUIANAS

DUTCH 7%

PORTUGUESE
32%

SOUTH
AMERICA

BRAZIL

Slaves were often bought and sold on the decks of the ship they traveled on, as in this painting from the 1770s (lower left). Note that the ship has put up a barricade (left side of the illustration) to keep slaves separate from the rest of the ship while the selling is proceeding. Africans found themselves in a variety of conditions in the Americas. Most toiled on plantations. Some, however, like these "watermen" along the James River in Virginia (upper left), claimed more independence. Still others ran away to maroon communities in the interior. This armed Maroon (a runaway slave; lower right) is from Dutch Guiana, where conditions on the plantations were particularly harsh.

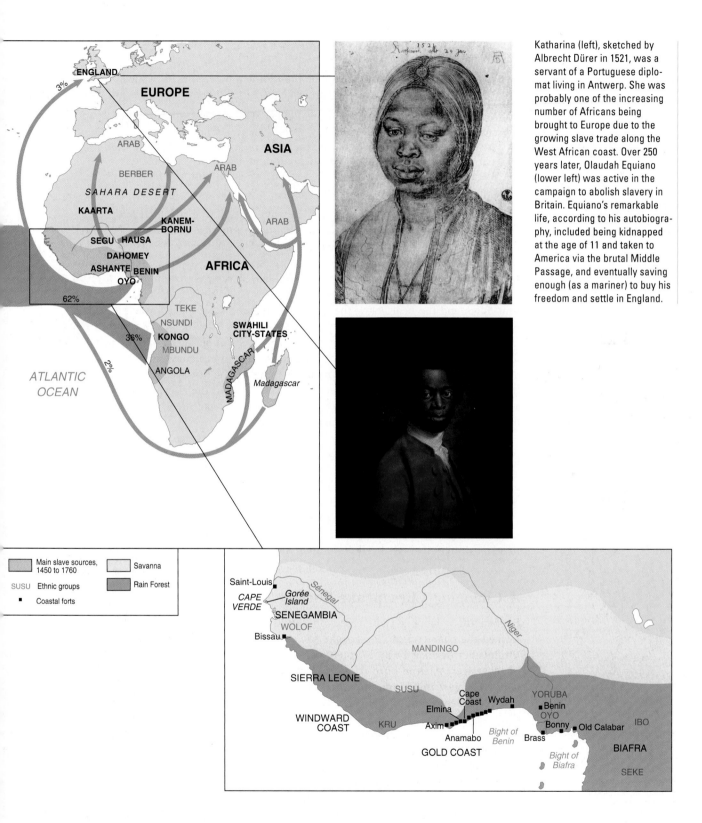

Katharina (left), sketched by Albrecht Dürer in 1521, was a servant of a Portuguese diplomat living in Antwerp. She was probably one of the increasing number of Africans being brought to Europe due to the growing slave trade along the West African coast. Over 250 years later, Olaudah Equiano (lower left) was active in the campaign to abolish slavery in Britain. Equiano's remarkable life, according to his autobiography, included being kidnapped at the age of 11 and taken to America via the brutal Middle Passage, and eventually saving enough (as a mariner) to buy his freedom and settle in England.

EUROPE

ENGLAND

3%

ASIA

ARAB

BERBER

SAHARA DESERT

KAARTA

ARAB

KANEM-BORNU

ARAB

SEGU HAUSA

DAHOMEY

ASHANTE BENIN

OYO

AFRICA

62%

TEKE

NSUNDI

KONGO

SWAHILI CITY-STATES

MBUNDU

36%

ANGOLA

MADAGASCAR

Madagascar

2%

ATLANTIC OCEAN

Main slave sources, 1450 to 1760

SUSU   Ethnic groups

■   Coastal forts

Savanna

Rain Forest

Saint-Louis

CAPE VERDE

Gorée Island

Senegal

SENEGAMBIA

WOLOF

Bissau

MANDINGO

Niger

SIERRA LEONE

SUSU

YORUBA

Cape Coast Wydah

Benin

Elmina

OYO

IBO

WINDWARD COAST

KRU

Axim

Bonny

Old Calabar

Anamabo

Bight of Benin

Brass

BIAFRA

GOLD COAST

Bight of Biafra

SEKE

65

on the Sierra Leone River, or perhaps marched into the gloomy underground slave-holds at the English fort at Cape Coast. Farther south, captives were held in marshy, fever-ridden lowlands along the Bight of Benin, waiting for a slaver to drop anchor. One African, Ottobah Cugoano, recalled finally being taken aboard ship:

> There was nothing to be heard but the rattling of chains, smacking of whips, and the groans and cries of our fellow-men. Some would not stir from the ground, when they were lashed and beat in the most horrible manner. . . . And when we found ourselves at last taken away, death was more preferable than life, and a plan was concerted amongst us that we might burn and blow up the ship and to perish altogether in the flames.

Middle Passage

Worse than the imprisonment was the voyage itself: the so-called Middle Passage, a journey of 5000 miles across the Atlantic to America. As many as 200 black men, women, and children were packed belowdecks, squeezed onto platforms built in tiers spaced so close that sitting upright was impossible. It was difficult to know whether the days or the nights were more hellish. Slaves were taken out and forced to exercise for their health for a few hours each day; the rest of the day, the sun beat down and the heat below the decks was "so excessive," one voyager recalled, that the doctors who went below to examine slaves "would faint away, and the candles would not burn." At night, the slaves "were often heard making a howling melancholy kind of noise, something expressive of extreme anguish," noted a doctor aboard another ship. When he made inquiries, he discovered it was because the slaves, in sleeping, had dreamed "they were back in their own country again, amongst their families and friends" and "when they woke up to find themselves in reality on a slave ship they began to bay and shriek."

After the numb, exhausted survivors of the Middle Passage reached American ports, they faced more challenges to staying alive. The first year in the colonies was the most deadly for new, unseasoned slaves. The sickle cell genetic trait gave blacks a greater immunity than white Europeans had to malaria, but slaves were highly susceptible to respiratory infections. One-quarter of all Africans died during their first year in the Chesapeake, and among Carolina and Caribbean slaves, mortality rates were even higher. In addition to the new disease environment, Africans were forced to adapt to lives without freedom in a wholly unfamiliar country and culture.

A Changing Chesapeake Society

Exchanging a labor system based on servitude for one based on slavery transformed the character of Chesapeake society. Most obviously, the number of black Virginians rose sharply. By 1740, 40 percent of all Virginians were black, and most of those were African-born. Unlike black men and women who had arrived earlier, these new inhabitants had little familiarity with English language and culture. This larger, more distinctively African community was also locked into a slave system that was becoming ever more rigid and demeaning. By the late decades of the seventeenth century, laws were in place making it more difficult for masters to free slaves. Other legislation systematically separated the races by prohibiting free black settlers from owning white servants and outlawing interracial marriages and sexual relationships. The legal code encouraged white contempt for black Virginians in a variety of other ways. While masters were prohibited from whipping their white servants on the bare back, slaves had no such protection. And "any Negro that shall presume to strike any white" was to receive 30 lashes for that rash act.

The new laws both reflected and encouraged racism among white colonists of all classes. Deepening racial hatred, in turn, made it unlikely that poor white planters, tenants, and servants would ever join with poor black slaves to challenge the privilege of great planters. Instead of identifying with the plight of the slaves, the Chesapeake's poorer white residents considered black Virginians their natural inferiors. They could pride themselves on sharing with wealthy white gentlemen the same skin color and on being their equals in the eyes of the law.

Racism

The leaders of the Chesapeake colonies cultivated unity among white inhabitants by improving economic prospects for freed servants and lesser planters. The Virginia assembly made provisions for freed servants to get a better start as independent farmers. It lowered taxes, allowing small planters to keep more of their earnings. New laws also gave most white male Virginians a vote in elections, allowing them an outlet to express their grievances. Economic trends toward the end of the seventeenth century contributed to the greater prosperity of small planters, because tobacco prices rose slightly and then stabilized. As a result of Bacon's savage campaign against the Virginia Indians, new land on the frontier became available. Even the domestic lives of ordinary people became more secure as mortality rates declined and the numbers of men and women in the white population evened out. As a result, virtually all men were now able to marry, and families were fragmented less often by the premature deaths of spouses and parents.

Opportunities for
white settlers

After 1700 the Chesapeake evolved into a more stable society. Gone were the bands of wild, landless, young bachelors one step ahead of the law, the small body of struggling lesser planters one step ahead of ruin, and the great mass of exploited servants one step away from rebellion. Virginia and Maryland became colonies of farming families, most of them small planters who owned between 50 and 200 acres. These families held no slaves, or at most two or three. And they accepted, usually without question, the social and political leadership of their acknowledged "superiors," great planters who styled themselves the "gentry."

The Chesapeake Gentry

The new Chesapeake gentry were the sons of well-to-do London merchant families, many of whom had intermarried with England's landed gentry. For both landed gentry and merchants, Virginia offered new prospects for land and commercial wealth. Enterprising fathers sent their sons to the Chesapeake between 1640 and 1670 to establish family interests in America by creating vast plantations. This new colonial generation of merchant-gentlemen did not plunge into the feverish gambling and exploitation practiced by the first planters along the Chesapeake. Instead, they and their coolly calculating descendants achieved status and power by shrewdly using their capital and influence and by skillfully managing their family estates.

The gentry's fortunes rested in part on the cultivation of tobacco on thousands of acres by hundreds of slaves. But the leading planters made even more money by marketing the tobacco of their humbler neighbors, selling them manufactured goods, supplying them with medical and legal services, lending money, and hiring out slaves. Unlike the rough-hewn barons of the early tobacco boom, the gentry

George Booth, the son of a wealthy planter family in Gloucester County, Virginia, was being raised for mastery. The young man's self-assured stance, the bow and arrows, the dog at his feet clutching the kill, the classical busts of women flanking his figure, and his family estate in the distance all suggest the gentry's concern for controlling the natural and social worlds.

did not owe their wealth to wringing work from poor whites. Instead they amassed great estates by wringing work from black slaves while converting their white "inferiors" into modestly prosperous small planters and paying clients.

But the gentry wanted more than money: they wanted the respect of lesser whites. On election days, when all the voters in the county assembled, each approached in his turn the gentleman candidate he preferred, publicly announced his vote, and sometimes made a brief, flattering speech about his choice. At militia musters, when every able-bodied man in the county over the age of 16 gathered, gentlemen officers led the military drills. On court days, defendants and plaintiffs testified before gentlemen justices of the peace, bedecked in wigs and robes and seated on raised benches. And every Sunday, when many in the county came to worship at the Anglican chapel, families filed soberly into the church in order of their social rank, with the gentlemen vestry heading the procession. The courthouse and church, the tavern and training field—all served as theaters in which the new Chesapeake gentry dramatized their superiority and lesser men deferred.

The plantation societies of Virginia and Maryland remained as unequal after 1700 as they had been a century earlier. Indeed, they were even more unequal because the rise of slavery sharpened economic distinctions within the white population. Those who owned slaves enjoyed a decided economic edge over those who did not. But while extreme economic inequality persisted, social tension between richer and poorer white settlers lessened. As racism unified all classes within white society and as economic and political gains eased discontent among small planters, the changing character of the Chesapeake's leaders also reduced social friction. The unscrupulous scoundrels who once dominated society had been replaced by gentlemen-planters who fancied themselves the "fathers" of their plantations and neighborhoods.

From the Caribbean to the Carolinas

During the same decade that the English invaded Powhatan's land, they began to colonize the Caribbean. A century earlier, Columbus had charted the route: ships picked up the trade winds off Madeira and the Canary Islands and headed west across the Atlantic to paradise. At journey's end the surf broke over shores rimmed with white sand beaches that rose sharply to coral terraces, then to broad plateaus or mountain peaks shrouded in rain forests.

Transformation of the Caribbean

Paradise was lost to the Indians of the Caribbean, or at least to those few remaining alive. European diseases, combined with Spanish exploitation, had eliminated virtually all the natives of Hispaniola by the 1520s. Over the next century the natives of Cuba, Puerto Rico, the Bahamas, the Lesser Antilles, and Jamaica would likewise be decimated. And the "paradise" that remained was filled with plants and animals that would have been strange to natives only a century earlier. Hogs and cattle, now wild, had been imported by Europeans, as had figs, oranges, pomegranates, and African yams. That ecological migration of flora and fauna would continue to transform the Americas in the century to come.

Paradise was lost to the English as well. At first they came to the Caribbean intending not to colonize but to steal from the Spanish. Even after 1604 when some English settled on the islands, few intended to stay. Yet not only did the English establish permanent plantation colonies in the West Indies, but their Caribbean settlements also became the jumping-off points for a new colony on the North American mainland—South Carolina. Because of the strong West Indian influence, South Carolina developed a social order in some ways distinct from that of the Chesapeake. Yet in other ways, the development of the Carolinas paralleled Virginia and Maryland's path from violence, high mortality, and uncertainty toward relative stability.

Paradise Lost

The English had traded and battled with the Spanish in the Caribbean since the 1560s. From those island bases English buccaneers conducted an illegal trade with Spanish settlements, sacked the coastal towns, and plundered silver ships bound for Seville. Weakened by decades of warfare, Spain could not hold the West Indies. The Dutch drove a wedge into Caribbean trade routes, and the French and the English began to colonize the islands.

In the 40 years after 1604, some 30,000 immigrants from the British Isles planted crude frontier outposts on St. Kitts, Barbados, Nevis, Montserrat, and Antigua. The settlers—some free, many others indentured servants, and almost all young men—devoted themselves to working as little as possible, drinking as much as possible, and returning to England as soon as possible. They cultivated for export a poor quality of tobacco, which returned just enough profit to maintain straggling settlements of small farms.

Then, nearly overnight, sugar cultivation transformed the Caribbean. In the 1640s Barbados planters learned from the Dutch how to process sugarcane. The Dutch also supplied African slaves to work the cane fields and marketed the sugar for high prices in the Netherlands. Sugar plantations and slave labor rapidly spread to other English and French islands as Europeans developed an insatiable sweet tooth for the once scarce commodity. Caribbean sugar made more money for England than the total volume of commodities exported by all the mainland American colonies.

Caribbean sugar

In 1650, when this map of Barbados was drawn, the sugar boom was only beginning. Most of the settlements lie on the leeward side of the island, away from the prevailing winds. The map's drawings indicate that, already, escaped slaves (upper left) were being hunted down in their mountain hideaways. Hogs (two are shown) ran wild everywhere on the island. They were an import from Europe that in a few short years had multiplied more rapidly than the humans who brought them.

Even though its great planters became the richest people in English America, they could not have confused the West Indies with paradise. Throughout the seventeenth century, disease took a fearful toll, and island populations grew only because of immigration. In the scramble for land, small farmers were pushed onto tiny plots that barely allowed them to survive.

Slavery in the Caribbean

The desperation of bound laborers posed another threat. After the Caribbean's conversion to cultivating sugar, black slaves gradually replaced white indentured servants in the cane fields. By the beginning of the eighteenth century, black inhabitants outnumbered white residents by four to one. Fear of servant mutinies and slave rebellions frayed the nerves of island masters. They tried to contain the danger by imposing harsh slave codes and inflicting brutal punishments on white and black laborers alike. But planters lived under a constant state of siege. One visitor to Barbados observed that whites fortified their homes with parapets from which they could pour scalding water on attacking servants and slaves. During the first century of settlement, seven major slave uprisings shook the English islands.

As more people, both white and black, squeezed onto the islands, some settlers looked for a way out. With all the land in use, the Caribbean no longer offered opportunity to freed servants or even planters' sons. It was then that the West Indies started to shape the history of the American South.

The Founding of the Carolinas

The colonization of the Carolinas began with the schemes of Virginia's royal governor, William Berkeley, and Sir John Colleton, a supporter of Charles I who had been exiled to the Caribbean at the end of England's civil war. Colleton saw that the Caribbean had a surplus of white settlers, and Berkeley knew that Virginians needed room to expand as well. Together the two men set their sights on the area south of Virginia. Along with a number of other aristocrats, they convinced Charles II to make them joint proprietors in 1663 of a place they called the Carolinas, in honor of the king.

North Carolina

A few hardy souls from Virginia had already squatted around Albemarle Sound in the northern part of the Carolina grant. The proprietors provided them with a governor and a representative assembly. About 40 years later, in 1701, they set off North Carolina as a separate colony. The desolate region quickly proved a disappointment. Lacking good harbors and navigable rivers, the colony had no convenient way of marketing its produce. North Carolina remained a poor colony, its sparse population engaged in general farming and the production of masts, pitch, tar, and turpentine.

South Carolina

The southern portion of the Carolina grant held far more promise, especially in the eyes of one of its proprietors, Sir Anthony Ashley Cooper, earl of Shaftesbury. In 1669 he sponsored an expedition of a few hundred English and Barbadian immigrants, who planted the first permanent settlement in South Carolina. By 1680 the colonists had established the center of economic, social, and political life at the confluence of the Ashley and the Cooper rivers, naming the site Charles Town (later Charleston) after the king.

Cooper had big plans for his Carolina colony. Charleston stood at the hub of a network of river routes, allowing for easy development of the region's commercial potential. Because the proprietors were offering liberal land grants and had promised religious toleration and a representative government, settlers would flock to the colony. These new inhabitants would enrich the proprietors by paying quitrents, a halfpenny per acre annually.

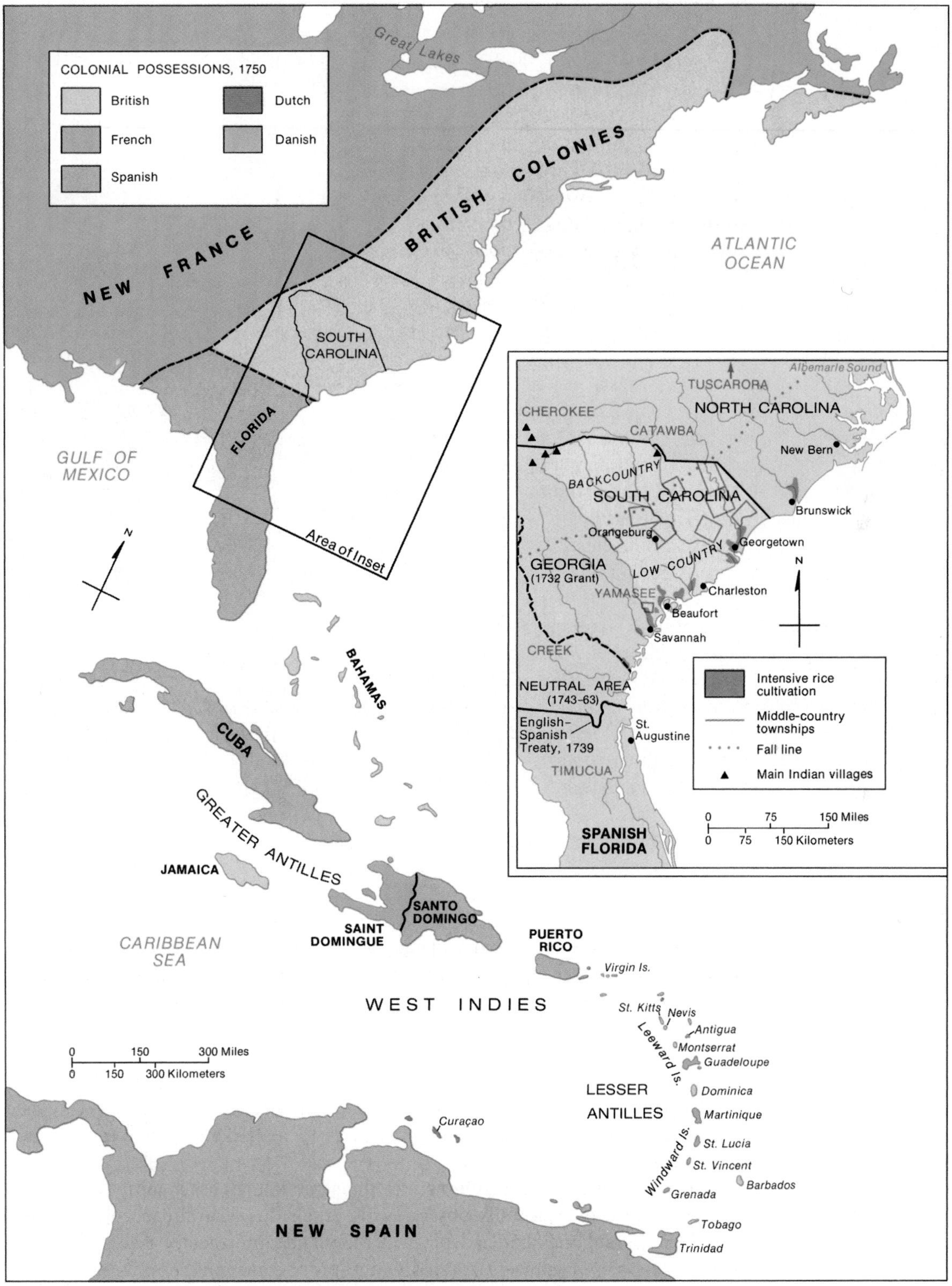
COLONIAL POSSESSIONS, 1750
British
French
Spanish
Dutch
Danish
Great Lakes
NEW FRANCE
BRITISH COLONIES
ATLANTIC OCEAN
SOUTH CAROLINA
FLORIDA
GULF OF MEXICO
Area of Inset
BAHAMAS
CUBA
GREATER ANTILLES
JAMAICA
SAINT DOMINGUE
SANTO DOMINGO
PUERTO RICO
CARIBBEAN SEA
Virgin Is.
WEST INDIES
St. Kitts
Nevis
Antigua
Montserrat
Guadeloupe
Leeward Is.
LESSER ANTILLES
Dominica
Martinique
St. Lucia
St. Vincent
Barbados
Windward Is.
Grenada
Tobago
Trinidad
Curaçao
NEW SPAIN
0 150 300 Miles
0 150 300 Kilometers
Albemarle Sound
TUSCARORA
NORTH CAROLINA
CHEROKEE
CATAWBA
New Bern
BACKCOUNTRY
SOUTH CAROLINA
Brunswick
Orangeburg
Georgetown
GEORGIA
(1732 Grant)
LOW COUNTRY
YAMASEE
Charleston
Beaufort
Savannah
CREEK
NEUTRAL AREA
(1743-63)
English-Spanish Treaty, 1739
St. Augustine
TIMUCUA
SPANISH FLORIDA
Intensive rice cultivation
Middle-country townships
Fall line
Main Indian villages
0 75 150 Miles
0 75 150 Kilometers

The Carolinas and the Caribbean The map underscores the geographic link between West Indian and Carolina settlements. Emigrants from Barbados dominated politics in early South Carolina, while Carolinians provided foodstuffs, grain, and cattle to the West Indies. As South Carolinians began growing rice, Caribbean slave ships found it an easy sail north and west to unload their cargoes in Charleston.

Daily Lives

FOOD/DRINK/DRUGS
A Taste for Sugar

It is said that shortly before his death in 735 C.E., the Venerable Bede, an English abbot, bequeathed a precious treasure to his brother monks. It consisted of a cache of spices, including a little stock of sugar. What separated Bede's world, in which sugar was a costly luxury, from twentieth-century Americans' world of ever-present sweetness was the discovery of America and the establishment of plantation economies in the Caribbean and Brazil.

Europeans first learned of sugar during an earlier surge of expansion—the Arab conquests in the Mediterranean, North Africa, and Spain during the seventh and eighth centuries. From then until the fourteenth century, Europe's merchants imported small quantities of sugar at great expense from Arab plantations as well as from distant Persia and India, countries that had produced sugar since 500 C.E.

Throughout the Middle Ages and the early modern era, only the royal and the rich of Europe could indulge their desire for sugar, and even those classes partook sparingly. Europeans classified sugar as a spice, like the equally scarce and exotic pepper, nutmeg, ginger, and saffron. Nobility valued sugar as a medicine for sore throats, stomach disorders, and infertility. It was also used as a remedy for the Black Death and tooth decay. The cooks of castle kitchens seasoned food and sauces with a pinch of sugar or sprinkled it on meat, fish, fowl, and fruit to preserve freshness— or to conceal rot. Only on great occasions did the confectioners of noble families splurge, fashioning for courtly feasts great baked sugar sculptures of knights and kings, horses and apes, called "subtleties."

The Sugar Mill.

Once harvested, sugarcane in the West Indies was crushed, as in this sugar mill. The juice was collected and channeled to the sugar works, where it was concentrated through boiling and evaporation. This neat diagrammatic picture belies the harsh conditions of labor and the high mortality that slaves experienced: sweetness came at a steep price.

Such plans were big enough to satisfy most of the Carolina proprietors, who regarded their venture simply as land speculation. But Cooper, like others before him, hoped to create an ideal society in America. Cooper's utopia was one in which a few landed aristocrats and gentlemen would rule with the consent of many smaller property holders. With his personal secretary, John Locke, Cooper drew up an intricate scheme of government, the Fundamental Constitutions. The design provided Carolina with a proprietary governor and a hereditary nobility who, as a Council of Lords, would recommend all laws to a Parliament elected by lesser landowners.

The Fundamental Constitutions

The Fundamental Constitutions met the same fate as other lordly dreams for America. Instead of peacefully observing its provisions, Carolinians plunged into the political wrangling that had plagued Maryland's proprietary rule. Assemblies resisted the sweeping powers granted to the proprietary governors. Ordinary settlers protested against paying quitrents claimed by the proprietors. Political unrest in North Carolina triggered three rebellions between 1677 and 1711. In South Carolina opposition to the proprietors gathered strength more slowly but finally exploded with equal force.

For the rest of Europe, life was not as sweet. While the rich and royal savored sugary treats, the diets of ordinary people ran to monotonous, meager starches. The staff of everyday life consisted of bread, peas, beans, and, in good years, a little milk, butter, and cheese. The occasional pig slaughtered, rabbit trapped, or fish caught supplied stray protein for the poor.

That pattern of consumption started to change as Europeans turned to African slave labor to grow sugar for them. Madeira and the Canary Islands became more than stepping-stones across the Atlantic for Spain and Portugal. The sugar plantations established there were a foretaste of veritable sugar factories created in the Caribbean colonies of England and France.

By the sixteenth and seventeenth centuries, Europe's merchant classes could imitate elite patterns of eating by pouring sugar into pastries and puddings. And by the middle of the eighteenth century, an increasingly large and inexpensive supply from the Caribbean was making sugar essential to the poorest Europeans. Among England's laboring classes, another colonial import—Indian tea, laced heavily with sugar—began to accompany an otherwise cold supper of bread. Sweet tea and bread constituted the entire diet of those at the bottom of English society. Cheaper, warmer, and more stimulating than milk or beer (its prime competitors), sugared tea won the loyalty of England's mass market and ranked as the non-alcoholic beverage of national choice. By the nineteenth century, English working families were also combining sugar and starch by pouring treacle (molasses) over porridge and spreading jams or marmalades on their bread.

Europe and America affected each other in many ways, but diet figured among the more fundamental conditions of life altered by colonization. More than coffee, chocolate, rum, or tobacco—indeed, more than any of the other "drug foods" produced by the colonies except tea—sugar provided a major addition to the diet of the English and other Europeans.

Even though sugar changed gradually from a scarce, coveted luxury to a mass-marketed basic foodstuff, its association with power persisted. But by the eighteenth century, it was no longer the *consumption* of sugar that bestowed status. On the contrary, as sweeteners found their way into the barest cupboards, the rich and royal probably used less sugar than the poor and powerless. Instead, after 1700 it was the *production* of sugar that conferred power. Planters who grew it, merchants who shipped and sold it, industrialists who refined it, and politicians who taxed it discovered in sugar sources of profit and distinction less perishable than the subtleties of noble banquets or the legacy of the Venerable Bede.

Early Instability

Immigrants from Barbados, the most numerous among the early settlers, came quickly to dominate South Carolina politics. Just as quickly, they objected to proprietary power. To offset the influence of the Barbadians, most of whom were Anglican, the proprietors encouraged the migration of French Huguenots and English Presbyterians and Baptists. The stream of newcomers only heightened tensions, splitting South Carolinians into two camps with competing political and religious loyalties.

Meanwhile, settlers spread out along the coastal plain. Searching for a profitable export, the first colonists raised grains and cattle, foodstuffs that they exported to the West Indies. South Carolinians also developed a large trade in deerskins with coastal tribes like the Yamasee and the Creeks and Catawbas of the interior. More numerous than the Indians of the Chesapeake and even more deeply divided, the Carolina tribes competed to become the favored clients of white traders. Southeastern Indian economies quickly became dependent on English guns, rum, and clothing. To repay their debts to white traders, Indians enslaved

Mulberry Plantation in South Carolina was first carved from coastal swamps in 1714. This photograph from 1935 suggests the way that the landscape may have looked. Stands of live oak draped with Spanish moss ringed the paddy fields, where African slaves skilled in rice cultivation oversaw the difficult and arduous task of properly irrigating the crop.

Yamasee War

The end of proprietary rule

and sold to white buyers large numbers of men, women, and children taken in wars waged against rival tribes.

Provisions, deerskins, and Indian slaves proved less profitable for South Carolinians than did rice, which became the colony's cash crop by the opening of the eighteenth century. Constant demand for rice in Europe made South Carolina the richest colony and South Carolina planters the richest people on the mainland of North America.

Unfortunately, South Carolina's swampy coast, so perfectly suited to growing rice, was less suited for human habitation. Weakened by chronic malaria, settlers died in epic numbers from yellow fever, smallpox, and respiratory infections. The white population grew slowly, through immigration rather than natural increase, and numbered a mere 10,000 by 1730.

Early South Carolinians had little in common but the harsh conditions of frontier existence. Most colonists lived on isolated plantations; early deaths fragmented families and neighborhoods. Immigration after 1700 only intensified the colony's ethnic and religious diversity, adding Swiss and German Lutherans, Scots-Irish Presbyterians, Welsh Baptists, and Spanish Jews. The colony's only courts were in Charleston; churches and clergy of any denomination were scarce. On those rare occasions when early Carolinians came together, they gathered at Charleston to escape the pestilential air of their plantations, to sue each other for debt and haggle over prices, or to fight over religious differences and proprietary politics.

White, Red, and Black: The Search for Order

By the opening decades of the eighteenth century, South Carolina seemed as strife-torn and unstable as the early Chesapeake colonies. In addition to internal tensions, external dangers threatened the very life of the Carolina settlements. The Spanish were rattling their sabers in Florida, the French were filtering into the Gulf region, and pirates were lurking along the North Carolina coast.

Most menacing were the Indians, and in 1715 they struck. The Yamasee of the coast allied themselves with the Creeks farther inland and launched a series of assaults that nearly pushed white Carolinians into the sea. All that saved the colony was an alliance with the Cherokee, another interior tribe who, in return for trading privileges, mounted a counterattack against their Indian rivals.

As colonists reeled from the Yamasee War, opposition mounted against the proprietors, who had done nothing to protect their vulnerable colony. Military expenses had also forced Carolinians to fall into greater debt, to pay higher taxes, and to struggle with an inflated currency that month by month was worth less. Even Presbyterians, Baptists, and Huguenots, who had once defended the proprietors, shifted their sympathies because they disapproved of more recent attempts to establish the Church of England as South Carolina's official religion. During the 1720s, mass meetings and riots so disrupted government that it all but ground to a halt. Finally, in 1729, the Crown formally established royal government; by 1730 economic recovery had done much to ease the strife. Even more important in bringing greater political stability, the white colonists of South Carolina came to realize that they must unite if they were to counter the Spanish in Florida and the French and their Indian allies to the southwest.

The growing black population gave white Carolinians another reason to maintain a united front. During the first decades of settlement, frontier conditions and the scarcity of labor had forced masters to allow enslaved Africans greater freedom within bondage. White and black laborers shared chores on small farms. On stock-raising plantations, called "cowpens," black cowboys ranged freely over the countryside. Black contributions to the defense of the colony also reinforced racial interdependence and muted white domination. Whenever the Spanish, the French, or the Indians threatened, black Carolinians were enlisted in the militia.

Slavery in South Carolina

White Carolinians depended on black labor even more after turning to rice as their cash crop. In fact, planters began to import slaves in larger numbers because of West African skill in rice cultivation. But whites harbored deepening fears of the black workers whose labor built planter fortunes. As early as 1708 black men and women had become a majority in the colony, and by 1730 they outnumbered white settlers by two to one. Like Caribbean planters, white Carolinians put into effect strict slave codes that converted their colony into an armed camp and snuffed out the freedoms that black settlers had enjoyed earlier.

The ever-present threat of revolt on the part of the black majority gave all white South Carolinians an incentive to cooperate, whatever their religion, politics, or ethnic background. To be sure, the colony's high death rates and cultural differences persisted, while local government and churches remained weak. Yet against all these odds, white South Carolinians prospered and political peace prevailed after 1730. Any course except harmony would have exacted too high a price.

The Founding of Georgia

After 1730 South Carolinians could take comfort not only from their new prosperity and new political harmony but also from the founding of a new colony on their southern border. South Carolinians liked Georgia a great deal more than the Virginians had liked Maryland, for the colony formed a defensive buffer between British North America and Spanish Florida.

Enhancing the military security of South Carolina was only one reason for the founding of Georgia. More important to General James Oglethorpe and other idealistic English gentlemen was the aim of aiding the "worthy poor" by providing them with land, employment, and a new start. They envisioned a colony of hardworking small farmers who would produce silk and wine, sparing England the need to import those commodities. That dream seemed within reach when George II made Oglethorpe and his friends the trustees of the new colony in 1732, granting them a charter for 21 years. At the end of that time Georgia would revert to royal control.

James Oglethorpe

The trustees did not, as legend has it, empty England's debtors' prisons to populate Georgia. They freed few debtors but recruited from every country in Europe paupers who seemed willing to work hard—and who professed Protestantism. They paid their passage and provided each with 50 acres of land, tools, and a year's worth of supplies. Settlers who could pay their own way were encouraged to come by granting them larger tracts of land. Much to the trustees' dismay, that generous offer was taken up not only by many hoped-for Protestants but also by several hundred Ashkenazim (German Jews) and Sephardim (Spanish and Portuguese Jews), who established a thriving community in early Savannah.

The trustees were determined to ensure that Georgia became a small farmers' utopia. Rather than selling land, the trustees gave it away, but none of the colony's

The Yuchi were neighbors of one of Georgia's early settlements, and one of the newly emigrated German colonists painted this watercolor of a Yuchi celebration. Judging from the guns hanging at the back of the shelter, these Indians were already trading with white settlers in the area.

Utopian designs

settlers could own more than 500 acres. The trustees also outlawed slavery and hard liquor in order to cultivate habits of industry and sustain equality among whites. This design for a virtuous and egalitarian utopia was greeted with little enthusiasm by Georgians. They pressed for a free market in land and argued that the colony could never prosper until the trustees revoked their ban on slavery. Because the trustees had provided for no elective assembly, settlers could express their discontent only by moving to South Carolina—which many did during the early decades.

As mounting opposition threatened to depopulate the colony, the trustees caved in. They revoked their restrictions on land, slavery, and liquor a few years before the king assumed control of the colony in 1752. Under royal control, Georgia continued to develop an ethnically and religiously diverse society, similar to that of South Carolina. Similarly, its economy was based on rice cultivation and the Indian trade.

Similarities among the plantation colonies

Although South Carolina and the English West Indies were both more opulent and more embattled societies than Virginia and Maryland, the plantation colonies stretching from the Chesapeake to the Caribbean had much in common. Everywhere planters depended on a single staple crop, which brought both wealth and political power to those commanding the most land and the most labor. Everywhere the biggest planters relied for their success on the very people whom they deeply feared—enslaved African Americans. Everywhere, that fear was reflected in the development of repressive slave codes and the spread of racism throughout all classes of white society.

The Spanish Borderlands

St. Augustine and Santa Fe

When the English founded Jamestown, Spanish settlement in the present-day United States consisted of one feeble fort in southeastern Florida and a single outpost in New Mexico. Hoping both to intimidate privateers who preyed on silver ships and to assert their sovereign claim to the Americas, Spain had established St. Augustine on the Florida coast in 1565. But for decades the place remained a squalid garrison town of a few hundred soldiers and settlers beleaguered by hurricanes, pirates, and Indians. Meanwhile, the Spanish planted a straggling settlement under azure skies and spectacular mesas near present-day Santa Fe in 1598. Their fervent desire was to create colonies in the Southwest that would prove more richly profitable than even those in Central and South America.

Defending both outposts proved so great a drain on royal resources that the Spanish government considered abandoning its precarious footholds in North America. Only the pleas of Catholic missionaries, who hoped to convert the native peoples, persuaded the Crown to sustain its support. But even by 1700, St. Augustine could boast only about 1500 souls, an assortment of Spaniards, black slaves, and Hispanicized Indians. New Mexico's colonial population amounted to fewer than 3000 Spanish ranchers, soldiers, and clergy scattered among the haciendas (cattle and sheep ranches), presidios (military garrisons), and Catholic missions along the Rio Grande. There, the native Pueblo Indians numbered some 30,000.

Still, during these years the Catholic clergy remained active, creating mission communities designed to incorporate native tribes into colonial society. In New Mexico, Franciscan friars supervised Pueblo women (who traditionally built their people's adobe homes) in the construction of more than 30 missions. By 1675 in Florida, perhaps 10,000 Indians were living in 35 villages in which the friars came to stay. Although the new churches were built with native materials, their rectangular forms contrasted sharply with the circular public halls preferred by the Indians of both New Mexico and Florida. Like the curves of a circle interrupted by the right angles of a square, Spanish and Indian cultures coexisted uneasily.

Mission communities

Unlike the English, the Spanish projected a place in their colonies for the Indians. Homes, workshops, granaries, and stables clustered around the church. The missionaries taught Indians European agricultural techniques and crafts. At mission schools, adults as well as children learned to say prayers, sing Christian hymns, and speak Spanish. In 1675, when the bishop of Cuba toured Florida's missions, he spoke enthusiastically of converts who embraced "with devotion the mysteries of our holy faith."

The Indians were selective, however, in the European "mysteries" they chose to adopt. Some natives regarded the friars' presence simply as a means of protecting themselves against the harsher treatment of Spanish soldiers and ranchers. Other Indians used the Spanish presence to give them the upper hand in dealing with rival tribes, just as Powhatan had used white Virginians to further his own designs. And in their religious ceremonies, many natives simply placed Jesus, Mary, and Christian saints beside the other deities they honored. They continued their own religious devotions, much to the frustration of the friars.

Indian and Spanish cultures bumped up against each other in material ways as well. When the Spanish at St. Augustine found the climate unsuitable for growing wheat, olives, and grapes, they turned to Indian maize, beans, and squash. Indians adopted domesticated animals from Europe—horses, cattle, sheep, mules, and donkeys. Watermelons and peach trees, brought to the Atlantic coast by the Spanish, spread quickly along Indian trade routes, often ahead of Europeans themselves.

To their dismay, Indians discovered that in the long run, becoming "civilized" usually meant learning to work for Spanish masters as docile servants. The labor was harsh enough to send many to an early death. European diseases, too, took a gruesome toll among mission Indians. As the population dropped sharply, the demand by Spanish colonists rose for increasingly scarce Indian labor. In theory, Spanish laws protected Indians from ruthless exploitation, but soldiers and settlers illegally forced natives to tend herds, till fields, and haul heavy loads. In New Mexico, captured Indians were sent south to be sold as slaves in the mines of New Spain.

This Native American drawing on a canyon wall in present-day Arizona represents the progress of the Spanish into the Southwest. The prominence of horses underscores their novelty to the Indians, an initial advantage enjoyed by the invaders. "The most essential thing in new lands is horses," one of Coronado's men emphasized. "They instill the greatest fear in the enemy and make the Indians respect the leaders of the army." Many Indian peoples soon put the horse to their own uses, however, and even outshone the Spanish in their riding skills.

As the abuses increased, so did the resentment. Indians regularly fled the mission settlements; others made life miserable for their "benefactors." One padre at Taos Pueblo was served corn tortillas laced with urine and mouse meat. From beyond Spanish lines, the Apache used the horses introduced from Europe to rustle Spanish cattle. On occasion discontent and anger ignited major insurrections. The most successful was the Pueblo Revolt of 1680, which drove the Spanish out of New Mexico for more than a decade. Popé, an Indian spiritual leader in Taos, coordinated an uprising of several Pueblo tribes that vented the full force of their hatred of Spanish rule. They killed 400 people in outlying haciendas and burned the Spanish-style houses and churches to the ground. The attack wiped out one-fifth of the Spanish population of 2500 and sent survivors scurrying for refuge down Dead Man's Road to El Paso, Texas.

Despite native opposition, the Spanish persisted, especially because they saw their European rivals making headway in North America. By the end of the seventeenth century, English settlements in South Carolina were well entrenched, which prompted the Spanish in Florida to offer freedom to any escaped slaves willing to defend the colony and convert to Catholicism. The black fugitives established a fortified settlement north of St. Augustine, Gracia Real de Santa Teresa de Mose, which served as a barrier against English attacks and as a base for raiding Carolina's plantations. Meanwhile the French were building forts at Biloxi and Mobile near the mouth of the Mississippi River, signaling their designs on the Gulf of Mexico. As a counterweight, the Spanish added a second military outpost in Florida at Pensacola and founded several missions in present-day Texas. And after 1769, to secure their claims to the Pacific coast from England and Russia, Spanish

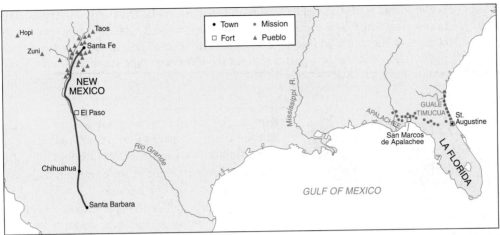

Town	Mission
Fort	Pueblo

Spanish Missions in North America, ca. 1675 From St. Augustine, Spanish missionaries spread north into Guale Indian villages in present-day Georgia and westward among the Indians of Timucua, Apalachee, and Apalachicola. In New Mexico, missions radiated outward from the Rio Grande, as distant as Hopi Pueblo in the west.

soldiers and missionaries began colonizing California. Led by the Franciscan friar Junípero Serra, they established 20 communities along the Pacific coastal plain.

Empire . . . utopia . . . independence. . . . For more than a century after the founding of Jamestown in 1607, those dreams inspired the inhabitants of the Chesapeake, the Carolinas and Georgia, the Caribbean, and the Spanish borderlands. The regions served as staging grounds where kings and commoners, free and unfree, men and women, red, white, and black played out their hopes. Most met only disappointment and many met disaster in the painful decades before the new colonies achieved a measure of stability.

The dream of an expanding empire faltered for the Spanish, who found no new El Dorado in the Southwest. The dream of empire failed, too, when James I and Charles I, England's early Stuart kings, found their power checked by Parliament. And the dream foundered fatally for Powhatan's successors, who were unable to resist both white diseases and land-hungry tobacco planters.

English lords had dreamed of establishing feudal utopias in America. But proprietors like the Calvert family in Maryland and Cooper in the Carolinas found themselves hounded by frontier planters and farmers who sought economic and political power. Georgia's trustees struggled in vain to nurture their dream of a utopia for the poor. The dream of a Spanish Catholic utopia brought by missionaries to the American Southwest dimmed with Indian resistance.

The dream of independence proved the most deceptive of all, especially for the inhabitants of England's colonies. Just a bare majority of the white servant immigrants to the Chesapeake survived to enjoy freedom. The rest were struck down by disease or worn down at the hands of tobacco barons eager for profit. Not only in the Chesapeake but also in the Caribbean and the Carolinas, real independence eluded the English planters. Poorer people—dependent on richer people for land and leadership—deferred to them at church and on election days and depended on them to buy crops or to extend credit. Even the richest planters were dependent on the English and Scottish merchants who supplied them with credit and marketed their crops, as well as on the English officials who made colonial policy.

And everywhere in the American South and Southwest, white people's lingering dreams were realized only through the labor of the least free members of colonial America. In the Southwest the Spanish made servants of the Indians. Along the southern Atlantic coast and in the Caribbean, English plantation owners (like the Spanish before them) turned for labor to the African slave trade. Only after slavery became firmly established as a social and legal institution did England's southern colonies begin to settle down and grow: during the late seventeenth century for the Chesapeake region and the early eighteenth for the Carolinas. That stubborn reality would haunt Americans of all colors who continued to dream of freedom and independence.

chapter summary

During the seventeenth century, plantation economies based on slavery gradually developed throughout the American South.

- Native peoples everywhere in the American South resisted white settlement, but their populations were drastically reduced by warfare, disease, and enslavement.

- Thriving monocultures were established throughout the region—tobacco in the Chesapeake, rice in the Carolinas, and sugar in the Caribbean.
- African slavery emerged as the dominant labor system in all the southern colonies.
- Instability and conflict characterized the southern colonies for most of the first century of their existence.
- As the English colonies took shape, the Spanish extended their empire in Florida and New Mexico, establishing military garrisons, missions, and cattle ranches.

interactive learning

The Primary Source Investigator CD-ROM offers the following materials related to this chapter:

- Interactive maps: **The Atlantic World, 1400–1850** (M2) and **Growth of the Colonies, 1610–1690** (M3)

- A collection of primary sources on the English colonization of North America, such as an engraving that illustrates the dress and customs of Native Americans living near Jamestown, letters and documents about the peace resulting from the marriage of Pocahontas and John Rolfe, and the terrible collapse of that peace captured in a contemporary engraving of the Indian massacre of Jamestown settlers. Also included are several sources on the origins of slavery in America: a document that presents one of the earliest restrictive slave codes in the British colonies, images of Portuguese slave trading forts on the coast of West Africa, and a sobering diagram of the human cargo holds of that era's slave-trading ships.

additional reading

The best treatment of early Virginia is Edmund S. Morgan, *American Slavery, American Freedom* (1975). A more intimate portrait of an early Virginia community can be found in Darrett and Anita Rutman's study of Middlesex County, *A Place in Time* (1984). Karen Kupperman offers an excellent overview of relations between whites and Indians not only in the early South but throughout North America in *Settling with the Indians* (1980), while James Merrell sensitively explores the impact of white contact on a single southern tribe in *The Indians' New World* (1989). Two other notable treatments of slavery and race relations in Britain's southern colonies are Richard Dunn's study of the Caribbean, *Sugar and Slaves* (1972), and Peter Wood's work on South Carolina, *Black Majority* (1974). And for the Spanish borderlands, see David J. Weber, *The Spanish Frontier in North America* (1992).

The Chesapeake has always drawn more notice from early American historians than South Carolina has, but in recent years some important studies have redressed that neglect. The best overview of that colony's development remains Robert Weir, *Colonial South Carolina* (1982); for fine explorations of more specialized topics, see Daniel C. Littlefield, *Rice and Slaves* (1981); Peter Colclanis, *The Shadow of a Dream* (1989); and Timothy Silver, *A New Face on the Countryside* (1990). For a fuller list of readings, see the Bibliography at www.mhhe.com/davidsonnation5.

significant events

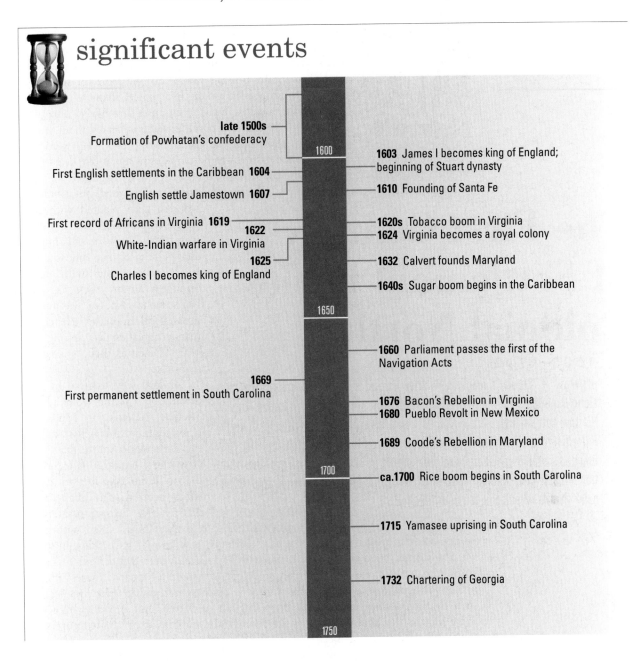

late 1500s
Formation of Powhatan's confederacy

1603 James I becomes king of England; beginning of Stuart dynasty

First English settlements in the Caribbean **1604**

English settle Jamestown **1607**

1610 Founding of Santa Fe

First record of Africans in Virginia **1619**

1620s Tobacco boom in Virginia

1622
White-Indian warfare in Virginia

1624 Virginia becomes a royal colony

1625
Charles I becomes king of England

1632 Calvert founds Maryland

1640s Sugar boom begins in the Caribbean

1660 Parliament passes the first of the Navigation Acts

1669
First permanent settlement in South Carolina

1676 Bacon's Rebellion in Virginia

1680 Pueblo Revolt in New Mexico

1689 Coode's Rebellion in Maryland

ca.1700 Rice boom begins in South Carolina

1715 Yamasee uprising in South Carolina

1732 Chartering of Georgia

1600
1650
1700
1750

Chapter 3

They came to her one night while she slept. Into her dreams drifted a small island, and on the island were tall trees and living creatures, one of them wearing the fur of a white rabbit. When she told of her vision, no one took her seriously, not even the wise men among her people, shamans and conjurers whose business it was to interpret dreams. No one, that is, until two days later, when the island appeared to all, floating toward shore. On the island, as she had seen, were tall trees, and on their branches—bears. Or creatures that looked so much like bears that the men grabbed their weapons and raced to the beach, eager for the good hunt sent by the gods. They were disappointed. The island was not an island at all but a strange wooden ship planted with the trunks of trees. And the bears were not bears at all but a strange sort of men whose bodies were covered with hair. Strangest among them, as she had somehow known, was a man dressed all in white. He commanded great respect among the bearlike men as their "shaman," or priest.

The First Century of Settlement in the Colonial North

1600–1700

preview • Europe's religious rivalries shaped seventeenth-century colonies along America's northern rim: the Protestant Reformation stamped English Puritan settlements from Maine to Long Island, and the Catholic Counter-Reformation encouraged the less numerous settlers of French Canada. New England's stable societies, with their strong family bonds and growing tradition of self-government, contrasted with the more prosperous and ethnically diverse colonies of the mid-Atlantic.

In that way, foretold by the dreams of a young woman, the Micmac Indians in 1869 recounted their tribe's first meeting with whites more than two centuries earlier. Uncannily, the traditions of other northern tribes record similar dreams predicting the European arrival: "large canoes with great white wings like those of a giant bird," filled with pale bearded men bearing "long black tubes." Perhaps the dreamers gave shape in their sleep to stories heard from other tribes who had actually seen white strangers and ships. Or perhaps, long before they ever encountered Europeans, these Indians imagined them, just as Europeans fantasized about a new world. The first whites seen by those tribes might have been English or Dutch. But probably, like the party met by the Micmacs, they were French, the most avid early adventurers in the northern reaches of the Americas.

Cartier and Champlain

For the time being, few French had dreams of their own about settling in the Americas. Jacques Cartier looked for a Northwest Passage to Asia in 1535 and instead discovered the St. Lawrence River. But not until 1605 did the French plant a permanent colony, at Port Royal in Acadia (Nova Scotia). Three years later, Samuel de Champlain shifted French interests to the St. Lawrence valley, where he founded Quebec. His plan was to follow the network of rivers and lakes leading from Quebec into the interior, exploring the continent for furs and a passage to the Pacific.

Over the next several decades the handful of soldiers, traders, and missionaries who came to New France established friendly relations with tribes of expert fishers and hunters. There were the Algonquin and Montagnais of the St. Lawrence valley; and in the fertile meadows and rich forests around Georgian Bay there was Huronia, a nation 25,000 strong. In return for French goods, these peoples traded

Converts of the French Jesuits, these women of the Caughnawaga tribe (right) are kneeling before a statue of the Virgin Mary, taking vows of celibacy. One cuts her hair, a symbol of banishing pride, in imitation of the practice of Catholic nuns like Marguerite Bourgeoys (left), who founded a religious community dedicated to the education of young girls. Women as well as men in religious orders dedicated their lives to missionary work in Canada.

beaver, otter, and raccoon they had trapped. The furs went to make fashionable European hats, while mink and marten were sent to adorn the robes of high-ranking European officials and churchmen. The French had a name for what New France had become by 1630—a *comptoir*, a storehouse for the skins of dead animals, not a proper colony.

That began to change when other French with their own dreams took responsibility for Canada. Louis XIII and his chief minister, Cardinal Richelieu, hoped that American wealth might be the making of France and its monarchs. In the 1630s they granted large tracts of land and a trading monopoly to a group of private investors, the Company of the Hundred Associates. The Associates brought a few thousand French farmers across the Atlantic and scattered them over 200 miles of company lands along the St. Lawrence.

Religious zeal, as much as the hope of profit, spurred France's renewed interest in colonization. Throughout Europe the Catholic church was enjoying a revival of religious piety as a result of the Counter-Reformation, an effort to correct those abuses that had prompted the Protestant Reformation. To reclaim members lost to Protestantism, the Counter-Reformation also launched an aggressive campaign of repression in Europe and missionary work abroad. In France the Catholic majority persecuted Protestant Huguenots and targeted Canada as a field for harvesting Indian converts.

The shock troops of these missions, not only in the Americas but also in India and Japan, were the Jesuits, members of the Society of Jesus. With Richelieu's encouragement Jesuit missionaries streamed into Canada to assist other French settlers in bringing the Indians the "right" kind of Christianity. At first, it seemed unlikely that the Jesuits would shake the Indians' strong belief in the superiority of their own cultures. In Indian eyes these spiritual soldiers were a joke—men encumbered by their

The Jesuits

effeminate robes, deformed by their "very ugly" beards, and forbidden physical pleasure by their vow of celibacy. The Jesuits were also a nuisance. Not content to preach at French settlements and Indian villages, they undertook "flying" missions to the nomadic tribes, tagging along with Indian trappers. Once in the wilderness the Jesuits were a disaster—tangling in their snowshoes as they tried to surmount wintry drifts, trying for a first and last time to stand in canoes, refusing to carry any weapons, and sponging off the Indians for food and shelter.

Some Indians gradually formed a better opinion of the French and their priests. French traders, known as *coureurs de bois*, and their soldiers often adopted the native way of life and married Indian women. More to the point, the French were still relatively few. Interested primarily in trade, they had no designs on Indian land. The Jesuits, too, won acceptance among some tribes. Their lack of interest in Indian land, furs, and women made them a novelty among white men, while their greater immunity to the diseases that killed many Indians confirmed their claims to superior power. And once the Jesuits mastered the native languages, they showed a talent for smooth talk that the Indians, who prized oratory, greatly admired.

Jesuit persistence slowly paid off. Christian factions formed in many tribes, especially those in which shamans or important families embraced the new religion. Part of the Jesuits' appeal was that they accepted and even appreciated much of Indian culture. The Jesuits never wavered in their zeal to replace Indian religions with Catholicism, but they did not try to transform the Indians into French men and women. If the natives chose to become Catholics in their religion while retaining the rest of their culture, it was all to the good—a good deal better than their becoming English and Protestant.

Throughout the seventeenth century, the French in North America remained relatively few. Instead, it was English Protestants who established the most populous settlements along the north Atlantic coast, challenging Indian dreams with religious visions of their own. Just as Jesuit crusaders of the Counter-Reformation shaped the culture of New France, so the zealous followers of John Calvin left their unmistakable imprint on New England.

The Founding of New England

The English regarded the northern part of North America as a place in which only the mad French could see possibility. English fisherfolk who strayed from Newfoundland to the coast of Acadia and New England carried home descriptions of the long, lonely coast, rockbound and rugged. Long winters of numbing cold melted into short summers of steamy heat. There were no minerals to mine, no crops suitable for export, no large native population available for enslaving. The Chesapeake, with its temperate climate and long growing season, seemed a much likelier spot.

But by 1620, worsening conditions at home instilled in some English men and women the mixture of desperation and idealism needed to settle an uninviting, unknown world. Religious differences among English Protestants became a matter of sharper controversy during the seventeenth century. Along with the religious crisis came mounting political tensions and continuing problems of unemployment and recession. Times were bad—so bad that the anticipation of worse times to come swept men and women to the shores of New England.

The Puritan Movement

The settlement of New England started with a king who chose his enemies unwisely. James I, shortly after succeeding Elizabeth I in 1603, vowed to purge England of all radical Protestant reformers. The radicals James had in mind were the Puritans, most of whom were either Presbyterians or Congregationalists. Although both groups of Puritan reformers embraced Calvin's ideas, they differed on the best form of church organization. Individual Presbyterian churches (or congregations) were guided by higher governing bodies of ministers and laypersons. Congregationalists, on the other hand, believed that each congregation should conduct its own affairs independently, answering to no other authority.

King James angered not only the Puritans but also members of Parliament, who objected to his attempts to levy taxes without their consent. The hostility of both Parliament and the Puritans did not bode well for James's reign. In Parliament he faced influential landowners and merchants who were convinced that the law was on their side. And in the Puritans he faced determined zealots who were convinced that God was on their side.

Like all Christians, Protestant and Catholic, the Puritans believed that God was all-knowing and all-powerful. And like all Calvinists, the Puritans emphasized that idea of divine sovereignty known as predestination. At the center of their thinking was the belief that God had ordained the outcome of history, including the eternal fate of every human being. The Puritans found comfort in their belief in predestination because it provided their lives with meaning and purpose. They felt assured that a sovereign God was directing the fate of individuals, nations, and all of creation. The Puritans strove to play their parts in that divine drama of history and to discover in their performances some signs of personal salvation.

The divine plan, as the Puritans understood it, called for reforming both church and society along the lines laid down by John Calvin. It seemed to the Puritans that England's government hampered rather than promoted religious purity and social order. It tolerated drunkenness, theatergoing, gambling, extravagance, public swearing, and Sabbath breaking. It permitted popular recreations rooted in pagan custom and superstition—sports like bear baiting and maypole dancing and festivals like the celebration of Christmas and saints' days.

What was worse, the state had not done enough to purify the English church of the "corruptions" of Roman Catholicism. The Church of England counted as its members everyone in the nation, saint and sinner alike. To the Puritans, belonging to a church was no birthright. They wished to limit membership and the privileges of baptism and communion to godly men and women. The Puritans also deplored the hierarchy of bishops and archbishops in the Church of England, as well as its elaborate ceremonies in which priests wore ornate vestments. Too many Anglican clergy were "dumb dogges" in Puritan eyes, too poorly educated to instruct churchgoers in the truths of Scripture or to deliver a decent sermon. In reformer John Foxe's vision of good and evil (page 86), Anglican priests on the right side of the drawing are shown in vestments and headdresses worshiping Satan before an altar. Anglican worshipers (bottom right) superstitiously count rosary beads and follow a priestly procession like so many dumb sheep. In contrast, Puritan worshipers (bottom left) conspicuously hold their Bibles and attend only to the word of God.

Because English monarchs had refused to take stronger measures to reform church and society, the Puritans became their outspoken critics. Elizabeth I had tolerated this opposition, but James I would not endure it and intended to rid England of these radicals. With some of the Puritans, known as the Separatists, he seemed to succeed.

Presbyterians and
Congregationalists

Predestination

Puritan calls for reform

John Foxe's *Actes and Monuments* (1563), a book revered by the Puritan founders of New England, arrayed the forces of righteousness (left side of the page) against a host of devils, priests, and their sheeplike followers within the Church of England at right. Under the Catholic Queen Mary, Protestants were regarded as heretics and some were burned at the stake (middle left).

The Pilgrim Settlement at Plymouth Colony

The Separatists were devout Congregationalists who concluded that the Church of England was too corrupt to be reformed. They abandoned Anglican worship and met secretly in small congregations. From their first appearance in England during the 1570s, the Separatists suffered persecution from the government—fines, imprisonment, and, in a few cases, execution. Always a tiny minority within the Puritan movement, the Separatists were people from humble backgrounds: craft-workers and farmers without the influence to challenge the state. By 1608 some had become so discouraged that they migrated to Holland, where the Dutch government permitted complete freedom of religion. But when their children began to adopt Dutch customs and other religions, some Separatists decided to move again, this time to Virginia.

It can only be imagined what fate would have befallen the unworldly Separatists had they actually settled in the Chesapeake during the tobacco boom. But a series of mistakes—including an error in charting the course of their ship, the *Mayflower*—landed the little band in New England instead. In November 1620, some 88 Separatist "Pilgrims" set anchor at a place they called Plymouth on the coast of present-day southeastern Massachusetts. They were sick with scurvy, weak from malnutrition, and shaken by a shipboard mutiny, and neither the site nor the season invited settlement. As one of their leaders, William Bradford, later remembered:

Early difficulties

> For summer being done, all things stand upon them with a weatherbeaten face, and the whole country, full of woods and thickets represented a savage hue. If they looked behind them, there was the mighty ocean which they had passed and was now as a main bar and gulf to separate them from all the civil parts of the world.

For some, the shock was too great. Dorothy Bradford, William's wife, is said to have fallen overboard from the *Mayflower* as it lay anchored off Plymouth. It is more likely that she jumped to her death.

Few Pilgrims could have foreseen founding the first permanent white settlement in New England, and many did not live long enough to enjoy the distinction. They had arrived too late to plant crops and had failed to bring an adequate supply of food. By the spring of 1621, half the immigrants had died. English merchants who had financed the *Mayflower* voyage failed to send supplies to the struggling colony.

Plymouth might have become another doomed colony had the Pilgrims not received better treatment from native inhabitants than they did from their English backers. Samoset and Squanto, two Indians who had learned to speak English from visiting fishermen, introduced the settlers to native strains of corn. They also arranged a treaty between the Pilgrims and the region's main tribe, the Wampanoags.

The Pilgrims also set up a government for their colony, the framework of which was the Mayflower Compact. That agreement provided for a governor and several assistants to advise him, all to be elected annually by Plymouth's adult males. In the eyes of English law, the Plymouth settlers had no clear basis for their land claims or their government, for they had neither a royal charter nor approval from the Crown. But English authorities, distracted by problems closer to home, left the tiny colony of farmers alone.

The Mayflower Compact

The Puritan Settlement at Massachusetts Bay

Among the Crown's distractions were two groups of Puritans more numerous and influential than the gentle Pilgrims. They included both the Presbyterians and the majority of Congregationalists who, unlike the Pilgrim Separatists, still considered the Church of England capable of being reformed. But the 1620s brought these Puritans only fresh discouragements. In 1625 Charles I inherited his father's throne and all his enemies. When Parliament attempted to limit the king's power, Charles

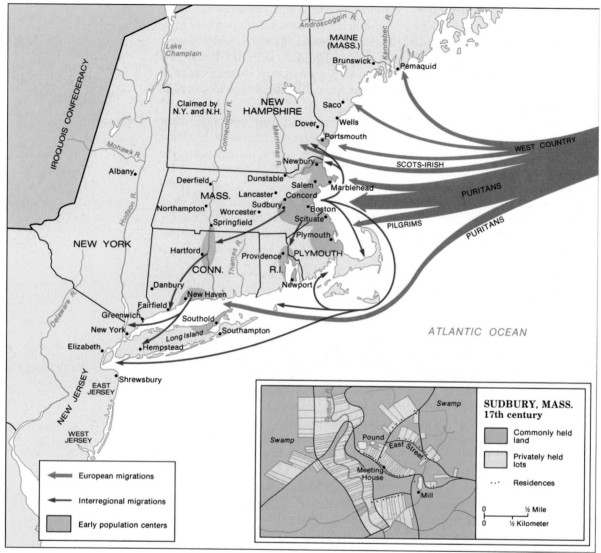

Early New England Despite some variety among emigrants to New England, the region remained relatively homogeneous and stable, with everyday life centered in small towns like Sudbury (located to the west of Boston). Most families lived close to one another in houses clustered around the meeting-house, in contrast to the decentralized plantations of the South. The privately held farm lots were mixed together as well, so that neighbors worked and lived in close contact with one another.

simply dissolved it, in 1629, and proceeded to rule without it. When Puritans pressed for reform, he supported a host of measures proposed by his archbishop, William Laud, for purging England's parishes of ministers with Puritan leanings.

This persecution swelled a second wave of Puritan migration that also drew from the ranks of Congregationalists. Unlike the humble Separatists, these emigrants included merchants, landed gentlemen, and lawyers who organized the Massachusetts Bay Company in 1629. Those able Puritan leaders aimed to build a better society in America, an example to the rest of the world. Unlike the Separatists, they had a strong sense of mission and destiny. They were not abandoning the English church, they insisted, but merely regrouping for another assault on corruption from across the Atlantic. They began organizing a mass migration to Massachusetts Bay that had the efficiency of a military maneuver and the martial spirit of a crusade. One of the immigrants, Edward Johnson, described his fellows as "Soldiers of Jesus Christ," who "for England's sake . . . are going from England to pray without ceasing for England."

Despite the company's Puritan leanings, it somehow obtained a royal charter confirming its title to most of present-day Massachusetts and New Hampshire. Advance parties in 1629 established the town of Salem on the coast well north of Plymouth. In 1630 the company's first governor, John Winthrop, sailed from England with a dozen other company stockholders and a fleet of men and women committed to the Puritan cause. Winthrop, a landed gentleman, was both a tough-minded lawyer and a visionary determined to set an example for the world. "We shall be as a city on a hill," he told his fellow passengers during the crossing on the ship *Arbella.*

Once established in the Bay Colony, Winthrop and the other stockholders transformed the charter for their trading company into the framework of government for a colony. The company's governor became the colony's chief executive, and the company's other officers became the governor's assistants. The charter provided for annual elections of the governor and his assistants by company stockholders, known as the freemen. But to create a broad base of support for the new government, Winthrop and his assistants expanded the freemanship in 1631 to include every adult male church member.

Establishing the colony's government

The governor, his assistants, and the freemen together made up the General Court of the colony, which passed all laws, levied taxes, established courts, and made war and peace. In 1634 the whole body of the freemen stopped meeting and instead each town elected representatives or deputies to the General Court. Ten years later, the deputies formed themselves into the lower house of the Bay Colony legislature, and the assistants formed the upper house. By refashioning a company charter into a civil constitution, Massachusetts Bay Puritans gained full control of their future, fulfilling their dream of shaping society, church, and state to their liking.

New England Communities

Contrary to expectations, New England proved more hospitable to the English than did the Chesapeake. The character of the migration itself gave New England settlers an advantage, for most arrived in family groups—not as young, single, indentured servants of the sort whose discontents unsettled Virginia society. The heads of New England's first households were typically free men—farmers, artisans, and merchants. Most were skilled and literate. Since husbands usually migrated with their wives and children, the ratio of men to women within the population was fairly evenly balanced.

Most immigrants, some 21,000, came in a cluster between 1630 and 1642. Thereafter new arrivals tapered off because of the outbreak of the English Civil War. This relatively rapid settlement fostered solidarity because immigrants shared a common past of persecution and a strong desire to create an ordered society modeled on Scripture.

The "Great Migration"

Stability and Order in Early New England

Puritan emigrants and their descendants thrived in New England's bracing but healthy climate. The first generation of colonists lived to an average age of 70, nearly twice as long as Virginians and 10 years longer than English men and women. With 90 percent of all children reaching adulthood, the typical family consisted of seven or eight children who came to maturity. Because of low death rates and high birthrates, the number of New Englanders doubled about every 27 years—while the populations of Europe and the Chesapeake barely reproduced themselves.

Long-lived New Englanders

By 1700, New England and the Chesapeake both had populations of approximately 100,000. But whereas the southern population grew because of continuing immigration, New England's expanded through natural increase.

As immigrants arrived in the Bay Colony after 1630, they carved out an arc of small villages around Massachusetts Bay. Within a decade settlers pressed into Connecticut, Rhode Island, and New Hampshire. Connecticut and Rhode Island received separate charters from Charles II in the 1660s, guaranteeing their residents the rights to land and government. New Hampshire, to which Massachusetts laid claim in the 1640s, did not become a separate colony until 1679. The handful of hardy souls settled along the coast of present-day Maine had also accepted the Massachusetts Bay Colony's authority.

Patterns of settlement

Early New Englanders planted most of their settlements with an eye to stability and order. Unlike the Virginians, who scattered across the Chesapeake to isolated plantations, most New Englanders established tightly knit communities like those they had left behind in England. In fact, migrating families from the same village or congregation back in England often petitioned the colony government for a tract of land to found their own new town. All prospective adult townsmen initially owned in common this free grant of land, along with the right to set up a local government. Townsmen gradually parceled out among themselves the land granted by the colony. Each family received a lot for a house along with about 150 acres of land in nearby fields. Farmers left many of their acres uncultivated as a legacy for future generations, for most had only the labor of their own families to work their land. While the Chesapeake abounded with servants and tenant farmers, almost every adult male in rural New England owned property.

The economy that supported most of New England's families and towns offered few chances for anyone to get rich. Farmers could coax a yield of food crops sufficient to feed their families, but the stony soil and long winters could not support cash crops like tobacco, rice, or sugar. With no resources for commercial agriculture, New England farmers also had no incentive to import large numbers of servants and slaves or to create large plantations.

Strong family institutions contributed to New England's order and stability. While the early deaths of parents regularly splintered Chesapeake families, two adult generations were often on hand to encourage order within New England households. Husbands and fathers exacted submission from wives and strict obedience from children. Land gave New England's long-lived fathers great authority over even their grown children, for sons and daughters relied on paternal legacies of farms in order to marry and establish their own families.

Hierarchy in village leadership

New Englanders also created, quite deliberately, a distinctive village leadership. Few members of the English upper class migrated to New England, but the Puritan colonists, like most other seventeenth-century English, believed that a stable society depended on some degree of inequality. Each town favored certain families in its land distribution, awarding them a little more than the average allotment. The heads of such families were often ministers or other men with university educations or artisans with skills useful to the community. Such men became the "town fathers" and took the lead in directing local affairs. The trust that most New Englanders invested in their leaders contrasts sharply with the attitudes of early Virginians, who constantly challenged the authority of their elites.

Congregational Church Order

Equally important in preserving local order was the church. Most settlers formed churches as quickly as they founded towns, and each congregation ran its own affairs, hiring and dismissing ministers, admitting and disciplining members.

Membership in New England's Congregational churches was voluntary, but it was not available for the asking. Those wishing to join had to satisfy the church that they had experienced "conversion." Puritans understood conversion to mean a turning of the heart and soul toward God, a spiritual rebirth that was reflected by a pious and disciplined life. In New England, believers who could credibly relate their conversions to the minister and other church members gained admission to membership. Most early New Englanders sought and received church membership, a status that entitled them to receive communion and to have their children baptized. Widespread membership also enabled the churches to oversee public morality. Although the churches of New England could not inflict corporal punishment or fines on their members, as church courts did in England, Puritan churches could and did censure and expel wayward members for misbehavior.

Everywhere in New England except Rhode Island, civil laws obliged everyone to attend worship services on the Sabbath and to pay taxes to support Congregationalist ministers. Although the separation between church and state was incomplete, it had progressed further in New England than in most nations of Europe. New England ministers did not serve as officers in the civil government, and the Congregational churches owned no property. In contrast, Catholic and Anglican church officials wielded real temporal power in European states, and the churches held extensive tracts of land.

Church membership

Separation of church and state

The interior of the Old Ship Meetinghouse, built in Hingham, Massachusetts, in 1681, expresses the importance of hierarchy among New England Puritans. Families with wealth and influence enjoyed the comfort of enclosed wooden pews on the ground floor, while those with slimmer means sat on rows of benches on the second-floor gallery. The raised pulpit at the front of the meetinghouse bespeaks the congregation's respect for the authority and learning of the clergy.

Colonial Governments

The last institution fostering order in daily life was the town meeting, the basis of local self-government. In every New England village, all white, male adult inhabitants met regularly at the meetinghouse to decide matters of local importance. Nearly all of them could vote for town officials. The town fathers generally set the meeting's agenda and offered advice, but the unanimous consent of townsmen determined all decisions. Reaching consensus was a practical necessity because the town fathers had no means of enforcing unpopular decisions.

Colony governments in early New England also evolved into representative and responsive institutions. Typically the central government of each colony, like the General Court of Massachusetts Bay, consisted of a governor and a bicameral legislature, including an upper house, or council, and a lower house, or assembly. All officials were elected annually by the freemen—white adult men entitled to vote in colony elections. Voting qualifications varied, but the number of men enfranchised made up a much broader segment of society than that in seventeenth-century England.

Communities in Conflict

Not every community in early New England was a small, self-sufficient farming village in which strong families, town fathers, and watchful churches pursued the ideals of Puritanism. Along the edges of settlement, several towns departed dramatically from the usual patterns.

Commerce and "company towns"

One such outpost was Marblehead, a fishing port on the Massachusetts coast settled by immigrant fisherfolk from every port in the British Isles. Most eked out a bare existence as suppliers and employees of Boston merchants, who managed Marblehead's fishery. Single men dominated the population, and their brawls and drunken cavorting often spilled out of the town's many taverns onto the streets. Local government remained weak for most of the seventeenth century, and inhabitants managed to avoid founding a local church for 50 years.

Similar problems plagued Springfield, Massachusetts, in the fertile Connecticut River valley. A single powerful family, the Pynchons, founded the town as a center of the fur trade and later developed a thriving commercial agriculture. Here, too, profit-minded merchants dominated local life and exploited the labor of most inhabitants—an assortment of Scottish convicts and English indentured servants.

The rest of Massachusetts tolerated chaotic "company towns" like Marblehead and Springfield because their inhabitants produced what few commodities New England could trade to the rest of the world. Marblehead's fish found a ready market in Catholic Spain and Portugal; Springfield's grain and livestock commanded a good price among Caribbean planters. In exchange, New Englanders acquired wine, sugar, molasses, textiles, and iron goods—commodities that they needed but could not produce.

Conflict over religious differences

More commonly, conflicts in New England towns were likely to arise over religious differences. Although most New Englanders called themselves Puritans and Congregationalists, the very fervency of their convictions often led them to disagree about how best to carry out the teachings of the Bible and the ideas of John Calvin. The Puritans of Plymouth Colony, for example, believed that religious purity required renouncing the Church of England, while those of the Bay Colony clung to the hope of reforming the Anglican church from within.

Even within Massachusetts Bay, Puritans differed among themselves about how to organize their churches. During the first decades of settlement, those differences led to the founding of new colonies in New England. In 1636 Thomas Hooker, the minister of Cambridge, Massachusetts, led part of his congregation to Connecticut, where they established the first English settlement. Somewhat more liberal than other Bay Puritans, Hooker favored more lenient standards for church membership. He also opposed the Bay's policy of limiting voting in colony elections to church members. In contrast, New Haven (a separate colony until it became part of Connecticut in 1662) was begun in 1638 by strict Congregationalists who found Massachusetts too liberal. Massachusetts recognized its southern neighbors, including Separatist Plymouth, as colonies within the Puritan fold, respectable suburbs of Winthrop's city on a hill.

Heretics

The same could not be said of Rhode Island, for that little colony on Narragansett Bay began as a ghetto for heretics. While voluntary migration formed Connecticut and New Haven, enforced exile filled Rhode Island with men and women whose radical ideas unsettled the rest of Massachusetts.

Roger Williams, Rhode Island's founder, had come to New England in 1631, serving as a respected minister of Salem. But soon Williams announced that he was a Separatist, like the Pilgrims of Plymouth. He encouraged the Bay Colony to break all ties to the corrupt Church of England. He also urged a more complete separation of church and state than most New Englanders were prepared to accept, and later in his career he endorsed full religious toleration. Finally, Williams denounced the Bay's charter—the legal document that justified Massachusetts's existence—on the grounds that the king had no right to grant land that he had not purchased from the Indians. When Williams made bold to suggest that Massachusetts actually inform the king of his mistake, angry authorities prepared to deport him. Instead Williams fled the colony in the dead of winter to live with the Indians. In 1636, he became the founder and first citizen of Providence, later to be part of Rhode Island.

Roger Williams

Another charismatic heretic from Massachusetts arrived soon after. Anne Hutchinson, a skilled midwife and the spouse of a wealthy merchant, came to Boston in 1634. Enthusiasm for her minister, John Cotton, started her on a course of explaining his sermons to gatherings of her neighbors—and then to elaborating ideas of her own in which many of the Bay's leaders detected the dangerous heresy of antinomianism.

Anne Hutchinson

The Bay Puritans, like all Calvinists, denied that men and women could "earn" salvation simply by obeying God's laws. They held that salvation came through divine grace, not human actions. But many Puritans believed that the ability to lead an upright life was a natural consequence of being saved. A minority in the Puritan movement, including Anne Hutchinson, rejected that notion. Hutchinson contended that outward obedience to God's laws indicated nothing whatsoever about the inward state of the soul. She was certain that those predestined for salvation knew it intuitively and could recognize the same grace in others.

When most of the Bay Colony's ministers rejected her views, Anne Hutchinson denounced them. Her attack on the clergy, along with the popularity of her preaching

Daily Lives

POPULAR ENTERTAINMENT

A World of Wonders and Witchcraft

Early in the 1680s the Reverend Increase Mather, a learned and devout Boston minister, was putting the finishing touches on a book. It would be a plump volume when published, its pages packed with remarkable occurrences that had taken place during the first 50 years of New England's settlement. Those occurrences dealt not with politics, nor even with the churches, but rather with "wonders"—interventions of the supernatural in the normal order of things. Ministers throughout New England contributed accounts of such wonders to Mather's book. Reverend John Higginson of Salem told of a "Conjuring Book," which filled readers with "a strange kind of Horror" and caused their hair to stand on end. From Newbury, Massachusetts, Reverend Joshua Moodey reported a house inhabited by evil spirits and a "monstrous birth." From Connecticut came the story of a phantom ship sighted sailing into New Haven harbor that suddenly disappeared. Other ministers related cases of bewitchment, appearances of the devil, and dire events forecast by comets, eclipses, earthquakes, and rainbows.

Mather's book of wonders became one of many available to New England readers—a numerous group, for literacy was almost universal. Accounts of marvelous events poured from presses in England, the Continent, and the colonies. Some were splashed across a single sheet by literary hacks; others, like Mather's book, filled the fat volumes written by learned men. The authors drew their reports of visions and voices, untimely deaths and natural disasters from ancient and early Christian authors, medieval chronicles, the Bible, and local lore collected by contemporaries, like Mather's network of New England ministers.

Most seventeenth-century New Englanders preferred to read religious books: the Bible, psalmbooks, sermons, stories of the sufferings of Protestant martyrs, and accounts of the battles against temptation waged by ordinary people. Even so, authors like Increase Mather recognized that a wider audience might be reached by volumes blending godly messages with sensational topics. Ministers recounted wonders to make the religious argument that the world was shot through with mystery and miracle and that men and women were at the mercy of God's will and the devil's wiles. At the same time, these books titillated readers with accounts of witches, apparitions, and freaks

Witchcraft trials and executions took place throughout Europe in the sixteenth and seventeenth centuries, occurring far more frequently and claiming many more victims than in colonial America. But, as this engraving of an English hanging of witches indicates, women composed a majority of those charged and executed on both sides of the Atlantic.

---

among many important merchant families, prompted the Bay Colony government to expel Hutchinson and her followers for sedition in 1638. She settled briefly in Rhode Island before moving on to Long Island, where she died in an Indian attack.

Colony leaders were especially critical of Hutchinson because she was a woman, and they believed that women should remain less assertive of their beliefs. In later religious controversies, the devil of dissent assumed the shape of a woman as well. The Quakers, one of the most radical religious groups produced by the Protestant Reformation in England, sent Ann Austin and Mary Fisher as their first missionaries to the Bay. Women were among the most active early converts, and one of them, Mary Dyer, was hanged for her persistence, along with three Quaker men, in 1656. Like the antinomians, the Quakers attached great

Quakers of New England

of nature. Published narratives of New Englanders taken captive by the Indians and the confessions of convicted murderers combined the same mixture of religion and sensationalism. The pious message that God prevailed over Satan and his servants was mixed with lurid depictions of violence and evildoing.

Knowing what early New Englanders liked to read offers a glimpse not only of their entertainments but of their inner world. Especially significant was their enduring fascination with wonders, which were believed to be true both by learned folks and by humble farmers and their wives. The popularity of wonder lore is powerful proof that all New Englanders inhabited an enchanted universe. Their world brimmed with invisible forces and supernatural beings that could interrupt the order of nature.

That widely shared belief made witchcraft a crime punishable by death and allowed for the unfolding of the notorious witchcraft trials in Salem Village. There, in the early months of 1692, a group of adolescent girls used the white of a raw egg suspended in a glass of water as a kind of crude crystal ball to divine what sorts of men their future husbands might be. Somehow, the seance went sour and the frightened adolescents began behaving in ways that other villagers took to be signs of bewitchment. Crying out in pain and terror, the afflicted women claimed to see taunting specters of witches, whom they recognized as fellow villagers. In the hysteria that ensued, hundreds of accusations of witchcraft led to the trial and execution of 20 innocent men and women. Only when Increase Mather and 14 other Massachusetts ministers publicly warned against the trials' excesses did the hangings stop.

Many historians have tried to explain the deeper causes behind the Salem episode. Some point to the Puritan mistrust of independent women, others to the bitter rivalries among Salem Village families. Still others have noted ties between accused witches and heretical groups like the Quakers. Whatever the source of Salem's particular troubles, the witchcraft charges there and elsewhere in seventeenth-century New England were rooted in the widespread belief in a world of wonders, at once terrible and fascinating.

significance to an inward state of grace, called the "Light Within." Through that inner light, the Quakers claimed, God revealed his will directly to believers, enabling men and women to attain spiritual perfection. Because they held that everyone had immediate access to God, the Quakers also dispensed with a clergy and the sacraments.

Goodwives and Witches

If Anne Hutchinson and Mary Dyer had been men, their ideas would still have been deemed heretical. On the other hand, if these women had been men, they might have found other ways to express their intelligence and magnetism. But life

The artist who sketched this Quaker meeting called attention to one of that sect's most controversial practices by placing a woman at the center of his composition. Women were allowed to speak in Quaker worship services and to preach and proselytize at public gatherings of non-Quakers. The Puritans roundly condemned this liberty as contrary to the teachings of St. Paul.

in colonial New England offered women, especially married women, little scope for their talents.

Most adult women were hardworking farm wives who cared for large households of children. Between marriage and middle age, most New England wives were pregnant except when breast-feeding. When they were not nursing or minding children, mothers were producing and preparing much of what was consumed and worn by their families. They planted vegetable gardens and pruned fruit trees, salted beef and pork and pressed cider, milked cows and churned butter, kept bees and tended poultry, cooked and baked, washed and ironed, spun, wove, and sewed. While husbands and sons engaged in farm work that changed with the seasons, took trips to taverns and mills, and went off to hunt or fish, housebound wives and daughters were locked into a humdrum routine with little time for themselves.

Legal barriers for women

Women suffered legal disadvantages as well. English common law and colonial legal codes accorded married women no control over property. Wives could not sue or be sued, they could not make contracts, and they surrendered to their husbands any property that they possessed before marriage. Divorce was almost impossible to obtain until the late eighteenth century. Only widows and a few single women had the same property rights as men, but they could not vote in colony elections.

The one arena in which women could attain something approaching equal standing with men was the churches. Women wielded their greatest influence among the Quakers. They could speak in Quaker meetings, preach as missionaries, and oversee the behavior of other female members in "women's meetings." Puritan women could not become ministers, but after the 1660s they made up the majority of church members. In some churches membership enabled them to vote for ministerial candidates and to voice opinions about admitting and disciplining members. Puritan doctrine itself rejected the medieval Catholic suspicion of women as "a necessary evil," seeing them instead as "a necessary good." Even so, the Puritan ideal of the virtuous woman was a chaste, submissive "helpmeet," a wife and mother who served God by serving men.

Communities sometimes responded to assertive women with accusations of witchcraft. Like most early modern Europeans, New Englanders believed in wizards and witches, men and women who were said to acquire supernatural powers by signing a compact with Satan. A total of 344 New Englanders were charged with witchcraft during the first century of settlement, with the notorious Salem Village episode of 1692 producing the largest outpouring of accusations and 20 executions. More than three-quarters of all accused witches were women, usually middle-aged and older, and most of those accused were regarded as unduly independent. Before they were charged with witchcraft, many had been suspected of heretical religious beliefs, others of sexual impropriety. Still others had inherited or stood to inherit property.

Witchcraft

Salem witchcraft crisis of 1692

Whites and Indians in Early New England

Most white settlers in New England, like those in the Chesapeake, condemned the "savagery" and "superstition" of the Indians around them. Unlike the French, however, the Puritans made only a few efforts to spread their faith to the Indians.

In truth, the "godly" New Englanders had more in common with the natives in the region than they might have cared to admit. Perhaps 100,000 Algonquin men and women lived in the area reaching from the Kennebec River in Maine to Cape Cod. Like the Puritans, they relied for food on fishing in spring and summer, hunting in winter, cultivating and harvesting food crops in spring and fall. And, to an even greater degree than among white settlers, Indian political authority was local. Within each village, a single leader known as the "sachem" or "sagamore" directed economic life, administered justice, and negotiated with other tribes and English settlers. As with New England's town fathers, a sachem's power depended on keeping the trust and consent of his people.

Similarities between Puritans and Indians

The Indians of New England shared one other characteristic with all Europeans: they quarreled frequently with neighboring nations. The antagonism among the English, Spanish, Dutch, and French was matched by the hostilities among the Abenaki, Pawtucket, Massachusett, Narragansett, and Wampanoag tribes of the north Atlantic coast. Rivalries kept different tribes from forging an effective defense against white colonials. New England settlers, like those in the Chesapeake, exploited Indian disunity.

The first New England natives to put up a strong resistance to Europeans were the Pequots, whom white settlers encountered when they began to push into Connecticut. Had the Pequots allied with their neighbors, the Narragansetts, they could have retarded English expansion. But the Narragansetts, bitter enemies of the Pequots, allied with the English instead. Together they virtually destroyed the Pequots in 1637. Then, in 1643, the English turned against their former allies; they joined forces with the Narragansetts' rivals, the Mohegans, and intimidated the Narragansetts into ceding much of their territory. Only a few whites objected to those ruthless policies, among them Roger Williams. "God Land," he warned one Connecticut leader, "will be (as it now is) as great a God with us English as God Gold was with the Spanish."

War

Playing one tribe off against another finally left the Wampanoags of Plymouth the only coastal tribe capable of resisting Puritan expansion. In 1675, their sachem Metacomet, whom the English called King Philip, organized an uprising that devastated white frontier settlements. By the spring of 1676, Metacomet's forces were closing in on the coast, raiding towns that lay within 20 miles of Boston.

Faced with shortages of food and ammunition, Metacomet called for assistance from the Abenaki, a powerful Maine tribe, and from the Iroquois of New York. But those tribes withheld their support, not wishing to jeopardize their trade with the English. In the summer of 1676 Metacomet met his death in battle, and the Indian offensive collapsed. In seventeenth-century New England, as in the Chesapeake, the clash between Indians and white settlers threatened the very survival of both groups. Perhaps 20,000 whites and Indians lost their lives in Metacomet's War.

Effect of Old World diseases

Even if the natives of New England had been able to unify against whites, they still would have had no defense against another deadly enemy—disease. Like all the Indians of the precolonial Americas, those in New England had been singularly free of the illnesses such as chicken pox and measles that most Europeans experienced in childhood. They were free, too, of the deadly epidemics that beset the Old World—smallpox, influenza, plague, malaria, yellow fever, and tuberculosis. But the absence of those pathogens in the pre-Columbian environment also meant that native Americans had built up no acquired immunity. For that reason, European microbes devastated Indian populations throughout the Americas. In New England, the total number of native Americans plummeted from 70,000 to fewer than 12,000 during the first 75 years of the seventeenth century.

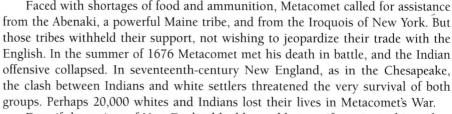

The Mid-Atlantic Colonies

The inhabitants of the mid-Atlantic colonies—New York, New Jersey, Pennsylvania, and Delaware—enjoyed more secure lives than most southern colonials. But they lacked the common bonds that lent stability to early New England. Instead, throughout the mid-Atlantic region a variety of ethnic and religious groups vied for wealth from farming and the fur trade and contended bitterly against governments that commanded little popular support.

The Founding of New Netherlands

New York was settled in 1624 as New Netherlands, an outpost of the Dutch West India Company. Far more impressed with the commercial potential of Africa and South America, the company limited its investment in North America to a few fur-trading posts along the Hudson, Connecticut, and Delaware rivers.

Ethnic and religious diversity

Intent only on trade, the Dutch had little desire to plant permanent colonies abroad because they enjoyed prosperity and religious freedom at home. Most of New Netherlands' few settlers clustered in the village of New Amsterdam on Manhattan Island at the mouth of the Hudson. One hundred and fifty miles upriver lay a fur-trading outpost, Fort Orange (Albany), and by the 1660s a few other farming villages dotted the west end of Long Island, upper Manhattan Island, Staten Island, and the lower Hudson valley. In all, there were fewer than 9000 New Netherlanders—a mixture of Dutch, Belgians, French, English, Portuguese, Swedes, Finns, and Africans. The first blacks had arrived in 1626, imported as slaves; some later became free, intermarried with whites, and even owned white indentured servants.

This ethnic diversity ensured a variety of religions. Although the Dutch Reformed church predominated, other early New Netherlanders included Lutherans, Quakers, and Catholics. There were Jews as well, refugees from Portuguese Brazil, who were required by law to live in a ghetto in New Amsterdam. Yet another religious group kept to themselves by choice: New England Congregationalists. Drawn by promises of cheap land and self-government, they planted farming communities on eastern Long Island during the 1640s.

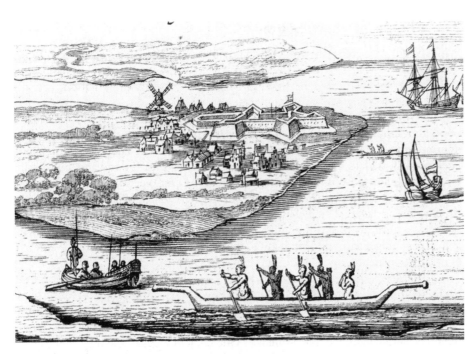

New Amsterdam (later New York City) in about 1626. Despite having this outpost in New Netherlands, the Dutch had far more interest in vying with the Portuguese for control of commerce with the Far East than in competing with the English for the fur trade in North America.

New Netherlanders knew that their cultural differences hampered the prospects for a stable social and political life. The Dutch West India Company made matters worse by appointing corrupt, dictatorial governors who ruled without an elective assembly. The company also provided little protection for its outlying settlers; when it did attack neighboring Indian nations, it did so savagely, triggering terrible retaliations. By the time the company went bankrupt in 1654, it had virtually abandoned its American colony.

New Englanders on Long Island, who had insisted on a free hand in governing their own villages, now began to demand a voice in running the colony as well. By the 1660s they were openly challenging Dutch rule and calling for English conquest of the colony.

English Rule in New York

Taking advantage of the disarray in New Netherlands, Charles II ignored Dutch claims in North America and granted his brother, James, the Duke of York, a proprietary charter there. It granted James all of New Netherlands to Delaware Bay as well as Maine, Martha's Vineyard, and Nantucket Island. In 1664 James sent an invading fleet, whose mere arrival caused the Dutch to surrender.

English management of the new colony, renamed New York, did little to ease ethnic tensions or promote political harmony. The Dutch resented English rule, and only after a generation of intermarriage and acculturation did that resentment fade. James also failed to win friends among Long Island's New Englanders. He grudgingly gave in to their demand for an elective assembly in 1683 but rejected its first act, the Charter of Liberties, which would have guaranteed basic political rights. The chronic political strife discouraged prospective settlers. By 1698 the colony numbered only 18,000 inhabitants, and New York City, the former New Amsterdam, was an overgrown village of a few thousand.

The League of the Iroquois

While New York's colonists wrangled, many of its native Indians succumbed to the same pressures that shattered the natives of New England and the Chesapeake. Only one tribe of Indians in New York's interior, the Iroquois nation, actually gained greater strength from its contacts with whites.

The Indian trade

Like the tribes of South Carolina, the Indians of northern New York became important suppliers of furs to white traders. As in the Carolinas, powerful tribes dominated the interior, far outnumbering white settlers. The handful of Dutch and, later, English traders had every reason to keep peace with the Indians. But the fur trade heightened tensions among interior tribes. At first the Mahicans had supplied furs to the Dutch. But by 1625 the game in their territory had been exhausted, and the Dutch had taken their business to the Iroquois. When the Iroquois faced the same extinction of fur-bearing animals in the 1640s, they found a solution. With Dutch encouragement and Dutch guns, the Iroquois virtually wiped out the neighboring Huron nation and seized their hunting grounds.

The destruction of the Huron made the Iroquois the undisputed power on the northern frontier. More successfully than Powhatan's confederacy in the Chesapeake, the League of the Iroquois welded different tribes into a coherent political unit. This union of the Five Nations (to become six after the Tuscaroras joined them in 1712) included the Mohawk, Oneida, Onondaga, Cayuga, and Seneca tribes and stretched from the lands around the upper Hudson in the east to the Genesee River in the west. Political strength enabled the Iroquois to deal effectively with their Algonquin rivals in New England as well as European newcomers. As the favored clients of the Dutch and, later, the English, they became opponents of the French.

Iroquois women

The League's strength rested on a remarkable form of political and social organization, one in which men and women shared authority. The most powerful women anywhere in colonial North America were the matriarchs of the Iroquois. Matrilineal kinship formed the basis of Iroquois society, as it did among the Pueblos of the Southwest. When men married, they joined their wives' families, households over

Many French colonials showed an abiding interest in and respect for Native American culture. Among them was George Heriot, an eighteenth-century Quebec-based painter, who produced a series of watercolor sketches of Iroquois ceremonies, including this portrayal of a calumet (or peace-pipe) dance.

which the eldest female member presided. But unlike Pueblo women, Iroquois matriarchs wielded political influence as well. The most senior Iroquois women selected
the confederation's council of chiefs, advised them, and "dehorned"—removed from
office—those deemed unfit. Throughout the eighteenth century, the League of the
Iroquois would continue to figure as a major force in North America.

The Founding of New Jersey

New Jersey took shape in the shadow of its stronger neighbors to the north. Its inhabitants were less united and powerful than the Iroquois, less wealthy and influential
than New Yorkers, and less like-minded and self-governing than New Englanders.

Confusion attended New Jersey's beginnings. The lands lying west of the
Hudson and east of the Delaware River had been part of the Duke of York's proprietary grant. But in 1664 he gave about 5 million of these acres to Lord Berkeley
and Sir George Carteret, two of his favorites who were already involved in the proprietary colonies of the Carolinas. New Jersey's new owners guaranteed settlers land,
religious freedom, and a representative assembly in exchange for a small quitrent,
an annual fee for the use of the land. The proprietors' terms promptly drew Puritan
settlers from New Haven, Connecticut. At the same time, unaware that James had
already given New Jersey to Berkeley and Carteret, New York's Governor Richard
Nicolls granted Long Island Puritans land there.

More complications ensued when Berkeley and Carteret decided to divide New
Jersey into east and west and sell both halves to Quaker investors—a prospect that
outraged New Jersey's Puritans. Although some English Quakers migrated to West
Jersey, the investors quickly decided that two Jerseys were less desirable than one
Pennsylvania and resold both East and West Jersey to speculators. In the end the
Jerseys became a patchwork of religious and ethnic groups. Settlers who shared a
common religion or national origin formed communities and established small
family farms. When the Crown finally reunited east and west as a single royal colony
in 1702, New Jersey was overshadowed by settlements not only to the north but
now, also, to the south and west.

Quaker Odysseys

Religious and political idealism similar to that of the Puritans inspired the settlement of Pennsylvania, making it an oddity among the mid-Atlantic colonies. The
oddity began with an improbable founder, William Penn. Young Penn devoted his
early years to disappointing his distinguished father, Sir William Penn, an admiral
in the Royal Navy. Several years after being expelled from college, he finally chose
a career that may have made the admiral yearn for mere disappointment: young
Penn undertook a lifelong commitment to put into practice Quaker teachings. By
the 1670s he had emerged as an acknowledged leader of the Society of Friends, as
the Quakers formally called themselves.

The Quakers behaved in ways and believed in ideas that most people regarded
as odd. They dressed in a deliberately plain and severe manner. They withheld from
their social superiors the customary marks of respect, such as bowing, kneeling,
and removing their hats. They refused to swear oaths or to make war. They allowed   *Quaker beliefs*
women public roles of religious leadership. That pattern of behavior reflected their
egalitarian ideals, the belief that all men and women shared equally in the "Light
Within." Some 40,000 English merchants, artisans, and farmers embraced Quakerism by 1660, and many suffered fines, imprisonment, and corporal punishment.

Since the English upper class has always prized eccentricity among its members, it is not surprising that Penn, despite his Quakerism, remained a favorite of Charles II. More surprising is that the king's favor took the extravagant form of presenting Penn in 1681 with all the land between New Jersey and Maryland. Perhaps the king was repaying Penn for the large sum that his father had lent the Stuarts. Or perhaps the king was hoping to export England's Quakers to an American colony governed by his trusted personal friend.

Penn envisioned that his proprietary colony would provide a refuge for Quakers while producing quitrents for himself. To publicize his settlement, he distributed pamphlets praising its attractions throughout the British Isles and Europe. The response was overwhelming: by 1700 its population stood at 21,000. The only early migration of equal magnitude was the Puritan colonization of New England.

Patterns of Settlement

Perhaps half of Pennsylvania's settlers arrived as indentured servants, while the families of free farmers and artisans made up the rest. The majority were Quakers from Britain, Holland, and Germany, but the colonists also included Catholics, Lutherans, Baptists, Anglicans, and Presbyterians. In 1682 when Penn purchased and annexed the Three Lower Counties (later the colony of Delaware), his settlement included the Dutch, Swedes, and Finns living there, about 1000 people.

Quakers from other colonies—West Jersey, Maryland, and New England—also flocked to the new homeland. Those experienced settlers brought skills and connections that contributed to Pennsylvania's rapid economic growth. Farmers sowed their rich lands into a sea of wheat, which merchants exported to the Caribbean. The center of the colony's trade was Philadelphia, a superb natural harbor situated at the confluence of the Delaware and Schuylkill rivers.

In contrast to New England's landscape of villages, the Pennsylvania countryside beyond Philadelphia was dotted with dispersed farmsteads. Commercial

The tidy, productive farmsteads of the Pennsylvania countryside were the basis of that colony's prosperity during the eighteenth century. Their produce fueled the growth of Philadelphia and sustained the expansion of sugar plantations on England's Caribbean islands.

agriculture required larger farms, which kept settlers at greater distances from one another. As a result, the county rather than the town became the basic unit of local government in Pennsylvania.

Another reason that farmers did not need to cluster their homes within a central village was that the coastal Indians, the Lenni Lenapes (also called Delawares by the English), posed no threat. Thanks to two of the odder Quaker beliefs—their commitment to pacifism and their conviction that the Indians rightfully owned their land—peace prevailed between native inhabitants and newcomers. Before Penn sold any land to white settlers, he purchased it from the Indians. He also prohibited the sale of alcohol to the tribe, strictly regulated the fur trade, and learned the language of the Lenni Lenapes. "Not a language spoken in Europe," he remarked, "hath words of more sweetness in Accent and Emphasis than theirs."

Quakers and Indians

"Our Wildernesse flourishes as a Garden," Penn declared late in 1683, and in fact, his colony lived up to its promises. New arrivals readily acquired good land on liberal terms, while Penn's Frame of Government instituted a representative assembly and guaranteed all inhabitants the basic English civil liberties and complete freedom of worship.

Quakers and Politics

Even so, Penn's colony suffered constant political strife. Rich investors whom he had rewarded with large tracts of land and trade monopolies dominated the council, which held the sole power to initiate legislation. That power and Penn's own claims as proprietor set the stage for controversy. Members of the representative assembly battled for the right to initiate legislation. Farmers opposed Penn's efforts to collect quitrents. The Three Lower Counties agitated for separation, their inhabitants feeling no loyalty to Penn or Quakerism.

Penn finally bought peace at the price of approving a complete revision of his original Frame of Government. In 1701 the Charter of Privileges, Pennsylvania's new constitution, stripped the council of its legislative power, leaving it only the role of advising the governor. The charter also limited Penn's privileges as proprietor to the ownership of ungranted land and the power to veto legislation. Thereafter an elective unicameral assembly, the only single-house legislature in the colonies, dominated Pennsylvania's government.

Penn's compromises

As Pennsylvania prospered, Philadelphia became the commercial and cultural center of England's North American empire. Gradually the interior of Pennsylvania filled with immigrants—mainly Germans and Scots-Irish—who harbored no "odd" ideas about Indian rights, and the Lenni Lenapes and other tribes were bullied into moving farther west. As for William Penn, he returned to England and spent time in a debtors' prison after being defrauded by his unscrupulous colonial agents. He died in 1718, an ocean away from his American utopia.

In the year 1685, from the city of London, a new English king surveyed his American domains. The former Duke of York, now James II, had hoped that America might contribute to the making of kings and queens. Like earlier Stuart monarchs, James hoped to ride to absolute power on a wave of colonial wealth, just as Spain's monarchs had during the previous century. To encourage colonial settlement, Stuart kings had chartered the private trading companies of Virginia, Plymouth,

Adjustment to Empire

England, in an effort to regulate colonial trade, required all ships bound from America to pass through British ports and pay customs duties. Places like Plymouth, Liverpool, and Bristol (shown here) thrived as a result. Contrast this large, bustling commercial center with the modest size of Plymouth 200 years earlier (illustration, page 27).

and Massachusetts Bay. They had rewarded their aristocratic favorites with huge tracts of land—Maryland, the Carolinas, New York, New Jersey, and Pennsylvania.

Yet to what end? Although North America now abounded in places named in honor of English monarchs, the colonies themselves lacked any strong ties to the English state. In only three colonies—New Hampshire, New York, and Virginia—did England exercise direct control through royally appointed governors and councils. Until Parliament passed the first Navigation Acts in 1660, England had not even set in place a coherent policy for regulating colonial trade. Even more disheartening, ungrateful colonists were resisting their duty to enrich the English state and the Stuarts. While Chesapeake planters grumbled over the customs duties levied on tobacco, New Englanders, the worst of the lot, ignored the Navigation Acts altogether and traded openly with the Dutch. New Yorkers were turning out just as badly, as James, the first proprietor of that colony, recalled all too well. Even in recently settled colonies like New Jersey, the Carolinas, and Pennsylvania, the stirrings of opposition to royally appointed proprietors did not bode well.

Control over the colonies tightened

What was needed, in James's view, was an assertion of royal authority over America, starting with Massachusetts. His brother, Charles II, had laid the groundwork in 1673 by persuading Parliament to authorize the placement of customs agents in colonial ports to suppress illegal trade. Charles also formed the Lords of Trade and Plantations, a committee to oversee colonial affairs. When reports of defiance continued to surface, the king delivered the decisive blow: an English court in 1684 revoked Massachusetts' original charter, leaving the Bay Colony without a legal basis for its claim to self-government.

The Dominion of New England

Charles died the following year, leaving James II to finish the job of reorganization. In 1686, at the king's urging, the Lords of Trade consolidated the colonies of Connecticut, Plymouth, Massachusetts Bay, Rhode Island, and New Hampshire into a single entity to be ruled by a royal governor and a royally appointed council. By 1688 James had added New York and New Jersey to that domain, now called the

Dominion of New England. Showing the typical Stuart distaste for representative government, James also abolished all northern colonial assemblies. The king's aim to centralize authority over such a large territory made the Dominion not only a royal dream but a radical experiment in English colonial administration.

Sir Edmund Andros, a tough professional soldier sent to Boston as the Dominion's royal governor, quickly came to rival his king for the title of most unpopular man north of Pennsylvania. Andros set in force policies that outraged every segment of New England society. He strictly enforced the Navigation Acts, which slowed down commerce and infuriated merchants and workers in the maritime trades. He commandeered a Boston meetinghouse for Anglican worship and immediately angered devout Congregationalists. He abolished all titles to land granted under the old charter, alarming farmers and speculators. He imposed arbitrary taxes, censored the press, and forbade all town meetings, thereby alienating almost everyone.

Edmund Andros

The Aftershocks of the Glorious Revolution

About the same time that northern colonials were reaching the end of their patience with Andros, the English decided they had taken enough from his royal master. James II had revealed himself to be yet another Stuart who tried to dispense with Parliament and who had embraced Catholicism besides. As it had before with Charles I, Parliament dispensed with the king. In a quick, bloodless coup d'état known as the Glorious Revolution, Parliament forced James into exile in 1688. In his place it elevated to the throne of England his daughter, Mary, and her Dutch husband, William of Orange. Mary was a distinctly better sort of Stuart. A staunch Protestant, she agreed to rule with Parliament.

The deposing of James II proved so popular among New Englanders that even before Parliament had officially proclaimed William and Mary king and queen, Boston's militia seized Governor Andros and sent him home in April 1689. William and Mary officially dismembered the Dominion and reinstated representative assemblies everywhere in the northern colonies. Connecticut and Rhode Island were restored their old charters, but Massachusetts received a new charter in 1691. Under its terms Massachusetts, Plymouth, and present-day Maine were combined into a single royal colony headed by a governor appointed by the Crown rather than elected by the people. The charter also made property ownership rather than church membership the basis of voting rights and imposed religious toleration.

The Dominion overthrown

Leisler's Rebellion

The new charter did not satisfy all New Englanders, but they soon adjusted to the political realities of royal rule. In contrast, the violent political infighting that plagued New York mirrored that colony's instability.

Word of revolution in England and rebellion in Massachusetts roused New Yorkers into armed opposition in May 1689. Declaring their loyalty to William and Mary, the New York City militia forced from office Andros's second-in-command, the Dominion's lieutenant governor. In his place they installed one of their own leaders, Jacob Leisler, a German merchant.

Because James II had won few friends in New York, the rebellion met no opposition. But Leisler could not win commanding support for his authority. Although Protestant Dutch farmers, artisans, and small shopkeepers stood by him, the leaders of the colony—an intermarried elite of English and Dutch merchants—considered Leisler an upstart who threatened their own influence. After royal rule was restored to New York in 1691, a jury composed of Englishmen convicted Leisler and his son-in-law, Jacob Milburne, of treason. Their executions guaranteed a long life to the bitter political rivalries that Leisler's Rebellion had fueled in New York.

Royal Authority in America in 1700

Closer regulation of trade

In the wake of upheaval at home and in North America, England focused its imperial policy on reaping maximum profit from the colonial trade. In 1696 Parliament enlarged the number of customs officials stationed in each colony to enforce the Navigation Acts. To help prosecute smugglers, Parliament established colonial vice-admiralty courts, tribunals without juries presided over by royally appointed justices. To keep current on all colonial matters, the king appointed a new Board of Trade to replace the old Lords of Trade. The new enforcement procedures generally succeeded in discouraging smuggling and channeling colonial trade through England.

That was enough for England and its monarchs for half a century thereafter. English kings and queens gave up any dreams of imposing the kind of centralized administration of colonial life that James II had attempted in his Dominion of New England. To be sure, royal control had increased over the previous half century. By 1700 royal governments had been established in Virginia, New York, Massachusetts, and New Hampshire. New Jersey, the Carolinas, and Georgia would shortly be added to the list. Royal rule meant that the monarch appointed governors and (everywhere except Massachusetts) also appointed their councils. Royally appointed councils could veto any law passed by a colony's representative assembly, royally appointed governors could veto any law passed by both houses, and the Crown could veto any law passed by both houses and approved by the governor.

The limits of royal power

Despite the ability to veto, the sway of royal power remained more apparent than real after 1700. The Glorious Revolution asserted once and for all that Parliament's authority—rule by the legislative branch of government—would be supreme in the governing of England. In the colonies members of representative assemblies grew more skilled at dealing with royal governors and more protective of their rights. They guarded most jealously their strongest lever of power—the right of the lower houses to levy taxes.

The political reality of the assemblies' power reflected a social reality as well. No longer mere outposts along the Atlantic, the colonies of 1700 were becoming more firmly rooted societies. Their laws and traditions were based not only on what they had brought from England but also on the conditions of life in America. That social reality had already blocked Stuart ambitions to shape the future of North America, just as it had thwarted the designs of lordly proprietors and the dreams of religious reformers.

Still, the dream of empire would revive among England's rulers in the middle of the eighteenth century—in part because the same dream had never died among the rulers of France. By 1663, Louis XIV had decided that kings could succeed where the enterprise of private French traders had failed: he placed New France under royal rule. Thereafter France's fortunes in America steadily improved. Soldiers strengthened Canada's defenses, colonists and traders expanded the scope of French influence, and the Jesuits made more converts among the tribes of the interior. Under the Sun King, as Louis was known to admiring courtiers, royal rule became absolute, and the hopes for empire grew absolutely. Louis and his heirs would continue their plans for the making of France by contending for empire with the English, both in the Old World and in the New.

chapter summary

While the Catholic Counter-Reformation encouraged the French colonization of Canada, the Protestant Reformation in England spurred the settlement of New England and Pennsylvania.

- During the seventeenth century, the French slowly established a fur trade, agricultural communities, and religious institutions in Canada.

- Over the same period, English Puritans planted more populous settlements between Maine and Long Island.

- The migration of family groups and a rough equality of wealth lent stability to early New England society, reinforced by the settlers' shared commitment to Puritanism and a strong tradition of self-government.

- The mid-Atlantic colonies also enjoyed a rapid growth of people and wealth, but political wrangling as well as ethnic and religious diversity made for a higher level of social conflict.

- Whereas New Englanders attempted to subdue native peoples, white settlers in the mid-Atlantic colonies enjoyed more harmonious relations with local Indian tribes.

- The efforts of the later Stuart kings to centralize England's empire ended with the Glorious Revolution in 1688, which greatly reduced tensions between the colonies and the parent country.

interactive learning

The Primary Source Investigator CD-ROM offers the following materials related to this chapter:

- Interactive maps: **The Atlantic World, 1400–1850** (M2) and **Salem Witchcraft** (M4)

- A short documentary movie on the Salem witchcraft crisis of 1692 (D1)

- A collection of primary sources about the development of the English colonies from hardscrabble outposts into thriving and complex societies: models of a colonial dwelling, an image of a New England garrison home, a poem describing life in servitude, and plans and maps of colonial urban centers. The expansion of European settlement did not come without resistance from Native Americans, and several sources shed light on those ever-deepening cultural tensions: an engraving of a Pequot village being destroyed by English colonists, a legal agreement between Indians and colonists, and Puritan William Bradford's remarks on the wilderness. A number of other sources examine the Salem witchcraft crisis.

additional reading

James Axtell, *The Invasion Within* (1985), offers a readable and fascinating account of relations between northern Indian tribes and French and English colonials. The best introductions to Puritanism are still Francis Bremer, *The Puritan Experiment* (1976); and Edmund S. Morgan, *The Puritan Dilemma* (1958), but David Hall, *Worlds of Wonder, Days of Judgment* (1989), provides the best coverage of the religious experiences and supernatural beliefs of ordinary New Englanders. There are many studies of individual New England communities, but the classic account of local political and social life remains Kenneth Lockridge, *A New England Town* (1970). Family life and women's experience in the early northern colonies are ably described by Laurel Ulrich, *Good Wives* (1982), and by Barry Levy's provocative study of Pennsylvania, *Quakers and the American Family* (1988). David Lovejoy, *The Glorious Revolution in America* (1972), provides a useful overview of that event, but the most thoughtful assessment of British imperial policy in the late seventeenth century is Richard R. Johnson, *Adjustment to Empire* (1981). For a fuller list of readings, see the Bibliography at www.mhhe.com/davidsonnation5.

The ethnic and religious diversity of the mid-Atlantic region offers an intriguing and instructive contrast to the relative homogeneity of early New England. Among the recent studies that render memorable portraits of those complex societies in early New York are Donna Merwick, *Possessing Albany, 1630–1710* (1990), and Joyce Goodfriend, *Before the Melting Pot* (1991). For Pennsylvania, see the fine overview of Joseph Illick, *Colonial Pennsylvania* (1976), and the topical essays in Richard Dunn and Mary Maples Dunn, eds., *The World of William Penn* (1986). For a fuller list of readings, see the Bibliography at www.mhhe.com/davidson5.

significant events

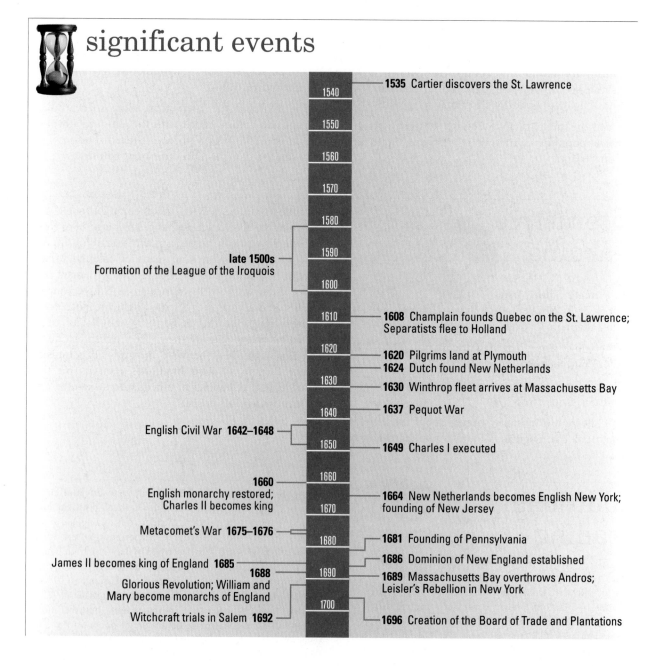

1535	Cartier discovers the St. Lawrence
late 1500s	Formation of the League of the Iroquois
1608	Champlain founds Quebec on the St. Lawrence; Separatists flee to Holland
1620	Pilgrims land at Plymouth
1624	Dutch found New Netherlands
1630	Winthrop fleet arrives at Massachusetts Bay
1637	Pequot War
1642–1648	English Civil War
1649	Charles I executed
1660	English monarchy restored; Charles II becomes king
1664	New Netherlands becomes English New York; founding of New Jersey
1675–1676	Metacomet's War
1681	Founding of Pennsylvania
1685	James II becomes king of England
1686	Dominion of New England established
1688	Glorious Revolution; William and Mary become monarchs of England
1689	Massachusetts Bay overthrows Andros; Leisler's Rebellion in New York
1692	Witchcraft trials in Salem
1696	Creation of the Board of Trade and Plantations

Chapter 4

bout 150 Iroquois sat facing the colonial commissioners in Albany, New York, on the morning of June 29, 1754. In front of the governor's house, servants had set up rows of long wooden planks upon which the delegates from the Six Nations of the Iroquois now sat. The commissioners themselves, 25 in all, were not about to make do with planks; each had his own chair. They represented seven colonies, from Massachusetts Bay in the north to Maryland in the south.

Governor James DeLancey of New York stood and read a proclamation of welcome, pledging to "brighten the Chain of Friendship" between the Iroquois and the English. As each paragraph of the governor's speech was translated, the Iroquois were presented with a decorative belt, to which they responded with a ceremonial "Yo-heigh-eigh," shouted in unison. The noise unsettled those colonials attuned to the subtleties of Iroquois diplomacy. Normally, each nation voiced its agreement individually: six Yo-heigh-eighs coming one after another. By mixing them together, noted one observer, the delegates "had a mind to disguise that all the Nations did not universally give their hearty assent" to uniting with the English.

The Mosaic of Eighteenth-Century America

1689–1771

preview • British colonials were such a diverse, contentious lot that any hope of political union seemed utterly impractical. The most bitter conflicts sprang from sectional disputes between the established East and the back-country West. The South became more embattled too, as resistance increased among enslaved African Americans. Yet despite such disagreements, a majority of white colonials took pride in their English traditions and in membership in a powerful empire.

Unity—and not merely the unity of the Iroquois—was much on the mind of one commissioner from Philadelphia. Several chairs to the left of Governor DeLancey sat the most influential member of the Pennsylvania delegation, Benjamin Franklin. He knew that the question of whether the Iroquois would unite in an alliance with British America was only half the issue for this gathering at Albany. Equally important was whether the British colonies themselves could unite to deal effectively with France's threat throughout North America. Franklin had a plan for bringing the colonies together, but whether they would pay any notice remained an open question.

Rivalry between France and England

In a sense that plan grew out of a lifetime of experience, for the imperial rivalry between England and France had begun well before Franklin's birth and had flared, on and off, throughout his adult years. In 1689 England had joined the Netherlands and the League of Augsburg (several German-speaking states) in a war against France. While the main struggle raged on the continent of Europe, French and English colonials, joined by their Indian allies, skirmished in what was known as King William's War. Peace returned in 1697, but only until 1702, when the Anglo-French struggle resumed again, four years before Franklin was born. It continued throughout his boyhood, until 1713.

For a quarter of a century thereafter, the two nations waged a kind of cold war, competing for position and influence. At stake was not so much control over people or even territory as control over trade. In North America, France and

In the mid–eighteenth century, Philadelphia became the largest city in the colonies and the second largest in all the British empire. Its busy harbor served not only as a commercial hub but also as the disembarkation point for thousands of immigrants.

England vied for access to the sugar islands of the Caribbean, a monopoly on supplying manufactured goods to New Spain, and title to the fur trade. The British had the advantage of numbers: nearly 400,000 subjects in the colonies in 1720, compared with only about 25,000 French spread along a thin line of fishing stations and fur-trading posts. Yet the French steadily strengthened their chain of forts, stretching from the mouth of the Mississippi north through the Illinois country and into Canada. The forts helped channel the flow of furs from the Great Lakes and the Mississippi River valley into Canada, thus keeping them out of the clutches of English traders. And the forts neatly encircled England's colonies, confining their settlement to the eastern seaboard.

When fighting again engulfed Europe and the colonies in 1744, the results were inconclusive. King George's War, as the colonials dubbed it, ended four years later, but peace did nothing to diminish the old rivalry. As English traders and settlers filtered steadily into the Ohio River valley, the French built a new line of forts in 1752, from south of Lake Erie to the Ohio River. Two years later they erected Fort Duquesne at the strategic forks of the Ohio, flush against the border of Franklin's Pennsylvania. That startled Pennsylvania and other colonies into sending commissioners to Albany in 1754 to coordinate efforts to deal with the worsening crisis. Franklin put the message plainly in his newspaper, the *Pennsylvania Gazette*, in a cartoon of a snake cut into segments. It was inscribed "Join, or Die."

Throughout those years of imperial maneuvering, the Iroquois League maintained a cool neutrality. The Six Nations had become uneasy at the prospect of a North America without the French. Without French competition for Indian furs, what would spur British colonials to offer fair prices and trade goods of high quality? Without the arc of French settlement encircling the British American colonies, what would halt the westward spread of white settlement? Increasingly, too, the Iroquois were impressed by the show of French military might.

For the time being, the commissioners at Albany could do little to satisfy Iroquois doubts except lavish as much hospitality as their budgets would allow. In the end the Iroquois made vague promises of loyalty and then hauled away 30 wagons full of presents.

The Albany Plan of Union

But would the colonies themselves unite? On the way to the Albany Congress Franklin had sketched out a framework for colonial cooperation. He proposed establishing "one general government" for British North America—a federal council composed of representatives from each colony, presided over by a president-general appointed by the Crown. The council would assume all responsibility for colonial defense and Indian policy, building forts and patrolling harbors with taxes levied on all Americans. The commissioners were bold enough to accept the plan, alarmed by the wavering Iroquois and the looming French threat.

But the union born at Albany was smothered by the jealous colonies, who were unwilling to sing "yo-heigh-eigh" either in unison or separately. Not a single assembly approved the Albany Plan of Union. And no American legislature was ready to surrender its cherished right to tax inhabitants of its own colony—not to a federal council or to any other body. "Everyone cries, a union is necessary," Franklin wrote Governor Shirley of Massachusetts in disgust; "but when they come to the manner and form of the union, their weak noodles are perfectly distracted." If the Albany Congress proved one thing, it was that American colonials were hopelessly divided.

Forces of Division

Franklin, of course, should have known better than to hope for an intercolonial union. A practical man not given to idle dreams, he recognized the many forces of division at work in America. He knew that the colonies were divided by ethnic and regional differences as well as racial and religious prejudices. Year after year small wooden ships brought a bewildering variety of immigrants to American seaports—especially Philadelphia, where Franklin had lived since 1723. From his efforts to reorganize the post office Franklin knew, too, that Americans were separated by vast distances, poor transportation, and slow communications. He knew how suspicious the frontier districts remained of seaboard communities and how the eastern seaboard disdained the backcountry. Taken all in all, the British settlements in America were, in the eighteenth century, a diverse and divided lot.

Immigration and Natural Increase

One of the largest immigrant groups—250,000 black men, women, and children—had come to the colonies from Africa not by choice but in chains. White arrivals included many English immigrants but also a quarter of a million Scots-Irish, the descendants of seventeenth-century Scots who had regretted settling in northern Ireland; perhaps 135,000 Germans; and a sprinkling of Swiss, Swedes, Highland Scots, and Spanish Jews. Most non-English white immigrants were fleeing lives torn by famine, warfare, and religious persecution. All the voyagers, English and non-English, risked the hazardous Atlantic crossing (see Daily Lives, pages 114–115). Many had paid for passage by signing indentures to work as servants in America.

High birthrate

The immigrants and slaves who arrived in the colonies between 1700 and 1775 swelled an American population that was already growing dramatically from natural increase. The birthrate in eighteenth-century America was triple what it is today. Most women bore between five and eight children, and most children survived to maturity. Indeed, the social and political consequences of this population explosion so intrigued Franklin that he wrote an essay on the subject in 1751. He recognized that ethnic and religious diversity, coupled with the hectic pace of westward expansion after 1700, made it hard for colonials to share any common identity. Far from fostering political union, almost every aspect of social development set Americans at odds with one another.

The Settlement of the Backcountry

To white immigrants from Europe weary of war or worn by want, the seaboard's established communities must have seemed havens of order and stability. But by the beginning of the eighteenth century, even the children of longtime settlers could not acquire land along the coast. In older New England towns, three and four generations were putting pressure on a limited supply of land, while wasteful farming practices had depleted the soil of its fertility. Farther south, earlier settlers had already snatched up the farmland of Philadelphia's outlying counties, the prime Chesapeake tobacco property, and low-country rice swamps.

With older rural communities offering few opportunities to either native-born or newly arrived white families, both groups were forced to create new communities on the frontier. The peopling of New England's frontier—Maine, New Hampshire, and Vermont—was left mainly to the descendants of old Yankee families. Better opportunities for new immigrants to acquire land at cheaper prices lay south of New York. By the 1720s German and Scots-Irish immigrants as well as native-born settlers were pouring into western Pennsylvania. Some settled permanently, but others streamed southward into the backcountry of Virginia and the Carolinas, where they encountered native-born southerners pressing westward.

This log cabin, built in the North Carolina backcountry in 1782, would have been dark inside, given its lack of windows. The spaces between the logs in such cabins were usually chinked with thin stones or wedges of wood and then daubed with mortar.

Daily Lives

TIME AND TRAVEL
Transatlantic Trials

A mountain of water swelled from the Atlantic, towered over the *Jamaica Packet,* then toppled onto the small wooden passenger ship. The impact hurled Janet Schaw and her maid about their cabin like rag dolls. As seawater surged in, the two women struggled to grasp something, anything, to keep from drowning. The ship pitched wildly, "one moment mounted to the clouds and whirled on the pointed wave," the next plunging prow first into the heaving ocean. Four sailors lashed to the helm fought for control, while the rest of the crew worked with their hands "torn to pieces by the wet ropes." The ship's provisions—hogsheads of water, coops of chickens, and barrels of salted meat—snapped from their fastenings and careened across the deck before bouncing overboard.

For more than two days the *Jamaica Packet* hurtled in the gale's grip. Then its foremast splintered, and the ship flipped onto its side. Passengers, crew, and furniture crashed "heels over head to the side the vessel had laid down on." Schaw found herself "swimming amongst joint-stools, chests, [and] tables" in her cabin and listening to the sound of "our sails fluttering into rags." It would have been the end of the *Jamaica Packet* if, at that moment, its masts had not washed overboard. With the weight of the masts gone, the ship righted itself.

Schaw, "a lady of quality," as she described herself, was traveling by the finest accommodations from Great Britain to America in the age of sail. For those passengers who could not pay for a private cabin on the *Jamaica Packet,* the storm was worse. Twenty-two or more indentured servants from Scotland in that year of 1774 were bound aboard ship for the West Indies. Those impoverished families of farmers and fisherfolk had agreed with British merchants to work for American masters in return for the costs of passage. Like thousands of others who came to America in the eighteenth century, they were consigned to steerage, the between-decks area or "upper hold."

Perhaps four to five feet high, that space was crowded with narrow wooden bunks arranged in tiers about two feet apart. It was impossible for most people to stand in steerage or to sit up in a bunk, where as many as four people huddled together at night. Sanitary facilities consisted of a few wooden buckets filled with seawater; candles and fish-oil lanterns supplied the only light. The sole source of air was the hatch opening onto the deck.

Isolation of the backcountry

Backcountry settlers endured greater isolation than did other colonials. From many farmsteads it was a day's ride to the nearest courthouse; taverns and churches were often just as distant. Isolation hindered the formation of strong social bonds, as did the rapid rate at which people came to and left western communities. Many families pulled up stakes three or four times before settling permanently. Houses reflected that transience: most families crowded into one-room shacks walled with mud, turf, or crude logs.

The backcountry meant economic isolation as well. Large portions of the interior were cut off from water transport because they were located above the fall line, where rivers flowing to the Atlantic became unnavigable. By 1755 several crude wagon roads linked western Pennsylvania and Virginia to towns farther east, including Philadelphia, but transporting crops and driving livestock overland proved prohibitively expensive. Cut off from outside markets, farmers grew only enough to feed their households. Most backcountry inhabitants could not afford to invest in a slave or even a servant, so they relied on family labor alone to cultivate a small fraction of their farms' total acreage. Those conditions made the frontier, more than anywhere else in America, a society of equals.

When the storm struck, the hatch was fastened tightly to keep the holds from filling with water. But as waves dashed over the decks, water streamed into steerage, forcing its occupants to stand, clutching their children to keep them from being crushed or suffocated as the storm tumbled everyone from one side of their dark, watery prison to the other. For nine days they stood in water, without a fire or any food except raw potatoes and moldy biscuits. And they were without light or fresh air, except for one young man and his pregnant wife. During the storm the woman miscarried, and her "absolutely distracted" husband, Schaw reported, somehow forced open the hatch and carried her up to the deck, reviving the unconscious woman and saving her life. When at last the servants were allowed to come up on deck, they discovered that all their belongings had been swept overboard.

What followed the servants up to the deck, to the horror of all, was a stench "sufficient to raise a plague aboard." But the luck of the *Jamaica Packet* held, for it escaped not only shipwreck but epidemic disease. Passengers on other transatlantic voyages were not so fortunate. Throughout the eighteenth century notices of ships "lost at sea" or of passengers who slipped overboard in storms filled colonial newspapers. Outbreaks of epidemic disease—smallpox, influenza, typhus, and diphtheria—were common. Although there are no reliable statistics for shipboard mortality during the eighteenth century, estimates range from 3 percent of all passengers to as high as 10 to 15 percent, a rate nearly comparable to that for slave ships during the Middle Passage across the Atlantic.

For all who ventured abroad, transatlantic travel was tedious and dirty at best, hazardous and horrific at worst. Those who risked the crossing routinely made out wills and sought the prayers of loved ones. But disease and danger at sea took the greatest toll from the poor, indentured servants and convict laborers who made up the majority of eighteenth-century emigrants.

What the frontier gained in equality it may have lost in stability. In the backcountry there were no southern gentlemen or northern town fathers to supply continuous, experienced local leadership. There was only a handful of farmers in each county set above their neighbors by owning a few extra acres or a single slave. To these inexperienced and poorly educated men fell the tasks of overseeing public order as justices of the peace or officers in the local militia or representatives to colonial assemblies. It was hard for those with so little authority over their fellows to police sprawling backcountry communities; not surprisingly, coarse and aggressive behavior dominated frontier life. Backcountry men and women mated out of wedlock, swore in public, drank to excess, and brawled at any provocation.

Nor were the churches much help in promoting law and order. Building churches lay beyond the means of many frontier communities, and few ministers were willing to endure the rigors of preaching from one backcountry neighborhood to another. While churches loomed large in the lives of Americans on the coast, most western families, although often deeply pious, had only occasional contact with organized religion.

Frontier women

Hard work dominated the lives of backcountry settlers. Besides doing the usual chores of farm women, western wives and daughters joined male family members in the fields. One traveler from the East expressed his astonishment at seeing German women in western Pennsylvania "at work abroad on the Farm mowing, Hoeing, Loading Dung into a Cart." Perhaps even more difficult to endure than the hard labor was the loneliness of many women's lives. The reactions of women to being resettled on the frontier can be imagined from the promise that one Scottish husband offered his wife: "We would get all these trees cut down . . . [so] that we would see from house to house."

Social Conflict on the Frontier

Despite the discomforts of frontier life, cheap land lured many families to the West. Benjamin Franklin had observed the hordes of Scots-Irish and German immigrants lingering in Philadelphia just long enough to scrape together the purchase price of a frontier farm. From Franklin's point of view, the backcountry performed a valuable service by siphoning off surplus people from congested eastern settlements. But he knew, too, that the frontier was an American Pandora's box. Once opened, the West unleashed discord, especially between the eastern seaboard and the backcountry.

The Paxton Boys

In Pennsylvania, Franklin himself mediated one such contest between East and West. In 1763 a band of Scots-Irish farmers known as "the Paxton Boys" protested the government's inadequate protection of frontier settlers by killing a number of Indians.

This cartoon supported the Paxton Boys by branding Quakers as treacherously sympathetic to frontier Indians. One Quaker, on the left, eagerly supplies Indians with tomahawks, while on the right another makes sexual advances to an Indian woman. Meanwhile Benjamin Franklin, center, offers a sack of money to buy off hostile Indians.

Then the Paxton Boys took their protests and their guns to Philadelphia, marching as far as Lancaster before Franklin intervened and promised redress of their grievances.

Strife between East and West was even deadlier and more enduring in North and South Carolina. In both colonies legislatures dominated by coastal planters refused to grant inland settlers equitable political representation or even basic legal institutions. In response to those injustices, two protest movements emerged in the Carolina interior, each known as the Regulation.

Farmers in the South Carolina backcountry organized their Regulation in the 1760s, after that colony's assembly refused to set up courts in the backcountry. Westerners were desperate for protection from outlaws who stole livestock, kidnapped and raped women, and tortured and murdered men. In the absence of courts the Regulators acted as vigilantes, meting out their own brand of grisly frontier justice against these criminals. Regulator threats to march on Charleston itself finally panicked eastern political leaders into extending the court system, but bitter memories lingered among westerners.

Regulation movements

Western North Carolinians organized their Regulation to protest not the absence of a legal system but the corruption of local government. Lawyers and merchants, backed by wealthy eastern planters, moved into the western parts of that colony and seized control of politics. Then they used those local offices to exploit frontier settlers, charging exorbitant fees for legal services, imposing high taxes, and manipulating debt laws. Western farmers responded to these abuses with the Regulation: they seized county courts and finally squared off against an eastern militia led by the governor. Easterners crushed the Regulators at the Battle of Alamance in 1771 but left frontier North Carolinians with an enduring hostility to the seaboard.

Ethnic differences heightened sectional tensions between East and West. People of English descent predominated along the Atlantic coast, whereas Germans, Scots-Irish, and other white minorities were concentrated in the interior. Many English colonials regarded these new immigrants as culturally inferior and politically subversive. Charles Woodmason, an Anglican missionary in the Carolina backcountry, lamented the arrival of "5 or 6000 Ignorant, mean, worthless, beggarly Irish Presbyterians, the Scum of the Earth, the Refuse of Mankind," who "delighted in a low, lazy, sluttish, heathenish, hellish life."

Ethnic conflicts

German immigrants were generally credited with having steadier work habits, as well as higher standards of sexual morality and personal hygiene. But like the clannish Scots-Irish, the Germans preferred to live, trade, and worship among themselves. By 1751 Franklin was warning that the Germans would retain their separate language and customs: the Pennsylvania English would be overrun by "the Palatine Boors."

Boundary Disputes and Tenant Wars

The settlement of the frontier also triggered disputes between colonies over their boundaries. At the root of the confusion were the old colonial charters and their vague definitions of western borders that allowed groups of settlers and speculators from different colonies to claim the same tract of land. The most serious of these border wars pitted New York against farmers from New England who had settled in present-day Vermont: Ethan Allen and the Green Mountain Boys. In the 1760s, New York, backed by the Crown, claimed land that Allen and his friends had already purchased from New Hampshire. When New York tried to extend its rule over Vermont, Allen led a successful guerrilla resistance, harassing Yorker settlers and officials, occupying Yorker courthouses, and setting up a competing judicial system in the Green Mountains.

Green Mountain Boys

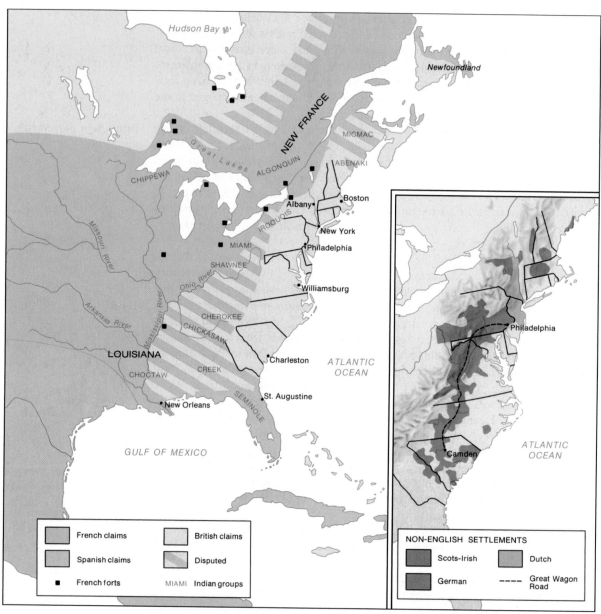

Patterns of Settlement in the Eighteenth Century The French, English, and Indian nations all jockeyed for power and position across North America during the eighteenth century. The French expanded their fur trade through the interior while English settlement at midcentury began to press the barrier of the Appalachians. Many non-English settlers spilled into the backcountry: the Scots-Irish and Germans followed the Great Wagon Road through the western parts of the middle colonies and southern colonies while the Dutch and Germans moved up the Hudson River valley. Albany, where Franklin journeyed in 1754 for the Albany Congress, was one natural pivotal point in the rivalry—a place where Iroquois, French, and English interests converged.

The spread of settlement also set the stage for mass revolts by tenants in those areas where proprietors controlled vast amounts of land. In eastern New Jersey, proprietors insisted that squatters pay quitrents on land that had become increasingly populated and therefore more valuable. When the squatters, many of them migrants from New England, refused to pay rents, buy the land, or move, the proprietors began evictions, touching off riots in the 1740s. Tenant unrest also raged in New York's Hudson River valley. In the 1680s the royal governor had granted several prominent merchant families large estates in that region. By the middle of the eighteenth century, there were about 30 manors around New York City and Albany, totaling some 2 million acres and worked by several thousand tenants. Newcomers from New England, however, demanded to own land and preached their ideas to Dutch and German tenants. Armed insurrection exploded in 1757 and again, more violently, in 1766. Tenants refused to pay rents, formed mobs, and stormed the homes of landlords.

Eighteenth-Century Seaports

While most Americans on the move settled on the frontier, others swelled the populations of colonial cities. By present-day standards such cities were small, harboring from 8000 to 22,000 citizens by 1750. The scale of seaports remained intimate, too: all of New York City was clustered at the southern tip of Manhattan Island, and the length of Boston or Charleston could be walked in less than half an hour.

All major colonial cities were seaports, their waterfronts fringed with wharves and shipyards. A jumble of shops, taverns, and homes crowded their streets; the spires of churches studded their skylines. By the 1750s, the grandest and most populous was Philadelphia, which boasted straight, neatly paved streets, flagstone sidewalks, and three-story brick buildings. Older cities like Boston and New York had a more medieval aspect: most of their dwellings and shops were wooden structures with tiny windows and low ceilings, rising no higher than two stories to steeply pitched roofs. The narrow cobblestone streets of Boston and New York also challenged pedestrians, who competed for space with livestock being driven to the butcher, roaming herds of swine and packs of dogs, clattering carts, carriages, and horses.

Commerce, the lifeblood of seaport economies, was managed by merchants who tapped the wealth of surrounding regions. Traders in New York and Philadelphia shipped the Hudson and Delaware valleys' surplus of grain and livestock to the West Indies. Boston's merchants sent fish to the Caribbean and Catholic Europe, masts to England, and rum to West Africa. Charlestonians exported indigo to English dyemakers and rice to southern Europe. Other merchants specialized in the import trade, selling luxuries and manufactured goods produced in England—fine fabrics, ceramics, tea, and farming implements. Wealth brought many merchants political power: they dominated city governments and shared power in colonial assemblies with lawyers and the largest farmers and planters.

Skilled craftworkers or artisans made up the middling classes of colonial cities. The households of master craftworkers usually included a few younger and less skilled journeymen working in other artisans' shops. Unskilled boy apprentices not only worked but also lived under the watchful eye of their masters. No large-scale domestic industry produced goods for a mass market: instead craft shops filled orders for specific items placed by individual purchasers. Some artisans specialized in the maritime trades as shipbuilders, blacksmiths, and sailmakers. Others, like butchers, millers, and distillers,

The commercial classes

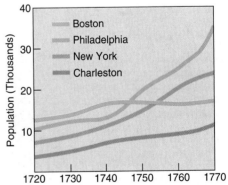

Estimated Population of Colonial Cities, 1720–1770 Although Boston's population remained stable after 1740, it was surpassed due to the sharp growth of New York and, especially, Philadelphia.

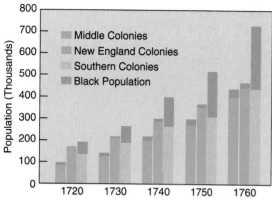

Estimated Population by Region, 1720–1760

processed and packed raw materials for export. Still others served the basic needs of city dwellers—the men and, occasionally, women who baked bread, mended shoes, combed and powdered wigs, and tended shops and taverns.

On the lowest rung of a seaport's social hierarchy were free and bound workers. Free laborers were mainly young white men and women—journeyman artisans, sailors, fishermen, domestic workers, seamstresses, and prostitutes. The ranks of unfree workers included apprentices and indentured servants doing menial labor in shops and on the docks.

Black men and women also made up a substantial part of the bound labor force of colonial seaports, not only in southern Charleston but in northern cities as well. Although the vast majority of slaves imported from Africa were destined for southern plantations, a smaller number were sold to urban merchants and craftworkers. Laboring as porters at the docks, as assistants in craft shops, or as servants in wealthy households, black residents made up almost 20 percent of the population in New York City and 10 percent in Boston and Philadelphia.

The character of slavery in northern seaports changed decisively during the mid–eighteenth century. When wars raging in Europe reduced the supply of white indentured servants, colonial cities imported a larger number of Africans. In the two decades after 1730, one-third of all immigrants arriving in New York harbor were black; by 1760, blacks constituted more than three-quarters of all bound laborers in Philadelphia. The preference for importing African men upset what had been an equal balance of black men and women in colonial seaports, making it difficult for the newcomers to establish families. Slaves from Africa also lacked immunity to American diseases, and many did not survive their first winter: the death rate among urban blacks was double that for whites.

But the survivors brought to urban black culture a new awareness of a common West African past. The influence of African traditions appeared most vividly in an annual event known as "Negro election day," celebrated in northern seaports.

Ashley Bowen, an eighteenth-century New Englander, made a drawing to commemorate his courtship of Dorothy Chadwick. Although she refused him at first (He: "Will thee consent to be my bride"; She: "Sir, I have not that Desire."), Bowen finally prevailed. Ashley's self-portrait, dominating both the sketch and the diminutive Dorothy, underscores colonial views of the relative status of men and women.

During the festival, similar to ones held in West Africa, some black men and women paraded in their masters' clothes or mounted on their horses. An election followed to choose black kings, governors, and judges who then held court and settled minor disputes among white and black members of the community. Negro election day did not challenge the established racial order with its temporary reversal of roles, but it did allow the black communities of seaports to honor their own leaders.

The availability of domestic workers, both black and white, made for leisured lives among women from wealthy white families. Even those city women who could not afford household help spent less time on domestic work than did farming wives and daughters. Although some housewives grew vegetables in backyard gardens or kept a few chickens, large markets stocked by outlying farmers supplied most of the food for urban families.

Women in cities

For women who had to support themselves, seaports offered a number of employments. Young single women from poorer families worked in wealthier households as maids, cooks, laundresses, seamstresses, or nurses. The highest-paying occupations for women, midwifery and dressmaking, both required long apprenticeships and expert skills. The wives of artisans and traders sometimes assisted their husbands and, as widows, often continued to manage groceries, taverns, and print shops. But most women were confined to caring for households, husbands, and children; fewer than 1 out of every 10 women in seaports worked outside their own homes.

Urban diversions and hazards

All seaport dwellers—perhaps 1 out of every 20 Americans—enjoyed a more stimulating environment than other colonials did. The wealthiest could attend an occasional ball or concert; those living in New York or Charleston might even see a play performed by touring English actors. The middling classes could converse with other tradespeople at private social clubs and fraternal societies. Men of every class found diversion in drink and cockfighting. Crowds of men, women, and children swarmed to tavern exhibitions of trained dogs and horses or the spectacular waxworks of one John Dyer, featuring "a lively Representation of Margaret, Countess of Herrinburg, who had 365 Children at one Birth."

But city dwellers, then as now, paid a price for their pleasures. Commerce was riddled with risk: ships sank and wars disrupted trade. When such disasters struck, the lower classes suffered most. The ups and downs of seaport economies, combined with the influx of immigrants, swelled the ranks of the poor in all cities by the mid–eighteenth century. Although the major seaports established workhouses to employ the able-bodied poor, city governments continued to aid most of the dependent with small subsidies of money, food, and firewood. Furthermore, epidemics and catastrophic fires occurred with greater frequency and produced higher mortality rates in congested seaports than in the countryside.

During the eighteenth century in both England and America, portraits of prominent white families and individuals sometimes included black slaves who served wealthy households. This portrait depicts a young child of New York's Van Rensselaer family and foretells his future mastery of both the young black male slave and, in the background, a fine estate in the Hudson River valley.

Social Conflict in Seaports

The swelling of seaport populations, like the movement of whites to the West, often churned up trouble. English, Scots-Irish, Germans, Swiss, Dutch, French, and Spanish jostled uneasily against one another in the close quarters of Philadelphia and New York. To make matters worse, religious differences heightened ethnic divisions. Jewish funerals in New York, for example, drew crowds of hostile and curious Protestants, who heckled the mourners.

Class resentment also stirred unrest. Some merchant families flaunted their wealth, building imposing town mansions and dressing in the finest imported fashions. During hard times, symbols of merchant wealth like expensive coaches and full warehouses became targets of mob vandalism. Crowds also gathered to intimidate and punish other groups who provoked popular hostility—unresponsive politicians, prostitutes, and "press gangs." Impressment, attempts to force colonials to serve in the British navy, triggered some of the most violent urban riots.

Slave Societies in the Eighteenth-Century South

Far starker than the inequalities and divisions among seaport dwellers were those between white and black in the South. By 1775 one out of every five Americans was of African ancestry, and more than 90 percent of all black Americans lived in the South, most along the seaboard. Here, on tobacco and rice plantations, slaves fashioned a distinctive African American society and culture. But they were able to build stable families and communities only late in the eighteenth century and against enormous odds.

The Chesapeake versus the Lower South

Whether a slave was auctioned off to the Chesapeake or to the Lower South shaped his or her future in important ways. Slaves in the low country of South Carolina and Georgia lived on large plantations with as many as 50 other black workers, about half of whom were African-born. They had infrequent contact with

Distribution of the American Population, 1775 The African American population expanded dramatically during the eighteenth century, especially in the southern colonies. The high volume of slave imports accounts for most of the growth in the first half of the century, but natural increase was responsible for the rising black population during later decades.

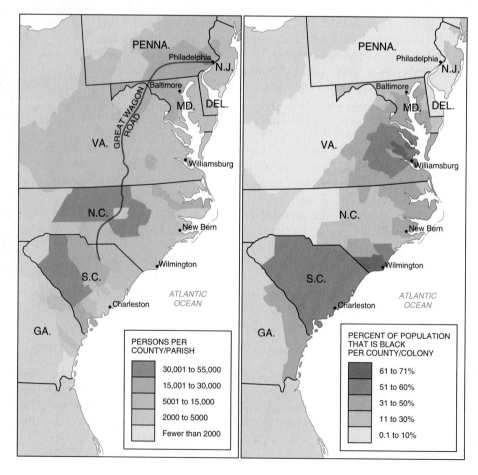

either their masters or the rest of the sparse white population. "They are as 'twere, a Nation within a Nation," observed Francis LeJau, an Anglican priest in the low country. And their work was arduous, for rice required constant cultivation. Black laborers tended young plants and hoed fields in the sweltering summer heat of the mosquito-infested lowlands. During the winter and early spring, they built dams and canals to regulate the flow of water into the rice fields. But the use of the "task system" rather than gang labor widened the window of freedom within slavery. When a slave had completed his assigned task for the day, one planter explained, "his master feels no right to call upon him."

Many Chesapeake slaves, like those in the Lower South, were African-born, but most lived on smaller plantations with fewer than 20 fellow slaves. Less densely concentrated than in the low country, Chesapeake slaves also had more contact with whites. Unlike Carolina's absentee owners, who left white overseers and black drivers to run their plantations, Chesapeake masters actively managed their estates and subjected their slaves to closer scrutiny.

The Slave Family and Community

The four decades following 1700 marked the heaviest years of slave importation into the Chesapeake and Carolina regions. Those Africans had survived the trauma of captivity, the Middle Passage, and sale at slave auctions only to be thrust into a bewildering new world: a sea of unfamiliar faces, a clamor of different languages, a host of demands from men and women who called themselves masters.

The newcomers also had to adjust to their fellow slaves. The "new Negroes" hailed from a number of diverse West African tribes, each with a separate language or dialect and distinctive cultures and kinship systems. Often, they had little in common with one another and even less in common with the American-born black minority. Native-born African Americans enjoyed better health, command of English, and experience in dealing with whites. They were also more likely to enjoy a family life, for their advantages probably made them the preferred partners of black women, who were outnumbered two to one by black men. And since immigrant women waited two or three years before marrying, some immigrant men died before they could find a wife, and many never married. Africans resented native-born men as rivals in the competition for wives, and some immigrants held in particular contempt native converts to Christianity.

African slaves versus American-born slaves

After the middle of the eighteenth century, a number of changes fostered the growth of black families and the vitality of slave communities. As slave importations began to taper off, the rate of natural reproduction among blacks started to climb. As the proportion of new Africans dropped and the number of native-born black Americans grew, the ratio of men to women in the slave community became more equal. Those changes and the appearance of more large plantations, even in the Chesapeake, created more opportunities for black men and women to find partners and form families. Elaborate kinship networks gradually developed, often extending over several plantations in a single neighborhood. And as the immigrant generations were replaced by native-born offspring, earlier sources of tension and division within the slave community disappeared.

Even so, black families remained vulnerable. If a planter fell on hard times, members of black families might be sold off to different buyers to meet his debts. When an owner died, black spouses, parents, and children might be divided among surviving heirs. Even under the best circumstances, fathers might be hired out to other planters for long periods or sent to work in distant quarters. The migration

The Old Plantation affords a rare glimpse of life in the slave quarters. At this festive gathering, both men and women dance to the music of a molo (a stringed instrument similar to a banjo) and drums. Below is a gudugudu drum, an instrument common throughout West Africa and similar to the drum depicted (far right) in the painting.

of slaveholders from the coast to the interior also disrupted black efforts to fashion domestic and communal bonds. Between 1755 and 1782, masters on the move resettled fully one-third of all adult African Americans living in Tidewater, Virginia. Most slaves forced to journey west were men and women in their teens and early twenties, who had to begin again the long process of establishing families and neighborhood networks far from kin and friends.

Black families struggling with terrible uncertainties were sustained by the distinctive African American culture evolving in the slave community. The high percentage of native Africans among the eighteenth-century American black population made it easier for slaves to retain the ways of their lost homeland. Christianity won few converts, in part because white masters feared that baptizing slaves might make them more rebellious but also because African Americans preferred their traditional religions. African influence appeared as well in the slaves' agricultural skills and practices, folktales, music, and dances.

Slavery and Colonial Society in French Louisiana

The experience of Africans unfolded differently in the lower Mississippi Valley, France's southernmost outpost in eighteenth-century North America. Louisiana's earliest colonial settlements were begun by a few thousand French soldiers, indentured servants, and free settlers who had straggled down from Canada, and by immigrants who came from France and Germany. When they founded New Orleans in 1718 the colonists, hoping to create prosperous plantations in the surrounding Mississippi delta, immediately clamored for bound laborers. A year later, French authorities bent to their demands, and the Company of the Indies, which managed France's slave trade, brought nearly 6000 slaves, overwhelmingly men, directly from Africa to Louisiana. Yet even with this influx of new laborers, the search for a cash crop eluded white planters, whose tobacco and, later, indigo proved inferior to the varieties exported from Britain's colonies.

Louisiana's socially mixed society is evident from this market scene: the buyers and sellers include Indians as well as colonials of French, Spanish, and African descent.

Instead of proving the formula for economic success, the sudden influx of Africans challenged French control. In 1729, with blacks already constituting a majority of the population, some newly arrived slaves joined forces with the Natchez Indians, who feared the expansion of white settlement. Their rebellion, the Natchez Revolt, left 200 French planters dead—more than 10 percent of the European population of Louisiana. The French retaliated in a devastating counterattack, enlisting both the Choctaw Indians, who were rivals of the Natchez, and other enslaved blacks, who were promised freedom in return for their support.

Natchez Revolt

The planters' costly victory persuaded French authorities to stop importing slaves into Louisiana, which helped to ensure that the colony did not develop a plantation economy until the end of the eighteenth century, when the cotton boom transformed its culture. In the meantime, blacks continued to make up a majority of all Louisianans, and by the middle of the eighteenth century, nearly all were native-born. The vast majority were slaves, but their work routines—tending cattle, cutting timber, producing naval stores, manning boats—afforded them greater freedom of movement than most slaves enjoyed elsewhere in the American South. They were also encouraged to market the produce of their gardens, hunts, and handicrafts, which became the basis of a thriving trade with both white settlers and the dwindling numbers of Native Americans. But the greatest prize—freedom—was awarded those black men who served in the French militia, defending the colony from the English and Indians as well as capturing slave runaways. The descendants of these black militiamen would become the core of Louisiana's free black community.

Greater freedom for blacks in Louisiana

Slave Resistance in Eighteenth-Century British North America

British North America had no comparable group of black soldiers, but it also had no shortage of African Americans who both resisted captivity and developed strategies for survival. Among newly arrived Africans, collective attempts at escape were most common. Groups of slaves, often made up of newcomers from the same tribe, fled inland and formed "Maroon" communities of runaways. These efforts were usually unsuccessful because the Maroon settlements were large enough to be easily detected.

More acculturated blacks adopted subtler ways of subverting slavery. Domestics and field hands alike faked illness, feigned stupidity and laziness, broke tools, pilfered from storehouses, hid in the woods for weeks at a time, or simply took off to visit other plantations. Other slaves, usually escaping bondage as solitary individuals, found a new life as craftworkers, dock laborers, or sailors in the relative anonymity of colonial seaports.

The Stono Rebellion

More infrequently, black rebellion took direct and violent form. Whites in communities with large numbers of blacks lived in gnawing dread of arson, poisoning, and insurrection. Four slave conspiracies were reported in Virginia during the first half of the eighteenth century. In South Carolina, more than two decades of abortive uprisings and insurrection scares culminated in the Stono Rebellion of 1739, the largest slave revolt of the colonial period. Nearly 100 African Americans, led by a slave named Jemmy, seized arms from a store in the coastal district of Stono and killed several white neighbors before they were caught and killed by the white militia.

But throughout the eighteenth century, slave rebellions occurred far less frequently on the mainland of North America than in the Caribbean or Brazil. Whites outnumbered blacks in all of Britain's mainland colonies except South Carolina, and only there did rebels have a haven for a quick escape—Spanish Florida. Faced with those odds, most slaves reasoned that the risks of rebellion outweighed the prospects for success—and most sought opportunities for greater personal freedom within the slave system itself.

Despite the growing rebelliousness of black slaves, southern planters continued to import Africans throughout the eighteenth century. The practice mystified Franklin, revealing at least one gap in his knowledge—the crucial importance of slavery in the southern economy. But unlike some of his Quaker neighbors in Pennsylvania, who were beginning to object to slavery on moral and humanitarian grounds, Franklin's reservations—like his opposition to German immigration—were overtly racist. "Why increase the sons of Africa by planting them in America," he asked, "where we have so fair an opportunity, by excluding all blacks and tawnys, of increasing the lovely white and red?"

Enlightenment and Awakening in America

The differences among eighteenth-century colonials resulted in more than clashes between regions, races, classes, and ethnic groups. Those differences also made for diversity in the ways that Americans thought and believed. City dwellers were more attuned to European culture than were people living in small villages or on the frontier. White males from well-to-do families of English ancestry were far more likely to receive college educations than were those from poorer or immigrant households. White women of every class and background were excluded from higher education, and slaves received no formal education at all. Where they lived, how well they lived, whether they were male or female, native-born or immigrant, slave or free—all these variables fostered among colonials distinctive worldviews, differing attitudes and assumptions about the individual's relationship to nature, society, and God.

The Enlightenment in America

The diversity of colonials' inner lives became even more pronounced during the eighteenth century because of the Enlightenment, an intellectual movement that started in Europe during the seventeenth century. The leading figures of the Enlightenment, the philosophes, stressed the power of human reason to promote progress by revealing the laws that governed both nature and society. In the American colonies the Enlightenment influenced some curious artisans in major seaports and some wealthy merchants, lawyers, and landowners with the leisure and education to read the latest books from Europe.

Like many devotees of the Enlightenment, Franklin was most impressed by its emphasis on useful knowledge and experimentation. He pondered air currents and then invented a stove that heated houses more efficiently. He toyed with electricity and then invented lightning rods to protect buildings in thunderstorms. Other amateur colonial scientists constructed simple telescopes, classified animal species native to North America, or sought to explain epidemics in terms of natural causes.

Higher education helped spread Enlightenment ideas among young colonials from affluent families. Although many Americans were still educated at English universities, six colleges had been established in the colonies by 1763. The founders of some of these institutions, such as Harvard (1636) and Yale (1701), had intended them primarily to train ministers, but by the eighteenth century their graduates included lawyers, merchants, doctors, and scientists. Most offered courses in mathematics and the natural sciences that taught students algebra and such advanced theories as Copernican astronomy and Newtonian physics.

Some clergy educated at American colleges were touched by the Enlightenment, adopting a more liberal theology that stressed the reasonableness of Christian beliefs. By the middle of the eighteenth century this "rational Christianity" commanded a small following among colonials, usually Anglicans or liberal Congregationalists. Their God was not the Calvinists' awesome deity but a benevolent creator who offered salvation to all, not just to a small, predestined elite. They believed that God's greatest gift to humankind was reason, which enabled all human beings to follow the moral teachings of Jesus. They muted the Calvinist emphasis on human sinfulness and the need for a soul-shattering conversion.

Rational versus traditional Christianity

Enlightenment philosophy and rational Christianity did not affect the outlook of most colonials. By the middle of the eighteenth century, more than half of all white men (and a smaller percentage of white women) were literate, but most colonial readers were not equipped to tackle the learned writings of Enlightenment philosophes. As a result, the outlook of most colonials contrasted sharply with that of the cosmopolitan few. The great majority of Americans still looked for ultimate truth in biblical revelation rather than human reason and explained the workings of the world in terms of divine providence rather than natural law.

Widespread attachment to traditional Christian beliefs was strengthened by the hundreds of new churches built during the first half of the eighteenth century. Church attendance ran highest in the northern colonies, where some 80 percent of the population turned out for public worship on the Sabbath. In the South, because of the greater distances involved and the shortage of clergy, about half of all colonials regularly attended Sunday services.

Despite the prevalence of traditional religious beliefs, many ministers expressed concern about the dangerous influence of rational Christianity. They also worried that the lack of churches might tempt many frontier families to abandon Christianity altogether. Exaggerated as these fears may have been, the consequence was a major religious revival that swept the colonies during the middle decades of the eighteenth century.

The First Great Awakening

The Great Awakening, as the revival came to be called, deepened the influence of older forms of Protestant Christianity and, specifically, Calvinism throughout British America. Participation in the revival was the only experience that a large number of people everywhere in the colonies had in common.

George Whitefield drew critics as well as admirers in both England and America. In this satirical English cartoon, he is depicted as a moneygrubbing evangelist who uncharitably condemns other ministers. His audience, which consists mainly of women, is taken in by his pose of sanctity and his youthful good looks.

The first stirrings of revival appeared in the 1730s among Presbyterians and Congregationalists in the Middle Colonies and New England. Many ministers in these churches preached an "evangelical" message, emphasizing the need for individuals to experience "a new birth" through religious conversion. Among them was Jonathan Edwards, the pastor of a Congregational church in Northampton, Massachusetts. Edwards's preaching combined moving descriptions of God's grace with terrifying portrayals of eternal damnation. "The God that holds you over the pit of hell, much as one holds a spider or some loathsome insect over the fire, abhors you and is dreadfully provoked," he declaimed to one congregation. "There is no other reason to be given, why you have not dropped into hell since you arise in the morning, but that God's hand has held you up."

These local revivals of the 1730s were mere tremors compared to the earthquake of religious enthusiasm that shook the colonies with the arrival in the fall of 1739 of George Whitefield. This handsome, cross-eyed "boy preacher" from England electrified crowds from Georgia to New Hampshire during his two-year tour of the colonies. He and his many imitators among colonial ministers turned the church into a theater, enlivening sermons with dramatic gestures, flowing tears, and gruesome depictions of hell's torments. The drama of such performances appealed to people of all classes, ethnic groups, and races. By the time Whitefield sailed back to England in 1741, thousands of awakened souls were joining older churches or forming new ones.

The Aftermath of the Great Awakening

Whitefield also left behind a raging storm of controversy. Many "awakened" church members now openly criticized their ministers as cold, unconverted, and uninspiring. To supply the missing fire, some laymen—"and even Women and Common Negroes"—took to "exhorting" any audience willing to listen. The most popular ministers became "itinerants," traveling like Whitefield from one town to another. Throughout the colonies the more rationalist and moderate clergy questioned the unrestrained emotionalism and the disorder that attended the gatherings of lay exhorters and itinerants.

Religious divisions

Although Americans had been fighting over religion well before the Great Awakening, the new revivals left colonials even more divided along religious lines. The largest single group of churchgoers in the northern colonies remained within the Congregational and Presbyterian denominations. But both these groups split into factions that either supported or condemned the revivals. Some conservative Presbyterians and Congregationalists, disgusted with the disorder, defected to the Quakers and the Anglicans, who had shunned the revival. On the other hand, the most radical converts joined forces with the warmest champions of the Awakening, the Baptists.

Evangelicalism on the frontier

While northern churches splintered and bickered, the fires of revivalism spread to the South and its backcountry. From the mid-1740s until the 1770s, scores of new Presbyterian and Baptist churches were formed, but conflict often accompanied religious zeal. Ardent Presbyterians in the Carolina backcountry disrupted Anglican worship by loosing packs of dogs in local chapels. In northern Virginia, Anglicans took the offensive against the Baptists, whose strict moral code sounded a silent reproach to the hard-drinking, high-stepping, horse-racing, slaveholding gentry. County officials, prodded by resentful Anglican parsons, harassed, fined, and imprisoned Baptist ministers.

While the West was turning toward evangelical Calvinism, the most powerful people on the southeastern coast remained Anglican and, in the Middle Colonies, Quaker. As a result, the seaboard and the backcountry often found themselves quarreling over religious as well as political and ethnic issues. Inevitably, civil governments were drawn into the fight. In colonies in which one denomination received state support, other churches lobbied legislatures for disestablishment, an end to the favored status of Congregationalism in Connecticut and Massachusetts and of Anglicanism in the southern colonies.

And so a diverse lot of Americans found themselves continually at odds with one another. Because of differences in religion and education, colonials quarreled over whether rational Christianity enlightened the world or emotional revivalists destroyed its order. Because of ethnic and racial tensions, Spanish Jews found themselves persecuted, and African Americans searched for ways to resist their white masters. Because of westward expansion, Carolina Regulators waged war against coastal planters while colonial legislatures from Massachusetts to Virginia quarreled over western boundaries.

Colonial diversity: a summary

Benjamin Franklin, a man who made it his business to know, surely understood the depth of those divisions as he made his way toward the Albany Congress in the spring of 1754. He himself had brooded over the boatloads of non-English newcomers. He had lived in two booming seaports and felt the explosive force of the frontier. He personified the Enlightenment—and he had heard George Whitefield himself preach from the steps of the Philadelphia courthouse.

Why, then, could Franklin, who knew how little held the colonials together, sustain his hopes for political unity? The answer may be that even in 1754, the majority of colonials were of English descent. And these free, white Americans liked being English. That much they had in common.

Anglo-American Worlds of the Eighteenth Century

Most Americans prided themselves on being English. When colonials named their towns and counties, they named them after places in their parent country. When colonials established governments, they turned to England for their political models. They frequently claimed "the liberties of freeborn Englishmen" as their birthright. Even in diet, dress, furniture, architecture, and literature, colonists adopted English standards of taste.

Yet American society had developed in ways significantly different from that of Great Britain.* Some differences made colonials feel inferior, ashamed of their simplicity when compared with London's sophistication. But colonials also came

*When England and Scotland were unified in 1707, the nation as a whole became known officially as Great Britain; its citizens, as British.

Coffeehouses such as this establishment in London were favorite gathering places for eighteenth-century Americans visiting Britain. Here merchants and mariners, ministers and students, lobbyists and tourists warmed themselves, read newspapers, and exchanged gossip about commerce, politics, and social life.

to appreciate the greater equality of their society and the more representative character of their governments. If it was good to be English, it was better still to be English in America.

English Economic and Social Development

The differences between England and America began with their economies. Large financial institutions like the Bank of England and influential corporations like the East India Company were driving England's commercial development. A growing number of textile factories and mines were deepening its industrial development. Although most English men and women worked at agriculture, it, too, had become a business. Members of the gentry rented their estates to tenants, members of the rural middle class. In turn, these tenants hired men and women from the swollen ranks of England's landless to perform the actual farm labor. In contrast, most colonial farmers owned their land, and most family farms were a few hundred acres. The scale of commerce and manufacturing was equally modest, limited by the preference of colonials to farm instead.

England's more developed economy fostered the growth of cities, especially London, a teeming colossus of 675,000 in 1750. In contrast, 90 percent of all eighteenth-century colonials lived in towns of fewer than 2000.

 ## The Consumer Revolution

But in another respect, England's more advanced economy drew the colonies and the parent country together, as a consumer revolution transformed the everyday lives of people on both sides of the Atlantic. By the beginning of the eighteenth century, small manufacturers throughout England were producing a newly large and enticing array of consumer goods—fine textiles and hats, ceramics and glassware, carpets and furniture. Americans proved as eager as Britons to acquire these commodities—so eager that the per capita consumption of imported manufactures among colonials rose 120 percent between 1750 and 1773. Only the wealthy could afford goods of the highest quality, but people of all classes demanded and indulged in small luxuries like a tin of tea, a pair of gloves, or a bar of Irish soap. In both England and its colonies, the spare and simple material life of earlier centuries was giving way to a new order in which even people of ordinary means owned a wider variety of things.

This tea caddy, owned by a Massachusetts colonial, was a new consumer luxury, as was the tea it held.

Inequality in England and America

Then there were people of no means, and in England, they were legion. London seethed with filth, crime, and desperate poverty. The poor and the unemployed as well as pickpockets and prostitutes crowded into its gin-soaked slums, taverns, and brothels. The contrast between the luxuries enjoyed by a wealthy few Londoners and the misery of the many disquieted colonial observers. Ebenezer Hazard, an American Quaker, knew for certain that he was not in Philadelphia, but instead in "a Sink of Sin."

Class distinctions

The opportunities for great wealth provided by England's more developed economy created deep class distinctions, as did the inherited privileges of its aristocracy. The members of the upper class, the landed aristocracy and gentry, made up less than 2 percent of England's population but owned 70 percent of its land. By right of birth, English aristocrats claimed membership in the House of Lords; by custom, certain powerful gentry families dominated the other branch of Parliament, the House of Commons. England's titled gentlemen shared power and wealth and often family ties with the rich men of the city—major merchants, successful lawyers, and lucky financiers. They too exerted political influence through the House of Commons.

The colonies had their own prominent families but no titled ruling class holding political privilege by hereditary right. And even the wealthiest colonial families lived in far less magnificence than did their English counterparts. Probably the finest mansion in eighteenth-century America, William Byrd's Westover plantation, was scarcely a tenth the size of the Marquis of Rockingham's country house, which was longer than two football fields.

If England's upper classes lived more splendidly, its lower classes were larger and worse off than those in the colonies. Less than a third of England's inhabitants belonged to the "middling sort" of traders, professionals, artisans, and tenant farmers. More than two-thirds struggled for survival at the bottom of society. In contrast, the colonial middle class counted for nearly three-quarters of the white population. With land cheap, labor scarce, and wages for both urban and rural workers 100 percent higher in America than in England, it was much easier for colonials to accumulate savings and then buy a farm of their own.

Ambivalent Americans

Colonials were both fascinated and repelled by English society. Benjamin Rush, a Philadelphia physician, felt in the House of Lords as if he "walked on sacred ground." He begged his guide for permission to sit on the throne therein, and then sat "for a considerable time." Other colonials gushed over the grandeur of aristocratic estates and imported suits of livery for their servants, tea services for their wives, and wallpaper for their drawing rooms. They exported their sons to Britain for college educations at Oxford and Cambridge, medical school at

This portrait of John Stuart, the third Earl of Bute (1713–1792), wearing the ceremonial robes of the House of Lords, epitomizes the opulence of Britain's ruling class in the eighteenth century.

England's balanced constitution

Tools for "managing" Parliament

Edinburgh, and legal training at London's Inns of Court.

But the aping of English ways made colonials uneasy, too. One Philadelphia Quaker ordered an elegant English coach complete with coat of arms—but then reconsidered and removed the crest. Second thoughts also plagued colonial parents when sons educated in England came home wearing dandified silks, affecting foppish manners, and spouting fashionable slang—"Split me, Madam!" "By Gad!" and "Dam me!" Such behavior mirrored the bad habits of some English gentlemen, whose large incomes from renting land encouraged idleness and extravagance.

Colonials recognized that England's ruling classes purchased their luxury and leisure at the cost of the rest of the nation. In his *Autobiography,* Benjamin Franklin painted a devastating portrait of the degraded lives of his fellow workers in a London printshop, who drowned their disappointments by drinking throughout the workday, even more excessively on the Sabbath, and then faithfully observing the holiday of "St. Monday's" to nurse their hangovers. Like Franklin, many colonials believed that gross inequalities of wealth would endanger liberty. They regarded the idle among England's rich and poor alike as ominous signs of a degenerate nation.

Politics in England and America

Colonials were also of two minds about England's government. While they praised the English constitution as the basis of all liberties, they were alarmed by the actual workings of English politics. In theory, England's "balanced constitution" was designed to give every order of English society some voice in the workings of government. While the Crown represented the monarchy and the House of Lords the aristocracy, the House of Commons represented the democracy, the people of England. In fact, the monarch's executive ministers had become dominant by creating support for their policies in Parliament through patronage—or, put more bluntly, bribery.

Over the course of the eighteenth century, a large executive bureaucracy had evolved in order to enforce laws, collect taxes, and wage the nearly constant wars in Europe and America. The power to appoint all military and treasury officials, customs and tax collectors, judges and justices of the peace lay with the monarch and his or her ministers. By the middle of the eighteenth century, almost half of all members of Parliament held such Crown offices or government contracts. Royal patronage was also used to manipulate parliamentary elections. The executive branch used money or liquor to bribe local voters into selecting their candidates. The small size of England's electorate fostered executive influence. Perhaps one-fourth of all adult males could vote, and many electoral districts were not adjusted to keep pace with population growth and resettlement. The notorious "rotten boroughs" each elected

This satirical rendering of an English election, by the English artist William Hogarth, mirrored the reservations of many Americans about the political culture of the mother country. The man seated in the foreground of the jostling crowd represents Hogarth's dark view of the typical English voter: much incapacitated by drink, he is being told for whom to vote by the man standing and whispering in his ear. In the background, the overturned carriage suggests that political corruption threatens the stability of England.

a member of Parliament to represent fewer than 500 easily bribable voters, while some large cities like Manchester and Leeds, newly populous because of industrial growth, had no representation in Parliament at all.

Americans liked to think that their colonial governments mirrored the ideal English constitution. In terms of formal structure, there were similarities. Most colonies had a royal governor who represented the monarch in America and a bicameral (two-house) legislature made up of a lower house (the assembly) and an upper house (or council). The democratically elected assembly, like the House of Commons, stood for popular interests, while the council, some of which were elected and others appointed, more roughly approximated the House of Lords.

Colonial governments

But these formal similarities masked real differences between English and colonial governments. On the face of it, royal governors had much more power than the English Crown. Unlike kings and queens, royal governors could veto laws passed by assemblies; they could dissolve those bodies at will; they could create courts and dismiss judges. However, governors who asserted their full powers quickly met opposition from their assemblies, who objected that such overwhelming authority endangered popular liberty. In any showdown with their assemblies, most royal governors had to give way, for they lacked the government offices and contracts that bought loyalty. The colonial legislatures possessed additional leverage, since all of them retained the sole authority to levy taxes.

Even if the governors had enjoyed greater patronage powers, their efforts to influence colonial legislatures would have been frustrated by the sheer size of the American electorate. There were too many voters in America to bribe. More than half and possibly as many as 70 percent of all white adult colonial men were enfranchised. Property requirements were the same in America as in England, but widespread ownership of land in the colonies allowed most men to meet the qualifications easily.

The colonial electorate was also more watchful. Representatives were required to reside in the districts that they served, and a few even received binding instructions from their constituents about how to vote. Representation was also apportioned according to population far more equitably than in England. Because they were so closely tied to their constituents' wishes, colonial legislators were far less likely than members of Parliament to be swayed by executive pressure.

Most Americans were as pleased with their inexpensive and representative colonial governments as they were horrified by the conduct of politics in England. John Dickinson, a young Pennsylvanian training as a lawyer in London, was scandalized by a parliamentary election he witnessed in 1754. The king and his ministers had spent over 100,000 pounds sterling to buy support for their candidates, he wrote his father, and "if a man cannot be brought to vote as he is desired, he is made dead drunk and kept in that state, never heard of by his family and friends, till all is over and he can do no harm."

The Imperial System before 1760

Colonials like Dickinson thought long and hard about the condition of England's society and politics. Meanwhile, the English thought about their colonies little, understood them less, and wished neither to think about them more nor to understand them better. It would be hard to exaggerate just how insignificant North America was in the English scheme of things. Those few Britons who thought about America at all believed that colonials resembled the "savage" Indians more than the "civilized" English. As a London acquaintance remarked to Thomas Hancock, it was a pity Mrs. Hancock had to remain in Boston when he could "take her to England and make her happy with Christians."

The same indifference contributed to England's haphazard administration of its colonies. The Board of Trade and Plantations, created from the Lords of Trade in 1696, gathered information about Atlantic trading and fishing, reviewed laws and petitions drawn up by colonial assemblies, and exchanged letters and instructions with royal governors. But the Board of Trade was only an advisory body, reporting to the king's ministers and passing on information to other government agencies.

Real authority over the colonies was divided among an array of other agencies. The Treasury oversaw customs and gathered other royal revenues; the Admiralty Board enforced regulations of trade; the War Office orchestrated colonial defense. But these departments spent most of their hours handling more pressing responsibilities. Colonial affairs stood at the bottom of their agendas. Most British officials in America seemed equally indifferent. Often enough, they had been awarded their jobs in return for political support, not in recognition of administrative ability.

The branch of England's government most indifferent to America was Parliament. Aside from passing an occasional law to regulate trade, restrict manufacturing, or direct monetary policy, Parliament made no effort to assert its authority in America. Its members assumed that Parliament's sovereignty extended over the entire empire, and nothing had occurred to make them think otherwise.

The benefits of benign neglect

For the colonies, this chaotic and inefficient system of colonial administration worked well enough. The very weakness of imperial oversight left Americans with a great deal of freedom. Even England's regulation of trade rested lightly on the shoulders of most Americans. Southern planters were obliged to send their rice, indigo, and tobacco to Britain only, but they enjoyed favorable credit terms and knowledgeable marketing from English merchants. Colonials were prohibited from finishing iron products and exporting hats and textiles, but they had scant interest in developing domestic industries. Americans were required to import all manufactured goods through England, but by doing so, they acquired high-quality goods

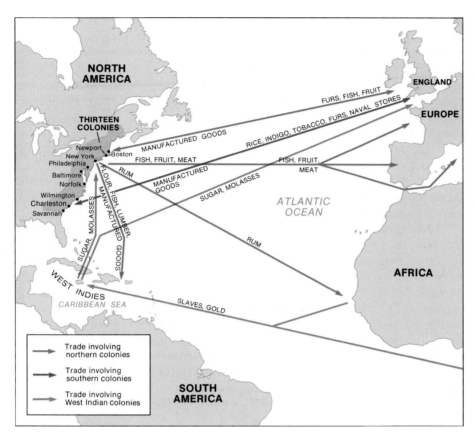

Overseas Trade Networks Commercial ties to Spain and Portugal, Africa, and the Caribbean sustained the growth of both seaports and commercial farming regions on the British North American mainland and enabled colonials to purchase an increasing volume of finished goods from England. The proceeds from exports in foodstuffs and lumber to the West Indies and trade in fish to Spain and Portugal enabled northern merchants and farmers to buy hardware and clothing from the mother country. Southern planters financed their consumption of English imports and their investment in African slaves with the profits from the sale of tobacco, rice, and indigo abroad.

at low prices. At little sacrifice, most Americans obeyed imperial regulations. Only sugar, molasses, and tea were routinely smuggled.

Following this policy of benign neglect the British empire muddled on to the satisfaction of most people on both sides of the Atlantic. Economic growth and political autonomy allowed most Americans to like being English, despite their misgivings about their parent nation. The beauty of it was that Americans could be English in America, enjoying greater economic opportunity and political equality. If imperial arrangements had remained as they were in 1754, the empire might have muddled on indefinitely. But because of the French and the Indians on the American frontier, the British empire began to change. And those changes made it increasingly hard for Americans to be English in America.

Toward the Seven Years' War

In the late spring of 1754, while Benjamin Franklin dreamed of unifying Americans, a young Virginian dreamed of military glory. As Franklin rode toward Albany, the young man, an inexperienced officer, led his company of Virginia militia toward Fort Duquesne, the French stronghold on the forks of the Ohio.

Less than a year earlier, the king's ministers had advised royal governors in America to halt the French advance into the Ohio country. The Virginia government organized an expedition against Fort Duquesne, placing at its head the young man who combined an imposing physique with the self-possession of an English gentleman. He wanted, more than anything, to become an officer in the regular British army.

Washington at Fort Necessity

But events in the Ohio country during that spring and summer did not go George Washington's way. French soldiers easily captured Fort Necessity, his crude outpost near Fort Duquesne. In early July, as the Albany Congress was debating, Washington was surrendering to a French force in the Pennsylvania backcountry and beating a retreat back to Virginia. By the end of 1754, Washington had resigned his militia command and retired to his plantation at Mount Vernon. The disaster at Fort Necessity had dashed his dreams of martial glory and a regular army commission. He had no future as a soldier.

With the rout of Washington and his troops, the French grew bolder and the Indians more restless. The renewal of war between England and France was certain by the beginning of 1755. This time the contest between the two powers would decide the question of sovereignty over North America. That, at least, was the dream of William Pitt, who was about to become the most powerful man in England.

The ambitions of William Pitt

Even by the standards of English politicians, William Pitt was an odd character. Subject to bouts of illness and depression and loathed for his opportunism and egotism, Pitt surmounted every challenge, buoyed by a strong sense of destiny—his own and that of England. He believed that England must seize the world's trade, for trade meant wealth and wealth meant power. As early as the 1730s, Pitt recognized that the only obstacle between England and its destiny was France—and that the contest between the two for world supremacy would be decided in America. During King George's War, Pitt had mesmerized the House of Commons and the nation with his spellbinding oratory about England's imperial destiny. But the mounting cost of fighting prompted the government to accept peace with France in 1748. In frustration Pitt retired from public life.

But while Pitt sulked in his library, the rivalry for the American frontier moved toward a showdown. The French pressed their front lines eastward; the English pushed for land westward; the Indians maneuvered for position. Heartened by the news from America, Pitt clung to his dream of English commercial dominion and French defeat. By the late spring of 1754, as Benjamin Franklin and George Washington rode toward their defeats, William Pitt knew that he would have his war with France and his way with the world.

Other dreams would wait longer for fulfillment. The Albany Congress had demonstrated that a few Americans like Franklin had seen beyond the diversity of a divided colonial world to the possibility of union, however unaccustomed and untried. But it would take another war, one that restructured an empire, before some Americans saw in themselves a likeness that was not English.

chapter summary

Over the course of the eighteenth century, British North Americans grew increasingly diverse, which made the prospect of any future colonial political union appear remote.

- Differences became more pronounced among whites because of the immigration of larger numbers of non-English settlers, the spread of settlement to the backcountry, and the growth of major seaports.

- Although disorder was not uncommon either on the frontier or in cities, the most serious social and political conflict drew its strength from sectional controversies between East and West.

- The South became more embattled, too, as a result of the massive importation of slaves directly from Africa during the first half of the eighteenth century and a rising tide of black resistance to slavery.

- After about 1750 the growth of a native-born population strengthened black communal and family life.

- Religious conflict among colonials was intensified by the spread of Enlightenment ideas and the influence of the first Great Awakening.

- Despite their many differences, a majority of white colonials took pride in their common English ancestry and in belonging to a powerful empire.

interactive learning

The Primary Source Investigator CD-ROM offers the following materials related to this chapter:

- Interactive maps: **The Atlantic World, 1400–1850** (M2) and **The Settlement of Colonial America, 1700–1763** (M5)

- A collection of primary sources exploring the development of the British empire in North America, such as a diagram of a slave ship, an image of a homespun garment, and a sermon from the famous itinerant preacher George Whitefield. Several sources illustrate the consequences of widespread slavery, including a poem by African American Phyllis Wheatley and a minister's description of racial slavery. In addition, several sources demonstrate how imperial expansion sparked internal problems: disputes with colonial governments and the Carolina Regulators movement, a portrait of the Iroquois go-between Mary Brant, and a political cartoon from Benjamin Franklin on the difficulties of uniting the colonies.

additional reading

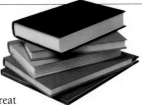

A number of excellent studies treat broad aspects of American development during the later colonial period. For a comprehensive treatment of economic development, see John McCusker and Russell Menard, *The Economy of British America, 1607–1787* (1985). For the evolution of political institutions, consult Bernard Bailyn, *The Origins of American Politics* (1968). On the subject of religious change, the book to read is Patricia Bonomi, *Under the Cope of Heaven* (1986). For family life, consult Philip Greven's *The Protestant Temperament* (1977). The best studies of the frontier are Charles Grant's work on western Connecticut, *Democracy in the Frontier Town of Kent* (1961), and Rachel Klein's account of the South Carolina backcountry, *The Unification of a Slave State* (1990). The evolution of major seaports is exhaustively chronicled in Gary Nash's *Urban Crucible* (1979), while relations between blacks and whites in the South are ably described by Allan Kulikoff, *Tobacco and Slaves* (1987); Rhys Isaac, *The Transformation of Virginia, 1740–1790* (1982); and Mechal Sobel, *The World They Made Together* (1987).

Understanding the impact of immigration and ethnic diversity is essential to appreciating the dynamism of eighteenth-century colonial society. Some especially vivid accounts include Bernard Bailyn, *Voyagers to the West* (1986); Bernard Bailyn and Philip D. Morgan, eds., *Strangers within the Realm* (1991); and Ira Berlin, "Time, Space, and the Evolution of Afro-American Society in British Mainland North America," *American Historical Review,* 85 (1980), 44–78. For a fuller list of readings, see the Bibliography at www.mhhe.com/davidsonnation5.

significant events

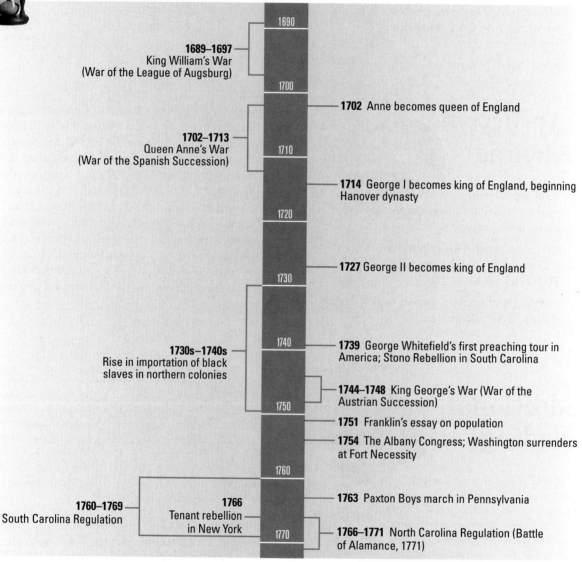

1689–1697
King William's War
(War of the League of Augsburg)

1690

1700

1702 Anne becomes queen of England

1702–1713
Queen Anne's War
(War of the Spanish Succession)

1710

1714 George I becomes king of England, beginning Hanover dynasty

1720

1727 George II becomes king of England

1730

1730s–1740s
Rise in importation of black
slaves in northern colonies

1740

1739 George Whitefield's first preaching tour in America; Stono Rebellion in South Carolina

1744–1748 King George's War (War of the Austrian Succession)

1750

1751 Franklin's essay on population

1754 The Albany Congress; Washington surrenders at Fort Necessity

1760

1760–1769
South Carolina Regulation

1766
Tenant rebellion
in New York

1763 Paxton Boys march in Pennsylvania

1770

1766–1771 North Carolina Regulation (Battle of Alamance, 1771)

THE CREATION OF A NEW REPUBLIC

As the shrewd Benjamin Franklin had observed in 1751, the population of British North America was doubling approximately every 25 years. This astonishing rate was quite possibly the fastest in the world at the time. Even so, the North American surge was merely one part of a more general global rise in population during the second half of the eighteenth century. In sheer numbers China led the way. Its population of 150 million in 1700 had doubled to more than 313 million by the end of the century. Europe's total rose from about 118 million in 1700 to about 187 million a century later, the greatest growth coming on its eastern and western flanks, in Great Britain and Russia. African and Indian populations seem to have increased as well, although historians have analyzed trends there less closely.

This worldwide rise, unprecedented in previous history, occurred for a variety of reasons. Climate may have been one. In Europe, at least, warmer and drier seasons produced generally better harvests. (The population of the already dry Middle East seems not to have expanded, and that region may have been hurt by the climate changes.) Furthermore, health and nutrition improved globally with the spread of Native American crops. Irish farmers discovered that a single acre planted with the lowly American potato could support an entire family. The tomato added crucial vitamins to the Mediterranean diet, while maize provided more calories per acre than any European or African

grain. In China the American sweet potato thrived in hilly regions where rice would not grow.

Not only plants but diseases were carried back and forth by European ships. As we have seen, contact between previously isolated peoples produced extreme mortality from epidemics, enabling invaders like Hernando Cortés to conquer populous civilizations. Similarly, the Pilgrims unwittingly blessed divine providence for allowing them to take over deserted fields that had been cleared and farmed by Indians only recently struck down by disease. By 1800 the more globally isolated peoples, such as the inhabitants of Australia or the North American plains, remained at risk. But after more than two centuries of sustained contact, Indians developed increased biological resistance to European and African illnesses. The frequent circulation of diseases worldwide led to a more stable environment in which populations began to swell.

During the years that Europeans explored the Atlantic frontiers of North and South America, Slavic and Romanian pioneers were moving eastward into the Eurasian steppes. There they turned sparsely settled pastoral lands into feudal manors and farms. In northern forests unsuitable for farming, Russian fur traders advanced eastward across Siberia until they reached the Pacific in the 1630s. By the 1780s Russian pioneers had pushed into Alaska and down the Pacific American coast, bumping up against western Europeans who were harvesting furs from Canada's forests and streams.

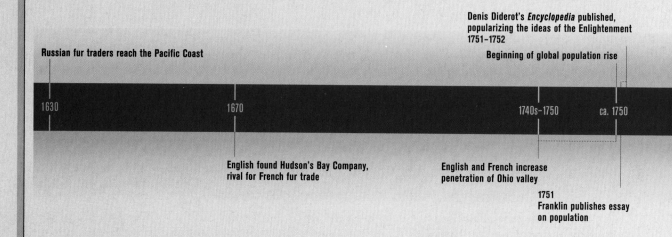

Russian fur traders reach the Pacific Coast

Denis Diderot's *Encyclopedia* published, popularizing the ideas of the Enlightenment 1751–1752

Beginning of global population rise

| 1630 | 1670 | 1740s–1750 | ca. 1750 |

English found Hudson's Bay Company, rival for French fur trade

English and French increase penetration of Ohio valley

1751 Franklin publishes essay on population

AMERICAN EVENTS

Both flanks of this European thrust often depended on forced labor, especially in agricultural settings. As we have seen, the institution of slavery in North America became increasingly restrictive over the course of the seventeenth century. Furthermore, the number of slaves imported to North America paled when compared to the thousands shipped by the Portuguese to the slave markets of Rio de Janeiro. Similarly, the plight of serfs worsened from 1500 to 1650, as the demand for labor increased in eastern Europe. In 1574 Polish nobles received the right to punish their serfs entirely as they pleased—including execution if they chose. By 1603, Russian peasants were routinely sold along with the land they worked.

The eighteenth-century Enlightenment penetrated eastern Europe too, as it had the urban centers of North America. Russia's Peter the Great absorbed many ideas when he traveled, sometimes incognito, to England and western Europe. As czar (1689–1725), he attempted to put them to use in westernizing Russia. Catherine the Great was even more influenced by the artistic currents of the Enlightenment. During her reign (1762–1796), she imported Western architects, sculptors, and musicians to grace her court.

But Catherine's limits to toleration were made brutally clear in 1773. The same year that a group of rowdy Americans were dumping tea into Boston harbor, a Cossack soldier named Emelian Pugachev launched a peasant rebellion. Grandly proclaiming himself emperor, Pugachev issued

decrees abolishing serfdom and taxes. Serfs in the Ural and Volga river valleys flocked to his ragtag army. Catherine ruthlessly imprisoned Pugachev (shown here jailed and chained) and then

GLOBAL EVENTS

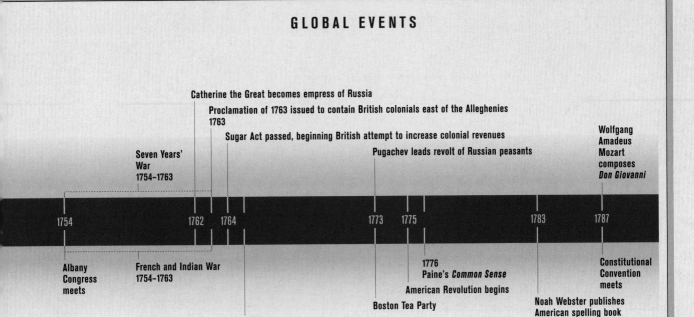

Catherine the Great becomes empress of Russia

Proclamation of 1763 issued to contain British colonials east of the Alleghenies
1763

Sugar Act passed, beginning British attempt to increase colonial revenues

Pugachev leads revolt of Russian peasants

Seven Years' War 1754–1763

Wolfgang Amadeus Mozart composes *Don Giovanni*

1754   1762   1764   1773   1775   1783   1787

Albany Congress meets

French and Indian War 1754–1763

1776
Paine's *Common Sense*

American Revolution begins

Boston Tea Party

Constitutional Convention meets

Noah Webster publishes American spelling book

1765
Stamp Act protests and riots

AMERICAN EVENTS

executed him and scattered his followers. In 1775 she granted Russian nobles even more absolute control over their serfs.

To make the obvious comparison—between a failed Russian revolution for liberty and the triumph of American colonials—would be too smug. Liberty-loving American merchants like John Hancock and genteel tobacco planters like George Washington were hardly in the position of serfs. A more appropriate link might be made between Russian serfs and American slaves, since both groups supplied the forced labor along the frontiers of European expansion. But the slaves, whose African homelands lay thousands of miles away, found the odds of a successful rebellion just as difficult as Russian serfs

did. Ironically, white Americans may have been able to fight so vigorously for their liberties precisely because they had made revolt by a class of forced laborers so difficult.

Americans rebelled in 1775 not out of a serf's desperation; quite the opposite. The Seven Years' War ended in 1763 with the French driven from North America and British colonials thriving, thanks to a wartime boom. Thomas Mayhew, a respected Boston minister, voiced the opinion of many when he envisioned a glorious empire spreading across the continent in the century to come. "I do not mean an independent one," he added carefully, but in 1763 the qualification was hardly necessary. Most white Americans were quite pleased with the prospect

of being English. With the significant exception of the slave class, the distance between the poorest and richest individuals was smaller in America than it was anywhere in Europe. And the British tradition of representative government ensured a broader involvement of citizens in colonial government. Thus, an American Revolution was hardly inevitable in 1776. Most certainly one did not appear likely in 1763. The timing of the break with Great Britain was the result of specific decisions made on both sides of the Atlantic.

America's isolated position on the edge of European expansion certainly created conditions that made separation likely at some point. Most colonials, used to relative social equality among white Americans, blanched at what

PART TWO

GLOBAL EVENTS

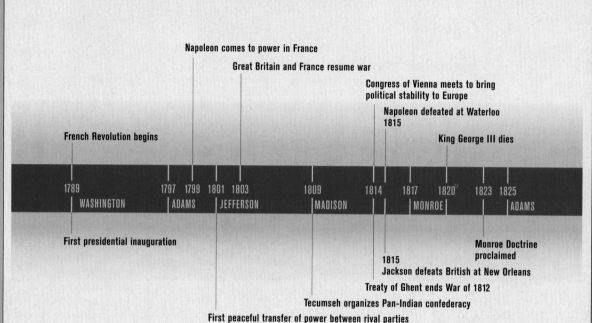

Napoleon comes to power in France

Great Britain and France resume war

Congress of Vienna meets to bring political stability to Europe

Napoleon defeated at Waterloo 1815

French Revolution begins

King George III dies

| 1789 | 1797 | 1799 | 1801 | 1803 | 1809 | 1814 | 1817 | 1820 | 1823 | 1825 |

WASHINGTON   ADAMS   JEFFERSON   MADISON   MONROE   ADAMS

First presidential inauguration

Monroe Doctrine proclaimed

1815
Jackson defeats British at New Orleans

Treaty of Ghent ends War of 1812

Tecumseh organizes Pan-Indian confederacy

First peaceful transfer of power between rival parties

AMERICAN EVENTS

they saw as English luxury and corruption. English governing elites, when they bothered to notice Americans, usually found them provincial and naive. Under different circumstances the move for independence might have come in 1800, or even 1867, as it did for Canada. But the break came earlier. American colonials, who in 1763 liked being English and gloried in the British empire, gradually came to think of themselves as independent Americans, subject neither to a British monarch nor to Parliament.

Chapter 5

mericans liked being English. They had liked being English from the beginning of colonial settlement, but they liked it more than ever for a few years after 1759. One wonderful day during those years—September 16, 1762—Bostonians turned out to celebrate belonging to the British empire. Soldiers mustered on the Common; bells pealed from the steeples of local churches; the charge of guns fired from the battery resounded through towns; strains of orchestra music from an outdoor concert floated through the city's crowded streets and narrow alleys. When darkness fell and bonfires illuminated the city, Bostonians consumed "a vast quantity of liquor," drinking "loyal healths" to their young king, George III, and in celebration of Britain's victory in the Seven Years' War.

When the great news of that triumph reached the North American mainland in the fall of 1762, similar celebrations broke out all over the colonies. And with good reason. France's empire in America, which only a few years earlier had appeared so formidable, was now vanquished. Great Britain had become master of Canada, thanks to the joint efforts of British and American colonial troops. In 1763 the Treaty of Paris ratified their victories, making Britain the largest and most powerful empire in the Western world. Americans were among His Majesty's proudest subjects.

Thirteen years after the celebration of 1762, Boston was a different place. Pride in belonging to the empire had shriveled to shrill charges that England conspired to enslave its colonies. Massachusetts led the way, drawing other colonies deep into resistance. Bostonians initiated many of the petitions and resolves against British authority. When words did not work, they ignited riots, harassed British officials, baited British troops, and destroyed British property. In 1775, they were laying plans for rebellion against the British empire.

Toward the War for American Independence

1754–1776

preview • Parliament passed the Sugar Act, Stamp Act, and other measures of the early 1760s in hopes of binding the American colonies more closely to the empire. Instead, once-loyal Americans became convinced that their constitutional rights were being violated: the right to consent to taxes, the right to a trial by jury, and the freedom from standing armies. With the passage of the harsh Coercive Acts of 1774, a break with Britain was not long in coming.

A process of disillusionment

An ironic fate overtook that generation of Americans who loved being English, boasted of their rights as Britons, and celebrated their membership in the all-conquering empire. That very pride drove colonials into rebellion, for the men who ran the British empire after 1763 would not allow Americans to be English. Even before the Seven Years' War, some colonials saw that diverging paths of social and political development made them different from the English. After the Seven Years' War, events demonstrated to even more colonials that they were not considered the political equals of the English who lived in England. As their disillusionment with the empire deepened, British North Americans from Massachusetts to Georgia slowly discovered a new identity as Americans and declared their independence from being English.

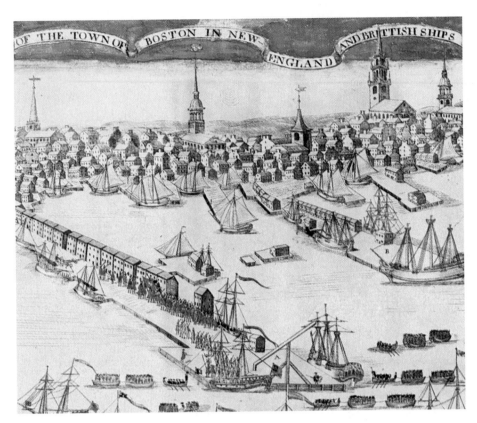

The Seven Years' War, which actually lasted nine years, pitted Britain and its

The Seven Years' War

ally, Prussia, against France, in league with Austria and Spain. The battle raged from 1754 until 1763, ranging over the continent of Europe, the coast of West Africa, India, the Philippines, the Caribbean, and North America.

The Years of Defeat

The war started in 1754 when Virginia sent George Washington and a company of militia into the Ohio River valley to halt French penetration into the area (pages 135–136). Washington's surrender at Fort Necessity only stiffened Britain's resolve to assert its own claims to the Ohio country. In the summer of 1755, as two British regiments led by Major General Edward Braddock approached the French outpost at Fort Duquesne on the forks of the Ohio, they were ambushed and cut to pieces by a party of French and Indians. Washington led the mortally wounded Braddock and the remnants of his army in a retreat.

Braddock's defeat

During the summer of Braddock's defeat, New Englanders fared somewhat better against French forces in Nova Scotia and deported 6000 farmers from that region. The Acadians, as they were known, professed to be neutral in the war between France and Britain. But their ancestors had been French, and the English worried that neighboring Quebec might still persuade them to rebel. Thus the Acadians had their land confiscated, and they were dispersed throughout the colonies.

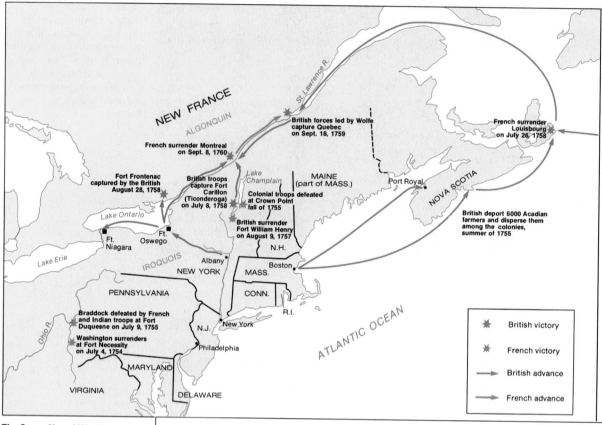

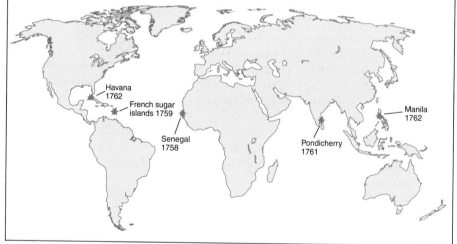

The Seven Years' War After Washington's surrender and Braddock's defeat in the Pennsylvania backcountry, the British and French waged their final contest for supremacy in North America in northern New York and Canada. But the rivalry for empire between France and Britain was worldwide, with naval superiority providing the needed edge to Britain. The British navy isolated French forces in India, winning a victory at Pondicherry, while English offensives captured the French sugar islands in the Caribbean and French trading posts along the West African coast. When Spain entered the war on the side of France, British fleets captured both Havana and the strategic port of Manila in the Philippines.

Still, deporting farmers did little to help win a war. During the opening years of the conflict, Britain mismanaged its forces disastrously. When England and France formally declared war in May 1756, John Campbell, the Earl of Loudoun, took command of the North American theater. American soldiers and colonial assemblies alike hated Lord Loudoun. They balked at his efforts to take command over colonial troops and dragged their heels at his demands for men and supplies. Meanwhile, the French appointed an effective new commanding general of their forces in Canada, Louis Joseph, the marquis de Montcalm. Montcalm drove southward, capturing key British forts and threatening the security of both New York and New England. While he prospered in America, the British were also taking a beating from the French in Europe and in India.

During the years when the French seemed unstoppable, the British looked for help from the strongest tribes of the interior—the Iroquois in the North and the Creek, Choctaw, and Cherokee in the South. Instead, Benjamin Franklin's worst fears were realized: most tribes adopted neutrality or joined the French. As France seemed certain to carry the continent, Indian attacks on English frontier settlements increased.

The Years of Victory

As British fortunes worsened throughout 1756 and 1757, William Pitt resumed his political career and took personal control over the war in his usual bold way. "I know that I can save this country and that no one else can," he announced. Leaving the fighting in Europe to the Prussians, Pitt focused the full strength of the British military on beating the French in America. Pitt also renewed colonial support for the war effort by replacing Lord Loudoun and giving his successor far more limited authority over colonial troops. And Pitt sent requests for men and money directly to each colonial assembly—accompanied by promises of reimbursement in gold and silver.

William Pitt turns the tide

With Pitt now in control, the tide of battle turned. In July of 1758, the British gained control of the St. Lawrence River when the French fortress at Louisbourg fell before the combined force of the Royal Navy and British and colonial troops. In August, a force of New Englanders strangled France's frontier defenses by capturing Fort Frontenac, thereby isolating French forts lining the Great Lakes and the Ohio valley. The Indians, seeing the French routed from the interior, switched their allegiance to the English.

The British succeeded even more brilliantly in 1759. In Canada, Brigadier General James Wolfe gambled on a daring stratagem and won Quebec from Montcalm. Under the cover of darkness, naval squadrons landed Wolfe's men beneath the city's steep bluffs, where they scaled the heights to a plateau known as the Plains of Abraham. Montcalm might have won by holding out behind the walls of his fortress and awaiting reinforcements. Instead, he matched Wolfe's recklessness and offered battle. Five days later both Wolfe and Montcalm lay dead, along with 1400 French soldiers and 600 British and American troops. Quebec had fallen to the British. A year later the French surrender of Montreal ended the fighting in North America, although it continued elsewhere in the world for another two years.

Wolfe and Montcalm battle for Quebec

The Treaty of Paris, signed in February 1763, ended the French presence on the continent of North America. The terms confirmed British title to all French territory east of the Mississippi as well as to Spanish Florida. (Spain had made the last-minute mistake of entering the war, against Britain, in 1762.) France ceded to its ally Spain all of its land lying west of the Mississippi and the port of New Orleans.

Postwar Expectations

Britain's victory gave rise to great expectations among Americans. The end of the war, they were sure, meant the end of high taxes. The terms of the peace, they were confident, meant that the fertile lands of the Ohio valley would be thrown open to English settlement. The prosperity of the war years alone made for a mood of optimism. British military spending and William Pitt's subsidies had made

Colonial pride and optimism

The British navy bombarded Quebec in a vain attempt to compel surrender. Both sides were struck by the devastation of the city, with many of its buildings razed to smoldering shells, which presaged the end of France's empire in North America.

money for farmers, merchants, artisans, and anyone else who had anything to do with supplying the army or navy. Colonials also took pride in their contributions of troops and money to the winning of the war. In view of that support, Americans expected to be given more consideration within the British empire. Now, as one anonymous pamphleteer put it, Americans would "not be thought presumptuous, if they consider[ed] themselves upon an equal footing" with English in the parent country.

English resentments

But most imperial officials in America thought that if Americans took pride in being English, they had done a poor job of showing it. British statesmen complained that colonial assemblies had been tightfisted when it came to supplying the army. British commanders charged that colonial troops had been lily-livered when it came to fighting the French. Such charges were unjust, but they stuck in the minds of many Britons, who concluded that the Americans were selfish and self-interested, unconcerned with the welfare of the empire as a whole. Britain had accumulated a huge national debt that would saddle the nation with high taxes for years to come. To make matters worse, some Britons suspected that, with the French removed from North America, the colonies would move toward independence. As early as 1755, Josiah Tucker, a respected English economist, had warned that "to drive the French out of all North America would be the most fatal step we could take." Ironically, independence entered the minds of some observers in England long before it was ever entertained by Americans.

Americans in 1763 were not, in truth, revolutionaries in the making. They were loyal British subjects in the flush of postwar patriotism. Americans in 1763,

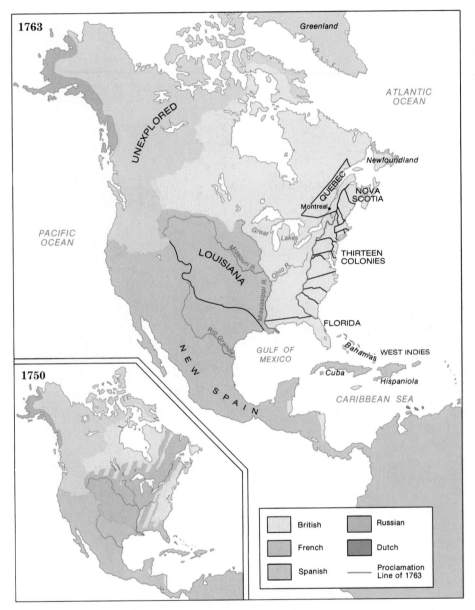

1763

European Claims in North America, 1750 and 1763 The British victory in the Seven Years' War secured Great Britain's title to a large portion of present-day United States and Canada. Colonials hoped to settle the newly won territory, but politicians in London intended to restrict westward movement with the Proclamation of 1763.

deeply divided among themselves, were not even "Americans." But most postwar English colonials did expect to enjoy a more equal status in the empire. And most Britons had no inclination to accord them that equality. The differing expectations of the colonies' place in the empire poised the postwar generation for crisis.

It was common sense. Great Britain had waged a costly war to secure its

The Imperial Crisis

empire in America; now it needed to consolidate those gains. The empire's North American territory needed to be protected, its administration tightened, and its colonies made as profitable as possible to the parent nation. In other words, the

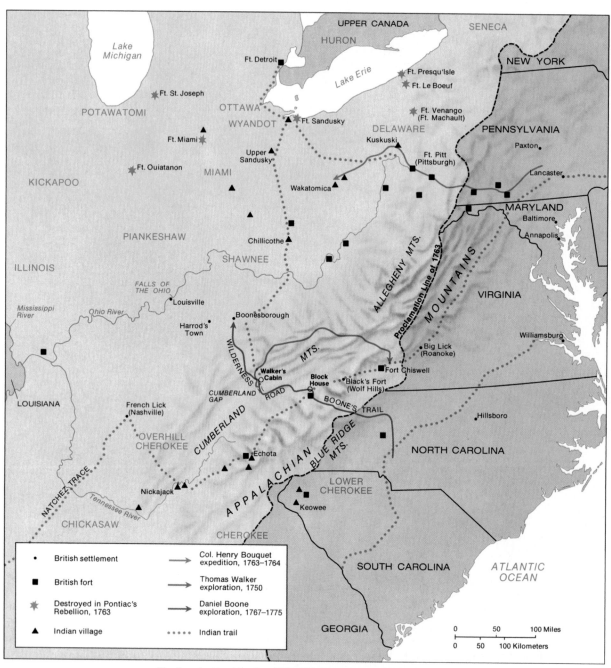

The Appalachian Frontier, 1750–1775 Made bold by the presence of British forts and soldiers, land-hungry colonials spilled into the West through the Cumberland Gap, a notch in the chain of mountains stretching the length of the North American interior. Only Indians and some white hunters knew of the Cumberland Gap before it was scouted in 1750 by Dr. Thomas Walker and a party of Virginians on behalf of a company of land speculators. In 1763, Indians led by Pontiac seized eight British forts before troops under Colonel Henry Bouquet stopped the offensive at Bushy Run, Pennsylvania. In 1775 Daniel Boone took the first large party of pioneers through the Cumberland Gap and established a fort at Boonesborough in present-day Kentucky.

empire needed to be centralized. That conclusion dictated Britain's decision to leave a standing army of several thousand troops in America after the Seven Years' War. The British army would prevent France from trying to regain its lost territory.

New Troubles on the Frontier

Keeping troops in North America made sense to the British because of the Indians, as well. With the French gone, English traders, speculators, and settlers would swarm into the West. Without the French as trading partners, Indian tribes were in a weaker position to deal with the British. No longer could they count on a steady supply of arms and ammunition from European rivals competing for their furs. The Indians were edgy, expecting the worst, and the British were worried.

Events bore out British fears. In the early 1760s a Lenni Lenape prophet, Neolin, began advising the tribes to return to their native ways and resist the spread of white settlement. Pontiac, an Ottawa chief, embraced Neolin's message of renaissance and rebellion. Other interior tribes joined Pontiac's offensive, and during the summer of 1763 they captured all the British outposts west of Pittsburgh. British troops and American militia finally smothered Pontiac's Rebellion.

Pontiac's Rebellion

Thereafter British administrators discovered another use for troops in America— to enforce the newly issued Proclamation of 1763. That order, issued by England's Board of Trade, prohibited white settlement past the crest of the Appalachian Mountains. Restricting westward movement might ease Indian fears, the British hoped, and so stave off future conflicts. It might also keep the colonials confined to the seaboard, where they were more easily subject to the control of the empire.

Proclamation of 1763

George Grenville's New Measures

A final reason for keeping troops in the colonies occurred to the British by 1764: an armed presence could enforce American acceptance of other new and sensible measures for tightening the empire. Those measures were the solutions of George Grenville, the first lord of the treasury, to the financial problems facing England after the Seven Years' War.

Britain's national debt had doubled in the decade after 1754. Adding to that burden was the drain of supporting troops in the colonies. As matters stood, heavy taxes were already triggering protests among hard-pressed Britons. Americans, in contrast, paid comparatively low taxes to their colonial governments and little in trade duties to the empire. Indeed, Grenville discovered that the colonial customs service paid out four times more in salaries to its collectors than it gathered in duties and was thereby operating at a net loss.

The income from customs duties was slim because colonial merchants evaded the Molasses Act of 1733. That tariff imposed a hefty duty of six pence on every gallon of molasses imported from the French and Dutch sugar islands. Parliament had designed the duty to encourage colonists to consume more British molasses, which carried a higher price but came duty-free. New England merchants, who distilled molasses into rum and then traded it to the southern colonies and to West Africa, claimed that the British sugar islands could not satisfy the demands of their distilleries. Regrettably, the merchants were forced to import more molasses from the French and Dutch. More regrettably, to keep their costs low and the price of their rum competitive, they had to bribe British customs officials. With the going rate for bribes ranging from a halfpenny to a penny and a half per gallon, the whole

Molasses Act of 1733

regrettable arrangement made handsome profits for both merchants and customs inspectors.

George Grenville reasoned that if Americans could pay out a little under the table to protect an illegal trade, they would willingly pay a little more to go legitimate. Parliament agreed. In April 1764 it passed the Revenue Act, commonly called the Sugar Act. The legislation actually lowered the duty on foreign molasses from six to three pence a gallon. This time, however, Grenville intended to enforce the new duty and to crack down on smugglers. To do so, the Sugar Act required shipmasters to submit papers listing every item in their cargoes when entering or clearing colonial ports. Even common sailors had to declare the contents of their sea chests. Those caught on the wrong side of the law were to be tried in admiralty courts, where verdicts were handed down by royally appointed judges rather than colonial juries more likely to sympathize with their fellow citizens.

By tightening customs enforcement, Grenville hoped to raise more revenue from the American trade. Unlike the earlier Navigation Acts, which imposed duties mainly to regulate trade, the Sugar Act's duties were intended mainly to yield revenue. Even so, Grenville regarded his demands as modest: he did not expect colonials to help reduce England's national debt or even to cover the entire cost of their defense.

Grenville made other modest proposals, all approved by Parliament. There was the Currency Act of 1764, which prohibited the colonies from making their paper money legal tender. That prevented Americans from paying their debts to British traders in currency that had fallen to less than its face value. There was the Quartering Act of 1765, which obliged any colony in which troops were stationed to provide them with suitable accommodations. That contributed to the cost of keeping British forces in America. Finally, in March of 1765, Parliament passed the Stamp Act.

The Stamp Act placed taxes on legal documents, customs papers, newspapers, almanacs, college diplomas, playing cards, and dice. After November 1, 1765, all these items had to bear a stamp signifying that their possessor had paid the tax. Violators of the Stamp Act, like those disobeying the Sugar Act, were to be tried without juries in admiralty courts. The English had been paying a similar tax for nearly a century, so it seemed to Grenville and Parliament that colonials could have no objections.

Every packet boat from London that brought news of Parliament passing another one of Grenville's measures dampened postwar optimism. For all of the differences between the colonies and England, Americans still held much in common with the English. Those shared ideas included firm beliefs about why the British constitution, British customs, and British history all served to protect liberty and the rights of the empire's freeborn citizens. For that reason the new measures, which seemed like common sense to Grenville and Parliament, did not make sense at all to Americans.

The Beginning of Colonial Resistance

Like other Britons, colonials in America accepted a maxim laid down by the English philosopher John Locke: property guaranteed liberty. Property, in this view, was not merely real estate, or wealth, or material possessions. It was the source of strength for every individual, providing the freedom to think and act independently. Protecting the individual's right to own property was the main responsibility of government, for if personal property was not sacred, then neither was personal liberty.

It followed from this close connection between property, power, and liberty that no people should be taxed without their consent or that of their elected

Sugar Act

Currency and Quartering Acts

Stamp Act

Locke on property and liberty

representatives. The power to tax was the power to destroy by depriving a person of property. Yet both the Sugar Act and the Stamp Act were taxes passed by members of Parliament, none of whom had been elected by colonials.

Like the English, colonials also prized the right of trial by jury as one of their basic constitutional liberties. Yet both the Sugar Act and the Stamp Act would prosecute offenders in the admiralty courts, not in local courts, thus depriving colonials of the freedom claimed by all other English men and women.

The concern for protecting individual liberties was only one of the convictions shaping the colonies' response to Britain's new policies. Equally important was their deep suspicion of power itself, a preoccupation that colonials shared with a minority of radical English thinkers. These radicals were known by a variety of names: the Country Party, the Commonwealthmen, and the Opposition. They drew their inspiration from the ancient tradition of classical republicanism, which held that representative government safeguarded liberty more reliably than either monarchy or oligarchy did. Underlying that judgment was the belief that human beings were driven by passion and insatiable ambition. One person (a monarch), or even a few people (an oligarchy), could not be entrusted with governing, because they would inevitably become corrupted by power and turn into tyrants. Even in representative governments, the people were obliged to watch those in power at all times. The price of liberty was eternal vigilance.

Visual imagery brought home the urgency of resistance to Americans who could not read political pamphlets or radical newspapers. This detail from an engraving by Paul Revere includes a liberty tree, from which is hung an effigy of the Boston stamp distributor, and a beast busily destroying the Magna Carta while trampling American colonials. The date on the tree, August 14, 1765, marked the first Stamp Act riot in Boston.

The Opposition believed that the people of England were not watching their rulers closely enough. During the first half of the eighteenth century, they argued, the entire executive branch of England's government—monarchs and their ministers—had been corrupted by their appetite for power. Proof of their ambition was the executive bureaucracy of civil officials and standing armies that steadily grew larger, interfered more with citizens' lives, and drained increasing amounts of money from taxpayers. Even more alarming, in the Opposition's view, the executive branch's bribery of members of Parliament was corrupting the representative branch of England's government. They warned that a sinister conspiracy originating in the executive branch of government threatened English liberty.

Opposition thinkers commanded little attention in England, where they were dismissed as a discontented radical fringe. But they were revered by political leaders in the American colonies. Especially popular were John Trenchard, a lawyer, and Thomas Gordon, a schoolteacher, who collaborated on a series of scathing essays against the political establishment. Too many "unhappy nations have lost that precious jewel *liberty*," Trenchard warned, because they "have permitted a standing army to be kept amongst them." Why, colonials worried, did Britain insist on keeping troops in America, just when Parliament was putting in place new taxes that had never been approved by American legislatures? Events seemed to confirm all too well the Opposition's description of how powerful rulers turned themselves into tyrants and reduced the people whom they ruled to slaves.

In sum, Grenville's new measures led some colonials to suspect that ambitious men ruling England might be conspiring against American liberties. At the very least, the new measures implied that colonials were not the political equals of the English living in England. They were not entitled to taxation by consent or to trial by jury. To be treated like second-class citizens wounded colonials' pride and mocked their postwar expectations. The heady dreams of the role that the colonies would play in the British empire evaporated, leaving behind the bitter dregs of disappointment.

Britain's determination to centralize its empire after 1763 was a disaster of timing, not just psychologically but also economically. By then, the colonies were in the throes of a recession. The boom produced in America by government spending during the war had collapsed once subsidies were withdrawn. Colonial merchants were left with stocks full of imported goods gathering dust on their shelves. Farmers lost the brisk and profitable market of the army.

Colonial response to the Sugar Act reflected the painful postwar readjustments. New England merchants led the opposition, objecting to the Sugar Act principally on economic grounds. But with the passage of the Stamp Act, the terms of the imperial debate widened, and resistance intensified within all the colonies. The Stamp Act hit all colonials, not just New England merchants. It took money from the pockets of anyone who made a will, filed a deed, traded out of a colonial port, bought a newspaper, consulted an almanac, graduated from college, took a chance at dice, or played cards. More important, the Stamp Act served notice that Parliament possessed the rightful authority to tax the colonies directly and for the sole purpose of raising revenue.

Riots and Resolves

That unprecedented assertion provoked an unprecedented development: the first display of colonial unity. A nearly unanimous chorus of outrage greeted Parliament's claim that it could tax the colonies. During the spring and summer of 1765, American assemblies passed resolves denying Parliament that authority. The right to tax Americans belonged to colonial assemblies alone, they argued, by the law of nature and by the liberties guaranteed in colonial charters and in the British constitution.

Virginia's assembly, the House of Burgesses, took the lead in protesting the Stamp Act, prodded by Patrick Henry. Just 29 years old in 1765, Henry had tried his hand at planting in western Virginia before recognizing his real talent—demagoguery. Blessed with the eloquence of an evangelical preacher, the dashing charm of a southern gentleman, and a mind uncluttered by much learning, Henry parlayed his popularity as a smooth-talking lawyer into a place among the Burgesses. He took his seat just 10 days before introducing the Virginia Resolves against the Stamp Act.

The Burgesses passed Henry's resolutions upholding their exclusive right to tax Virginians. They stopped short of adopting those resolves that called for outright resistance to the Stamp Act. When news of Virginia's stand spread to the rest of the colonies, other assemblies followed suit, affirming that the sole right to tax Americans resided in their elected representatives. But some colonial newspapers deliberately printed a different story—that the Burgesses had approved all of Henry's resolves, including one that sanctioned disobedience to any parliamentary tax. That prompted a few assemblies to endorse resistance. In October 1765 delegates from nine colonies convened in New York, where they prepared a joint statement of the American position and petitioned the king and Parliament to repeal both the Sugar Act and the Stamp Act.

Meanwhile, colonial leaders turned to the press to arouse popular opposition to the Stamp Act. Disposed by the writings of the English Opposition to think of politics in conspiratorial terms, they warned that Grenville and the king's other ministers schemed to deprive the colonies of their liberties by unlawfully taxing

Impact of postwar recession

Patrick Henry's resolves

This idealized likeness of Patrick Henry, by the American artist Thomas Sully, conveys the subject's intensity. Henry's eloquence and passion as an orator made a vivid impression on his contemporaries.

their property. The Stamp Act was only the first step in a sinister plan to enslave Americans.

Whether or not dark fears of a ministerial conspiracy haunted most colonials in 1765, many resisted the Stamp Act. The merchants of Boston, New York, and Philadelphia agreed to stop importing English goods in order to pressure British traders to lobby for repeal. In every colony, organizations emerged to ensure that the Stamp Act, if not repealed, would never be enforced.

The new resistance groups, which styled themselves the "Sons of Liberty," **Sons of Liberty** consisted of traders, lawyers, and prosperous artisans. With great success, they organized the lower classes of seaports in opposition to the Stamp Act. The sailors, dockworkers, poor artisans, apprentices, and servants who poured into the streets resembled mobs that had been organized from time to time earlier in the century. Previous riots against houses of prostitution, merchants who hoarded goods, or supporters of smallpox inoculation had not been spontaneous, uncontrolled out-bursts. Crowds chose their targets and their tactics carefully and then carried out the communal will with little violence.

In every colonial city, the mobs of 1765 burnt the stamp distributors in effigy, insulted them on the streets, demolished their offices, and attacked their homes. One hot night in August 1765, a mob went further than the Sons of Liberty had planned. They vandalized the stately mansion of Thomas Hutchinson, the unpop-ular lieutenant governor of Massachusetts and the brother-in-law of the colony's stamp distributor. By morning Hutchinson's home had been all but leveled. The destruction stunned Bostonians, especially the Sons of Liberty, who resisted Britain in the name of protecting private property. Thereafter they took care to keep crowds under tighter control. In most cases, the mere show of popular force was sufficient: by the first of November, the day that the Stamp Act took effect, most of the stamp distributors had resigned.

Repeal of the Stamp Act

Meanwhile, the repeal of the Stamp Act was already in the works back in England. The man who came—unintentionally—to America's relief was George III. The young king was a good man, industrious and devoted to the empire, but he was also immature and not particularly bright. Insecurity made the young king an irk-some master, and he ran through ministers rapidly. By the end of 1765, George had dismissed Grenville for reasons unrelated to the uproar in America and appointed a new first minister, the Marquis of Rockingham. Rockingham had opposed the Stamp Act from the outset, and he had no desire to enforce it. He received support from London merchants, who were beginning to feel the pinch of the American nonimportation campaign, and secured repeal of the Stamp Act in March 1766.

The Stamp Act controversy demonstrated to colonials how similar in politi-cal outlook they were to one another and how different they were from the British. Americans had found that they shared the same assumptions about the meaning of representation. To counter colonial objections to the Stamp Act, Grenville and his supporters had claimed that Americans *were* represented in Par-liament, even though they had elected none of its members. Americans were virtually represented, Grenville insisted, for each member of Parliament stood for **Virtual versus actual** the interests of the whole empire, not just those of the particular constituency **representation** that had elected him.

Colonials could see no virtue in the theory of virtual representation. After all, the circumstances and interests of colonials, living an ocean away, were so different from those of Britons. The newly recognized consensus among Americans was that colonials could be truly represented only by those whom they had elected. Their view, known as actual representation, emphasized that elected officials were directly accountable to their constituents.

Americans also had discovered that they agreed about the extent of Parliament's authority over the colonies: it stopped at the right to tax. Colonials conceded Parliament's right to legislate and to regulate trade for the good of the whole empire. But taxation, in their view, was the free gift of the people through their representatives—who were not sitting in Parliament.

Declaratory Act

Members of Parliament had brushed aside colonial petitions and resolves, all but ignoring their constitutional argument. To make its own authority perfectly clear, Parliament accompanied the repeal of the Stamp Act with a Declaratory Act, asserting that it had the power to make laws for the colonies "in all cases whatsoever." In fact, the Declaratory Act clarified nothing. Did Parliament understand the power of legislation to include the power of taxation?

This 1766 porcelain of *Lord Chatham and America* attests to the popularity of William Pitt, Earl of Chatham, among Americans who resisted the Stamp Act. The artist's representation of "America" as a black kneeling in gratitude echoes the colonists' association of taxation with slavery.

The Townshend Acts

In the summer of 1766 George III—again inadvertently—gave the colonies what should have been an advantage by changing ministers again. The king replaced Rockingham with William Pitt, who enjoyed great favor among colonials for his leadership during the Seven Years' War and for his opposition to the Stamp Act. Almost alone among British politicians, Pitt had grasped and approved the colonists' constitutional objections to taxation. During Parliament's debate over repeal of the Stamp Act, Grenville asked sarcastically, "Tell me when the colonies were emancipated?" Pitt immediately shot back, "I desire to know when they were made slaves!"

If the man who believed that Americans were "the sons not the bastards of England" had been well enough to govern, matters between Great Britain and the colonies might have turned out differently. But almost immediately after Pitt took office, his health collapsed, and power passed into the hands of Charles Townshend, the chancellor of the exchequer, who wished only to raise more revenue from the Americans. In 1767 he persuaded Parliament to tax the lead, paint, paper, glass, and tea that Americans imported from Britain.

In addition, Townshend was determined to curb the power of the upstart American assemblies. To set a bold example, he singled out for punishment the New York legislature, which was refusing to comply with provisions of the Quartering Act of 1765. The troops that were left on the western frontier after the Seven Years' War had been pulled back into colonial seaports in 1766. In part their movement was meant to economize on costs, but royal officials also hoped the troops' presence would help quiet agitation over the Stamp Act. When the largest contingent came to New York, that colony's assembly protested, claiming that the cost of quartering the troops constituted a form of indirect taxation. But Townshend was determined, and Parliament backed him, suspending the New York assembly in 1767 until it agreed to obey the Quartering Act.

Townshend also dipped into the revenue from his new tariffs in order to make royal officials less dependent on the assemblies. Governors and other officers like customs collectors and judges had previously received their salaries from colonial legislatures. The assemblies lost that crucial leverage when Townshend used the revenues to pay those bureaucrats directly. Finally, in order to ensure more effective enforcement of all the duties on imports, Townshend created an American Board of Customs Commissioners, who appointed a small army of new customs collectors. He also established three new vice-admiralty courts in Boston, New York, and Charleston to bring smugglers to justice.

The Resistance Organizes

In Townshend's efforts to centralize the administration of the British empire, Americans saw new evidence that they were not being treated like the English. In newspapers and pamphlets colonial leaders repeated their earlier arguments against taxation. The most widely read publication, "A Letter from a Farmer in Pennsylvania," was the work of John Dickinson—who was, in fact, a Philadelphia lawyer. He urged Americans to protest the Townshend duties with a show of superior virtue—hard work, thrift, simplicity, and home manufacturing. By consuming fewer imported English luxuries, Dickinson argued, Americans would advance the cause of repeal.

John Dickinson and Samuel Adams

As Dickinson's star rose over Philadelphia, the Townshend Acts also shaped the destiny of another man, farther north. By the 1760s Samuel Adams was a leader in the Massachusetts assembly. In some ways his rise had been unlikely. Adams's earlier ventures as a merchant ended in bankruptcy; his stint as a tax collector left all of Boston in the red. But he proved a consummate political organizer and agitator, a man who knew how to exploit every advantage. First his enemies and later his friends claimed that Adams had decided on independence for America as early as 1768. In that year he persuaded the assembly to send to other colonial legislatures a circular letter condemning the Townshend Acts and calling for a united American resistance.

As John Dickinson and Samuel Adams whipped up public outrage, the Sons of Liberty again organized the opposition in the streets. Customs officials, like the stamp distributors before them, became targets of popular hatred. But the customs collectors gave as good as they got. Using the flimsiest excuses, they seized American vessels for violating royal regulations. With cold insolence they shook down American merchants for what amounted to protection money. The racketeering in the customs service brought tensions in Boston to a flash point in June 1768 after officials seized and condemned the *Liberty,* a sloop belonging to one of the city's biggest merchants, John Hancock. Several thousand Bostonians vented their anger in a night of rioting, searching out and roughing up customs officials.

The new secretary of state for the colonies, Lord Hillsborough, responded to the *Liberty* riot by sending two regiments of troops to Boston. In the fall of 1768 the redcoats, like a conquering army, paraded into town under the cover of warships lying off the harbor. (See Paul Revere's illustration on page 145.) In the months that followed, citizens bristled when challenged on the streets by armed soldiers. Even more disturbing to Bostonians was the execution of British military justice on the Common. British soldiers were whipped savagely for breaking military discipline, and desertion was punished by execution.

John Dickinson, a moderate who defended American rights but hoped for reconciliation

Daily Lives

PRIVATE SPACE/ PUBLIC SPACE
Street Theater

On the first night of November 1765 the narrow, winding streets of New York glowed with unaccustomed light. The Stamp Act was to have taken effect on that date, but the colony's stampmaster had long since resigned his office. What had frightened him into resignation could be seen in the moving shadows of men, women, and children, hundreds of them. The flaring torches and flickering candles that they carried aloft through the city's crooked byways cast on storefronts and doorways dark images of a crowd protesting the "death of Liberty."

Bringing up the rear of the procession was a seaman, bearing atop his head an old chair in which was seated a paper effigy. It represented Cadwallader Colden, "the most hated man in the province," and as New York's temporary governor, the local representative of British authority. The crowd marched to the center of town, shouting insults at Colden's figure and peppering it with pistol shots. When some of the marchers decided that their

effigy should evoke the Roman Catholic pope, the chief symbol of tyrannical power to colonial Americans, they broke into Colden's stable and stole his fine coach for a proper papal throne. A second group joined the crowd, bearing their own piece of portable political theater—a gallows illuminated with two lanterns. Hanging from the gallows were effigies of Colden and the devil, the "grand Deceiver of Mankind." The entire assembly climaxed the evening by burning the effigies in a bonfire and then vandalizing the homes of several Stamp Act supporters.

Similar protests had been staged in seaports all over the

colonies, following Boston's rioting against the Stamp Act. Some crowds held mock trials of unpopular British officials and then tarred and feathered, beat, hung, or burned their effigies. Other crowds enacted mock funerals, parading effigies in carts or coffins to the accompaniment of tolling church bells. Certain symbols appeared repeatedly: devils and gallows, lanterns and the paraphernalia of papal authority. The "people-out-of-doors," as such crowds were called in the eighteenth century, were making their views known—and their collective power felt.

The frequency and the political focus of street protests were new

A Pope's Day parade in mid-eighteenth-century Boston. Dressed as the devil's imps, boys accompany a cart bearing an effigy of the pope.

The *Liberty* riot and the arrival of British troops in Boston pushed colonial assemblies to coordinate their resistance more closely. Most legislatures endorsed the Massachusetts circular letter sent to them by Samuel Adams. They promptly adopted agreements not to import or to consume British goods. The reluctance among some merchants to revive nonimportation in 1767 gave way to greater enthusiasm by 1768, and by early 1769, such agreements were in effect throughout the colonies.

The Stamp Act crisis had also called forth intercolonial cooperation and tactics like nonimportation. But the protests against the Townshend Acts raised the stakes by creating new institutions to carry forward the resistance. Subscribers to the nonimportation agreements established "committees of inspection" to enforce

to the decade preceding the Revolution. Still, the actions taken resembled those of earlier colonial crowds in their direction and restraint.

Equally striking, the resistance after 1765 drew on rituals and symbols surrounding traditional forms of protest, punishment, and celebration. For centuries before the Revolution, for example, crowds on both sides of the Atlantic had meted out to prostitutes, adulterers, or henpecked husbands punishments known in England as "rough music." After being tarred and feathered, the targets of rough music were often ridden "skimmington": placed on the back of a donkey, pelted with mud and dung, and driven through the streets to the accompaniment of hooting laughter and beating drums.

An even more important inspiration for resistance rituals came from Pope's Day, an elaborate annual outdoor celebration of anti-Catholic sentiment that started in Boston early in the eighteenth century. Craftworkers and apprentices from both the North End and the South End of town fashioned a cart bearing a lantern, effigies of the pope and the devil, and signs reading "The devil take the pope" and "North [or South] End Forever." Local boys with blackened faces and jester's caps played the part of the "devil's imps," taunting the pope's effigy as laboring people from both ends of town paraded their carts through the streets. Each group tried to destroy the other's creation before the final bonfire at the end of the evening.

As colonials adopted the symbols of the past for their street theater of political resistance, the borrowing took an odd twist. Pope's Day, the model for later protests, was in fact a colonial adaptation of an English celebration of monarchy, Guy Fawkes Day. In 1605 Fawkes, a Catholic, had been foiled in his attempt to assassinate James I, a failure that the English annually commemorated with a parade ending with burning the conspirator in effigy. In colonial America an effigy of the pope took the place of the Catholic Fawkes; in resistance rituals after 1765 hated British officials took the place of the pope. Beginning in 1776 Americans celebrated public readings of the Declaration by parading, burning, and burying effigies of George III. Strangely enough, Americans had converted symbols and ceremonies designed to honor monarchy to represent the killing of a king.

the ban on trade with Britain. The committees publicly denounced merchants who continued to import, vandalized their warehouses, forced them to stand under the gallows, and sometimes resorted to tar and feathers.

After 1768 the resistance also brought a broader range of colonials into the politics of protest. Artisans, who recognized that nonimportation would spur domestic manufacturing, began to organize as independent political groups. In many towns, women took an active part in opposing the Townshend duties. The "Daughters of Liberty" took to heart John Dickinson's advice: they wore homespun clothing instead of English finery, served coffee instead of tea, and boycotted shops selling British goods.

The International Sons of Liberty

The resistance after 1768 grew broader in another sense as well. Many of its supporters in the American colonies felt a new sense of kinship with freedom fighters throughout Europe and increasingly regarded themselves as part of a transatlantic network of the friends of liberty. They eagerly read about the doings of men like Charles Lucas, an Irish newspaper editor and member of the Irish Parliament, and John Wilkes, a London journalist and a leading politician of the Opposition, both of whom charged the king's ministers with corrupting the political life of the British Isles. The triumphs and setbacks of those combating tyrannical regimes even in distant Poland and Turkey engaged colonial sympathies. But perhaps the cause abroad that proved dearest to the hearts of liberty's friends in America during the late 1760s was the fate of Corsica.

Colonials follow Paoli's struggle

For years, the state of Genoa had been trying to impose its rule on this tiny island off the coast of Italy. Led by Pascal Paoli, the Corsicans had for decades waged what one New York newspaper touted as a "glorious struggle" against Genoese rule, an insurgency "interesting to every friend of liberty." In 1768, Genoa sold its title to the island to France, prompting many in the British Empire to hope that England would rally to defend Corsica's freedom, if only to keep France from seizing this strategic point in the Mediterranean. But British statesmen had no intention of going to war with France over mere Corsica, and when French troops routed his rebel army, Paoli fled to exile in England in 1769. To add insult to injury, Paoli, once lionized by the colonial resistance as "the greatest man of earth," snubbed Opposition leaders like John Wilkes, hobnobbed with the likes of the Duke of Grafton, the minister of the treasury, and even accepted a pension of 1,000 pounds a year from George III.

The moral of this sad story, one closely followed by the readers of colonial newspapers, was that the British ministry's corruption pervaded not only the empire, but all of Europe. Merely by doing nothing, the king's ministers had snuffed out the Corsican resistance. And by doling a mere thousand pounds annually, they had bought the compliance of its leader, the great Paoli himself. In the fate of Corsica and its sons of liberty, many colonials saw the threat that ambitious men posed to popular liberty—and a disturbing portent for America's future.

The Boston Massacre

Meanwhile, the situation in Boston deteriorated steadily. British troops found themselves regularly cursed by citizens and occasionally pelted with stones, dirt, and human excrement. The British regulars were particularly unpopular among Boston's laboring classes because they competed with them for jobs. Off-duty soldiers moonlighted as maritime laborers, and they sold their services at cheaper rates than the wages paid to locals. By 1769, brawls between British regulars and waterfront workers broke out with unsettling frequency.

With some 4000 redcoats enduring daily contact with some 15,000 Bostonians under the sway of Samuel Adams, what happened on the night of March 5, 1770, was nearly inevitable. A crowd gathered around the customshouse for the sport of heckling its guard of 10 soldiers. The redcoats panicked and fended off insults and snowballs with live fire, hitting 11 rioters and killing 5. Adams and other propagandists seized upon the incident. Labeling the bloodshed "the Boston Massacre," they publicized that "atrocity" throughout the colonies. The radical *Boston Gazette* framed its account in an eye-catching black-bordered edition headed with a drawing of five coffins.

A British grenadier

While Townshend's policies spurred the resistance in America, the obvious finally dawned on Parliament. They recognized that Townshend's duties only discouraged sales to colonials and encouraged them to manufacture at home. The argument for repeal was overwhelming, and the way had been cleared by the unexpected death of Townshend shortly after Parliament adopted his proposals. In 1770 his successor, Lord North, convinced Parliament to repeal all the Townshend duties except the one on tea, allowing that tax to stand as a source of revenue and as a symbol of Parliament's authority.

Resistance Revived

Repeal of the Townshend duties took the wind from the sails of American resistance for more than two years. But the controversy between England and the colonies had not been resolved. Colonials still paid taxes on molasses and tea, taxes to which they had not consented. They were still subject to trial in admiralty courts, which operated without juries. They

While the new political activism of some American women often amused male leaders of the resistance, it inspired the scorn of some partisans of British authority. When the women of Edenton, North Carolina, renounced imported tea, this British cartoon mocked them.

still lived with a standing army in their midst. Beneath the banked fires of protest smoldered the live embers of Americans' political inequality. Any shift in the wind could fan those embers into flames.

The wind did shift, quite literally, on Narragansett Bay in 1772, running aground the *Gaspee,* a British naval schooner in hot pursuit of Rhode Island smugglers. Residents of nearby Providence quickly celebrated the *Gaspee*'s misfortune with a bonfire built on the ship's deck. Outraged British officials sent a special commission to look into the matter, intending once again to bypass the established colonial court system. The arrival of the *Gaspee* Commission reignited the imperial crisis, and in America, once again, resistance flared.

It did so through an ingenious mechanism, the committees of correspondence. Established in all the colonies by their assemblies, the committees drew up statements of American rights and grievances, distributed those documents within and among the colonies, and solicited responses from towns and counties. The brainchild of Samuel Adams, the committee structure formed a new communications network, one that fostered an intercolonial agreement on resistance to British measures. The strategy succeeded, and not only among colonies. The committees spread the scope of the resistance from colonial seaports into rural areas, engaging farmers and other country folk in the opposition to Britain.

Committees of correspondence

The committees had much to talk about when Parliament passed the Tea Act in 1773. The law was an effort to bail out the bankrupt East India Company by granting that corporation a monopoly on the tea trade to Americans. Because the company could use agents to sell its product directly, cutting out the middlemen, it could offer a lower price than that charged by colonial merchants. Thus, although the Tea Act would hurt American merchants, it promised to make tea cheaper for ordinary Americans. Still, many colonials saw the act as Parliament's attempt to trick them into accepting its authority to tax the colonies. They set out to deny that power once and for all.

In early winter of 1773 the tempest over the Tea Act peaked in Boston, with popular leaders calling for the cargoes to be returned immediately to England. On the evening of December 16, thousands of Bostonians, as well as farmers from the surrounding countryside, packed into the Old South Meetinghouse. Some members of the audience knew what Samuel Adams had on the evening's agenda, and they awaited their cue. It came when Adams told the meeting that they could do nothing more to save their country. War whoops rang through the meetinghouse, the crowd spilled onto the streets and out to the waterfront, and the Boston Tea Party commenced. From the throng emerged 50 men dressed as Indians to disguise their identities. The party boarded three vessels docked off Griffin's Wharf, broke open casks containing 90,000 pounds of tea, and brewed a beverage worth 10,000 pounds sterling in Boston harbor.

The Empire Strikes Back

The Boston Tea Party proved to British satisfaction that the colonies aimed at independence. Lord North's assessment was grim: "We are now to dispute whether we have, or have not, any authority in that country." To reassert its authority, Parliament passed the Coercive Acts, dubbed in the colonies the "Intolerable Acts." The first of these came in March 1774, two months after hearing of the Tea Party, when Parliament passed the Boston Port Bill, closing that harbor to all oceangoing traffic until such time as the king saw fit to reopen it. And George, Parliament announced, would not see fit until colonials paid the East India Company for their losses.

Coercive Acts

During the next three months, Parliament approved three other "intolerable" laws designed to punish Massachusetts. The Massachusetts Government Act handed over the colony's government to royal officials. Even convening town meetings would require royal permission. The Impartial Administration of Justice Act permitted any royal official accused of a crime in Massachusetts to be tried in England or in another colony. The Quartering Act allowed the housing of British troops in private homes—not only in Massachusetts but in all the colonies.

Many colonials saw the Coercive Acts as proof of a plot to enslave the colonies. In truth, the taxes and duties, laws and regulations of the past decade *were* part of a deliberate design—a commonsensical plan to centralize the administration of the British empire. But those efforts by the king's ministers and Parliament to run the colonies more efficiently and profitably were viewed by more and more Americans as a sinister conspiracy against their liberties.

Fear of conspiracy

For colonials, the study of history confirmed that interpretation, especially their reading of the histories written by the English Opposition. The Opposition's favorite historical subject was the downfall of republics, whether those of ancient Greece and Rome or more recent republican governments in Venice and Denmark. The lesson of their histories was always the same: power overwhelmed liberty. Those who had power would always seek more, and ambitious politicians would always pursue the same strategies to replace representative government and popular freedom with tyranny. In all places and at all times in the past, the Opposition warned, the conspiracy against liberty unfolded in predictable stages.

First, the people of a republic were impoverished by costly wars—something the colonists could well appreciate after the Seven Years' War. Then the government loaded the people with taxes to pay for those wars—as in the case of the Sugar Act or the Stamp Act or the Townshend duties. Next the government stationed a standing army in the country, pretending to protect the people but actually lending military force to those in power. And, of course, troops had been unloaded in Boston harbor, were quartered in New York, and were making trouble wherever they appeared. Then wicked men were favored with public offices and patronage to secure their loyalty and support for the foes of liberty. And how else could one describe the royal governors, customs collectors, and judges who now received salaries from the revenues of the Townshend duties? Those in power also deliberately promoted luxury, idleness, and extravagance to weaken the moral fiber of the people—like the consumption encouraged by the low prices ensured by the Tea Act. Finally, those in power attempted to provoke the people to violent action in order to justify new oppression.

Week after week in the spring of 1774, reports of legislative outrages came across the waters. Shortly after approving the Coercive Acts, Parliament passed the Quebec Act, which established a permanent government in what had been French Canada. Ominously, it included no representative assembly. Equally ominous to Protestant colonials, the Quebec Act officially recognized the Roman Catholic church and extended the bounds of the province to include all land between the Mississippi and Ohio rivers. Suddenly New York, Pennsylvania, and Virginia found themselves bordering a British colony whose subjects had no voice in their own government.

Quebec Act

With the passage of the Coercive Acts, many more colonials came to believe not only that ambitious men plotted to enslave the colonies but also that those conspirators included almost all British political leaders. At the time of the Stamp Act and again during the agitation against the Townshend Acts, most colonials had confined their suspicions to the king's ministers. By 1774 members of Parliament were also implicated in that conspiracy—and a few radicals were wondering aloud about George III.

As alarm deepened in the wake of the Coercive Acts, one colony after another called for an intercolonial congress—like the one that had met during the Stamp Act crisis—to determine the best way to defend their freedom. But many also remained unsettled about where the logic of their actions seemed to be taking them: toward a denial that they were any longer English.

First Continental
Congress called

Toward the Revolution

By the beginning of September 1774, when 55 delegates to the First Continental Congress gathered in Philadelphia, the news from Massachusetts was bad. The colony verged on anarchy, it was reported, as its inhabitants resisted the enforcement of the Massachusetts Government Act.

In the midst of this atmosphere of crisis, the members of Congress also had to take one another's measure. Many of the delegates had not traveled outside their own colonies. (All but Georgia sent representatives.) Although the delegates encountered a great deal of diversity, they quickly discovered that they esteemed the same traits of character, attributes that they called "civic virtue." These traits included simplicity and self-reliance, industry and thrift, and above all, an unselfish commitment to the public good. Most members of the Congress also shared a common mistrust of England, associating the mother country with vice, extravagance, and corruption.

Still, the delegates had some misgivings about those from other colonies. Massachusetts in particular brought with it a reputation—well deserved, considering that Samuel Adams was along—for radical action and a willingness to use force to accomplish its ends.

Samuel Adams, a radical who masterminded colonial resistance tactics

The First Continental Congress

As the delegates settled down to business, their aim was to reach agreement on three key points. How were they to justify the rights they claimed as American colonials? What were the limits of Parliament's power? And what were the proper tactics for resisting the Coercive Acts? Congress quickly agreed on the first point. The delegates affirmed that the law of nature, the colonial charters, and the British constitution provided the foundations of American liberties. This position was what most colonials had argued since 1765. On the two other issues, Congress charted a middle course between the demands of radicals and the reservations of conservatives.

Since the time of the Stamp Act, most colonials had insisted that Parliament had no authority to tax the colonies. But later events had demonstrated that Parliament could undermine colonial liberties by legislation as well as by taxation. The suspension of the New York legislature, the *Gaspee* Commission, and the Coercive Acts all fell into this category. Given those experiences, the delegates adopted a Declaration of Rights and Grievances on October 14, 1774, asserting the right of the colonies to tax and legislate for themselves. The Declaration of Rights thus limited Parliament's power over Americans more strictly than colonials had a decade earlier.

Joseph Galloway's plan

By denying Parliament's power to make laws for the colonies, the Continental Congress blocked efforts of the most conservative delegates to reach an accommodation with England. Their leading advocate, Joseph Galloway of Pennsylvania, proposed a plan of union with Britain similar to the one set forth by the Albany Congress in 1754. Under it, a grand council of the colonies would handle all common concerns, with any laws it passed subject to review and veto by Parliament. For its part, Parliament would have to submit for the grand council's approval any acts it passed affecting America. A majority of delegates judged that Galloway's proposal left Parliament too much leeway in legislating for colonials, and they rejected his plan.

Although the Congress denied Parliament the right to impose taxes or to make laws, delegates stopped short of declaring that it had no authority at all in the colonies. They approved Parliament's regulation of trade, but only because of the interdependent economy of the empire. And although some radical pamphleteers were attacking the king for plotting against American liberties, Congress acknowledged the continuing allegiance of the colonies to George III. In other words, the delegates called for a return to the situation that had existed in the empire before 1763, with Parliament regulating trade and the colonies exercising all powers of taxation and legislation.

The Association

On the question of resistance, Congress satisfied the desires of its most radical delegates by drawing up the Continental Association, an agreement to cease all trade with Britain until the Coercive Acts were repealed. They agreed that their fellow citizens would immediately stop drinking East India Company tea and that by December 1, 1774, merchants would no longer import goods of any sort from Britain. A ban on the export of American produce to Britain and the West Indies would go into effect a year later, during September 1775—the lag being a concession to southern rice and tobacco planters, who wanted to market crops already planted.

Revere and the Suffolk Resolves

The Association provided for the total cessation of trade, but Samuel Adams and other radicals wanted bolder action. They received help from Paul Revere, a Boston silversmith who had long provided newspapers with many lurid engravings showing British abuses. On September 16, Revere galloped into Philadelphia bearing a copy of resolves drawn up by Bostonians and other residents of Suffolk

County. The Suffolk Resolves, as they were called, branded the Coercive Acts as unconstitutional and called for civil disobedience to protest them. Congress endorsed the resolves, as Adams had hoped. But it would not approve another part of the radicals' agenda—preparing for war by authorizing proposals to strengthen and arm colonial militias.

Thus the First Continental Congress steered a middle course. Although determined to bring about repeal of the Coercive Acts, it held firm in resisting any revolutionary course of action. If British officials had responded to its recommendations and restored the status quo of 1763, the war for independence might have been postponed—perhaps indefinitely. On the other hand, even though the Congress did not go to the extremes urged by the radicals, its decisions drew colonials farther down the road to independence.

The Last Days of the British Empire in America

Most colonials applauded the achievements of the First Continental Congress. They expected that the Association would bring about a speedy repeal of the Coercive Acts. But fear that the colonies were moving toward a break with Britain led others to denounce the doings of the Congress. Conservatives were convinced that if independence was declared, chaos would ensue. Colonials, they argued, would quarrel over land claims and sectional tensions and religious differences, as they had so often in the recent past. Without Britain to referee such disputes, they feared, the result would be civil war, followed by anarchy.

The man in America with the least liking for the Continental Congress sat in the hottest seat in the colonies, that of the governor of Massachusetts. General Thomas Gage now watched as royal authority crumbled in Massachusetts and the rebellion spread to other colonies. In June 1774 a desperate Gage dissolved the Massachusetts legislature, only to see it re-form, on its own, into a Provincial Congress. That new body assumed the government of the colony in October and began arming the militia. Gage then started to fortify Boston and pleaded for more troops—only to find his fortifications damaged by saboteurs and his requests for reinforcements ignored by Britain.

Thomas Gage in Boston

Outside Boston, royal authority fared no better. Farmers in western Massachusetts forcibly closed the county courts, turning out royally appointed justices and establishing their own tribunals. Popularly elected committees of inspection charged with enforcing the Association took over towns everywhere in Massachusetts, not only restricting trade but also regulating every aspect of local life. The committees called upon townspeople to display civic virtue by renouncing "effeminate" English luxuries like tea and fine clothing and "corrupt" leisure activities like dancing, gambling, and racing. The committees also assigned spies to report on any citizen unfriendly to the resistance. "Enemies of American liberty" risked being roundly condemned in public or beaten and pelted with mud and dung by hooting, raucous mobs.

Collapse of royal authority

Throughout the colonies a similar process was under way. During the winter and early spring of 1775, provincial congresses, county conventions, and local committees of inspection were emerging as revolutionary governments, replacing royal authority at every level. As the spectacle unfolded before General Gage, he concluded that only force could subdue the colonies. It would take more than he had at his command, but reinforcements might be on the way. In February of 1775, Parliament had approved an address to the king declaring that the colonies were in rebellion.

The Fighting Begins

As spring came to Boston, the city waited. A band of artisans, organized as spies and express riders by Paul Revere, watched General Gage and waited for him to act. Gage waited for reinforcements from Lord North and watched the hostile town. On April 14 word from North finally arrived: Gage was to seize the leaders of the Provincial Congress. That would behead the rebellion, North said. Gage knew better than to believe North—but he also knew that he had to do something.

On the night of April 18 the sexton of Boston's Christ Church hung two lamps from its steeple. It was a signal that British troops had moved out of Boston and were marching toward the arms and ammunition stored by the Provincial Congress in Concord. As the lamps flashed the signal, Revere and a comrade, William Dawes, rode out to arouse the countryside.

Lexington and Concord   When the news of a British march reached Lexington, its Minuteman militia of about 70 farmers, chilled and sleepy, mustered on the Green at the center of the small rural town. Lexington Green lay directly on the road to Concord. At about four in the morning 700 British troops massed on the Green, and their commander, Major John Pitcairn, ordered the Lexington militia to disperse. The townsmen, outnumbered and overawed, began to obey. Then a shot rang out—whether the British or the Americans fired first is unknown—and then two volleys burst from the ranks of the redcoats. With a cheer the British set off for Concord, five miles distant, leaving eight Americans dead on Lexington Green.

By dawn, hundreds of Minutemen from nearby towns were surging into Concord. The British entered at about seven in the morning and moved, unopposed, toward their target, a house lying across the bridge that spanned the Concord River. While three companies of British soldiers searched for American guns and ammunition, three others, posted on the bridge itself, had the misfortune to find those American arms—borne by the rebels and being fired with deadly accuracy. By noon, the British were retreating to Boston.

An unknown artist depicted the arrival of British troops in Concord, Massachusetts, just before their fateful encounter with the Minutemen on the North Bridge.

The narrow road from Concord to Boston's outskirts became a corridor of carnage. Pursuing Americans fired on the column of fleeing redcoats from the cover of fences and forests. By the end of April 19, the British had sustained 273 casualties; the Americans, 95. It was only the beginning. By evening of the next day, some 20,000 New England militia had converged on Boston for a long siege.

Common Sense

The bloodshed at Lexington Green and Concord's North Bridge committed colonials to a course of rebellion—and independence. That was the conclusion drawn by Thomas Paine, who urged other Americans to do the same.

Paine himself was hardly an American at all. He was born in England, first apprenticed as a corsetmaker, appointed later a tax collector, and fated finally to become midwife to the age of republican revolutions. Paine came to Philadelphia late in 1774, set up as a journalist, and made the American cause his own. "Where liberty is, there is my country," he declared. In January 1776 he wrote a pamphlet to inform colonials of their identity as a distinct people and their destiny as a nation. *Common Sense* enjoyed tremendous popularity and wide circulation, selling 120,000 copies within three months of its publication.

After Lexington and Concord, Paine wrote, as the imperial crisis passed "from argument to arms, a new era for politics is struck—a new method of thinking has arisen." That new era of politics for Paine was the age of republicanism. He denounced monarchy as a foolish and dangerous form of government, one that violated the dictates of reason as well as the word of the Bible. By ridicule and remorseless argument, he severed the ties of colonial allegiance to the king. *Common Sense* scorned George III as "the Royal Brute of Britain," who had enslaved the chosen people of the new age—the Americans.

Thomas Paine argues for independence

Nor did Paine stop there. He rejected the idea that colonials were or should want to be English. The colonies occupied a huge continent an ocean away from the tiny British Isles—clear proof that nature itself had fashioned America for independence. England lay locked in Europe, doomed to the corruption of an Old World. America had been discovered anew to become an "asylum of liberty."

Many Americans had liked being English, but being English hadn't worked. Perhaps that is another way of saying that over the course of nearly two centuries colonial society and politics had evolved in such a way that the identity between the Americans and the English no longer fit. By the end of the Seven Years' War, the colonies had established political institutions that made the rights of "freeborn Britons" more available to ordinary citizens in America than in the nation that had created those liberties. Perhaps, then, most Americans had succeeded *too* well at becoming English, regarding themselves as political equals entitled to basic constitutional freedoms. In the space of less than a generation, the logic of events made clear that despite all that the English and Americans shared, in the distribution of political power they were fundamentally at odds. And the call to arms at Lexington and Concord made retreat impossible.

Thomas Paine, author of *Common Sense*

On that point Paine was clear. It was the destiny of Americans to be republicans, not monarchists. It was the destiny of Americans to be independent, not subject to British dominion. It was the destiny of Americans to be American, not English. That, according to Thomas Paine, was common sense.

chapter summary

Resistance to British authority grew slowly but steadily in the American colonies during the period following the Seven Years' War.

- The new measures passed by Parliament in the early 1760s—the Proclamation of 1763, the Sugar Act, the Stamp Act, the Currency Act, and the Quartering Act—were all designed to bind the colonies more closely to the empire.

- These new measures deflated American expectations of a more equal status in the empire and also violated what Americans understood to be their constitutional and political liberties—the right to consent to taxation, the right to trial by jury, and the freedom from standing armies.

- Although Parliament repealed the Stamp Act, it reasserted its authority to tax Americans by passing the Townshend Acts in 1767.

- With the passage of the Coercive Acts in 1774, many Americans concluded that all British actions in the past decade were part of a deliberate plot to enslave Americans by depriving them of property and liberty.

- When the First Continental Congress convened in September 1774, delegates resisted both radical demands to mobilize for war and conservative appeals to reach an accommodation.

- The First Continental Congress denied Parliament any authority in the colonies except the right to regulate trade; it also drew up the Continental Association, an agreement to cease all trade with Britain until the Coercive Acts were repealed.

- When General Thomas Gage sent troops from Boston in April 1775 to seize arms being stored at Concord, the first battle of the Revolution took place.

interactive learning

The Primary Source Investigator CD-ROM offers the following materials related to this chapter:

- Interactive maps: **The Atlantic World, 1400–1850** (M2) and **The Settlement of Colonial America, 1700–1763** (M5)

- A collection of primary sources examining the age of the American Revolution, including the imperial acts that outraged American colonists, a selection from Thomas Paine's seminal work *Common Sense,* and a gazette article describing the Boston Massacre.

additional reading

The most balanced and readable account of the entire revolutionary era is still Edmund S. Morgan, *The Birth of the Republic* (1956). His study entitled *The Stamp Act Crisis* (1953), coauthored with Helen M. Morgan, remains the clearest and most vivid description of the issues, events, and people involved in that defining moment of the imperial crisis. Good coverage of later developments can be found in Pauline Maier, *From Resistance to Revolution* (1972). To understand the impact of the Seven Years' War on the attitudes toward Britain among ordinary men in Massachusetts, consult Fred Anderson's excellent *A People's Army* (1984); two equally imaginative interpretations of how the logic of resistance took shape among colonials are Timothy Breen, *Tobacco Culture* (1985); and Robert A. Gross, *The Minutemen and Their World* (1976). Bernard Bailyn, *The Ideological Origins of the American Revolution* (1967), demonstrates the influence of the English opposition in the evolution of colonial political thought. The most important book on British politics in this period is John Brewer, *Party Ideology* and *Popular Politics at the Accession of George III* (1976), but for a lively treatment of the monarchy, see J. H. Plumb, *The First Four Georges* (1956).

Biographies shed light on not only their subjects but also the times in which they lived. Some of the best biographies chronicle the careers of eighteenth-century Americans who led—or opposed—the resistance to Britain. For the rebels, see Richard R. Beeman, *Patrick Henry* (1974); Eric Foner, *Tom Paine and Revolutionary America* (1976); Pauline Maier, *The Old Revolutionaries* (1980); and Dumas Malone, *Jefferson the Virginian* (1948). For sympathetic treatment of one American loyalist, see Bernard Bailyn, *The Ordeal of Thomas Hutchinson* (1974). For a fuller list of readings, see the Bibliography at www.mhhe.com/davidsonnation5.

significant events

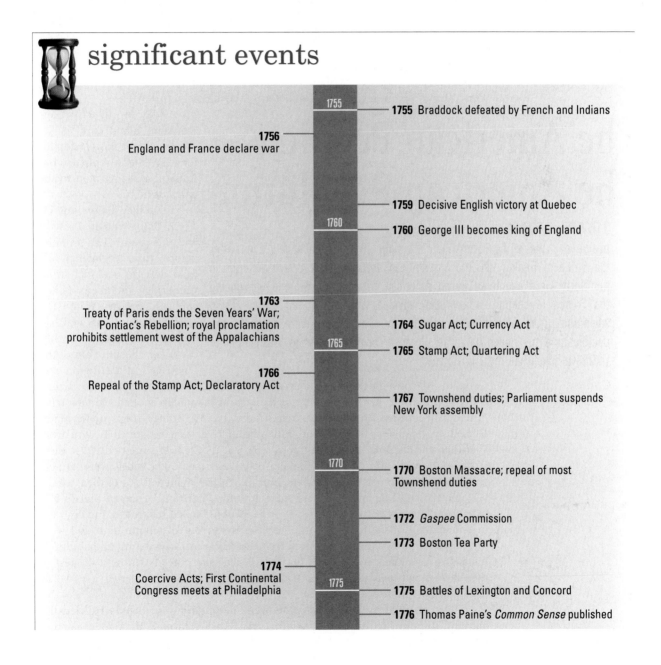

1756 — England and France declare war

1763 — Treaty of Paris ends the Seven Years' War; Pontiac's Rebellion; royal proclamation prohibits settlement west of the Appalachians

1766 — Repeal of the Stamp Act; Declaratory Act

1774 — Coercive Acts; First Continental Congress meets at Philadelphia

1755

1760

1765

1770

1775

1755 Braddock defeated by French and Indians

1759 Decisive English victory at Quebec

1760 George III becomes king of England

1764 Sugar Act; Currency Act

1765 Stamp Act; Quartering Act

1767 Townshend duties; Parliament suspends New York assembly

1770 Boston Massacre; repeal of most Townshend duties

1772 *Gaspee* Commission

1773 Boston Tea Party

1775 Battles of Lexington and Concord

1776 Thomas Paine's *Common Sense* published

Chapter 6

F rom a high place somewhere in the city—Beacon Hill, perhaps, or Copse Hill—General Thomas Gage looked down on Boston. Through a spyglass his gaze traveled over the church belfries and steeples, the roofs of brick and white frame houses. Finally he fixed his sights on a figure far in the distance across the Charles River. The man was perched atop a crude fortification on Breed's Hill, an elevation lying just below Bunker Hill on the Charlestown peninsula. Gage took the measure of his enemy: an older man, past middle age, a sword swinging beneath his homespun coat, a broad-brimmed hat shading his eyes. As he passed the spyglass to his ally, an American loyalist, Gage asked Abijah Willard if he knew the man on the fort. Willard peered across the Charles and identified his own brother-in-law, Colonel William Prescott. A veteran of the Seven Years' War, Prescott was now a leader in the rebel army laying siege to Boston.

The American People & The American Revolution

1775–1783

preview • Would Americans actually fight for independence? Even after the Battle of Bunker Hill, the answer was not clear. But British victories in the North were countered by an American triumph at Saratoga, convincing the French to commit to a crucial alliance with the United States. Then, when the British attempted to conquer the South, they were foiled by the Continental Army under Nathanael Greene. Their surrender to Washington at Yorktown astonished most of Europe.

Battle of Bunker Hill

"Will he fight?" Gage wondered aloud.

"I cannot answer for his men," Willard replied, "but Prescott will fight you to the gates of hell."

Fight they did on June 17, 1775, both William Prescott and his men. The evening before, three regiments had followed the colonel from Cambridge to Breed's Hill— soldiers drawn from the thousands of militia who had swarmed to surround British-occupied Boston after the bloodshed at Lexington and Concord. All through the night, they dug deep trenches and built up high earthen walls atop the hill. At the first light of day, a British warship spotted the new rebel outpost and opened fire. By noon barges were ferrying British troops under Major General William Howe across the half mile of river that separated Boston from Charlestown. The 1600 raw rebel troops tensed at the sight of scarlet-coated soldiers streaming ashore, glittering bayonets grasped at the ready. The rebels were farmers and artisans, not professional soldiers, and they were frightened out of their wits.

But Prescott and his men held their ground. The British charged Breed's Hill twice, and Howe watched in horror as streams of fire felled his troops. Finally, during the third British frontal assault, the rebels ran out of ammunition and were forced to withdraw. Redcoats poured into the rebel fort, bayoneting its handful of remaining defenders. By nightfall the British had taken Breed's Hill and the rest of the Charlestown peninsula. They had bought a dark triumph at the cost of 228 dead and 800 wounded.

The cost came high in loyalties as well. The fighting on Breed's Hill fed the hatred of Britain that had been building since April. Throughout America, preparations for war intensified: militia in every colony mustered; communities stockpiled arms and ammunition. Around Charlestown civilians fled the countryside, abandoning homes and shops set afire by the British shelling of Breed's Hill. "The roads filled with frightened women and children, some in carts with their tattered

Eleven years after the event, the American artist John Trumbull painted *Battle of Bunker's Hill* (1786), a canvas executed in the currently fashionable mode of grand historical painting, designed to commemorate (and elevate) an occasion of note.

furniture, others on foot fleeing into the woods," recalled Hannah Winthrop, one of their number.

The bloody, indecisive fight on the Charlestown peninsula known as the Battle of Bunker Hill actually took place on Breed's Hill. And the exchange between Thomas Gage and Abijah Willard that is said to have preceded the battle may not have taken place at all. But the story has persisted in the folklore of the American Revolution. Whether it really happened or not, the conversation between Gage and Willard raised the question that both sides wanted answered. Were Americans willing to fight for independence from British rule? It was one thing, after all, to oppose the British ministry's policy of taxation. It was another to support a rebellion for which the ultimate price of failure was hanging for treason. And it was another matter entirely for men to wait nervously atop a hill as the seasoned troops of their own "mother country" marched toward them with the intent to kill.

Will they fight? This Pennsylvania regimental flag gives one reason why some did.

Indeed, the question "will they fight?" was revolutionary shorthand for a host of other questions concerning how ordinary Americans would react to the tug of loyalties between long-established colonial governments and a long-revered parent nation and monarch. For slaves, the question revolved around their allegiance to masters who spoke of liberty or to their masters' enemies who promised liberation. For those who led the rebels, it was a question of strengthening the resolve of the undecided, coordinating resistance, instilling discipline—translating the *will* to fight into the ability to do so. And for those who believed the rebellion was a madness whipped up by artful politicians, it was a question of whether to remain silent or risk speaking out, whether to take up arms for the king or flee. All these

Americans react to the Revolution

questions were raised, of necessity, by the act of revolution. But the barrel of a rifle shortened them to a single, pointed question: will you fight?

The Decision for Independence

The delegates to the Second Continental Congress gathered at Philadelphia on May 10, 1775, just one month after the battles at Lexington and Concord. They had to determine whether independence or reconciliation offered the best way to protect the liberties of their colonies.

For a brash, ambitious lawyer from Braintree, Massachusetts, British abuses dictated only one course. "The Cancer [of official corruption] is too deeply rooted," wrote John Adams, "and too far spread to be cured by anything short of cutting it out entire." Yet during the spring and summer of 1775, even strong advocates of independence did not openly seek a separation from Britain. If the radicals' objective of independence was ever to be achieved, greater agreement among Americans had to be attained. Moderates and conservatives harbored deep misgivings about independence: they had to be brought along slowly.

The Second Continental Congress

To bring them along, Congress adopted the "Olive Branch Petition" in July 1775. Drawn up by Pennsylvania's John Dickinson, the document affirmed American loyalty to George III and asked the king to disavow the policies of his principal ministers. At the same time Congress issued a declaration denying that the colonies aimed at independence. Yet, less than a month earlier, Congress had authorized the creation of a rebel military force, the Continental Army, and had issued paper money to pay for the troops.

Aggressive British response

A Congress that sued for peace while preparing for war was a puzzle that British politicians—least of all, Lord George Germain—did not even try to understand. A tough-minded statesman now charged with overseeing colonial affairs, Germain was determined to subdue the rebellion by force. George III proved just as stubborn: he refused to receive the Olive Branch Petition. By the end of that year Parliament had shut down all trade with the colonies and had ordered the Royal Navy to seize colonial merchant ships on the high seas. In November 1775 Virginia's royal governor, Lord Dunmore, offered freedom to any slaves who would join the British. During January of the next year, he ordered the shelling of Norfolk, Virginia, reducing that town to a smoldering rubble.

British belligerence withered the cause of reconciliation within Congress and the colonies. Support for independence gained more momentum from the overwhelming reception of *Common Sense* in January 1776. Radicals in Congress realized that the future was theirs and were ready to act. In April 1776 the delegates opened American trade to every nation in the world except Great Britain; a month later Congress advised the colonies to establish new state governments. And on June 7 Virginia's Richard Henry Lee offered the motion "that these United Colonies are, and of right ought to be, free and independent States . . . and that all political connection between them and the State of Great Britain is, and ought to be, totally dissolved."

The Declaration

Congress postponed a final vote on Lee's motion until July. Some opposition still lingered among delegates from the middle colonies, and a committee appointed to write a declaration of independence needed time to complete its work. That committee included some of the leading delegates in Congress: John Adams, Benjamin Franklin, Connecticut's Roger Sherman, and New York's Robert Livingston. But the man who did most of the drafting was a young planter and lawyer from western Virginia.

Thomas Jefferson was just 33 years old in the summer of 1776 when he withdrew to his lodgings on the outskirts of Philadelphia, pulled a portable writing desk onto his lap, and wrote the statement that would explain American independence to a "candid world." In the document's brief opening section, Jefferson set forth a general justification of revolution that invoked the "self-evident truths" of human equality and "unalienable rights" to "life, liberty, and the pursuit of happiness." These natural rights had been "endowed" to all persons "by their Creator," the Declaration pointed out; thus there was no need to appeal to the narrower claim of the "rights of Englishmen."

Thomas Jefferson

While the first part of the Declaration served notice that Americans no longer considered themselves English, its second and longer section denied England any authority in the colonies. In its detailed history of American grievances against the British empire, the Declaration referred only once to Parliament. Instead, it blamed George III for a "long train of abuses and usurpations" designed to achieve "absolute despotism." Unlike *Common Sense,* the Declaration denounced only the reigning king of England; it did not attack the institution of monarchy itself. But like *Common Sense,* the Declaration affirmed that government originated in the consent of the governed and upheld the right of the people to overthrow oppressive rule.

Blaming George III

Later generations have debated what Jefferson meant by the "pursuit of happiness" and whether he had either women or black Americans in mind when he wrote the famous phrase "all men are created equal." His own contemporaries in Congress did not pause to consider those questions and surely would have found themselves divided if they had. No matter. By firmly grounding the Declaration on the natural rights due all people, Jefferson placed equality at the center of the new nation's identity, setting the framework for a debate that would continue over the next two centuries. Congress adopted the Declaration of Independence on July 4, 1776.

This painting, which commemorated the signing of the Declaration of Independence, shows Benjamin Franklin (seated center), obviously weighing the consequences of the action he and his colleagues are about to undertake. John Hancock, the president of the Congress, is reported to have remarked, "We must be unanimous; there must be no pulling different ways; we must all hang together." Franklin is said to have rejoined, "Yes, we must indeed all hang together, or most assuredly, we shall all hang separately."

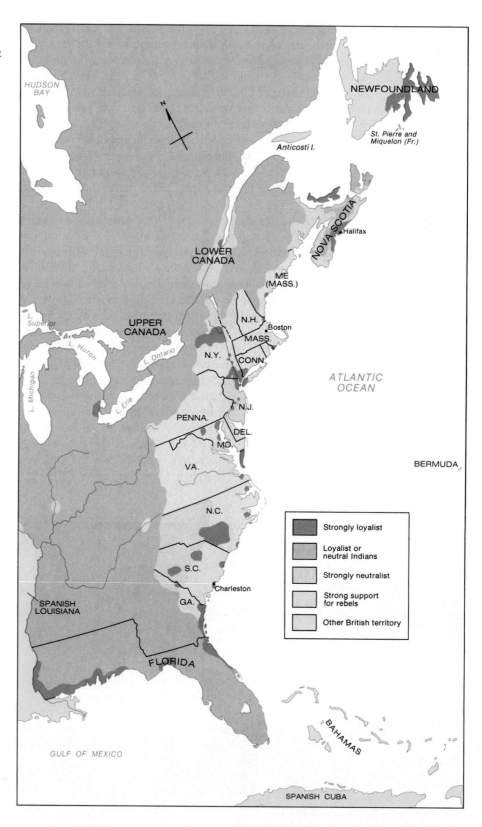

Patterns of Allegiance While most New Englanders rallied behind the rebel cause, support for the Revolution was not as widespread in the middle colonies and southern colonies.

HUDSON BAY

NEWFOUNDLAND

St. Pierre and Miquelon (Fr.)

Anticosti I.

NOVA SCOTIA

• Halifax

LOWER CANADA

ME (MASS.)

N.H.

• Boston

MASS.

UPPER CANADA

L. Superior

L. Huron

L. Michigan

L. Ontario

L. Erie

N.Y.

CONN.

ATLANTIC OCEAN

N.J.

PENNA.

DEL.

MD.

VA.

BERMUDA

N.C.

Strongly loyalist

Loyalist or neutral Indians

Strongly neutralist

Strong support for rebels

Other British territory

S.C.

Charleston

GA.

SPANISH LOUISIANA

FLORIDA

BAHAMAS

GULF OF MEXICO

SPANISH CUBA

174

American Loyalists

But the sentiment for independence was not universal. Americans who would not back the rebellion, supporters of the king and Parliament, numbered perhaps one-fifth of the population in 1775. While they proclaimed themselves "loyalists," their rebel opponents dubbed them "tories"—"a thing whose head is in England, whose body is in America, and whose neck ought to be stretched." That division made the Revolution a conflict pitting Americans against one another as well as the British. In truth, the war for independence was the first American civil war.

Predictably, the king and Parliament commanded the strongest support in colonies that had been wracked by internal strife earlier in the eighteenth century. In New York, New Jersey, Pennsylvania, and the Carolinas, not only did memories of old struggles sharpen worries of future upheaval, but old enemies often took different sides in the Revolution. The Carolina backcountry emerged as a stronghold of loyalist sentiment because of influential local men who cast their lot with Britain. To win support against Carolina's rebels, whose ranks included most wealthy coastal planters, western loyalist leaders played on ordinary settlers' resentments of privileged easterners. Grievances dating back to the 1760s also influenced the revolutionary allegiances of former land rioters of New York and New Jersey. If their old landlord opponents opted for the rebel cause, the tenants took up loyalism.

Other influences also fostered allegiance to Britain. Government officials who owed their jobs to the empire, major city merchants who depended on British trade, and Anglicans living outside the South retained strong ties to the parent country. Loyalists were also disproportionately represented among recent emigrants from the British Isles. The inhabitants of Georgia, the newest colony, inclined toward the king, as did the Highland Scots, many of whom had arrived in the colonies as soldiers during the Seven Years' War or had worked for a short time in the southern backcountry as tobacco merchants and Indian traders.

In any case, although a substantial minority, loyalists never became numerous enough anywhere to pose a serious menace to the Revolution. A more formidable threat was posed by the British army. And the greatest threat of all was posed by those very Americans who claimed that they wanted independence. For the question remained: would they fight?

Sources of loyalist support

The Fighting in the North

In the summer of 1775 Americans who wished to remain neutral probably outnumbered either loyalists or rebels. From the standpoint of mere survival, staying neutral made more sense than fighting for independence. Even the most ardent advocates of American rights had reason to harbor doubts, given the odds against the rebel colonists defeating the armed forces of the British empire.

Perhaps no friend of American liberty saw more clearly how slim the chances of a rebel victory were than George Washington. But Washington's principles, and his sense of honor, prevailed. June of 1775 found him, then 43 years old, attending the deliberations of the Second Continental Congress and dressed—a bit conspicuously—in his officer's uniform. The other delegates listened closely to his opinions on military matters, for Washington was the most celebrated American veteran of the Seven Years' War who remained young enough to lead a campaign. Better still, as a southerner he could bring his region into what thus far had

George Washington, general

George Washington

"Regulars" versus
the militia

remained mostly New England's fight. Congress readily appointed him commander
in chief of a newly created Continental Army.

The Two Armies at Bay

Thus did Washington find himself, only a month later, looking to bring some order
to the rebel forces massing around Boston. He knew he faced a formidable foe.

Highly trained, ably led, and efficiently equipped, the king's troops were seasoned professionals. Rank-and-file soldiers, men drawn mainly from the bottom of
British society, were drilled rigorously and disciplined (often savagely) by an aristocratic officer corps. At the height of the campaign in America, reinforcements
brought the number of British troops to 50,000, strengthened by some 30,000
Hessian mercenaries from Germany and the support of half the ships in the British
navy, the largest in the world.

Washington was more modest about the army under his command, and he had
much to be modest about. At first Congress recruited his fighting force of 16,600
rebel "regulars," the Continental Army, from the ranks of local New England militia bands. Although enlistments swelled briefly during the patriotic enthusiasm of
1775, for the rest of the war Washington's Continentals suffered chronic shortages
of men and supplies. Even strong supporters of the Revolution hesitated to join the
regular army, with its low pay and strict discipline and the constant threat of disease and danger. Most men preferred to fight instead as members of local militia
units, the "irregular" troops who turned out to support the regular army whenever
British forces came close to their neighborhoods.

The general reluctance to join the Continental Army created a host of difficulties for its commander and for Congress. Washington wanted and needed an army
whose size and military capability could be counted on in long campaigns. He
could not create an effective fighting force out of civilians who mustered occasionally with the militia or enlisted for short stints in the Continental Army.
Washington's desire for a professional military establishment clashed with the preferences of most republican leaders. They feared standing armies and idealized
"citizen-soldiers"—men of selfless civic virtue who volunteered whenever
needed—as the backbone of the common defense. "Oh, that I was a soldier,"
chubby John Adams fantasized in 1775. "Everyone must and will and shall be a
soldier."

But everyone did not become a soldier, and the dwindling number of volunteers gradually overcame republican fears of standing armies. In September 1776
Congress set terms in the Continental Army at a minimum of three years or for
the duration of the war and assigned each state to raise a certain number of troops.
They offered every man who enlisted in the army a cash bounty and a yearly clothing issue; enlistees for the duration were offered 100 acres of land as well. Still the
problem of recruitment persisted. Less than a year later, Congress recommended
that the states adopt a draft, but Congress had no authority to compel the states
to meet their troop quotas.

Even in the summer of 1775, before enlistments fell off, Washington was worried. As his Continentals laid siege to British-occupied Boston, he measured them
against the adversary and found them wanting. Inexperienced officers provided no
real leadership, and the men under their command shirked the most basic responsibilities of soldiers. They slipped away from camp at night; they left sentry duty
before being relieved; they took potshots at the British; they tolerated filthy conditions in their camps.

While Washington strove to impose discipline on his Continentals, he also attempted, without success, to rid himself of "the Women of the Army." When American men went off to fight, their wives usually stayed at home. To women then fell the sole responsibility for running farms and businesses, raising children, and keeping households together. They helped to supply the troops by sewing clothing, making blankets, and saving rags and lead weights for bandages and bullets. Other women on the home front organized relief for the widows and orphans of soldiers and protests against merchants who hoarded scarce commodities.

But the wives of poor men who joined the army were often left with no means to support their families. Thousands of such women—1 for every 15 soldiers—drifted after the troops. In return for half-rations, they cooked and washed for the soldiers; and after battles, they nursed the wounded, buried the dead, and scavenged the field for clothing and equipment. An even larger number of women accompanied the redcoats: their presence was the only thing that Washington did not admire about the British army and could barely tolerate in his own. But the services that they performed were indispensable, and women followed the troops throughout the war.

Women of the Army

Laying Strategies

At the same time that he tried to discipline the Continentals, Washington designed a defensive strategy to compensate for their weakness. To avoid exposing raw rebel troops on "open ground against their Superiors in number and Discipline," he planned to fight the British from strong fortifications. With that aim in mind, in March 1776, Washington barricaded his army on Dorchester Heights, an elevation commanding Boston harbor from the south. That maneuver, which allowed American artillery to fire on enemy warships, confirmed a decision already made by the British to evacuate their entire army from Boston and sail for Halifax, Nova Scotia.

Britain had hoped to reclaim its colonies with a strategy of strangling the resistance in Massachusetts. But by the spring of 1776 it saw clearly that more was required than a show of force against New England. Instead Britain's leaders chose to wage a conventional war in America, capturing major cities and crushing the Continental forces in a decisive battle. Military victory, the British believed, would enable them to restore political control and reestablish imperial authority.

British assumptions

The first target was New York City. General William Howe and Lord George Germain, the British officials now charged with overseeing the war, chose that seaport for its central location and—they hoped—its large loyalist population. They planned for Howe's army to move from New York City up the Hudson River, meeting ultimately with British troops under General Sir Guy Carleton coming south from Canada. Either the British drive would lure Washington into a major engagement, crushing the Continentals, or, if unopposed, the British offensive would cut America in two, smothering resistance to the south by isolating New England.

Unfortunately for the British, the strategy was sounder than the men placed in charge of executing it. General Howe took to extremes the conventional wisdom of eighteenth-century European warfare, which aimed as much at avoiding heavy casualties as at winning victories against the enemy. Concern for preserving troops addicted Howe to caution, when daring more would have carried the day. Howe's brother, Admiral Lord Richard Howe, the head of naval operations in America, also stopped short of pressing the British advantage, owing to his personal desire for reconciliation. The reluctance of the Howe brothers to fight became the formula for British frustration in the two years that followed.

Howe brothers

Daily Lives

CLOTHING AND FASHION
Radical Chic and the Revolutionary Generation

Women and men of revolutionary America sought to invest themselves with virtue as they escaped British "corruption." The most zealous partisans of colonial rights took that "investiture" to a literal extreme: they made and wore particular clothing as an emblem of political commitment. In the 1760s "homespun," any coarse cloth made in America, became a badge of opposition to British colonial policy.

Clothes sewn from domestic textiles identified the men and women who wore them as friends of liberty, freed from the vanity of British fashion and the humiliating dependence on British imports. As early as 1766 the radical press called for increased domestic industry to offset American reliance on English cloth. It aimed its pleas particularly at the women who managed colonial households.

By 1769 radical propaganda had produced a new ritual of American resistance, the patriotic spinning competition. Wives and daughters from some of the wealthiest and most prominent families, women who had heretofore vied to outdo each other in acquiring the latest English finery, were the featured players in this new form of political theater. Its setting was usually the home of a local minister, where, early in the morning, "respectable" young ladies, all dressed in homespun, assembled with their spinning wheels. They spent the day spinning furiously, stopping only to sustain themselves with "American produce . . . which was more agreeable to them than any foreign Dainties and Delicacies" and to drink herbal tea. At the end of the day the minister accepted their homespun and delivered an edifying sermon to all present. That was a large group, often including from 20 to 100 "respectable" female spinners as well as hundreds of other townsfolk who had come to watch the competition or to provide food and entertainment.

Women reveled in the new attention and value that the male resistance movement and the

Hunting shirts like the one worn by this rifleman (second from right) captured the imagination of the French army officer in America who made these watercolor sketches of revolutionary soldiers. The enlistment of blacks (infantryman at the far left) drew his attention as well.

The Campaigns in New York and New Jersey

However cautiously, British forces landed on Staten Island in New York harbor during July 1776. The Continentals marched from Boston and fortified Brooklyn Heights on Long Island, the key to the defenses of New York City on Manhattan Island. By mid-August, 32,000 British troops, including 8000 Hessians, the largest expeditionary force of the eighteenth century, faced Washington's army of 23,000.

At dawn on August 22 the Howe brothers moved on Long Island and easily pushed the rebel army back across the East River to Manhattan. After lingering on Long Island for a month, the Howes again lurched into action, ferrying their forces to Kip's Bay, just a few miles south of Harlem. When the British landed, the handful of rebel defenders at Kip's Bay fled—straight into the towering wrath of Washington, who happened on the scene during the rout. For once the general

British capture New York City

radical press now attached to a common and humdrum domestic task. By the beginning of 1769 New England newspapers were highlighting spinning bees and their female participants, sometimes termed the "Daughters of Liberty." Front pages overflowed with praise of female patriotism: "The industry and frugality of American ladies must exalt their character in the Eyes of the World and serve to show how greatly they are contributing to bring about the political salvation of a whole Continent."

Spinning competitions and the vogue of wearing homespun served two political purposes. First, the bees actively enlisted American women in the struggle against Britain. Wives and daughters from families of every rank were made to feel that they could play an important role in the resistance by imitating the elite women showcased in public spinning spectacles. Every woman could display her devotion to liberty by encouraging industry and frugality in her own household. Many women took pride in the new political importance that radical propaganda attributed to domestic pursuits. Writing to her English cousin, Charity Clarke of New York City cast herself as one of America's "fighting army of amazones . . . armed with spinning wheels."

Spinning bees and "dressing down" in homespun also contributed to the solidarity of the resistance by narrowing the visible distance between rich and poor Americans. In accounts of spinning competitions, the radical press emphasized that even the daughters of the elite sacrificed for the cause of resistance by embracing domestic economy and simplicity.

And what genteel women wove, leading men wore. On public occasions throughout the revolutionary crisis, radical leaders appeared in homespun, displaying both their patriotic virtue and their identification with poorer Americans who could not afford British finery. When they returned to their home counties to muster local militia companies, many southern gentlemen adopted homespun "hunting shirts," long, loose, full-sleeved frocks that reached past the thigh. This dress of the frontier united the gentry with ordinary men of the backcountry while declaring their superiority to the corrupt mother country.

lost his habitual self-restraint, flogged both officers and men with his riding crop, and came close to being captured himself. But the Howes remained reluctant to hit hard, letting Washington's army escape from Manhattan to Westchester County.

Throughout the fall of 1776 General Howe's forces followed as Washington's fled southward into New Jersey. By mid-November, as the British advance picked up speed, the rebels stepped up their retreat and crossed the Delaware River into Pennsylvania on December 7. There Howe stopped, pulling back most of his army to winter in New York City and leaving the Hessians to hold the British line of advance along the New Jersey side of the Delaware River.

Although the retreat through New York and New Jersey had shriveled rebel strength to only 3000 men, Washington decided that the campaign of 1776 was not over. On a snowy Christmas night, the Continentals floated back across the Delaware, picked their way across roads iced with sleet and finally slid into

Rebel victories at Trenton and Princeton

179

At the Battle of Princeton, British troops bayoneted the rebel general Hugh Mercer, an assault later commemorated in this painting by George Washington Parke Custis, the adopted step-grandson of George Washington. This rendering draws attention not only to Mercer's courage but also to the savagery of the redcoats, both of which helped the rebels gain civilian support.

Hessian-held Trenton at eight in the morning. One thousand German soldiers, still recovering from their spirited Christmas celebration and caught completely by surprise, quickly surrendered. Washington's luck held when, on January 3, 1777, the Continentals defeated British troops on the outskirts of Princeton, New Jersey.

During the winter of 1776–1777 the British lost more than battles: they alienated the very civilians whose loyalties they had hoped to ensure. In New York City the presence of the main body of the British army brought shortages of food and housing and caused constant friction between soldiers and city dwellers. In the New Jersey countryside still held by the Hessians, the situation was more desperate. Forced to live off the land, the Germans aroused resentment among local farmers by seizing "hay, oats, Indian corn, cattle, and horses, which were never or but very seldom paid for," as one loyalist admitted. The Hessians ransacked and destroyed homes and churches; they kidnapped and raped young women.

Many neutrals and loyalists who had had enough of the king's soldiers now took their allegiance elsewhere. Bands of militia on Long Island, along the Hudson River, and all over New Jersey rallied to support the Continentals.

Capturing Philadelphia

In the summer of 1777 General Howe still hoped to entice the Continentals into a decisive engagement or to seize a major seaport and its surrounding countryside. But he had now decided to goad the Americans into battle by capturing Philadelphia.

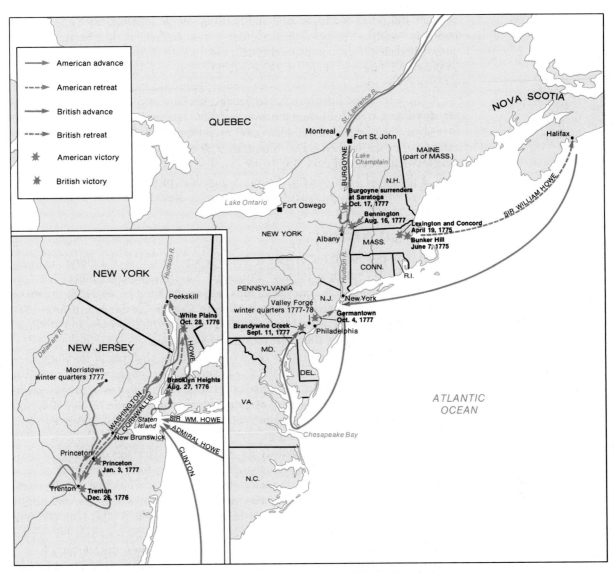

The Fighting in the North, 1775–1777 After the British withdrew from Boston in 1775, they launched an attack on New York City the following year. Washington was forced to retreat northward, then across the Hudson and south into New Jersey and Pennsylvania, before surprising the British at Trenton and Princeton. Burgoyne's surrender at Saratoga in 1777 marked a turning point in the war.

Rather than risk his army on a march through hostile New Jersey, he approached the rebel capital by sea. In early August the redcoats disembarked on the Maryland shore and headed for Philadelphia, 50 miles away. Washington had hoped to stay on the strategic defensive, holding his smaller army together and harassing the enemy but avoiding full-scale battles. Howe's march on Philadelphia made that impossible: Washington's army hurried south from New Jersey to protect the new nation's capital. Washington engaged Howe twice: in September at Brandywine Creek and in October in an early dawn attack at Germantown, but both times the rebels were beaten back. He had been unable to prevent the British occupation of Philadelphia.

Still, the rebels could take satisfaction from the troubles that beset the British even in victory. In Philadelphia, as in New York, British occupation jacked up

Brandywine and Germantown

demand and prices for food, fuel, and housing. While inflation hit hardest at the poor, the wealthy resented British officers who became their uninvited house guests. Philadelphians complained of redcoats looting their shops, trampling their gardens, and harassing them on the streets. Elizabeth Drinker, the wife of a Quaker merchant, confided in her diary that "I often feel afraid to go to bed."

Even worse, the British march through Maryland and Pennsylvania had outraged civilians, who fled before the army and then returned to find their homes and barns bare, their crops and livestock gone. Everywhere Howe's men went in the mid-Atlantic, they left in their wake Americans with compelling reasons to support the rebels. Worst of all, just days after Howe marched his occupying army into Philadelphia in the fall of 1777, another British commander in North America was surrendering his entire army to rebel forces at Saratoga, New York.

Disaster at Saratoga

The calamity that befell the British at Saratoga was the doing of a glorymongering general, John "Gentleman Johnny" Burgoyne. After his superior officer, Sir Guy Carleton, bungled a drive into New York during the summer of 1776, Burgoyne won approval to command another attack from Canada. At the end of June 1777 he set out from Quebec with a force of 9500 redcoats, 2000 women and children, and an elaborate baggage train that included the commander's silver dining service, his dress uniforms, and numerous cases of his favorite champagne. As Burgoyne's huge entourage lumbered southward, it was slowed by a rough, winding road that was broken by boulders, felled trees, and ramshackle bridges that swayed over yawning ravines. Meanwhile, a handful of Continentals and a horde of New England militia assembled several miles below Saratoga at Bemis Heights under the command of General Horatio Gates.

Burgoyne surrenders at Saratoga

On September 19 Gates's rebel scouts, nested high in the trees on Bemis Heights, spied the glittering bayonets of Burgoyne's approaching force. Benedict Arnold, a brave young officer, led several thousand rebels into the surrounding woods, meeting Burgoyne's men in a clearing at Freeman's Farm. At the end of the day British reinforcements finally pushed the rebels back from a battlefield piled high with the bodies of soldiers from both sides. Burgoyne tried to flee back to Canada but got no farther than Saratoga, where he surrendered his army to Gates on October 17.

Saratoga changed everything. Burgoyne had not just been nipped in a skirmish; he had lost his entire army. The triumph was enough to convince Britain's old rival France that, with a little help, the Americans might well reap the fruits of victory.

The Turning Point

France had been waiting for revenge against Britain since its humiliating defeat in the Seven Years' War. Over the previous decade, as France's agents in America sent home reports of a rebellion brewing, a scheme for evening the score had been taking shape in the mind of the French foreign minister, Charles Gravier de Vergennes. He reckoned that France might turn discontented colonials into willing allies against Britain.

The American Revolution Becomes a Global War

Vergennes approached the Americans cautiously. He wanted to make certain that the rift between Britain and its colonies would not be reconciled and that the rebels in America stood a fighting chance. Although France had been secretly supplying the Continental Army with guns and ammunition since the spring of 1776, Vergennes would go no further than covert assistance.

Congress approached its former French enemies with equal caution. Would France, the leading Catholic monarchy in Europe, make common cause with the republican rebels? A few years earlier American colonials had fought against the French in Canada. Only recently they had renounced a king. For centuries they had overwhelmingly adhered to Protestantism.

The string of defeats dealt the Continental Army during 1776 convinced Congress that they needed the French enough to accept both the contradictions and the costs of such an alliance. In November Congress appointed a three-member commission to negotiate not only aid from France but also a formal alliance. Its senior member was Benjamin Franklin, who enchanted all of Paris when he arrived in town sporting a simple fur cap and a pair of spectacles (something no fashionable Frenchman wore in public). Hailed as a homespun sage, Franklin played the role of American innocent to the hilt and watched as admiring Parisians stamped his face on everything from the top of commemorative snuffboxes to the bottom of porcelain chamber pots.

Still, Franklin understood that mere popularity could not produce the alliance sought by Congress. It was only news that Britain had surrendered an entire army at Saratoga that finally convinced Vergennes that the rebels could actually win. In February 1778 France signed a treaty of commerce and friendship and a treaty of alliance, which Congress approved in May. Under the terms of the treaties, both parties agreed to accept nothing short of independence for America. France pledged to renounce all future claims in continental North America and to give back any territory captured in the war. The alliance left the British no choice other than to declare war on France. Less than a year later Spain joined France, hoping to recover territory lost to England in earlier wars.

The French public's infatuation with Benjamin Franklin knew no bounds. They particularly delighted in his rustic dress and styled him a representative of "frontier" America. He appears in this guise on a snuffbox along with two revered French philosophers, Voltaire and Rousseau.

Winding Down the War in the North

The Revolution widened into a global war after 1778. Preparing to fight France and Spain dictated a new British strategy in America. No longer could the British concentrate on crushing the Continental Army. Instead they would disperse their forces to fend off challenges all over the world. In May Sir Henry Clinton replaced William Howe as commander in chief and received orders to withdraw from Philadelphia to New York City. There, and in Newport, Rhode Island, Clinton was to maintain defensive bases for harrying northern coastal towns.

Only 18 miles outside of Philadelphia, at Valley Forge, Washington and his Continentals were assessing their own situation. Some 11,000 rebel soldiers had passed a harrowing winter in that isolated spot, starving for want of food, freezing for lack of clothing, huddling in miserable huts, and hating the British who lay so close and yet so comfortably in Philadelphia. The army also cursed their fellow citizens, for the misery of the soldiers resulted from congressional weakness and disorganization and from civilian corruption and indifference. Congress lacked both money to pay and maintain the army and an efficient system for dispensing provisions to the troops. Most farmers and merchants preferred to supply the British, who could pay handsomely, than to do business with a financially strapped Congress and the Continentals. What little did reach the army often was food too rancid to eat or clothing too rotten to wear. Perhaps 2500 perished at Valley Forge, the victims of cold, hunger, and disease.

The soldiers in this 1777 illustration condemn civilian neglect and the profiteering of private contractors who supplied the Continental Army. Such grievances would provoke mutinies within the army before the end of the fighting.

First Soldier: "Keep up courage, my boys, we will soon bring those villains to terms."

Second Soldier: "These d[amne]d Extortioners are the worst enemies to the country."

Third Soldier: "I serve my country for sixteen pence a day, pinched with cold."

Army uprisings

Why did civilians who supported the rebel cause allow the army to suffer? Probably because by the winter of 1777, the Continentals came mainly from social classes that received little consideration at any time. The respectable, propertied farmers and artisans who had laid siege to Boston in 1775 had stopped enlisting. Serving in their stead were single men in their teens and early twenties, some who joined the army out of desperation, others who were drafted, still others who were hired as substitutes for the more affluent. The landless sons of farmers, unemployed laborers, drifters, petty criminals, vagrants, indentured servants, slaves, even captured British and Hessian soldiers—all men with no other means and no other choice—were swept into the Continental Army. The social composition of the rebel rank and file had come to resemble that of the British army. It is the great irony of the Revolution: a war to protect liberty and property was waged by those Americans who were poorest and least free.

The beginning of spring in 1778 brought a reprieve. Supplies arrived at Valley Forge, and so did a fellow calling himself Baron von Steuben, a penniless Prussian soldier of fortune. Although Washington's men had shown spirit and resilience ever since Trenton, they still lacked discipline and training. Those defects and more von Steuben began to remedy. Barking orders and spewing curses in German and French, the baron (and his translators) drilled the rebel regiments to march in formation and to handle their bayonets like proper Prussian soldiers. By the summer of 1778, morale had rebounded as professional pride fused solidarity among Continental ranks in the crucible of Valley Forge.

Spoiling for action after their long winter, Washington's army, now numbering nearly 13,500, set out to harass Clinton's army as it marched overland from Philadelphia to New York. The Continentals caught up with the British force on June 28 at Monmouth Courthouse, where a long, confused battle ended in a draw. After both armies retired for the night, Clinton's forces slipped away to safety in New York City. Washington pursued, longing to launch an all-out assault on New York City, but he lacked the necessary numbers.

While Washington waited outside New York City, his army started to come apart. During the two hard winters that followed, resentments mounted among the rank and file over spoiled food, inadequate clothing, and arrears in pay. The army retaliated with mutinies. Between 1779 and 1780 officers managed to quell uprisings in three New England regiments. But in January 1781 both the Pennsylvania and New Jersey lines mutinied outright and marched on Philadelphia, where Congress had reconvened. Order returned only after Congress promised back pay and provisions and Washington put two ringleaders in front of a firing squad.

War in the West

Trouble also loomed on the western frontier. There both the British and the rebels sought support from the Indians because the most powerful tribes determined the balance of power. Most of the tribes remained neutral, but those tribes who took sides most often joined the British, who had tried to stem the tide of colonials taking Indian lands.

While George Rogers Clark and his few hundred rebel troops helped contain British and Indian raids in the Old Northwest, General John Sullivan led an expedition against the Iroquois in upstate New York. Loyalists under Major John Butler and Iroquois fighters under a Mohawk chief, Thayendanegea (called Joseph Brant by the English), had conducted a series of raids along the New York and Pennsylvania frontiers. Sullivan's expedition routed the marauders and burned more than 40 Indian villages.

The Home Front in the North

Although in 1779 most northern civilians on the seaboard enjoyed a respite from the war, the devastation lingered. Since the outbreak of the fighting at Lexington and Concord, every rumor of approaching enemy troops had pitched the inhabitants of imperiled neighborhoods into a panic. Refugees on foot and in hastily packed carts filled the roads, fleeing the advancing armies. Those who remained to protect their homes and property might be caught in the crossfire of contending forces or cut off from supplies of food and firewood. Loyalists who remained in areas occupied by rebel troops faced harassment, imprisonment, or the confiscation of their property. Rebel sympathizers met similar fates in regions held by the British. Disease, however, disregarded political allegiances: military camps and occupied towns spawned epidemics of dysentery and smallpox that devastated civilians as well as soldiers, rebels and loyalists alike.

While plundering armies destroyed civilian property wherever they marched, military demands disrupted family economies throughout the northern countryside. The seasons of intense fighting drew men off into military service just when their labor was most needed on family farms. Wives and daughters were left to assume the work of husbands and sons while coping with loneliness, anxiety, and grief. Often enough, the disruptions, flight, and loss of family members left lasting scars. Two years after she fled before Burgoyne's advance into upstate New York, Ann Eliza Bleecker confessed to a friend, "Alas! the wilderness is within: I muse so long on the dead until I am unfit for the company of the living."

Women and the war

Despite these hardships, many women vigorously supported the revolutionary cause in a variety of ways. The Daughters of Liberty joined in harassing opponents to the rebel cause. One outspoken loyalist found himself surrounded by angry women who stripped off his shirt, covered him with molasses, and plastered him with flower petals. In more genteel fashion, groups of well-to-do women collected not only money but medicines, food, and pewter to melt for bullets.

Women's perspectives on the War for Independence

Between the autumn of 1778 and the summer of 1781, while Washington and ## The Struggle in the South

his restless army waited outside New York City, the British opened another theater in the American war. Despite their armed presence in the North, the British had come to believe that their most vital aim was to regain their colonies in the mainland South. The Chesapeake and the Carolinas were more profitable to the empire and more strategically important, being so much closer to rich British sugar islands in the West Indies. That new "southern strategy" prompted Clinton to dispatch forces

Britain's southern strategy

to the Caribbean and Florida. In addition, the British laid plans for a new offensive drive into the Carolinas and Virginia.

English politicians and generals believed that the war could be won in the South. Loyalists were numerous, they believed, especially in the backcountry. Resentment of the seaboard, a rebel stronghold, would breed readiness among frontier folk to take up arms for the king at the first show of British force. And southern rebels—especially the vulnerable planters along the coast—could not afford to turn their guns away from their slaves. So, at least, the British theorized. All that was needed, they concluded, was for the British army to establish a beachhead in the South and then, in league with loyalists, drive northward, pacifying the population while pressing up the coast.

The Siege of Charleston

The southern strategy worked well for a short time in a small place. In November 1778 Clinton sent 3500 troops to Savannah, Georgia. The resistance in the tiny colony quickly collapsed, and a large number of loyalists turned out to help the British. Encouraged by that success, the British moved on to South Carolina.

During the last days of 1779, an expedition under Clinton himself set sail from New York City. Landing off the Georgia coast, his troops mucked through malarial swamps to the peninsula lying between the Ashley and Cooper rivers. At the tip of that neck of land stood Charleston, and the British began to lay siege. By then, an unseasonably warm spring had set in, making the area a heaven for mosquitoes and a hell for human beings. Sweltering and swatting, redcoats weighted down in their woolen uniforms inched their siege works toward the city. By early May Clinton's army had closed in, and British shelling was setting fire to houses within the city. On May 12 Charleston surrendered.

Clinton sailed back to New York at the end of June 1780, leaving behind 8300 redcoats to carry the British offensive northward to Virginia. The man charged with leading that campaign was his ambitious and able subordinate, Charles, Lord Cornwallis.

The Partisan Struggle in the South

Cornwallis's task in the Carolinas was complicated by the bitter animosity between rebels and loyalists there. Many Carolinians had taken sides years before Clinton's conquest of Charleston. In the summer and fall of 1775 the supporters of Congress and the new South Carolina revolutionary government mobbed, tortured, and imprisoned supporters of the king in the backcountry. These attacks only hardened loyalist resolve: roving bands seized ammunition, broke their leaders out of jail, and besieged rebel outposts. But within a matter of months, a combined force of rebel militias from the coast and the frontier managed to defeat loyalist forces in the backcountry.

Rebels and loyalists battle for the backcountry

With the fall of Charleston in 1780, the loyalist movement on the frontier returned to life. Out of loyalist vengefulness and rebel desperation issued the brutal civil war that seared the southern backcountry after 1780. Neighbors and even families fought and killed each other as members of roaming rebel and tory militias. The intensity of partisan warfare in the backcountry produced unprecedented destruction. Loyalist militia plundered plantations and assaulted local women; rebel militias whipped suspected British supporters and burned their farms; both sides committed brutal assassinations and tortured prisoners. All of society, observed one minister, "seems to be at an end. Every person keeps close on his own plantation. Robberies and murders are often committed on the public roads. . . . Poverty, want, and hardship appear in almost every countenance."

Cornwallis, when confronted with the chaos, erred fatally. He did nothing to stop his loyalist allies or his own troops from mistreating civilians. A Carolina loyalist admitted that "the lower sort of People, who were in many parts originally attached to the British Government, have suffered so severely . . . that Great Britain has now a hundred enemies, where it had one before." Although rebels and loyalists alike plundered and terrorized the backcountry, Cornwallis's forces bore more of the blame and suffered the consequences.

A growing number of civilians outraged by the behavior of the king's troops cast their lot with the rebels. That upsurge of popular support enabled Francis Marion, the "Swamp Fox," and his band of white and black raiders to cut British lines of communication between Charleston and the interior. It swelled another rebel militia led by "the Gamecock," Thomas Sumter, who bloodied loyalist forces throughout the central part of South Carolina. It mobilized the "over-the-mountain men," a rebel militia in western Carolina who claimed victory at the Battle of Kings Mountain in October 1780. By the end of 1780, these successes had persuaded most civilians that only the rebels could restore order.

If rebel fortunes prospered in the partisan struggle, they faltered in the conventional warfare being waged at the same time in the South. In August of 1780 the Continentals commanded by Horatio Gates lost a major engagement to the British force at Camden, South Carolina. In the fall of 1780 Congress replaced Gates with Washington's candidate for the southern command, Nathanael Greene, an energetic 38-year-old Rhode Islander and a veteran of the northern campaigns.

British victory at Camden

Greene Takes Command

General Nathanael Greene

Greene bore out Washington's confidence by grasping the military situation in the South. He understood the needs of his 1400 hungry, ragged, and demoralized troops and instructed von Steuben to lobby Virginia for food and clothing. He understood the importance of the rebel militias and sent Lieutenant Colonel Henry "Lighthorse Harry" Lee to assist Marion's raids. He understood the weariness of southern civilians and prevented his men from plundering the countryside.

Above all, Greene understood that his forces could never hold the field against the whole British army. That led him to break the first rule of conventional warfare: he divided his army. In December 1780 he dispatched to western South Carolina a detachment of 600 men under the command of Brigadier General Daniel Morgan of Virginia.

Back at the British camp, Cornwallis worried that Morgan and his rebels, if left unchecked, might rally the entire backcountry against the British. On the other hand, Cornwallis reckoned that he could not commit his entire army to the pursuit of Morgan's men, for then Greene and his troops might retake Charleston. The only solution, unconventional to be sure, was for Cornwallis to divide *his* army. That he did, sending Lieutenant Colonel Banastre Tarleton and 1100 men west after Morgan. Cornwallis had played right into Greene's hands: the rebel troops might be able to defeat a British army split into two pieces. For two weeks Morgan led Tarleton's troops on a breakneck chase across the Carolina countryside. In January 1781 at an open meadow called Cowpens, Morgan routed Tarleton's force.

Cowpens

The Fighting in the South, 1780–1781 In December 1780 Nathanael Greene made the crucial decision to split his army, sending Daniel Morgan west, where he defeated the pursuing Banastre Tarleton at Cowpens. Meanwhile Greene regrouped and replenished at Cheraw, keeping Cornwallis off balance with a raid (dotted line) toward Charleston and the coast. Then, with Cornwallis in hot pursuit, Greene and Morgan rejoined at Salisbury, retreating into Virginia. Cornwallis was worn down in this vain pursuit and lost three-quarters of the troops he began with before finally abandoning the Carolina campaign.

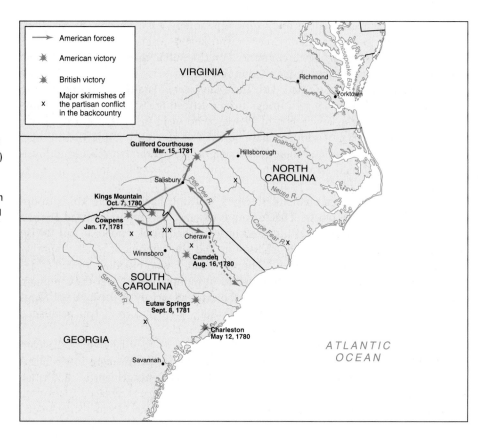

Value of the militia

Now Cornwallis took up the chase. Morgan and Greene joined forces and agreed to keep going north until the British army wore out. Cornwallis finally stopped at Hillsboro, North Carolina, but few local loyalists responded to his call for reinforcements. To ensure that loyalist ranks remained thin, Greene decided to make a show of force near the tiny village of Guilford Courthouse. On a brisk March day the two sides joined battle, each sustaining severe casualties before Greene was forced to retreat. But the high cost of victory convinced Cornwallis that he could not put down the rebellion in the Carolinas. "I am quite tired of marching about the country in quest of adventures," he informed Clinton.

Although Nathanael Greene's command provided the Continentals with effective leadership in the South, it was the resilience of rebel militia that thwarted the British offensive in the Carolinas. Many Continental Army officers complained about the militia's lack of discipline, its habit of melting away when homesickness set in or harvest approached, and its record of cowardice under fire in conventional engagements. But when set the task of ambushing supply trains and dispatch riders, harrying bands of local loyalists, or making forays against isolated British outposts, the militia came through. Many southern civilians refused to join the British or to provide the redcoats with food and information because they knew that once the British army left their neighborhoods, the rebel militia would always be back. The Continental Army in the South lost many conventional battles, but the militia kept the British from restoring political control over the backcountry.

African Americans in the Age of Revolution

The British also lost in the Carolinas because they did not seek greater support from those southerners who would have fought for liberty *with* the British—African American slaves.

Black Americans, virtually all in bondage, made up one-third of the population between Delaware and Georgia. Since the beginning of the resistance to Britain, white southerners had worried that the watchwords of *liberty* and *equality* would spread to the slave quarters. Gripped by the fear of slave rebellion, southern revolutionaries began to take precautions. Marylanders disarmed black inhabitants and issued extra guns to the white militia. Charlestonians hanged and then burned the body of Thomas Jeremiah, a free black who was convicted of spreading the word to others that the British "were come to help the poor Negroes."

Southern whites fully expected the British to turn slave rebelliousness to their strategic advantage. As early as 1775, Virginia's royal governor, Lord Dunmore, confirmed white fears by offering to free any slave who joined the British. When Clinton invaded the South in 1779, he renewed that offer. According to Janet Schaw, an English woman visiting her brother's North Carolina plantation, her brother's neighbors had heard that loyalists were "promising every Negro that would murder his master and family he should have his Master's plantation" and that "the Negroes have got it amongst them and believe it to be true."

White fears of rebellion

But in Britain there was overwhelming opposition to organizing support among African Americans. British leaders dismissed Dunmore's ambitious scheme to raise a black army of 10,000 and another plan to create a sanctuary for black loyalists on the southeastern coast. Turning slaves against masters, they recognized, was not the way to conciliate southern whites.

Even so, southern fears of insurrection made the rebels reluctant to enlist black Americans as soldiers. At first, Congress barred African Americans from the Continental Army. But as the rebels became more desperate for manpower, policy changed. Northern states actively encouraged black enlistments, and in the Upper

Rebel Americans were able to hold the southern backcountry because of the determination of militias such as the one depicted in this detail of a nineteenth-century painting. Francis Marion's company was unusual among southern militias because it included blacks.

African American quests
for liberty

South, some states allowed free men of color to join the army or permitted slaves to substitute for their masters.

Slaves themselves sought freedom from whichever side seemed most likely to grant it. In 1775 more than 800 took up Dunmore's offer and deserted their masters, and thousands more flocked to Clinton's forces after the fall of Charleston. For many runaways the hope of liberation proved an illusion. Although some served the British army as laborers, spies, and soldiers, many died of disease in army camps or were sold back into slavery in the West Indies. An estimated 5000 black soldiers served in the revolutionary army in the hope of gaining freedom. In addition, the number of runaways to the North soared during the Revolution. All told, some 55,000 slaves fled to freedom, some escaping behind British lines, others into the North.

The slave revolts so dreaded by southern whites never materialized. Possibly the boldest slaves were drawn off into the armies; possibly greater white precautions discouraged schemes for black rebellions. In South Carolina, where the potential for revolt was greatest, most slaves chose to remain on plantations rather than risk a collective resistance and escape in the midst of the fierce partisan warfare.

The World Turned Upside Down

Despite his losses in the Carolinas, Cornwallis still believed that he could score a decisive victory against the Continental Army. The theater he chose for that showdown was the Chesapeake. During the spring of 1781, he had marched his army to the Virginia coast and joined forces with the hero of Saratoga and newly turned loyalist, Benedict Arnold. Embarrassed by debt and disgusted by Congress's shabby treatment of the Continental Army, Arnold had started exchanging rebel secrets for British money in 1779 before defecting outright in the fall of 1780. By June of 1781 Arnold and Cornwallis were fortifying a site on the tip of the peninsula formed by the York and James rivers, a place called Yorktown.

Meanwhile, Washington and his French ally, the comte de Rochambeau, met in Connecticut to plan a major attack. Rochambeau urged a coordinated land-sea assault on the Virginia coast. Washington insisted instead on a full-scale offensive against New York City. Just when the rebel commander was about to have his way, word arrived that a French fleet under the comte de Grasse was sailing for the Chesapeake to blockade Cornwallis by sea. Washington's Continentals headed south.

On September 30, 1780, a wagon bearing this two-faced effigy was drawn through the streets of Philadelphia. The effigy represents Benedict Arnold, who sits between a gallows and the devil. Note the similarities between this piece of street theater and the demonstrations mounted on Pope's Day several decades earlier, shown on page 158.

Surrender at Yorktown

By the end of September, 7800 Frenchmen, 5700 Continentals, and 3200 militia had sandwiched Yorktown between the devil of an allied army and the deep blue sea of French warships. "If you cannot relieve me very soon," Cornwallis wrote to Clinton, "you must expect to hear the worst." The British navy did arrive—but seven days after Cornwallis surrendered to the rebels on October 19, 1781. When Germain carried the news from Yorktown to the king's first minister, Lord North replied, "Oh, God, it is over." Then North resigned, Germain resigned, and even George III murmured something about abdicating.

It need not have ended at Yorktown, but timing made all the difference. At the end of 1781 and early in 1782, the British army received setbacks in the other theaters of the war: India, the West Indies, and Florida. The French and the Spanish were everywhere in Europe as well, gathering in the English Channel, planning a major offensive against Gibraltar. The cost of the fighting was already enormous. British leaders recognized that the rest of the empire was at stake and set about cutting their losses in America.

The Treaty of Paris, signed on September 3, 1783, was a diplomatic triumph for the American negotiators: Benjamin Franklin, John Adams, and John Jay. They dangled before Britain the possibility that a generous settlement might weaken American ties to France. The British jumped at the bait. They recognized the independence of the United States and agreed to ample boundaries for the new nation: the Mississippi River on the west, the 31st parallel on the south, and the present border of Canada on the north. American negotiators then persuaded a skeptical France to approve the treaty by arguing that, as allies, they were bound to present a united front to the British. When the French finally persuaded Spain, the third member of the alliance, to reduce its demands on Britain for territorial concessions, the treaty became an accomplished fact. The Spanish settled for Florida and Minorca, an island in the Mediterranean.

Treaty of Paris

The Significance of a Revolution

If the Treaty of Paris marked both the end of a war and the recognition of a new nation, the surrender at Yorktown captured the significance of a revolution. Those present at Yorktown on that clear autumn afternoon in 1781 watched as the British second in command to Cornwallis (who had sent word that he was "indisposed") surrendered his superior's sword. He offered the sword first, in a face-saving gesture, to the French commander, Rochambeau, who politely refused and pointed to Washington. But the American commander in chief, out of a mixture of military protocol, nationalistic pride, and perhaps even wit, pointed to *his* second in command, Benjamin Lincoln.

Some witnesses recalled that British musicians arrayed on the Yorktown green played "The World Turned Upside Down." Their recollections may have been faulty, but the story has persisted as part of the folklore of the American Revolution—and for good reasons. The world had, it seemed, turned upside down with the coming of American independence. The colonial rebels shocked the British with their answer to the question: would they fight?

The answer had been yes—but on their own terms. By 1777 most propertied Americans avoided fighting in the Continental Army. Yet whenever the war reached their homes, farms, and businesses, many Americans gave their allegiance to the new nation by turning out with rifles or supplying homespun clothing, food, or

Citizen-soldiers fight on their own terms

The world turned upside down:
the British lay down their arms
at Yorktown.

ammunition. They rallied around Washington in New Jersey, Gates in upstate New York, Greene in the Carolinas. Middle-class American men fought, some from idealism, others out of self-interest, but always on their own terms, as members of the militia. These citizen-soldiers turned the world upside down by defeating professional armies.

Of course, the militia did not bear the brunt of the fighting. That responsibility fell to the Continental Army, which by 1777 drew its strength from the poorest ranks of American society. Yet even the Continentals, for all their desperation, managed to fight on their own terms. Some asserted their rights by raising mutinies, until Congress redressed their grievances. All of them, as the Baron von Steuben observed, behaved differently than European soldiers. Americans followed orders only if the logic of commands was explained to them. The Continentals, held in contempt by most Americans, turned the world upside down by sensing their power and asserting their measure of personal independence.

Thus did a revolutionary generation turn the world upside down. Descended from desperate, idealistic, and self-interested men and women who settled colonies

named for kings and queens—ruled by kings and queens who aimed to increase the wealth and power of their dynasties and their nations—these Americans rebelled against a king. They wanted more than a monarch. But what more did they want? What awaited in a world turned upside down by republican revolutionaries?

chapter summary

The American Revolution brought independence to Britain's former colonies after an armed struggle that began in 1775 and concluded with the Treaty of Paris in 1783.

- When the Second Continental Congress convened in the spring of 1775, many of the delegates still hoped for reconciliation—even as they approved the creation of the Continental Army.

- The Second Continental Congress adopted the Declaration of Independence on July 4, 1776, hoping that they could count on a majority of Americans to support the Revolution.

- The British scored a string of victories in the North throughout 1776 and 1777, capturing both New York and Philadelphia.

- The British suffered a disastrous defeat at the Battle of Saratoga in early 1778, which prompted France to openly ally with the American rebels soon thereafter.

- By 1780 Britain aimed to win the war by claiming the South, and captured both Savannah, Georgia, and Charleston, South Carolina.

- The Continental Army in the South, led by Nathanael Greene, foiled the British strategy, and Cornwallis surrendered to Washington after the Battle of Yorktown in 1781.

- Except during the first year of fighting, the rank and file of the Continental Army were drawn from the poorest Americans, whose needs for food, clothing, and shelter were neglected by the Continental Congress.

interactive learning

The Primary Source Investigator CD-ROM offers the following materials related to this chapter:

- Interactive map: **The American Revolution, 1775–1781** (M6)

- A short documentary movie on women's perspectives on the War for Independence (D2)

- A collection of primary sources concerning the colonies' struggle for independence, including several drafts of the Declaration of Independence, paintings memorializing fallen heroes, and Thomas Paine's *common sense*. Other sources illustrate the important role of African Americans and Native Americans in the American Revolution, including Lord Dunmore's proclamation freeing slaves in Virginia to fight on the side of the British empire. Still others explore the role of women in the American Revolution, such as Molly Pitcher's recollection of her experiences in the Continental Army and a letter from Abigail Adams to John Adams.

additional reading

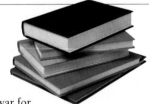

Two superb overviews of the war for independence are Don Higginbotham, *The American War for Independence* (1971); and Robert Middlekauff, *The Glorious Cause, 1763–1789* (1982). Both provide a wealth of detail about battles, the contending armies, and the roles of the militia and the civilian population. Two particularly thoughtful accounts of the relationship between the war and American society are Charles Royster, *A Revolutionary People at War* (1979); and John Shy, *A People Numerous and Armed* (1976). Sylvia Frey offers a fine account of African Americans throughout the years of revolutionary crisis in *Water from the Rock* (1991), and the role of women in wartime America is treated most comprehensively by Mary Beth Norton, *Liberty's Daughters* (1980). An intimate account of the impact of the war on one Connecticut family is Joy Day Buel and Richard Buel Jr., *The Way of Duty* (1984).

Many excellent studies probe the impact of the American Revolution on the institution of slavery and the lives of African Americans. Among the best are Ira Berlin and Ronald Hoffman, eds., *Slavery and Freedom in the Age of the American Revolution* (1983); David Brion Davis, *The Problem of Slavery in the Age of Revolution* (1975); and Gary B. Nash, *Race and Revolution* (1990). For a fuller list of readings, see the Bibliography at www.mhhe.com/davidsonnation5.

significant events

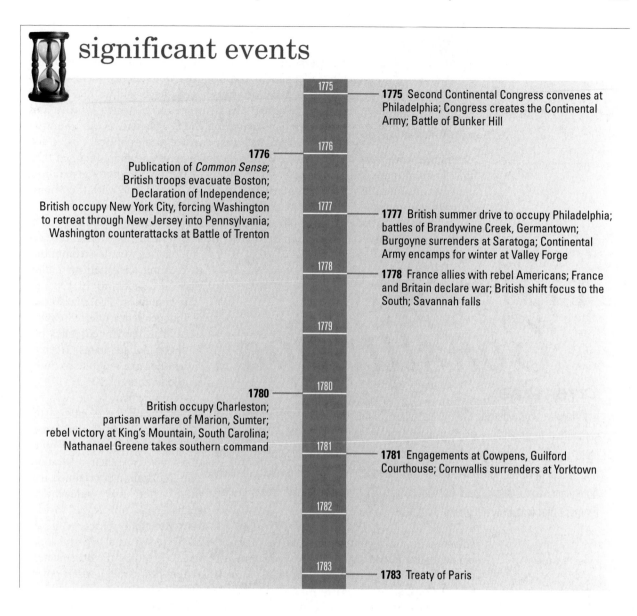

1775 Second Continental Congress convenes at Philadelphia; Congress creates the Continental Army; Battle of Bunker Hill

1776
Publication of *Common Sense*;
British troops evacuate Boston;
Declaration of Independence;
British occupy New York City, forcing Washington
to retreat through New Jersey into Pennsylvania;
Washington counterattacks at Battle of Trenton

1777 British summer drive to occupy Philadelphia; battles of Brandywine Creek, Germantown; Burgoyne surrenders at Saratoga; Continental Army encamps for winter at Valley Forge

1778 France allies with rebel Americans; France and Britain declare war; British shift focus to the South; Savannah falls

1780
British occupy Charleston;
partisan warfare of Marion, Sumter;
rebel victory at King's Mountain, South Carolina;
Nathanael Greene takes southern command

1781 Engagements at Cowpens, Guilford Courthouse; Cornwallis surrenders at Yorktown

1783 Treaty of Paris

Chapter 7

"I am not a Virginian, but an American," Patrick Henry declared in the Virginia House of Burgesses. Most likely he was lying. Certainly no one listening took him seriously, for the newly independent colonists did not identify themselves as members of a nation. They would have said, as did Thomas Jefferson, "Virginia, Sir, is my country." Or as John Adams wrote to another native son, "Massachusetts is our country." Jefferson and Adams were men of wide political vision and experience: both were leaders in the Continental Congress and more inclined than most to think nationally. But like other members of the revolutionary generation, they identified deeply with their home states and even more deeply with their home counties and towns.

It followed that allegiance to the states, not the Union, determined the shape of the first republican political experiments. For a decade after independence, the revolutionaries were less committed to creating an American nation than to organizing 13 separate state republics. The Declaration of Independence referred explicitly not to *the* United States but to *these* United States. It envisioned not one republic so much as a federation of 13.

Crisis & *Constitution*

1776–1789

preview • For a decade after independence, American revolutionaries were less committed to creating a single national republic than to organizing 13 separate state republics, united only loosely under the Articles of Confederation. By the mid-1780s, however, the weakness of the Confederation seemed evident to many Americans. The Constitutional Convention of 1787 produced a new frame of government that was truly national in scope.

Only when peace was restored during the decade of the 1780s were Americans forced to face some unanswered questions raised by their revolution. The Declaration proclaimed that these "free and independent states" had "full power to levy war, conclude peace, contract

How close a union?

alliances, establish commerce." Did that mean that New Jersey, as a free and independent state, could sign a trade agreement with France, excluding the other states? If the United States was to be more than a loose federation, how could it assert power on a national scale? Similarly, American borderlands to the west presented problems. If these territories were settled by Americans, would they eventually join the United States? Go their own ways as independent nations? Become new colonies of Spain or England?

Such problems were more than political; they were rooted in social realities. For a political union to succeed, the inhabitants of 13 separate states had to start thinking of themselves as Americans. When it came right down to it, what united a Vermont farmer working his rocky fields and a South Carolina gentleman presiding over a vast rice plantation? What bonds existed between a Kentuckian rafting the Ohio River and a Salem merchant sailing to China for porcelain?

And in a society in which all citizens were said to be "created equal," the inevitable social inequalities had to be confronted. How could women participate in the Revolution's bid for freedom if they were not free to vote or to hold property? How could black Americans feel a bond with white Americans when so often the

The portraits of Captain and Mrs. Samuel Chandler, a New England couple, project the virtuous rectitude of the new republican era. Husband and wife share the same direct, disarming gaze, a mixture of wariness and resolution.

only existing bonds had been forged with chains? To these questions there were no final answers in 1781. And as the decade progressed, the sense of crisis deepened. Americans worried that factions and selfish interest groups would pull "these" United States apart. The new republican union, which spread out over so many miles, constituted a truly unprecedented venture. A good deal of experimenting would be needed if it was to succeed.

After independence was declared in July 1776, many of America's best political # Republican Experiments

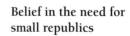

minds turned to drawing up constitutions for their individual states. Thomas Jefferson deserted the Continental Congress, leaving the conduct of the war and national affairs to other men, for the more important business of creating Virginia's new government.

In truth, the state constitutions were crucial republican experiments, the first efforts at establishing a government of and by the people. All the revolutionaries agreed that the people—not a king or a few privileged aristocrats—should rule. Yet they were equally certain that republican governments were best suited to small territories. They believed that the new United States was too sprawling and its people too diverse to be safely consolidated into a single national republic. They feared, too, that the government of a large republic would inevitably grow indifferent to popular concerns, being distant from many of its citizens. Without being under the watchful eye of the people, representatives would become less accountable to the electorate and turn tyrannical. A federation of small state republics, they reasoned, would stand a far better chance of enduring.

Belief in the need for small republics

The State Constitutions

The new state constitutions retained the basic form of their old colonial governments, all except Georgia and Pennsylvania providing for a governor and a bicameral legislature. But while most states did not alter the basic structure of their governments, they changed dramatically the balance of power among the different branches of government.

Curbing executive power

From the republican perspective in 1776, the greatest problem of any government lay in curbing executive power. What had driven Americans into rebellion was the abuse of authority by the king and his appointed officials. To ensure that the executive could never again threaten popular liberty, the new states either accorded almost no power to their governors or abolished that office entirely. The governors had no authority to convene or dissolve the legislatures. They could not veto the legislatures' laws, grant land, or erect courts. Most important from the republican point of view, governors had few powers to appoint other state officials. All these limits were designed to deprive the executive of any patronage or other form of influence over the legislature. By reducing the governors' power, Americans hoped to preserve their states from the corruption that they deplored in British political life.

Strengthening legislative powers

What the state governors lost, the legislatures gained. Sam Adams, the Boston rebel leader, expressed the political consensus when he declared that "every legislature of every colony ought to be the sovereign and uncontrollable Power within its own limits of territory." To ensure that those powerful legislatures truly represented the will of the people, the new state constitutions called for annual elections and required candidates for the legislature to live in the districts they represented. Many states even asserted the right of voters to instruct the men elected to office how to vote on specific issues. Although no state granted universal manhood suffrage, most reduced the amount of property required of qualified voters. Finally, state supreme courts were also either elected by the legislatures or appointed by elected governors.

Americans responded to independence with rituals of "killing the king," like the one enacted by this New York crowd in 1776 as it pulls down a statue of George III. Americans also expressed their mistrust of monarchs and their ministers by establishing new state governments with weak executive branches.

By investing all power in popular assemblies, Americans abandoned the British system of mixed government. In one sense, that change was fairly democratic. A majority of voters within a state could do whatever they wanted, unchecked by governors or courts. On the other hand, the arrangement opened the door for legislatures to turn as tyrannical as governors. The revolutionaries brushed that prospect aside: republican theory assured them that the people possessed a generous share of civic virtue, the capacity for selfless pursuit of the general welfare.

In an equally momentous change, the revolutionaries insisted on written state constitutions. Whenever government appeared to exceed the limits of its authority, Americans wanted to have at hand the written contract between rulers and ruled. When eighteenth-century Britons used the word *constitution,* they meant the existing arrangement of government—not an actual document but a collection of parliamentary laws, customs, and precedents. But Americans believed that a constitution should be a written code that stood apart from and above government, a yardstick against which the people measured the performance of their rulers. After all, they reasoned, if Britain's constitution had been written down, available for all to consult, would American rights have been violated?

Written constitutions

From Congress to Confederation

While Americans lavished attention on their state constitutions, the national government nearly languished during the decade after 1776. With the coming of independence, the Second Continental Congress conducted the common business of the federated states. It created and maintained the Continental Army, issued currency, and negotiated with foreign powers.

But while Congress acted as a central government by common consent, it lacked any legal basis for its authority. To redress that need, in July 1776 Congress appointed a committee to draft a constitution for a national government. The more urgent business of waging and paying for the war made for delay, as did the consuming interest in framing state constitutions. Congress finally approved the first national constitution in November 1777, but it took four more years for all the states to ratify these Articles of Confederation.

The Articles of Confederation provided for a government by a national legislature—essentially a continuation of the Second Continental Congress. That body had the authority to declare war and make peace, conduct diplomacy, regulate Indian affairs, appoint military and naval officers, and requisition men from the states. In affairs of finance it could coin money and issue paper currency. Extensive as these responsibilities were, Congress could not levy taxes or even regulate trade. The crucial power of the purse rested entirely with the states, as did the final power to make and execute laws. Even worse, the national government had no distinct executive branch. Congressional committees, constantly changing in their membership, not only had to make laws but had to administer and enforce them as well. With no executive to carry out the policies of finance, war, and foreign policy, the federal government's influence was extremely limited.

Articles of Confederation

Those weaknesses of the federal government appear more evident in hindsight. For Congress in 1777 it was no easy task to frame a new government in the midst of a war. Besides that distraction, most American leaders of the 1770s had given little thought to federalism, the organization of a United States. Political leaders had not yet recognized the need for dividing power between the states and the national government. With the new nation in the midst of a military crisis, Congress assumed—correctly in most cases—that the states did not have to be forced to contribute men and money to the common defense. To have given significant powers to the national government would only have aroused opposition among the states, each jealous of its independence. Creating a strong national government would also have antagonized many Americans, who after all had just rebelled against the distant, centralized authority of Britain's king and Parliament.

Guided by republican political theory and by their colonial experience, American revolutionaries created a loose confederation of 13 independent state republics under a nearly powerless national government. They succeeded so well that the United States almost failed to survive the first decade of its independence. The problem was that republican theory and lessons from the colonial past were not always useful guides to postwar realities. Only when events forced Americans to think nationally did they begin to consider the possibility of reinventing "these United States"—this time under the yoke of a truly federal republic.

The Temptations of Peace

The surrender of Cornwallis at Yorktown in 1781 marked the end of military crisis in America. But as the threat from Britain receded, so did the source of American unity. The many differences among Americans, most of which lay submerged during the struggle for independence, surfaced in full force. Those domestic divisions, combined with challenges to the new nation from Britain and Spain, created conflicts that neither the states nor the national government proved equal to handling.

The Temptations of the West

The greatest opportunities and the greatest problems for postwar Americans awaited in the rapidly expanding West. With the boundary of the new United States now set at the Mississippi River, more settlers spilled across the Appalachians, planting farmsteads and raw frontier towns throughout Ohio, Kentucky, and Tennessee. By 1790 places that had been almost uninhabited by whites in 1760 held more than 2.25 million people, one-third of the nation's population.

After the Revolution, as before, western settlement fostered intense conflict. American claims that its territory stretched all the way to the Mississippi were by no means taken for granted by European and Indian powers. The West also confronted Americans with questions about their own national identity. Would the newly settled territories enter the nation as states on an equal footing with the original 13 states? Would they be ruled as dependent colonies? Could the federal government reconcile conflicting interests, cultures, and traditions over so great an area? The fate of the West, in other words, constituted a crucial test of whether "these" United States could grow and still remain united.

Foreign Intrigues

Both the British from their base in Canada and the Spanish in Florida and Louisiana hoped to chisel away at American borders. Their considerable success in the 1780s exposed the weakness of Confederation diplomacy.

Before the ink was dry on the Treaty of Paris, Britain's ministers were secretly instructing Canadians to maintain their forts and trading posts inside the United States' northwestern frontier. They reckoned—correctly—that with the Continental Army disbanded, the Confederation could not force the British to withdraw.

The British also made mischief along the Confederation's northern borders, mainly with Vermont. For decades, Ethan Allen and his Green Mountain Boys had waged a war of nerves with neighboring New York, which claimed Vermont as part of its territory. After the Revolution the Vermonters petitioned Congress for statehood, demanding independence of both New York and New Hampshire. When Congress dragged its feet, the British tried to woo Vermont into their empire as a province of Canada. That flirtation with the British pressured Congress into granting Vermont statehood in 1791.

The loyalty of the southwestern frontier was even less certain. By 1790 more than 100,000 settlers had poured through the Cumberland Gap to reach Kentucky and Tennessee. Along with the farmers came speculators, who bought up large tracts of land from the Indians. But the commercial possibilities of the region depended entirely on access to the Mississippi and the port of New Orleans, since it was far too costly to ship southwestern produce over the rough trails east across the Appalachians. And the Mississippi route was still dominated by the Spanish, who controlled Louisiana as well as forts along western Mississippi shores as far north as St. Louis. The Spanish, seeing their opportunity, closed the Mississippi to American navigation in 1784. That action prompted serious talk among southwesterners about seceding from the United States and joining Spain's empire.

The Spanish also tried to strengthen their hold on North America by making common cause with the Indians. Of particular concern to both groups was protecting Florida, which had reverted to Spain's possession, from the encroachment of American settlers filtering south from Georgia. Florida's governor alerted his superiors back in Spain to the threat posed by those backwoods folk who were "nomadic like Arabs and . . . distinguished from savages only in their color, language, and the superiority of their depraved cunning and untrustworthiness." So Spanish colonial officials responded eagerly to the overtures of Alexander McGillivray, a young Indian leader whose mother was of French-Creek descent and whose father was a Scots trader. His efforts brought about a treaty of alliance between the Creeks and

Spanish designs on the Southwest

Rivalries flared along the southwestern frontier of the United States as Spain vied to win the allegiance of Indians by supplying them with British trade goods. The Indians welcomed such goods (note the shovel, at left, the plow, center, and European clothing worn by some of the Indians). Here a white man, probably the American Indian agent Benjamin Hawkins, visits an Indian village during the 1790s.

the Spanish in 1784, quickly followed by similar alliances with the Choctaws and the Chickasaws. What cemented such treaties were the trade goods that the Spanish agreed to supply the tribes, for, as McGillivray explained, "Indians will attach themselves to and serve them best who supply their necessities." Securing European gunpowder and guns had become essential to southeastern Indians, because their entire economies now revolved around hunting and selling deerskins to white traders. So eager were the Spanish to "serve" the Indians in that matter that they even permitted British merchants, who could command a steady supply of manufactured goods, to monopolize the Indian trade. The largest dealers, William Panton and John Leslie, two loyalists who had fled to Florida in the wake of the Revolution, developed a trading network with southeastern tribes that reached all the way to the Mississippi by the 1790s. This flood of British merchandise sustained the alliance between the Spanish and the Indians, while British guns enabled the Creeks to defend their hunting territory from American invaders.

Disputes among the States

As if foreign intrigues were not divisive enough, the states continued to argue among themselves over western land claims. The old royal charters for some colonies had extended their boundaries all the way to the Mississippi and beyond. (See the map

Western Land Claims, 1782–1802 The Confederation's settlement of conflicting western land claims was an achievement essential to the consolidation of political union. Some states asserted that their original charters extended their western borders to the Mississippi River. A few states, like Virginia, claimed western borders on the Pacific Ocean.

on pg. 202.) But the charters were often vague, granting both Massachusetts and Virginia, for example, undisputed possession of present-day Wisconsin. In contrast, other charters limited state boundaries to within a few hundred miles of the Atlantic coast. "Landed" states like Virginia wanted to secure control over the large territory granted them by their charters. "Landless" states (which included Maryland, Delaware, Pennsylvania, Rhode Island, and New Jersey) called on Congress to restrict the boundaries of landed states and to convert western lands into a domain administered by the Confederation.

Landed versus landless states

The landless states argued that the landed states enjoyed an unfair advantage from the money they could raise selling their western claims. That revenue would allow landed states to reduce taxes, and lower taxes would lure settlers from the landless states. Meanwhile, landless states would have to raise taxes to make up for the departed taxpayers, causing even more residents to leave. Speculators were also eager to see Congress control the western lands. Before the Revolution, many prominent citizens of landless Pennsylvania, Maryland, and New Jersey had purchased tracts in the West from Indians. These speculators now joined forces with the political leaders of the landless states to lobby for congressional ownership of all western lands—except those tracts that they had already purchased from the Indians.

The landless states lost the opening round in the contest over ownership of the West. The Articles of Confederation acknowledged the old charter claims of the landed states. Then Maryland, one of the smallest landless states, retaliated by refusing to ratify the Articles. Since every state had to approve the Articles before they were formally accepted, the fate of the United States hung in the balance. One by one the landed states relented. The last holdout, Virginia, in January 1781 ceded its charter rights to land north of the Ohio River. In a moment of uncharacteristic modesty, the Virginians conceded that they might have trouble extending a republican government over the entire territory allotted them in their charter—a substantial portion of the North American continent. Once Virginia ceded, Maryland ratified the Articles in February 1781, four long years after Congress had first approved them.

The More Democratic West

More bitterly disputed than western land claims was the issue concerning the sort of men westerners elected to political office. The state legislatures of the 1780s were both larger and more democratic in their membership than the old colonial assemblies. Before the Revolution no more than a fifth of the men serving in the assemblies were middle-class farmers or artisans. Government was almost exclusively the domain of the wealthiest merchants, lawyers, and planters. After the Revolution twice as many state legislators were men of moderate wealth. The shift was more marked in the North, where middle-class men predominated among representatives. But in every state, some men of modest means, humble background, and little formal education attained political power.

State legislatures became more democratic in their membership mainly because as backcountry districts grew, so too did the number of their representatives. Since western districts tended to be less developed economically and culturally, their leading men were less rich and cultivated than the eastern seaboard elite. Wealthy, well-educated gentlemen thus became a much smaller and less powerful group within the legislatures because of greater western representation and influence.

Changing composition of state legislatures

But many republican gentlemen, while endorsing government by popular consent, doubted whether ordinary people were fit to rule. The problem, they contended, was that the new western legislators concerned themselves only with the

This sketch of a new cleared farm idealizes many aspects of life on the late-eighteenth-century frontier. Although western farmers first sought to "improve" their acreage by felling trees, as the stumps dotting the landscape indicate, their dwellings were far less substantial than those depicted in the background above. And while Indians sometimes guided parties of white surveyors and settlers into the West, as shown in the foreground, Indians more often resisted white encroachment. For that reason, dogs, here perched placidly in canoes, were trained to alert their white masters to the approach of Indians.

narrow interests of their constituents, not with the good of the whole state. As Ezra Stiles, the president of Yale College, observed, the new breed of politicians were those with "the all-prevailing popular talent of coaxing and flattering," who "whenever a bill is read in the legislature . . . instantly thinks how it will affect his constituents." And if state legislatures could not rise above petty bickering and narrow self-interest, how long would it be before civic virtue and a concern for the general welfare simply withered away?

The Northwest Territory

Such fears of "democratic excess" also influenced policy when Congress finally came to decide what to do with the Northwest Territory. Carved out of the land ceded by the states to the national government, the Northwest Territory comprised the present-day states of Ohio, Indiana, Illinois, Michigan, and Wisconsin. With so many white settlers moving into these lands, Congress was faced with a crucial test of its federal system. If an orderly way could not be devised to expand the confederation of states beyond the original 13 colonies, the new territories might well become independent countries or even colonies of Spain or Britain. Congress dealt with the issue of expansion by adopting three ordinances.

Jefferson's plan for the Northwest

The first, drafted by Thomas Jefferson in 1784, divided the Northwest Territory into 10 states, each to be admitted to the Union on equal terms as soon as its population equaled that in any of the existing states. In the meantime, Jefferson provided for democratic self-government of the territory by all free adult males. A second ordinance of 1785 set up an efficient mechanism for dividing and selling public lands. The Northwest Territory was surveyed into townships six miles square. Each township was then divided into 36 lots of one square mile, or 640 acres.

Congress waited in vain for buyers to flock to the land offices it established. The cost of even a single lot—$640—was too steep for most farmers. Disappointed by the shortage of buyers and desperate for money, Congress finally accepted a proposition submitted by a private company of land speculators who offered to buy

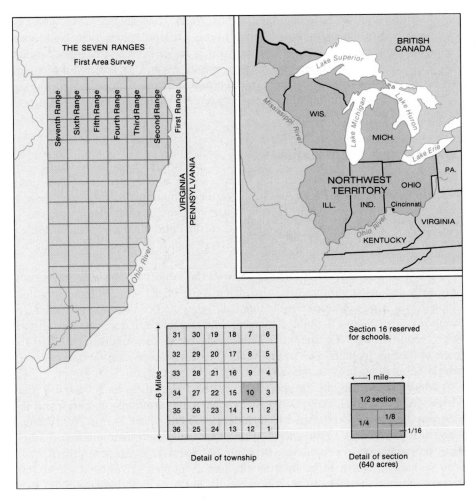

THE SEVEN RANGES
First Area Survey

Seventh Range | Sixth Range | Fifth Range | Fourth Range | Third Range | Second Range | First Range

VIRGINIA
PENNSYLVANIA

Ohio River

BRITISH CANADA

Lake Superior

Mississippi River

WIS.

Lake Michigan

Lake Huron

MICH.

Lake Erie

PA.

NORTHWEST TERRITORY   OHIO

ILL.   IND.   Cincinnati

VIRGINIA

Ohio River

KENTUCKY

6 Miles

31	30	19	18	7	6
32	29	20	17	8	5
33	28	21	16	9	4
34	27	22	15	10	3
35	26	23	14	11	2
36	25	24	13	12	1

Detail of township

Section 16 reserved for schools.

←——1 mile——→

1/2 section

1/4   1/8

1/16

Detail of section
(640 acres)

The Ordinance of 1785 Surveyors entered the Northwest Territory in September of 1785, imposing on the land regular grids of six square miles to define new townships, as shown on this range map of a portion of Ohio. Farmers purchased blocks of land within townships, each one mile square, from the federal government or from land speculators. This pattern was followed in mapping and settling public lands all the way to the Pacific coast.

some 6 million acres in present-day southeastern Ohio. That several members of Congress numbered among the company's stockholders no doubt added to enthusiasm for the deal.

The transaction concluded, Congress calmed the speculators' worries that incoming settlers might enjoy too much self-government by scrapping Jefferson's democratic design and substituting the Northwest Ordinance of 1787. That ordinance provided for a period in which Congress held sway in the territory through its appointees—a governor, a secretary, and three judges. When the population reached 5000 free adult males, a legislature was to be established, although its laws required the governor's approval. A representative could sit in Congress but had no vote. When the population reached 60,000, the inhabitants might apply for statehood, and the whole Northwest Territory was to be divided into not less than three or more than five states. The ordinance also guaranteed basic rights—freedom of religion and trial by jury—and provided for the support of public education.

Congress's plan completely ignored the rights of the Shawnee, Chippewa, and other Indian peoples who lived in the region. And in terms of Jefferson's democratic ideals for white inhabitants, the ordinance of 1787 also fell short. Still, Congress had succeeded in extending republican government to the West and incorporating the frontier into the new nation. Congress also outlawed slavery throughout the territory.

Northwest Ordinance

That decision had an unexpected, almost ironic consequence. The Northwest Ordinance went a long way toward establishing a federal system that would minimize tensions between the East and the West, a major source of postwar conflict. The Republic now had a peaceful, orderly way to expand its federation of states. Yet by limiting the spread of slavery in the northern states, Congress deepened the critical social and economic differences between North and South, evident already in the 1780s.

Slavery and Sectionalism

When white Americans declared their independence, they owned nearly half a million black Americans. African Americans of the revolutionary generation, most of them enslaved, constituted 20 percent of the total population of the colonies in 1775, and nearly 90 percent of them lived in the South. Yet few political leaders directly confronted the issue of whether slavery should be permitted to exist in a truly republican society.

Republicanism and
slavery

When political discussion did stray toward the subject of slavery, southerners—especially ardent republicans—bristled defensively. Theirs was a difficult position, riddled with contradictions. On the one hand, they had condemned parliamentary taxation as tantamount to political "slavery" and had rebelled, declaring that all men were "created equal." On the other hand, enslaved African Americans formed the basis of the South's plantation economy. To surrender slavery, southerners believed, would be to usher in economic ruin.

Some planters in the Upper South resolved the dilemma by freeing their slaves. Such decisions were made easier by changing economic conditions in the Chesapeake. As planters shifted from tobacco toward wheat, a crop demanding a good deal less labor, Virginia and Maryland liberalized their manumission statutes, laws providing for freeing slaves. Between 1776 and 1789, most southern states also joined the North in prohibiting the importation of slaves, and a few antislavery societies appeared in the Upper South. But no southern state legally abolished slavery. Masters defended their right to hold human property in the name of republicanism.

Eighteenth-century republicans regarded property as crucial, for it provided a man and his family with security, status, and wealth. More important, it provided a measure of independence: to be able to act freely, without fear or favor of others. People without property were dangerous, republicans believed, because the poor could never be politically independent. Southern defenders of slavery thus argued that free, propertyless black people would pose a political threat to the liberty of propertied white citizens. Subordinating the human rights of blacks to the property rights of whites, southern republicans reached the paradoxical conclusion that their freedom depended on keeping African Americans in bondage.

The North followed a different course. Because its economy depended far less on slave labor, black emancipation did not run counter to powerful economic interests. Antislavery societies, the first founded by the Quakers in 1775, spread throughout the northern states during the next quarter century. Over the same period the legislatures of most northern states provided for the immediate or gradual abolition of slavery. Freedom for most northern African Americans came slowly, but by 1830 there were fewer than 3000 slaves out of a total northern black population of 125,000.

The Revolution, which had been fought for liberty and equality, did little to change the status of most black Americans. By 1800 more enslaved African

Negro Methodists Holding a Meeting in a Philadelphia Alley evokes the vibrancy of African American religious life in the city that became a haven for free blacks. The artist, until recently believed to be a visiting Russian, Pavel Petrovich Svinin, is now thought to be the American John Lewis Krimmel.

Americans lived in the United States than had lived there in 1776. Slavery continued to grow in the Lower South as the rice culture of the Carolinas and Georgia expanded and as the new cotton culture spread westward.

Still, a larger number of slaves than ever before became free during the war and in the following decades, whether through military service, successful escape, manumission, or gradual emancipation. All these developments fostered the growth of free black communities, especially in the Upper South and in northern cities. By 1810 free African Americans made up 10 percent of the total population of Maryland and Virginia. The composition of the postwar free community changed as well. Before independence most free blacks had been either mulattoes—the offspring of interracial unions—or former slaves too sick or aged to have value as laborers. In contrast, the free population of the 1780s became darker skinned, younger, and healthier. This group injected new vitality into black communal life, organizing independent schools, churches, and mutual benefit societies for the growing number of "free people of color."

Growth of the free black community

After the Revolution slavery ceased to be a national institution. It became the "peculiar institution" of a single region, the American South. The isolation of slavery in one section set North and South on radically different courses of social development, sharpening economic and political divisions.

Free black sailors

Wartime Economic Disruption

With the outbreak of the Revolution, Americans had suffered an immediate economic loss. Formerly, Britain had supplied manufactured goods, markets for American exports, and credit that enabled commerce to flourish. The war changed all that. Hardest hit were southern planters, who had to seek new customers for their tobacco, cotton, and rice as well as find new sources of capital to finance production. Northerners too faced difficulties, for their major seaports were occupied for a time by British troops, whose presence disrupted commercial activity.

Public and private debt

Matters did not improve with the coming of peace. France and Britain flooded the new states with their manufactures, and postwar Americans, eager for luxuries, indulged in a most unrepublican spending spree. The flurry of buying left some American merchants and consumers as deeply in debt as their governments. When loans from private citizens and foreign creditors like France proved insufficient to finance the fighting, both Congress and the states printed paper money—a whopping total of $400 million. The paper currency was backed only by the government's promise to redeem the bills with money from future taxes, because legislatures balked at the unpopular alternative of levying taxes during the war. For the bills to be redeemed, the United States had to survive, so by the end of 1776, when Continental forces sustained a series of defeats, paper money started to depreciate dramatically. By 1781 it was virtually without value, and Americans coined the expression "not worth a Continental."

Postwar inflation

The printing of paper money, combined with a wartime shortage of goods, triggered an inflationary spiral. As goods became scarcer and scarcer, they cost more and more worthless dollars. In this spiral, creditors were gouged by debtors, who paid them back with depreciated currency. At the same time soaring prices for food and manufactured goods eroded the buying power of wage earners and small farmers. And the end of the war brought on demands for prompt repayment from the new nation's foreign creditors as well as from soldiers seeking back pay and pensions.

Congress could do nothing. With no power to regulate trade, it could neither dam the stream of imported goods rushing into the states nor stanch the flow of gold and silver to Europe to pay for these items. With no power to prohibit the states from issuing paper money, it could not halt depreciation. With no power to regulate wages or prices, it could not curb inflation. With no power to tax, it could not reduce the public debt. Efforts to grant Congress greater powers met with determined resistance from the states. They refused Congress any revenue of its own, fearing the first steps toward "arbitrary" government.

Political divisions over economic policy

Within states, too, economic problems aroused discord. Some major merchants, creditors, and large commercial farmers had profited handsomely during the war by selling supplies to the American, British, and French armies at high prices or by preying on enemy vessels as privateers. Eager to protect their windfall, they lobbied state legislatures for an end to inflationary monetary policies. They pushed for the passage of high taxes to pay wartime debts, a paper currency that was backed up with gold and silver, and an active policy to encourage foreign trade.

Less affluent men fought back, pressing legislatures for programs that met their needs. Western farmers, often in debt, urged the states to print more paper money and to pass laws lowering taxes and postponing the foreclosure of mortgages. Artisans opposed merchants by calling for protection from low-priced foreign imports that competed with the goods they produced. They set themselves against farmers as well by demanding price regulation of the farm products they consumed. In the continuing struggle, the state legislatures became the battleground of competing economic factions, each bent on gaining its own particular advantage.

As the 1780s wore on, conflicts mounted. As long as the individual states remained sovereign, the Confederation was crippled—unable to conduct foreign affairs effectively, unable to set coherent economic policy, unable to deal with

discontent in the West. Equally dismaying was the discovery that many Americans, instead of being selflessly concerned for the public good, selfishly pursued their private interests.

The war for independence transformed not only America's government and econ- **Republican Society**
omy but also its society and culture. Inspired by the Declaration's ideal of equality, some Americans rejected the subordinate position assigned to them under the old colonial order. Westerners, newly wealthy entrepreneurs, urban artisans, and women all claimed greater freedom, power, and recognition. The authority of the traditional leaders of government, society, and the family came under a new scrutiny; the impulse to defer to social superiors became less automatic. The new assertiveness demonstrated how deeply egalitarian assumptions were taking root in American culture.

The New Men of the Revolution

The Revolution gave rise to a new sense of social identity and a new set of ambitions among several groups of men who had once accepted a humbler status. The more democratic society of the frontier emboldened westerners to believe themselves the equals of easterners. As one Kentuckian explained to James Madison, the western migrants "must make a very different mass from one which is composed of men born and raised on the same spot. . . . They see none about them to whom or to whose families they have been accustomed to think themselves inferior."

Gilbert Stuart's *The Skater* captures one American gentleman's characteristic sense of mastery over himself, nature, and society. But the Revolution instilled in many people of humbler status a new sense of pride and potential. Typical of such groups were New York's Society of Pewterers, whose banner proclaimed them "solid and pure"—the equals of those gentlemen who prided themselves on being society's "natural leaders."

The war also offered opportunities to aspiring entrepreneurs everywhere, and often they were not the same men who had prospered before the war. At a stroke, independence swept away the political prominence of loyalists, whose ranks included an especially high number of government officials, large landowners, and major merchants. And while loyalists found their properties confiscated by revolutionary governments, other Americans grew rich. Many northern merchants gained newfound wealth from privateering or military contracts. Commercial farmers in the mid-Atlantic states prospered from the high food prices caused by wartime scarcity and army demand.

The Revolution effected no dramatic redistribution of wealth. Indeed, the gap between rich and poor increased during the 1780s. But those families newly enriched by the Revolution came to demand and receive greater social recognition and political influence. The republican ideal of "an aristocracy of merit" justified their ambitions.

Urban artisans

City craftworkers pushed for recognition too. Their experience in organizing boycotts against British goods during the imperial crisis gave artisans a greater taste of politics. With the Revolution accomplished, they clamored for men of their own kind to represent them in government. Their assertiveness came as a rude shock to gentlemen like South Carolina's William Henry Drayton, who balked at sharing power with men "who never were in a way to study" anything except "how to cut up a beast in the market to the best advantage, to cobble an old shoe in the neatest manner, or to build a necessary house."

While master craftworkers competed for political office, the laborers who worked for them also exhibited a new sense of independence. As domestic manufacturing expanded after the Revolution, journeymen and even apprentices moved out of their masters' households and away from the supervision of their masters. Recognizing that their interests were often distinct from those of masters, journeymen formed new organizations to secure higher wages. Between 1786 and 1816 skilled urban laborers organized the first major strikes in American history.

The New Women of the Revolution

Not long after the fighting with Britain had broken out, Margaret Livingston of New York wrote to her sister Catherine, "You know that our Sex are doomed to be obedient in every stage of life so that we shant be great gainers by this contest." By war's end, however, Eliza Wilkinson from rural South Carolina was complaining boldly to a woman friend: "The men say we have no business with political matters . . . it's not our sphere. . . . [But] I won't have it thought that because we are the weaker Sex (as to bodily strength my dear) we are Capable of nothing more, than minding the Dairy . . . surely we may have enough sense to give our Opinions."

What separated Margaret Livingston's resignation from Eliza Wilkinson's assertion of personal worth and independence was the Revolution. Eliza Wilkinson had managed her parents' plantation during the war and defended it from British marauders. Other women discovered similar reserves of skill and resourcefulness. When soldiers returned home, some were surprised to find their wives and daughters, who had been running family farms and businesses, less submissive and more self-confident.

Exclusion of women from politics

But American men had not fought a revolution for the equality of American women. In fact, male revolutionaries gave no thought whatsoever to the role of women in the new nation, assuming that those of the "weaker sex" were incapable of making informed and independent political decisions. Most women of the revolutionary generation agreed that the proper female domain was the home, not the public arena of politics. Still, the currents of the Revolution occasionally left gaps that allowed women to display their keen political interests. When a loosely worded provision in the New Jersey state constitution gave the vote to "all free inhabitants" owning a specified amount of property, white widows and single women went to the polls. Only in 1807 did the state legislature close the loophole.

Mary Wollstonecraft's *Vindication*

In the wake of the Revolution there also appeared in England a book that would become a classic text of modern feminism, Mary Wollstonecraft's *A Vindication of the Rights of Women* (1792). Attracting a wide, if not widely approving, readership in America as well, it called not only for laws to guarantee women civil and political equality but also for educational reforms to ensure their social and economic equality.

Like many young, single English women with more wit than fortune, Wollstonecraft started her working life as a governess and a school's headmistress. Then she turned to writing for her livelihood, producing book reviews, translations, a novel, and a treatise on women's education before dashing off *Vindication* in six short months. She charged that men deliberately conspired to keep women in "a state of perpetual childhood" by giving them inferior, frivolous educations. That encouraged young girls to fixate on fashion and flirtation and made them "only anxious to inspire love, when they ought to cherish a nobler ambition, and by their abilities and virtues exact respect." Girls, she proposed, should receive the same education as boys, including training that would prepare them for careers in medicine, politics, and business. No woman should have to pin her hopes for

Contrast the portrait of Mary Wollstonecraft rendered just before her death in 1797 with a strikingly masculinized rendering in a book published in the United States in 1809, which placed her in the company of "actresses, adventurers, authoresses, fortunetellers, gipsies, dwarfs, swindlers, and vagrants."

financial security on making a good marriage, Wollstonecraft argued. On the contrary, well-educated and resourceful women capable of supporting themselves would make the best wives and mothers, assets to the family and the nation.

Vindication might have been written in gunpowder rather than ink, given the reaction it aroused on both sides of the Atlantic. Even so, Wollstonecraft at first won many defenders among both men and women, who sometimes publicly and more often privately expressed their agreement with her views. This favorable reception ended abruptly after her death in childbirth in 1797, when a memoir written by her husband revealed that she had lived out of wedlock with him—and before him, with another lover. Even so, Wollstonecraft's views found some admirers in America. Among them were Aaron Burr, the future vice president, who dubbed *Vindication* "a work of genius" and promised to read it aloud to his wife, and the Philadelphia Quaker Elizabeth Drinker, who confided to her diary that "In very many of her sentiments, she . . . *speaks my mind.*"

Republican Motherhood and Education

Wollstonecraft's ideas also lent support to the leading educational reformers in the revolutionary generation. Her sentiments echo in the writings of Judith Sargent Murray, a New Englander who urged the cultivation of women's minds to encourage self-respect and celebrated "excellency in our sex." Her fellow reformer, the Philadelphian Benjamin Rush, agreed that only educated and independent-minded women could raise the informed and self-reliant citizens that a republican government required. Their view, known as "republican motherhood," contributed to the most dramatic change in the lives of women after the war—the spread of female literacy.

Improved schooling and literacy rates

Between 1780 and 1830 the number of American colleges and secondary academies rose dramatically, and some of these new institutions were devoted to educating women. Not only did the number of schools for women increase, but these schools also offered a solid academic curriculum. By 1850—for the first time in American history—there were as many literate women as there were men. To counter popular prejudices, the defenders of female education contended that schooling for women would produce the ideal republican mother.

Women's legal status

The Revolution also prompted some states to reform their marriage laws, making divorce somewhat easier, although it remained extremely rare. But while women won greater freedom to divorce, courts became less concerned with enforcing a widow's traditional legal claim to one-third of her spouse's real estate. And married women still could not sue or be sued, make wills or contracts, or buy and sell property. Any wages that they earned went to their husbands; so did all personal property that wives brought into a marriage; so did the rents and profits of any real estate they owned. Despite the high ideals of republican motherhood, most women remained confined to the domestic sphere of the home and deprived of the most basic legal and political rights.

The Attack on Aristocracy

Why wasn't the American Revolution more revolutionary? Independence secured the full political equality of white men who owned property, but women were still deprived of political rights, African Americans of human rights. Why did the revolutionaries stop short of extending equality to the most unequal groups in American society—and with so little sense that they were being inconsistent?

In part, the lack of concern was rooted in republican ideas themselves. Republican ideology viewed property as the key to independence and power. Lacking property, women and black Americans were easily consigned to the custody of husbands and masters. Then, too, prejudice played its part: the perception of women and blacks as naturally inferior beings.

Republican view of equality

But revolutionary leaders also failed to press for greater equality because they conceived their crusade in terms of eliminating the evils of a European past dominated by kings and aristocrats. They believed that the great obstacle to equality was monarchy—kings and queens who bestowed hereditary honors and political office on favored individuals and granted legal privileges and monopolies to favored churches and businesses. These artificial inequalities posed the real threat to liberty, most republicans concluded. In other words, the men of the Revolution were intent on attaining equality by leveling off the top of society. It did not occur to most republicans that the cause of equality could also be served by raising up the bottom—by attacking the laws and prejudices that kept African Americans enslaved and women dependent.

The most significant reform of the republican campaign against artificial privilege was the dismantling of state-supported churches. Most states had a religious establishment. In New York and the South, it was the Anglican church; in New England, the Congregational church. Since the 1740s, dissenters who did not worship at state churches had protested laws that taxed all citizens to support the clergy of established denominations. After the Revolution dissenters argued that equality required ending such privileges. As more dissenters became voters, state legislators gradually abolished state support for Anglican and Congregational churches.

Disestablishment

Not only in religious life but in all aspects of their culture, Americans rejected inequalities associated with a monarchical past. In that spirit reformers attacked the Society of Cincinnati, a group organized by former officers of the Continental Army in 1783. The society, which was merely a social club for veterans, was forced to disband for its policy of passing on its membership rights to eldest sons. In this way, critics charged, the Cincinnati was creating artificial distinctions and perpetuating a hereditary warrior nobility.

Society of Cincinnati

Today, many of the republican efforts at reform seem misdirected. While only a handful of revolutionaries worked for the education of women and the emancipation of slaves, enormous zeal went into fighting threats from a monarchical past that had never existed in America. Yet the threat from kings and aristocrats was real to the revolutionaries—and indeed remained real in many parts of Europe. Their determination to sweep away every shred of formal privilege ensured that these forms of inequality never took root in America. And if eighteenth-century Americans did not extend equality to women and racial minorities, it was a failure that they shared with later revolutionary movements that promised more.

From Confederation to Constitutions

While Americans in many walks of life sought to realize the republican commitment to equality, leaders in Congress wrestled with the problem of preserving the nation itself. With the new republic slowly rending itself to pieces, some political leaders concluded that neither the Confederation nor the state legislatures were able to remedy the basic difficulties facing the nation. But how could the states be convinced to surrender their sovereign powers? The answer came in the wake of two events—one foreign, one domestic—that lent momentum to the cause of strengthening the central government.

Daily Lives

FOOD/DRINK/ DRUGS

The Spirits of Independence

If God had intended man to drink water, Ben Franklin remarked, he would not have made him with an elbow capable of raising a wine-glass. Colonials from all across America agreed with Franklin on the virtues of drink. The ruddy glow of colonial cheeks (still visible in the portraits hung in museums) reflected not only good health and ardent republican virtue but also substantial daily doses of alcohol. Colonials consumed about twice as much alcohol as Americans today, though in different forms. Beer was not popular, the only sort consumed being a weak, homemade "small beer" containing about one percent alcohol. Only the wealthy, like Franklin, could afford imported Madeira and port wines. On the other hand, the produce of apple orchards allowed Americans northward from Virginia to drink their fill of hard cider. Far and away the most popular distilled liquor was rum, a potent 90 proof beverage (45 percent alcohol) that they sipped straight or mixed with water and sugar to make "toddies."

Special occasions were particularly convivial. The liquor flowed freely at ministerial ordinations in New England towns, at court days in the South, at house-raisings, corn-huskings, and quilting bees on the frontier, and at weddings, elections, and militia musters everywhere in the colonies. But Americans did not confine their drinking to occasional celebrations. Some, like John Adams, started the day with a tankard of hard cider. Others, merchants and craftworkers, broke the boredom of late mornings and early afternoons by sending the youngest apprentice in the shop out for spirits. Laborers in seaport docks and shipyards, fishermen and sailors at sea, and farm workers in the countryside commonly received a daily allotment of liquor as part of their wages. And at night, men of every class enjoyed a solitary glass at home or a sociable one at a local tavern.

Socialization into the drinking culture started in childhood. Parents permitted youngsters to sip the sweet dregs of a glass of rum, and when young men entered their teens, they joined their fathers at the tavern. Women drank too, although more often at home, and they sometimes explained their use of distilled liquor as serving some "medicinal" purpose. Slaves got around laws restricting their consumption of alcohol by stealing from masters or bartering with white peddlers.

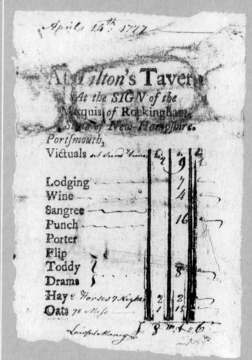

This tavern bill from New Hampshire indicates that in 1777 whiskey was still too rare to be listed.

The Jay-Gardoqui Treaty

The international episode that threatened to leave the Confederation in shambles was a debate over a proposed treaty with Spain. In 1785 southwesterners still could not legally navigate the Mississippi and were still threatening to secede from the union and annex their territory to Spain's American empire. To shore up southwestern loyalties, Congress instructed its secretary of foreign affairs, John Jay, to negotiate an agreement with Spain preserving American rights to navigate on the Mississippi River. But the Spanish emissary, Don Diego de Gardoqui, sweet-talked Jay into accepting a treaty by which the United States would give up all rights to the Mississippi for 25 years. In return, Spain agreed to grant trading privileges to American merchants.

Jay, a New Yorker, knew more than a few northern merchants who were eager to open new markets. But when the proposed treaty became public knowledge,

Until the middle of the eighteenth century, most colonials (and Europeans) considered spirits a source of physical strength and an essential supplement to their diet, as well as a remedy for colds, fevers, snakebite, and, ironically, depression. They did not condone public drunkenness, but they saw nothing amiss in the regular use of alcohol or even in occasional intoxication.

The easy acceptance of drinking prevailed for most of the colonial period for two reasons. First, until about the 1760s, frequent access to the strongest spirits, rum, lay beyond the means of most Americans. Second, the leaders of local communities were able to oversee most public drinking and to keep disorder to a minimum. But by the middle of the eighteenth century, some Americans developed misgivings about the drinking culture. Increased production and importation led the price of rum to drop so sharply that an ordinary laborer could earn enough in a day to stay "drunk as a lord" for the rest of the week. Taverns proliferated, making it impossible for community leaders to monitor the popular consumption of alcohol.

The new concern that the drinking of rum fostered crime and social disruption prompted the first steps toward temperance reform. By the 1770s, Quakers like Anthony Benezet were urging that alcohol, like slavery, was an "unrepublican vice," for both forms of bondage deprived their victims of liberty and the capacity for rationality and self-control. Some members of the medical profession, most notably Benjamin Rush, also joined early temperance ranks.

Although the advocates of more moderate consumption won support among some educated elites, most Americans altered their drinking habits by consuming *more* hard liquor. Rum, the liquor of choice before the Revolution, lost much of its ground to a new rival, whiskey. Whiskey was democratic and cheap, for it could be made in the lowliest backcountry farmhouse. It was patriotic, since it did not depend on imports from the Caribbean. Gradually these "spirits of independence" supplanted rum not only in the frontier West but also in the urban East. Consumption of alcohol was on a steady rise that would finally result, half a century after the Revolution, in louder calls for temperance reform.

southwesterners denounced it as nothing short of betrayal. The treaty was never ratified, but the hostility stirred up during the debate revealed the strength of sectional feelings.

Shays's Rebellion

On the heels of this humiliation by Spain came an internal conflict that challenged the notion that individual states could maintain order in their own territories. The trouble erupted in western Massachusetts, where many small farmers were close to ruin. By 1786 farm wages and prices had fallen sharply and farmers were selling little produce. Yet they still had to pay mortgages on their farms and other debts. In 1786 the lower house of the Massachusetts legislature obliged the farmers with a package of relief measures. But creditors in eastern Massachusetts, determined to safeguard their own investments, persuaded the upper house to defeat the measures.

In the summer of 1786 western farmers responded, demanding that the upper house of the legislature be abolished and that the relief measures go into effect. That autumn 2000 farmers rose in armed rebellion, led by Captain Daniel Shays, a veteran of the Revolution. They closed the county courts to halt creditors from foreclosing on their farms and marched on the federal arsenal at Springfield. The state militia quelled the uprising by February 1787, but the insurrection left many in Massachusetts and the rest of the country thoroughly shaken.

Response to agrarian unrest

Alarmed conservatives saw Shays's Rebellion as the consequence of radical democracy. "The natural effects of pure democracy are already produced among us," lamented one republican gentleman; "it is a war against virtue, talents, and property carried on by the dregs and scum of mankind." He was wrong. The rebels with Daniel Shays were no impoverished rabble. They were reputable members of western communities who wanted their property protected and believed that government existed to provide that protection. The Massachusetts state legislature had been unable to safeguard the property of farmers from the inroads of recession or to protect the property of creditors from the armed debtors who closed the courts. It had failed, in other words, to fulfill the most basic aim of republican government.

What if such violent tactics spread? Other states with discontented debtors feared what the example of western Massachusetts might mean for the future of the Confederation itself. But by 1786 Shays's Rebellion supplied only the sharpest jolt to a movement for reform that was already under way. Even before the rebellion, a group of Virginians had proposed a meeting of the states to adopt a uniform system of commercial regulations. Once assembled at Annapolis in September 1786, the delegates from five states agreed to a more ambitious undertaking. They called for a second, broader meeting in Philadelphia, which Congress approved, for the "express purpose of revising the Articles of Confederation."

Framing a Federal Constitution

It was the wettest spring anyone could remember. The 55 men who traveled over muddy roads to Philadelphia in May 1787 arrived drenched and bespattered. Fortunately, most of the travelers were men in their thirties and forties, young enough to survive a good soaking. Since most were gentlemen of some means—planters, merchants, and lawyers with powdered wigs and prosperous paunches—they could recover from the rigors of their journey in the best accommodations offered by America's largest city.

The delegates came from all the states except Rhode Island. The rest of New England supplied shrewd backroom politicians—Roger Sherman and Oliver Ellsworth from Connecticut and Rufus King and Elbridge Gerry, Massachusetts men who had learned a trick or two from Sam Adams. The middle states marshaled much of the intellectual might: two Philadelphia lawyers, John Dickinson and James Wilson; one Philadelphia financier, Robert Morris; and the aristocratic Gouverneur Morris. From New York there was Alexander Hamilton, the mercurial and ambitious young protégé of Washington. South Carolina provided fiery orators Charles Pinckney and John Rutledge.

It was "an assembly of the demi-gods," gushed Thomas Jefferson, who, along with John Adams, was serving as a diplomat in Europe when the convention met. In fact, the only delegate who looked even remotely divine was the convention's presiding deity. Towering a full half foot taller than most of his colleagues, George Washington displayed his usual self-possession from a chair elevated on the speaker's platform in the Pennsylvania State House, where the delegates met. At first glance, the delegate of least commanding presence was Washington's fellow Virginian, James Madison. Short and slightly built, the 36-year-old Madison had no profession except hypochondria; he read a great deal and dressed in black. But he was an astute politician and a brilliant political thinker who, more than anyone else, shaped the framing of the federal Constitution.

The delegates from 12 different states had two things in common. They were all men of considerable political experience, and they all recognized the need for a stronger national union. So when the Virginia delegation introduced Madison's outline for a new central government, the convention was ready to listen.

The Virginia and New Jersey Plans

What Madison had in mind was a truly national republic, not a confederation of independent states. His "Virginia Plan" proposed a central government with three branches: legislative, executive, and judicial. Furthermore, the legislative branch, Congress, would possess the power to veto all state legislation. In place of the Confederation's single assembly, Madison substituted a bicameral legislature, with a lower house elected directly by the people and an upper house chosen by the lower, from nominations made by state legislatures. Representatives to both houses would be apportioned according to population—a change from practice under the Articles, in which each state had a single vote in Congress. Madison also revised the structure of government that had existed under the Articles by adding an executive, who would be elected by Congress, and an independent federal judiciary.

James Madison, the scholar and statesman whose ideas and political skill shaped the Constitution

After two weeks of debate over the Virginia Plan, William Paterson, a lawyer from New Jersey, presented a less radical counterproposal. Although his "New Jersey Plan" increased Congress's power to tax and to regulate trade, it kept the national government as a unicameral assembly, with each state receiving one vote in Congress under the policy of equal representation. The delegates took just four days to reject Paterson's plan. Most endorsed Madison's design for a stronger central government.

Paterson's New Jersey Plan

Even so, the issue of apportioning representation continued to divide the delegates. While smaller states pressed for each state having an equal vote in Congress, larger states backed Madison's provision for basing representation on population. Underlying the dispute over representation was an even deeper rivalry between southern and northern states. While northern and southern populations were nearly equal in the 1780s, and the South's population was growing more rapidly, the northern states were more numerous. Giving the states equal votes would put the South at a disadvantage. Southerners feared being outvoted in Congress by the northern states and felt that only proportional representation would protect the interests of their section.

That division turned into a deadlock as the wet spring burned off into a blazing summer. Delegates suffered the daily torture of staring at a large sun painted on the speaker's chair occupied by Washington. The stifling heat was made even worse because the windows remained shut to keep any news of the proceedings from drifting out into the Philadelphia streets.

The Deadlock Broken

Finally, as the heat wave broke, so did the political stalemate. On July 2 a committee headed by Benjamin Franklin suggested a compromise. States would be equally represented in the upper house of Congress, each state legislature appointing two senators to six-year terms. That satisfied the smaller states. In the lower

Compromise over representation

house of Congress, which alone could initiate money bills, representation was to be apportioned according to population. Every 30,000 inhabitants would elect one representative for a two-year term. A slave was to count as three-fifths of a free person in the calculation of population, and the slave trade was to continue until 1808. That satisfied the larger states and the South.

By the end of August the convention was prepared to approve the final draft of the Constitution. The delegates agreed that the executive, now called the president, would be chosen every four years. Direct election seemed out of the question—after all, how could citizens in South Carolina know anything about a presidential candidate who happened to live in distant Massachusetts, or vice versa? But if voters instead chose presidential electors, those eminent men would likely have been involved in national politics, have known the candidates personally, and be prepared to vote wisely. Thus the Electoral College was established, with each state's total number of senators and representatives determining its share of electoral votes.

An array of other powers ensured that the executive would remain independent and strong. He would have command over the armed forces, authority to conduct diplomatic relations, responsibility to nominate judges and officials in the executive branch, and the power to veto congressional legislation. Just as the executive branch was made independent, so too the federal judiciary was separated from the other two branches of government. Madison believed that this clear separation of powers was essential to a balanced republican government.

Madison's only real defeat came when the convention refused to give Congress veto power over state legislation. Still, the new bicameral national legislature enjoyed much broader authority than Congress had under the Confederation, including the power to tax and to regulate commerce. The Constitution also limited the powers of state legislatures, prohibiting them from levying duties on trade, coining money or issuing paper currency, and conducting foreign relations. The Constitution and the acts passed by Congress were declared the supreme law of the land, taking precedence over any legislation passed by the states. And changing the Constitution would not be easy. Amendments could be proposed only by a two-thirds vote of both houses of Congress or in a convention requested by two-thirds of the state legislatures. Ratification of amendments required approval by three-quarters of the states.

On September 17, 1787, thirty-nine of the forty-two delegates remaining in Philadelphia signed the Constitution. It was fortunate that the signatories included

Electoral College

Separation of powers

Amending the Constitution

As the Constitution is signed, Benjamin Franklin (second from left) looks on; Washington presides. "The business being closed," Washington wrote, "the members adjourned to the City Tavern, dined together and took cordial leave of each other."

so many lawyers, for the summer's proceedings had been of such dubious legality that many skilled attorneys would be needed to make them seem otherwise. Charged only to revise the Articles, the delegates had instead written a completely new frame of government. And to speed up ratification, the convention decided that the Constitution would go into effect after only nine states had approved it, overlooking the fact that even a revision of the Articles would have required the assent of all state legislatures. They further declared that the people themselves— not the state legislatures—would pass judgment on the Constitution in special ratifying conventions. To serve final notice that the new central government was a republic of the people and not merely another confederation of states, Gouverneur Morris of Pennsylvania hit on a happy turn of phrase to introduce the Constitution. "We the People," the document begins, "in Order to form a more perfect Union . . ."

Ratification

With grave misgivings on the part of many, the states called for conventions to decide whether to ratify the new Constitution. Those Americans with the gravest misgivings—the Anti-Federalists as they came to be called—voiced familiar republican fears. Older and less cosmopolitan than their Federalist opponents, the Anti-Federalists drew upon their memories of the struggle with England to frame their criticisms of the Constitution. Expanding the power of the central government at the expense of the states, they warned, would lead to corrupt and arbitrary rule by new aristocrats. Extending a republic over a large territory, they cautioned, would separate national legislators from the interests and close oversight of their constituents.

The Anti-Federalists

Madison responded to these objections in *The Federalist Papers,* a series of 85 essays written with Alexander Hamilton and John Jay during the winter of 1787–1788. He countered Anti-Federalist concerns over the centralization of power by pointing out that each separate branch of the national government would keep the others within the limits of their legal authority. That mechanism of checks and balances would prevent the executive from oppressing the people while preventing the people from oppressing themselves.

The Federalist Papers

To answer Anti-Federalist objections to a national republic, Madison drew on the ideas of an English philosopher, David Hume. In his famous tenth essay in *The Federalist Papers,* Madison argued that in a great republic, "the Society becomes broken into a greater variety of interests, of pursuits, of passions, which check each other." The larger the territory, the more likely it was to contain multiple political interests and parties, so that no single faction could dominate. Instead, each would cancel out the others.

The one Anti-Federalist criticism Madison could not get around was the absence of a national bill of rights. Opponents insisted on an explicit statement of rights to secure the freedoms of individuals and minorities from being violated by the federal government. Madison finally promised to place a bill of rights before Congress immediately after the Constitution was ratified.

Bill of Rights

Throughout the early months of 1788, Anti-Federalists continued their opposition. But they lacked the articulate and influential leadership that rallied behind the Constitution and commanded greater access to the public press. In the end, too, Anti-Federalist fears of centralized power proved less compelling than Federalist prophecies of the chaos that would follow if the Constitution was not adopted.

Ratification of the Constitution

State	Date	Vote For	Vote Against
Delaware	December 8, 1787	30	9
Pennsylvania	December 12, 1787	46	23
New Jersey	December 18, 1787	38	0
Georgia	January 2, 1788	26	0
Connecticut	January 9, 1788	128	40
Massachusetts	February 16, 1788	187	168
Maryland	April 26, 1788	63	11
South Carolina	May 23, 1788	149	73
New Hampshire	June 21, 1788	57	47
Virginia	June 25, 1788	89	79
New York	July 26, 1788	30	27
North Carolina	November 21, 1789	194	77
Rhode Island	May 29, 1790	34	32

By the end of July 1788 all but two states had voted in favor of ratification. The last holdout—Rhode Island, to no one's surprise—finally came aboard in May 1790, after Madison had carried through on his pledge to submit a bill of rights to the new Congress. Indeed, these 10 amendments proved to be the Anti-Federalists' most impressive legacy.

Changing Revolutionary Ideals

Within the life span of a single generation, Americans had declared their independence twice. In many ways the political freedom claimed from Britain in 1776 was less remarkable than the intellectual freedom that Americans achieved by agreeing to the Constitution. The Constitution represented both a triumph of imagination and common sense and a rejection of some older, long-cherished republican beliefs.

Rejected republican beliefs

Americans thought long and hard before changing their minds, but many did. Committed at first to limiting executive power by making legislatures supreme, they at last ratified a constitution that provided for an independent executive and a balanced government. Committed at first to preserving the sovereignty of the states, they at last established a national government with authority independent of the states. Committed at first to the proposition that a national republic was impossible, they at last created an impossibility that still endures.

Behavior shaped by interest rather than virtue

What, then, became of the last tenet of the old republican creed—the belief that civic virtue would sustain popular liberty? The hard lessons of the war and the crises of the 1780s withered confidence in the capacity of Americans to sacrifice their private interests for the public welfare. Many came to share Washington's sober view that "the few . . . who act upon Principles of disinterestedness are, comparatively speaking, no more than a drop in the Ocean." The Constitution reflected the new recognition that interest rather than virtue shaped the behavior of most people most of the time and that the clash of diverse interest groups would remain a constant of public life.

Yet Madison and many other Federalists did not believe that the competition between private interests would somehow result in policies fostering public welfare. That goal would be met instead by the new national government acting as "a disinterested and dispassionate umpire in disputes between different passions and interests in the State." The Federalists looked to the national government to fulfill that role because they trusted that a large republic, with its millions of citizens, would yield more of that scarce resource—disinterested gentlemen dedicated to serving the public good. Such gentlemen, in Madison's words, "whose enlightened views and virtuous sentiments render them superior to local prejudices," would fill the small number of national offices.

Not all the old revolutionaries agreed. Anti-Federalists drawn from the ranks of ordinary Americans still believed that common people were more virtuous and gentlemen more interested than the Federalists allowed. "These lawyers and men of learning, and moneyed men, that talk so finely," complained one Anti-Federalist, would "get all the power and all of the money into their own hands, and then they will swallow up all us little folks." Instead of being dominated by enlightened gentlemen, the national government should be composed of representatives from every social class and occupational group.

The narrow majorities by which the Constitution was ratified reflected the continuing influence of such sentiments, as well as fear that the states were surrendering too much power. That fear made Patrick Henry so ardent an Anti-Federalist that he refused to attend the Constitutional Convention in 1787, saying that he "smelt a rat." "I am not a Virginian, but an American," Henry had once declared. Most likely he was lying. Or perhaps Patrick Henry, a southerner and a slaveholder, could see his way clear to being an "American" only as long as sovereignty remained firmly in the hands of the individual states. Henry's convictions, 70 years hence, would rise again to haunt the Union.

chapter summary

Leading Americans would give more thought to federalism, the organization of a United States, as the events of the postrevolutionary period revealed the weaknesses of the state and national governments.

- For a decade after independence, the revolutionaries were less committed to creating a single national republic than to organizing 13 separate state republics, each dominated by popularly elected legislatures.

- The Articles of Confederation provided for a government by a national legislature but left the crucial power of the purse, as well as all final power to make and execute laws, entirely to the states.

- Many conflicts in the new republic were occasioned by westward expansion, which created both international difficulties with Britain and Spain and internal tensions over the democratization of state legislatures.

- In the wake of the Revolution, ordinary Americans struggled to define republican society; workers began to organize, some women claimed a right to greater political, legal, and educational opportunities, and religious dissenters called for disestablishment.

- In the mid-1780s the political crisis of the Confederation came to a head, prompted by the controversy over the Jay-Gardoqui Treaty and Shays's Rebellion.

- The Constitutional Convention of 1787 produced an entirely new frame of government that established a truly national republic and provided for a separation of powers among a judiciary, a bicameral legislature, and a strong executive.

- The Anti-Federalists, opponents of the Constitution, softened their objections when promised a bill of rights after ratification, which was accomplished by 1789.

interactive learning

The Primary Source Investigator CD-ROM offers the following materials related to this chapter:

- A short documentary movie on free black sailors (D4)

- A collection of primary sources allowing exploration of the founding of the United States, including the Northwest Ordinance, several arguments from the Federalist Papers, and the Virginia Constitution. Other sources include paintings illustrating key moments in the founding of the nation, and the originals of America's most important founding documents, including the Constitution and the Declaration of Independence. Other documents explore the effects of the Revolution on Native Americans and western lands.

additional reading

Gordon Wood's two books, *The Creation of the American Republic* (1969) and *The Radicalism of the American Revolution* (1992), tell a compelling story about the transformation of American society, culture, and politics in the latter half of the eighteenth century. Forrest MacDonald's accounts of the Confederation period and the Constitution, *E Pluribus Unum* (1965) and *Novus Ordo Seclorum* (1985), are also excellent, as is Linda Kerber's study of the relevance of republicanism for American women, *Women of the Republic* (1980). The liveliest account of the framing of the Constitution is still Clinton Rossiter, *1787: The Grand Convention* (1973), while the best single introduction to the Anti-Federalists remains Cecilia Kenyon's "Men of Little Faith: The Anti-Federalists and the Nature of Representative Government," *William and Mary Quarterly,* 12 (1955).

Historians are developing a new and deeper appreciation for the ways in which the Revolutionary era transformed society and politics in the early republic, particularly in the North. For a vivid sense of how that change affected a single community in western Massachusetts, see John Brooke, *The Heart of the Commonwealth* (1991), and, for a fascinating tale of how the Revolution made one ordinary man's life extraordinary, see Alan Taylor, *William Cooper's Town* (1995). Probably the best single account of how the Revolution's legacy affected one African American community in the North is Shane White, *Somewhat More Independent* (1991). For a fuller list of readings, see the Bibliography at www.mhhe.com/davidsonnation5.

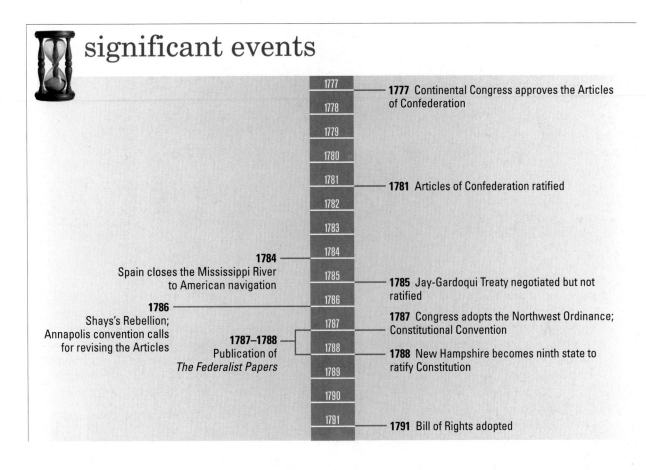

significant events

1777 Continental Congress approves the Articles of Confederation

1781 Articles of Confederation ratified

1784 Spain closes the Mississippi River to American navigation

1785 Jay-Gardoqui Treaty negotiated but not ratified

1786 Shays's Rebellion; Annapolis convention calls for revising the Articles

1787 Congress adopts the Northwest Ordinance; Constitutional Convention

1787–1788 Publication of *The Federalist Papers*

1788 New Hampshire becomes ninth state to ratify Constitution

1791 Bill of Rights adopted

White and Black Southerners Worshiping Together

During the 50 years before 1800, evangelicals introduced southerners to new ways of being religious. Those attending their worship services were men and women drawn into the earliest southern Baptist, Methodist, and Presbyterian churches by the First Great Awakening and other local revivals that followed in its wake. Some of these early services were held in private homes, others in crudely constructed churches, and still others in open fields. In such settings, evangelical preachers stressed the importance of being "reborn" by faith in Jesus Christ—and some southerners responded. They wept and confessed their sins; they encouraged one another with hopeful words and warm embraces. Those who came to such gatherings engaged in the most intimate kind of sharing and self-revelation.

But what made these services even more extraordinary is that some who participated were white, and some were black. These religious fellowships were truly biracial, and so they remained until after the

Civil War. That remarkable fact has intrigued historians. Evangelical churches were one of the few southern institutions that brought blacks and whites together rather than keeping them apart. How did members behave toward each other daily? Were born-again converts from both races treated equally? How was authority within such churches distributed among black and white members?

The questions are tantalizing, but the answers by no means easy to come by. Some letters and diaries survive from the last half of the eighteenth century, among them the daily journals and correspondence of ministers. A few preachers even published autobiographies of their experiences. But even more valuable information can be gathered from what might seem at first a rather drab source. There are scores of church records dating from this period, most of them kept by Virginia Baptists. The members of each Baptist church elected a clerk, always a white male "brother," whose duty it was to record all the business transacted at their monthly meetings, often in a ledger-sized bound volume called the "church book." Church books provide an insight into relations between whites and blacks in part because their clerks are *not* consciously trying to write about race relations. They are simply recording the everyday business of churches, week in, week out.

Sometimes practical concerns dominated the meeting. Should the church building be repaired? Who among the brethren will be permitted to preach? (Many Baptist churches boasted several preachers besides the pastor.) On other occasions, members debated about what the Bible taught was the holiest way to govern their churches. But at most meetings, members fixed their attention on admitting new converts to their fellowship and "disciplining" older members suspected of sexual misconduct or theft, slander or swearing, drinking or fighting. Church clerks duly noted all those accepted as new members, as well as the names of wayward brothers and sisters—and whether they were merely scolded for their faults or expelled.

Such records offer the most direct and vivid sense of African Americans' presence and participation in early evangelical churches. First, they show that blacks made up a substantial minority—perhaps one-fifth to one-quarter—of the members in most churches. In a few, they constituted a majority. Many churches, too, authorized at least one African American brother to preach, sometimes permitting him that "liberty" only among other blacks but in other instances allowing him to address racially mixed gatherings. There were even a few predominantly white churches in early Virginia that black preachers served as pastors.

In some churches, too, black men and, more rarely, black women were permitted to vote in meetings; and in all, African American members could participate in deliberations and give testimony in discipline cases. Indeed, there are several instances of masters being disciplined after slave members complained of being abused. Black members, too, were sometimes charged with wrongdoing,

but white men were far more likely than any other group of members to be hauled before the church for reported misdeeds. In short, evangelical churches like these Baptist fellowships were among the most racially egalitarian institutions in early southern society. They offered African Americans unusual opportunities to hold positions of authority, to voice their opinions, and to gain leverage over their masters.

Churchbook record: "Names of Black Members"

Note the treatment of black names.

Yet these same church records also reveal the limits of racial equality among early evangelicals. Like all evidence mined by historians, the sources yield data that are sometimes complex and contradictory.

Records of those meetings at which members discussed the mundane matter of church repair reveal, for example, that the Baptists segregated seating at public worship. African Americans were consigned to the least choice spots at the back of the church or in "sheds" attached to the side. Moreover, when white members filled every available seat, black members were ordered outdoors to listen from underneath open windows. The attitude that such practices convey—that whites regarded African Americans as "second-class" members—is also suggested by the manner in which many clerks recorded new church members. While they always entered the full names of white converts, new African American members were usually listed last and often collectively as "several Negroes."

Church discussions about who might preach also show a growing concern on the part of white members to restrict the activities of black preachers. Increasingly after 1750 those allowed that "liberty"

"Uncle Jack," shown in this 1849 engraving, preaches informally to a white congregation. He began his career as a minister in the 1790s and continued until 1832.

were given ever stricter instructions about whom they might preach to, at which times, and from what texts of the Bible. At meetings in which the rules of conducting church business were discussed, white members also began to express concern about whether African American members should be allowed to vote. Most churches revoked that right before the end of the eighteenth century. Tracing how churches dealt with black members accused of misbehavior suggests a similar anxiety among white members, which increased over time. Although African Americans continued to make up only a tiny minority of church members suspected of misbehavior, those convicted of wrongdoing were far more likely than white members to be expelled rather than to receive a milder punishment.

In other words, a closer inspection of church records suggests that white evangelicals drifted toward more racially restrictive policies over the latter half of the eighteenth century. Why? The numbers in the church books are suggestive. After the Revolution, increasing numbers of African Americans were entering Baptist (and other evangelical) churches. As the percentage of black members rose, white evangelicals feared that the "freedoms" given to black worshipers might detract from the church's ability to win converts among slaveholders.

Clearly, evangelicals were winning converts among African Americans. Yet other evidence suggests that black members were left unsatisfied by their treatment in white churches. The diaries and letters of white evangelicals reveal that many black members of biracial churches had also begun conducting their own separate devotions. Even by the 1790s, African American Christians were meeting nightly in the slave quarters to pray, sing, and hear the sermons of black preachers. Such "shadow churches" served as the crucible of Afro-Christianity, a melding of evangelical Protestant and West African religious traditions. John Antrobus's painting *Plantation Burial* (page 227, also on page 393) reflects the situation that prevailed by the mid–nineteenth century. Although blacks attended white services in greater numbers, their most vital worship often took place elsewhere. White masters and preachers were like the shadowy couple Antrobus painted on the right: divorced from the Christian worship of their slaves.

BIBLIOGRAPHY Historians disagree about the extent to which early evangelical churches were

egalitarian. The strongest arguments in favor are presented by Mechal Sobel, *The World They Made Together* (1987); the most forceful challenge to Sobel is Jewel Spangler, "Salvation Was Not Liberty: Baptists and Slavery in Revolutionary Virginia," *American Baptist Quarterly*, 13 (1994). Other studies that treat the dynamics of these early biracial churches and the experience of the first black southern evangelicals are Albert J. Raboteau, *Slave Religion* (1978), the best introduction to this subject; Sylvia R. Frey, *Water from the Rock* (1991), which usefully updates Raboteau; and, most recently, Christine Leigh Heyrman, *Southern Cross* (1997). The evolving views of race and slavery among early white evangelicals is thoughtfully analyzed in James Essig, *The Bonds of Wickedness* (1982), while the most eloquent descriptions of Afro-Christianity in the slave quarters appear in Eugene Genovese, *Roll, Jordan, Roll* (1972) and Lawrence Levine, *Black Culture and Black Consciousness* (1977).

Chapter 8

ne spring evening in 1794 General John Neville was riding home from Pittsburgh with his wife and granddaughter. While going up a hill his wife's saddle started to slip, so Neville dismounted to tighten the girth. As he adjusted the strap, he heard the clip-clop of approaching horses. A rider galloped up and in a gruff voice asked, "Are you Neville the excise officer?"

"Yes," Neville replied, without turning around.

"Then I must give you a whipping!" cried the rider as he leaped from his horse. He grabbed the startled Neville by the hair and lunged at his throat, and the two began tussling. Breaking free, Neville finally managed to knock the man down and subdue him. He recognized his assailant as Jacob Long, a local farmer. After Long fled, the badly shaken Neville resumed his journey.

John Neville was not accustomed to such treatment. As one of the wealthiest men in the area, Neville expected respect from those of lower social rank. And he had received it—at least he had until becoming embroiled in a controversy over the new "whiskey tax" on distilled spirits. In a frontier district like western Pennsylvania, farmers regularly distilled their grain into whiskey for barter and sale. Not surprisingly, the excise tax, passed by Congress in 1791, was notoriously unpopular. Still, Neville had accepted an appointment to be one of the tax's regional inspectors. For three years he had endured threats as he tried to enforce the law, but this roadside assault clearly indicated that popular hostility was rising.

The REPUBLIC LAUNCHED

1789–1801

preview • In 1789 Americans could be divided into those who were rural, largely self-sufficient farmers and those tied more closely to the world of commerce. Politics in the early republic was rooted in this fundamental social division. Hamilton's Federalists, active in the commercial markets, believed in order, hierarchy, and an active central government. Jefferson's Republicans, champions of the self-sufficient farmer, feared aristocracy and wealth and wanted a less active government.

As spring turned to summer, the grain ripened, and so did the people's anger. In mid-July, a federal marshal arrived to serve summonses to a number of farmer-distillers who had not paid taxes. One, William Miller, squinted at the paper and was amazed to find the government ordering him to set aside "all manner of business and excuses" and appear in court—hundreds of miles away in Philadelphia—in little more than a month. Even worse, the papers claimed he owed $250.

And there, next to this unknown federal marshal, stood the stiff-backed, unyielding John Neville.

"I felt myself mad with passion," recalled Miller. "I thought $250 would ruin me; and . . . I felt my blood boil at seeing General Neville along to pilot the sheriff to my very door." Meanwhile word of the marshal's presence brought 30 or 40 laborers swarming from a nearby field. Armed with muskets and pitchforks, they were both angry and well liquored. When a shot rang out, Neville and the marshal beat a hasty retreat.

Within hours, news of Neville's doings spread to a nearby militia company. Enraged by what they considered this latest trampling on individual liberty, the militia marched to Neville's estate, Bower Hill, the next morning. A battle ensued, and the general, aided by his slaves, beat back the attackers. A larger group,

Frontier farmers in Pennsylvania tar and feather a federal tax collector during the Whiskey Rebellion. The political violence of the 1790s led Americans to wonder whether the new government would succeed in uniting a socially diverse nation.

numbering 500 to 700, returned the following day to find Neville fled and his home garrisoned by a group of soldiers from nearby Fort Pitt. The mob burned down most of the outbuildings and, after the soldiers surrendered, torched Neville's well-furnished home.

Throughout the region that summer, marauding bands roamed the countryside, burning homes, banishing individuals, and attacking tax collectors and other enemies. To many citizens who learned of the disturbances, such echoes of the revolutionary 1760s and 1770s were deeply distressing. In the space of only 15 years, Americans had already overturned two governments: England's colonial administration and the Articles of Confederation. As the aged Benjamin Franklin remarked in 1788, although Americans were quite skilled at overthrowing governments, it remained to be seen whether they were any good at sustaining them. Now, Franklin's warning seemed prophetic.

Yet Federalists—supporters of the Constitution—had recognized from the beginning how risky it was to unite a territory as large as the United States' 890,000 square miles. Yankee merchants living along Boston wharves had economic interests and cultural traditions quite different from those of backcountry farmers who raised hogs, tended a few acres of corn, and distilled whiskey. Even among farmers, there was a world of difference between a South Carolina planter who shipped tons of rice to European markets and a New Hampshire family whose stony fields yielded barely enough to survive. Could the new government established by the Constitution provide a framework strong enough to unite such a socially diverse nation?

1789: A Social Portrait

When the Constitution went into effect, the United States stretched from the Atlantic Ocean to the Mississippi River. The first federal census, compiled in 1790, counted approximately 4 million people, divided about evenly between the northern and southern states. The Republic's population was overwhelmingly concentrated along the eastern seaboard. Only about 100,000 settlers lived beyond the Appalachians in the Tennessee and Kentucky territories, which were soon to become states. In limited parts of this region, commercial agriculture based on slavery had begun to take root. But full-scale operations could not develop in the trans-Appalachian West as long as Spain controlled the mouth of the Mississippi River. The area north of the Ohio River was virtually unsettled by whites.

Within the Republic's boundaries were two major racial groups that lacked effective political influence: African Americans and Indians. In 1790 black Americans numbered 750,000, almost one-fifth the total population. More than 90 percent lived in the southern states from Maryland to Georgia; most were slaves who worked on tobacco and rice plantations. But there were free blacks as well, their numbers increased by the ideals of the Revolution. Indeed, the free black population in 1790 was larger, relative to the total African American population, than it would be at any other time before the Civil War. The census did not count the number of Indians living east of the Mississippi. North of the Ohio, the powerful Miami Confederacy discouraged settlement, while to the south, five strong, well-organized tribes—the Creeks, Cherokees, Chickasaws, Choctaws, and Seminoles—dominated the region from the Appalachians to the Mississippi River.

Population growth   That situation would change, however, as the white population continued to double approximately every 22 years. Immigration contributed only a small part to this astonishing growth. On average, fewer than 10,000 Europeans arrived annually between 1790 and 1820. The primary cause was natural increase, since, on average, American white women gave birth to nearly eight children. As a consequence, the United States had an unusually youthful population: in 1790 almost half of all white Americans were under 16 years old.* The age at first marriage was about 25 for men, 24 for women; but it was significantly lower in newly settled areas (on average perhaps 21 for males and younger for females), which contributed to the high birthrate.

This youthful, growing population remained overwhelmingly rural. Only 24 towns and cities boasted 2500 or more residents, and 19 out of 20 Americans lived outside them. In fact, in 1800 more than 80 percent of American families were engaged in agriculture. In such a rural environment the movement of people, goods, and information was slow. Few individuals used the expensive postal system, and most **Poor transportation**   roads were still little more than dirt paths hacked through the forest, with stumps cut off at 16 inches (so axles would just clear them) and large trees sometimes left in the roadway. The roads were choked with dust during dry spells and overflowed with mud when it rained. In 1790 the country had 92 newspapers, published weekly or semiweekly, mostly in towns and cities along major avenues of transportation. Americans off the beaten path only occasionally heard news of the outside world.

---

*Because the 1790 census did not include significant data on the black population, many of the statistical figures quoted for this era apply only to white Americans.

Life in isolated regions contrasted markedly with that in bustling urban centers like New York and Philadelphia. But the most basic division in American society was not between the cities and the countryside, important as that was. What would divide Americans most broadly over the coming decades was the contrast between semisubsistence and commercial ways of life. Semisubsistence farmers lived on the produce of their own land and labor. Americans in the commercial economy were tied more closely to the larger markets of a far-flung world. As the United States began its life under the new federal union, the distinction between a semisubsistence economy and a commercial economy was a crucial one.

The Semisubsistence Economy of Crèvecoeur's America

Most rural white Americans lived off the produce of their own land in a barter economy. It was this world that a French writer, Hector St. John de Crèvecoeur, described so well.

Crèvecoeur arrived in the British colonies in 1759 and almost immediately began wandering: riding over the rutted roads that led to the farms of New England and New York, fording the streams between the scattered settlements of Ohio and Kentucky, knocking the dust of Virginia off his clothes, stopping to talk at taverns along the roads to Philadelphia, and finally settling for a number of years as a farmer in the Hudson River valley. He published in 1783 his *Letters from an American Farmer,* asking in them the question that had so often occurred to him: "What then is the American, this new man?"

For Crèvecoeur what distinguished American society was the widespread equality of its people, especially the rural farmers. Americans were hostile to social pretensions and anything that smacked of aristocratic privilege. Furthermore, the conditions of the country promoted equality. Land was abundant and widely distributed, citizens lived decently, and the population was not divided into the wealthy few and the desperate many. (Like most of his contemporaries, Crèvecoeur glided

Equality

He that by the plough would thrive — Himself must either hold or drive

Work in semisubsistence rural families was done by both sexes and often involved cooperation among neighbors. While a woman milks the cow, a group of men assist in the difficult labor of burning felled trees and plowing a new field with an eight-ox team.

rather quickly over the plight of black slaves.) "We are the most perfect society now existing in the world," he boasted.

Although Crèvecoeur waxed romantic about the conditions of American life, he painted a reasonably accurate portrait of most of the interior of the northern states and the backcountry of the South. Wealth in those areas, while not distributed equally, was spread fairly broadly. And subsistence remained the goal of most white families. "The great effort was for every farmer to produce anything he required within his own family," one European visitor noted. In such an economy women played a key role. Wives and daughters had to be skilled in making articles such as candles, soap, clothing, and hats, since the cost of buying such items was steep.

Barter economy

With labor scarce and expensive, farmers also depended on the help of their neighbors in clearing fields, building homes, and harvesting crops. If a farm family produced a small surplus, they usually exchanged it locally rather than selling it for cash in a distant market. In this barter economy money was seldom seen and was used primarily to pay taxes and purchase imported goods. "Instead of money going incessantly backwards and forwards into the same hands," a French traveler recorded, residents in the countryside "supply their needs . . . by direct reciprocal exchanges. . . . They write down what they give and receive on both sides and at the end of the year they settle a large variety of exchanges with a very small quantity of coin."

Indian economies were also based primarily on subsistence. In the division of labor women raised crops, while men fished or hunted—not only for meat but also for skins to make clothing. Indians did not domesticate cattle, sheep, or pigs, but they managed and "harvested" deer by burning the surrounding forests once or twice a year to produce an environment free of underbrush, full of large, well-spaced trees and open meadows. Because Indians followed game more seasonally than did white settlers, their villages were moved to several different locations over the course of a year. But both whites and Indians in a semisubsistence economy moved periodically to new fields after the old ones were exhausted. Indians exhausted agricultural lands less quickly because they planted beans, corn, and squash in the same field, a technique that better conserved soil nutrients.

Despite the popular image of both the independent "noble savage" and the self-reliant yeoman farmer, virtually no one in the backcountry operated within a truly subsistence economy. Although farmers tried to grow most of the food their families ate, they normally bought salt, sugar, and coffee, and they often traded with their neighbors for food and other items. In addition, necessities such as iron, glass, lead, and gunpowder had to be purchased, usually at a country store, and many farmers hired artisans to make items such as shoes and to weave cloth. Similarly, Indians quickly became enmeshed in the wider world of European commerce, exchanging furs for iron tools or clothing and ornamental materials.

The Commercial Economy of Franklin's America

Outside the backcountry, Americans were tied much more closely to a commercial economy. Here, merchants, artisans, and even farmers did not subsist on what they produced but instead sold goods or services in a wider market and lived on their earnings. Cities and towns, of course, played a key part in the commercial economy. But so did the agricultural regions near the seaboard and along navigable rivers.

For commerce to flourish, goods had to move from producers to market cheaply enough to reap profits. Water offered the only cost-effective transportation over any distance; indeed, it cost as much to ship goods a mere 30 miles over primitive roads as to ship by boat 3000 miles across the Atlantic to London.

Cost-effective transportation was available to the planters of the Tidewater South, and city merchants used their access to the sea to establish trading ties to the West Indies and Europe. But urban artisans and workers were also linked to this market economy, as were many farm families in the Hudson valley, southeastern Pennsylvania, and southern New England. Where transportation was limited or prohibitively expensive, farmers had no incentive to increase production, and an economy of barter and semisubsistence persisted.

Commercial society differed from Crèvecoeur's world in another important way: its wealth was less equally distributed. By 1790, the richest 10 percent of Americans living in cities and in the plantation districts of the Tidewater South owned about 50 percent of the wealth. In the backcountry the top 10 percent was likely to own 25 to 35 percent of the wealth.

Inequality of wealth

Crèvecoeur argued that the American belief in equality sustained this society of small farm families, bound together in a community of relative equals. But he failed to see how much that equality rested on isolation. Without access to market, one could aspire only so high. Where the market economy operated more fully, however, Americans were more acquisitive and materialistic. Europeans were struck by Americans' desire for wealth. "Man here weighs everything, calculates everything, and sacrifices everything to his interest," one foreign visitor reported. Although semisubsistence farm families were eager to rise in life and acquire material goods, only those in the commercial economy could realistically pursue these dreams.

The man who gained international renown as a self-made citizen of commercial America was Benjamin Franklin. In his writings and in the example of his own life, Franklin offered a vision of the new nation that contrasted with Crèvecoeur's ideal of a subsistence America. Franklin had arrived in Philadelphia as a runaway apprentice who by hard work and talent rose to be one of the leading citizens of his adopted city. The preface to Franklin's popular *Poor Richard's Almanack*, as well as his countless essays, spelled out simple maxims for Americans seeking the upward path. "The way to wealth is as plain as the way to market," he noted. "It depends chiefly on two words, industry and frugality." Those anxious to succeed

Commercial values

Philadelphia was the largest and most prosperous city in the country in 1789. Its growth fueled the development of commercial agriculture in the surrounding countryside, as more and more farmers hauled their surplus to town for sale in the city's busy markets. In this scene, both men and women buy fresh foods on the streets. Indians, pictured here, also participated in the commercial economy.

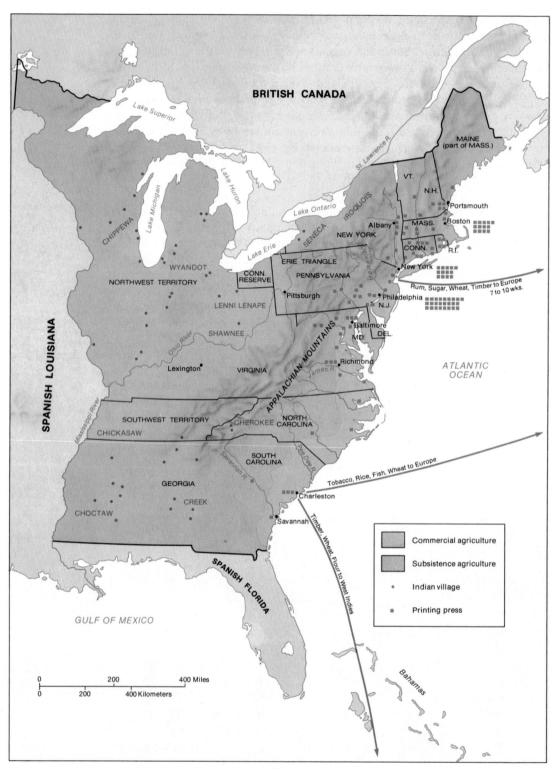

Semisubsistence and Commercial America, 1790 To prosper, a commercial economy demanded relatively cheap transportation to move goods. Thus in 1790 American commerce was confined largely to settled areas along the coast and to navigable rivers below the fall line. Because commerce depended on an efficient flow of information and goods, newspapers flourished in these areas.

should "remember that time is money." The kind of success he preached depended on taking advantage of commerce and a wider market. As a printer, Franklin was able to lead a life of acquisition and social mobility because he could distribute his almanacs and newspapers to ever-greater audiences.

The ethics of Franklin's marketplace, which looked forward to the opening up of opportunity in American society, threatened to destroy Crèvecoeur's egalitarian America. At the time of Franklin's death in 1790, the ideal that Crèvecoeur had so eloquently described still held sway across much of America. But the political debate of the 1790s showed clearly that Franklin's world of commerce and markets was slowly transforming the nation.

The Constitution and Commerce

In many ways the fight over ratification of the Constitution represented a struggle between the commercial and the subsistence-oriented elements of American society. Urban merchants and workers as well as commercial farmers and planters generally rallied behind the Constitution. They took a broader, more cosmopolitan view of the nation's future, and they had a more favorable view of government power. Franklin, predictably, supported the Constitution. So did Madison and Washington, both planters whose wealth depended on trade and commerce.

Americans who remained a part of the semisubsistence barter economy tended to oppose the Constitution. More provincial in outlook, they feared concentrated power, were suspicious of cities and commercial institutions, opposed aristocracy and special privilege, and in general just wanted to be left alone. They were a majority of the population, but they were not easily mobilized, lacked prestigious leaders, and did not have the access to communication that their opponents enjoyed. In defeat they remained suspicious that a powerful government would tax them to benefit the commercial sectors of the economy.

And so in 1789 the United States embarked on its new national course, with two rival visions of the direction that the fledgling Republic should take. Which vision would prevail—a question that was as much social as it was political—increasingly divided the generation of revolutionary leaders during the 1790s.

Whatever the Republic was to become, Americans agreed that George Washington personified it. When the first Electoral College cast its votes, Washington was unanimously elected, the only president in history so honored. John Adams became vice president.

The New Government

The Federalists—supporters of the Constitution—called the new government "the great experiment." They were intensely aware that throughout history democratic republics had in the end degenerated into quarreling factions, as with the city-states of ancient Greece, or ushered in dictatorships, as had happened in Cromwell's England. No republic—not England, or Rome, or the Swiss city-states—had stretched over a territory as large as the United States. Loyalty to the new Republic, with its untried form of government and diversity of peoples and interests, rested to a great degree on the trust and respect Americans gave Washington.

Failure of past republics

Washington's Character

Time has transformed Washington from a man into a monument: remote and unknowable, stiff, unbowing, impenetrable. Even during his own life, he had no close

Washington's trip from Virginia to New York City to assume the presidency was a triumphant procession as Americans enthusiastically greeted him with cheers and even flowers strewn along his path.

friends in public life and discouraged familiarity. "I could never be on familiar terms with the General—a man so cold, so cautious," one foreigner testified after visiting Mount Vernon. Washington learned with age to control his temper and tried to endure criticism patiently, yet he bitterly resented it. In an age of brilliant political thinkers, Washington was intellectually cautious and deliberate. As president he usually asked for written advice and made his decision only after weighing the options carefully.

The president also provoked criticism by the pomp with which he conducted the government. Washington, who was one of the richest men in America, enjoyed the luxuries that wealth brought. Critics complained about his formal public receptions, the large number of servants, and the coach emblazoned with his coat of arms—all aristocratic habits. Still, as much as Washington craved honor and military fame, he did not hunger for power and accepted the office of the presidency only reluctantly.

Organizing the Government

Washington realized that as the first occupant of the executive office, everything he did was fraught with significance. "I walk on untrodden ground," he commented. "There is scarcely any part of my conduct which may not hereafter be drawn into precedent."

The cabinet

The Constitution made no mention of a cabinet. Yet the drafters of the Constitution, aware of the experience of the Continental Congress under the Articles of Confederation, clearly assumed that the president would have some system of advisers. Congress authorized the creation of four departments—War, Treasury, State, and Attorney General—whose heads were to be appointed with the consent of the Senate. Washington's most important choices were Alexander Hamilton as secretary of the treasury and Thomas Jefferson to head the State Department. At first the president did not meet regularly with his advisers as a group, but the idea of a cabinet that met to discuss policy matters eventually evolved. Washington gradually excluded Adams from cabinet discussions, and any meaningful role for the vice president, whose duties were largely undefined by the Constitution, soon disappeared.

The Constitution created a federal Supreme Court but beyond that was silent about the court system. The Judiciary Act of 1789 set the size of the Supreme Court at 6 members; it also established 13 federal district courts and 3 circuit courts of appeal. Supreme Court justices spent much of their time serving on these circuit courts, a distasteful duty whose long hours "riding the circuit" caused one justice to grumble that Congress had made him a "traveling postboy." The Judiciary Act made it clear that federal courts had the right to review decisions of the state courts and specified cases over which the Supreme Court would have original jurisdiction. Washington appointed John Jay of New York, a staunch Federalist, as the first chief justice.

Federal judiciary

The Bill of Rights

Congress also confronted the demand for a bill of rights, which had become an issue during the debate over ratification. At that time, nearly 200 amendments had been put forward in one form or another. Supporters of the Constitution were particularly alarmed over proposals to restrict the federal power to tax. As leader of the Federalist forces in the House of Representatives, James Madison moved to head off any large-scale changes that would weaken federal power by submitting a bill of rights that focused on civil liberties.

Ultimately Congress sent 12 amendments to the states. By December 1791, 10 had been ratified and incorporated into the Constitution.* Their passage by Congress helped persuade North Carolina (1789) and Rhode Island (1790), the two holdouts, to join the Union. At the same time, the advocates of strong federal power, such as Hamilton, were relieved that "the structure of the government, and the mass and distribution of its powers," remained unchanged.

These first 10 amendments, known as the Bill of Rights, were destined to be of crucial importance in defining personal liberty in the United States. Among the rights guaranteed were freedom of religion, the press, and speech, as well as the right to assemble and petition and the right to bear arms. The amendments also established clear procedural safeguards, including the right to a trial by jury and protection against illegal searches and seizures. They prohibited excessive bail, cruel and unusual punishment, and the quartering of troops in private homes. The last two amendments were intended to calm fears about the federal government having unlimited power. Madison was careful, however, to phrase these particular amendments in very general terms. At the same time, an attempt in Congress to apply these same guarantees to state governments failed, and almost a century would pass before Congress moved, during Reconstruction, to prevent states from interfering with certain basic rights.

Protected rights

Hamilton's Financial Program

Before adjourning, Congress called on Alexander Hamilton, as secretary of the treasury, to prepare a report on the nation's finances. Hamilton undertook the assignment eagerly, for he did not intend to be a minor figure in the new administration.

Hamilton never forgot that he was a self-made man. His father was a Scottish merchant of noble birth, but his parents never married, and his father soon

---

*Of the two proposed amendments that were not initially approved, one was ratified in 1992 as the Twenty-seventh Amendment. It stipulates that there must be an intervening election before a congressional pay raise goes into effect.

Hamilton's character

abandoned the family. Hamilton grew up on the islands of the West Indies, scarred by the stigmas of poverty and illegitimacy. To compensate, he was driven constantly to seek respectability and money. He served as a military aide to Washington during the Revolution, and marriage to the daughter of a wealthy New York politician gave him influential connections he could draw on in his political career. Nevertheless, his haughty manner, jealousy, and penchant for intrigue made him many enemies. He was a brilliant thinker, yet he felt out of place in the increasingly democratic society emerging around him. "All communities divide themselves into the few and the many," he declared. "The first are rich and wellborn, the other the mass of the people. . . . The people are turbulent and changing; they seldom judge or determine right."

While Hamilton was not a monarchist, his experience in the army, which impressed on him the necessity of a vigorous government, made him more inclined than most of his colleagues to use force. Convinced that human nature was fundamentally selfish, Hamilton believed that the government needed to appeal to the self-interest of the rich and wellborn in order to succeed. "Men," he observed succinctly, "will naturally go to those who pay them best." He took as his model Great Britain, whose greatness he attributed to its system of public finance and its preeminence in commerce and manufacturing. Thus Hamilton set out to achieve two goals. He intended to use federal power to encourage manufacturing and commerce in order to make the United States economically strong and independent of Europe. And he was determined to link the interests of the wealthy with those of the new government.

Neither goal could be achieved until the federal government solved its two most pressing financial problems: revenue and credit. Without revenue it could not be effective. Without credit—the faith of merchants and other nations that the government would repay its debts—it would lack the ability to borrow. Hamilton proposed that all $52 million of the federal debt be paid in full (or funded). He also recommended that the federal government assume responsibility for the remaining $25 million in debts that individual states owed. He intended with these twin policies to put the new federal government on a sound financial footing and enhance its power by increasing its need for revenue and making the wealthy look to the national government, not the states. Hamilton also proposed a series of excise taxes, including a controversial 25 percent levy on whiskey, to help meet government expenses.

Funding and assumption

Location of the capital

After heated debate, Congress deadlocked over funding and assumption. Finally, over dinner with Hamilton, Jefferson and Madison of Virginia agreed to support his proposal if, after 10 years in Philadelphia, the permanent seat of government was

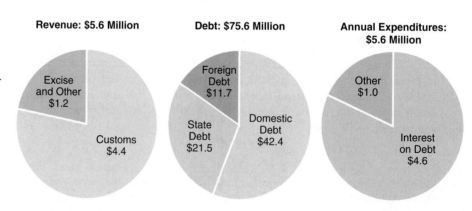

Hamilton's Financial System
Under Hamilton's financial system, more than 80 percent of federal revenues went to pay the interest on the national debt. Note that most of the revenue came from tariff duties.

Revenue: $5.6 Million
Excise and Other $1.2
Customs $4.4

Debt: $75.6 Million
Foreign Debt $11.7
State Debt $21.5
Domestic Debt $42.4

Annual Expenditures: $5.6 Million
Other $1.0
Interest on Debt $4.6

located in the South, on the Potomac River between Virginia and Maryland. Aided by this understanding, funding and assumption passed Congress. In 1791 Congress also approved a 20-year charter for the first Bank of the United States. The bank would hold government deposits and issue banknotes that would be received in payment of all debts owed the federal government. Congress proved less receptive to the rest of Hamilton's program, although a limited tariff to encourage manufacturing and several excise taxes, including the one on whiskey, won approval.

Opposition to Hamilton's Program

The passage of Hamilton's program caused a permanent rupture among supporters of the Constitution. Madison, who had collaborated closely with Hamilton in the 1780s, broke with his former ally over funding and assumption. Jefferson finally went over to the opposition when Hamilton announced plans for a national bank. Eventually the two warring factions organized themselves into political parties: the Republicans, led by Jefferson and Madison, and the Federalists, led by Hamilton and Adams.* But the division emerged slowly over several years.

Hamilton's program promoted the commercial sector at the expense of semi-subsistence farmers. Thus it rekindled many of the concerns that had surfaced during the struggle over ratification of the Constitution. The ideology of the Revolution had stressed that republics inevitably contained groups who sought power in order to destroy popular liberties and overthrow the republic. To some Americans,

A study in contrasts, Jefferson and Hamilton increasingly came into conflict in Washington's administration. Despite his aristocratic upbringing, Jefferson (left) was awkward, loose-jointed, reserved, and ill at ease in public. Testifying before a congressional committee, he casually lounged in a chair and spoke in a rambling, nonstop manner. "Yet he scattered information wherever he went," conceded Senator William Maclay of Pennsylvania, "and some even brilliant sentiments sparkled from him." Hamilton (right), though short of stature, cut a dashing figure with his erect bearing, strutting manner, meticulous dress, and carefully powdered hair. Declared the wife of the British ambassador: "I have scarcely ever been more charmed with the vivacity and conversation of any man."

*The Republican party of the 1790s, sometimes referred to as the Jeffersonian Republicans, is not to be confused with the modern-day Republican party, which originated in the 1850s.

Fears of a financial aristocracy

Hamilton's program seemed a clear threat to establish a privileged and powerful financial aristocracy—perhaps even a monarchy.

Who, after all, would benefit from the funding proposal? During and after the Revolution, the value of notes issued by the Continental Congress dropped sharply. Speculators had bought up most of these notes for a fraction of their face value from small farmers and workers. If the government ultimately redeemed the debt, speculators would profit accordingly. Equally disturbing, members of Congress had been purchasing the notes before the adoption of Hamilton's program. Nearly half the members of the House owned U.S. securities. Madison urged that only the original holders of the debt be reimbursed in full, but Hamilton rejected this idea, since commercial speculators were precisely the class of people he hoped to bind to the new government.

Similarly, when stock in the Bank of the United States went on sale, speculators snapped up all the shares in an hour. The price of a share skyrocketed from $25 to $300 in two months. Jefferson was appalled by the mania Hamilton's program encouraged. "The spirit of gambling, once it has seized a subject, is incurable," he asserted. "The taylor who has made thousands in one day, tho he has lost them the next, can never again be content with the slow and moderate earnings of his needle."

System of corruption

The national bank struck its critics as a dangerous mimicking of English corruption. Indeed, in Great Britain the Bank of England played a powerful role. Its investments not only helped fuel the economy; its loans to many members of Parliament gave it great political influence. Jefferson warned that the same thing would happen in the United States. English-style corruption seemed to be taking root as "paper men" became rich not by producing anything substantial with their own hard work but by shuffling paper, trading notes, and benefiting from the financial legislation they themselves passed. These fears were heightened because Americans had little experience with banks: only three existed in the country when the Bank of the United States was chartered. One member of Congress expressed a common attitude when he said that he would no more be caught entering a bank than a house of prostitution.

Then, too, banks and commerce were a part of the urban environment that rural Americans so distrusted. Although Hamilton's opponents generally granted that a certain amount of commerce was necessary, they believed that it should remain subordinate. Hamilton's program, in contrast, encouraged manufacturing and urbanization, developments that history had shown to be incompatible with liberty and equality. Moreover, the tariff favored one group in society—manufacturers—at the expense of other groups.

After Congress approved the bank bill, Washington hesitated to sign it. When he consulted his cabinet, Jefferson stressed that the Constitution did not specifically authorize Congress to charter a bank. Both he and Madison upheld the idea of strict construction—that the Constitution should be interpreted narrowly and the federal government restricted to powers expressly delegated to it. Otherwise, the federal government would be the judge of its own powers, and there would be no safeguard against the abuse of power.

Hamilton countered that the Constitution contained implied as well as enumerated powers. He particularly emphasized the clause that permitted Congress to make all laws "necessary and proper" to carry out its duties. A bank would be useful in carrying out the enumerated powers of regulating commerce and maintaining the public credit; therefore, Congress had a right to decide whether to establish one. Because the Constitution could not anticipate all future developments, the government needed flexibility to meet its responsibilities. In the end Washington accepted Hamilton's forceful arguments and signed the bill.

The Specter of Aristocracy

The threat posed by a powerful bank heightened the fears of Hamilton's opponents that an aristocracy was developing in the United States. While Americans did not insist on an equal division of property and wealth, they were hostile to any haughtiness among the upper classes and to Europe's aristocratic traditions. Because Hamilton's program deliberately aided the rich and created a class of citizens whose wealth derived from the federal government, it strengthened these traditional fears. "Money will be put under the direction of government," charged Philip Freneau, a leading Republican editor, "and the government will be put under the direction of money."

Many who opposed Hamilton's financial program had also been against the Constitution, but leadership of the opposition fell to Jefferson and Madison, who had staunchly worked for ratification. Although Jefferson and Madison were planters, well accustomed to the workings of the marketplace, they still distrusted cities and commerce and Hamilton's aristocratic ways.

Economically Hamilton's program was a success. The government's credit was restored, and the national bank ended the inflation of the previous two decades and created a sound currency. At the same time the administration demonstrated that the federal government would not be paralyzed as it had been under the Articles. In addition, Hamilton's theory of implied powers and broad construction gave the nation the flexibility necessary to respond to unanticipated crises.

Hamilton's success

Expansion and Turmoil in the West

In the peace treaty of 1783, Britain ceded to the United States the territory between the Appalachian Mountains and the Mississippi River. Even so, British troops continued to hold the forts in the Northwest and Indian tribes controlled most of this region. To demonstrate the government's effectiveness, Washington moved to extend control over the West.

The Resistance of the Miami

In principle, the United States recognized the rights of Indians to their lands. Furthermore, it had promised that any purchase of Indian land would be made only by treaty and not through private purchases by land companies and individual settlers. Nevertheless, the government was determined to buy out Indian titles in order to promote white settlement.

By 1790 the United States had negotiated purchase of Indian lands in most of Kentucky and about one-quarter of Tennessee. North of the Ohio, however, the Miami Confederacy (composed of eight western tribes headed by the Miami) stoutly refused to sell territory and soundly defeated two American military expeditions. In response, Washington dispatched an army of 2000, commanded by "Mad Anthony" Wayne, an accomplished general and hero of the Revolution, to the Ohio Valley. At the Battle of Fallen Timbers in August 1794 Wayne won a decisive victory, breaking the Indians' hold on the Northwest. In the Treaty of Greenville (1795), he forced the tribes to cede the southern two-thirds of the area between Lake Erie and the Ohio River, thus opening up the Northwest to white settlement.

Treaty of Greenville

The Whiskey Rebellion

Westerners approved of the administration's military policy against the Indians. They were far less pleased that in 1791 Congress had passed a new excise tax on distilled liquors. In the barter economy west of the Appalachians, barrels of whiskey were sometimes used as currency. Furthermore, about the only way farmers could profitably export surplus grain was to distill it and bring the liquor to market. So the whiskey tax brought the question of federal power quite directly to the attention of the ordinary citizen.

Western society

The West during the 1790s was a society in turmoil. Most property owners along the frontier found it hard to make ends meet. In response, a number were forced to sell their land and fell into the ranks of tenant farmers. Thus wealth became more concentrated in the hands of fewer individuals. While the whiskey tax was unpopular in many rural areas, frontier settlers resisted most fiercely, since for them the sale of whiskey made the greatest difference in providing a bit of extra income. Tenant farmers, resentful of the more commercially minded larger landowners of their region, protested loudly too. Many of these poor farmers turned out at mass meetings to condemn the tax and protest against having to support government officials and the burdensome national debt. Beset by economic dislocation, they directed their resentment not just at the authorities but also at wealthy landowners and merchants.

Farmers in the western districts of several states defied federal officials and refused to pay, launching a "whiskey rebellion." The greatest unrest flared in western Pennsylvania, where General Neville was burned out of his home (pages 228–229). That summer an even larger gathering of impoverished farmers threatened to march on Pittsburgh. For rural residents, the city had become a symbol of the corrupt cosmopolitan influences that threatened their liberty. Many in the crowd relished the idea of looting the property of wealthy residents. "I have a bad hat now, but I expect to have a better one soon," shouted one of the mob.

Collapse of resistance

To distant easterners, the Whiskey Rebellion at first appeared serious. Hamilton, who had pushed the whiskey tax in order to demonstrate the power of the new government, saw the matter as a question of authority. "Shall there be government, or no government?" he asked. An alarmed Washington led an army of 13,000 men—larger than he had commanded at Yorktown—into the Pennsylvania countryside to overawe the populace and subdue the rebels. Hamilton soon took charge, but to his disappointment the troops met no organized resistance. "An insurrection was announced and proclaimed and armed against, but could never be found," Jefferson scoffed. Even some of Hamilton's allies conceded that he had overreacted. "Elective rulers can scarcely ever employ the physical force of a democracy," one remarked, "without turning the moral force, or the power of public opinion, against the government."

Pinckney's Treaty

Navigation of the Mississippi

Western unhappiness was also eased somewhat when Washington sent Thomas Pinckney to negotiate a treaty with Spain. That nation still controlled Florida and the mouth of the Mississippi and had never agreed to a northern boundary between its possessions and the United States. Pinckney's Treaty, which the Senate unanimously ratified in 1796, set the 31st parallel as the southern boundary of the United States and granted Americans free navigation of the Mississippi, with the right to deposit goods at New Orleans for reshipment to ports in the East and abroad. No longer could Spain try to detach the western settlements from American control by promising to open the Mississippi to their trade.

The Emergence of Political Parties

Members of the Revolutionary generation fervently hoped that political parties would not take root in the United States. "If I could not go to heaven but with a party, I would not go at all," remarked Jefferson. Influenced by radical English republican thought, American critics condemned parties as narrow interest groups that routinely placed selfishness and party loyalty above a concern for the public good. In fact, many members of Britain's Parliament did in effect sell their votes in return for offices, pensions, and profitable contracts. Yet despite Americans' distrust of such institutions, the United States became the first nation to establish truly popular parties.

Social conditions encouraged the rise of parties. Because property ownership was widespread, the nation had a broad suffrage. Furthermore, during the Revolution legislatures lowered property requirements in many states, increasing the number of voters still further. If party members hoped to hold office, they had to offer a program attractive to the broader voting public. When parties acted as representatives of economic and social interest groups, they became one means by which a large electorate could make its feelings known. In addition, the United States had the highest literacy rate in the world and the largest number of newspapers, further encouraging political interest and participation. Finally, the fact that well-known patriots of the Revolution headed both the Federalists and the Republicans helped defuse the charge that either party was hostile to the Revolution or the Constitution.

Social conditions and parties

Americans and the French Revolution

While domestic issues first split the supporters of the Constitution, it was a crisis in Europe that served to push Americans toward political parties. Americans had hoped that their revolution would spark similar movements for liberty on the European continent, and in fact the American Revolution was only one of a series of revolutions in the late eighteenth century that shook the Western world, the most important of which occurred in France. There a rising population, the growth of a popular press, the failure of reform, the collapse of government finances, and widespread discontent with France's constitutional system sparked a challenge to royal authority that became a mass revolution. Eventually the French revolutionary ideals of "liberty, equality, and fraternity" would spill across the continent, carried by the French army.

When news of the Revolution arrived in the United States in 1789, Americans hailed it as the first stirring of liberty on the European continent. Each new ship from overseas brought exciting news: the Bastille prison had been stormed in July; the new National Assembly had abolished feudal privileges and adopted the Declaration of the Rights of Man. By 1793, however, American enthusiasm for the Revolution had cooled after radical elements instituted a reign of terror, executing the king and queen and many of the nobility. The French republic even out-

The execution of King Louis XVI, by guillotine, left Americans divided over the value of the French Revolution.

lawed Christianity and substituted the worship of Reason. Finally in 1793 republican France and monarchical England went to war. Americans were deeply divided over whether the United States should continue its old alliance with France or support Great Britain.

Hamilton and his allies viewed the French Revolution as sheer anarchy. Its leaders seemed to be destroying the very institutions that held civilization together: the

Differing views of the Revolution

church, social classes, property, law and order. The United States, Hamilton argued, should renounce the 1778 treaty of alliance with France and side with Britain. "Behold France, an open hell," warned Fisher Ames, a member of Congress from Massachusetts, ". . . still smoking with suffering and crimes, in which we see perhaps our future state." For Jefferson and his followers, the issue was republicanism versus monarchy. France was a sister republic and, despite deplorable excesses, its revolution was spreading the doctrine of liberty. Britain remained repressive and corrupt, presided over by the same tyrannical king who had made war on the colonies. Jefferson argued that the United States should maintain its treaty of alliance with France and insist that, as neutrals, Americans had every right to trade with France as much as with England.

As tempers flared, each faction suspected the worst of the other. To the Jeffersonians, Hamilton and his friends seemed part of a monarchist conspiracy. "The ultimate object of all this," Jefferson said of Hamilton's policies, "is to prepare the way for a change, from the present republican forms of Government, to that of a monarchy." As for the Hamiltonians, they viewed Jefferson and his faction as disciples of French radicals, conspiring to establish mob rule in the United States. Years later, when calm reflection was possible, John Adams conceded that both parties had "excited artificial terrors." But during the 1790s, each side believed that the destiny of the American republic was threatened by events abroad.

Washington's Neutral Course

Washington, for his part, was convinced that in order to prosper, the United States must remain independent of Europe and its unending quarrels and wars. Thus the

France, like Great Britain, put pressure on the United States to abandon its neutrality. The French minister to America, "Citizen" Edmond Genêt, went so far as to have broadsides like this one printed, encouraging Americans to fight for the French republic. Note the appeal to newcomers from Ireland, who were known to dislike the British. Genêt embarrassed even the friends of France like Jefferson, and Washington angrily demanded his recall.

Philadelphia, Auguſt, 1793.

ALL able bodied ſeamen who are willing to engage in the cauſe of Liberty, and in the ſervice of the French Republic, will pleaſe to apply to the French Conſul, at No. 132, North Second-ſtreet.

Particular attention will be paid to the generous and intrepid natives of Ireland, who, it is preſumed, will act like thoſe warlike troops from that oppreſſed country, who took refuge in France about a century ago, and performed prodigies of valor under the old government of that country.

president issued a proclamation of American neutrality and tempered Jefferson's efforts to support France.

Neutral rights

Under international law, neutrals could trade with belligerents—nations at war—as long as the trade had existed before the outbreak of hostilities and did not involve war supplies. But both France and Great Britain refused to respect the rights of neutrals in the midst of their desperate struggle. They began intercepting American ships and confiscating cargoes. In addition, Britain, which badly needed manpower to maintain its powerful navy, impressed into service American sailors it suspected of being British subjects. Despite these abuses, Hamilton continued to support a friendly policy toward Britain. He recognized, as did Washington, that the United States was not strong enough to challenge Britain militarily.

Moreover, Hamilton's domestic program depended on trade with the British, who purchased 75 percent of America's exports (mostly foodstuffs and naval supplies) as well as providing 90 percent of imports. With Europe torn by war, the demand for American grains rose sharply, driving up the price on the world market. During the decade, American exports nearly quadrupled, and American ships almost completely took over the carrying trade between the United States and Europe. All parts of the commercial economy shared in this unprecedented prosperity, not only merchants but also urban workers and businesspeople, sailors, the shipbuilding industry, and farmers who sold their surplus at high prices.

In addition to violating neutral rights and impressment, Great Britain continued to maintain the western forts it had promised to evacuate in 1783, and it closed the West Indies, a traditional source of trade, to American ships. Washington sent John Jay to Britain as a special minister to negotiate the differences between the two countries. In the end, Jay persuaded the British only to withdraw their troops from the Northwest. With the West Indies still closed to American shipping, Jay's Treaty in essence reinforced the United States' position as an economic satellite of Britain. Only reluctantly did a disappointed Washington submit it to the Senate.

Jay's Treaty

The treaty debate was extremely bitter. Republicans denounced Jay and hanged him in effigy while a mob stoned Hamilton in the streets. In June 1795 the Senate finally approved Jay's Treaty by a vote of 20 to 10, the bare two-thirds margin required.

The Federalists and Republicans Organize

Thus events in Europe contributed directly to the rise of parties in the United States by stimulating fears over the course of American development. The war, Jefferson commented, "kindled and brought forward the two parties with an ardour which our own interests merely, could never excite." By the mid-1790s both sides were organizing on a national basis. Hamilton took the lead in coordinating the Federalist party, which grew out of the voting bloc in Congress that had enacted his economic program. Increasingly, Washington drew closer to Federalist advisers and policies and became the symbol of the party, although he clung to the vision of a nonpartisan administration and never recognized the extent to which he had become a party leader.

The guiding genius of the opposition movement was Hamilton's onetime colleague James Madison. Jefferson, who resigned as secretary of state at the end of 1793, became the symbolic head of the party, much as Washington headed the Federalists. Even so, Jefferson was unconvinced of the wisdom and necessity of such

Organization of an opposition party

a party and was reluctant to lead it. But Madison acted more vigorously, conferring over strategy and lining up the Republican voting bloc in the House. The disputes over Jay's Treaty and the whiskey tax in 1794 and 1795 gave the Republicans popular issues, and they began organizing on the state and local levels. Unlike the Federalists, who cloaked themselves in Washington's mantle and claimed to uphold the government and the Constitution, the Republicans had to overcome the ingrained idea that an opposition party was seditious and therefore illegitimate. Because of broad support for the Constitution, Republican leaders had to be careful to distinguish between opposing the administration and opposing the Constitution. Indeed, it was by no means clear that an opposition party could arise without threatening the government itself.

As more and more members of Congress allied themselves with one faction or the other, voting became increasingly partisan. In the first two Congresses, party votes occurred mostly on Hamilton's economic program and organization of the government. In the third and fourth Congresses, party questions included foreign affairs and domestic issues, such as the Whiskey Rebellion. By 1796 even minor matters were decided by partisan votes. Gradually, party organization filtered downward to local communities.

The 1796 Election

As long as Washington remained head of the Federalists, they enjoyed an insurmountable advantage. But in 1796 the weary president, stung by the abuse heaped on him by the opposition press, announced he would not accept a third term, thereby setting a two-term precedent that other presidents would follow until Franklin Roosevelt. In his Farewell Address Washington warned against the dangers of parties and urged a return to the earlier nonpartisan system. But that vision had become obsolete: parties were an effective way of expressing the interests of different social and economic groups within the nation. When the Republicans chose Thomas Jefferson to oppose John Adams, the possibility of a nonparty constitutional system ended.

The framers of the Constitution did not anticipate that political parties would run competing candidates for both the presidency and the vice presidency. Thus they provided that, of the candidates running for president, the one with the most electoral votes would win and the one with the second highest number would become vice president. But Hamilton strongly disliked both Adams and Jefferson. Ever the intriguer, he tried to manipulate the electoral vote so that the Federalist vice presidential candidate, Thomas Pinckney of South Carolina, would be elected president. In the ensuing confusion, Adams won with 71 electoral votes, and his rival, Jefferson, gained the vice presidency with 68 votes.

Support for the two parties

The fault line between the two parties reflected basic divisions in American life. Geographically, the Federalists were strongest in New England, with its commercial ties to Great Britain and its powerful tradition of hierarchy and order. Moving farther south, the party became progressively weaker. Of the southernmost states, the Federalists enjoyed significant strength only in aristocratic South Carolina. The Republicans won solid support in semisubsistence areas like the West, where Crèvecoeur's farmers were only weakly involved with commerce. The middle states were closely contested, although the most cosmopolitan and commercially oriented elements remained the core of Federalist strength.

The Republicans won over most of the old Anti-Federalist opponents of the Constitution as well as a number of Americans who had firmly backed the new union. These supporters included some commercial farmers in the North and planters in the South and, increasingly, urban workers and small shopkeepers who were repelled by the aristocratic tone of the Federalists. The Republicans were often led by ambitious men of new wealth who felt excluded by the entrenched Federalist elite. For similar reasons Jefferson attracted the support of immigrants from France and Ireland, who felt culturally excluded, as well as members of religious sects such as the Baptists and Methodists, who resented the power and privileges of New England's established Congregational church.

Federalist and Republican Ideologies

In different ways, each party looked both forward and backward: toward certain traditions of the past as well as toward newer social currents that would shape America in the nineteenth century.

Most Federalists viewed themselves as a kind of natural aristocracy making a last desperate stand against the excesses of democracy. They clung to the notion that the upper class should rule over its social and economic inferiors. In supporting the established social order, most Federalists opposed unbridled individualism. They believed that society's needs were more important than the individual's. In their view, government should regulate individual behavior for the good of society and protect property from the violent and unruly. Pessimistic about human nature, Federalists were almost obsessed by fear of the "mob." In a republic, they argued, government had to restrain popular power.

Federalist ideas

Although the Federalists resolutely opposed the rising tide of democracy and individualism, they were remarkably forward-looking in their economic ideas. They sensed that the United States would become the major economic and military power of their vision only by prospering through commerce and economic development. To that end, they argued, the government ought to use its power actively, to encourage the growth of commerce and manufacturing.

The Republicans, in contrast, looked backward to the traditional Revolutionary fear that government power threatened liberty. Over and over Republicans emphasized the threat of corruption. The Treasury, they warned, was corrupting Congress, the army would enslave the people, and broad construction of the Constitution would make the federal government all-powerful. To them, Federalist attitudes and policies illustrated the corruption eating away at American morals, just as England had become corrupt before 1776.

Republican ideas

Nor did their economic ideals anticipate future American development. For Republicans, agriculture and not commerce stood as the centerpiece of American liberty and virtue. To be sure, leaders like Jefferson and Madison recognized that some commercial activity was necessary, especially to sell America's agricultural surplus abroad. But Jefferson and his followers believed that republican values would be preserved only by limiting commerce and promoting household manufacturing instead of industry. Furthermore, Republicans failed to appreciate the role of financial institutions in promoting economic development. Instead, Republicans focused on the abuses of "paper wealth" and those who manipulated it—speculators, bank directors, and holders of the public debt. Economically, they rejected the forward-looking ideals of urban commerce and industry that would dominate American society in the nineteenth century.

On the other hand, the Jeffersonians were more farsighted in matters of equality and personal liberty. Their faith in the people put them in tune with the emerging egalitarian temper of society. Eagerly they embraced the virtues of individualism, hoping to reduce government to the bare essentials in order to free individuals to develop their potential without interference. And they looked to the West—the land of small farms and a more equal society—as the means to preserve opportunity and American values.

The Presidency of John Adams

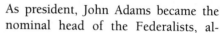

As president, John Adams became the nominal head of the Federalists, although in many ways he was out of step with his party. Unlike Hamilton, Adams felt no pressing need to aid the wealthy, nor was he fully committed to Hamilton's commercial-industrial vision. As a crusty revolutionary leader who in the 1780s had served as American minister to England, Adams also opposed any alliance with Britain.

Increasingly Adams and Hamilton clashed over policies and party leadership. Part of the problem stemmed from personalities. Adams was so abrasive and thin-skinned that it was difficult for anyone to get along with him, and Hamilton's intrigues in the 1796 election had not improved relations between the two men. Although Hamilton had resigned from the Treasury Department in 1795, key members of Adams's cabinet regularly turned to the former secretary for advice. Indeed, they opposed Adams so often that the frustrated president sometimes dealt with them, according to Jefferson, "by dashing and trampling his wig on the floor." The feud between the two rivals did not bode well for the Federalist party.

John Adams, who believed that pageantry and pomp were essential to government, aroused fears of monarchy and European corruption by proposing in 1789 that the president's title be "His Highness the President of the United States and Protector of the Rights of the Same." Of distinctly unmilitary bearing, he wore this sword at his inauguration in the vain hope that it would lend dignity. Sarcastic Republicans, noting his paunchy figure, gleefully bestowed a title of their own: "His Rotundity."

XYZ Affair

The Naval War with France

Adams began his term trying to balance relations with both Great Britain and France. Because the terms of Jay's Treaty were so favorable to the British, the French in retaliation set their navy and privateers to raiding American shipping. To resolve the conflict, Adams dispatched three envoys to France in 1797, but the French foreign minister demanded a bribe before negotiations could even begin. The American representatives refused, and when news of these discussions became public, it was known as the XYZ Affair (because in the official documents the Adams administration substituted the letters X, Y, and Z for the names of the French officials involved). A tremendous outcry ensued.

Confronted with such deeply felt anger, Federalist leaders saw a chance to retain power by exploiting the national emergency and going to war with France. With war fever running high, Congress in 1798 repudiated the French treaty of 1778 and enlarged the army and navy. Republicans suspected that the real purpose of the army was not to fight the French army—none existed in North America—but to crush the opposition party and establish a military despotism. All that remained was for Adams to whip up popular feeling and lead the nation into war.

But Adams hesitated, afraid he would become a scapegoat if his policies failed. Furthermore, he distrusted standing armies and preferred the navy as the nation's primary defense. So an unofficial naval war broke out as ships in each navy openly and freely raided the fleets of the other, while Britain continued to impress American sailors and seize ships suspected of trading with France.

Undeclared naval war

Eager for war, Hamilton dreamed of using the army to seize Louisiana and Florida from Spain, France's ally. He even toyed with provoking resistance in Virginia in order to justify suppression of the Republican party. Urging that Virginia be put "to the test of resistance," he disclosed that he was ready to use the army "to subdue a *refractory and powerful State.*" Hamilton's hotheaded behavior, however, only helped to cool Adams's willingness to go to war.

Suppression at Home

Meanwhile, Federalist leaders attempted to suppress disloyalty at home. In the summer of 1798 Congress passed several measures known together as the Alien and Sedition Acts. The Alien Act authorized the president to arrest and deport aliens suspected of "treasonable" leanings. Although never used, the act directly threatened nonnaturalized immigrants, many of whom were prominent Jeffersonians. To limit the number of immigrant voters—again, most of them Republicans—the Naturalization Act increased the period of residence required to become a naturalized citizen from 5 to 14 years. But the most controversial law was the Sedition Act, which established heavy fines and even imprisonment for writing, speaking, or publishing anything of "a false, scandalous and malicious" nature against the government or any officer of the government. To cries that such censorship violated the First Amendment's guarantees of freedom of speech and the press, Federalists replied that sedition and libel were not protected by the Constitution.

Alien and Sedition Acts

Because of the heavy-handed way it was enforced, the Sedition Act quickly became a symbol of tyranny. Federalists convicted and imprisoned a number of prominent Republican editors, and several Republican papers ceased publication. The act even brought to justice one unfortunate tippler who had proclaimed his fervent hope that a cannonball might hit the president in his rear. In all, 25 were arrested under the law and 10 convicted and imprisoned, including Matthew Lyon, a Republican member of Congress from Vermont. Unpopular by any measure, the Sedition Act became doubly obnoxious because Federalists used it in such a partisan manner.

The crisis over the Sedition Act forced Republicans to develop a broader conception of freedom of the press. Previously, most Americans had agreed that newspapers should not be restrained before publication but that they could be punished afterward for sedition. Jefferson and others now argued that the American government was uniquely based on the free expression of public opinion, and thus criticism of the government was not a sign of criminal intent. Only overtly seditious acts, not opinions, should be subject to prosecution. The courts eventually endorsed this view, adopting a new, more absolute view of freedom of speech guaranteed by the First Amendment.

Freedom of the press

The Republican-controlled legislatures of Virginia and Kentucky each responded to the crisis of 1798 by passing a set of resolutions. Madison secretly wrote those for Virginia, and Jefferson those for Kentucky. These resolutions proclaimed that the Constitution was a compact among sovereign states that delegated strictly limited powers to the federal government. When the government exceeded those

Virginia and Kentucky resolutions

Daily Lives

POPULAR ENTERTAINMENT

Exploring the Wondrous World

In 1786 Charles Willson Peale, painter and jack-of-all-trades, opened a museum of natural history in his home on Lombard Street in Philadelphia. Americans had always been fascinated by freaks of nature and "remarkable providences" (see Daily Lives, "A World of Wonders and Witchcraft," on pages 94–95). But unlike seventeenth-century colonials, Peale was not searching for signs of the supernatural in everyday life. A student of the Enlightenment, Peale intended his museum to be "a school of useful knowledge" that would attract men and women of all ages and social ranks. By studying natural history, Peale believed, citizens would gain an understanding of themselves, their country, and the world and thereby help sustain civilization in the United States. The sign over the door read, "Whoso would learn wisdom, let him enter here!"

Inside, the visitor found a wide assortment of items from around the world. Peale displayed nearly a hundred paintings he had completed of leading Americans, stuffed birds and animals, busts of famous scientists, cases of minerals, and wax figures representing the races of the world. Among the technological innovations that were showcased, a machine called a *physiognotrace* produced precise silhouettes. Moses Williams, a former slave, operated the machine and did a thriving business, selling 8880 profiles in the first year. Peale's backyard soon contained a zoo with a bewildering assortment of animals, including two grizzly bear cubs, an eagle, numerous snakes, monkeys, and a hyena. Prominent acquaintances such as Benjamin Franklin, George Washington, and Thomas Jefferson sent specimens, and the collection eventually totaled some 100,000 items.

Peale's most famous exhibit was a skeleton of a mastodon (he misnamed it a mammoth, thereby adding a synonym for *huge* to the American vocabulary). Assembled from several digs he had conducted with great publicity in upstate New York, it stood 11 feet high at the shoulder and was the first complete mastodon skeleton ever mounted. Billed "the ninth wonder of the world," it was housed in a special "Mammoth Room" that required a separate admission fee.

In gathering and mounting his specimens, Peale sought "to bring into one view a world in miniature." He carefully labeled plants, animals, insects, and birds and

In this self-portrait, Charles Willson Peale lifts a curtain to reveal the famous Long Room of his museum. Partially visible on the right behind Peale is the great mastodon skeleton, at which a woman gazes in awe, while in the rear a father instructs his son on the wonders of nature.

limits and threatened the liberties of citizens, states had the right to interpose their authority.

But Jefferson and Madison were not ready to rend a union that had so recently been forged. The two men intended for the Virginia and Kentucky resolutions only to rally public opinion to the Republican cause. They opposed any effort to resist federal authority by force. Furthermore, other states openly rejected the doctrine of "interposition." During the last year of the Adams administration, the Alien and Sedition Acts quietly expired. Once in power, the Republicans repealed the Naturalization Act.

arranged them according to accepted scientific classifications. He also pioneered the grouping of animals in their natural habitat. Stuffed tigers and deer stood on a plaster mountainside, while below, a glass pond was filled with fish, reptiles, and birds. For the safety of visitors who could not resist handling the exhibits, the birds, whose feathers were covered with arsenic, were eventually put in glass-fronted cases with painted habitats behind them.

Peale refused to indulge the popular taste for spectacles and freaks. He hesitated before accepting a five-legged cow with two tails, fearing it would lower the institution's dignity and compromise its serious purpose. He declined to display a blue sash belonging to George Washington because it had no educational value, and only after Peale's death was it exhibited. He put curiosities away in cabinets and showed them only on request.

Peale's museum was an expression of its founder's republican ideals of order, stability, and harmony. It was, in his mind, an institute of eternal laws, laid bare for the masses to see and understand. Peale hoped the museum would instill civic responsibility in its patrons, and he often told the story of how two hostile Indian chiefs, meeting by accident in the museum, were so impressed with its harmony that they agreed to sign a peace treaty.

The museum attracted thousands of curious customers and prospered in its early years. It was one of the major attractions in Philadelphia and became famous throughout the nation. Yet Peale's vast collection soon overwhelmed his scientific classification scheme, and his grandiose plans always outran his funds and soon his space as well. Refusing to slow his collection efforts, Peale moved his museum in 1794 to Philosophical Hall, and then in 1802 he took over the second floor of Independence Hall.

Before he retired in 1810, Peale tried vainly to interest the national government in acquiring his collection and creating a national museum. Under the direction of his son, the museum struggled on, but it was unable to satisfy the growing popular appetite for showmanship rather than education. The museum finally closed its doors in 1850, but during the Republic's formative years it offered thousands of Americans a unique opportunity, as the ticket of admission promised, to "explore the wondrous world."

The Election of 1800

With a naval war raging on the high seas and the Alien and Sedition Acts sparking debate at home, Adams suddenly shocked his party by negotiating a peace treaty with France. It was a courageous act, for Adams not only split his party in two but also ruined his own chances for reelection by driving Hamilton's pro-British wing of the party into open opposition. The nation benefited, however, for France signed a peace treaty ending its undeclared war. Adams, who bristled with pride and independence, termed this act "the most disinterested, the most determined and the most successful of my whole life."

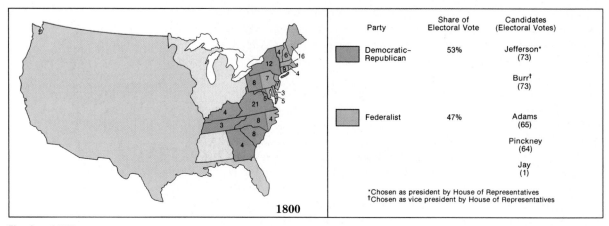

Party	Share of Electoral Vote	Candidates (Electoral Votes)
Democratic-Republican	53%	Jefferson* (73)
		Burr† (73)
Federalist	47%	Adams (65)
		Pinckney (64)
		Jay (1)

*Chosen as president by House of Representatives
†Chosen as vice president by House of Representatives

1800

Election of 1800

With the Federalist party split, Republican prospects in 1800 were bright. Again the party chose Jefferson to run against Adams, along with Aaron Burr for vice president. The Republicans' efficient party organization mobilized supporters, whereas the Federalists' high-handed policies and disdain for the "mob" doomed them in a republic where so many citizens could vote. The political journalist Noah Webster put his finger on the problem of his fellow Federalists when he commented, "They have attempted to resist the force of public opinion, instead of falling into the current with a view to direct it."

Sweeping to victory, the Republicans won control of both houses of Congress for the first time. Adams ran ahead of his party, but Jefferson outdistanced him, 73 electoral votes to 65. Once again, the election demonstrated the fragility of the fledgling political system. Jefferson and Burr received an equal number of votes, but the Constitution, with no provision for political parties, did not distinguish between the votes for president and vice president. With the election tied, the decision lay with the House of Representatives, where each state was allotted one vote. Because Burr refused to step aside for Jefferson, the election remained deadlocked for almost a week, until the Federalists eventually decided that Jefferson represented the lesser of two evils. They allowed his election on the thirty-sixth ballot. In 1804 the Twelfth Amendment corrected the problem, specifying that electors were to vote separately for president and vice president.

Political Violence in the Early Republic

It had been a tense moment: the leadership of the Republic hanging on bitter party votes in the House. Some Federalists even swore they would "go without a constitution and take the risk of civil war." Indeed, it is easy to forget how violent and unpredictable the politics of the 1790s had been.

Some of the violence was physical. The leading Republican newspaper editor in Philadelphia plunged into a street brawl with his Federalist rival; Representatives Matthew Lyon and Roger Griswold slugged it out on the floor of Congress. Mobs threatened the leaders of both parties, and at the height of the crisis of 1798–1799, President John Adams actually smuggled guns into his home for protection. The political rhetoric of the era was equally abusive and violent. Republicans accused patriots like Washington and Hamilton of being British agents and monarchists; Federalists portrayed Jefferson as an irreligious radical and the Republicans as "blood-drinking cannibals." Washington complained that he was abused

"in such exaggerated and indecent terms as could scarcely be applied . . . to a common pickpocket." By 1797, reported Jefferson sadly, "men who have been intimate all their lives, cross the streets to avoid meeting, and turn their heads another way, lest they should be obliged to touch their hats."

What accounted for this torrent of violence—both real and rhetorical—in the first decade of the Republic? For one thing, Federalists and Republicans alike recognized how fragile a form of government republicanism had proved over the long course of history. Its repeated failure left political leaders uneasy and uncertain about the American experiment. Then, too, the ideology of the American Revolution stressed the need to guard constantly against conspiracies to subvert liberty. All too quickly, turbulent foreign events like the French Revolution heightened domestic suspicions.

Ideology of republicanism

In such overheated circumstances, both Republicans and Federalists readily assumed the worst of one another. Neither side grasped that political parties were essential in a democracy to express and resolve peacefully differences among competing social, geographic, and economic interests. Instead, each party considered the other a faction and therefore illegitimate. Each longed to reestablish a one-party system. Not until after 1815 did a political ideology develop that recognized the need for parties.

As John Adams prepared to leave office, he looked back with mixed feelings on the 12 years that the Federalist party had held power. Under Washington's firm leadership and his own, his party had made the Constitution a workable instrument of government. The Federalists had proved that republicanism was compatible with stability and order, and they had established economic policies and principles of foreign affairs that even their opponents would continue. The Union had been strengthened, the Constitution had been accepted, and prosperity had returned.

Federalist achievements

But most Federalists took no solace in such reflections, for the forces of history seemed to be running against them. As the champions of order and hierarchy, of government by the wellborn, of a society in which social betters guided their respectful inferiors, they had waged one last desperate battle to save their disintegrating world—and had lost. Power had fallen into the hands of the ignorant and unwashed rabble, led by that demagogue Thomas Jefferson. Federalists shared fully the view of the British minister who concluded in 1800 that the entire American political system was "tottering to its foundations."

The great American experiment in republicanism had failed. Of this most Federalists were certain. And surely, if history was any judge, the destruction of liberty and order would soon follow.

chapter summary

Politics in the early Republic was rooted in a fundamental social division between the commercial and semisubsistence areas of the country. Commercially oriented Americans were tied to international trade and depended on the widespread exchange of goods and services, whereas families in the semisubsistence economy produced most of what they consumed and did not buy and sell in an extensive market.

- The first party to organize in the 1790s was the Federalists, led by Alexander Hamilton and George Washington. They were opposed by the Republicans, led by James Madison and Thomas Jefferson.

- Divisions over Hamilton's policies as secretary of the treasury stimulated the formation of rival political parties.

- The commercially minded Federalists believed in order and hierarchy, supported loose construction of the Constitution, and wanted a powerful central government to promote economic growth.

- The Republican party, with its sympathy for agrarian ideals, endorsed strict construction of the Constitution, wanted a less active federal government, and harbored a strong fear of aristocracy.

- The French Revolution and foreign policy also stimulated the formation of parties in the 1790s.

  – The Federalists supported England, and the Jeffersonians supported France.

  – The major events of John Adams's presidency—the XYZ Affair, the naval war, and the Alien and Sedition Acts—were all linked to the debate over foreign policy.

- In the presidential election of 1800, Thomas Jefferson became the first leader of an opposition party to be elected president.

- The Federalists demonstrated that the new government could be a more active force in American society, but their controversial domestic and foreign policies, internal divisions, and open hostility to the masses eventually led to their downfall.

interactive learning

The Primary Source Investigator CD-ROM offers the following materials related to this chapter:

- Interactive map: **Election of 1800** (M7)

- A collection of primary sources exploring the Jeffersonian era and the Revolution of 1800, including the U.S. Constitution and the Treaty of Greenville. Other documents investigate social unrest in the new republic, such as the insightful diaries of Quakers Elizabeth Drinker and John Woolman. Also included are key sources that illuminate the foreign policy of the young United States: Jay's Treaty and the Alien and Sedition Acts.

additional reading

Once the subject of considerable controversy, political developments in this period have attracted less attention from historians in recent years. Much of the scholarship, while older, is nevertheless sound. The most recent overview is Stanley Elkins and Eric McKitrick's massively detailed study, *The Age of Federalism* (1993). James Roger Sharp, *American Politics in the Early Republic* (1993), is a brief, up-to-date survey. Jacob E. Cooke, *Alexander Hamilton* (1982), is a good short biography, while Stephen G. Kurtz, *The Presidency of John Adams* (1957), analyzes the growing split in the party under Adams. Some of the most imaginative work has focused on the ideology of republicanism. Lance Banning, The *Jeffersonian Persuasion* (1978), and Drew R. McCoy, *The Elusive Republic* (1980), are both excellent treatments of the ideology of the Jeffersonians. There is no equivalent study of Federalist ideology. The best account of the Republican party's formation is Noble Cunningham, *The Jeffersonian Republicans* (1963).

Historians are beginning to examine American society in these years. Useful works include Jack Larkin, *The Reshaping of Everyday Life, 1790–1840* (1988); Reginald Horsman, *The Frontier in the Formative Years, 1783–1815* (1970); Howard Rock, *Artisans of the New Republic* (1979); and Laurel Thatcher Ulrich, *A Midwife's Tale* (1990). Crèvecoeur's and Franklin's writings are available in many editions. For a fuller list of readings, see the Bibliography at www.mhhe.com/davidsonnation5.

significant events

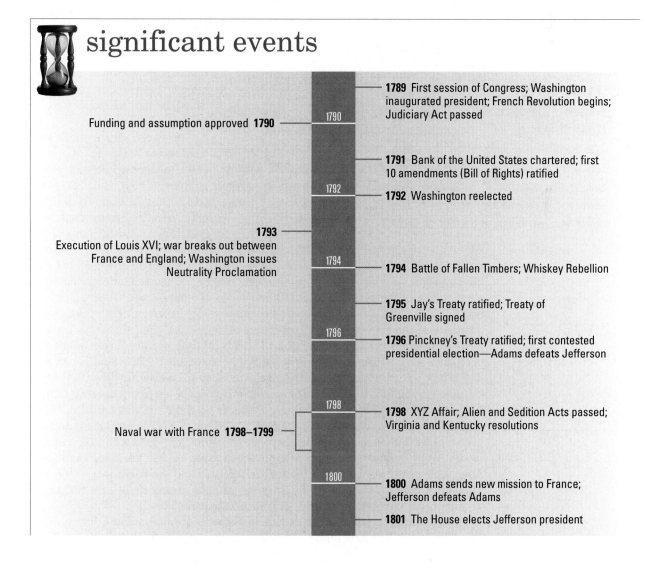

Funding and assumption approved 1790

1790

1789 First session of Congress; Washington inaugurated president; French Revolution begins; Judiciary Act passed

1791 Bank of the United States chartered; first 10 amendments (Bill of Rights) ratified

1792

1792 Washington reelected

1793
Execution of Louis XVI; war breaks out between France and England; Washington issues Neutrality Proclamation

1794

1794 Battle of Fallen Timbers; Whiskey Rebellion

1795 Jay's Treaty ratified; Treaty of Greenville signed

1796

1796 Pinckney's Treaty ratified; first contested presidential election—Adams defeats Jefferson

1798

1798 XYZ Affair; Alien and Sedition Acts passed; Virginia and Kentucky resolutions

Naval war with France 1798–1799

1800

1800 Adams sends new mission to France; Jefferson defeats Adams

1801 The House elects Jefferson president

Chapter 9

O n September 29, 1800, following a rather rocky courtship, Margaret Bayard married Samuel H. Smith. Even though Samuel was well educated and from a socially prominent family, Margaret's father consented to the marriage reluctantly, for the Bayards were staunch Federalists and Smith was an ardent Republican. Indeed, Thomas Jefferson had asked Smith, an editor in Philadelphia, to follow the government to Washington, D.C., and establish a Republican newspaper in the new capital. After the wedding, the couple traveled to the new seat of government on the banks of the Potomac River.

When the Smiths arrived in Washington, they found a raw village of 3200 souls. Samuel began publishing the *National Intelligencer,* the first national newspaper in the United States, while Margaret's social charm and keen intelligence made their home a center of Washington society. When she met Jefferson about a month after her arrival, she found herself captivated by his gracious manners, sparkling conversation, and gentlemanly bearing. Whatever remained of her Federalist sympathies vanished, and she became (perhaps as her father feared) a devoted supporter of the Republican leader.

In eager anticipation she went to the Senate on March 4, 1801, to witness Jefferson's inauguration. The chamber was packed, but the members of Congress nonetheless reserved one side for the ladies present. To

The Jeffersonian Republic
1801–1824

preview • Jefferson supported his agrarian principles by acquiring the Louisiana Territory. But increasingly he abandoned his earlier ideals of limited government in favor of a more active nationalism. Nationalism was also served by the stronger federal courts led by Chief Justice John Marshall and by the expansion of white Americans westward. The growth in national power and pride was not halted, either by a Pan-Indian alliance under Tecumseh or by Great Britain in the War of 1812.

Jefferson's inauguration

emphasize the change in attitude of the new administration, the president-elect walked to the Capitol with only a small escort. Absent were the elaborate ceremonies of the years of Federalist rule. Because Jefferson delivered his inaugural address in almost a whisper, few in the assembled crowd heard much of what he said. Then Chief Justice John Marshall, a Virginian but a Federalist whom Jefferson deeply distrusted, administered the oath of office. When the swearing-in was completed, the new president returned to his lodgings at Conrad and McMunn's boardinghouse, where he declined a place of honor and instead took his accustomed seat at the foot of the table. Only several weeks later did he finally move to his official residence.

As Margaret Smith proudly watched the proceedings, she could not help thinking of the most striking feature of this transfer of power: it was peaceful. "The changes of administration," she commented, "which in every government and in every age have most generally been epochs of confusion, villainy and bloodshed, in our happy country take place without any species of distraction, or disorder." After the fierce controversies of the previous decade and the harsh rhetoric of the election of 1800, to see the opposition party take power peacefully—the first such occurrence in the nation's history—was indeed remarkable.

Once in power, Jefferson set out to reshape the government and society into closer harmony with Republican principles. He later referred to his election as "the

We Owe Allegiance to No Crown, by John A. Woodside, reflects the growing nationalism in American life after 1815. Significantly, however, Woodside portrays a sailor and sailing ship, for during these years war on the seas challenged the independence of the United States.

Revolution of 1800," asserting that it "was as real a revolution in the principles of our government as that of 1776 was in its form." That statement is an exaggeration, perhaps. But the rule of the Republican party during the following two decades set the nation on a distinctly more democratic tack. And in working out its relationship with Britain and France, as well as with the Indian nations of the

West, America achieved a sense of its own nationhood that came only with time and with the passing of the Revolutionary generation.

Jefferson in Power

Thomas Jefferson was the first president to be inaugurated in the new capital, Washington, D.C. In 1791 George Washington had commissioned Pierre Charles L'Enfant, a French architect and engineer who had served in the American Revolution, to draw up plans for the new seat of government. L'Enfant designed a city with broad avenues, statues and fountains, parks and plazas, and a central mall. Because the Federalists believed that government was the paramount power in a nation, they had intended that the city would be a new Rome—a cultural, intellectual, and commercial center of the Republic.

The New Capital City

The new city, however, fell far short of this grandiose dream. It was located in a swampy river bottom near the head of navigation on the Potomac, and the surrounding low-lying hills rendered the spot oppressively hot and muggy during the summer. Removed from the thriving commercial centers of the country, the capital had no business or society independent of the government. The streets were filled with tree stumps and became impenetrable seas of mud after a rain. Much of the District was wooded, and virtually all of it remained unoccupied.

When the government moved to its new residence in 1800, the Senate chamber, where Jefferson took the oath of office, was the only part of the Capitol that had been completed. The executive mansion was unfinished as well, although it had been occupied since November, when the Adamses had moved in for the last few months of John Adams's presidency. Except for its classical architecture, the city gave no hint of imitating the great centers of antiquity. A British diplomat grumbled at having to leave Philadelphia, the previous capital, with its bustling commerce, regular communication with the outside world, and lively society, to conduct business in "a mere swamp."

Washington in 1800 barely resembled L'Enfant's grand design. When Jefferson was inaugurated, only one wing of the Capitol was complete, and a primitive Pennsylvania Avenue ran more than a mile through the woods before it connected with the unfinished executive mansion.

Yet the isolated and unimpressive capital reflected the new president's attitude toward government. Distrustful of centralized power of any kind, Jefferson deliberately set out to remake the national government into one of limited scope that touched few people's daily lives. He took as his ideal precisely what the Federalists had striven to avoid—a government, in Hamilton's words, "at a distance and out of sight," which commanded little popular attention.

Jefferson's Character and Philosophy

Jefferson himself reflected that vision of modesty. Even standing nearly 6 feet, 3 inches, the 57-year-old president lacked an imposing presence. He dressed so carelessly in frequently ill-fitting clothes that William Plumer, a New Hampshire Federalist, mistook him for a servant when he called at the executive mansion. Despite his wealth and genteel birth into Virginia society, Jefferson disliked pomp and maintained an image of republican simplicity. His informal manners and habit of conducting business in a frayed coat and slippers dismayed dignitaries who called on him decked out in ribbons and lace.

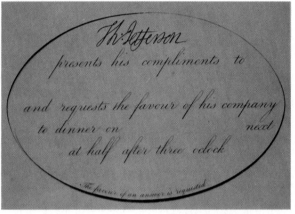

Jefferson was a product of the Enlightenment, with its faith in the power of human reason to improve society and decipher the universe. While afflicted with occasional bouts of despair, he was on the whole an unshakable optimist. "I steer my bark with Hope in the head," he once declared, "leaving fear astern." An elegant writer but ineffective public speaker, he preferred to accomplish his political business in private conferences or at his renowned dinner parties, where he charmed his guests with his stimulating conversation.

Thomas Jefferson's invitations to dinner may strike readers today as formal, but Jefferson was actually attempting to set a tone of democratic informality. One Federalist did not miss the implication and complained, "It is *Th:Jefferson* not the *President* that invites—& yet were he not the President I presume I should not be invited."

Jefferson considered "the will of the majority" to be "the only sure guardian of the rights of man," which he defined as "life, liberty, and the pursuit of happiness." Although he conceded that the masses might err, he was confident they would soon return to correct principles. His faith in human virtue exceeded that of most of the founding generation, yet in good republican fashion, he feared those in power, even if they had been elected by the people. Government seemed to Jefferson at best a necessary evil.

To Jefferson, agriculture was a morally superior way of life. "Those who labour in the earth are the chosen people of God, if ever he had a chosen people," he wrote in *Notes on the State of Virginia* (1787). Like Crèvecoeur, Jefferson praised rural life for nourishing the honesty, independence, and virtue so essential in a republic. Government would "remain virtuous . . . as long as [the American people] are chiefly agricultural," he assured James Madison. Rather than encouraging large-scale factories, Jefferson wanted to preserve small household manufacturing, which was an essential part of the rural economy. Commerce should exist primarily to sell America's agricultural surplus. He was never able to overcome his earlier belief, rooted in the republican ideology of the Revolution, that cities and commerce promoted speculation, greed, and useless luxury and self-indulgence.

Agrarian values

Although Jefferson asserted that "the tree of liberty must be refreshed from time to time by the blood of patriots and tyrants," his reputation as a radical was undeserved. While he wanted to extend the suffrage to a greater number of Americans, he clung to the traditional republican idea that voters should own property and thus be economically independent. One of the largest slaveholders in the country, he

Jefferson's radicalism exaggerated

increasingly muffled his once-bold condemnation of slavery, and in the last years of his life he reproached critics of the institution who sought to prevent it from expanding westward. Nor did his belief in free speech mean that he had any qualms about state governments punishing political criticism.

Slaveholding aristocrat and apostle of democracy, lofty theorist and pragmatic politician, Jefferson was an exceedingly complex, at times contradictory, personality. But like most politicians, he was flexible in his approach to problems and tried to balance means and ends. And like most leaders, he quickly discovered that he confronted very different problems in power than he had in opposition.

Republican Principles

Limited government

Once Jefferson had settled into the executive mansion, he took steps to return the government to the republican ideals of simplicity and frugality. The states rather than the federal government were "the most competent administrators for our domestic concerns," he asserted in his inaugural address. Ever the individualist, he recommended a government that left people "free to regulate their own pursuits of industry and improvement."

Jefferson also went out of his way to soothe the feelings of defeated Federalists. Acknowledging Hamilton's fiscal policies, he promised to uphold the government's credit and protect commerce as the "handmaiden" of agriculture—both Federalist concerns. Agreeing with Washington, he proposed friendship with all nations and "entangling alliances" with none. Finally, he called on Americans to unite for the common good: "We have called by different names brethren of the same principles. We are all republicans—we are all federalists."

The election of 1800 established the legitimacy of an opposition party in American politics, and Jefferson, in his inaugural address, seemed to endorse the validity of a party system. In reality, however, he hoped to restore one-party rule by winning over moderate and honest Federalists and isolating the party's extremists, whom he still attacked as monarchists.

Jefferson's Economic Policies

But what would Jefferson do about Hamilton's economic program? As he promised in his inaugural address, the new president proceeded to cut spending, reduce the size of the government, and begin paying off the national debt. Unless the debt was paid, he warned Albert Gallatin, his talented secretary of the treasury, "we shall be committed to the English career of debt, corruption and rottenness, closing with revolution." He abolished the internal taxes enacted by the Federalists, including the controversial levy on whiskey, and thus was able to get rid of all tax collectors and inspectors. "What farmer, what mechanic, what laborer, ever sees a tax gatherer in the United States?" boasted Jefferson in 1805. Land sales and the tariff duties would supply the funds needed to run the scaled-down government.

The most serious spending cuts were made in the military branches. Jefferson slashed the army budget in half, decreasing the army to 3000 men. In a national emergency, he reasoned, the militia could defend the country. Jefferson reduced the navy even more, halting work on powerful frigates authorized during the naval war with France and replacing them with a fleet of small gunboats, which captured Jefferson's fancy because they were cheap. In the long term, however, they proved totally inadequate to defend the nation's coasts in war.

By such steps, Jefferson made significant progress toward paying off Hamilton's hated national debt. He lowered it from $83 million to only $57 million by the end of his two terms in office, despite the added financial burden of the Louisiana Purchase (page 263). Still, Jefferson did not entirely dismantle the Federalists' economic program. Funding and assumption could not be reversed—the nation's honor was pledged to paying these debts, and Jefferson fully understood the importance of maintaining the nation's credit. The tariff had to be retained as a source of revenue to meet government expenses. More surprising, Jefferson argued that the national bank should be left to run its course until 1811, when its charter would expire. In reality, he expanded the bank's operations and, in words reminiscent of Hamilton, advocated tying banks and members of the business class to the government by rewarding those who supported the Republican party.

Failure to abolish Hamilton's program

In effect, practical politics had triumphed over agrarian economics. Throughout his presidency, Jefferson often put pragmatic considerations above unyielding principles. As he himself expressed it, "What is practicable must often control what is pure theory."

John Marshall and Judicial Review

Having lost both the presidency and control of Congress in 1800, the Federalists took steps to shore up their power before Jefferson took office. They did so by expanding the size of the federal court system, the one branch of the federal government that they still controlled. The Judiciary Act of 1801 created 6 circuit courts and 16 new judgeships, along with a number of marshals, attorneys, and clerks. Federalists justified these "midnight appointments" (executed by Adams in the last weeks of his term) on the grounds that the expanding nation required a larger judiciary.

Jefferson, however, saw matters differently. "The Federalists, defeated at the polls, have retired into the Judiciary," he fumed, "and from that barricade . . . hope to batter down all the bulwarks of Republicanism." In 1802, by a strict party vote, Congress repealed the 1801 law and eliminated the new courts and their officers.

Among Adams's last-minute appointments was that of William Marbury as justice of the peace for the District of Columbia. When James Madison assumed the office of secretary of state under the new administration, he found a batch of undelivered commissions, including Marbury's. Wishing to appoint loyal Republicans to these posts, Jefferson instructed Madison not to hand over the commissions, whereupon Marbury sued under the Judiciary Act of 1789. Since that act gave the Supreme Court original jurisdiction in cases against federal officials, the case of *Marbury v. Madison* went directly to the Court in 1803.

Marbury v. Madison

Chief Justice John Marshall, a Federalist and one of Adams's late-term appointments, seized on this case to affirm the Court's greatest power, the right to review statutes and interpret the meaning of the Constitution. "It is emphatically the province of and duty of the judicial department to say what the law is," he wrote in upholding the doctrine of judicial review. This idea meant that the Court "must of necessity expound and interpret" the Constitution and the laws when one statute conflicted with another or when a law violated the framework of the Constitution. Marshall found that the section of the Judiciary Act of 1789 that granted the Supreme Court original jurisdiction in the case was unconstitutional. Because the Constitution specified those cases in which the Court had such jurisdiction, they could not be enlarged by statute. *Marbury v. Madison* was so critical to the development of the American constitutional system that it has been called the keystone of the constitutional arch.

John Marshall

Judicial review

Marshall and his colleagues later asserted the power of the Court to review the constitutionality of state laws in *Fletcher v. Peck* (1810) when it struck down a Georgia law. It also brought state courts under the scrutiny of the Supreme Court in *Martin v. Hunter's Lessee* (1816), denying the claim of the Virginia Supreme Court that it was not subject to the authority of the federal judiciary, and in *Cohens v. Virginia* (1821), in which it asserted its right to review decisions of state courts on issues arising under the Constitution. In fact, during his tenure on the bench, Marshall extended judicial review to all acts of government. It took time for the doctrine to be accepted, but since Marshall's time the Supreme Court has successfully defended its position as the final judge of the meaning of the Constitution.

The Jeffersonian Attack on the Judiciary

Having disposed of the bulk of Adams's recent appointments, the Republicans proceeded to attack Federalist judges who had been particularly obnoxious during the party battles of the 1790s. Jefferson argued that impeachment was not limited to criminal acts but was an appropriate political device to remove any judge who proved unacceptable to two-thirds of the Senate. In 1803, after the House had impeached federal district judge John Pickering of New Hampshire, who was both insane and an alcoholic, he was convicted and removed by the Senate.

Encouraged by this success, the administration turned its attention to Associate Justice Samuel Chase of the Supreme Court. An ultra-Federalist, Chase had interpreted the Sedition Act in a blatantly partisan fashion to ensure convictions against Republicans. After the House impeached Chase, a majority of senators voted to convict, but since a two-thirds vote was necessary for removal, Chase was acquitted. In the end, Republicans decided to wait for death and retirement to give them eventual control of the remaining branch of the government through presidential appointments.

Jefferson and Western Expansion

The Federalists feared the West as a threat to social order and stability. Frontiersmen, sneered New Englander Timothy Dwight, were "too idle; too talkative; too passionate . . . and too shiftless to acquire either property or character." Farther south, another observer referred to squatters on western lands as "ragged, dirty, brawling, browbeating monsters, six feet high, whose vocation is robbing, drinking, fighting, and terrifying every peaceable man in the community." Thus when Federalists passed an act in 1796 authorizing the sale of federal land, they viewed it as a revenue measure rather than the means to develop the country and kept the price of land high. It sold for a minimum of $2 an acre, with a required purchase of at least 640 acres, over four times the size of the typical American farm.

Empire of liberty

Jefferson, on the other hand, viewed the West as the means to preserve the values of an agrarian republic. He anticipated that as settled regions of the country became crowded, many rural residents would migrate to the cities in search of work unless cheap land beckoned farther west. America's vast spaces provided land that would last for a thousand generations, he predicted in his inaugural address, enough to transform the United States into "an empire of liberty."

In 1801 the Republican Congress reduced the minimum tract that buyers could purchase to 320 acres and also offered sale on credit. The intention was to encourage rapid settlement of the interior, and in fact, land sales boomed under the new law. Most sales, however, were to speculators and land companies rather than

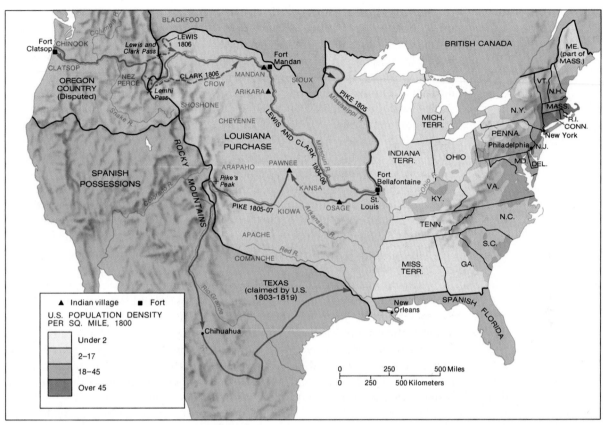

individual settlers. Even so, the West remained strongly Republican. The admission of new western states strengthened Jefferson's party and hastened the decline of the Federalists. From Jefferson's perspective, western expansion was a blessing economically, socially, and politically.

The Louisiana Purchase

Because Spain's colonial empire was disintegrating, Americans were confident that before long they would gain control of Florida and the rest of the Mississippi, either through purchase or by military occupation. This comforting prospect was shattered, however, when Spain ceded Louisiana—the territory lying between the Mississippi River and the Rocky Mountains—to France. Under the leadership of Napoleon Bonaparte, France had become the most powerful nation on the European continent, with the military might to protect its new colony and block American expansion. American anxiety intensified when Spain, while still in control of Louisiana, abruptly revoked Americans' right to navigate the lower Mississippi guaranteed by Pinckney's Treaty. Western farmers, who were suddenly denied access to the sea, angrily protested Spain's high-handed action.

Jefferson dispatched James Monroe to Paris to join Robert Livingston, the American minister, to negotiate the purchase of New Orleans and West Florida from the French and thus secure control of the Mississippi. "There is on the globe one single spot, the [possessor] of which is our natural and habitual enemy," Jefferson reminded them. "It is New Orleans."

Exploration and Expansion: The Louisiana Purchase The vast, largely uncharted Louisiana Purchase lay well beyond the most densely populated areas of the United States. The Lewis and Clark expedition, along with Lieutenant Zebulon Pike's exploration of the upper Mississippi River and the Southwest, opened the way for westward expansion.

Sale of Louisiana

In the meantime, however, Napoleon lost interest in Louisiana. With war looming again in Europe, he needed money, and so in April 1803 he offered to sell not just New Orleans but all of Louisiana to the United States. This proposal flabbergasted Livingston and Monroe. Their instructions said nothing about acquiring all of Louisiana, and they had not been authorized to spend what the French demanded. On the other hand, here was an unprecedented opportunity to expand dramatically the boundaries of the United States. Pressed for an immediate answer, Livingston and Monroe wanted to consult Jefferson but worried that the French might withdraw the offer as suddenly as they had made it. So the American ministers took a deep breath and, after haggling over a few details, agreed to purchase Louisiana for approximately $15 million.

The millions of acres of fertile farmland, untold natural resources, and control of the vital Mississippi River and its tributaries were one of the most extraordinary bargains in the history of the United States. In one fell swoop, the American negotiators had doubled the country's size by adding some 830,000 square miles. "From this day," Livingston asserted, "the United States take their place among the powers of the first rank."

Jefferson's pragmatism

Jefferson, naturally, was immensely pleased at the prospect of acquiring so much territory, which seemed to guarantee the survival of his agrarian republic. At the same time, as someone who favored the doctrine of strict construction, he found the legality of the act deeply troubling. The Constitution, after all, did not specifically authorize the acquisition of territory by treaty. Livingston and Monroe urged haste, however, and in the end, Jefferson sent the treaty to the Senate for ratification, noting privately, "The less we say about constitutional difficulties the better." Once again pragmatism had triumphed over theory.

The purchase of Louisiana was generally popular, and the Senate ratified the treaty 24 to 7. West Florida, which bordered part of the lower Mississippi, remained in Spanish hands, and Jefferson's efforts to acquire this region were unsuccessful. Nevertheless, western commerce could flow down the Mississippi unhindered to the sea. The Louisiana Purchase would rank as the greatest achievement of Jefferson's presidency.

Lewis and Clark

Early in 1803, even before the Louisiana Purchase was completed, Congress secretly appropriated $2500 to send an exploring party up the Missouri River to the Pacific. This expedition was led by Meriwether Lewis, Jefferson's secretary, and William Clark, a younger brother of Revolutionary War hero George Rogers Clark.

Jefferson instructed Lewis and Clark to map the region and make detailed observations of the soil, climate, rivers, minerals, and plant and animal life. They were also to investigate the practicability of an overland route to the Pacific and engage in diplomacy with the Indians along the way. Equally important, by pushing onward to the Pacific, Lewis and Clark would strengthen the American title to Oregon, which several nations claimed but none effectively occupied.

Exploration of the West

In the spring of 1804 Lewis and Clark left St. Louis and headed up the Missouri with 48 men. They laboriously pushed their boats up the Missouri River to present-day North Dakota, where they spent the winter with the Mandan Indians. The next spring, they headed west again. Only with great difficulty did the expedition pass the rugged mountains ahead of the winter snows and then float down first the Snake and then the Columbia River to the Pacific.

After spending a bleak winter in Oregon, vainly awaiting a ship that would take them back, the company returned in 1806 over the Rockies. Having traveled across half the continent in both directions, navigated countless rapids, and conducted negotiations with numerous tribes, Lewis and Clark arrived in St. Louis in September, two and a half years after they had departed. The expedition fired the imagination of Americans about the exotic lands of the newly acquired Louisiana Purchase as well as the Pacific Northwest. Lewis and Clark had collected thousands of useful plant and animal specimens, discovered several passes through the Rockies, and produced a remarkably accurate map, their most valuable contribution to western exploration.

Whites and Indians on the Frontier

In February 1803, as American diplomats prepared to leave for France in hopes of gaining title to western lands, another delegation was visiting Washington with a similar purpose. Black Hoof, a Shawnee chief from the Ohio River valley, asked the secretary of war to issue a deed to the lands that legally belonged to the Shawnees in western Ohio. The deed, said Black Hoof, would ensure that his people could "raise good Grain and cut Hay for our Cattle" and guarantee "that nobody would take advantage" of them. The astonished secretary was not about to give the Shawnee any document that would strengthen their title to land in Ohio. But he did promise to provide some plows and cattle.

Unlike many Shawnees, Black Hoof had decided that the best way to get along with white Americans was to adopt their ways. For a number of years he and his tribe settled along the Auglaize River, built log houses, wore garments like those of whites, cleared land to raise corn, potatoes, cabbage, and turnips, and even planted an apple orchard. But in 1808, after the government refused to pay a Quaker missionary who was providing technical support, Black Hoof's followers became increasingly dependent on government payments. Even Black Hoof admitted, "The white people . . . have been our ruin."

Indian attempts at assimilation

The Shawnees along the Auglaize were only one of many Indian tribes forced to make hard choices as white Americans streamed into the fertile lands of the Ohio River valley. In 1790 only about 100,000 whites lived in the West. By 1800 that number had jumped to almost 400,000 and, a decade later, to more than a million. By 1820 more than 2 million whites lived in a region they had first entered only 50 years earlier.

In this backcountry, where white and Indian cultures mixed and often clashed, both peoples experienced the breakdown of traditional cultural systems. White immigrants pushing into Indian territory often lacked the structures of community such as churches, schools, and legal institutions. But Indian cultures were also severely stressed by the availability of white trade goods and by the more settled agricultural ways of white farmers, with their domesticated animals and fenced-in fields. Above all, Indians had to deal with the unceasing hunger of whites for Indian lands.

The Course of White Settlement

Following the Treaty of Greenville in 1795, white settlers poured into the Ohio Territory by wagon and flatboat. "From what I have seen and heard," one girl wrote while crossing Pennsylvania bound for the West, "I think the State of Ohio will be well fill'd before winter,—Waggons without number, every day go on." The pattern of settlement remained the same: in the first wave came backwoods families who laboriously cleared a few acres of forest by girdling the trees, removing the brush, and planting corn between the dead trunks. Their isolated one-room log cabins were crude, dark, and windowless, with mud stuffed between the chinks; the furniture and utensils were sparse and homemade. Such settlers were mostly squatters without legal title to their land. As a region began to fill up, these restless pioneers usually sold their improvements and headed west again.

Maturing society

Many of the settlers who replaced them were young unmarried men who left crowded regions in the East seeking new opportunities. Their migration, which relieved population pressures back home, contributed to the imbalance of males and females on the frontier. Once established, they quickly married and started families. Like the pioneers before them, most engaged in semisubsistence agriculture. As their numbers increased and a local market developed, they switched to surplus agriculture, growing and making much of what the family needed while selling or exchanging the surplus to obtain essential items. "The woman told me that they spun and wove all the cotton and woolen garments of the family, and knit all the stockings," a visitor to an Ohio farm wrote. "Her husband, though not a shoemaker by trade, made all the shoes. She manufactured all the soap and candles they used." The wife sold butter and chickens to get money to buy coffee, tea, and whiskey.

A Changing Environment

The inrush of new settlers significantly reduced the amount of original forest west of the Appalachian Mountains. Americans, who equated clearing the forest with progress, "have an unconquerable aversion to trees," one observer noted, "and whenever a settlement is made they cut away all before them without mercy; not one is spared; all share the same fate and are involved in the same general havoc." By 1850 they had cleared at least 100 million acres. In newly cleared areas the resulting landscape was often bleak, according to one traveler. "The trees are cut over at the height of three or four feet from the ground and the stumps are left for many years till the roots rot;—the edge of the forest, opened for the first time to the light of the sun looks cold and raw;—the ground rugged and ill-dressed . . . as if nothing could ever be made to spring from it."

Effects of deforestation

This rapid cutting of the forest altered plant and animal life in significant ways. Large animals, such as the deer and bears, became scarce, and the bison soon disappeared east of the Mississippi River. The loss of forest cover, combined with the new plowing of the land, increased the amount of runoff after rains, which lowered the water table and caused many streams to dry up for a good part of the year. At the same time increased runoff made rivers more destructive and floods more common. Clearing the land also produced serious soil erosion, particularly on hillsides, and silted many previously navigable streams and rivers. The climate changed as well: it was hotter in the summer and the winds blew more fiercely, causing erosion in the summer and chilling gusts in the winter.

Deforestation also made the Ohio valley more unhealthy. Malaria was not unknown in the region previously, but the growing population density and the cutting of forests made the disease more common. In clearing the land, settlers often created wasteland with pools of stagnant water from the increased runoff, which became breeding places for mosquitoes that spread the disease. Observers remarked on the greater prevalence of malaria and other summer diseases in the region as the forests came down.

The Second Great Awakening

It was the sparsely settled regions that became famous for a second wave of revivals, known collectively as the Second Great Awakening, that swept across the nation beginning in the late 1790s. Like the first national outpouring of religious enthusiasm

50 years earlier, these revivals were fanned by ministers who traveled the countryside preaching to groups anywhere they could. Beginning in the late 1790s Congregationalists, Presbyterians, and Baptists all participated. The Methodists, however, had the most effective organization for spreading the gospel in remote areas with their system of circuit riders. One competing Presbyterian minister ruefully noted that "into every hovel I entered I learned that the Methodist missionary had been there before me."

News of several revivals in Kentucky in the summer of 1800 quickly spread, and people came from 50 and 100 miles around, camping in makeshift tents and holding services out of doors. This new form of worship, the camp meeting, reached its climax at Cane Ridge, Kentucky, in August 1801. At a time when the largest city in the state had only 2000 people, more than 10,000 gathered for a week to hear dozens of ministers.

Cane Ridge

Men and women earnestly examined their hearts; scoffers came, half-mocking, half-fearful of what they might see. For rural folk accustomed to going to bed soon after dark, the sight of hundreds of campfires flickering throughout the woods far into the night, reinforced by the endless singing, praying, and crying, was a powerful tonic indeed. "The vast sea of human beings seemed to be agitated as if by storm," recalled one skeptic, who himself was converted at Cane Ridge.

> I counted seven ministers all preaching at once. . . . Some of the people were singing, others praying, some crying for mercy in the most piteous accents. . . . At one time I saw at least 500 swept down in a moment as if a battery of a thousand guns had been opened upon them, and then immediately followed shrieks and shouts that rent the very heavens.

Although the clergy at camp meetings were male, women played prominent roles, often pressing husbands to convert. In the overwhelming emotion of the moment, converts might dance, bark, laugh hysterically, or jerk uncontrollably, hair flying, the whole body shaking, as they sought to gain assurance of their salvation. (See Daily Lives, "The Frontier Camp Meeting," pages 268–269.)

Men and women witness the baptism of a female worshiper. A European observer said of such baptisms, "Barefoot and bareheaded, with flowing hair, they step solemnly into the river, while a choir sings." Like camp meetings and revivals, such scenes were an emotional experience for the congregation as well as the converts. Several members kneel in prayer or shout praises to the Lord while the rest of the group gaze with rapt attention.

Daily Lives

PUBLIC SPACE/ PRIVATE SPACE
The Frontier Camp Meeting

The Cane Ridge revival, one of the earliest along the frontier, was a chaotic, disorganized affair. But as western clergy became more experienced with outdoor camp meetings, they standardized the format. About a week in advance, organizers chose a forest clearing, removed nearby underbrush, erected pulpits, and constructed benches. Usually the camp went up near an established church, which provided lodging for the ministers. Since a water supply was essential, camps were located near springs, creeks, or rivers. A good site needed dry ground, shade so worshipers could escape the blazing sun, and pasturage for the horses.

The site might be laid out in a horseshoe, a rectangle, or, most popularly, a broad circle. In each case the tents of the worshipers formed a ring around the outdoor auditorium where services were held. As participants arrived, a supervisor directed drivers where to park wagons, tether animals, and pitch tents. At large meetings, where as many as 200 tents covered the site, tents were set up in several rows with streets in between to allow easy access. To help people find their lodgings, the streets were sometimes even named. This outer perimeter constituted the meeting's private space. Here, beneath tents of sailcloth or even shelters patched together from old blankets and sheets, individuals could withdraw from the larger group to find relative solitude, cook meals in front of campfires, and sleep on rude beds of straw or simply on the ground.

Worshipers were naturally drawn toward the central public space, where they filled bench after bench at the periodic call of a bugle. Rising above the listeners, at one or both ends of the clearing, stood the preachers' pulpit. Sometimes it was merely a 10-foot-square platform on stilts; other times it was more elaborate, with several levels and a roof. Services were held in the open, and neither rain nor thunderstorms would interrupt them. At night, the dancing light and shadows produced by the candles, torches, campfires, and fire altars (earthen-covered platforms) at each corner heightened the feeling of awe.

The democracy of the frontier did not automatically break down customary social constraints. For reasons of authority as well as practicality, the ministers' pulpit rose above the congregation. And the audience itself was segregated: women on one side of the clearing, men on the other. In the South, black worshipers were

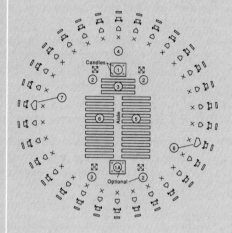

CODE
- ✕ Cooking fires—illumination also from candles in trees
- ⌂ Tents
- 🛏 Wagons
- ⊖ Horses
1. Speakers' stand—candles for illumination
2. Earthen covered fire platforms
3. Mourners' bench
4. Blacks' worship area
5. Seats—women's side
6. Seats—men's side
7. Preachers' tent
8. Boarding tent

Source: Adapted from Charles A. Johnson, *The Frontier Camp Meeting: Religion's Harvest Time* (Dallas: SMU Press, 1955), pp. 43 and 47.

African Americans and revivals

In the South, African Americans, including slaves, attended camp meetings and enthusiastically participated in the tumultuous services. Indeed, revivals were a major force in spreading Christianity to African Americans and producing slave conversions. Revivalists' clear and vivid speech, their acceptance of the moral worth of every individual regardless of race, and their emphasis on the conversion experience rather than abstract theology had the same appeal to black listeners, who had little formal schooling, as they did to poorly educated white churchgoers. Blacks worshiped separately from and sometimes together with whites. The revivals also produced black preachers, who exhorted white as well as black audiences. Some slaveholders, especially in eastern plantation districts, worried that camp meetings might foster racial egalitarianism, but revivalists concentrated on bringing slaves to Christ rather than questioning society's institutions. As was the case

seated in an area behind the pulpit, where they set up their own camp and conducted separate services.

Since the purpose of camp meetings was to "revive" religion and stir listeners' hearts, several rows of planks were set aside directly in front of the pulpit as an "anxious bench," for those whose souls struggled in the agony of conversion. The design of the space thus focused the attention of both congregation and ministers on the "mourners," who were exhorted and prayed over in hopes that they would receive a new birth in Christ. As camp meetings became increasingly organized, separate mourning tents were set up on the edge of the arena near the anxious benches. (Again, curtains separated the male and female sections, and black participants had their own mourning tents.)

But the social boundaries between public and private, male and female, and even black and white could be broken down. As excitement grew, several services might be held at once, some people praying, others singing, shouting, or listening to ministers who stood on wagons or makeshift platforms of felled trees. And when formal services ended, men and women often continued singing and exhorting in small groups, going into the woods to pray, and searching one another's souls by campfires late into the night. Indeed, the social mixing and spontaneous excitement were great enough that meeting sponsors quickly learned that supervision was necessary to prevent unseemly activities. The nearby forest, the numerous tents, and nightfall all offered temptations for drinking, carousing, or lovemaking. Therefore, official patrols were set up to regularly investigate suspicious activities and to monitor sleeping arrangements.

On the final day white and black worshipers joined together in a singing and marching festival before disbanding to their more humdrum daily routines. Successful camp meetings depended on more than the talents of the clergy and the enthusiasm of participants. In their layout they were carefully planned and regulated communities in the forest, designed to reduce the distance between public and private space and thereby instill a sense of religion into all the activities that took place in the meeting as well as those that would be resumed in the regular world.

with white worshipers, the Baptist and Methodist churches received the bulk of African American converts.

The revivals quickly found critics, who decried the emotionalism and hysteria they produced. For a time Presbyterians and Baptists withdrew from camp meetings, leaving the field to the Methodists. Eventually even the Methodists sought to dampen excessive emotion by restricting admittance and patrolling the meeting grounds.

Revivals like Cane Ridge provided an emotional release from the hard, isolated life on the frontier. Pioneers could momentarily forget the drabness of their lives, the pains and sorrows they endured as they struggled to carve an existence out of the forest. For families with few neighbors, camp meetings offered a chance to participate in a wider social gathering while relieving pent-up emotions. And for those

Attraction of revivals

at the bottom of the social hierarchy, the revivalists' message emphasized an individual's ability to gain personal triumph and salvation regardless of his or her station in life. In the swiftly changing borderlands north and south of the Ohio River, where society seemed constantly in flux, revivals brought a sense of uplift and comfort.

Pressure on Indian Lands and Culture

As white settlers continued to flood into the backcountry, the pressure to acquire Indian lands increased. Jefferson endorsed the policy that Indian tribes would either have to assimilate into American culture by becoming farmers and abandoning their seminomadic hunting or would have to move west of the Mississippi River. There, isolated from white settlement, the Indians could gradually develop the skills and values necessary to fit into American society. Jefferson defended these alternatives as in the best interests of the Indians, because he believed that otherwise they faced extermination. But he also recognized that by becoming farmers they would need less land. "While they are learning to do better on less land," he noted, "our increasing numbers will be calling for more land."

The hard truth about white policies toward Indians was that however enlightened some individuals might be, the demographic pressure of high birthrates and aggressive expansion ensured conflict between the two cultures. Anglo-Americans never doubted the superiority of their ways. As William Henry Harrison, governor of the new Indiana Territory, confessed in 1801, "A great many of the Inhabitants of the Fronteers consider the murdering of the Indians in the highest degree meritorious." Even a disciple of the Enlightenment, such as Jefferson, could become cynical and encourage the policy of selling goods on credit in order to lure Indians into debt. "When these debts get beyond what the individuals can pay," the president observed, "they become willing to lop them off by a cession of lands." Between 1800 and 1810 whites pressed Indians into ceding more than 100 million acres in the Ohio River valley.

Destruction of Indian cultures

The loss of so much land to white settlement devastated traditional Indian cultures by reducing hunting grounds and making game and food scarce. "Stop your people from killing our game," the Shawnees complained in 1802 to federal Indian agents. "They would be angry if we were to kill a cow or hog of theirs, the little game that remains is very dear to us." Tribes also became dependent on white trade to obtain blankets, guns, metal utensils, alcohol, and decorative beads. To pay for these goods with furs, Indians often overtrapped, which forced them to invade the lands of neighboring tribes, provoking wars. The destructive effects of alcohol, which Indians turned to as a means of coping with cultural stress, were especially marked during these years, and increased production in white backcountry settlements during the 1790s and early 1800s made whiskey readily available. Indeed, white consumption of alcohol was also rising during these years, a symptom of the adjustment of white society to cultural stress.

Among the Shawnees in the Ohio River valley, the strain produced by white expansion led to alcoholism, growing violence among tribe members, family disintegration, and the collapse of the clan system designed to regulate relations among different villages. These problems might have been lessened by separation from white culture, but the Shawnees had become dependent on trade for articles they could not produce themselves. The question of how to deal with white culture became a matter of anguished debate. Black Hoof, as we have seen, attempted to take up farming and accommodate to white ways. But for most Indians, the course of assimilation proved unappealing and fraught with risk.

The Prophet, Tecumseh, and the Pan-Indian Movement

Other Shawnees decided not to adopt white ways but to revitalize their culture by severing all ties with the white world. In such efforts Indian religion often played a central role. During the 1790s a revival of religious fervor led by Handsome Lake took hold among the Iroquois, following the loss of most of the Iroquois lands and the collapse of their military power in western New York. Subsequently, Lalawethika, also known as the Prophet, sparked a religious revival among the Shawnees. The Prophet's early life was undistinguished: he was a poor hunter and as a child accidentally blinded himself in the right eye with an arrow. His portly build and homely looks reinforced his unsightly appearance, and the ridicule of his fellow tribe members drove him to alcoholism. Then, suddenly, in April 1805 he lapsed into a trance so deep that he was given up for dead. When he revived, he spoke of having died and been reborn. In this vision and others he later received, he outlined a new creed for the Shawnees. Renouncing alcohol, he took a new name, Tenskwatawa (the Open Door), to express his mission to "reclaim the Indians from bad habits and to cause them to live in peace with all mankind."

Tenskwatawa urged the Shawnees to renounce whiskey and white goods and return to their old ways of hunting with bows and arrows, eating customary foods such as corn and beans, and wearing traditional garb. Seeking to revitalize Shawnee culture, the Prophet condemned intertribal violence, promoted monogamous marriage, and denounced the idea of private instead of communal property. Except for guns, which could be used in self-defense, his followers were to discard all items made by whites.

Not only was trade forbidden with white settlers, but so was intermarriage. Indian wives of white men were to leave their husbands and return to the tribe, and children of mixed parentage were to be barred from the village. Setting up headquarters at the newly built village of Prophetstown in Indiana in 1808, Tenskwatawa led a religious revival among the tribes of the Northwest, who were increasingly concerned about the loss of their lands. Just as thousands of white settlers traveled to Methodist

Prophet's message

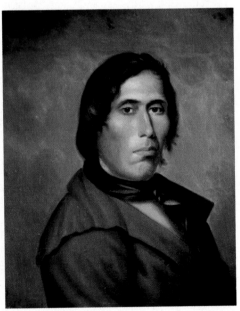

Tenskwatawa (left), "the Open Door," shown in traditional dress, led a religious movement to revitalize Shawnee culture and attracted a large following among the northwestern tribes. After the Battle of Tippecanoe, he was supplanted as leader of the Indian revitalization movement by his brother Tecumseh (right), who advocated political unity to preserve Indian lands and cultures. Tecumseh was the dominant figure among the western tribes until he died fighting alongside the British in the War of 1812.

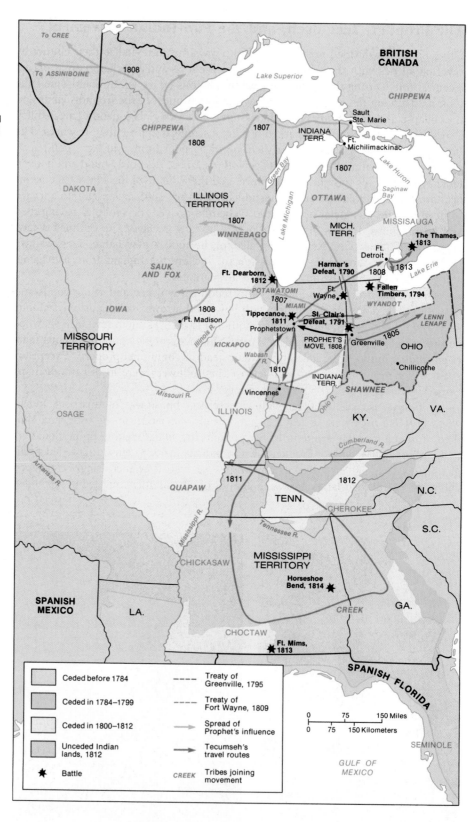

The Indian Response to White Encroachment With land cessions and white western migration placing increased pressure on Indian cultures after 1790, news of the Prophet's revival fell on eager ears. It spread especially quickly northward along the shores of Lake Michigan and westward along Lake Superior and the interior of Wisconsin. Following the Battle of Tippecanoe, Tecumseh eclipsed the Prophet as the major leader of Indian resistance, but his trips south to forge political alliances met with less success.

or Baptist camp meetings in the woods, where preachers denounced the evils of liquor and called for a return to a purer way of life, so thousands of Indians from northern tribes traveled to the Prophet's village for inspiration.

Whereas Tenskwatawa's strategy of revitalization was primarily religious, his older brother Tecumseh turned to political and military solutions. William Henry Harrison described Tecumseh as "one of those uncommon geniuses which spring up occasionally to produce revolutions and overturn the established order of things." Tall and athletic, an accomplished hunter and a renowned warrior, Tecumseh became active in 1809, after the Lenni Lenape and Miami tribes ceded yet another 3 million acres in Indiana and Illinois under the Treaty of Fort Wayne. Repudiating the treaty, he traveled throughout the Northwest, urging tribes to forget their ancient rivalries and unite under his leadership to protect their lands from white incursions. Tecumseh's confederacy brought together the Wyandot, Chippewa, Sauk and Fox, Winnebago, Potawatomi, and other tribes. As Tecumseh began to overshadow the Prophet, William Harrison aptly termed him "really the efficient man—the Moses of the family."

Tecumseh's movement

Tecumseh's message of Pan-Indian unity and centralized authority ran counter to many facets of traditional Indian cultures. He asked villages to pay less attention to their local leaders and join his larger movement; he also called on tribes to unite with their traditional enemies in a common cause. Although the amount of support he received was impressive, his following never matched that of the Prophet's earlier revivals. After recruiting allies among the northwestern tribes, Tecumseh in 1811 headed south, where he encountered greater resistance. In general, the southern tribes were more prosperous, were more acculturated, and felt less immediate pressure on their land from whites. In addition, the Choctaws and Chickasaws refused to forget long-standing feuds with northern tribes. So Tecumseh's southern mission ended largely in failure.

Tecumseh's failure in the South

To compound Tecumseh's problems, while he was away a force of Americans under Governor Harrison defeated the Prophet's forces at the Battle of Tippecanoe in November and then destroyed Prophetstown. As a result, Tecumseh became convinced that the best way to contain white expansion was to play off the Americans against the British in the Great Lakes region. Indeed, by 1811, the two nations were on the brink of war.

As Tecumseh worked to overcome obstacles to a Pan-Indian alliance, Jefferson encountered his own difficulties in trying to achieve American political unity.

The Second War for American Independence

The president's goal was to woo all but the most extreme Federalists into the Republican camp. His reelection in 1804 showed how much progress he had made, as he defeated Federalist Charles Cotesworth Pinckney and carried 15 of 17 states. With the Republicans controlling three-quarters of the seats in Congress, Jefferson's goal of one-party rule seemed at hand.

But events across the Atlantic complicated the efforts to unite Americans. Only two weeks after Napoleon agreed to sell Louisiana to the United States, war broke out between France and Great Britain. As in the 1790s, the United States again found itself caught between the world's two greatest powers. Jefferson insisted that the nation should remain neutral in a European war that did not concern Americans. But the controversial policies he proposed to maintain American neutrality brought out the divisions in American society and momentarily revived the two-party system.

The Barbary Pirates and Cultural Identities

In seeking a common national identity, citizens of the United States often found it easier to define themselves in terms of what they were not. As conflict increased along the nation's western frontiers, most Americans believed they were not like the Indians, whom they perceived as nomadic and wild. As France and England harassed U.S. ships on the high seas, Americans insisted they should not be like the nations of Europe, where "Favoritism as well as Corruption prevails," as one American diplomat complained. And Americans drew another sharp cultural contrast during these decades: they protested they were not like the "Barbary pirates" of North Africa, who also preyed on American ships.

The Barbary states of North Africa—Algiers, Morocco, Tripoli, and Tunis—lay along the Mediterranean Sea's southern coast. During the seventeenth and eighteenth centuries their corsairs—light, maneuverable sailing vessels—plundered enemy ships, confiscating cargo and enslaving the captured crews. In doing so, the Barbary states behaved much like European nations along the Mediterranean, whose ships over the years had swept up North African cargo and crews. Indeed, the slavery imposed by the Barbary states was neither as harsh nor as extensive, in sheer numbers, as the slave trade engaged in by Europeans and Americans along the West African coast.

The United States and the Barbary States, 1801–1815 The young United States, like many European powers, found its trading vessels challenged by the Barbary states of Morocco, Algiers, Tunisia, and Tripoli. When the pasha of Tripoli declared war on the United States in 1801, Jefferson dispatched a force that blockaded Tripoli to bring the war to an end in 1805. Tribute paid to the other Barbary States continued until 1816, after a new naval force, led by Captain Stephen Decatur, forced the ruler of Algiers to end the practice.

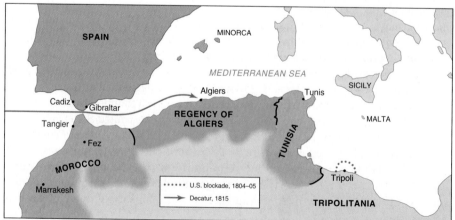

Corsairs, light, maneuverable ships sailing out of Barbary ports like Tripoli (shown here), were well fitted for their purpose. As one historian noted, "Like stinging insects, their light, rapid vessels were designed to strike at unarmed or lightly armed merchantmen, while being able to flee very speedily at the mere approach of a warship."

But the Barbary states were Muslim; and to American (and European) eyes, that made the tyranny of their rulers particularly objectionable. A biography of Islam's prophet, Muhammad, published in the United States in 1802, was typical in its condemnation. Muhammad's whole life had been an "imposture" and his teachings a "system of blasphemy and iniquity" by which the followers of Islam had been "degraded to the rank of brutes." More powerful European nations, like Britain, France, and Holland, found it convenient to pay tributes to the Barbary states so their ships could sail unmolested. But both Jefferson and John Adams disliked that idea. The "policy of Christendom" of paying tribute, complained Adams, "has made Cowards of all their Sailors before the Standard of Mahomet." In Adams's eyes, the cultural and religious differences clearly added insult to the injuries inflicted by the Barbary corsairs.

For their part, the Barbary states bore no special hostility toward Americans; indeed, in 1778 Morocco was among the first states to recognize the fledgling United States and to request that it send an ambassador. Congress, however, was so weak and distracted with its own affairs that for many years it could spare neither the money for bribes nor even the diplomats to open negotiations with the Barbary states. By the time John Adams became president, he had subdued his outrage, and he agreed to tributes. But when Tripoli increased its demands in 1801, President Jefferson sent a small squadron of American ships to force a settlement. In 1803 Tripoli captured the *U.S.S. Philadelphia,* the second largest frigate in the navy, which caused Federalists to mock the president for having neglected the navy for so long. The following year, however, Lieutenant Stephen Decatur retrieved the situation by sneaking into Tripoli's harbor and burning the *Philadelphia.* The American blockade that followed forced Tripoli to sue for peace and give up any further demands for tribute. Even so, the United States continued paying tribute to the other Barbary states until 1816.

American perceptions of Islamic culture

Neutral Rights

Both France and Britain found that paying tribute to the Barbary states gave their ships a competitive advantage over those of less powerful nations, like the United States, who could not afford the demands. But Americans soon found their commerce in more danger from the warring nations of France and Britain.

At first the war benefited American trade because it disrupted European agriculture, increasing the demand for American foodstuffs and other raw materials. As the fighting drove most nonneutral ships from the seas, American foreign trade doubled between 1803 and 1805. But after 1805 the British navy began seizing American ships with increasing frequency, as it tightened its blockade of Europe.

Impressment

Adding to American anger, the British navy also resumed its impressment of sailors and even passengers from American ships. British authorities refused to recognize the right of its citizens to emigrate and become American citizens, insisting that even if naturalized by the United States they remained subjects of the Crown. Anywhere from 4000 to 10,000 sailors were impressed by British naval officers, who did not always bother to distinguish naturalized from native-born Americans.

Isaac Clark, for example, was a native of Randolph, Massachusetts, yet he was taken from the American ship *Jane* in June 1809 after it was stopped by the British. When he presented papers attesting to his American citizenship, the English captain tore them up and threw them overboard. Refusing to work, Clark was put in irons and given a daily allowance of a biscuit and a pint of water, and once a week he received two dozen lashes. Finally, half-starved and physically broken, Clark gave in. He served in the British navy for more than two and a half years until wounded in action against a French frigate. While in a hospital he was freed through the intervention of the American consul. Voicing American indignation, John Quincy Adams characterized impressment as an "authorized system of kidnapping upon the ocean."

American ships seized

By 1805, the war had demonstrated the British navy's clear superiority at sea, while Napoleon's army enjoyed a decisive edge on land. Adopting a strategy of attrition, each country began to raid America's ocean commerce with the other side. Between 1803 and 1807, Britain seized more than 500 American ships; France, more than 300. Britain issued new regulations in 1807, known as the Orders in Council,

Orders in Council

that required any ship trading with France or its satellites to put in first at a British port, pay a duty, and get a license. Napoleon retaliated with the Milan Decree of 1807, which announced that any ship that stopped in Britain in conformity with the Orders in Council would be treated as a British ship, subject to seizure. American merchants, caught in the middle, saw the number of seized ships again increase. An irate Jefferson complained of France and England, "The one is a den of robbers, the other of pirates." When in June 1807 a British frigate fired on the U.S. warship *Chesapeake* in American waters and seized four deserters from the Royal Navy, public opinion clamored for military retaliation.

The Embargo

Yet Jefferson shrank from declaring war. He announced instead a program of "peaceable coercion," designed to protect neutral rights without war. The plan not only prohibited American ships from trading with foreign ports but also stopped the export of all American goods. Jefferson was confident that American exports were so essential to the two belligerents that they would quickly agree to respect American neutral rights. In December 1807 Congress passed the Embargo Act.

The president had seriously miscalculated. France did not depend on American trade and so managed well enough, while British ships quickly took over the carrying trade as American vessels lay idle. Under the embargo, American exports plunged from $108 million in 1807 to a mere $22 million a year later. At the same time, imports fell from almost $145 million to about $58 million. As the center of American shipping, New England port cities were hurt the most and protested the loudest. And when their merchants were not protesting, they were smuggling behind American officials' backs. During his last months in office Jefferson simply gave up trying to enforce the act.

Madison and the Young Republicans

Following Washington's example, Jefferson did not seek a third term. A caucus of Republican members of Congress selected James Madison to run against Federalist Charles Cotesworth Pinckney. Although Madison triumphed easily, Pinckney swept all of New England, where feeling against the embargo was highest, and the Federalists picked up 24 seats in Congress. The party seemed on the verge of a revival.

Few men have assumed the presidency with more experience than James Madison. A leading nationalist in the 1780s, the father of the Constitution, a key floor leader in Congress, the founder of the Republican party, Jefferson's secretary of state and closest adviser, Madison had spent over a quarter of a century in public life. Yet his tenure as president proved disappointing, for despite his intellectual brilliance, he lacked the force of leadership and the inner strength to impose his will on less capable men. *Madison's character*

With a president reluctant to fight for what he wanted, leadership passed from the executive branch to Congress. The elections of 1810 swept in a new generation of Republicans, led by the adroit and magnetic 34-year-old Henry Clay of Kentucky, who gained the rare distinction of being elected Speaker in his first term. These younger Republicans were much more nationalistic than the generation led by Jefferson and Madison. They sought an ambitious program of economic development and were aggressive expansionists, especially those from frontier districts. Their feisty willingness to go to war earned them the name of War Hawks. Though they numbered fewer than 30 in Congress, they quickly became the driving force in the Republican party. *War Hawks*

The Decision for War

During Jefferson's final week in office in early 1809, Congress repealed the Embargo Act. To encourage the two great powers to respect neutral rights, a new act reopened trade with all nations except Britain and France and authorized the president to resume trade with either nation if it withdrew its restrictions. The following year Congress authorized trade with France and England but decreed that if one of the two belligerents agreed to stop interfering with American shipping, trade with the other would be prohibited.

In this situation, Napoleon cleverly outmaneuvered the British by announcing that he would set aside the French trade regulations. Madison eagerly took the French emperor at his word and reimposed a ban on trade with England. But as French raiders continued to seize American ships, it became clear that Napoleon's words were not matched by French deeds. Madison, who had boxed himself into a corner, refused to rescind his order unless the British revoked the Orders in Council. In the disputes that followed, American anger focused on the British, who seized many more ships than the French and continued to impress American sailors.

Declaration of war

The embargo produced hard times in Britain, and finally, on June 16, 1812, the British ministry suspended the Orders in Council. But it was too late. Two days earlier, unaware of the change in policy, Congress granted Madison's request for a declaration of war against Britain. The vote was 79 to 49 in the House and 19 to 13 in the Senate, mostly along party lines, with every Federalist voting against war. As the representatives of commercial interests, particularly in New England, Federalists were convinced that war would ruin American commerce. They also still identified with Britain as the champion of order and conservatism. The handful of Republicans who joined the Federalists represented coastal districts, which were most vulnerable to the Royal Navy.

Clearly, the vote for war could not be explained as a matter of outraged Americans protecting neutral rights. The coastal areas, which were most affected, preferred trade over high principle. On the other hand, members of Congress from the South and the West, regions that had a less direct interest in the issue, clamored most strongly for war. Their constituents were consumed with a desire to seize additional territory in Canada or in Florida (owned by Britain's ally Spain). In addition, they accused the British of stirring up hostility among the Indian tribes.

Perhaps most important, the War Hawks were convinced that Britain had never truly accepted the verdict of the American Revolution. To them, American independence—and with it republicanism—hung in the balance. For insecure Americans, hungering for acceptance in the community of nations, nothing rankled more than being treated by the British as colonials. John Quincy Adams expressed this point of view when he declared: "In this question something besides dollars and cents is concerned and no alternative [is] left but war or the abandonment of our rights as an independent nation."

National Unpreparedness

With Britain preoccupied by Napoleon, the War Hawks expected that the United States would win an easy victory. In truth, the United States was totally unprepared for war. Crippled by Jefferson's cutbacks, the navy was unable to lift the British blockade of the American coast, which bottled up the country's merchant marine and most of its navy. As for the U.S. army, it was small and poorly led. When Congress moved to increase its size to 75,000, even the most hawkish states failed to meet their quotas. Congress was also reluctant to levy taxes to finance the war.

Battle of Lake Erie

A three-pronged American invasion of Canada from Detroit, Niagara, and Lake Champlain failed dismally in 1812. Americans fared better the following year, as both sides raced to build a navy on the strategically located Lake Erie. Led by Commander Oliver Hazard Perry, American forces won a decisive victory at Put-In Bay in 1813. Perry's triumph gave the United States control of Lake Erie and greatly strengthened the American position in the Northwest.

"A Chance Such as Will Never Occur Again"

As the United States struggled to organize its forces, Tecumseh sensed that his long-awaited opportunity had come to drive Americans out of the western territories. "Here is a chance . . . such as will never occur again," he told a war council, "for us Indians of North America to form ourselves into one great combination." Joining

During the Battle of New Orleans, American troops under Jackson entrenched behind breastworks, while their artillery raked the advancing British forces with deadly fire. The ladders needed to scale the American works quickly became entangled in the disorganized British assault.

up with the British, Tecumseh traveled south in the fall to talk again with his Creek allies. To coordinate a concerted Indian offensive for the following summer, he left a bundle of red sticks with eager Creek soldiers. They were to remove one stick each day from the bundle and attack when the sticks had run out.

A number of the older Creeks were more acculturated and preferred an American alliance. But about 2000 younger "Red Stick" Creeks launched a series of attacks, climaxed by the destruction of Fort Mims along the Alabama River in August 1813. Once again, the Indians' lack of unity was a serious handicap, as warriors from the Cherokee, Choctaw, and Chickasaw tribes, traditional Creek enemies, allied with the Americans. At the Battle of Horseshoe Bend in March 1814, General Andrew Jackson and his Tennessee militia soundly defeated the Red Stick Creeks. Jackson promptly dictated a peace treaty under which the Creeks ceded 22 million acres of land in the Mississippi Territory. They and the other southern tribes still retained significant landholdings, but Indian military power had been broken in the Southwest.

Defeat of the Creeks

Farther north, in October 1813 American forces under General William Henry Harrison defeated the British and their Indian allies at the Battle of the Thames. In the midst of heavy fighting Tecumseh was slain—and with him died any hope of a Pan-Indian movement.

Tecumseh's death

The British Invasion

As long as the war against Napoleon continued, the British were unwilling to divert army units to North America. But in 1814 Napoleon was at last defeated. Free to concentrate on America, the British devised a coordinated strategy to invade the United States in the northern, central, and southern parts of the country. The main army headed south from Montreal but was checked when Captain Thomas Macdonough destroyed the British fleet on Lake Champlain.

Meanwhile, a smaller British force captured Washington and burned several public buildings, including the Capitol and the president's home. To cover the scars of this destruction, the executive mansion was painted with whitewash and became

The War of 1812 After the American victory on Lake Erie and the defeat of the western Indians at the Battle of the Thames, the British adopted a three-pronged strategy to invade the United States, climaxing with an attempt on New Orleans. But they met their match in Andrew Jackson, whose troops marched to New Orleans after fighting a series of battles against the Creeks and forcing them to cede a massive tract of land.

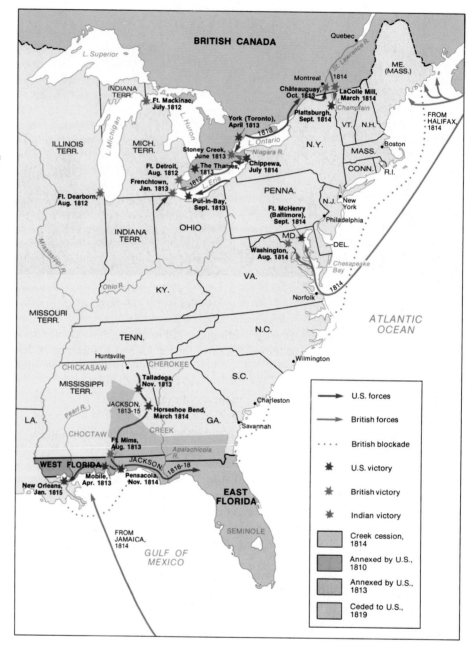

known as the White House. The burning of the capital was a humiliating event; President Madison and his wife, Dolley, were abruptly forced to flee, leaving their dinner to be eaten by the British. But the defeat had little military significance. The principal British objective was Baltimore, where for 25 hours their fleet bombarded Fort McHenry in the city's harbor. When he saw the American flag still flying above the fort at dawn, Francis Scott Key hurriedly penned the verses of "The Star Spangled Banner," which was eventually adopted as the national anthem.

The third British target was New Orleans, where a formidable army of 7500 British troops was opposed by a hastily assembled American force commanded by Major General Andrew Jackson. The Americans included regular soldiers; frontiersmen from Kentucky and Tennessee; citizens of New Orleans, including several companies of free African Americans; Choctaw Indians; and—for an added dash of color—a group of pirates. Jackson's outnumbered and ill-equipped forces won a stunning victory, which made the general an overnight hero. The Battle of New Orleans enabled Americans to forget the war's many failures and to boast that once again the United States had humbled the world's greatest military power.

Jackson's victory at New Orleans

The Hartford Convention

In December 1814, while Jackson was organizing the defense of New Orleans, New England Federalists met in Hartford to map strategy against the war. Yankee merchants, contemptuous of "Mr. Madison's War," had continued to trade with the enemy, while New England governors declined to make available the state militias. Finally the Massachusetts legislature called for a convention to discuss New England's grievances. Massachusetts, Connecticut, and Rhode Island sent delegates, but only three counties in New Hampshire and one in Vermont were represented.

Rejecting calls for secession, the delegates endorsed a series of proposed amendments to the Constitution that showed their displeasure with the government's economic policies and their resentment of the South's national political power. To their dismay, however, the committee sent to Washington to present the convention's demands arrived in the capital just as news of Andrew Jackson's victory was being trumpeted on the streets. The burst of national pride following Jackson's victory badly undercut the Hartford Convention's position, as did news from across the Atlantic that American negotiators in Ghent, Belgium, had signed a treaty ending the war. Hostilities had ceased, technically, on Christmas Eve 1814, two weeks before the Battle of New Orleans.

Like the war itself, the Treaty of Ghent accomplished little. All the major issues between the two countries, including impressment, neutral rights, trade, and the boundary between the United States and Canada, were either ignored or referred to future commissions for settlement. As John Quincy Adams commented, "Nothing was adjusted, nothing was settled—nothing in substance but an indefinite suspension of hostilities was agreed to." Both sides were simply relieved to end the conflict.

Treaty of Ghent

Adams was right in concluding that, in terms of international relations, the war

America Turns Inward

had settled nothing. Psychologically, however, the nation's mood had changed perceptibly. "Let any man look at the degraded condition of this country before the war," declaimed young Henry Clay, a leading War Hawk. "The scorn of the universe, the contempt of ourselves. . . . What is our present situation? Respectability and character abroad—security and confidence at home." Indeed, the return of peace hard on the heels of Jackson's victory sparked a new confidence in their country's destiny. "We have stood the contest, single-handed, against the conqueror of Europe," wrote Supreme Court justice Joseph Story to a friend, "and we are at peace, with all our blushing victories thick crowding on us."

National pride

The upsurge in national pride after the War of 1812 is reflected in the proud demeanor of these American soldiers, as portrayed by John Lewis Krimmel. Fourth of July parades routinely allowed soldiers to parade, drums beating and flags flying for the entertainment of civilians.

The upsurge in nationalism sounded the death knell of the Federalist party. The resistance of New England Federalists to the embargo and their disloyalty during the war had already weakened the party elsewhere, and the Hartford Convention tainted it with disunion and treason. Although the party had made its best showing in years in 1812, when Madison narrowly defeated his Federalist opponent, its support collapsed in the 1816 election. Madison's secretary of state, James Monroe, resoundingly defeated Federalist Rufus King of New York. Four years later Monroe ran for reelection unopposed.

The Missouri Crisis

The optimism of the era, however, was undercut by sectional rivalries that flared in 1819, when the Missouri Territory applied for admission as a slave state. Before the controversy over Missouri erupted, slavery had not been a major issue in American politics. Congress had debated the institution when it prohibited the African slave trade in 1808, the earliest year this step could be taken under the Constitution. In the absence of any specific federal legislation, however, slavery had crossed the Mississippi River into the Louisiana Purchase. Louisiana entered the Union in 1812 as a slave state, and in 1818 Missouri, which had about 10,000 slaves in its population, asked permission to come in too.

In 1818 the Union contained 11 free and 11 slave states. As the federal government became stronger and more active, both the North and the South became increasingly anxious about maintaining their political power. The North's greater population gave it a majority in the House of Representatives, 105 to 81. The Senate, of course, was evenly balanced, because each state had two senators regardless of population. But Maine, which previously had been part of Massachusetts, requested admission as a free state. That would upset the balance unless Missouri came in as a slave state.

Representative James Tallmadge of New York disturbed this delicate state of affairs when in 1819 he suddenly introduced an amendment designed to establish a program of gradual emancipation in Missouri. The debate that followed was bitter, as for the first time Congress directly debated the morality of slavery. The House approved the Tallmadge amendment, but the Senate refused to accept it, and the two houses deadlocked.

Missouri Compromise

When Congress reconvened in 1820, Henry Clay of Kentucky promoted what came to be known as the Missouri Compromise. Under its terms Missouri was admitted as a slave state and Maine as a free state. In addition, slavery was forever prohibited in the remainder of the Louisiana Purchase north of 36°30′ (the southern boundary of Missouri). Clay's proposal, the first of several sectional compromises he would engineer in his long career, won congressional approval and Monroe signed the measure, ending the crisis. But southern fears for the security of slavery and northern fears about its spread remained. As Thomas Jefferson had gloomily

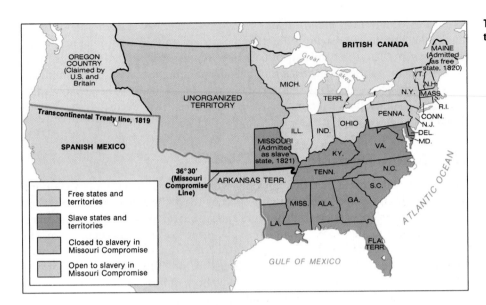

predicted, "A geographical line, coinciding with a marked principle, moral and political, once conceived and held up to angry passions of men, will never be obliterated; and every new irritation will mark it deeper and deeper."

Monroe's Presidency

The spirit of postwar harmony produced the so-called Era of Good Feelings, presided over by James Monroe, the last president of the Revolutionary generation. Monroe, like Jefferson before him, hoped to eliminate political parties, which he considered unnecessary in a free government. Like Washington, he thought of himself as the head of the nation rather than of a party.

Monroe's greatest achievements were diplomatic, accomplished largely by his talented secretary of state, John Quincy Adams, the son of President John Adams. An experienced diplomat, Adams thought of the Republic in continental terms and was intent on promoting expansion to the Pacific. Such a vision required dealing with Spain, which had never recognized the legality of the Louisiana Purchase. In addition, between 1810 and 1813 the United States had occupied and unilaterally annexed Spanish West Florida.

Spain, however, was preoccupied with events farther south in the Americas. In the first quarter of the nineteenth century, its colonies one after another had revolted and established themselves as independent nations. These revolutions increased the pressure on the Spanish minister to America, Luis de Onís, to come to terms with the United States. Furthermore, in 1818 Andrew Jackson marched into East Florida and captured several Spanish forts. Jackson had exceeded his instructions, but Adams understood well enough the additional pressure this aggression put on Onís and refused to disavow it.

Fearful that the United States might next invade Texas or other Spanish territory, Spain agreed to the Transcontinental, or Adams-Onís, Treaty in February 1819. Its terms set the boundary between American and Spanish territory all the way to the Pacific (map, above). Spain not only gave up its claims to the Pacific Northwest but also ceded Florida; in exchange, the U.S. government

Transcontinental Treaty

assumed $5 million in claims against Spain by American citizens. In order to obtain the line to the Pacific, the United States abandoned its contention that Texas was part of the Louisiana Purchase. Adams had wanted Texas, but he wanted the line to the Pacific even more. Understanding the strategic commitment to expanding across the continent, Adams wrote in his diary, "The acknowledgement of a definite line of boundary to the South Sea [the Pacific] forms a great epoch in our history."

The Monroe Doctrine

Improved relations with Britain

The United States came to terms not only with Spain but, even more important, with Great Britain as well. Following the War of 1812, the British abandoned their connections with the western Indian tribes and no longer attempted to block American expansion to the Rocky Mountains. In a growing spirit of cooperation, the Rush-Bagot Agreement in 1817 limited naval forces on the Great Lakes and on Lake Champlain. In 1818 the countries agreed to the 49th parallel as the northern boundary of the Louisiana Purchase and also to joint control of the Oregon Territory for 10 years, subject to renewal.

In this atmosphere of good will, George Canning, the British foreign secretary, proposed in August 1823 that the United States and Britain issue a joint statement disavowing any expansionist aims in Latin America and opposing the transfer of Spain's colonies to any foreign power. Monroe was inclined to accept the British offer, and both Jefferson and Madison urged him to do so. But John Quincy Adams forcefully argued that the United States should not make any pledge against acquiring territory in the future, particularly in Texas, Mexico, and the Caribbean. Adams also worried that in any joint statement the United States would appear to be merely a junior partner, coming along "as a cock-boat in the wake of a British man-of-war." Monroe finally agreed to make an independent statement.

Monroe Doctrine

He included it in his annual message to Congress, on December 2, 1823. Monroe reaffirmed that the United States would not intervene in European affairs, a principle of American foreign policy since Washington's Farewell Address. And he also announced that the United States would not interfere with already-established European colonies in the Western Hemisphere. But any intervention, he warned, in the new republics of Latin America would be considered a hostile act: "The American continents . . . are henceforth not to be considered as subjects for future colonization by any European powers." The essence of this policy, which was Adams's handiwork, was the concept of two worlds, one old and one new, each refraining from interfering in the other's affairs.

American public opinion hailed Monroe's statement and then promptly forgot it. Only years later would it be referred to as the Monroe Doctrine. Still, it represented the culmination of the American quest since 1776 for independence and sovereignty. The very fact that Britain had proposed a joint declaration demonstrated that, at last, the parent nation recognized its offspring as a legitimate and sovereign nation. Monroe's declaration underlined the United States' determination not to act in world affairs as a satellite of Britain. Ever since the adoption of the Constitution, the issue of independence had been at the center of American politics. It had surfaced during the 1790s, in Hamilton's quarrel with Jefferson over whether to favor Britain or France and in the differing responses of Americans to the French Revolution. It colored the debates over the embargo and finally once again came to a head in 1812 with the second war for American independence.

The End of an Era

The growing reconciliation with Great Britain ended the external threat to the Republic. Isolated from Europe and protected by the British fleet, the United States was free to turn its attention inward, to concentrate on expanding across the vast continent and on developing its resources. Yet how would the nation be developed? Jefferson had dreamed of an "empire of liberty," delighting in western expansion as the means to preserve a nation of small farmers like those Crèvecoeur had written about during the 1780s.

End of foreign threat

Younger, more nationalistic Republicans had a different vision. They spoke of internal improvements, protective tariffs to help foster American industries, better roads and canals to link farmers with towns, cities, and wider markets. The tone of these new Republicans was not aristocratic; they were not like the Federalists of old. Still, their dream of a national, commercial republic resembled Franklin's and Hamilton's more than Jefferson's. They looked to profit from speculation in land, from the increasing market for cotton, from the new methods of industrial manufacturing. If they represented the rising generation, what would be the fate of Crèvecoeur's semisubsistence farm communities? The answer was not yet clear.

In one of those remarkable coincidences that Americans hailed as a sign of Providence's favor, Thomas Jefferson and John Adams died within hours of each other on July 4, 1826, the fiftieth anniversary of the adoption of the Declaration of Independence. The lives of these two giants of the Revolution—Jefferson, the ever-hopeful, self-styled Revolutionary Virginia gentleman, and Adams, the prickly, independent Federalist of Braintree—intertwined with one another in the fabric of the nation's development. Partners in the struggle to secure American independence, these Revolutionary colleagues had become bitter foes in the heated party battles of the 1790s and resumed a warm friendship only after they had retired from public life. Their reconciliation was in tune with the surge of American nationalism, but their time was past. Leadership belonged now to a new generation of Americans, who confronted different problems and challenges. Revolutionary America had passed from the scene. The dawn of a new nation was at hand.

chapter summary

As president, Thomas Jefferson increasingly abandoned his earlier ideals in favor of nationalism, a trend that continued under his successors, James Madison and James Monroe.

- Before becoming president, Jefferson advocated the principles of agrarianism, limited government, and strict construction of the Constitution.

- Once in power, however, he failed to dismantle Hamilton's economic program and promoted western expansion by acquiring Louisiana from France despite his constitutional principles.

- The growth of nationalism was also reflected as the judiciary emerged as an equal branch of government.

  - Chief Justice John Marshall proclaimed that the courts were to interpret the meaning of the Constitution (judicial review).

- Many northern Indian tribes rallied to a religious movement led by the Shawnee prophet Tenskwatawa, which aimed to revive traditional Indian cultures.

  - The Prophet's brother Tecumseh advocated a political and military confederacy to protect Indians' lands, but a number of important tribes refused to support him.

  - Tecumseh's movement collapsed with his death during the War of 1812.

- France and Britain both interfered with neutral rights, and the United States went to war against Britain in 1812.
- In the years after 1815 there was a surge in American nationalism.
  - The Transcontinental Treaty with Spain (1819) foreshadowed American expansion by drawing a boundary line to the Pacific.

- The Monroe Doctrine (1823) barred European intervention in the Western Hemisphere.
- Britain's recognition of American sovereignty after 1815 ended the threat of foreign interference in America's internal affairs.
- But the Missouri crisis was an early indication of growing sectional rivalries.

interactive learning

The Primary Source Investigator CD-ROM offers the following materials related to this chapter:

- Interactive maps: **Indian Expulsion, 1800–1890** (M8); **Exploration of America's Far West, 1803–1807** (M9); and **The War of 1812** (M10)

- A collection of primary sources investigating the early national period: paintings depicting the War of 1812, "Mad Tom" (Jefferson) in a rage, and the resolutions of the secessionist Hartford Convention. Other sources include the Barbary treaties, paintings of women quilting and a country wedding, and an Iroquois Nation creation story.

additional reading

A good survey of the presidencies of Jefferson and Madison is Marshall Smelser, *The Democratic Republic* (1968). Drew R. McCoy, *The Elusive Republic* (1980), skillfully analyzes the dilemmas Jefferson and Madison confronted in power. An important study of the Federalist party is David Hackett Fischer, *The Revolution of American Conservatism* (1965). For the origins of the War of 1812, see Roger H. Brown, *The Republic in Peril* (1964). The biographies of Jefferson and Madison, listed in the Bibliography, examine political developments in this period in detail.

Malcolm J. Rohrbough, *The Trans-Appalachian Frontier* (1978), traces the process of western settlement, while other aspects of western society are treated in John Boles, *The Great Revival in the South* (1972); and R. David Edmunds, *The Shawnee Prophet* (1983). Donald Jackson, *Thomas Jefferson and the Stony Mountains: Exploring the West from Monticello* (1979), is a fascinating analysis of western exploration in this period. The journals of the Lewis and Clark expedition, which have been published in several editions, are invaluable; a recent history is Stephen E. Ambrose, *Undaunted Courage* (1996).

The first part of George Dangerfield, *The Awakening of American Nationalism* (1965), capably covers Monroe's administration. Samuel F. Bemis traces American foreign policy during and after the war in *John Quincy Adams and the Foundations of American Foreign Policy* (1949). Ernest R. May, *The Making of the Monroe Doctrine* (1976), is the best study of the subject. For a fuller list of readings, see the Bibliography at www.mhhe.com/davidsonnation5.

significant events

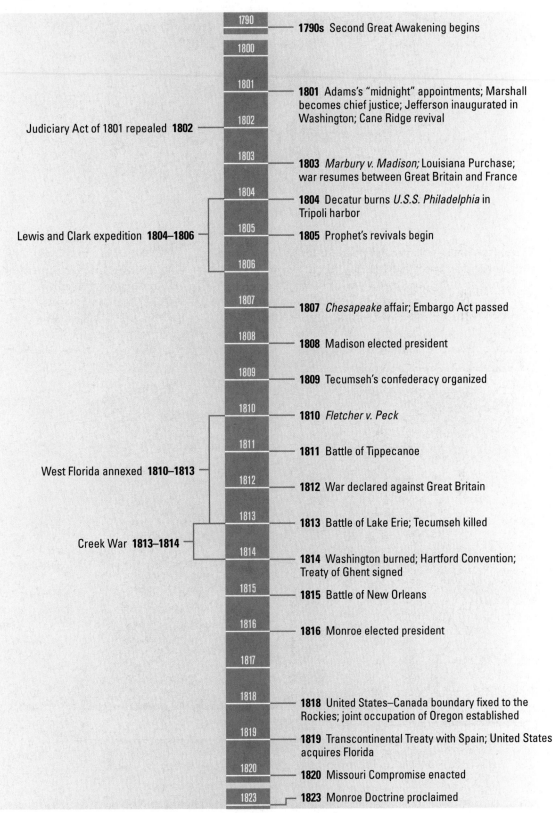

1790	**1790s** Second Great Awakening begins
1800	
1801	**1801** Adams's "midnight" appointments; Marshall becomes chief justice; Jefferson inaugurated in Washington; Cane Ridge revival
Judiciary Act of 1801 repealed **1802**	
1803	**1803** *Marbury v. Madison;* Louisiana Purchase; war resumes between Great Britain and France
1804	**1804** Decatur burns *U.S.S. Philadelphia* in Tripoli harbor
Lewis and Clark expedition **1804–1806**	**1805** Prophet's revivals begin
1807	**1807** *Chesapeake* affair; Embargo Act passed
1808	**1808** Madison elected president
1809	**1809** Tecumseh's confederacy organized
1810	**1810** *Fletcher v. Peck*
1811	**1811** Battle of Tippecanoe
West Florida annexed **1810–1813**	**1812** War declared against Great Britain
1813	**1813** Battle of Lake Erie; Tecumseh killed
Creek War **1813–1814**	**1814** Washington burned; Hartford Convention; Treaty of Ghent signed
1815	**1815** Battle of New Orleans
1816	**1816** Monroe elected president
1818	**1818** United States–Canada boundary fixed to the Rockies; joint occupation of Oregon established
1819	**1819** Transcontinental Treaty with Spain; United States acquires Florida
1820	**1820** Missouri Compromise enacted
1823	**1823** Monroe Doctrine proclaimed

Sally Hemings and Thomas Jefferson

The rumors began in Albemarle County, Virginia, more than two hundred years ago; they came to the notice of a journalist by the name of James Callender. A writer for hire, Callender had once lent his pen to the Republicans, but turned from friend into foe when the party failed to reward him with a political appointment. When his story splashed onto the pages of the *Recorder*, a Richmond newspaper, the trickle of rumor turned into a torrent of scandal. Callender alleged that Thomas Jefferson, during his years in Paris as the American minister, had contracted a liaison with one of his own slaves. The woman was the president's mistress even now, he insisted, in 1802. She was kept at

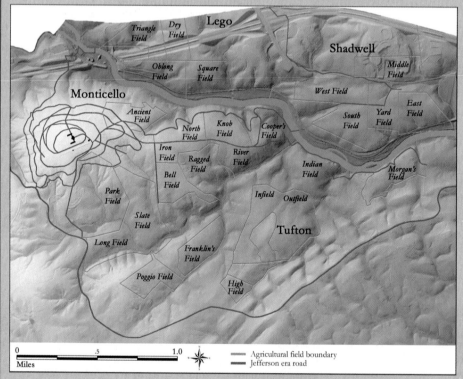

Jefferson owned 5000 acres of land in Albemarle County, Virginia, his "home farm" of Monticello and three "quarter farms"—Lego, Tufton, and Shadwell. Sally Hemings and her children lived at the Monticello plantation.

Monticello, and Jefferson had fathered children with her. Her name was Sally Hemings.

Solid information about Sally Hemings is scarce. She was one of six children, we know, born to Betty Hemings and her white master, John Wayles, a Virginia planter whose white daughter, Martha Wayles Skelton, married Jefferson in 1772. We know that Betty Hemings was the child of an African woman and an English sailor, which means Betty's children with Wayles, Sally among them, were quadroons—light-skinned men and women whose ancestry was one-quarter African. We know that Sally accompanied one of Jefferson's daughters to Paris as her maid in 1787 and that, upon returning to Virginia a few years later, she performed domestic work at Monticello. We know that she had six children and that the four who survived to adulthood escaped from slavery into freedom: Jefferson assisted her two eldest children, Beverly and Harriet, in leaving Monticello in 1822, and her two younger children, Madison and Eston, were freed by Jefferson's will in 1827. We know that shortly after Jefferson's death, his daughter, Martha Jefferson Randolph, freed Sally Hemings and that she lived with her two younger sons in Charlottesville until her own death in 1835.

We know, too, that Jefferson's white descendants stoutly denied (and, to this day, some still deny) any familial connection with the descendants of Sally Hemings. Even though Callender's scandal

This view of Monticello was painted shortly after Jefferson's death. It portrays his white descendants surrounded by a serene landscape.

quickly subsided, doing Jefferson no lasting political damage, his white grandchildren were still explaining away the accusations half a century later. In the 1850s, Jefferson's granddaughter, Ellen Coolidge Randolph, claimed that her brother, Thomas Jefferson Randolph, had told her that one of Jefferson's nephews, Samuel Carr, fathered Hemings's children. In the 1860s, Henry Randall, an early biographer of Jefferson, recalled a conversation with Thomas Jefferson Randolph in the 1850s in which he attributed paternity to another nephew, Samuel's brother Peter Carr.

Until the end of the twentieth century, most scholars resolved the discrepancy of this dual claim by suggesting that one of the Carr nephews had fathered Sally Hemings's children. And all of Jefferson's most eminent twentieth-century biographers—Douglass Adair, Dumas Malone, John Chester Miller, and Joseph J. Ellis—contended that a man of Jefferson's character and convictions could not have engaged in a liaison with a slave woman. After all, Jefferson was a Virginia gentleman and an American philosophe who believed that reason should rule over passion; he was also an eloquent apostle of equality and democracy and an outspoken critic of the tyrannical power of masters over slaves. And despite his opposition to slavery, Jefferson argued in his *Notes on the State of Virginia* (1785) for the likelihood that peoples of African descent were inferior intellectually and artistically to those of European descent. Because of that conviction, he warned of the dire consequences that would attend the mixing of the races.

The official version of events did not go unchallenged. Madison Hemings, a skilled carpenter who, a year after his mother's death, moved from Virginia to southern Ohio, publicly related an oral tradition repeated among his family. When interviewed by a Pike County, Ohio, newspaper in 1873, Madison reported that his mother had been Thomas Jefferson's "concubine" and that Jefferson had fathered all of her children. Even so, nearly a century passed before Madison Hemings's claims won wider attention. In 1968, the historian Winthrop Jordan noted that Sally Hemings's pregnancies coincided with Jefferson's stays at Monticello. In 1975, Fawn Brodie's best-selling "intimate history" of Jefferson portrayed his relationship with Sally Hemings as an enduring love affair; four years later, the African American novelist Barbara Chase-Rimboud set Brodie's findings to fiction.

An even more powerful case for Jefferson's paternity of all of Hemings's children was made in 1997 by Annette Gordon-Reed, an African American scholar. Gordon-Reed drew on her legal training to subject the handling of the evidence by Jefferson's biographers to a close and telling cross-examination. While they had dismissed Madison Hemings's recollections as mere family lore and wishful thinking, Gordon-Reed argued that such oral testimony was, in fact, no more or less reliable than the oral testimony of Jefferson's white Randolph descendants.

One year later, Gordon-Reed's arguments crested on a tidal wave of new revelations: A team of DNA research scientists headed by Eugene A. Foster discovered an exact match on the Y-chromosome markers between Thomas Jefferson's line and the descendants of Eston Hemings. (Eston was Sally's youngest child and the only one who left male-line descendants whose DNA could be tested.) Since the chance of such a match occurring randomly was less than one in a thousand, the DNA evidence made it highly probable that Thomas Jefferson fathered at least one of Sally Hemings's children. In addition, Foster's team found no DNA match between the Hemings line and the Carr family, thus discrediting the assertions of Jefferson's white descendants. Intrigued by these findings, the historian Fraser D. Neiman undertook a sophisticated statistical analysis of Hemings's conceptions and Jefferson's returns to Monticello (where he spent about half his time), which established a 99 percent probability that he had fathered all of Hemings's children.

Taken together, this new evidence has persuaded most historians that Thomas Jefferson conducted a monogamous liaison with Sally Hemings over thirty-eight years and that their union produced at least one and most likely all six of her children. Even scholars who still question whether Jefferson fathered all of Hemings's children now agree that the burden of proof has decisively shifted to those who doubt his paternity. As a result, the debate among historians has moved on to explore questions left unresolved by the new scientific findings.

One such question bears on how historians should assess the credibility of their sources. Specifically, how reliable are the oral traditions passed down through families? Both the DNA and statistical evidence bear out Madison Hemings's recollections. Surely that outcome, as Annette Gordon-Reed has urged, should prompt future historians to scrutinize the oral testimony of white masters like the Jeffersons and the Randolphs as closely as they do the narratives of slaves and the oral traditions of their descendants. But does it follow that historians should regard the recollections of nonliterate peoples as possessing a superior claim to being accurate recoveries of the past? Gordon-Reed and a host of other historians warn against that conclusion, arguing that all oral testimony must be tested against the findings yielded by the documentary record and scientific research. Their caution is warranted by the fact that the DNA findings to date have failed to show a match between the Jefferson line and that of Thomas Woodson, another Monticello slave whose African American descendants have long cited their own family's oral tradition as evidence of a biological connection to Jefferson.

An equally intriguing question concerns the character of the relationship between Sally Hemings and Thomas Jefferson. Was it forced and exploitative or

The names of Sally Hemings and her sons appear on this list of Thomas Jefferson's slaves.

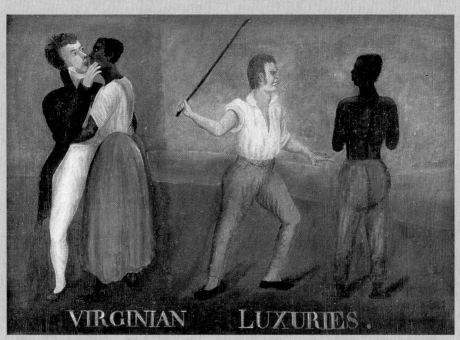

consensual and even affectionate? On the one hand, the long duration of their liaison suggests that it may have been based on a shared emotional intimacy. (If Jefferson fathered all of Hemings's children, their involvement began in Paris during the late 1780s and endured at least until the birth of Eston Hemings in 1808.) As Annette Gordon-Reed points out, even stronger support for this interpretation is that Sally Hemings and all of her children were the only nuclear slave family at Monticello who finally attained their freedom. Furthermore, biographers have never doubted Jefferson's affection for his first wife, Martha Wayles Skelton, before she died in 1782. Is it not likely that Jefferson felt similarly toward Sally, who was in fact Martha's unacknowledged half-sister?

This bell once belonged to Martha Wayles Jefferson, the wife of Thomas Jefferson. According to Hemings family tradition, she gave the bell to Sally Hemings, who was her half-sister.

On the other hand, the sexual exploitation of black women was common among white masters in the Chesapeake, the Carolinas, and the Caribbean. Like them, Jefferson may have availed himself of the privileges of ownership to compel sexual favors over many years from a slave whom he fancied. Or perhaps Sally Hemings submitted to Jefferson's sexual demands because she hoped to win better treatment—and, in the end, freedom—for herself and her children. Many bondswomen (among them, perhaps, Sally's mother, Betty Hemings, and her grandmother) used that strategy to protect their children from the ravages of slavery. What lends added support to either of those interpretations is the testimony of Madison Hemings, who recalled that while Jefferson was affectionate with his white Randolph grandchildren, he was "not in the habit of showing partiality or fatherly affection" to his children with Sally Hemings.

In the last analysis, the significance of Sally Hemings's relationship with Thomas Jefferson may reside in its power to reveal the complexity of southern plantation societies between the American Revolution and the Civil War. In that place and time, the American South was not starkly divided into whites and blacks; instead it was a culture in which the races had been mingling for generations, yielding

VIRGINIAN LUXURIES.

This painting was discovered on the reverse side of a portrait of a Virginia gentleman. Experts believe that it dates from the early national period and the artist, still unknown, evidently shared Jefferson's criticisms of slavery.

many people of mixed ancestry like Sally Hemings. Israel Jefferson, who passed part of his life in slavery at Monticello, remembered her as being "mighty near white," with "long straight hair down her back." Because of their shared bonds of blood, such light-skinned slaves sometimes enjoyed greater privileges and freedoms from their masters, but they also had to negotiate more complicated relationships with them and with less favored members of the slave community.

BIBLIOGRAPHY The best study of the Jefferson-Hemings controversy that predates the DNA discoveries in 1998 is Scot A. French and Edward L. Ayers, "The Strange Career of Thomas Jefferson," in *Jeffersonian Legacies*, ed. Peter S. Onuf (1993). Among those published after the DNA findings, the most informed and comprehensive are a "Forum" piece in the *William and Mary Quarterly*, 57 (2000), entitled "Thomas Jefferson and Sally Hemings Redux" (which includes Fraser D. Neiman's important statistical study); and an anthology of essays edited by Jan Lewis and Peter S. Onuf, *Sally Hemings and Thomas Jefferson* (1999). Readers who wish to pursue the subject in more depth should consult Fawn Brodie's provocative biography, *Thomas Jefferson: An Intimate History* (1974); Annette Gordon-Reed's pathbreaking challenge to the existing scholarship, *Thomas Jefferson and Sally Hemings* (1997); and the November 5, 1998, issue of *Nature*, the British scientific journal in which Eugene A. Foster and his research team first published their DNA findings. Equally intriguing are the ways in which fiction writers and filmmakers have depicted the liaison between Jefferson and Hemings: the best place to begin is with Barbara Chase-Rimboud's novel, *Sally Hemings* (1979), and the Merchant-Ivory film of 1995, *Jefferson in Paris*—the cinematography is gorgeous, the dialogue is sensitive and intelligent, and the actress Thandie Newton shines as Sally Hemings.

THE REPUBLIC TRANSFORMED AND TESTED

Two remarkable transformations began sweeping the world in the late eighteenth century. So wrenching and far-reaching were these changes that both have been called revolutions. The first was a cascade of political revolts that led to increased democratic participation in the governing of many nation-states. The other was the application of machine labor and technological innovation to agricultural and commercial economies, known as the industrial revolution.

Proclaiming the values of liberty and equality, Americans in 1776 led the way with their own democratic revolution. As we have seen, the act of revolution itself did not solve the question of how regional and economic antagonisms could be adjusted peacefully in the new nation-state. Not until the Republicans succeeded the Federalists was a tradition of peaceful political change established within the framework of the Constitution. And not until a new generation of leaders arrived on the scene during the second war for independence did a national consciousness fully bloom.

These were notable milestones, but internationally, the center of revolutionary attention had shifted in 1789 to France. There, as in America, the ideals of the Enlightenment played a part in justifying the rejection of rule by monarchy. French liberals like the marquis de Lafayette were inspired by the example of the United States. Still, the crowds

marching through the streets of Paris adopted a more radical and violent stance, reflecting the burdens on peasants and workers of the harsh feudal system as well as other social pressures. The worldwide rise in population of the previous half century had left the French capital overcrowded, underfed, and thoroughly unruly.

The French citizenry proved that much more willing to arm themselves and march on the Bastille, on the palace at Versailles, against any perceived enemies of the Revolution. The countryside, too, suffering from a series of bad harvests, rose up in protest, sometimes brutally. Paradoxically, the population pressure that had pushed matters to a crisis was relieved as the Revolution gave way to the emperor Napoleon, whose wars of conquest killed almost as many French soldiers as the natural increase of the nation's population. When Napoleon was at last defeated at the Battle of Waterloo in 1815, Louis XVIII reestablished the French monarchy.

In Latin America, however, movements of democracy and nationalism spread. Just as Great Britain had attempted to pay for its colonial defenses with additional revenue from its colonies, so the Spanish Crown raised taxes in the Americas, with predictable results. The Creole class—Spanish who had been born in America—resented the preferential treatment and administrative positions given the *peninsulares*—colonial residents born in Spain. Although the Spanish colonies lacked the tradition of representative assemblies found in North America, the writings of Jefferson and Thomas Paine circulated, as did translations of the French *Declaration of the Rights of Man*. From 1808 to

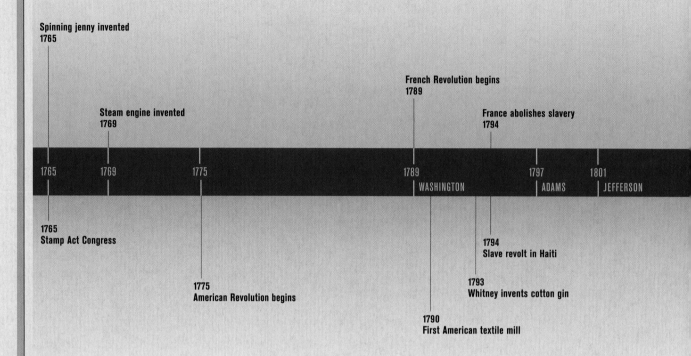

GLOBAL EVENTS

Spinning jenny invented
1765

Steam engine invented
1769

French Revolution begins
1789

France abolishes slavery
1794

1765   1769   1775   1789   1797   1801

WASHINGTON   ADAMS   JEFFERSON

1765
Stamp Act Congress

1794
Slave revolt in Haiti

1775
American Revolution begins

1793
Whitney invents cotton gin

1790
First American textile mill

AMERICAN EVENTS

1821 Spain's American provinces declared their independence one by one. Democracy did not always root itself in the aftermath of these revolutions, but democratic ideology remained a powerful social catalyst.

The industrial revolution was less violent but no less dramatic in its effects. It began in Great Britain, where canals built toward the end of the eighteenth century improved the transportation network, just as they would in the United States during the 1820s and 1830s. In Britain, too, James Watt in 1769 invented an engine that harnessed the power of steam, while innovations in textile production led to the use of water and later steam power to drive mechanical looms. At about the same time, steam power, along with other innovations,

made it possible for coal mining and the manufacture of iron to be accomplished on a larger scale. (The British miner shown here was drawn in 1814.)

As steam power was applied to ships and rail locomotives, the reach of commercial markets widened. Regular shipping made it possible to bring Egyptian cot-

ton from Alexandria to factories in British Manchester and American cotton from the Arkansas Red River country to New England. Just as skilled workers such as Samuel Slater smuggled the new technology out of England to the United States, others such as William Cockerill set up factories in Europe as the capabilities of steam and industrial manufacturing spread to the continent.

In many ways the narrative of the young American republic is the story of how one nation worked out the implications of these twin revolutions, industrial and democratic. It was only after the War of 1812 that a market economy began rapidly to transform the agricultural practices of Crèvecoeur's semisubsistence America. Urban areas of the North became more diversified and industrial as young

294

GLOBAL EVENTS

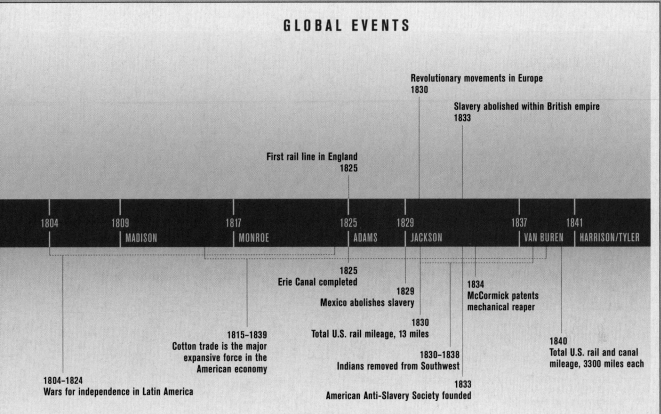

Revolutionary movements in Europe
1830

Slavery abolished within British empire
1833

First rail line in England
1825

1804	1809	1817	1825	1829	1837	1841
	MADISON	MONROE	ADAMS	JACKSON	VAN BUREN	HARRISON/TYLER

1825
Erie Canal completed

1829
Mexico abolishes slavery

1834
McCormick patents
mechanical reaper

1815–1839
Cotton trade is the major
expansive force in the
American economy

1830
Total U.S. rail mileage, 13 miles

1840
Total U.S. rail and canal
mileage, 3300 miles each

1804–1824
Wars for independence in Latin America

1830–1838
Indians removed from Southwest

1833
American Anti-Slavery Society founded

AMERICAN EVENTS

women took jobs in textile mills and young men labored in flour mills processing grain to be shipped east. The impact of industry on the North is probably clear enough in the popular imagination.

What is sometimes less appreciated is how the industrial revolution transformed the rural South. Cotton would never have become king there without the demand for it created by textile factories or without the ability to "gin" the seeds out of cotton by Eli Whitney's invention. (The "gin" in *cotton gin* is a clipped southern pronunciation of the word "engine.") Nor could cotton production have flourished without industrial advances in transportation, which allowed raw materials and factory goods to be shipped worldwide.

As the industrial and democratic revolutions developed side by side, the United States had to resolve the conflicts that the two presented each other. On the one hand, the advances in industry and commerce made it possible for resourceful entrepreneurs to reap profits on a scale that Americans of Crèvecoeur's day could never have imagined. They also created a labor force more impoverished than most Americans had been. In the North, factory workers found the conditions of labor increasingly harsh as the century progressed. In the South, the institution of slavery became even more economically entrenched because of the profits to be made using slave labor to raise cotton. The industrial revolution, in other words, made possible a society in which Americans could

become both richer and poorer than they had ever been before— a society more stratified and more unequal. On the other hand, the democratic revolution spreading across America was calling for greater equality among all citizens. This potential contradiction was one Americans wrestled with throughout the era.

The industrial revolution thus transformed both the North and the South—but in conflicting ways. Although the economies of the two regions depended on one another, slavery came increasingly to be the focus of disputes between them. The industrial revolution's demand for cotton increased both southern profits and the demand for slave labor. Yet the spread of democratic ideology worldwide was creating increased pressure to abolish

PART THREE

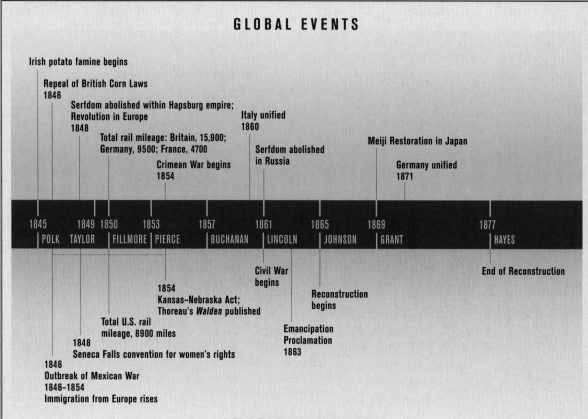

GLOBAL EVENTS

Irish potato famine begins

Repeal of British Corn Laws
1846

Serfdom abolished within Hapsburg empire;
Revolution in Europe
1848

Total rail mileage: Britain, 15,900;
Germany, 9500; France, 4700

Italy unified
1860

Serfdom abolished
in Russia

Crimean War begins
1854

Meiji Restoration in Japan

Germany unified
1871

| 1845 | 1849 | 1850 | 1853 | 1857 | 1861 | 1865 | 1869 | 1877 |
| POLK | TAYLOR | FILLMORE | PIERCE | BUCHANAN | LINCOLN | JOHNSON | GRANT | HAYES |

End of Reconstruction

Civil War
begins

Reconstruction
begins

1854
Kansas–Nebraska Act;
Thoreau's *Walden* published

Total U.S. rail
mileage, 8900 miles

Emancipation
Proclamation
1863

1848
Seneca Falls convention for women's rights

1846
Outbreak of Mexican War
1846–1854
Immigration from Europe rises

AMERICAN EVENTS

slavery everywhere. In France the revolutionary government struck it down in 1794. The British empire outlawed it in 1833, about the time that American abolitionists, influenced by their British friends, became more active in opposing it. In eastern Europe the near slavery of feudal serfdom was being eliminated as well: in 1848 within the Hapsburg em-

pire; in 1861 in Russia; in 1864 in Romania.

If the purpose of a democratic republic is to resolve conflicts among its members in a nonviolent manner, then in 1861 the American republic failed. It took four years of bitter fighting to reconcile the twin paths of democracy and industrial development. Given the massive size of the

territory involved and the depth of sectional divisions, it is perhaps not surprising that a union so diverse did not hold without the force of arms. That the separation was not final—that, in the end, reunion emerged out of conflict—is perhaps one reason why the tale is so gripping.

296

Chapter 10

The Opening of America

1815–1850

In the years before the Civil War, the name of Chauncey Jerome could be found traced in neat, sharp letters in a thousand different places across the globe: everywhere from the fireplace mantels of southern planters to the log cabins of Illinois prairie farmers and even in Chinese trading houses in Canton. Chauncey Jerome was a New England clockmaker whose clever, inexpensive, and addictive machines had conquered the markets of the world.

Jerome, the son of a Connecticut blacksmith, had apprenticed himself to a carpenter during his boyhood, but after serving in the War of 1812 he decided to try his luck as a clockmaker. For several years he eked out a living peddling his products from farmhouse to farmhouse. Then in 1824 his career took off thanks to a "very showy" bronze looking-glass clock. The new model he had designed sold as fast as the clocks could be manufactured. Between 1827 and 1837 Jerome's factory produced more clocks than any other in the country. But when the Panic of 1837 struck, Jerome had to scramble to avoid financial ruin.

Looking for a new opportunity, he set out to produce an inexpensive brass "one-day" clock—so called because its winding mechanism kept it running that long. Traditionally, the works of these clocks were made of wood, and the wheels and teeth had to be painstakingly cut by hand. Furthermore, wooden clocks could not be exported overseas because the humidity on board ship swelled the wood and ruined them. Jerome's brass version proved more accurate than earlier types and cheaper to boot. Costs came down further when he began to use interchangeable parts and combined his operations for making cases and movements within a single factory in New Haven, Connecticut. By systematically organizing the production process, Jerome brought the price of a good clock within the reach of ordinary people. So popular were the new models that desperate competitors began attaching Jerome labels to their own inferior imitations.

Disaster struck again in 1855, when Jerome went into partnership with several unreliable associates. Within a few years his business faltered, then failed. At the age of 62, the once-prominent business leader found himself working again in a clock factory as an ordinary mechanic. He lived his last years in poverty.

Jerome rose higher than most Americans of his generation, and he fell further. Yet his fellow citizens shared his dreams of success, just as they were haunted by the fear of losing everything. For Jerome, it wasn't only material comforts that vanished; so did respect. "One of the most trying things to me now," he confessed in his autobiography, "is to see how I am looked upon by the community since I lost my property. I never was any better when I owned it than I am now, and never behaved any better. But how different is the feeling towards you, when your neighbors can make nothing more out of you. . . . You are passed by without notice."

preview • In the quarter century after 1815 a market revolution transformed the United States into a boom-and-bust, geographically mobile society defined above all by materialism and wealth. New transportation networks encouraged entrepreneurs to sell to wider markets. Factories appeared, first in the textile industry, employing young women from rural families. As factory discipline structured time in more precise and demanding ways, workers protested by forming labor unions.

Chauncey Jerome's life spanned the transition from the master-apprentice system of production to the beginnings of mechanization and the rise of the factory system. Crèvecoeur's vision of independent American farmers living mainly on what they themselves produced had, by 1850, become a dream of the past. In its place stood a commercial republic in which a full-blown national market drew together most settled areas of the country.

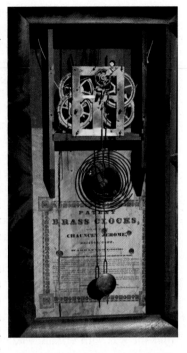

Chauncey Jerome's brass clock revolutionized clock-making and made him wealthy. The label displaying Jerome's name, the equivalent of a modern trademark, is visible inside the case.

The concept of the market is crucial here. Americans tied themselves to one another eagerly, even aggressively, through the mechanism of the free market. They sold cotton or wheat and bought manufactured cloth or brass one-day clocks. They borrowed money not merely to buy a house or farm but also to speculate and profit. They relied, even in many rural villages, on cash and paper money instead of bartering for goods and services. American life moved from less to more specialized forms of labor. It moved from face-to-face local dealings to impersonal, distant transactions. It shifted from the mechanically simple to the technologically complex and from less dense patterns of settlement on farms to more complex arrangements in cities and towns. Such were the changes Chauncey Jerome witnessed—indeed, changes he helped to bring about himself, with his clocks that divided the working days of Americans into more disciplined, orderly segments.

As these changes occurred about him, Jerome sensed that society had taken on a different tone—that the marketplace and its ethos had become dominant. "It is all money and business, business and money which make the man now-a-days," he complained. "Success is every thing, and it makes very little difference how, or what means he uses to obtain it." The United States, according to one foreign traveler, had become "one gigantic workshop, over the entrance of which there is the blazing inscription '*No admission here except on business.*'"

The Market Revolution

In 1844 John Burrows heard that potatoes were selling for $2.00 a bushel in New Orleans. Potatoes fetched less than 50 cents a bushel in Davenport in the Iowa Territory where Burrows was a small merchant, so he loaded 2500 bushels on a flatboat and started down the Mississippi River. Along the way, he learned that other merchants, acting on the same information, had done the same and that the market in New Orleans was now glutted with potatoes. When he reached his destination 6 weeks later, he could not sell his load at all. Desperate, he finally swapped his potatoes at 8 cents a bushel, taking a load of coffee in return. He made nothing on the transaction, since it had cost him that much to ship the load to New Orleans.

Burrows's experience demonstrated that a national market economy required not just the efficient movement of goods but also rapid communications. Looking back many years later on the amazing transformation that had occurred in his lifetime, Burrows commented, "No one can realize the difficulties of doing a produce business in those days."

A truly national system of markets began to grow following the War of 1812, when the United States entered a period of unprecedented economic expansion. As it grew, the economy became varied enough to sustain and even accelerate its growth. Before the war it had been tied largely to international trade. The United States exported staples like cotton, wheat, tobacco, and timber; if the nations that bought these commodities suddenly stopped doing so, the domestic economy suffered. That happened during the European wars of the 1790s and again after 1803. Because so many Americans remained rural and primarily self-sufficient, they could not absorb any increase in goods produced by American manufacturers.

Growth of a domestic market

But the War of 1812 marked the turning point in the creation and expansion of a domestic market. First the embargo and then the war itself stimulated the growth of manufacturing, particularly in textiles. In 1808 the United States had 8000 spindles spinning cotton thread; by the end of the war the number had jumped to around 130,000. In addition, war had also bottled up capital in Europe. When peace was restored, this capital flowed into the United States, seeking investments. Finally, the war experience led the federal government to adopt policies designed to spur economic expansion.

The New Nationalism

After the war with Britain, leadership passed to a new generation of the Republic— younger men like Henry Clay, John C. Calhoun, and John Quincy Adams. All were ardent nationalists eager to use federal power to promote rapid development of the nation. Increasingly dominant within the Republican party, they advocated the "New Nationalism," a set of economic policies designed to foster the prosperity of all regions of the country and bind the nation more tightly together.

National bank

Even James Madison saw the need for increased federal activity, given the problems the government experienced during the war. The national bank had closed its doors in 1811 when its charter expired. Without it the country had fallen into financial chaos. Madison had opposed Hamilton's national bank in 1791, but now with his approval, Congress in 1816 chartered the Second Bank of the United States for a period of 20 years. Madison also agreed to a mildly protective tariff to aid budding American industries by raising the price of competing foreign goods.

Protective tariff

Passed in 1816, it set an average duty of 20 percent on imported woolen and cotton cloth, iron, and sugar. The measure enjoyed wide support in the North and West, but a number of southern representatives voted against it because most of its benefits went to northern manufacturers.

Madison also recommended that the government promote internal improvements such as roads, canals, and bridges. The war had demonstrated how cumbersome it was to move troops or supplies overland. Although Madison did not believe that federal funds could be used for merely local projects, he was willing to support projects broader in scope. His successor, James Monroe, approved additional ones.

The Cotton Trade

Cotton proved to be the key to American economic development after 1815. By the end of the eighteenth century, southern planters had discovered that short-fiber cotton would grow in the lower part of the South. But the cotton contained sticky green seeds that could not be easily separated from the lint by hand. The needed breakthrough came in 1793 when Eli Whitney invented the cotton gin, a mechanical device that removed the seeds from the lint. The gin allowed a laborer to clean 50 pounds of cotton a day, compared with only 1 pound by hand. With prices high on the world market, cotton production in the Lower South soared. By 1840 the South produced more than 60 percent of the world supply, which accounted for almost two-thirds of all American exports.

Whitney's cotton gin

The cotton trade was the major expansive force in the economy until the depression of 1839. Northern factories increasingly made money by turning raw cotton into cloth, while northern merchants reaped profits from shipping the cotton and then reshipping the textiles. Planters used the income they earned to purchase foodstuffs from the West and goods and services from the Northeast.

The Transportation Revolution

To become truly national, a market economy needed an efficient transportation network linking various regions of the nation. The economy had not become self-sustaining earlier partly because the only means of transporting goods cheaply was by water. Thus trade was limited largely to coastal and international markets, for even on rivers, bulky goods moved easily in only one direction—downstream.

All that changed, however, after 1815. From 1825 to 1855—the span of a single generation—the cost of transportation on land fell 95 percent while its speed increased fivefold. As a result, new regions were drawn quickly into the market.

The Canal Age

Canals attracted considerable investment capital, especially after the success of the wondrous Erie Canal. Built between 1818 and 1825, the canal stretched 364 miles from Albany on the Hudson River to Buffalo on Lake Erie. Its construction by the state was an act of faith, for in 1816 the United States had only 100 miles of canals, none longer than 28 miles. Then, too, the proposed route ran through forests, disease-ridden swamps, and unsettled wilderness. The canal's engineers lacked experience, but they made up for that by sheer ingenuity. Improving on European tools, they devised a cable and screw that allowed one man to pull down even the largest trees and a stump-puller that removed up to 40 stumps a day.

Erie Canal

The project paid for itself within a few years. The Erie Canal reduced the cost of shipping a ton of goods from Buffalo to New York City from more than 19 cents a mile to less than 3 cents a mile. By 1860 the cost had fallen to less than a penny a mile. Where its busy traffic passed, settlers flocked, and towns like Rochester and Lockport sprang up and thrived by moving goods and serving markets. "Everything in this bustling place appears to be in motion," wrote one English traveler about Rochester in 1827. The steady flow of goods eastward gave New York City the dominant position in the scramble for control of western trade.

New York's commercial rivals, like Philadelphia and Baltimore, were soon frantically trying to build their own canals to the West. Western states like Ohio and Indiana, convinced that prosperity depended on cheap transportation, constructed canals to link interior regions with the Great Lakes. By 1840 the nation had completed more than 3300 miles of canals—a length greater than the distance from New York City to Seattle—at a cost of about $125 million. Almost half of that amount came from state governments.

The Erie Canal promoted urban growth, economic development, and feverish activity along its route. Here boaters guiding their craft past busy laborers on the shore provide an indication of the commerce that quickly flourished on the waterway.

End of canal era

By 1850 the canal era was over. The depression of 1839 caused several states to halt or slow their construction, especially since many poorly planned canals lost money. Still, whether profitable or not, canals sharply reduced transportation costs and stimulated economic development in a broad belt along their routes.

Steamboats and Railroads

Because of its vast expanse, the United States was particularly dependent on river transportation. But shipping goods downstream from Pittsburgh to New Orleans took 6 weeks, and the return journey required 17 weeks or more. Steamboats reduced the time of a trip from New Orleans to Louisville from 90 to 8 days while cutting upstream costs by 90 percent.

Western steamboats

Robert Fulton demonstrated the commercial possibilities of propelling a boat with steam when his ship, the *Clermont*, traveled in 1807 from New York City to Albany on the Hudson River. But steamboats had the greatest effect on transportation on western rivers, where the flat-bottomed boats could haul heavy loads even when the water level was low. The number of steamboats operating in those waters jumped from 17 in 1817 to 727 in 1855. Since steamboats could make many more voyages annually, the carrying capacity on the western rivers increased 100-fold between 1820 and 1860.

Governments did not invest heavily in steamboats as they had in canals; instead their main assistance was removing fallen trees and other obstacles to navigation. Although railroads would end the steamboat's dominance by 1860, it was the major form of western transportation during the years in which the national market economy grew up, and it proved the most important factor in the rise of manufacturing in the Ohio and upper Mississippi valleys.

Railroads' later influence

In 1830 the nation had only 13 miles of railroad track, and most of the lines constructed in the following decade served as feeder lines to canals. But soon enough, cities and towns saw that their economic future depended on having good rail links, so that by 1840 railroad and canal mileage were almost exactly equal (3325 miles). By 1850, the nation had a total of 8879 miles of track. Railroad rates were usually higher than canal or steamboat charges, but the new iron roads operated year-round, offered more direct routes, and moved goods about twice as fast. Even so, not until the 1850s did they come to dominate the transportation system.

Agriculture in the Market Economy

The new forms of transportation had a remarkable effect on Crèvecoeur's yeoman farm families: they became linked ever more tightly to a national market system. Before the canal era, wheat could be shipped at a profit no farther than 50 miles. But given cheap transportation, farmers eagerly grew more grain and sold the surplus in distant markets.

In this shift toward commercial agriculture, farmers began cultivating more acres, working longer hours, and adopting scientific farming methods, including crop rotation and the use of manures as fertilizer. Instead of bartering goods with friends and neighbors, they more often paid cash or depended on banks to extend them credit. Instead of taking the crops to market themselves, they began to rely on regional merchants, intermediaries in a far-flung distribution system. Like southern planters, western wheat farmers increasingly sold in a world market. Banks and distributors advanced credit to farmers, who more and more competed in a market controlled by impersonal forces centered in distant locations.

Commercial agriculture

As transportation and market networks connected more areas of the nation, they encouraged regional specialization. The South increasingly concentrated on staple crops for export, and the West grew foodstuffs, particularly grain. By 1850, Wisconsin and Illinois were major wheat-producing states. Eastern farmers,

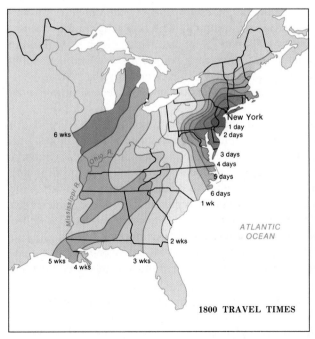

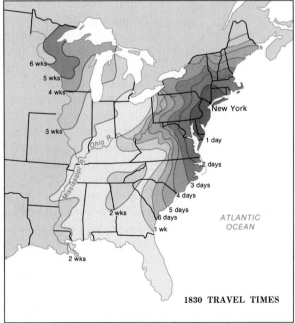

Travel Times, 1800 and 1830

unable to compete with wheat yields from fertile western farms, shifted to grazing sheep or producing fruits, vegetables, and dairy products for rapidly growing urban areas.

Although foreign commerce expanded too, it was overshadowed by the dramatic growth in domestic markets, which absorbed more and more of the goods and services being produced. The cities of the East no longer looked primarily to the sea for their trade; they looked to southern and western markets. That, indeed, was a revolution in markets.

John Marshall and the Promotion of Enterprise

For a national market system to flourish, a climate favorable to investment had to exist. Under the leadership of Chief Justice John Marshall the Supreme Court became the branch of the federal government most aggressive in protecting the new forms of business central to the growing market economy.

Marshall, who presided over the Court from 1801 to 1835, at first glance seemed an unlikely leader. Informal in manners and almost sloppy in dress, he was nonetheless a commanding figure: tall and slender, with twinkling eyes and a contagious, hearty laugh. His forceful intellect was reinforced by his genial ability to persuade. Time after time he convinced his colleagues to uphold the sanctity of private property and the power of the federal government to promote economic growth.

Constitutionality of the national bank

In the case of *McCulloch v. Maryland* (1819) the Court upheld the constitutionality of the Second Bank of the United States. Maryland had levied a tax on the Baltimore branch of the national bank, which the bank refused to pay, and the case went to the Supreme Court. The Court struck down the tax. Just as Alexander Hamilton had argued in the debate over the first national bank, Marshall emphasized that the Constitution gave Congress the power to make all "necessary and proper" laws to carry out its delegated powers. If Congress believed that a bank would help it meet its responsibilities, such as maintaining the public credit and regulating the currency, then it was constitutional. The bank only had to be useful, not essential. "Let the end be legitimate," Marshall wrote, "let it be within the scope of the Constitution, and all means which are appropriate, which are plainly adapted to that end, which are not prohibited . . . are constitutional." By upholding Hamilton's doctrine of implied powers, Marshall enlarged federal power to an extraordinary degree.

Interstate commerce

He also encouraged a more freewheeling commerce in *Gibbons v. Ogden* (1824). Under a New York law Aaron Ogden held a monopoly on steamboat traffic on the Hudson River between New Jersey and New York City. Thomas Gibbons, who had a federal license to operate a steamboat, set up a competing line and Ogden sued. The case gave Marshall a chance to define the greatest power of the federal government in peacetime, the right to regulate interstate commerce. In striking down a steamboat monopoly granted by the state of New York, the chief justice gave the term *commerce* the broadest possible definition, declaring that it covered all commercial dealings and that Congress's power over interstate commerce could be "exercised to its utmost extent." The result was increased business competition throughout society.

Protection of contracts

At the heart of most commercial agreements were private contracts, made between individuals or companies. Marshall took an active role in defining contract law, which was then in its infancy. The case of *Fletcher v. Peck* (1810) showed

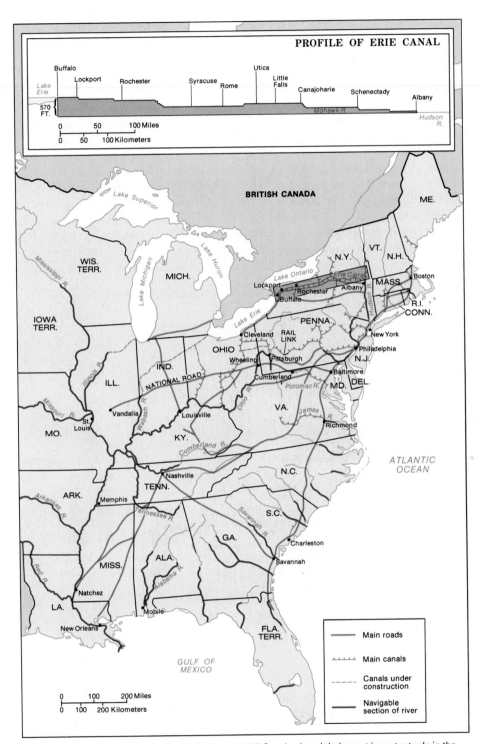

PROFILE OF ERIE CANAL

Buffalo
Lockport
Rochester
Syracuse
Rome
Utica
Little Falls
Canajoharie
Schenectady
Albany

Lake Erie

570 FT.

Mohawk R.

Hudson R.

0   50   100 Miles
0   50   100 Kilometers

BRITISH CANADA

ME.

Lake Superior

WIS. TERR.

Lake Michigan

Lake Huron

MICH.

N.Y.

VT.

N.H.

Lake Ontario

Erie Canal

Lockport

Rochester

Albany

MASS.

Boston

R.I.

CONN.

Buffalo

Lake Erie

IOWA TERR.

PENNA.

Cleveland

RAIL LINK

New York

OHIO

Wheeling

Pittsburgh

Philadelphia

N.J.

IND.

Mississippi R.

ILL.

NATIONAL ROAD

Cumberland

Baltimore

MD.

DEL.

Ohio R.

Potomac R.

Illinois R.

Missouri R.

St. Louis

Vandalia

Louisville

VA.

James R.

Richmond

MO.

KY.

Cumberland R.

N.C.

ATLANTIC OCEAN

ARK.

Arkansas R.

Nashville

TENN.

Memphis

Tennessee R.

S.C.

Savannah R.

Wabash R.

MISS.

ALA.

GA.

Charleston

Alabama R.

Savannah

Red R.

LA.

Natchez

Mobile

FLA. TERR.

New Orleans

GULF OF MEXICO

0   100   200 Miles
0   100   200 Kilometers

——— Main roads
++++++ Main canals
- - - - Canals under construction
——— Navigable section of river

The Transportation Network of a Market Economy, 1840 Canals played their most important role in the Northeast, where they linked eastern cities to western rivers and the Great Lakes. On the Erie Canal, a system of locks raised and lowered boats in a series of steps along the route. Steamboats were most crucial in the extensive river systems of the South and the West.

Daily Lives

TIME AND TRAVEL

Floating Palaces of the West

Plying the Mississippi River and its tributaries, the steamboat carried both freight and passengers, but it won its greatest fame as a mode of travel. The most luxurious boats, dubbed floating palaces, offered accommodations far beyond the experience of the average American. Steamboats also provided the cheapest form of inland transportation up to the Civil War. By midcentury, cabin passage for the 1400-mile trip from Louisville to New Orleans was only $12 to $15.

On the earliest steamboats passengers were housed on the main deck along with the cargo, but as the boats became larger, designers added a second, or boiler, deck (which, despite its name, was not where the boilers were located). Eventually a third level was added, the hurricane or texas, with additional accommodations. The boiler deck's saloon was the center of society, with the ladies' parlor at one end and the barroom at the other. Besides serving as a dining room and lounge, the saloon sometimes provided the sleeping quarters for men. Berths were arranged in two tiers on both sides and, at least on the better boats, contained bedding and a mattress. Women entered the saloon only for meals.

Steamboats also offered passage on the main deck for about one-fifth the price of a regular ticket. These passengers received no living quarters or toilet facilities and had to provide their own food. Then, too, boiler explosions, collisions, and sinkings from a snag took a much higher loss of life among lower-deck passengers, who were primarily the poor, immigrants, and African Americans. Between 1811 and 1851, 44 steamboats collided, 166 burned, 209 exploded, and 576 hit obstructions and sank, costing thousands of lives.

The steamboat was, as many travelers remarked, a "world in miniature," conveying slaves and planters, farmers and manufacturers, merchants and frontier families, soldiers and Indians, ministers and professional gamblers. As fares steadily dropped, people of widely different wealth and position were thrown together in the main cabin and mingled with democratic familiarity. Women spent

The luxurious saloon furnishings of a Mississippi steamboat, the *Princess*

how far he was willing to go to protect private property. The justices unanimously struck down a Georgia law taking back a land grant that a group of speculators had obtained by bribing members of the legislature. A grant was a contract, Marshall declared, and because the Constitution forbade states to impair "the obligation of contracts," the legislature could not interfere with the grant once it had been made. Although the framers of the Constitution probably meant *contracts* to refer only to agreements between private parties, Marshall made no distinction between public and private agreements, thereby greatly expanding the meaning of the contract clause.

their time talking, sewing, caring for children, and strolling the deck. Men passed the time in conversation about politics, the weather, business, and crops. The bar was the center of their social world, and gambling was rife.

The most famous vessels on the rivers boasted intricately carved gingerbread facings, painted a glistening white and trimmed in gold leaf—an architectural style known as "Steamboat Gothic." For all their luxurious veneer, however, steamboats lacked many amenities. Most six-by-six staterooms had two narrow shelves to sleep on and no lighting or heat. The washrooms in the main cabin contained tin basins and pitchers of cold water, a comb and brush, and a communal toothbrush. One traveler complained that there were only two towels for 70 men on one boat. Water, for both drinking and washing, came directly from the river and was laden with silt. Steamboat food was ample but often poorly prepared and saturated with grease. Furthermore, the average riverboat hardly lived up to the standards of the most famous packets. In 1843 John James Audubon journeyed from Louisville to St. Louis on what he described as "the very filthiest of all filthy old rattraps I ever traveled in." He grumbled particularly about a leaky roof, threadbare sheets, and pillows filled with corn husks.

In maintaining law and order, the captain was aided by the passengers, who in the tradition of the frontier sometimes formed their own courts to deal with those charged with minor offenses. Travelers accused of theft, illicit sexual relations, or cheating at gambling might find themselves flogged or put ashore at some desolate spot. In one case, when a young man and woman traveling together as "cousins" aroused suspicion, the passengers insisted on an investigation by the boat's officers, who discovered the pair sharing a berth. At the next stop, while the boat waited, indignant passengers marched the couple ashore, rounded up a minister, and compelled them to get married.

Despite the discomforts of swarming mosquitoes, heat from the boilers, and noisy engines at all hours of the night, observers agreed that journeying by steamboat was far more pleasant than taking a stagecoach, the principal alternative in the West before 1850. With their churning paddlewheels, gingerbread decks, and belching smokestacks, these gaudy vessels became the grandest showpieces of life along the commercial waterways of the Mississippi.

The most celebrated decision Marshall wrote on the contract clause was in *Dartmouth College v. Woodward*, decided in 1819. This case arose out of the attempt by New Hampshire to alter the college's charter granted by George III in 1769. The Court overturned the state law on the grounds that state charters were also contracts and could not be altered by later legislatures. By this ruling Marshall intended to protect corporations, which conducted business under charters granted by individual states.

Thus the Marshall Court encouraged economic risk taking. Its decisions protected property and contracts, limited state interference in business affairs, and created a climate of business confidence.

General Incorporation Laws

Importance of
corporations

Corporations were not new in American business, but as the economy expanded, they grew in numbers. Corporations had the advantage of continuing beyond the lives of the individuals who created them. By pooling investors' resources, they also provided a way to raise capital for large-scale undertakings. Then, too, corporations offered the advantage of limited liability: that is, an investor was liable only for the amount he or she had invested, which limited a person's financial risk. Small and medium-sized businesses continued to be run as partnerships and individual ventures, but ventures such as banks, insurance companies, railroads, and manufacturing firms—which all required a large amount of capital—increasingly were incorporated.

Originally, state legislatures were required to approve a special charter for each new corporation. Beginning in the 1830s, states adopted general incorporation laws that automatically granted a corporation charter to any applicant who met certain minimum qualifications. This reform made it much easier and faster to secure a charter and stimulated organization of the national market.

A Restless Temper

"Eating on the first of May," commented one New York City resident, "is entirely out of the question." That day was "moving day," when all the leases in the city expired. On that date nearly everyone, it seemed, moved to a new residence or place of business. Bedlam prevailed as furniture and personal belongings cluttered the sidewalks and people, movers, and horses crowded the streets. To Frances Trollope, it looked as if the whole population was "flying from the plague." Whereas in Europe millions of ordinary folk had never ventured beyond their local village, a Boston paper commented in 1828, "here, the whole population is in motion."

A People in Motion

Between 1815 and 1850, the nation reverberated with almost explosive energy. "An American . . . wants to perform within a year what others do within a much longer period," observed Francis Lieber, a noted political scientist who emigrated from Germany. The famous French commentator Alexis de Tocqueville was astonished, like most Europeans, at the restless mobility of the average American. "Born often under another sky, placed in the middle of an always moving scene, . . . the American . . . grows accustomed only to change, and ends by regarding it as the natural state of man."

A high-speed society

This emphasis on speed affected nearly every aspect of American life. Americans ate so quickly that one disgruntled European insisted food was "pitchforked down." Steamboat captains risked boiler explosions for the honor of having the fastest boat on the river, prompting the visiting English novelist Charles Dickens to comment that traveling under these conditions was like taking up "lodgings on the first floor of a powder mill." American technology emphasized speed over longevity on the assumption that the present design would soon be obsolete. Unlike European railroads, American railroads were lightweight, were hastily constructed, and paid little heed to the safety or comfort of passengers. Even so, Americans quickly embraced this new mode of transportation because of its speed. Eighteen-year-old Caroline Fitch of Boston likened her first ride on a railroad to a

"lightning flash": "It was 'whew!' and we were there, and 'whew!' and we were back again."

Even within railroad cars Americans were too fidgety to adapt to the European system of individual passenger compartments. Instead, American cars had a center aisle, allowing ever-restless passengers to wander the length of the train. Riding the rails in Texas, an English visitor was astounded that the passengers were "constantly jumping on and off whilst the train is in motion, and larking from one car to the other."

Horatio Greenough, a sculptor who returned to the United States in 1836 after an extended stay abroad, was amazed and a bit frightened by the pace he witnessed. "Go ahead! is the order of the day," he observed. "The whole continent presents a scene of scrambling and roars with greedy hurry." In the economic arena, the growth of a national market increased the sense of motion and restlessness. But social factors also contributed to this high-speed society.

Population Growth

The American population continued to double about every 22 years—more than twice the birthrate of Great Britain. The census, which counted fewer than 4 million Americans in 1790, surpassed 23 million in 1850. Although the birthrate peaked in 1800, it declined only slowly before 1840. During the 1840s, as urban areas grew rapidly, it dropped about 10 percent, the first significant decrease in American history. In cities, families were smaller, in part because the labor of children was not as critical to the family's economic welfare.

At the same time, many basic population characteristics changed little throughout the first half of the nineteenth century. Life expectancy did not improve significantly, the population remained quite young, and early marriage remained the norm, especially in rural areas.

From 1790 to 1820 natural increase accounted for virtually all the country's population growth. But immigration, which had been disrupted by the Napoleonic Wars in Europe, revived after 1815. In the 1830s some 600,000 immigrants arrived, more than double the number in the quarter century after 1790. And

Immigration rises after 1830

these newcomers proved to be merely a foretaste of the flood of immigrants that reached America beginning in the late 1840s.

The Federal Land Rush

The vast areas of land available for settlement absorbed much of the growing population. By 1850 almost half of all Americans lived outside the original 13 states. Well over 2 million lived beyond the Mississippi River. As settlers streamed west, speculation in western lands reached frenzied proportions. In the single year of 1818, at the peak of land-buying fever, the United States sold 3.5 million acres of its public domain. (In contrast, only 68,000 acres were sold in 1800.)

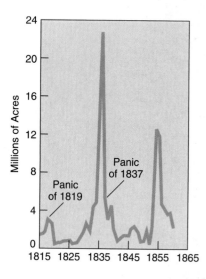

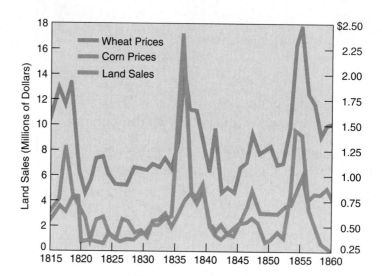

Purchase of Public Land

Year	Price per Acre	Minimum Acreage	Terms of Sale
1785	$1.00	640	Cash
1796	2.00	640	One-half cash; 1 year to pay balance
1800	2.00	320	Payment over 4 years
1804	2.00	160	Payment over 4 years
1820	1.25	80	Cash
1832	1.25	40	Cash
1841	Preemption (squatter could buy up to 160 acres at minimum price of $1.25 per acre)		
1854	Graduation (price of unsold lands reduced over time to a minimum of 12.5 cents per acre)		

Western Land Sales and the Price of Corn and Wheat Western farmers' expectations of future income were tied to the price of corn and wheat. As commodity prices rose, farmers eagerly bought land on credit, anticipating that future profits would enable them to pay off their mortgages. As the graph illustrates, when wheat and corn prices fell sharply in the Panic of 1819, land sales plummeted, and many farmers who had purchased on credit found themselves unable to pay their debts; a similar pattern is apparent in the 1830s. In the South there was a comparable relationship between land sales and the price of cotton. In order to encourage settlement, the terms to purchase public land (table, bottom) were made increasingly favorable, so that eventually a squatter could acquire the traditional 80-acre family farm on good land for only $100. Nevertheless, speculators continued to hold vast tracts of the public domain.

The Panic of 1819 sent sales and prices crashing, and in the depression that followed many farmers lost their farms. Congress reacted by abolishing credit sales and demanding payment in cash, but it tempered this policy by lowering the price of the cheapest lands to $1.25 an acre. (The best lands, sold at auction, fetched considerably higher prices, however.) The government also reduced the minimum tract to 80 acres, which meant that an ordinary farm could be purchased for $100.

Even so, speculators purchased most of the public lands sold, since the law put no limit on how many acres an individual or a land company could buy. These land speculators played a leading role in settlement of the West. To hasten sales, they usually sold land partially on credit—a vital aid to poorer farmers. They also provided loans to purchase needed tools and supplies, since the cost of establishing a farm was beyond the means of many young men. Many farmers became speculators themselves, buying up property in the neighborhood and selling it to latecomers at a tidy profit. "Speculation in real estate has been the ruling idea and occupation of the Western mind," one Englishman reported in the 1840s. "Clerks, labourers, farmers, storekeepers merely followed their callings for a living while they were speculating for their fortunes."

Speculators help settle western lands

Geographic Mobility

Given such rapid settlement, geographic mobility became one of the most striking characteristics of the American people. The 1850 census revealed that nearly half of all native-born free Americans lived outside the state where they had been born. In Boston from 1830 to 1860 perhaps one-third of the inhabitants changed their place of residence each year. Some owners, dissatisfied with their location, moved their houses instead. An astonished Charles Dickens recounted he once met a house "coming downhill at a good round trot, drawn by some twenty oxen!" The typical American "has no root in the soil," visiting Frenchman Michel Chevalier observed, but "is always in the mood to move on, always ready to start in the first steamer that comes along from the place where he had just now landed." Indeed, Americans were so mobile that Chevalier thought the national emblem should be a steamboat or locomotive.

On the road again

It was the search for opportunity, more than anything else, that accounted for such restlessness. An American moved, noted one British observer, "if by so doing he can make $10 where before he made $8." Often, the influence of the market uprooted Americans too. In 1851, a new railroad line bypassed the village of Auburn, Illinois, on the way to Springfield. "It seemed a pity," wrote one resident, "that so pretty a site as that of the old town should be abandoned for so unpromising a one . . . much of it mere swamp—but railroad corporations possess no bowels of compassion, the practical more than the beautiful being their object." After residents quickly moved to the new town that sprang up around the depot, a neighboring farmer purchased the site and plowed up the streets, and Auburn reverted to a cornfield.

Urbanization

Even with the growth of a national market, the United States remained a rural nation. Nevertheless, the four decades after 1820 witnessed the fastest rate of urbanization in American history. In 1820 there were only 12 cities with a population of more than 5000; by 1850 there were nearly 150. The 1820 census classified only about 9 percent of the American people as urban (living in towns with a population of 2500 or more). Forty years later the number had risen to 20 percent.

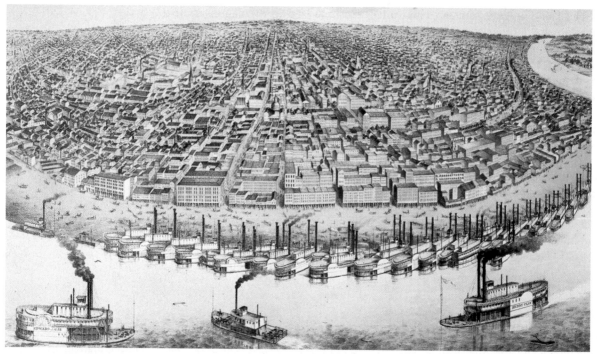

St. Louis, a major urban center that developed in the West, depended on the steamboat to sustain its commerce, as this 1859 illustration makes clear.

Urban centers, old and new

As a result, the ratio of farmers to city dwellers steadily dropped from 15 to 1 in 1800 to 5.5 to 1 in 1850. Improved transportation, the declining productivity of many eastern farms, the beginnings of industrialization, and the arrival of immigrants all stimulated the growth of cities.

The most heavily urbanized area of the country was the Northeast, where in 1860 more than a third of the population lived in cities.* The nation's largest city was New York, with more than half a million people, and older cities like Philadelphia, Boston, Baltimore, and New Orleans continued to be major urban centers. Equally significant, important urban centers such as St. Louis and Cincinnati arose in the West. Remarkably, by the century's midpoint, 40 percent of the nation's total urban population resided in interior cities. The South, with only 10 percent of its people living in cities, was the least urbanized region.

All these changes—the amazing growth of the population, the quickening movement westward, and the rising migration to the cities—pointed to a fundamental reorientation of American development. Expansion was the keynote of the new America, and the prospects it offered both excited and unsettled Americans.

The Rise of Factories

It was an isolated life, growing up in rural, hilly Vermont. But stories of the textile factories that had sprung up in Lowell and other towns in Massachusetts reached even small villages like Barnard. Fifteen-year-old Mary Paul was working there as a domestic servant when she asked her father for permission to move to Lowell. "I am in need of clothes which I cannot get about here," she explained. In

*The Northeast included New England and the mid-Atlantic states (New York, Pennsylvania, and New Jersey). The South comprised the slave states plus the District of Columbia.

1845 two friends from Barnard helped her find a job at the Lowell mills, from which she earned $128 in 11 months. After four years she returned home but now found "countryfied" life too confining. This time she left her rural hometown for good. She moved about and supported herself at several occupations before finally marrying and settling down in nearby Lynn.

Mary Paul was one of thousands of rural Americans whose lives were fundamentally altered by the economic transformation of the young republic. The changes in her lifestyle and her working habits demonstrated that the new factories and industries needed more than technological innovation to run smoothly. Equally crucial, the labor used to manufacture these goods needed to be reorganized.

Technological Advances

Before 1815 manufacturing had been done in homes or shops by skilled artisans who turned out a small number of finished goods, often made to order for local customers. As master craftworkers, they taught their trades to apprentices and journeymen. In addition, women often worked in their homes part-time under the putting-out system, making finished articles from raw material supplied by merchant capitalists. During the winter months many farm families manufactured items such as brooms and fans to supplement their income.

Small-scale manufacturing

After 1815 this older form of manufacturing began to give way to factories with machinery tended by unskilled or semiskilled laborers. Cheap transportation networks, the rise of cities, and the availability of capital and credit all stimulated the shift to factory production.

From England came many of the earliest technological innovations. But Americans often improved on the British machines or adapted them to more extensive uses. In contrast to the more traditional societies of Europe, "everything new is quickly introduced here," one visitor commented in 1820. "There is no clinging to old ways; the moment an American hears the word 'invention' he pricks up his ears." From 1790 to 1860 the United States Patent Office granted more patents than England and France combined.

Acceptance of technology

To protect their economic advantage, the British forbade the export of any textile machinery or emigration of any craftworker trained in their construction. But in 1790 a mill worker named Samuel Slater slipped past English authorities and built the first textile mill in America. Two decades later, the Boston merchant Francis Cabot Lowell imitated British designs for a power loom and then improved on them.

The first machines required highly skilled workers to both build and repair them. Eli Whitney had a better idea. Having won a contract to produce 10,000 muskets for the government, he developed machinery that would mass-produce parts that were interchangeable from one gun to another. Such parts had to be manufactured to rigid specifications that Whitney had difficulty attaining, but once the process was perfected after his death, a worker could assemble a musket quickly with only a few tools. Simeon North applied the same principle to the production of clocks, and Chauncey Jerome followed North's example and soon surpassed him.

Interchangeable parts

What rail and steam engines did for transportation, Samuel F. B. Morse's telegraph did for communications. Morse patented a device that sent electrical pulses over a wire in 1837, and before long, telegraph lines fanned out in all directions, linking various parts of the country instantaneously. By 1860 there were more than

Communication

50,000 miles of telegraph lines laid. The new telegraph sped business information, helped link the transportation network, and allowed newspapers to provide readers with up-to-date news.

Indeed, the invention of the telegraph and the perfection of a power press (1847) by Robert Hoe and his son Richard revolutionized journalism. The mechanical press sharply increased the speed with which sheets could be printed over the old hand method. Mass-produced newspapers, often selling for only a penny, gained huge circulations since ordinary families could afford them. Hoe's press had a similar impact on book publishing, as thousands of copies could be printed at affordable prices.

The Postal System

The development of a national market economy depended on mass communications that transmitted commercial information and brought into contact producers and sellers separated by great distances. While postage was relatively expensive, the American postal system subsidized the distribution of newspapers and disseminated other forms of information widely. Indeed, in the years before the Civil War, the postal system had more employees than any other enterprise in the country. While the postal system's primary purpose was to promote commerce, it had a profound social impact by accustoming people to long-range and even impersonal communication. By 1840, the post office handled almost 41 million letters and 39 million newspapers.

When traveling in the United States in 1831, Tocqueville was amazed at the scope of the postal system. "There is an astonishing circulation of letters and newspapers among these savage woods," he reported from the Michigan frontier. There was hardly a village or town in the country, no matter how remote, that was not connected with the rest of the country through the postal system. Nothing in Europe, he noted, could match it. While the British and French post offices handled a greater volume of mail, the United States throughout these years had a much more extensive postal system. In 1828, there were almost twice as many post offices in the United States as in Great Britain, and over five times as many as in France.

In the Americas, the Canadian postal system was so limited that merchants and even government officials routinely used the United States postal system to get mail to other provinces, while by midcentury Mexico had only 49 post offices and no regularized service for the whole country. In China, the government maintained a very efficient military-courier system for official communications, but foreigners developed the first private postal system, mainly for business correspondence; it was not until the twentieth century that a mass-based postal system was established. Most countries had no true postal system in these years, since literacy was so limited.

Textile Factories

The factory system originated in the Northeast, where capital, water power, and transportation facilities were available. In New England, as in England, the production of cloth was the first manufacturing process to make significant use of the new technology on a large scale. Eventually all the processes of manufacturing cloth were brought together in a single location, from opening the cotton bales to weaving the cloth, and machines did virtually all the work.

In 1813 a group of wealthy Boston merchants chartered the Boston Manufacturing Company and established the first fully integrated textile factory at Waltham, Massachusetts. Expanding their highly profitable operations, these investors, known as the Boston Associates, set up operations in 1820 at Chelmsford, Massachusetts, which they renamed Lowell. Intended as a model community, Lowell soon became the nation's most famous center of textile manufacturing.

Lowell

Its founders sought to avoid the wretched misery that characterized the factory system in England by combining paternalism with high profits. Instead of relying primarily on child labor or a permanent working class, the Lowell mills employed daughters of New England farm families. Thus women were the first factory workers in the United States. They lived in company boardinghouses under the watchful eye of a matron. To its many visitors, Lowell presented an impressive sight: huge factories, well-kept houses, bustling shops. Female employees were encouraged to attend lectures and use the library. They even published their own magazine, the *Lowell Offering*.

In reality, however, factory life involved strict rules and long hours of tedious, repetitive work. At Lowell, for example, workers could be fined for lateness or misconduct, including talking on the job. Alcohol, cards, and gambling were forbidden in the shop or mill yard. The women's morals in the boardinghouses were strictly guarded; male visitors were supervised, and there was a 10 P.M. curfew. Work typically began at 7 A.M. (earlier in the summer) and continued until 7 at night, six days a week. With only 30 minutes for the noon meal, many workers had to run to the boardinghouse and back to avoid being late. Winter was the "lighting up" season, when work began before daylight and ended after dark. The only light after sunset came from whale oil lamps that filled the long rooms with smoke. Even in summer the factories were poorly lit and badly ventilated.

Hard work in the mills

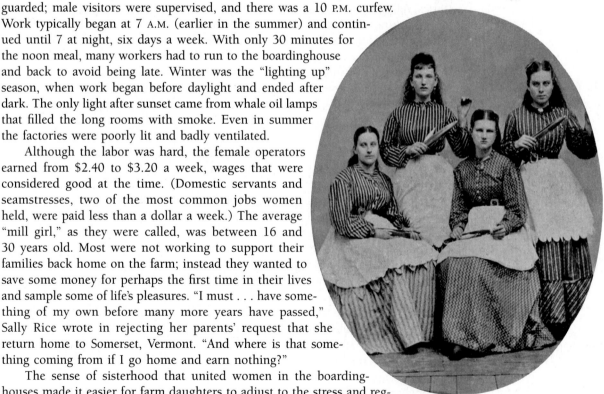

Mill workers, Lowell

Although the labor was hard, the female operators earned from \$2.40 to \$3.20 a week, wages that were considered good at the time. (Domestic servants and seamstresses, two of the most common jobs women held, were paid less than a dollar a week.) The average "mill girl," as they were called, was between 16 and 30 years old. Most were not working to support their families back home on the farm; instead they wanted to save some money for perhaps the first time in their lives and sample some of life's pleasures. "I must . . . have something of my own before many more years have passed," Sally Rice wrote in rejecting her parents' request that she return home to Somerset, Vermont. "And where is that something coming from if I go home and earn nothing?"

The sense of sisterhood that united women in the boardinghouses made it easier for farm daughters to adjust to the stress and regimen the factory imposed on them. So did their view of the situation as temporary rather than permanent, for most women worked in the mills no more than five years before getting married.

As competition in the textile industry intensified, factory managers sought ways to raise productivity. In the mid-1830s the mills began to increase the workloads and speed up the machinery. Even these changes failed to maintain previous profits, and on several occasions factories cut wages. The ever-quickening pace of work finally provoked resistance among the mill workers. Several times in the 1830s wage cuts sparked strikes in which a minority of workers walked out. Management retaliated by firing strike leaders, hiring new workers, and blacklisting women who refused to return. In the 1840s workers' protests focused on the demand for a 10-hour day.

Transformation of Lowell

The quest for profits also undercut the owners' paternalism. As the mills expanded, a smaller proportion of the workers lived in company boardinghouses and moral regulations were relaxed. But the greatest change was a shift in the workforce from native-born women to Irish immigrants. In 1845 the Irish made up only 8 percent of the Lowell workforce. By 1860 they amounted to almost half, many of them men and children. Because these new workers were poor and desperate for work, wages declined further. And because they did not view their situation as temporary, a permanent working class began to take shape.

Lowell and the Environment

Lowell was a city built on water power. Early settlers had used the power of the Merrimack River to run mills, but never on the scale used by the new textile factories. As the market spread, Americans came to link progress with the fullest use of the natural resources of the environment. Just as they had done in Lowell itself, the Boston Associates sought to impose a sense of order and regularity on the surrounding physical environment in order to efficiently use its natural resources. In the process, they fundamentally reshaped the area's waterscape.

Reshaping the area's waterscape

As more and more mills were built, the Boston Associates sought to harness water for energy. By 1836, Lowell had seven canals, with a supporting network of locks and dams, to govern the Merrimack's flow and distribute water to the city's twenty-six mills. The Associates also built dams at several points along the river to store water and divert it into power canals for factories. At Lawrence, they constructed the largest dam in the world at the time, a 32-foot-high granite structure that spanned 1600 feet across the river. But even dammed, the Merrimack's waters proved insufficient. So the Associates gained control of a series of lakes in New Hampshire covering more than 100 square miles that fed into the river system. By damming these lakes, they could provide a regular flow of water down the river, especially in the drier summer months. In the course of establishing this elaborate water-control system, they came to see water as a form of property, divorced from the ownership of land along the river. Water became a commodity that was measured in terms of its power to operate a certain number of spindles and looms.

Damaging effects

By regulating the river's waters, the Boston Associates made the Merrimack Valley the greatest industrial center in the country in the first half of the nineteenth century. But not all who lived in the valley benefited. By raising water levels, the dams flooded farm lands, blocked the transportation of logs downstream, and damaged mills upstream by reducing the current and creating backwater that impeded waterwheels. The dams also devastated the fish population by preventing upstream spawning, while factories routinely dumped their wastes into the river to be carried downstream. These wastes, combined with sewage from the growing population, eventually contaminated water supplies. Epidemics of typhoid, cholera, and dysentery occurred with increasing frequency, so that by midcentury Lowell had a reputation as a particularly unhealthy community.

In the end, the factory system fundamentally transformed the environment. Far from existing in harmony with its rural surroundings, Lowell, with its clattering

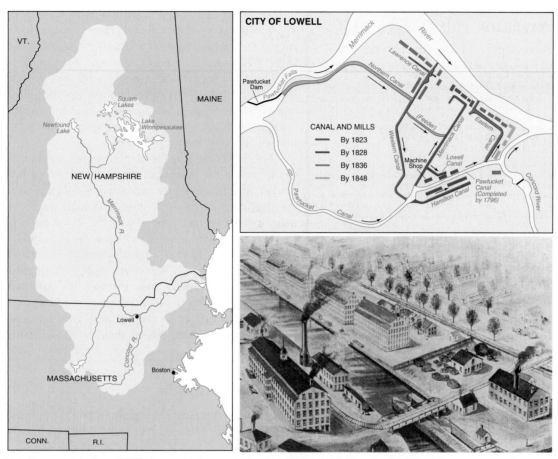

Development of the Lowell Mills As more mills were built at Lowell, the demand increased for water to power them. By 1859 the mills drew water from lakes 80 to 100 miles upstream, including Winnipesaukee, Squam, and Newfound. The map at left shows the watersheds affected. In the city of Lowell (right), a system of canals was enlarged over several decades. In the painting (done in 1845), the machine shop can be seen at left, with a row of mills alongside a canal. Rail links tied Lowell and Boston together.

machines and dammed rivers, presented a glaring contrast to rural life. The founding vision of Lowell had disappeared.

Industrial Work

For most workers, adaptation to the disciplined work routine of the factory did not happen easily. Traditionally, artisans had worked within the home. Apprentices were considered part of the family, and masters were responsible not only for teaching their apprentices a trade but also for providing them some education and for supervising their moral behavior. Journeymen took pride in their work, knowing that if they perfected their skill, they could become respected master artisans with their own shops. Skilled artisans worked not by the clock, at a steady pace, but rather in bursts of intense labor alternating with more leisurely time.

Artisan system

The factory changed that. Factory-produced goods were not as finished or elegant as those done by hand, and pride in craftsmanship gave way to rates of productivity. At the same time, workers were required to discard old habits, for

Transformation of work

TIME TABLE OF THE LOWELL MILLS,

To take effect on and after Oct. 21st, 1851.

The Standard time being that of the meridian of Lowell, as shown by the regulator clock of JOSEPH RAYNES, 43 Central Street.

	From 1st to 10th inclusive.			From 11th to 20th inclusive.			From 21st to last day of month.		
	1st Bell	2d Bell	3d Bell	Eve. Bell	1st Bell	2d Bell	3d Bell	Eve. Bell	1st Bell	2d Bell	3d Bell	Eve. Bell
January,	5.00	6.00	6.50	*7.30	5.00	6 00	6.50	*7.30	5.00	6.00	6.50	*7.30
February,	4.30	5.30	6.40	*7.30	4.30	5.30	6.25	*7.30	4.30	5.30	6.15	*7.30
March,	5.40	6.00		*7.30	5.20	5.40		*7.30	5.05	5.25		6.35
April,	4.45	5.05		6.45	4.30	4.50		6.55	4.30	4.50		7.00
May,	4 30	4.50		7.00	4.30	4.50		7.00	4.30	4.50		7 00
June,	"	"		"	"	"		"	"	"		"
July,	"	"		"	"	"		"	"	"		"
August,	"	"		"	"	"		"	"	"		"
September,	4.40	5.00		6.45	4.50	5.10		6.30	5.00	5.20		*7.30
October,	5.10	5.30		*7.30	5.20	5.40		*7.30	5.35	5.55		*7.30
November,	4.80	5.30	6.10	*7.30	4.80	5.30	6.20	*7.30	5.00	6.00	6.35	*7.30
December,	5.00	6.00	6.45	*7.30	5.00	6.00	6.50	*7.30	5.00	6 00	6.50	*7.30

* Excepting on Saturdays from Sept. 21st to March 20th inclusive, when it is rung at 20 minutes after sunset.

YARD GATES,

Will be opened at ringing of last morning bell, of meal bells, and of evening bells; and kept open Ten minutes.

MILL GATES.

Commence hoisting Mill Gates, Two minutes before commencing work.

WORK COMMENCES,

At Ten minutes after last morning bell, and at Ten minutes after bell which "rings in" from Meals.

BREAKFAST BELLS.

During March "Ring out".........at....7.30 a. m.........."Ring in" at 8.05 a. m.
April 1st to Sept. 20th inclusive.....at....7 00 " " .... " " at 7.35 " "
Sept. 21st to Oct. 31st inclusive.....at....7.30 " " .... " " at 8.05 " "
Remainder of year work commences after Breakfast.

DINNER BELLS.

" Ring out" ....12.30 p. m........."Ring in".... 1.05 p. m.

In all cases, the *first* stroke of the bell is considered as marking the time.

Long hours and punctuality: that is the message of this Lowell timetable. Often accustomed to a less regimented life on a farm, machine operators complained of the pace of the machines and the tyranny of the factory bell that summoned and dismissed them each day. A song, "The Lowell Factory Girl," described factory life:

> "The factory bell begins to ring,
> and we must all obey,
> And to our old employment go,
> or else be turned away."

Lynn as the center of shoemaking

industrialism demanded a worker who was sober, dependable, and self-disciplined. The machines, whirring and clacking away, set a strict schedule that had to be followed. Absenteeism, lateness, and drunkenness hurt productivity and, since work was specialized, disrupted the regular factory routine. Thus industrialization not only produced a fundamental change in the way work was organized but transformed the very nature of work.

For newcomers to industrial ways, the factory clock became the symbol of the new order. One mill worker who finally quit complained of "obedience to the ding-dong of the bell—just as though we are so many living machines." Along with the loss of personal freedom came the loss of standing in the community. Whereas the master-apprentice relationship was a close bond, factories sharply separated workers from management. Few workers rose through the ranks to supervisory positions, and even fewer could achieve the artisan's dream of setting up one's own business. Even well-paid workers sensed their decline in status.

The Shoe Industry

Shoemaking illustrated the industrial process at work. Traditionally, a skilled cobbler knew how to judge the quality of leather, cut out the various parts of a shoe, and stitch and glue the parts together. He then sold the shoes in the same shop where he and his apprentices made them. Unlike the textile industry, shoemaking was not rapidly transformed in this period by a shift to heavy machinery. Even so, expanding national markets fundamentally altered the business.

Following in his father's footsteps, Micajah Pratt, a cobbler from Lynn, Massachusetts, began selling shoes in 1812 to customers in New England. He found, however, that there were ready markets in the South and West for cheaply made shoes. So he hired workers to produce shoes in larger and larger central shops. Pratt cut costs further by using new production techniques, such as standardized patterns and sole-cutting machines. He eventually employed as many as 500 men and women and produced about a quarter million pairs of shoes annually. Other shoe manufacturers adopted similar strategies, and Lynn soon became the nation's shoe-manufacturing center.

With the shoe industry booming, Lynn's population doubled every 20 years. Yet so great was the national market that manufacturers could not keep pace with demand. Increasingly they hired nearby farmers, fishermen, and their families to do part-time work at home. Women and girls sewed the upper parts of a shoe, men and boys attached the bottoms. While slow, this mode of production allowed wages to be reduced still further. A few highly paid workers performed critical tasks like cutting the leather, but most work was done either in large central shops or in homes. With workers no longer able to make an entire shoe, in little more than a generation shoemaking ceased to be a craft. Though not organized in a factory setting, it had become essentially an assembly-line process.

The Labor Movement

In this newly emerging economic order, workers sometimes organized to protect their rights and traditional ways of life. Craftworkers like carpenters, printers, and tailors formed unions, and in 1834 individual unions came together in the National Trades' Union.

The leaders of these groups argued that labor was degraded in America: workers endured long hours, low pay, and low status. Workers were not being rewarded according to the value of their labor, they argued; instead, the idle rich lived off the industrious poor. Unlike most American social thinkers of the day, a number of labor leaders accepted the idea of conflict between different classes. They did not believe that the interests of workers and employers could be reconciled, and they blamed the plight of labor on monopolies, especially banking and paper money, and on machines and the factory system.

If the unions' rhetoric sounded radical, the solutions they proposed were moderate. Reformers agitated for public education and abolition of imprisonment for debt to provide better opportunities for workers. Leaders saw effective unions and political action as the means to restore labor to its former honored position. Proclaiming the republican virtues of freedom and equality, they attacked special privilege and decried workers' loss of independence.

The labor movement gathered some momentum in the decade before the Panic of 1837, but in the depression that followed, its strength collapsed. During hard times, few workers were willing to strike or engage in collective action. Nor did skilled craftworkers, who spearheaded the union movement, feel a particularly strong bond with semiskilled factory workers and unskilled laborers. More than a decade of agitation did finally gain the 10-hour day for some workers by the 1850s, and the courts also recognized workers' right to strike, but these gains had little immediate impact.

Workers were united in resenting the industrial system and their loss of status. But they found themselves divided by a host of other factors: ethnic and racial antagonisms, gender, conflicting religious perspectives, occupational differences, party loyalties, and disagreements over tactics. For most workers, the factory and industrialism were not agents of opportunity but reminders of their loss of independence and a measure of control over their lives.

Farmers, workers, and merchants—all these Americans were affected, as individuals, by the revolution in markets.

Social Structures of the Market Society

Equally critical, the market revolution restructured American society as a whole. It created greater extremes between the rich and the poor, contributed to the rise of a growing middle class, placed greater emphasis on material goods, and even changed the way Americans thought about time.

Economic Specialization

To begin with, the spread of the market produced greater specialization. As we have seen, transportation networks made it possible for farmers to concentrate on producing certain crops, while factories could focus on making a single item such as cloth or shoes. Within factories, the division of labor broke down the manufacture of an item into smaller, more specialized (and less skilled) tasks. As we have seen, no longer did one cobbler produce a pair of shoes from start to finish.

This process evolved at different rates. Textiles and milling were completely mechanized. Other sectors of the economy, like shoes and men's clothing, depended little on machinery. Indeed, large factories were the exception rather than the rule. Much manufacturing was still done in smaller shops with few employees. Even so, the tendency was toward more technology, greater efficiency, and increasing specialization.

Decline of women's traditional work

Specialization had consequences at home as well. The average eighteenth-century American woman produced thread, cloth, clothing, and candles in the home for family use. With the growth of factories, however, household manufacturing all but disappeared. As a result, women lost many of the economic functions they had once performed at home. Again, textiles are a striking example. Between 1815 and 1860, the price of cotton cloth fell from 18 to 2 cents a yard. Because manufactured cloth was also smoother and more brightly colored than homespun, most women purchased cloth rather than make it themselves. Similarly, the new ready-made men's clothing reduced the amount of sewing women did, especially in cities, where more men purchased clothing from retail stores. As Chapter 12 will make clearer, the growth of industry led to an economic reorganization of the family and a new definition of women's role in society.

Materialism

Europeans who visited the United States during these years were struck by how hard Americans worked and how preoccupied they were with material goods and achievements. The new generation did not invent materialism, but the spread of the market after 1815 made it much more evident. "I know of no country, indeed," Tocqueville commented, "where the love of money has taken stronger hold on the affections of men." And in 1836 the American writer Washington Irving coined the classic phrase that captured the spirit of the age when he spoke, in one of his stories, of "the almighty dollar, that great object of universal devotion throughout the land."

Wealth and status

In a nation that had no legally recognized aristocracy, no established church, and class lines that were only informally drawn, wealth became the most obvious symbol of status. Dismissing birth as "a mere idea," one magazine explained, "Wealth is something substantial. Everybody knows that and feels it." Materialism reflected more than a desire for goods and physical comfort. It represented a quest for respect and recognition. "Americans boast of their skill in money making," one contemporary observed, "and as it is the only standard of dignity and nobility and worth, they endeavor to obtain it by every possible means."

The emphasis on money and material goods left its mark on the American character. Often enough, it encouraged sharp business practices and promoted a greater tolerance of wealth acquired by questionable means. Families were rated by the size, not the source, of their fortunes. Americans also emphasized practicality over theory. The esteem of the founding generation for intellectual achievement was mostly lost in the scramble for wealth that seemed to consume the new generation.

The Emerging Middle Class

In the years after 1815, a new middle class took shape in American society. A small class of shopkeepers, professionals, and master artisans had existed earlier, but the creation of a national market economy greatly expanded its size and influence. As specialization increased, manual and nonmanual labor were more often physically separated. Office work and selling became removed from the production and handling of merchandise. More frequently, businesspeople, professionals, storekeepers, clerks, office workers, and supervisors began to think of themselves as a distinct social group. "In America it is customary to denominate as 'clerk' all young men engaged in commercial pursuits," wrote one observer at midcentury. "Of course, the term is not applied to those engaged in mechanical trades." Members of the growing middle class had access to more education and enjoyed greater social mobility. They were paid not only more but differently. A manual worker might earn $300 a year, paid as wages computed on an hourly basis. White-collar employees received a yearly salary and might make $1000 a year or more.

Separation of middle class from manual laborers

Middle-class neighborhoods, segregated along income and occupational lines, also began to develop in towns and cities. Moreover, in large urban areas the separation of work from place of residence combined with improvements in transportation made it possible for many middle-class residents to live in surrounding suburbs and commute to work. Leisure also became segregated as separate working-class and middle-class social organizations and institutions emerged.

During these years, a distinct middle-class way of life evolved based in part on levels of consumption. Greater wealth meant the ability to consume more.

Material goods as emblems of success

This traffic jam in New York City conveys the rapid pace and impatient quality of American life in the first half of the nineteenth century. "In the streets all is hurry and bustle," one European visitor to the city reported. "Carts, instead of being drawn by horses at a walking pace, are often met at a gallop, and always in a brisk trot. . . . The whole population seen in the streets seem to enjoy this bustle and add to it by their own rapid pace, as if they were all going to some place of appointment, and were hurrying on under the apprehension of being too late."

Someone like Joseph Engles, a Philadelphia publishing agent, might boast a house furnished with not one but two sofas, a looking glass, thirteen chairs, five yards of ingrain carpet on the floors, and even a piano and stool. Material goods became emblems of success and status—as clockmaker Chauncey Jerome sadly discovered when his business failed and his wealth vanished. Indeed, this materialistic ethos was most apparent in the middle class, as they strove to set themselves apart from other groups in society.

The rise of a middle class would soon launch far-reaching changes in American society, as we will see in Chapter 12. The middle class came to embrace a new concept of marriage, the family, and the home. Along with occupation and income, moral outlook also marked class boundaries during this period.

The Distribution of Wealth

As American society became more specialized and differentiated, greater extremes of wealth appeared. After 1815, local tax records reveal a growing concentration of wealth at the top of the social pyramid. The concentration was greatest in large eastern cities and in the cotton kingdom of the South, but everywhere the tendency was for the rich to get richer and own a larger share of the community's total wealth. In New York, Brooklyn, Boston, and Philadelphia, the top 1 percent of the wealth holders owned a quarter of the total wealth in 1825; by 1850 they owned half. Similar trends appeared in western cities, such as Cincinnati and St. Louis. By 1860, 5 percent of American families owned more than 50 percent of the nation's wealth.

In contrast, those at the base of the social pyramid held a smaller percentage of a community's wealth. In Connecticut towns between 1831 and 1851 the number of inhabitants listed as having no property increased by 33 percent. In Cincinnati the lower half of the city's taxpayers held 10 percent of the wealth in 1817; in 1860 their share had dropped to less than 3 percent.

In a market society, the rich were able to build up their assets because those with capital were in a position to increase it dramatically by taking advantage of new investment opportunities. Although a few men, such as Cornelius Vanderbilt and John Jacob Astor, vaulted from the bottom ranks of society to the top, most of the nation's richest individuals came from wealthy families.

Social Mobility

The existence of great fortunes is not necessarily inconsistent with the idea of social mobility or property accumulation. Although the gap between the rich and the poor widened after 1820, even the incomes of most poor Americans rose, because the total amount of wealth produced in America had become much larger. From about 1825 to 1860 the average per capita income almost doubled to $300. Voicing the popular belief, a New York judge proclaimed, "In this favored land of liberty, the road to advancement is open to all."

Limits of social mobility   Social mobility existed in these years, but not as much as contemporaries boasted. Most laborers—or more often their sons—did manage to move up the social ladder, but only a rung or two. Few unskilled workers rose higher than to a semiskilled occupation. Even the children of skilled workers normally did not escape the laboring classes and enter the middle-class ranks of clerks, managers, or lawyers. For most workers, improved status came in the form of a savings account or home ownership, which gave them some security during economic downswings and in old age.

A New Sensitivity to Time

It was no accident that Chauncey Jerome's clocks spread throughout the nation along with the market economy. The new methods of doing business involved a new and stricter sense of time. Factory life required a more regimented schedule in which work began at the sound of a bell, workers kept machines going at a constant pace, and the day was divided into hours and even minutes.

Clocks began to invade private as well as public space. Before Jerome and his competitors began using standardized parts, only the wealthy owned clocks, but with mass production ordinary families could afford them. Even farmers became more sensitive to time as they became integrated into the marketplace. As one frontier traveler reported in 1844, "In Kentucky, in Indiana, in Illinois, in Missouri, and here in every dale in Arkansas, and in cabins where there was not a chair to sit on, there was sure to be a Connecticut clock."

The Market at Work: Three Examples

To sense how much America was leaving behind Crèvecoeur's vision of a land of subsistence farmers, consider three examples of the new market economy, from a small city on the East Coast to the distant frontier of the Rocky Mountains.

In 1820 Kingston, New York, was a small, rural-oriented community of 1000 people, located along the Hudson River halfway between New York City and Albany. But in 1828 the Delaware and Hudson Canal linked Kingston with the Pennsylvania coal fields, jolting the town out of its economic lethargy. The rise of the coal trade stimulated local commerce and greatly increased the number of banks and the variety of businesses. The rhythm of life in Kingston now focused on the docks, stores, and canal boats rather than on planting and harvest. By 1850 Kingston had a population of 10,000, ten times that in 1820.

The market transforms Kingston, New York

Its landscape changed too. In 1820 most storekeepers and craftworkers had conducted business from their homes. By 1850 a commercial district boasted specialized stores, some handling china and glassware, others dry goods, clothing, or jewelry and watches. In addition, most manufacturing facilities were confined to two sections on the city's outskirts. Residential areas were separate from the commercial center and had become segregated along class lines, with different neighborhoods for the elite of the community, for skilled workers, and for unskilled laborers. By midcentury, street signs and gas lamps were going up, and numbers were being assigned to buildings. Kingston had become an urban center.

A thousand miles west lay the small prairie settlement of Sugar Creek, Illinois. The first white settlers had moved to Sugar Creek in 1817, as the market revolution was getting under way. The village's pioneers were primarily concerned about simply surviving. The land they plowed was on the edge of the forest, where girdled trees often remained standing among the crops until they could be cleared. The roads to larger towns like Springfield were mere cart paths, winding hither and yon among the trees.

Sugar Creek, Illinois

By the 1840s and 1850s the market economy had made inroads at Sugar Creek. True, a farmer like Eddin Lewis might still keep an account book noting that James Wilson came by for "six days work planting corn [$]3.00." That was the traditional barter system in action, for no cash actually changed hands. Lewis was simply keeping tabs, noting also when he helped Wilson, so that eventually the account could be balanced. But Lewis had also begun to drive hogs to St. Louis, where he received cash in return. By 1848 he was shipping south 6000 pounds of barreled pork, as well as lard and 350 bushels of corn. Wealth had become more concentrated in Sugar Creek, too. The richest farmers concentrated on a few money-making crops and rented their surplus land to poorer tenants; their wives no longer had to produce large amounts of butter for market to make ends meet. Sugar Creek, in other words, was becoming more specialized, more stratified in its wealth, and more tied into regional and national markets.

Mountain men and the fur trade

Another thousand miles west a different sort of American roamed, who might at first seem unconnected to the bustle of urban markets. These were the legendary mountain men. Traveling across the Great Plains, along upland streams, and over the passes of the Rockies, hard-bitten outdoorsmen like Jim Bridger, Jedediah Smith, and James Walker wore buckskin hunting shirts, let their unkempt hair grow to their shoulders, and stuck pistols and tomahawks in their belts. In good times they feasted on raw buffalo liver and roasted hump; when game was scarce, some were not above holding their hands "in an anthill until they were covered with ants, then greedily [licking] them off," as one trapper recalled. Wild and exotic, the mountain men quickly became romantic symbols of the American quest for individual freedom.

Yet these wanderers too were tied to the market. During their heyday, from the mid-1820s to the early 1840s, they trapped beaver, whose pelts were shipped east and turned into fancy hats for gentlemen. The fur trade was not a sporting event but a business, dominated by organizations like John Jacob Astor's American Fur Company, and the trapper was part of a vast economic structure that stretched from the mountains to the eastern cities and on to Europe. The majority of these men went into the wilderness not to flee civilization but to make money. Their ultimate goal was to accumulate capital in order to set themselves up in society. Of those

Thomas Hicks's painting, *Calculating,* captures the spirit of the United States as the market revolution unfolded. Americans, one foreign visitor reported, were a "guessing, reckoning, expecting and calculating people." During this period the phrase "I calculate" came to mean "I think." The man carefully going over his figures wears a beaver hat, the end product of the fur trade. Indeed, business attitudes shaped and controlled the fur trade, and many mountain men ended up as calculating businessmen.

who survived the fur trade, almost none remained permanently outside the bounds of civilization; most returned and took up new careers. Far from repudiating society's values, the mountain men sought respectability and success as defined by the society they had temporarily left. They, like farmers, were expectant capitalists for whom the West was a land of opportunity.

The mountain men, the farmers of Sugar Creek, and the workers of Kingston

Prosperity and Anxiety

were all alert to the possibilities of the market. As Americans saw their nation's frontiers expand and its economy grow, many began to view history in terms of an inevitable and continuous improvement. The path of commerce, however, was not steadily upward. Rather it advanced in a series of wrenching boom-bust cycles: accelerating growth and overheated expansion, followed by a crash and then depression.

The country remained extraordinarily prosperous from 1815 until 1819, only to sink into a depression that lasted from 1819 to 1823. During the next cycle, slow economic expansion in the 1820s gave way to almost frenzied speculation and investment in the 1830s. Then came the inevitable contraction in 1837, and the country suffered an even more severe depression from 1839 to 1843. The third cycle again followed the familiar pattern: gradual economic growth during the 1840s, frantic expansion in the 1850s, and a third depression that began in 1857 and lasted until the Civil War. In each of these depressions, thousands of workers were thrown out of work, overextended farmers lost their farms, and many businesses closed their doors.

Boom-bust cycle

The impact of the boom-bust cycle can be seen in the contrasting fates of two Americans who moved west in search of opportunity. In 1820, 17-year-old Benjamin Remington left Hancock, Massachusetts, for western New York, which was just being opened to white settlement. Possessing little money and no property, he tried his hand at several jobs before purchasing on credit a 150-acre farm near the growing city of Rochester. Remington's timing was ideal. In 1823, two years after his arrival, the new Erie Canal was completed as far as Rochester. Wheat prices rose, flour shipments from the region shot up, and Remington prospered supplying food for eastern markets. Over the years, he added to his acreage, built a comfortable house for his family, and was elected town supervisor. For Remington, the West was indeed a land of opportunity.

Somewhat younger, Addison Ward moved west when he came of age in 1831, leaving Virginia for Indiana. Unfortunately, by the time Ward arrived in Greene County, the best land had already been claimed. All he could afford was 80 acres of rough government land, which he bought in 1837 largely on credit. The region lacked adequate transportation to outside markets, but the economy was booming, land values were soaring, and the state had begun an ambitious internal improvements program. Ward's timing, however, could not have been worse. Almost immediately the country entered a depression, driving farm prices and land values downward. Overwhelmed by debts, Ward sold his farm and fell into the ranks of tenant farmers. He eventually moved on but never recovered financially. Catching the wrong end of the boom-bust cycle, Ward never achieved economic success and social respectability. As his experience demonstrated, the market revolution wore a double face, and the bright side did not shine on everyone.

In such an environment, prosperity, like personal success, seemed all too fleeting. Because Americans believed that the good times would not last—that the bubble would burst and another "panic" would set in—their optimism was often

Popular anxiety

tinged by insecurity and anxiety. They knew too many individuals like Chauncey Jerome, who had been rich and then lost all their wealth in a downturn.

The Panic of 1819

The initial shock of this boom-and-bust psychology came with the Panic of 1819, the first major depression in the nation's history. From 1815 to 1818 cotton had commanded truly fabulous prices on the Liverpool market, reaching 32.5 cents a pound in 1818. In this heady prosperity, the federal government extended liberal credit for land purchases, and the new national bank encouraged merchants and farmers to expand their operations by borrowing in order to catch the rising tide.

National depression

But in 1819 the price of cotton collapsed and took the rest of the economy with it. Once the inflationary bubble burst, land values, which had been driven to new heights by the speculative fever, plummeted 50 to 75 percent almost overnight. As the economy went slack, so did the demand for western foodstuffs and eastern manufactured goods and services, pushing the nation into a severe depression.

Because the market economy had spread to new areas, the downturn affected not only city folk but rural Americans as well. Many farmers, especially in newly settled regions, had bought their land on credit, and farmers in established areas had expanded their operations, looking to future profits. When prices fell, both groups were hard-pressed to pay their debts. New cotton planters in the Southwest, who were most vulnerable to the ups and downs of the world market, were especially hard hit.

The panic's economic stresses stirred sectional tensions, but the downturn affected the political life of the nation in even more direct ways. As the depression deepened and hardship spread, Americans viewed government policies as at least partly to blame. The postwar nationalism, after all, had been based on the belief that government should stimulate economic development through a national bank and protective tariff, by improving transportation, and by opening up new lands. As Americans struggled to make sense of their new economic order, they looked to take more direct control of the government that was so actively shaping their lives. During the 1820s, the popular response to the market and the Panic of 1819 produced a strikingly new kind of politics in the Republic.

---

chapter summary

By uniting the country in a single market, the market revolution transformed the United States during the quarter century after 1815.

- The federal government promoted the creation of a market through a protective tariff, a national bank, and internal improvements.

- The development of new forms of transportation, including canals, steamboats, and eventually railroads, allowed goods to be transported cheaply on land.

- The Supreme Court adopted a pro-business stance that encouraged investment and risk taking.

- Economic expansion generated greater national wealth, but it also brought social and intellectual change.

  - Americans pursued opportunity, embraced a new concept of progress, viewed change as normal, developed a strong materialist ethic, and considered wealth the primary means to determine status.

  - Entrepreneurs reorganized their operations to increase production and sell in a wider market.

- The earliest factories were built to serve the textile industry, and the first laborers in them were young women from rural families.
  - Factory work imposed on workers a new discipline based on time and strict routine.
  - Workers' declining status led them to form unions and resort to strikes, but the depression that began in 1837 destroyed these organizations.
- The market revolution distributed wealth much more unevenly and left Americans feeling alternately buoyant and anxious about their social and economic status.
  - Social mobility still existed, but it was more limited than popular belief claimed.
  - The economy lurched up and down in a boom-bust cycle.
  - In hard times, such as the Panic of 1819, Americans looked to the government to relieve economic distress.

interactive learning

The Primary Source Investigator CD-ROM offers the following materials related to this chapter:

- Interactive maps: **Slavery and the Cotton Kingdom** (M11) and **The Transportation Revolution, 1830–1890** (M12)

- A collection of primary sources, including many exploring the massive economic expansion that occurred in this period. Other documents demonstrate social changes connected to the rise of the Cotton Kingdom, including an illustration of domestic slaves and servants, patent diagrams of the cotton gin, and advertisements selling western land investment opportunities. Also read about the building of the National Road.

additional reading

Charles Sellers, *The Market Revolution* (1991), is the most ambitious synthesis of social, economic, and political developments in this period, but it is marred by an overly romantic view of preindustrial society and a pronounced ideological bias. For a critique of Sellers's interpretation, see William E. Gienapp, "The Myth of Class in Jacksonian America," *Journal of Policy History,* 6 (1994), 232–281, with comments and a rejoinder. Additional assessments are offered in Melvin Stokes and Stephen Conway, eds., *The Market Revolution in America* (1996). Insightful discussions of a number of relevant topics can be found in Mary Kupiec Cayton et al., eds., *Encyclopedia of American Social History* (3 vols., 1993), a superb and wide-ranging collection based on the latest scholarship.

A very important overview of economic change is Douglass C. North, *The Economic Growth of the United States, 1790–1860* (1961). George Rogers Taylor, *The Transportation Revolution, 1815–1860* (1951), is the classic survey, while John Larson, *Internal Improvements* (2001), is an excellent recent study. Many of the social consequences of the new market economy are described in Jack Larkin, *The Reshaping of Everyday Life, 1790–1840* (1988), and more analytically in Christopher Clark, *The Roots of Rural Capitalism* (1990). Significant community studies include Stuart M. Blumin, *The Urban Threshold* (1976) and John Mack Faragher, *Sugar Creek* (1986). Workers' experiences are sympathetically examined in Thomas Dublin, *Women at Work* (1979); Paul G. Faler, *Mechanics and Manufacturers in the Early Industrial Revolution* (1981); and Sean Wilentz, *Chants Democratic: New York City and the Rise of the American Working Class, 1788–1850* (1984). Stuart Blumin's *The Emergence of the Middle Class* (1989) is an excellent treatment of a critical subject. For a fuller list of readings, see the Bibliography at www.mhhe.com/davidsonnation5.

significant events

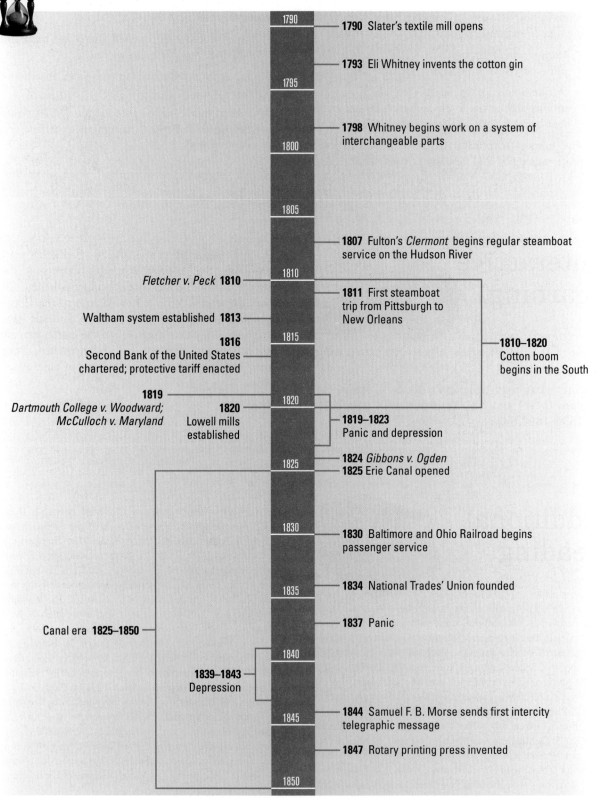

1790	**1790** Slater's textile mill opens
	1793 Eli Whitney invents the cotton gin
1795	
	1798 Whitney begins work on a system of interchangeable parts
1800	
1805	
	1807 Fulton's *Clermont* begins regular steamboat service on the Hudson River
Fletcher v. Peck **1810** — **1810**	**1811** First steamboat trip from Pittsburgh to New Orleans
Waltham system established **1813**	
1816 Second Bank of the United States chartered; protective tariff enacted **1815**	**1810–1820** Cotton boom begins in the South
1819	
Dartmouth College v. Woodward; McCulloch v. Maryland **1820** Lowell mills established	**1819–1823** Panic and depression
	1824 *Gibbons v. Ogden*
1825	**1825** Erie Canal opened
1830	**1830** Baltimore and Ohio Railroad begins passenger service
1835	**1834** National Trades' Union founded
	1837 Panic
Canal era **1825–1850** **1840**	
1839–1843 Depression	
1845	**1844** Samuel F. B. Morse sends first intercity telegraphic message
	1847 Rotary printing press invented
1850	

The notice, printed in a local newspaper, made the rounds in the rural Pearl River district of Mississippi. A traveler, the advertisement announced, had lost a suitcase while fording the Tallahala River. The contents included "6 ruffled shirts, 6 cambric handkerchiefs, 1 hair-brush, 1 tooth-brush, 1 nail-brush, . . ."

As the list went on, the popular reaction would inevitably shift from amusement to disdain: "1 pair curling tongs, 2 sticks poma-tum . . . 1 box pearl powder, 1 bottle Cologne, 1 [bottle] rose-water, 4 pairs silk stockings, and 2 pairs kid gloves." The howls of derision that filled the air could only have increased upon learning that anyone find-ing said trunk was requested to contact the owner—Mr. Powhatan Ellis of Natchez.

Powhatan Ellis was no ordinary backcountry traveler. Born into a genteel Vir-ginia family, Ellis had moved in 1816 to the raw Southwest to increase his for-tune. With his cultivated tastes, careful dress, and stately dig-nity, he upheld the tradition of the gentleman politician. In Virginia he would have com-manded respect: indeed, in Mis-sissippi he had been appointed district judge and U.S. senator. But for the voters along the Pearl River, the advertisement for his trunk of ruffled shirts, hair oils, and fancy "skunkwa-ter" proved to be the political kiss of death. His opponents branded him an aristocrat and a dandy, and his support among the piney woods farmers evaporated faster than a morning mist along Old Muddy on a sweltering summer's day.

The Rise of DEMOCRACY

1824–1840

preview • In the 1820s and 1830s a new democratic political culture champi-oned the wisdom of the people and the need for political parties. Andrew Jack-son personified the new spirit, expanding the power of the presidency by reject-ing South Carolina's doctrine of states' rights and by humbling the national bank. Paradoxically, democratic politics intensified racism, as Indians east of the Mis-sissippi were forced from their lands and free African Americans met increased discrimination.

No one was more satisfied with this outcome than the resourceful Franklin E. Plummer, one of Ellis's political enemies. In truth, while the unfortunate Powhatan Ellis had lost a trunk fording a stream, he had never placed the advertisement try-ing to locate it. That was the handiwork of Plummer, who well understood the new playing field of American politics in the 1820s. If Powhatan Ellis typified the passing political world of the Revolutionary era, Plummer was a product of the raucous democratic system emerging in its place. Leaving his home in New En-gland, Plummer had made his way as a young man to the new state of Mississippi, where he set himself up as an attorney, complete with a law library of three books. Plummer's shrewdness and oratorical talent made up for his lack of legal training, however, and he was quickly elected to the legislature.

Champion of the people

In 1830 Plummer's ambition led him to announce a run for Congress. At first few observers took his candidacy seriously. But Plummer boldly portrayed himself as the champion of the people battling against the aristocrats of Natchez. Con-trasting his humble background with that of his wealthy opponent, Plummer pro-claimed: "We are taught that the highway to office, distinction and honor, is as free to the *meritorious poor* man, as to the *rich;* to the man who has risen from obscu-rity by his own individual exertions, as to him who has inherited a high and ele-vated standing in society. . . ." Taking as his slogan "Plummer for the People, and the People for Plummer," he was easily elected.

By 1840 the new style of democratic politics was in full swing. This rally in Knoxville, Tennessee, uses a camp meeting–style platform in the woods to rally supporters. The makeup of this audience underscores another feature of Jacksonian democracy: the vote went only to adult white males.

On the campaign trail Plummer knew how to affect the common touch. Once, while canvassing the district with his opponent, the pair stopped at a farmhouse. When his opponent, seeking the farmer's vote, kissed the daughter, Plummer lifted up a toddling boy and began picking red bugs off him, telling the enchanted mother, "They are powerful bad, and mighty hard on babies." On another occasion, while his opponent slept, Plummer rose at dawn to help milk the family's cow—and won another vote.

As long as Plummer maintained his image as one of the people, fighting their battles against aristocrats, he remained invincible. But in 1835 when he became a candidate for the U.S. Senate, his touch deserted him. Borrowing money from a Natchez bank, he purchased a stylish coach, put his servant in a uniform, and campaigned across the state. Aghast at such pretensions, his followers promptly abandoned him, and he was soundly defeated. He died in 1852 in obscurity and poverty. Ah, Plummer! Even the staunchest of nature's noblemen may stumble, prey to the temptations of power and commerce!

Franklin Plummer was being pulled two ways by the forces transforming American society. As the previous chapter explained, the growth of commerce and new markets opened up opportunities for more and more Americans during these years. *Opportunity* was one of the bywords of the age. Through his connections with bankers and the well-to-do, Plummer saw the opportunity to accumulate wealth and to gain status and respect.

Yet at the same time that new markets were producing a more stratified, unequal society, the nation's politics were becoming more democratic. The new political system that developed after 1820 differed strikingly from that of the early Republic. Just as national markets linked the regions of America economically, the new system of national politics with its mass electioneering techniques involved more voters than ever before and created a new class of politicians. Plummer's world reflected that new political culture. And its central feature—another byword

Daily Lives

CLOTHING AND FASHION

The Plain Dark Democracy of Broadcloth

The emergence of democracy in American life was accompanied by a dramatic change in men's clothing. In the eighteenth century clothing was a prime indicator of social rank and set members of the upper class apart from ordinary citizens. A gentleman's finely tailored apparel—ruffled shirts, lace cuffs, silk stockings, decorative garters, and buckled shoes—was a mark of status because only elites could afford these expensive items. Because of the cost and extensive labor involved, most Americans owned only a few clothes, and these usually were made out of homespun—cloth woven from thread spun in the household. With a quick glance an observer could tell a person's social rank.

In the Jacksonian era, however, fashionable clothing became cheaper and much more widely available, and as a result dress no longer revealed social standing. By significantly lowering the cost, textile mills made good-quality cloth accessible to ordinary families. "All sorts of cotton fabrics are now so cheap that there is no excuse of any person's not being well provided," commented *The Young Lady's Friend* in 1836. Poor families and slaves did not share in this abundance, but most Americans' basic wardrobe expanded: now women usually owned more than a couple of dresses, and men ordinarily had more than a single jacket and one or two pairs of pants.

The colorful shirts, rude trousers, leather aprons, frocks, and heavy boots and shoes worn by farmers and mechanics while working were readily distinguishable from the coats and trousers of middle-class merchants, professionals, managers, and clerks. Outside the workplace, however, differences in clothing style, if not tailoring quality, largely disappeared. British traveler John Fowler in 1831 was amazed to see American workers, decked out in their Sunday best, walking the streets wearing "sleek coats, glossy hats, watchguards, and deerskin gloves!" Unlike men in the eighteenth century, these Americans dressed in somber colors. By the 1830s "black was the prevailing color," one New Yorker recalled. "It was worn for promenade, parlor, church, ball, business," and "in such uniformity of style, as effectively to destroy all individuality."

As this nattily dressed butcher suggests, clothes were not much help in sorting out social status in America. Although the clothing of the upper class was often made of finer material and was more skillfully tailored, by the 1820s less-prosperous Americans wore similar styles. "The washerwoman's Sunday attire is now as nearly like that of the merchant's wife as it can be," commented one astonished observer.

on everyone's lips—was equality. In truth, the relationship between the new equalities of politics and the new opportunities of the market was an uneasy one.

Equality and Opportunity

Middle- and upper-class Europeans who visited the United States during these decades were especially sensitive to the egalitarian quality of American life. Coming from the more stratified society of Europe, they were immediately struck by the "democratic spirit" that had become "infused into all the national habits and all the customs of society." Europeans spent only a few days traveling American roads before the blunt contours of Franklin Plummer's world were brought home to them.

The emergence after 1840 of the ready-made clothing industry also had a decisive impact on men's fashions. A growing number of men in middle-class positions were anxious to create a proper image but could not afford the expert tailoring required to make a business suit. In response to this demand, tailors developed standardized patterns and a proportional sizing system and began mass-producing affordable ready-made clothing. Decently made, fashionable suits could be purchased off the rack, and thus clerks began wearing clothing identical in style to that worn by their employer. By eliminating the distinction between homemade apparel and that sewed by a tailor, ready-made clothing further democratized men's attire.

New ways of dressing began with the urban middle class and gradually spread throughout most of society. Ill-fitting clothes were increasingly a sign not of poverty but of isolation from the main avenues of transportation, commerce, and information.

Rather than distinguishing one class from another, democratic fashions increasingly set men apart from women. Fashion came to be considered a female concern, and ornamentation and bright colors now were associated with women's clothing. Ready-made clothing was not available for women, because female apparel required a close fit in the bodice. Nevertheless, the style of women's clothing also became standardized. American women sought to keep abreast of the latest Paris fashions, and if they could not afford a dressmaker's fitting, they sewed their own clothing. Illustrated magazines such as *Godey's Lady's Book* publicized the latest fashions, and even young women working in the mills at Lowell joined together to buy a subscription.

An English visitor reported that in the United States "men dress after the same type, differing only in finer or coarser material; every man would wear, if he could, a black satin waistcoat and a large diamond pin stick in the front of his shirt, as he certainly has a watch or a gild or gold chain of some sort or other. The mean white affects the style of the large proprietor of . . . capital as closely as he can. . . ." As one newspaper commented, Americans in the Jacksonian era were citizens of the "plain dark democracy of broadcloth."

To begin with, they discovered that only one class of seats was available on stagecoaches and rail cars. These were filled according to the rough-and-ready rule of first come, first served. In steamboat dining rooms or at country taverns, everyone ate at a common table, sharing food from the same serving plates. As one upper-class gentleman complained, "The rich and the poor, the educated and the ignorant, the polite and the vulgar, all herd on the cabin floor, feed at the same table, sit in each others laps, as it were."

Indeed, the democratic "manners" of Americans seemed positively shocking. In Europe social inferiors would speak only if spoken to. But Americans felt free to strike up a conversation with anyone, including total strangers. Frances Trollope was offended by the "coarse familiarity of address" between classes, while another visitor complained that in a nation where every citizen felt free to shake the hand of another, it was impossible to know anyone's social station. This informality—a forward, even *rude* attitude—could also be seen in the American custom of chewing tobacco and spitting everywhere: in taverns, courts, and hospitals, even in private homes. Fanny Kemble, an English actress, reported that on an American steamboat "it was a perfect shower of saliva all the time."

Americans were self-consciously proud of such democratic behavior, which they viewed as a valued heritage of the Revolution. The keelboaters who carried the future King Louis-Philippe of France on a trip down the Mississippi made their republican feelings plain when the keelboat ran aground. "You kings down there!" bellowed the captain. "Show yourselves and do a man's work, and help us three-spots pull off this bar!" The ideology of the Revolution made it clear that, in the American deck of cards at least, "three-spots" counted as much as jacks, kings, and queens. Kings were not allowed to forget that—and neither was Franklin Plummer.

The Tension between Equality and Opportunity

Opportunity and inequality of wealth

Although Americans praised both opportunity and equality, a fundamental tension existed between the two values. Inevitably, widespread opportunity would produce inequality of wealth. In Crèvecoeur's America, a rough equality of wealth and status had prevailed because of the lack of access to the market. In 1800 shoemakers in Lynn, with no way to ship large quantities of shoes across the country, could not become wealthy. Without steamboats or canals, farmers in Jefferson's day could not market surplus grain for profit. But by the 1820s and 1830s, as the opportunities of the market expanded, wealth became much more unevenly distributed. Thus the new generation had to confront contradictions in the American creed that their parents had been able to conveniently ignore.

Meaning of equality

By equality, Americans did not mean equality of wealth or property. "I know of no country where profounder contempt is expressed for the theory of permanent equality of property," Alexis de Tocqueville wrote. Nor did equality mean that all citizens had equal talent or capacity. Americans realized that individuals possessed widely differing abilities, which inevitably produced differences in wealth. "Distinctions in society will always exist under every just government," Andrew Jackson declared. "Equality of talents, or education, or of wealth cannot be produced by human institutions."

In the end, what Americans upheld was the equality of opportunity, not equality of condition. "True republicanism requires that every man shall have an equal chance—that every man shall be free to become as unequal as he can," one American commented. In an economy that could go bust as well as boom, Americans agreed that one primary objective of government was to safeguard opportunity. Thus the new politics of democracy walked hand in hand with the new opportunities of the market.

The New Political Culture of Democracy

The stately James Monroe, with his powdered hair and buckled shoes and breeches, was not part of the new politics. In 1824 as he neared the end of his second term, a host of new leaders in the Republican party looked to succeed him. Traditionally, a congressional caucus selected the party's presidential nominee, and the Republican caucus finally settled on Secretary of Treasury William H. Crawford of Georgia. Condemning "King Caucus" as undemocratic, three other Republicans, all ardent nationalists, refused to withdraw

Death of the caucus system

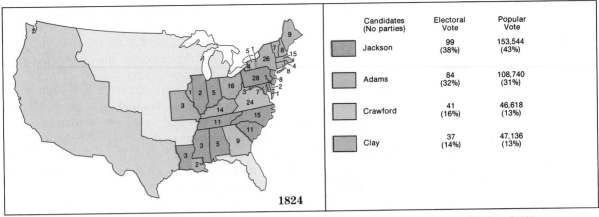

Candidates (No parties)	Electoral Vote	Popular Vote
Jackson	99 (38%)	153,544 (43%)
Adams	84 (32%)	108,740 (31%)
Crawford	41 (16%)	46,618 (13%)
Clay	37 (14%)	47,136 (13%)

1824

Election of 1824

from the race: Secretary of State John Quincy Adams; John C. Calhoun, Monroe's secretary of war; and Henry Clay, the Speaker of the House.

None of these men bargained on the sudden emergence of another Republican candidate, Andrew Jackson, the hero of the Battle of New Orleans. Because of his limited political experience, no one took Jackson's candidacy seriously at first, including Jackson himself. But soon the general's supporters and rivals began receiving reports of his unusual popularity. From Cincinnati an observer wrote, "Strange! Wild! Infatuated! All for Jackson!" Savvy politicians soon flocked to his standard, but it was the people who first made Jackson a serious candidate.

The Election of 1824

Calhoun eventually dropped out of the race, but that still left four candidates, none of whom received a majority of the popular vote. Jackson led the field, however, and finished first in the Electoral College with 99 votes. Adams had 84, Crawford 41, and Clay 37. Under the Twelfth Amendment, the House was to select a president from the top three candidates. Clay, though himself eliminated, held enough influence as Speaker of the House to name the winner. After he met privately with Adams, he rallied the votes in the House needed to put Adams over the top.

Two days later, Adams announced that Clay would be his new secretary of state, the usual steppingstone to the presidency. Jackson and his supporters promptly charged that there had been a "corrupt bargain" between Adams and Clay. Before Adams had even assumed office, the 1828 race was under way.

Corrupt bargain

Even more significant, the election of 1824 shattered the old party system. Henry Clay and John Quincy Adams began to organize a new party, known as the National Republicans, to distinguish it from Jefferson's old party. Jackson's disappointed supporters eventually called themselves Democrats. To muddy the political waters even further, a third party arose out of a controversy that erupted in 1826 over a secret organization known as the Freemasons.

Anti-Masonry and the Defense of Equality

The Freemasons (or simply Masons) were a secret fraternal group whose chapters had spread through Europe and America during the eighteenth century. Members like George Washington and Benjamin Franklin shared the Enlightenment's belief in the power of reason and the idea of progress while also embracing the Masons' moral commitment to temperance, charity, and hard work. By 1826 the 150,000 American Masons were predominantly business leaders, manufacturers, and professionals. While Masons were often above average in wealth, their power and prestige stemmed more from the number of public offices they held.

Origins of the Anti-Masonic movement

It was in western New York along the Erie Canal that William Morgan, a disgruntled Mason, announced in 1826 that he intended to publish a book exposing the secrets of the order. Not long after, he was seized by a group of Masons, forced into a closed carriage, and spirited off. Morgan was never seen again, and little doubt exists that he was murdered, allegedly near Niagara Falls. When prominent Masons used their power to thwart any investigation, the Anti-Masonic movement began. Anti-Masons demanded that the Masonic order be rooted out and eliminated. By 1830, they had organized in 10 states as a political party. Two years later they ran a presidential ticket.

Appeal of Anti-Masonry

In national terms Morgan's disappearance was a relatively minor incident, but it touched raw nerves in an egalitarian society. The shadowy Masons seemed a sinister threat to equality and opportunity, since the members swore an oath to advance a "brother's" interests over those of nonmembers. Confronted with the power of such an "aristocratic" order, how could ordinary citizens compete? "The direct object of freemasonry," one Anti-Masonic writer charged, "is to benefit the few at the expense of the many, by creating a privileged class, in the midst of a community entitled to enjoy equal rights and privileges." The Anti-Masons undertook to reform society by arousing public opinion and involving more citizens in politics.

As a rule, Anti-Masonry was strongest in populous, rapidly developing, market-oriented towns. Poor farmers who lacked access to markets and desired new roads or canal lines were often suspicious of Masonic officeholders. So were farmers in newly opened areas who had become dependent on city banks and merchants for credit. By attacking Masonry as an infidel society that exalted reason over traditional religion, the Anti-Masonic movement also represented a fervent desire to Christianize society. As such it represented a protest against the increasingly secular aspects of American life, which the spread of the market had strengthened.

Second party system

The new parties were one indication of how much the political system was in flux. By the mid-1830s, the National Republicans gave way to the Whigs, a new party that absorbed many members of the fading Anti-Masons. The Democrats, the other major party, came together under the leadership of Andrew Jackson. Once established, this second American party system dominated the nation's politics until the 1850s.

Social Sources of the New Politics

New attitudes toward government

Why was it that a new style and new system of politics emerged in the 1820s? We have already seen that a revolution in markets, stimulated by new transportation networks, was under way. We have seen, too, that the scramble to bring western lands into the market generated a speculative land boom that collapsed in the Panic of 1819. The rise of the new political culture was rooted in these social conditions. During the sharp depression that followed, many Americans became convinced that government policy had aggravated, if not actually produced, hard times. As a result, they decided that the government had a responsibility to relieve distress and promote prosperity.

For the first time, large numbers of Americans saw politics as relevant to their daily lives. Agitation mounted, especially at the state level, for government to enact relief for those in debt and provide other forms of assistance. Elections soon became the means through which the majority expressed its policy preferences by voting for candidates pledged to specific programs. The older idea that representatives should be independent and vote according to their best judgment gave way to the notion that representatives were to carry out the will of the people, as expressed in the outcomes of elections.

With more citizens championing the "will of the people," pressure mounted to open up the political process. Most states eliminated property qualifications for voting in favor of white manhood suffrage, under which all adult white males were allowed to vote. Similarly, property requirements for officeholders were reduced or dropped.

Democratic reforms

Presidential elections became more democratic as well. By 1832 South Carolina was the only state in which the legislature rather than the voters still chose presidential electors. The Anti-Masons pioneered a convention as a more democratic method of nominating party candidates and approving a platform, and the other parties soon followed suit. And because a presidential candidate had to carry a number of states in different sections of the country, the backing of a national party, with effective state and local organizations, became essential.

These democratic winds of change affected European societies and eventually other areas of the world as well. In no other major country, however, were such reforms achieved as early, and with as little resistance, as in the United States. Suffrage provides a good example. In Britain, in response to growing demonstrations and the cautionary example of the French monarchy's overthrow in 1830, Parliament approved the Reform Bill of 1832, which enfranchised a number of property holders and gave Britain the broadest electorate in Europe. Yet in fact, only about 15 percent of the adult males in Britain enjoyed the right of suffrage after the bill's passage. In France the figure was less than one percent.

Male suffrage in Europe and Latin America

The democratic revolutions of 1848 championed universal male suffrage in France and Prussia. Yet this ideal soon suffered setbacks. By 1852 the French republic had been replaced by a monarchy under the emperor Louis Napoleon. And in Prussia, the new constitution essentially negated universal male suffrage by dividing the electorate into three classes according to wealth, a formula that enabled 5 percent of the voters to elect one-third of parliament. Belgium, which had the most liberal constitution in Europe, did not approximate manhood suffrage until 1848. Even the second Reform Act (1867) in Britain enfranchised only about one-third of the adult males.

Likewise, the Latin American republics established in the 1820s and 1830s imposed property requirements on voting or, like Uruguay, excluded certain occupational groups such as servants and peasants from the suffrage. One exception was Mexico, where a number of states adopted an extremely broad suffrage. A new constitution in 1836, however, established a much more centralized state and sharply limited voting rights. The most restricted suffrage existed in the republic of Haiti, where only army officers and a few other privileged individuals enjoyed the franchise. When the revolution of 1843 brought a new constitution with mass-based suffrage, it met widespread resistance among elites, and the government quickly failed.

As the new reforms went into effect, voter turnout soared. Whereas in the 1824 presidential election only 27 percent of eligible voters bothered to go to the

Voter turnout

polls, four years later the proportion had more than doubled to 56 percent. In 1840, 78 percent of eligible voters cast ballots, probably the highest turnout in American history.

The Acceptance of Parties

Rise of the professional politician

All these developments worked to favor the rise of a new type of politician: one whose life was devoted to party service and who often depended for his living on public office. As the number of state-sponsored internal improvement projects increased during the 1820s, so did the number of government jobs that could support party workers. No longer was politics primarily the province of the wealthy, who spent only part of their time on public affairs. Instead, political leaders were more likely to come from the middle ranks of society, especially outside the South. Many became economically established after entering politics, but as Franklin Plummer demonstrated, large sums of money were not required to conduct a campaign. Indeed, a successful politician now had to mingle with the masses and voice their feelings—requirements that put the wealthy elite at a disadvantage.

Van Buren champions the party system

In many ways, Martin Van Buren epitomized the new breed of politician. The son of a New York tavern keeper, Van Buren lacked great oratorical skills or a magnetic personality. But he was a master organizer and tactician, highly skilled at using the new party system. His abilities eventually carried him to the Senate and even the White House. Unlike the older Revolutionary generation, who regarded political parties as dangerous and destructive, Van Buren argued that they were not only "inseparable from free governments" but "in many and material respects . . . highly useful to the country." While conceding that political parties were subject to abuse, he stressed that competing parties would watch each other and check abuses at the same time that they kept the masses informed.

The Politics of the Common Man

New style of politics

Andrew Jackson was one of the first political leaders to grasp the new politics in which the ordinary citizen was celebrated as never before. "Never for a moment believe that the great body of the citizens . . . can deliberately intend to do wrong," he proclaimed. Party leaders everywhere avoided aristocratic airs when on the stump. "I have always dressed chiefly in *Home spun* when among the people," one North Carolina member of Congress explained. "If a Candidate be dressed Farmerlike he is well received and kindly remembered by the inmates of the Log Cabin, and there is no sensation among the children or the *chickens.*"

Politics became mass entertainment, in which campaign hoopla often overshadowed the issues. Parades, glee clubs, massive rallies, and barbecues were used to rouse voters, and treating to drinks became an almost universal campaign tactic. ("The way to men's hearts is down their throats," quipped one Kentucky vote-getter.) Although politicians often talked about principles, political parties were pragmatic organizations, intent on gaining and holding power.

Limitations of the democratic political system

The Jacksonian era has been called the Age of the Common Man, but such democratic tendencies had distinct limits. Women and slaves were not allowed to vote, nor could free African Americans (except in a few states) and Indians. Nor did the parties always deal effectively with (or even address) basic problems in society. Still, Van Buren's insight was perceptive. Popular political parties provided an essential mechanism for peacefully resolving differences among competing interest groups, regions, and social classes.

"The Will of the People the Supreme Law" reads the banner at this county election. One of the few occasions when most of the men would assemble at the village, Election Day remained an all-male event as well as a time of excitement, heated debate, and boisterous celebration. As citizens give their oath to an election judge, diligent party workers dispense free drinks, solicit support, offer party tickets, and keep a careful tally of who has voted. Liquor and drinking are prominently featured: one elector enjoys another round, a prospective voter who is too drunk to stand is held up by a faithful party member, and on the right a groggy partisan sports a bandage as a result of a political brawl.

Jackson's Rise to Power

The new democratic style of politics first appeared on the state and local levels: Van Buren deftly working behind the scenes in New York; Amos Kendall of Kentucky campaigning in favor of debtor relief; Davy Crockett of Tennessee carefully dressed in frontier garb and offering voters a drink from a jug of whiskey and a chew from a large plug of tobacco. The national implications of these changes, however, were not immediately clear.

John Quincy Adams's Presidency

When he assumed the presidency in 1825, John Quincy Adams might have worked to create a mass-based party. But Adams, a talented diplomat and a great secretary of state, possessed hardly a political bone in his body. Cold and tactless, he could build no popular support for the ambitious and often farsighted programs he proposed. His plans for the federal government to promote not only manufacturing and agriculture but also the arts, literature, and science left his opponents aghast.

Nor would Adams take any steps to gain reelection, though he earnestly desired it. Despite urgent pleas from Henry Clay and other advisers, he declined to remove from federal office men who actively opposed him. Since Adams refused to be a party leader, Clay undertook to organize the National Republicans. But with a reluctant candidate at the top of the ticket, Clay labored under serious handicaps. The new style of politics came into its own nationally only when Andrew Jackson swept to power at the head of a new party, the Democrats.

Jackson's election

Building a new party was a tricky business. Because Jackson's coalition was made up of conflicting interests, "Old Hickory" remained vague about his own position on many issues. Thus the campaign of 1828 soon degenerated into a series of personal attacks, splattering mud on all involved. Aided by enormous majorities in the South, Jackson won handily.

In one sense, the significance of the election was clear. It marked the beginning of politics as Americans have practiced it ever since, with two disciplined national parties actively competing for votes, an emphasis on personalities over issues, and the resort to mass electioneering techniques. Yet in terms of public policy, the meaning of the election was anything but clear. The people had voted for Jackson as a national hero without any real sense of what he would do with his newly won power.

President of the People

Certainly the people looked for change. "I never saw such a crowd here before," Daniel Webster wrote as inauguration day approached. "Persons have come 500 miles to see General Jackson, and they really seem to think that the country is rescued from some dreadful danger!" Some 15,000 supporters cheered wildly after Jackson was sworn in.

Jackson's stubborn determination shines through clearly in this portrait by Asher Durand, painted in 1835. "His passions are terrible," Jefferson noted. "When I was President of the Senate, he was Senator, and he could never speak on account of the rashness of his feelings. I have seen him attempt it repeatedly, and as often choke with rage. His passions are, no doubt, cooler now; he has been much tried since I knew him, but he is a dangerous man."

At the White House reception pandemonium reigned. Elbowing aside the invited dignitaries, thousands of ordinary citizens pushed inside to catch a glimpse of their idol. The new president had to flee after being nearly crushed to death by well-wishers. The crowd trampled on the furniture, broke glass, smashed mirrors, and ruined carpets and draperies. "It was a proud day for the people," boasted Amos Kendall, one of the new president's advisers. "General Jackson is their own president." Supreme Court Justice Joseph Story was less enraptured: "I never saw such a mixture. The reign of King Mob seemed triumphant."

Jackson's character

Whether loved as a man of the people or hated as a demagogue leading the mob, Jackson was the representative of the new democracy. The first president from west of the Appalachians, he moved as a young lawyer to the Tennessee frontier.

He had a quick mind but limited schooling and little use for learning; after his death a family friend acknowledged that the general had never believed that the Earth was round. A man of action, his decisiveness served him well as a soldier and also in the booming economy around Nashville, where he established himself as a large landowner and slaveholder. Tall and wiry, with flowing white hair, Jackson carried himself with a soldier's bearing. His troops had nicknamed him Old Hickory out of respect for his toughness, but that strength sometimes became arrogance, and he could be vindictive and a bully. He was not a man to provoke, as his reputation for dueling demonstrated.

For all these flaws, Jackson was a shrewd politician. He knew how to manipulate men and could be affable or abusive as the occasion demanded. He would sometimes burst into a rage to get his way with a hostile delegation, only to chuckle afterward, "They thought I was mad." He also displayed a keen sense of public opinion, skillfully reading the shifting national mood.

As the nation's chief executive, Jackson defended the spoils system, under which public offices were awarded to political supporters, as a democratic reform. Rotation in office, he declared, would guard against insensitive bureaucrats who presumed that they held their positions by right. The cabinet, he believed, existed more to carry out his will than to offer counsel, and throughout his term he remained a strong executive who insisted on his way—and usually got it.

Spoils system

The Political Agenda in the Market Economy

Jackson took office at a time when the market economy was spreading through America and the nation's borders were expanding geographically. The three major problems his administration faced were directly caused by the resulting growing pains.

First, the demand for new lands put continuing pressure on Indians, whose valuable cornfields and hunting grounds could produce marketable commodities like cotton and wheat. Second, as the economies of the North, South, and West became more specialized, their rival interests forced a confrontation over the tariff. And finally, the booming economy focused attention on the role of credit and banking in society and on the new commercial attitudes that were a central part of the developing market economy. The president attacked all three issues in his characteristically combative style.

As a planter, Jackson benefited from the **Democracy and Race** international demand for cotton that was drawing new lands into the market. He had gone off to the Tennessee frontier in 1788, a rowdy, ambitious young man who could afford to purchase only one slave. Caught up in the get-rich-quick mania of the frontier, he became a prominent land speculator, established himself as a planter, and by the time he became president owned nearly 100 slaves. His popularity derived not only from defeating the British but also from opening extensive tracts of valuable Indian lands to white settlement. Through military fighting and treaty negotiating, he was personally responsible for obtaining about a third of Tennessee for the United States, three-quarters of Florida and Alabama, a fifth of Georgia and Mississippi, and a tenth of Kentucky and North Carolina.

Even so, in 1820 an estimated 125,000 Indians remained east of the Mississippi River. In the Southwest the Choctaws, Creeks, Cherokees, Chickasaws, and

Seminoles retained millions of acres of prime agricultural land in the heart of the cotton kingdom. Led by Georgia, southern states demanded that the federal government clear these titles. In response, Monroe in 1824 proposed to Congress that the remaining eastern tribes be relocated west of the Mississippi River.

As white pressure for removal intensified, a shift in the attitude toward Indians and race increasingly occurred. Previously whites had generally attributed cultural differences among whites, blacks, and Indians to the environment. After 1815 the dominant white culture stressed "innate" racial differences that could never be erased. A growing number of Americans began to argue that the Indian was a permanently inferior savage who blocked progress.

Accommodate or Resist?

The new, more aggressive attitudes among white Americans placed Indians and other minorities in the Old Southwest in a difficult position. During the seventeenth and eighteenth centuries the region reflected a multiracial character because Indians, Spanish, French, and Africans had all settled there. The intermixture of cultures could be seen in the garb of the Creek Indian chief William McIntosh (below), who adopted a style of dress that reflected both his Indian and white heritage. McIntosh's father was a Scot, his mother a Creek, his wife a Cherokee—and McIntosh himself had allied his people with Andrew Jackson's forces during the War of 1812. But not long after he signed a treaty for the cession of Creek lands in 1825, he was murdered by a rival faction of the tribe, who regarded the cession as an act of betrayal.

William McIntosh's attire reflects the multicultural nature of the Old Southwest. He wears the ruffled shirt and cravat of a white gentleman, but his robe, sash, leggings, and moccasins display with pride his Creek heritage.

As southern whites increased their clamor for Indian removal, similar tensions among various tribal factions increased.

Among the Seminoles, mixed-bloods (those with white as well as Indian ancestry) took the lead in urging military resistance to any attempt to expel them. In the Cherokee nation, on the other hand, mixed-bloods led by John Ross advocated a program of accommodation by adopting white ways to prevent removal. After a bitter struggle Ross prevailed, and in 1827 the Cherokees adopted a written constitution modeled after that of the United States. They also enacted the death penalty for any member who sold tribal lands to whites without consent of the governing general council. Developing their own alphabet, they published a bilingual newspaper, the *Cherokee Phoenix*. Similarly, the neighboring Creeks moved to centralize authority by strengthening the power of the governing council at the expense of local towns. They too made it illegal for individual chiefs to sell any more land to whites.

The division between traditionalists and those favoring accommodation reflected the fact that Indians too had been drawn into a web of market relationships. As more Cherokee families began to sell their surplus crops, they ceased to share property communally as in the past. Cherokee society became more stratified and unequal, just as white society had, and economic elites dominated the tribal government. Women's traditional economic role was transformed as well, as men now took over farming operations, previously a female responsibility. Nor were the Cherokees untouched by the cotton boom. Some of the tribe's leaders, particularly half-bloods who could deal easily with white culture, became substantial planters who owned large numbers of black slaves and thousands of acres of cotton land. Largely of mixed ancestry, slaveholders were wealthier, had investments in other enterprises such as gristmills and ferries, raised crops for market, were more likely to read English, and were the driving force behind acculturation.

Changing nature of Cherokee society

As cotton cultivation expanded among the Cherokees, slavery became harsher and a primary means of determining status, just as in southern white society. The general council passed several laws forbidding intermarriage with African Americans and excluding African Americans and mulattoes from voting or holding office. Ironically, at the same time that white racial attitudes toward Indians were deteriorating, the Cherokees' racial attitudes toward blacks were also hardening, paralleling the increased racism among white Americans.

Trail of Tears

As western land fever increased and racial attitudes sharpened, Jackson prodded Congress to provide funds for Indian removal. He watched sympathetically as the Georgia legislature overturned the Cherokee constitution, declared Cherokee laws null and void, and decreed that tribal members would be tried in state courts. In 1830 Congress finally passed a removal bill.

Pressure for Indian removal

But the Cherokees brought suit in federal court against Georgia's actions. In 1832 in the case of *Worcester v. Georgia*, the Supreme Court sided with the Cherokees. Indian tribes had full authority over their lands, wrote Chief Justice John Marshall in the opinion. Thus Georgia had no right to extend its laws over Cherokee territory. Pronouncing Marshall's decision "stillborn," Jackson ignored the Court's edict and went ahead with plans for removal.

Although Jackson assured Indians that they could be removed only voluntarily, he paid no heed when state governments harassed tribes into surrendering lands. Under the threat of coercion, the Choctaws, Chickasaws, and Creeks reluctantly agreed to move to tracts in present-day Oklahoma. In the process, Indians unaccustomed to white law and notions of property fell victim to shameful frauds, as land-hungry schemers cheated countless tribal members out of their lands. As much as 90 percent of the land allotments may have fallen into the hands of speculators.

Indian removal along the Trail of Tears

The Cherokees held out longest, but to no avail. In order to deal with more pliant leaders of the tribe, Georgia authorities kidnapped Chief John Ross, who led the resistance to relocation, and threw him into jail. Ross was finally released but not allowed to negotiate the treaty, which stipulated that the Cherokees leave their lands no later than 1838. When that time came, most refused to go. In response, President Martin Van Buren had the U.S. Army round up resistant members and force them, at bayonet point, to join the westward march. Of the 15,000 who traveled this Trail of Tears, approximately one-quarter died along the way of exposure, disease, and exhaustion, including Ross's wife. As for the western tracts awaiting the survivors, they were smaller and generally inferior to the rich lands that had been taken from the Cherokees.

Removal of the Cherokees

Indian Removal During Jackson's presidency, the federal government concluded nearly 70 treaties with Indian tribes, in the Old Northwest as well as in the South. Under their terms, the United States acquired approximately 100 million acres of Indian land.

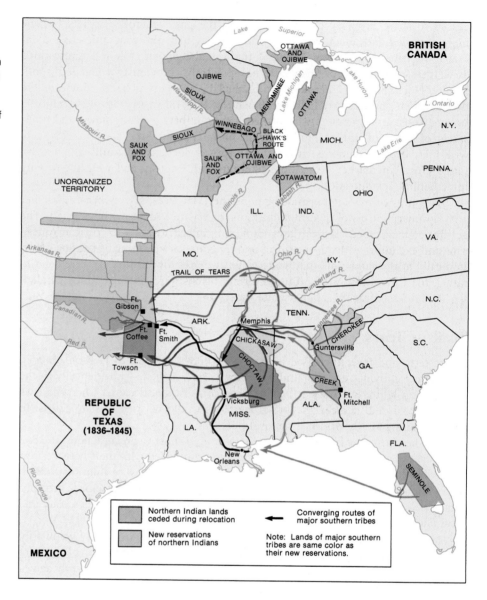

Military resistance

Some Indians chose resistance. In the Old Northwest a group of the Sauk and Fox led by Black Hawk recrossed the Mississippi into Illinois in 1832 and were crushed by federal troops and the militia. More successful was the military resistance of a minority of Seminoles under the leadership of Osceola. Despite his death, they held out until 1842 in the Everglades of Florida before being subdued and removed. In the end, only a small number of southern tribe members were able to escape removal. Most were shunted off onto worthless lands that whites did not want.

Except for a few missionaries and eastern reformers, Americans expressed little regret over the treatment of the eastern tribes. In his Farewell Address in 1837, Jackson defended his policy by piously asserting that the eastern tribes had been finally "placed beyond the reach of injury or oppression, and that [the] paternal care of the General Government will hereafter watch over them and protect them."

Indians, however, knew the bitter truth of the matter. Without effective political power, they found themselves at the mercy of the pressures of the marketplace and the hardening racial attitudes of white Americans.

Free Blacks in the North

Unlike Indian removal, the rising discrimination against free African Americans during this period did not depend directly on presidential action. Still, it was Jackson's Democratic party, which was in the vanguard of promoting white equality, that was also the most strongly proslavery and the most hostile to black rights. The intensifying racism that accompanied the emergence of democracy in American life bore down with particular force on free African Americans. "The policy and power of the national and state governments are against them," commented one northerner. "The popular feeling is against them—the interests of our citizens are against them. Their prospects . . . are dreary, and comfortless."

In the years before the Civil War, the free black population remained small: only about 171,000 in the North in 1840, about a quarter of whom were mulattoes. Although those numbers amounted to less than 2 percent of the North's population, most states enacted laws to keep African Americans in an inferior position. (For a discussion of free African Americans in the South, see Chapter 13.)

Most black northerners lacked meaningful political rights. Black men could vote on equal terms with whites in only five New England states. New York imposed a property requirement only on black voters, which disfranchised the vast majority. Moreover, in New Jersey, Pennsylvania, and Connecticut, African American men lost the right to vote after having previously enjoyed that privilege.

Discrimination against free blacks

Black northerners were also denied basic civil rights that whites enjoyed. Five states prohibited them from testifying against whites, and either law or custom excluded African Americans from juries everywhere except Massachusetts. In addition, several western states passed black exclusion laws prohibiting free African Americans from immigrating into the state. These laws were seldom enforced, but they were available to harass the African American population in times of social stress.

Segregation, or the physical separation of the races, was widely practiced in the free states. African Americans were assigned to separate sections on public transportation. Throughout the North they could not go into most hotels and restaurants, and if permitted to enter theaters and lecture halls, they sat in the corners and balconies. In white churches, they were put in separate pews and took communion after white members. In virtually every community, black children were excluded from the public schools or forced to attend overcrowded and poorly funded separate schools. Commented one English visitor: "We see, in effect, two nations—one white and another black—growing up together . . . but never mingling on a principle of equality."

Black poverty

Discrimination pushed African American males into the lowest-paying and most unskilled jobs in society: servants, sailors, waiters, and common laborers. In Philadelphia in 1838, 80 percent of employed black males were unskilled laborers, and three of five black families had less than $60 total wealth. African American women normally continued working after marriage, mostly as servants, cooks, laundresses, and seamstresses, because their wages were critical to the family's economic survival. Blacks were willing strikebreakers, because white workers, fearing economic competition and loss of status, were overtly hostile and excluded them from trade unions. A number of antiblack riots erupted in northern cities during these years. "Whenever the interests of the white man and the black come into collision,"

The Spread of White Manhood Suffrage White manhood suffrage became the norm during the Jacksonian era, but in a number of states free black males who had been voting by law or by custom lost the right to vote. After 1821 a $250 property requirement disfranchised about 90 percent of adult black males in New York.

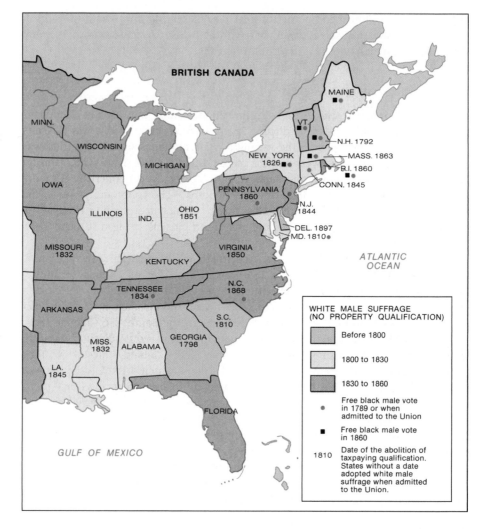

WHITE MALE SUFFRAGE
(NO PROPERTY QUALIFICATION)

Before 1800

1800 to 1830

1830 to 1860

• Free black male vote in 1789 or when admitted to the Union

■ Free black male vote in 1860

1810 Date of the abolition of taxpaying qualification. States without a date adopted white male suffrage when admitted to the Union.

one foreign observer noted, "the black man goes to the wall. It is certain that, wherever labor is scarce, there he is readily employed; when it becomes plentiful, he is the first to be discharged." Driven into abject poverty, free blacks in the North suffered from an inadequate diet, were more susceptible to disease, and in 1850 had a life expectancy 8 to 10 years less than that of whites.

"None but those who experience it can know what it is—this constant, galling sense of cruel injustice and wrong," grieved Charlotte Forten, a free African American from Philadelphia.

The African American Community

African Americans responded to this oppression by founding self-help societies, and the black community centered on institutions such as black churches, schools, and mutual aid societies. They also agitated against slavery in the South and for equal rights in the North. After 1840 black frustration generated a nationalist movement that emphasized racial unity, self-help, and, for some, renewal of ties with Africa.

Because of limited economic opportunity, the African American community was not as diversified as white society in terms of occupation and wealth. There were distinctions, nevertheless, that rested on wealth and skin color. In general, mulattoes (lighter-skinned blacks) had greater opportunities to become more literate and skilled, were better off economically, and were more likely to be community leaders. Mulattoes' feelings of superiority were reflected in marriage choices, as they usually shunned darker-skinned blacks. "They have as much caste among themselves as we have," lamented the abolitionist Sarah Grimké, "and despise the poor as much I fear as their pale brethren."

The Minstrel Show

The racist attitudes of the day were very much reflected in popular culture, nowhere more than in minstrel shows, the most popular form of entertainment in Jacksonian America. Originating in the 1830s and 1840s and playing to packed houses in cities and towns throughout the nation, minstrel shows featured white actors performing in blackface. They dealt in the broadest of racial stereotypes, ridiculing blacks as physically different and portraying them as buffoons.

Appeal of minstrelsy

Although popular throughout the country, minstrelsy's primary audience was in northern cities. Its basic message was that African Americans could not cope with freedom and therefore did not belong in the North. Enslaved African Americans were portrayed as happy and contented, whereas free black Americans were caricatured either as strutting dandies or as helpless ignoramuses. Drawing its patrons from workers, Irish immigrants, and the poorer elements in society, minstrelsy assured these white champions of democracy that they remained superior.

The unsettling economic, social, and political changes of the Jacksonian era heightened white Americans' fear of failure, which stimulated racism. The popular yet unrealistic expectation was that any white man might become rich. Yet in fact, 20 percent or more of white adult males of this era never accumulated any property. Their lack of success encouraged them to relieve personal tensions through increased hostility to their black neighbors. Subjecting black Americans to legal

Deepening racism

Minstrel sheet music (left) illustrates the racist attitudes that pervaded Jacksonian democracy. Blacks, played by whites, were made to appear ridiculous through grotesque physical features, exaggerated poses, and pretentious airs. In contrast, the confident expression of this African American (right), who had this daguerreotype taken around 1856, evidences the dignity free blacks maintained in the face of unrelenting hostility and discrimination.

disabilities ensured that even the poorest whites would enjoy an advantage in the race for wealth and status. "The prejudice of race appears to be stronger in the states that have abolished slavery than in those where it still exists," Tocqueville noted, "and nowhere is it so intolerant as in those states where servitude has never been known." The power of racism in Jacksonian America stemmed, at least in part, from the fact that equality remained part of the nation's creed while it steadily receded as a social reality.

The Nullification Crisis

Indian removal and antiblack discrimination provided one answer to the question of who would be given equality of opportunity in America's new democratic society. Indians and African Americans would not. The issue of nullification raised a different, equally pressing question. As the market revolution propelled the economies of the North, South, and West toward increased specialization, how would various regions or interest groups accommodate their differences?

The Growing Crisis in South Carolina

South Carolina had been particularly hard hit by the depression of 1819. When prosperity returned to the rest of the nation, many of the state's cotton planters remained economically depressed. With lands exhausted from years of cultivation, they could not compete with the fabulous yields of frontier planters in Alabama and Mississippi.

Increasingly, South Carolinians viewed federal tariffs as the cause of their miseries. When Congress raised the duty rates in 1824, they assailed the tariff as an unfair tax that raised the prices of goods they imported while benefiting other regions of the nation. Other southern states opposed the 1824 tariff as well, though none so vehemently as South Carolina.

The one southern state in which black inhabitants outnumbered whites, South Carolina had also been growing more sensitive about the institution of slavery. In 1822 a slave conspiracy led by Denmark Vesey, a free black carpenter in Charleston, had been thwarted only at the last moment. A brilliant leader, literate, and well traveled, Vesey argued that slavery violated the principles of both republicanism and Christianity. He devised a well-coordinated plan to seize control of the city and raise the standard of black liberty, but several slaves betrayed the conspiracy at the last moment. Charleston authorities hurried to arrest Vesey and his lieutenants, who were tried, convicted, and either executed or banished. Even so, white South Carolinians were convinced that other undetected conspirators lurked in their midst.

Denmark Vesey's conspiracy

As an additional measure of security, the state's leaders pushed for stronger constitutional protection of slavery. After all, supporters of high tariffs had already claimed that the "implied powers" of the Constitution gave them the right to promote manufacturing. What was to stop this same broad interpretation from being used to end slavery? "In contending against the tariff, I have always felt that we were combatting against the symptom instead of the disease," argued Chancellor William Harper of South Carolina. "Tomorrow may witness [an attempt] to relieve . . . your slaves."

When Congress raised the duty rates still higher in 1828 with the so-called Tariff of Abominations, South Carolina's legislature published the *South Carolina*

Exposition and Protest, which outlined for the first time the theory of nullification. Only later was it revealed that its author was Jackson's own vice president, John C. Calhoun.

Calhoun's Theory of Nullification

Educated at Yale and at the most distinguished law school in the country, Calhoun was the most impressive intellect of his political generation. During the 1820s the South Carolina leader made a slow but steady journey away from nationalism toward an extreme states' rights position. When he was elected Jackson's vice president, South Carolinians assumed that tariff reform would soon be enacted. But Jackson and Calhoun quarreled, and Calhoun lost all influence in the administration.

In his theory of nullification, Calhoun addressed the problem of how to protect the rights of a minority in a political system based on the rule of the majority. The Union, he argued, was a compact between sovereign states. Thus the people of each state, acting in special popular conventions, had the right to nullify any federal law that exceeded the powers granted to Congress under the Constitution. The law would then become null and void in that state. In response, Congress could either repeal the law or propose a constitutional amendment expressly giving it the power in question. If the amendment was ratified, the nullifying state could either accept the decision or exercise its ultimate right as a sovereign state and secede from the Union.

Minority rights versus majority rule

As Daniel Webster outlines his nationalist theory of the Constitution and the Union, Senator Robert Hayne of South Carolina sits (front, left) with his hands together. The Senate gallery is filled, with most of the seats occupied by women, evidence of the widespread interest in politics.

Nationalists' theory of the Union

When Senator Robert Hayne of South Carolina outlined Calhoun's theory in the Senate in 1830, Senator Daniel Webster of Massachusetts replied sharply that the Union was not a compact of sovereign states. The people and not the states, he argued, had created the Constitution. "It is the people's constitution, the people's government, made for the people, made by the people, and answerable to the people." Webster also insisted that the federal government did not merely act as the agent of the states but had sovereign powers in those areas in which it had been delegated responsibility. Finally, Webster endorsed the doctrine of judicial review, which gave the Supreme Court authority to determine the meaning of the Constitution.

The Nullifiers Nullified

When Congress passed another tariff in 1832 that failed to give the state any relief, South Carolina's legislature called for the election of delegates to a popular convention, which overwhelmingly adopted an ordinance in November that declared the tariffs of 1828 and 1832 "null, void, and no law, nor binding upon this state, its officers or citizens" after February 1, 1833.

Idea of a perpetual Union

Jackson, who had spent much of his life defending the nation, was not about to tolerate any defiance of his authority or the federal government's. In his Proclamation on Nullification, issued in December 1832, he insisted that the Union was perpetual. Under the Constitution, there was no right of secession. Surprisingly, it had taken 40 years since the adoption of the Constitution to develop this point. To reinforce Jackson's announced determination to enforce the tariff laws, Congress passed the Force Bill, reaffirming the president's military powers.

Compromise of 1833

Yet Jackson was also a skillful politician. At the same time that he threatened South Carolina, he urged Congress to reduce the tariff rates. By holding out the hope of tariff reform, he managed to isolate South Carolina from the rest of the southern states. With no other state willing to follow South Carolina's lead, Calhoun reluctantly agreed to a compromise tariff, which Jackson signed on March 1, 1833, the same day he signed the Force Bill. South Carolina's convention repealed the nullifying ordinance, and the crisis passed.

Calhoun's doctrine had proved too radical for the rest of the South. Yet at the same time the controversy convinced many southerners that they were becoming a permanent minority. "It is useless and impracticable to disguise the fact," concluded nullifier William Harper, "that we are divided into slave-holding and non-slaveholding states, and this is the broad and marked distinction that must separate us at last." As that feeling of isolation grew, it was not nullification but the threat of secession that ultimately became the South's primary weapon.

The Bank War

Jackson understood well the political ties that bound the nation. He grasped much less firmly the economic and financial connections that linked different regions of the country through banks and national markets. In particular, the president was suspicious of the national bank and the power it possessed. His clash with the Second Bank of the United States brought on the greatest crisis of his presidency.

The National Bank and the Panic of 1819

Chartered by Congress in 1816 for a 20-year period, the Second Bank of the United States suffered initially from woeful mismanagement. At first it helped fuel the speculative pressures in the economy. Then it turned about-face and sharply contracted credit by calling in loans when the depression hit in 1819. The Bank regained a sound financial footing, but William Gouge, a Philadelphia journalist and economist, charged, "The Bank was saved and the people were ruined." Critics viewed the Bank's policies not as a consequence but as the cause of the financial downswing. To many Americans, the Bank had already become a monster.

Monster bank

The psychological effects of the Panic of 1819 were almost as momentous as the economic. In the midst of dizzying prosperity and unbounded optimism, Americans were suddenly plunged into privation, despair, and economic depression. That shock convinced many uneasy farmers and workers that the hard times were punishment for having lost sight of the old virtues of simplicity, frugality, and hard work. For them banks became a symbol of the commercialization of American society and the rapid passing of a simpler way of life.

Biddle's Bank

In 1823 Nicholas Biddle, a rich 37-year-old Philadelphia businessman, became president of the national bank. Biddle was intelligent and thoroughly familiar with the banking system, but he was also impossibly arrogant and had an inflated view of his importance. Seeking boldly to restore the Bank's damaged reputation, he set out to use the Bank to regulate the amount of credit available in the economy and thereby provide the nation with a sound currency.

Function as a central bank

Government revenues were paid largely in banknotes (paper money) issued by state-chartered banks. Because the Treasury Department regularly deposited U.S. funds in the national bank, the notes of state banks from all across the Union came into its possession. If Biddle believed that a state bank was overextended and had issued more notes than was safe, he presented them to that bank and demanded they be redeemed in specie (gold or silver). Because banks did not have enough specie reserves to back all the paper money they issued, the only way a state bank could continue to redeem its notes was to call in its loans and reduce the amount of its notes in circulation. This action had the effect of lessening the amount of credit in the economy.

On the other hand, if Biddle felt that a bank's credit policies were reasonable, he simply returned the state banknotes to circulation without presenting them for redemption. Being the government's official depository gave Biddle's bank enormous power over state banks and over the economy. As Biddle tactlessly admitted, "There are very few [state banks] which might not have been destroyed by an exertion of the powers of the bank." Under Biddle's direction the Bank became a financial colossus: it had 29 branches and made 20 percent of the country's loans, issued one-fifth of the total banknotes, and held fully a third of all deposits and specie. Yet for the most part, Biddle used the Bank's enormous power responsibly to provide the United States a sound paper currency, which the expanding economy needed.

Although the Bank had strong support in the business community, workers complained that they were often paid in depreciated state banknotes. Such notes could be redeemed for only a portion of their face value, a practice that in effect cheated

Opposition to paper money

workers out of part of their wages. They called for a "hard money" currency of only gold and silver. Hard money advocates viewed bankers and financiers as profiteers who manipulated the paper money system to enrich themselves at the expense of honest, hardworking farmers and laborers.

The Clash between Jackson and Biddle

Jackson's own experiences left him with a deep distrust of banks and paper money. In 1804 his Tennessee land speculations had brought him to the brink of bankruptcy, from which it took years of painful struggle to free himself. Reflecting on his personal situation, he became convinced that banks and paper threatened to corrupt the Republic.

As president, Jackson called for reform of the banking system from time to time, but Biddle refused even to consider curbing the Bank's powers. Already distracted by the nullification controversy, Jackson warned Biddle not to inject the bank issue into the 1832 campaign. When Biddle went ahead and applied for a renewal of the Bank's charter in 1832, four years early, Jackson was furious. "The Bank is trying to kill me," he stormed to Van Buren, "*but I will kill it.*"

Jackson's veto

Despite the president's opposition, Congress passed a recharter bill in the summer of 1832. Immediately Jackson vetoed it as unconstitutional (rejecting Chief Justice Marshall's ruling in favor of the Bank in *McCulloch v. Maryland*). The president went on to condemn the Bank as an agent of special privilege and as inconsistent with the republican principle of equality, because it made "the rich richer and the potent more powerful." Holding up the national bank as a symbol of aristocracy, the president pledged to protect "the humble members of society—the farmer, mechanics, and laborers"—against "the advancement of the few at the expense of the many." The message completely ignored the Bank's vital services in the economy.

As Jackson's veto message revealed, the struggle over the national bank tended to pit traditional farmers and workers against the world of commerce and national markets. Jackson's strongest supporters were workers and farmers outside the commercial economy and those who were disturbed by the changes that the market produced in their lives. Individuals who were more comfortable with the new commercial ethos rallied to the Bank's defense. In the end, most of them would wind up as members of the opposing Whig party.

The Bank Destroyed

When Congress failed to override Jackson's veto, the recharter of the Bank became a central issue of the 1832 campaign. Jackson's opponent was Henry Clay, a National Republican who eagerly accepted the financial support of Biddle and the national bank. Clay went down to defeat, and once reelected, Jackson was determined to destroy the Bank. He believed that as a private corporation the Bank wielded a dangerous influence over government policy and the economy, and he was justly incensed over its heavy-handed attempt to influence the election.

Removal of the deposits

To cripple the Bank, the president simply ordered all the government's federal deposits withdrawn. Because such an act clearly violated federal law, Jackson was forced to transfer one secretary of the treasury and fire another before he finally found in Roger Taney someone willing to take the job and carry

In this Bank War cartoon, Jackson boxes Biddle as Webster and Clay urge Biddle on and Van Buren shouts instructions from Old Hickory's corner. The heavyset woman holding a bottle of port (an upper-class beverage) represents the national bank, bloated with privilege and wealth, while a plain American in frontier garb keeps watch over Jackson's bottle of whiskey, the drink of the masses.

out the edict. Taney (pronounced "Taw-ney") began drawing against the government's funds to pay its debts while depositing new revenues in selected state banks.

Biddle fought back by deliberately precipitating a brief financial panic in 1833. "Go to Biddle," Jackson snapped to businesspeople seeking relief. "I never will restore the deposits. I never will recharter the United States Bank, or sign a charter for any other bank." Eventually Biddle had to relent, and Jackson's victory was complete. When the Bank's charter expired in 1836, no national banking system replaced it. Instead, Jackson continued depositing federal revenues in selected state banks. A large majority of these "pet banks" were controlled by Democrats.

Jackson's Impact on the Presidency

Jackson approached the end of his administration in triumph. Indian removal was well on its way to completion, the nullifiers had been confounded, and the "Monster Bank" had been destroyed. In the process, Jackson immeasurably enlarged the power of the presidency. "The President is the direct representative of the American people," he lectured the Senate when it opposed him. "He was elected by the people, and is responsible to them." With this declaration, Jackson redefined the character of the presidential office and its relationship to the people.

Jackson also converted the veto into an effective presidential power. During his two terms in office, he vetoed 12 bills, compared with only 9 for all previous presidents combined. Moreover, where his predecessors had vetoed bills only on strict constitutional grounds, Jackson felt free to block laws simply because he thought them bad policy. The threat of such action became an effective way to

Strengthening of
presidential powers

shape pending legislation to his liking, which fundamentally strengthened the power of the president over Congress. The development of the modern presidency began with Andrew Jackson.

Van Buren and Depression

With the controls of the national bank removed, state banks rapidly expanded the amount of paper money in circulation. The total value of banknotes jumped from $82 million in January 1835 to $120 million in December 1836. As the currency expanded, so did the number of banks: from 329 in 1829 to 788 in 1837. A spiraling inflation set in as prices rose 50 percent after 1830 and interest rates by half as much.

As prices rose sharply, so did speculative fever. By 1836 land sales, which had been only $2.6 million four years earlier, approached $25 million. Almost all of these lands were bought entirely on credit with banknotes, many of which had little value. Settlers seeking land poured into the Southwest, and as one observer wryly commented, "under this stimulating process prices rose like smoke." In an attempt to slow the economy, Jackson issued the Specie Circular in July 1836, which decreed that the government would accept only specie for the purchase of public land. Land sales drastically declined, but the speculative pressures in the economy were already too great.

Specie Circular

This Whig cartoon blames the Democratic party for the depression that began during Van Buren's administration. Barefoot workers go unemployed, and women and children beg and sleep in the streets. Depositors clamor for their money from a bank that has suspended specie payments, while the pawnbroker and liquor store do a thriving business and the sheriff rounds up debtors.

"Van Ruin's" Depression

During Jackson's second term, his opponents had gradually come together in a new party, the Whigs. Led by Henry Clay, they charged that "King Andrew I" had dangerously concentrated power in the presidency. The Whigs also embraced Clay's "American System," designed to spur national economic development and particularly manufacturing. To do this the Whigs advocated a protective tariff, a national bank, and federal aid for internal improvements. In 1836 the Democrats nominated Martin Van Buren, who triumphed over three Whig sectional candidates.

Whig party

Van Buren had less than two months in office to savor his triumph before the speculative mania collapsed, and with it the economy. After a brief recovery, the bottom fell out of the international cotton market in 1839 and the country entered a serious depression. Arising from causes that were worldwide, the depression demonstrated how deeply the market economy had penetrated American society. It was not until 1843 that the economy revived.

Depression

Public opinion identified hard times with the policies of the Democratic party. Because he strongly opposed a new national bank, Van Buren instead persuaded Congress in 1840 to create an Independent Treasury to keep the government's funds. Its offices were forbidden to accept paper currency, issue any banknotes, or make any loans. The government's money would be safe, but it would also remain unavailable to banks to make loans and stimulate the economy.

Independent Treasury

As the depression deepened, thousands of workers were unemployed and countless businesses failed. Urban workers and their families were among the hardest hit. Nationally wages fell 30 to 50 percent. "Business of all kinds is completely at a stand," wrote one business leader in 1840, "and the whole body politic sick and infirm, and calling aloud for a remedy."

The Whigs' Triumph

The Whigs had done much to strengthen their party's national organization, and with the nation stuck in the worst depression of the century, they approached the election of 1840 in high spirits. To oppose Van Buren, they turned to William Henry Harrison, the military leader who had won fame defeating the Shawnee Indians at Tippecanoe. Using the democratic electioneering techniques that Jackson's supporters had first perfected, they portrayed Harrison as a man of the people while painting Van Buren as an aristocrat who wore a corset, ate off gold plates with silver spoons, and used cologne. Shades of Franklin Plummer!

First modern presidential campaign

This Illinois marching club benefited from the support of women.

Whig rallies featured hard cider and log cabins to reinforce Harrison's image as a man of the people. Ironically, Harrison had been born into one of Virginia's most aristocratic families and was living in a 16-room mansion in Ohio. But the Whig campaign, by portraying the election as a contest between aristocracy and democracy, was perfectly attuned to the prevailing national spirit.

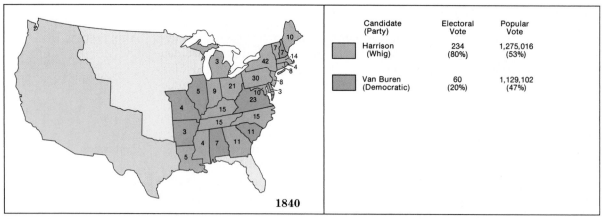

Candidate (Party)	Electoral Vote	Popular Vote
Harrison (Whig)	234 (80%)	1,275,016 (53%)
Van Buren (Democratic)	60 (20%)	1,129,102 (47%)

1840

Election of 1840

Women take a new political role

Both parties used parades, barbecues, liberty pole raisings, party songs, and mass meetings to stir up enthusiasm. But the Whigs pioneered a new aspect of mass political campaigning: they prominently involved women. Deeming themselves the party of morality, Whigs appealed directly to women for support, urging them to become politically informed in order to morally instruct their husbands. Women attended Whig rallies, conducted meetings, made speeches, and wrote campaign pamphlets, activities that before had been solely the duties of men. "I never took so much interest in politics in my life," Mary Steger of Richmond confessed to a friend. Uncertain what to make of this new Whig tactic, one Democrat observed, "This way of making politicians of their women is something new under the sun." Democrats had no choice but to eventually follow suit. Women's role in national politics began in 1840, and within a few years their presence at party rallies was commonplace.

Just as the Panic of 1819 had roused the voters to action, the depression and the two parties' response to it sparked mass interest. The result was a record turnout, as some 900,000 new voters were mobilized between 1836 and 1840 and nearly four-fifths of the eligible voters went to the polls. Although the popular vote was fairly close (Harrison led by about 150,000 votes out of 2.4 million cast), in the Electoral College Harrison won an easy victory, 234 to 60.

The "log cabin" campaign marked the final transition from the deferential politics of the Federalist era to the egalitarian politics that had emerged in the wake of the Panic of 1819. "We have been sung down, lied down, drunk down!" protested one indignant Democratic journal. As the *Democratic Review* conceded after the Whigs' victory in 1840, "We have taught them how to conquer us."

The Jacksonian Party System

It is easy, given the hoopla of democratic campaigning, to be distracted from the central fact that the new political system was directly shaped by the social and economic strains of an expanding nation. Whigs and Democrats held different attitudes toward the changes brought about by the market, banks, and commerce.

Democrats, Whigs, and the Market

Democratic ideology

The Democrats tended to view society as a continuing conflict between "the people"—farmers, planters, and workers—and a set of greedy aristocrats. The latter were not Europe's landed aristocrats, of course, but a "paper money aristocracy" of bankers, stock jobbers, and investors. This new class manipulated the banking system for its own profit, Democrats claimed, and sapped the nation's virtue by encouraging speculation and the desire for quickly gained, unearned wealth. For Democrats, the Bank War became a battle to restore the old Jeffersonian Republic with its values of simplicity, frugality, hard work, and independence. This attempt to retain those values is what Jackson was referring to when he said that removal of the deposits from Biddle's Bank would "preserve the morals of the people."

Jackson understood the dangers that private banks posed to a democratic society. Yet Democrats, in effect, wanted the rewards of the market without sacrificing the features of a simple agrarian republic. They wanted the wealth and goods that the market offered without the competitive, changing society, the complex dealings, the dominance of urban centers, and the loss of independence that came with it.

Whigs, on the other hand, were more comfortable with the market. For them, commerce and economic development were agents of civilization. Nor did the Whigs envision any conflict in society between farmers and mechanics on the one hand and businesspeople and bankers on the other. Economic growth would benefit everyone by creating jobs, stimulating demand for agricultural products, raising national income, and expanding opportunity. The government's responsibility was to provide a well-regulated economy that guaranteed opportunity for citizens of ability. In such an economy, banks and corporations were not only useful but necessary. A North Carolina Whig well expressed the party's vision of society: "All should be mutual friends and helpers to each other, and who ever aids and assists his fellow men from good motives, by lending money, by affording employment by precept or example, is a benefactor to his fellow men."

Whig ideology

Whigs and Democrats differed not only in their attitudes toward the market but also in their view of how active government should be. Despite Andrew Jackson's inclination to be a strong president, Democrats as a rule believed in limited government. Government's role in the economy was to promote competition by destroying monopolies and special privileges. As one New Jersey Democratic newspaper declared, "All Bank charters, all laws conferring special privileges, with all acts of incorporation, for purposes of private gain, are monopolies, in as much as they are calculated to enhance the power of wealth, produce inequalities among the people and to subvert liberty."

Democrats' belief in limited government

In *Charles River Bridge v. Warren Bridge* (1837) the Supreme Court strengthened the vision of an expanding capitalistic society undergirded by free competition. The opinion was written by Chief Justice Roger Taney, whom Jackson had appointed in 1835 to succeed John Marshall. At issue was whether in authorizing construction of a free bridge Massachusetts violated the rights of the owners of an adjacent toll bridge. Declaring that the public interest was the overriding concern, Taney's opinion struck down the idea of implied monopolies. In this decision, the Court sought to promote equality of opportunity and economic progress.

Opposition to monopolies

In keeping with this philosophy of limited government, Democrats also rejected the idea that moral beliefs were the proper sphere of government action. Religion and politics, they believed, should be kept clearly separate, and they generally opposed humanitarian legislation as an interference with personal freedom. On the other hand, they supported debtor relief, which in their view curbed the wealthy aristocrats who tyrannized the common worker.

The Whigs, in contrast, viewed government power positively. They believed that it should be used to protect individual rights and public liberty and that it

Whigs' belief in active government

had a special role where individual effort was ineffective. By regulating the economy and competition, the government could ensure equal opportunity. Indeed, for Whigs the concept of government promoting the general welfare went beyond the economy. Northern Whigs in particular also believed that government power should be used to foster the moral welfare of the country. They were much more likely to favor temperance or antislavery legislation and aid to education. Whigs portrayed themselves not only as the party of prosperity but also as the party of respectability and proper behavior.

The Social Bases of the Two Parties

In some ways the social makeup of the two parties was similar. To be competitive, Whigs and Democrats both had to have significant support among farmers, the largest group in society, and workers. Neither party could carry an election by appealing exclusively to the rich or the poor.

Attitudes toward the market economy

The Whigs, however, enjoyed disproportionate strength among the business and commercial classes, especially following the Bank War. Whigs appealed to planters who needed credit to finance their cotton and rice trade in the world market, to farmers who were eager to sell their surpluses, and to workers who wished to improve their social position. Democrats attracted farmers isolated from the market or uncomfortable with it, workers alienated from the emerging industrial system, and rising entrepreneurs who wanted to break monopolies and open the economy to newcomers like themselves. The Whigs were strongest in the towns, cities, and rural areas that were fully integrated into the market economy, whereas Democrats dominated areas of semisubsistence farming that were more isolated and languishing economically. Attitude toward the market, rather than economic position, was more important in determining party affiliation.

Religious and ethnic factors

Religion and ethnic identities also shaped partisanship. As the self-proclaimed "party of respectability," Whigs attracted the support of high-status native-born church groups, including the Congregationalists and Unitarians in New England and Presbyterians and Episcopalians elsewhere. The party also attracted immigrant groups that most easily merged into the dominant Anglo-Protestant culture, such as the English, Welsh, and Scots. Democrats, on the other hand, recruited more Germans and Irish, whose more lenient observance of the Sabbath and (among Catholics) use of parochial schools generated native-born hostility. Democrats appealed to the lower-status Baptists and Methodists, particularly in states where they earlier had been subjected to disabilities. Both parties also attracted freethinkers and the unchurched, but the Democrats had the advantage because they resisted demands for temperance and sabbatarian laws, such as the prohibition of Sunday travel. In states where they could vote, African Americans were solidly Whig in reaction to the Democratic party's strong racism and hostility to black rights.

The Triumph of the Market

Clearly, Jacksonian politics evolved out of the social and economic dislocation produced by rapidly expanding economic opportunity. Yet efforts to avoid the costs of the market while preserving its benefits were doomed to failure. In states where the Democrats eliminated all banks, so much hardship and financial chaos ensued that some system of banking was soon restored. The expansion of the economy after 1815 had caught farmers as well as urban residents in an international network of trade and finance, tying them with a tightening grip to the price of cotton in Liverpool or the interest rates of the Bank of England. There was no rolling back the market in a return to the ideals of Crèvecoeur.

Still, Americans had evolved a system of democratic politics to deal with the conflicts that the new order produced. The new national parties—like the new markets spreading across the nation—had become essential structures uniting the American nation. They advanced an ideology of equality and opportunity, which stood as a goal for the nation even though women, African Americans, and Indians were excluded. The new politics developed a system of truly national parties, competing with one another, involving large numbers of ordinary Americans resolving differences through compromise and negotiation. Along with the market, democracy had become an integral part of American life.

chapter summary

Beginning in the 1820s, the United States experienced a democratic revolution that was identified with Andrew Jackson.

- The rise of democracy was stimulated by the Panic of 1819, which caused Americans to look toward both politicians and the government to address their needs.

- The new political culture of democracy included the use of conventions to make nominations, the celebration of the wisdom of the people, the adoption of white manhood suffrage, and the acceptance of political parties as essential for the working of the constitutional system.

- The new politics had distinct limits, however. Women were not given the vote, and racism intensified.

  - The eastern Indian tribes were forced to move to new lands west of the Mississippi River.

  - Free African Americans found themselves subject to increasingly harsh discrimination and exclusion.

- In politics, Andrew Jackson came to personify the new democratic culture. Through his forceful lead-

ership, he significantly expanded the powers of the presidency.

  - Jackson threatened to use force against South Carolina when it tried to nullify the federal tariff using John C. Calhoun's theory of nullification, that is, that a state convention could nullify a federal law.

  - In response, nationalists advanced the idea of the perpetual Union. A compromise, which gradually lowered the tariff, ended the crisis (Compromise of 1833).

  - Jackson vetoed a bill to recharter the Second Bank of the United States and destroyed the Bank by removing its federal deposits.

- Under President Martin Van Buren, the nation entered a severe depression.

- Capitalizing on hard times and employing the democratic techniques pioneered by the Democrats, the Whigs gained national power in 1840.

- By 1840 the two parties had developed different ideologies.

  - The Whigs were more comfortable with the mechanisms of the market and linked commerce with progress.

  - The Democrats were uneasy about the market and favored limited government.

interactive learning

The Primary Source Investigator CD-ROM offers the following materials related to this chapter:

- Interactive maps: **Election of 1824** (M7), **Election of 1840** (M7), and **Indian Expulsion, 1800–1890** (M8)

- A short documentary movie on Indian removal along the Trail of Tears (D6)

- A collection of primary sources including Andrew Jackson's response to the Nullification issue, a cartoon satirizing the Jackson administration, and a caricature of Martin Van Buren. Several sources illustrate the Indian expulsion: audio clips of slave songs and field hollers, the orders to remove the Cherokees, the Treaty at Echota, a memorial from the ladies of Steubenville protesting the Indian removal, and a physician's report of emigrating Cherokees at Fort Payne, Alabama.

additional reading

Arthur M. Schlesinger Jr., *The Age of Jackson* (1945), marks the beginning of modern historiography on the Jacksonian era. Locating the main sources of Jacksonianism among eastern workers, Schlesinger emphasized the banking and currency issue as the defining issue of Jacksonian politics. Lightly researched, over-written, and partisan in its analysis, Schlesinger's book provoked a flurry of works challenging its interpretation. Among the most important is the chapter on Jackson in Richard Hofstadter, *The American Political Tradition* (1948). Despite this withering criticism, Schlesinger is not without defenders. Charles Sellers, *The Market Revolution* (1991), offers an updated—and equally flawed—version of Schlesinger's argument.

A good recent interpretation of Jacksonian politics is Harry Watson, *Liberty and Power* (1990). Robert Remini places the features of the new democratic political system in bold relief in *The Election of Andrew Jackson* (1963). Important discussions of party ideologies include Marvin Meyers, *The Jacksonian Persuasion* (1957); Daniel Walker Howe, *The Political Culture of the American Whigs* (1979); and Lawrence Frederick Kohl, *The Politics of Individualism* (1988). For the Whig party, see Michael F. Holt's *The Rise and Fall of the American Whig Party* (1999), which provides a full and detailed account of the party's history. The best account of the nullification crisis is William W. Freehling, *Prelude to Civil War* (1966), and Robert Remini offers a succinct analysis of the banking issue in *Andrew Jackson and the Bank War* (1967). Paul Goodman, *Towards a Christian Republic* (1988), is the most valuable study of Anti-Masonry. For differing views on Indian removal, see Michael D. Green, *The Politics of Indian Removal* (1982), which deals with Creek society, and Robert Remini, *The Legacy of Andrew Jackson* (1988). For a fuller list of readings, see the Bibliography at www.mhhe.com/davidsonnation5.

significant events

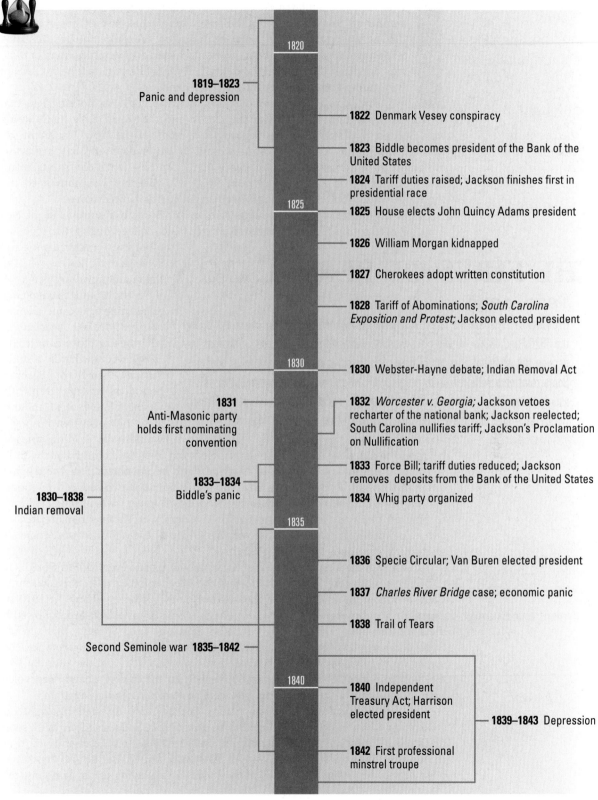

1819–1823
Panic and depression

1820

1822 Denmark Vesey conspiracy

1823 Biddle becomes president of the Bank of the United States

1824 Tariff duties raised; Jackson finishes first in presidential race

1825

1825 House elects John Quincy Adams president

1826 William Morgan kidnapped

1827 Cherokees adopt written constitution

1828 Tariff of Abominations; *South Carolina Exposition and Protest;* Jackson elected president

1830

1830 Webster-Hayne debate; Indian Removal Act

1831
Anti-Masonic party holds first nominating convention

1832 *Worcester v. Georgia;* Jackson vetoes recharter of the national bank; Jackson reelected; South Carolina nullifies tariff; Jackson's Proclamation on Nullification

1833–1834
Biddle's panic

1833 Force Bill; tariff duties reduced; Jackson removes deposits from the Bank of the United States

1834 Whig party organized

1830–1838
Indian removal

1835

1836 Specie Circular; Van Buren elected president

1837 *Charles River Bridge* case; economic panic

1838 Trail of Tears

Second Seminole war **1835–1842**

1840

1840 Independent Treasury Act; Harrison elected president

1839–1843 Depression

1842 First professional minstrel troupe

Chapter 12

I n 1826 the Reverend Lyman Beecher was probably the most celebrated minister of the Republic, and the pulpit of Hanover Street Church was his to command. Beecher looked and spoke like a pious farmer, but every Sunday he was transformed when he mounted the pulpit of Boston's most imposing church. From there, he would blaze forth denunciations of dancing, drinking, dueling, or "infidelity," all the while punctuating his sermon with pump-handle strokes of the right hand.

Nor were Beecher's ambitions small. His goal was nothing less than to bring the kingdom of Christ to the nation and the world. Like many ministers, Beecher had studied the intriguing final book of the New Testament, the Revelation to John. The Revelation foretold in Latter days of Earth a glorious millennium—a thousand years of peace and triumph—when the saints would rule and evil would be banished from the world. Beecher was convinced that the long-awaited millennium might well begin in the United States.

Personal experience reinforced this optimism. Born to a sturdy line of New England blacksmiths in 1775, Beecher entered Yale College during the high tide of postwar nationalism—and, some said, the lowest ebb of religion among young people. In the revivals of the Second Great Awakening that came to many colleges in 1802, Beecher had been one of those converted.

THE FIRES OF PERFECTION

1820–1850

preview • The Second Great Awakening unleashed a cascade of reform during the 1820s and 1830s. Middle-class women were prominent in these campaigns, reflecting the profound changes in their social roles wrought by the market economy. Some reformers withdrew from everyday life to create utopian communities; others sought humanitarian reforms such as temperance, educational improvement, women's rights, and—most disruptive to the political system—the abolition of slavery.

But he was hardly a stodgy Puritan. Much of Beecher's boundless energy went into raising a family of 11 children, every one of whom he prayed would take leading roles in bringing the kingdom of God to America. He loved to wrestle on the floor with his sons, climb the highest trees, or go "berrying" with his daughters. Still, the religious dimension of their lives was constant. The family attended two services on Sunday, a weekly prayer meeting, and a monthly "concert of prayer," where the devout met to pray for the conversion of the world. Beecher's son Thomas remembered his father commanding: "Overturn and overturn till He whose right it is shall come and reign, King of nations and King of saints."

To usher in the kingdom of God entire communities and even nations would have to be swept with a divine fire. Toward that end Beecher joined other Protestant ministers in supporting a host of religious reforms and missionary efforts. In 1810 the American Board of Commissioners for Foreign Missions was established, followed by the American Bible Society (1816) and the American Tract Society (1825), whose Bibles and religious pamphlets blanketed every sleepy hamlet in the country. Societies sprang up to promote Sunday schools and minister to sailors and the poor. By 1830 the most important of these organizations made up the loosely united "Benevolent Empire." To Beecher these organizations were signs of the coming kingdom.

As the new pastor at Hanover Street, Beecher also directed his righteous artillery on a host of evils that seemed to be obstructing God's kingdom. With scorn he attacked Unitarians, whose liberal, rational creed rejected the divinity of Jesus. In Boston, Unitarians were mainly upper class and cultured. But he also denounced what he viewed as sinful pastimes of the lower class: playing cards, gambling, and

Lyman Beecher (center) with his family in 1855. Five of his six sons, all of whom were ministers, stand in back. In front, daughters Catharine (holding his arm to steady it for the long exposure) and Isabella are on the left; Harriet, the author of *Uncle Tom's Cabin,* is at the far right.

drinking. And he denounced Roman Catholic priests and nuns as superstitious, devious agents of "Antichrist."

Beecher's efforts at "moral reform" antagonized many immigrants and other working people who enjoyed liquor or lotteries. Thus when a blaze broke out in the basement of his church in 1830, unsympathetic local firefighters stood by while the splendid structure burned to the ground. The fires of spiritual reform had been halted, temporarily, by a blaze of a literal sort.

Any fire, real or spiritual, is unpredictable as it spreads from one scrap of tinder to the next. That proved to be the case with reform movements of the 1820s and 1830s, as they moved in diverging, sometimes contradictory, ways. What did it mean, after all, to bring in Christ's kingdom? The goals of the early reform societies were moral rather than social. Leaders like Beecher sought to convert individuals and to church the unchurched, with the help of religious revivals and benevolent associations. Their conservative aim, as he expressed it, was to restore America to "the moral government of God."

Other Christians, however, began to focus on social issues like slavery, the inequality of women, and the operation of prisons. To these problems they demanded more radical solutions. Ironically, many of Beecher's children went well beyond his more conservative strategies for hastening the millennium. They spoke out for abolition, women's rights, and education in ways that left their father distinctly uncomfortable. In their activities the Beechers reflected the diversity of the reform impulse itself.

Revivalism and the Social Order

Society during the Jacksonian era was undergoing deep and rapid changes. The revolution in markets brought both economic expansion and periodic depressions, as its citizens competed—often anxiously—for status and wealth. In a nation where fortunes could be won and lost almost overnight, some reformers sought stability and moral order in religious community. The bonds of unity created by a revival brought a sense of peace in the midst of a society in change. Revivals could reinforce strength and discipline, too, in an emerging industrial culture that demanded sobriety and regular working habits.

Other reformers, however, sought to check the excesses of Jacksonian America by radically remaking institutions or devising utopian, experimental ways of living and working together. The drive for renewal, in other words, led reformers sometimes to preserve social institutions, other times to overturn them. It led them sometimes to liberate, other times to control. And the conflicting ways in which these dynamics operated could be seen in the electric career of Charles Grandison Finney.

Finney's New Measures

In 1821, as a young man, Finney experienced a soul-shattering conversion that led him to give up his law practice to become an itinerant minister. Eventually he was ordained in the Presbyterian church, although he lacked any formal theological training. He first attracted national attention when in the mid-1820s and early 1830s he conducted a series of spectacular revivals in the booming port cities along the new Erie Canal.

Charles Finney, about 1834

Like George Whitefield before him, Finney had an entrancing voice that carried great distances. His power over an audience was such that when he described the descent of a sinner into hell, those in the back of the hall rose to witness the final plunge. His success, however, resulted also from his use of special techniques—"the new measures"—and his casual attitude toward religious doctrine.

These new measures had been developed during the frontier revivals of the Second Great Awakening (page 266). Finney's contribution was to popularize the techniques and use them systematically. He held "protracted meetings" night after night to build up excitement. Speaking boldly and bluntly, he prayed for sinners by name, encouraged women to testify in public gatherings, and placed those struggling with conversion on the "anxious bench" at the front of the church. "A revival is not a miracle," he coolly declared, "it is a purely scientific result of the right use of constituted means."

Conversion experience

Finney and other evangelical* revivalists stressed the need for individuals to undergo an emotionally wrenching conversion experience and be reborn. Not all conversion experiences, however, occurred during revivals, prayer meetings, and religious gatherings. The slave Mortimer, for example, first heard a voice calling his name while he was in the field plowing. As he started to run, the cry "I am blessed but you are damned!" reverberated around him. Begging for mercy, Morte began to pray when a soft voice reassured him, "You are this day made alive and freed from hell." Deeply impressed by Morte's experience, his master told him henceforth he could preach on the plantation, and Morte thus commenced his lifelong career as a preacher. Like Mortimer, born-again Christians could describe in detail their feelings and experiences when they were reborn. And, as in his case, religion could bring both peace and a sense of purpose in one's life.

---

*The word *evangelical* derives from a Greek word meaning the bringing of good news—in this case the Gospel. Protestant evangelicals stressed the need for individual conversion and rebirth stemming from an awareness of sinful guilt and Christ's act of atoning, through his death, for their sins.

The Philosophy of the New Revivals

Finney also rejected many religious doctrines of Calvinism, including predestination, which maintained that God had already determined which individuals were destined to be saved or damned and that no human effort could change this decision. But by the 1820s such a proposition seemed unreasonable to a generation that condemned hereditary distinctions, celebrated personal dignity, and praised human ability and activity. Leaving the Lord little role in the drama of human deliverance, Finney embraced the doctrine of free will. All men and women who wanted to could be saved. To those anxious about their salvation, he thundered, "Do it!" Finney's approach also made emotion paramount. His revivals were not as tumultuous as those on the southern frontier, but agonized prayers, groans, and uncontrolled crying often resounded through the hall.

Free will and perfectionism

With salvation within reach of every individual, what might be in store for society at large? "If the church would do her duty," Finney confidently predicted, "the millennium may come in this country in three years." By the 1830s Finney had taken to preaching not merely faith in human progress but something more—human perfectibility. Embracing this new theology of "perfectionism," he boldly asserted that all Christians should "aim at being holy and not rest satisfied until they are as perfect as God." And a true Christian would not rest until society was made perfect as well.

By preaching an optimistic message of free will and salvation to all, Finney and his eager imitators transformed Protestantism. But not all clergy applauded. For Lyman Beecher, as well as for many supporters of the Second Great Awakening, Finney's new measures went too far in generating excessive emotionalism, while his theology of perfectionism verged on heresy. Undaunted by such criticism, Finney continued his revivals. As for Lyman Beecher, he decided in 1832 to outflank his adversaries by moving west to become the president of Lane Seminary in Cincinnati. There he planned to train the right sort of revivalists to save the frontier for true religion and to bring about the kingdom of God in America.

In *The Way of Good and Evil* devout Christians are all helped on the path (right) to millennial perfection by the virtues of family, religion, education, and hard work. Sinners on the left, however, take the path of disobedience, intemperance, and lying—straight to hell.

Religion and the Market Economy

Revival audiences responded to the call for reform partly because they were unsettled by the era's rapid social changes. In the North, evangelical religion proved strongest not in isolated backwaters but in frontier areas just entering the market economy. Rochester, New York, a booming flour-milling center on the Erie Canal, epitomized that social environment.

<table>
<tr><td>Finney's Rochester
revival</td><td>

When Charles Finney came to town in the winter of 1830–1831, Rochester was a community in crisis. It had grown in a decade and a half from a village of 300 souls to a commercial city of more than 20,000. That wrenching expansion produced sharp divisions among the town's leaders, a large working class that increasingly lived apart from employers and beyond their moral control, and a rowdy saloon culture catering to canal boatmen and other transients.

Finney preached almost daily in Rochester for six months. He was assisted by local ministers with his revivals, which brought thousands to accept his message of voluntary salvation and doubled church membership. Religion helped bring order to what had been a chaotic and fragmented city.
</td></tr>
</table>

Finney's Rochester revival

When Charles Finney came to town in the winter of 1830–1831, Rochester was a community in crisis. It had grown in a decade and a half from a village of 300 souls to a commercial city of more than 20,000. That wrenching expansion produced sharp divisions among the town's leaders, a large working class that increasingly lived apart from employers and beyond their moral control, and a rowdy saloon culture catering to canal boatmen and other transients.

Finney preached almost daily in Rochester for six months. He was assisted by local ministers with his revivals, which brought thousands to accept his message of voluntary salvation and doubled church membership. Religion helped bring order to what had been a chaotic and fragmented city.

Revivalism's appeal to the middle class

Although revivals like Finney's Rochester triumph drew converts from all segments of American society, they appealed especially to the middle class. Lawyers, merchants, retailers, and manufacturers all played central roles in the larger market economy and invested in factories and railroads. The market put intense pressure on these upwardly mobile citizens. They viewed success as a reflection of moral character, yet they also feared that with the ups and downs of the economy—boom, then bust—they would lose their wealth. Religion provided a way in which to cope with the tensions and uncertainties of their own lives.

Workers and church membership

Workers, too, were among the converted. Conversions among workers dramatically increased during the depression that began in 1839, as revivalists preached from street corners and held meetings in the workplace and homes. The Methodist church, which lacked the social respectability of some of the other evangelical churches, was particularly important in instilling the values of sobriety, frugality, and hard work in the urban working class.

Among other things, joining a church reflected a desire to get ahead in the new economy by accepting moral self-discipline. To a striking degree, social mobility and church membership were linked. In Rochester two-thirds of the male workers who were church members improved their occupational status in a decade. In contrast, workers who did not join a church rarely stayed in town more than a few years, and those who stayed were likely to decline in status.

Revivalists like Finney were interested in saving souls, not money, and their converts were most concerned with their spiritual state. Even so, evangelical Protestantism reinforced values needed to succeed in the new competitive economy. Churchgoers embraced the values of hard work, punctuality, and sobriety; they internalized the demand for self-control. In that sense, religion was one means of social control in a disordered society. And many employers put pressure on workers to give up their drinking habits, on and off the job, and to embrace religion.

The Rise of African American Churches

Independent black churches grew in size and importance as well because African Americans in urban areas increasingly resented being treated as second-class worshipers. In 1787, only a month after the close of the Constitutional Convention in Philadelphia, Richard Allen was praying at St. George's Church. Allen was not only a devout churchgoer but also a popular black preacher. But this Sunday morning his prayers were interrupted. "You must get up—you must not kneel here," a white usher whispered to Allen, who was not in the area reserved for black parishioners. Several white ushers roughly pulled him to his feet. Allen and other black members of the congregation walked out. In 1794 he organized the Bethel Church, where African Americans would be free to worship without discrimination.

In the early nineteenth century, similar tensions led to the formation of black Methodist and Baptist churches in a number of northern and southern cities. The most important was the African Methodist Episcopal (AME) Church. Growing fears for the security of slavery caused southern white communities, especially in the Deep South, to suppress independent black churches after 1820. But these churches, which were strongly evangelical, continued to grow in the North. In 1836 the AME Church, first organized in 1816, had 7,500 members. Twenty years later its membership was about 20,000. As with the black Baptist church, however, its major growth lay in the future and in the South following emancipation.

The Significance of the Second Great Awakening

As a result of the Second Great Awakening, the dominant form of Christianity in America became evangelical Protestantism. Membership in the major Protestant churches—Congregational, Presbyterian, Baptist, and Methodist—soared during the first half of the nineteenth century. By 1840 an estimated half of the adult population was nominally connected to some church, with the Methodists emerging as the largest Protestant denomination in both the North and the South.

Evangelicalism was in harmony with the basic values of early-nineteenth-century Americans. Its emphasis on the ability of everyone to bring about his or her salvation upheld the American belief in individualism. By catering to a mass audience without social distinctions, the revivals reinforced the American belief in democracy and equality. And Finney's invincibly optimistic doctrine of perfectionism was exactly attuned to the spirit of the age.

Evangelicalism bolsters individualism and equality

But not all—or even a majority—of Americans who flocked to revivals or

Women's Sphere

joined reform societies were men. On the contrary, female converts outnumbered males by about three to two. Usually the initial convert in a family was a woman, and many men who converted were related to women who had come forward earlier.

Women and Revivalism

Women played such an important role in the Awakening partly because of changes in their own social universe. Instead of parents arranging the marriages of their children, couples were beginning to wed more often on the basis of affection. Under such conditions, a woman's prospects for marriage became less certain, and in older areas like New England, the migration of so many young men to the West compounded this uncertainty. Yet marriage was deemed important for a woman's happiness, and it remained essential for her economic security.

Women's changing lives

The unpredictability of these social circumstances drew young women toward religion. Women between the ages of 12 and 25 were especially susceptible to conversion. Joining a church heightened a young woman's feeling of initiative and gave her a sense of purpose. By establishing respectability and widening her social circle of friends, church membership also enhanced her chances of marriage.

The Ideal of Domesticity

The era's changing economic order brought other pressures to bear on wives and mothers. Most men now worked outside the home, while the rise of factories led

As business affairs grew increasingly separate from the family in the nineteenth century, the middle-class home became a female domain. A woman's role as a wife and mother was to dispense love and moral guidance to her husband and her children. As this domestic scene makes clear, she was at the very center of the world of the family.

"Sisterhood" and social networks

to a decline in part-time work such as spinning, which women had once performed to supplement family income. Moreover, except on the frontier, home manufacturing was no longer essential, for the family purchased articles that women previously had made, such as cloth, soap, and candles. "The transition from mother-and-daughter power to water-and-steam power," one New England minister noted, produced "a complete revolution of domestic life."

This growing separation of the household from the workplace meant that the home took on a new social identity. It was idealized as a place of "domesticity," a haven away from the competitive, workaday world, with the mother firmly at its center. This new view of women's role was elaborated largely by clergy and female authors in sermons, advice manuals, and pieces of sentimental fiction for an urban middle-class audience. But the ideal's significance and acceptance had far-reaching consequences. The idea of domesticity was based on the notion of separate sexual spheres. If men's sphere was the world of factories, offices, and fields, women's sphere was the home, where they were to dispense love and comfort and teach moral values to husbands and children. "Love is our life our reality, business yours," Mollie Clark told one suitor.

Women, who were considered morally stronger, were also held to a higher standard of sexual purity. A man's sexual infidelity, while hardly condoned, brought no lasting shame. But a woman who engaged in sexual relations before marriage or was unfaithful afterward was threatened with everlasting disgrace. Under this double standard, women were to be passive and submerge their identities in those of their husbands.

Most women of the era did not see this ideology as a rationale for male dominance. On the contrary, women played an important role in creating the ideal of domesticity, none more than Lyman Beecher's daughter Catharine. Like the earlier advocates of "republican motherhood," Catharine Beecher argued that women exercised power as moral guardians of the nation's future. The proper care of a middle-class household was also a crucial responsibility, and Beecher wrote several books on efficient home management. "There is no one thing more necessary to a housekeeper in performing her varied duties, than a habit of system and order," she told readers. "For all the time afforded us, we must give account to God."

Catharine Beecher was also a leading advocate of giving women greater educational opportunities so that they could become schoolteachers. Conceiving of the school as an extension of the home, she maintained that teachers, like mothers, should instill sound moral values in children. She argued that women's naturally pious character and their affection for children made them ideally suited to be teachers.

Women also exerted their moral authority through the growing number of benevolent organizations, which fostered close friendships among women. Women gave emotionally much more to other family members than they received in exchange, and they turned to other women for comfort and support. This "sisterhood"—the common sense of identity and shared experiences—helped sustain reform movements launched by women to aid females of the lower classes.

The ideal of domesticity was not unique to the United States. The middle class became increasingly important in Europe, so that after 1850 it was culturally dominant and formulated society's values. Employment opportunities expanded for women as industrialization accelerated, yet the social expectation among the middle class was that women would not be employed outside the home. This redefinition of women's roles was more sweeping in Europe because previously, middle-class women had left the task of child-raising largely to hired nurses and governesses. By midcentury, these mothers devoted much more time to domestic duties, including rearing the children. Family size also declined, both in France and in England. The middle class was most numerous in England; indeed, the importance of the middle class in Britain during Queen Victoria's reign gave these ideals the label *Victorianism*.

Domesticity in Europe

The majority of white women hardly had time to make the ideal of domesticity the center of their lives. Farmers' wives had to work constantly, whereas lower-class families could not get by without the wages of female members. Still, most middle-class women tried to live up to the ideal, though many found the effort confining. "The great trial is that I have nothing to do," one complained. "Here I am with abundant leisure and capable, I believe, of accomplishing some good, and yet with no object on which to expend my energies."

Women's socially defined role as guardians of morality helps explain their prominence among revival converts. Religious activity was one way that women could exert influence over society and one area where wives need not be subordinate to their husbands. For some male critics, Finney's policy of giving women a prominent role in revivals threatened to bring about a dangerous equality between the sexes. One unhappy man in Rochester complained about the effect of Finney's visit to his home: "He *stuffed* my wife with tracts, and alarmed her fears, and nothing short of meetings, night and day, could atone for the many fold sins my poor, simple spouse had committed." Then, getting to the heart of the matter, he added, "She made the miraculous discovery, that she had been 'unevenly yoked.' From this unhappy period, peace, quiet, and happiness have fled from my dwelling, never, I fear, to return."

The Middle-Class Family in Transition

As the middle-class family adapted to the pressures of competitive society by becoming a haven of moral virtue, it developed a new structure and new set of attitudes closer in spirit to those of the modern family. One basic change was the rise of privacy. The family was increasingly seen as a sheltered retreat from the outside world. (See Daily Lives, "Privacy Begins at Home," pages 370–371.) In addition, the pressures to achieve success led middle-class young adults to delay marriage, since a husband was expected to have the financial means to support his wife.

Smaller family size was a result of the delay in marriage as well, since wives began bearing children later. But especially among the urban middle class, women began to use birth control to space children further apart and minimize the risks of pregnancy. In addition, it has been estimated that before 1860 one abortion was performed for every five or six live births. These practices contributed to a decline in the birthrate, from slightly more than 7 children per family in 1800 to 5.4 in 1850—a 25 percent drop. And over that 50-year period the decline became more abrupt beginning in the 1830s. Family size was directly related to the success ethic. On the farm, children working in the fields and around the house were an economic asset. In the new, market-oriented urban society, in contrast, children needed an extended education and special training in order to succeed. Thus they were a greater financial burden on their parents.

Decline in the birthrate

Daily Lives

PUBLIC SPACE/ PRIVATE SPACE
Privacy Begins at Home

In 1831 Olive Walkley made a significant decision: she moved the bed in which she and her husband, Stephen, slept out of the parlor and replaced it with a carpet. She also had the unfinished upstairs plastered and partitioned into bedrooms for their children. The Walkleys were farmers in Southington, Connecticut, but like middle-class urban families they were influenced by the new movement to separate public and private space in the home.

When the Walkleys were married in 1811, Americans were accustomed to living in close quarters, for most houses had few rooms. Further, the limited light and heat forced members to congregate together. Parents and sometimes the entire family slept in the parlor, where visitors were also entertained and where the family's most valuable possessions, including its best bed, were proudly displayed. Even in the wealthiest households, usually only the parents enjoyed separate sleeping quarters, and in most homes beds could be found in virtually every room.

In the years after 1820, however, the American home was reshaped to create specialized regions of privacy, service, and socializing. While houses increasingly faced the road, new designs provided greater privacy by creating an entry hall that served as a transition space from the outside world to the various parts of the house and by separating living and cooking quarters from areas for entertainment.

A sitting room was for the family's everyday use, whereas the parlor was reserved for public activity, including receiving company, giving recitals, and performing ceremonies such as weddings and funerals. As Americans developed a new sense of privacy, the parents' bed and the intimate activities associated with it were placed out of sight. In more prosperous homes an upholstered mahogany sofa replaced the bed in the parlor, and the floor was covered with a carpet, as much a symbol of the family's refinement as the mantel clock was of its modern outlook.

Food preparation and domestic work were done in a separate kitchen and adjoining back rooms. While rural families often continued to eat in the sitting room, houses more frequently contained a separate dining room. Stoves, which enlarged usable space by radiating heat, became common in more affluent homes, while the hearth and its fire—once the main source of food, heat, and light—ceased to be the center of

An architect confers with builders about the plans as a new house goes up in the background

---

With smaller families, however, parents could tend more carefully to their children's success. Increasingly middle-class families took on the expense of additional education to prepare their sons for a career in business. They also frequently equalized inheritances rather than favoring the eldest son or favoring sons over daughters.

American Romanticism

The rational-minded Unitarians in Boston had become accustomed to being attacked by evangelical ministers like Lyman Beecher. They were less prepared to be criticized by one of their own—and on their own home ground, no less. Yet that was what happened when a Unitarian minister named Ralph Waldo Emerson addressed the students of Harvard Divinity School on a warm summer evening in July 1838.

the family's life together. In addition, sleeping space became increasingly private and individual. Larger homes now contained bedrooms, normally on the second floor, and if space permitted, adolescent and grown unmarried children were given separate bedrooms, where they could withdraw from the rest of the family. Smaller family size as well as higher income enabled middle-class families to create new private space within the home.

The newer homes projected a sense of order as well, in sharp contrast to the run-down appearance of older houses, especially in the countryside. These were rarely painted, doors often did not fit, broken windows were patched with rags, and front yards remained unenclosed. Often enough, trash and garbage were simply tossed out the nearest window or door. However, as middle-class families (especially in the North) became increasingly sensitive to the home's exterior public face, they began to paint their houses and keep them in good repair. They also erected white-washed fences around their front yards, planted ornamental trees and shrubs, trimmed the grass, and put their refuse in pits.

The new standards of domestic life also emphasized cleanliness and decoration. Lydia Maria Child's popular *The American Frugal Housewife* offered families of modest means numerous tips on cleaning and scouring as well as decorating. The market for brooms soared as wives sought to keep their homes clean. In 1798 only a few hundred broomcorn brooms were manufactured; in 1840 almost 2 million were sold. At the same time, women increasingly decorated their homes with mass-produced carpets, wallpaper, mirrors, lithographs, and curtains (which enhanced privacy from passersby).

A home's floor plan and furnishings not only determined comfort but also defined a family's status and aspirations. These signs of refinement were most often found in homes of professionals, prosperous farmers, and upwardly mobile skilled workers. The new domestic ideal of the home, which required additional floor space and the ownership of consumer goods, widened the gap between the middle and poorer ranks of society.

Emerson warned his listeners that the true church seemed "to totter to its fall, almost all life extinct." Outside, nature's world was alive and vibrant: "The grass grows, the buds burst, the meadow is spotted with fire and gold in the tint of flowers." But from the pulpits of too many congregations came lifeless preaching. "In how many churches, by how many prophets, tell me," Emerson demanded, "is man made sensible that he is an infinite Soul?" Leaving the shocked audience to ponder his message, Emerson and his wife drove home beneath a night sky illuminated by the northern lights.

Emerson's Divinity School Address glowed much like that July aurora. The address lacked the searing fire of Finney's revivals, yet it was bold in its own way because it reflected a second major current of thought that shaped the reform movements of the era. That current was the intellectual movement known as Romanticism.

Romantic movement

Romanticism began in Europe as a reaction against the Enlightenment. The Enlightenment had placed reason at the center of human achievement; Romanticism instead emphasized the importance of emotion and intuition as sources of truth. It gloried in the unlimited potential of the individual, who might soar if freed from the restraints of institutions. Romanticism extolled humanitarianism and sympathized with the oppressed.

In elevating inner feelings and heartfelt convictions, Romanticism reinforced the emotionalism of religious revivals. Philosophically, its influence was strongest among intellectuals who took part in the Transcendental movement and in the dramatic flowering of American literature. And like revivalism, Romanticism offered its own paths toward perfectionism.

Emerson and Transcendentalism

Above all, Romanticism produced individualists. Thus Transcendentalism is difficult to define, for its members resisted being lumped together. It blossomed in the mid-1830s, when a number of Unitarian clergy like George Ripley and Ralph Waldo Emerson resigned their pulpits, loudly protesting the church's smug, lifeless teachings. The new "Transcendentalist Club" attracted a small following among other discontented Boston intellectuals, including Margaret Fuller, Bronson Alcott, and Orestes Brownson.

Transcendentalist ideas

Like European Romantics, American Transcendentalists emphasized feeling over reason, seeking a spiritual communion with nature. By *transcend* they meant to go beyond or to rise above—specifically above reason and beyond the material world. As part of creation, every human being contained a spark of divinity, Emerson avowed. Transcendentalists also shared in Romanticism's glorification of the individual. "Trust thyself. Every heart vibrates to that iron string," Emerson advised. "The root and seed of democracy is the doctrine, judge for yourself." If freed from the constraints of traditional authority, the individual had infinite potential. So optimistic

In the summer of 1858 members of the cultural Saturday Club of Boston made an excursion to the Adirondacks to observe nature. In *Philosopher's Camp,* painted by William J. Stillman, who organized the expedition, a group on the left dissects a fish under the supervision of the famous scientist Louis Agassiz, while on the right others practice firing rifles. Symbolically, Ralph Waldo Emerson stands alone in the center contemplating the world in solitude.

was Transcendentalism in its view of human nature that it essentially denied the existence of evil.

Transcendentalism had much in common with Jacksonian America—optimism, individualism, and an egalitarian spirit. Like the devout at Finney's revivals, who sought to perfect themselves and society, listeners who flocked to Emerson's lectures were infused with the spirit of optimistic reform.

As the currents of Romanticism percolated through American society, the country's literature came of age. In 1820 educated Americans still tended to ape the fashions of Europe and read English books. But as the population grew, education increased, and the country's literary market expanded, American writers looked with greater interest at the customs and character of their own society. Improved printing presses made possible cheaper, mass-produced American books, and better transportation led to a wider distribution of printed material. By 1850 for every British book, two American books were sold in the United States.

Emergence of American literature

Emerson's address "The American Scholar" (1837) constituted a declaration of literary independence. "Our long dependence, our long apprenticeship to the learning of other lands draws to a close," he proclaimed. "Events, actions arise, that must be sung, that will sing themselves."

The Clash between Nature and Civilization

At the time Emerson spoke, James Fenimore Cooper was already making his mark as the first distinctive American novelist. In the Leatherstocking Tales, a series of five novels written between 1823 and 1841, he focused on the clash between nature and civilization. Cooper clearly admired his hero, Natty Bumppo, a self-reliant frontiersman who represented the nobility and innocence of the wilderness. At the same time, the novels portrayed the culture of the frontier as a threat to the civilization Cooper prized so highly.

Cooper and wilderness

In one scene in *The Pioneers* (1823), as frontier villagers slaughter thousands of pigeons, Leatherstocking laments the wanton destruction, only to hear a townsman express surprise that anyone would "grumble at the loss of a few pigeons. . . . If you had to sow your wheat twice, and three times, as I have done," he continues, "you wouldn't be so massyfully feeling'd toward the devils." As Americans began to exploit the resources of the hinterlands, many of the country's new Romantic writers betrayed a concern that the advance of civilization, with its market economy and crowded urban centers, might destroy the natural simplicity of the land. Natty Bumppo stood halfway between the savage and civilized worlds, not comfortable embracing either.

Henry David Thoreau, too, used nature as a backdrop to explore the conflict between the unfettered individual and the constraints of society. Thoreau grew up in Concord, Massachusetts, where he became part of Emerson's circle. In 1845 he built a cabin on the edge of Walden Pond, living in relative solitude for 16 months to demonstrate the advantages of self-reliance. His experiences became the basis for one of the classics in American literature, *Walden* (1854).

Thoreau and individualism

Thoreau argued that only in nature could one find true independence. By living simply, it was possible to master oneself and the world. Thoreau's own isolation, however, was less than total. When lonely or hungry, he walked to Emerson's home nearby for conversation and a slice of Lidia Emerson's apple pie, and most of the materials he used to build his "wilderness" cabin were store-bought. Still, *Walden* eloquently denounced Americans' frantic competition for material goods and wealth. "Money is not required to buy one necessity of the soul," Thoreau maintained.

"I see my townsmen, whose misfortune it is to have inherited farms, houses, barns, cattle, and farming tools. . . . Who made them serfs of the soil?" It seemed only too clear that "the mass of men lead lives of quiet desperation."

Thoreau's individualism was so extreme that he rejected any institution that contradicted his personal sense of right. "The only obligation which I have a right to assume, is to do at any time what I think right," he wrote in his essay "On Civil Disobedience." Voicing the anti-institutional impulse of Romanticism, he took individualism to its antisocial extreme.

Songs of the Self-Reliant and Darker Loomings

In contrast to Thoreau's exclusiveness, Walt Whitman was all-inclusive, embracing American society in its infinite variety. A journalist and laborer in the New York City area, Whitman was inspired by the common people, whose "manners, speech, dress, friendships . . . are unrhymed poetry." In taking their measure in *Leaves of Grass* (1855), he pioneered a new, modern form of poetry, unconcerned with meter and rhyme and filled with frank imagery and sexual references.

Conceiving himself the representative of all Americans, Whitman exuberantly titled his first major poem "Song of Myself."

> I am your voice—It was tied in you—In me it began to talk.
> I celebrate myself to celebrate every man and woman alive.

Walt Whitman, poet of democracy

Emerson and other critics were put off by his rough-hewn methods, but Whitman, like the Transcendentalists, exalted the emotions, nature, and the individual. At the same time, he endowed these ideas with a more joyous, democratic spirit.

More brooding in temperament was Nathaniel Hawthorne, who lived for a time in Concord. Unable to partake of Emerson's sunny optimism and repelled by the self-centered outlook of Thoreau, Hawthorne wrote of the power of the past to shape future generations and the consequences of pride, selfishness, envy, and secret guilt. In *The Scarlet Letter* (1850), set in New England's Puritan era, Hawthorne spun the tale of Hester Prynne, who bore an illegitimate child, and of the Puritan neighbors who harshly condemned her. Like the Puritans, Hawthorne had no illusions about creating a world without evil, and he rejected the American belief that a person or nation could free itself from the past.

Melville and nature's destructive power

Hawthorne found a soul mate in Herman Melville, whose dark masterpiece, *Moby-Dick* (1851), drew on his youthful experiences aboard a whaling ship. The novel's Captain Ahab relentlessly drives his ship in pursuit of the great white whale Moby-Dick. In Melville's telling, Ahab becomes a powerful symbol of American character: the prototype of the ruthless businessman despoiling nature's resources in his pursuit of success. "Swerve me?" he asks at one point. "The path to my fixed purpose is laid with iron rails, whereon my soul is grooved to run. Over unsound gorges, through the rifled hearts of mountains, under torrents' beds, unerringly I rush!" Ahab is Emerson's self-reliant man, but in him, self-reliance is transformed into a monomania that eventually destroys his ship, its crew, and himself.

Herman Melville

More clearly than any other writer, Melville recognized the dilemma created by Romanticism's emphasis on the individual. Liberated from institutional restraints, human possibilities seemed unlimited to Romantic philosophers. Yet as older traditions and institutions dropped away, the new individualism also led to a competitive materialism devoid of the older sense of community. How, Melville asked, could American society be made perfect, if it was based on self-interested materialism and individualism?

But awash in the many opportunities opening before them, most Americans were not attuned to such searching criticism. They preferred to celebrate, with Emerson, the glories of democracy and the individual's quest for perfection.

The Age of Reform

In the glowing fires of a fervent camp meeting, the quest for perfection often proved hard to control. At the Cane Ridge revival of 1801, the Methodist Peter Cartwright had his hands full trying to stop less orthodox preachers from gathering converts. Quite a few worshipers had joined a group known as the Shakers. Cartwright had to ride around the neighborhood "from cabin to cabin" trying to cure people of the Shaker "delusion."

The Shakers were only one group that demonstrated more radical possibilities for democratic change. While the mainline benevolent societies aimed at a more conservative reformation of individual sinners, the more radical offshoots of Romanticism and perfectionism sought to remake society at large.

Some schemers and dreamers for a better world harbored decidedly eccentric notions. Sylvester Graham, who argued that diet determined character, won lasting fame by inventing the cracker named after him. While he gained a small following, most Americans ignored him—except commercial bakers, who, knowing a threat when they saw one, mobbed this champion of homemade bread. Other reformers, however, decided that the best way to test untried ideas was to withdraw from the everyday world in order to demonstrate the possibilities of perfection.

Utopian Communities

Utopian communities aimed at reforming the world through example. They looked to replace the competitive individualism of American society with a purer spiritual unity and group cooperation. Some were directly linked to religion, but even the secular communities shared the optimism of perfectionism and millennialism.

Dancing was an integral part of the Shakers' religion, as this picture of a service at Lebanon, New York, indicates. In worshiping, men and women formed separate lines with their hands held out and moved back and forth in rhythm while singing religious songs. One Shaker hymn proclaimed, "With ev'ry gift I will unite, / And join in sweet devotion / To worship God is my delight, / With hands and feet in motion." Note the presence of African Americans in the community.

The Shakers

The Shakers proved to be one of the most long-lived utopian experiments. Ann Lee, the illiterate daughter of an English blacksmith, believed that God had a dual nature, part male and part female. Through a series of religious visions Lee became convinced that her own life would reveal the female side of the divinity, just as Christ had come to earth exemplifying the male side. In 1774 she led a small band of followers to America.

The Shaker movement's greatest growth, however, came after Lee's death, when her followers recruited converts at revivals like Cane Ridge. The new disciples founded about 20 communal settlements based on the teachings of Mother Ann, as she was known. Her followers sometimes shook in the fervent public demonstration of their faith—hence the name Shakers. Convinced that the end of the world was at hand and that there was no need to perpetuate the human race, Shakers practiced celibacy, separating the sexes as far as practical. Men and women normally worked apart, ate at separate tables in silence, entered separate doorways, and had separate living quarters.

Shaker communities accorded women unusual authority and equality. Community tasks were generally assigned along sexual lines, with women performing household chores and men laboring in the fields. Leadership of the church, however, was split equally between men and women. By the mid–nineteenth century, a majority of members were female.

Property in Shaker settlements was owned communally and controlled by the church hierarchy. The sect's members worked hard, lived simply, and impressed outsiders with their cleanliness and order. Lacking any natural increase, however, membership began to decline after 1850, from a peak of about 6000 members.

The Oneida Community and complex marriage

The Oneida Community, founded by John Humphrey Noyes, also set out to alter the relationship between the sexes, though in a markedly different way. Noyes, a convert of Charles Finney, took the doctrine of perfection to extremes. Whereas Finney argued that men and women should strive to achieve perfection, Noyes announced that he had actually reached this blessed state. Settling in Putney, Vermont, and, after 1848, in Oneida, New York, Noyes set out to create a community organized on his religious ideals.

In pursuit of greater freedom, Noyes relieved women of what he termed "kitchen slavery." Female members cooked only at breakfast and thereafter were free from household duties until the next morning. Noyes's ideas of liberation, however, went beyond the kitchen. Under his doctrine of "complex marriage," commune members were permitted to have sexual relations with one another, but only with the approval of the community and after a searching examination of the couple's motives. Noyes eventually undertook experiments in planned reproduction by selecting "scientific" combinations of parents to produce morally perfect children.

Under his charismatic leadership the Oneida Community grew to more than 200 members in 1851. But in 1879 an internal dispute drove him from power, and without his guiding hand the community soon fell apart. In 1881 its members reorganized as a business enterprise.

The Mormon Experience

The Church of Jesus Christ of Latter-day Saints, whose members are generally known as Mormons, was founded by a young man named Joseph Smith in Palmyra, in western New York, where the religious fires of revivalism flared up regularly. The son of a poor farmer, Smith was robust, charming, almost hypnotic in his appeal. In 1827, at the age of only 22, he announced that he had discovered a set of golden tablets on which was written the *Book of Mormon*. The tablets, which

Smith claimed to have translated, told the story of a band of Hebrews who in biblical times journeyed to America, splitting into two groups, the Nephites and Lamanites. The Nephites established a Christian civilization, only to be exterminated by the Lamanites, whose descendants are said to be the Indians of the Americas. Proclaiming that he had a commission from God to reestablish the true church, Smith gathered about him a group of devoted followers.

Like Charles Finney's more liberal theology, Mormonism placed little emphasis on predestination and proclaimed that salvation was available to all. Moreover, Mormon culture upheld the middle-class values of hard work, thrift, and self-control. It partook of the optimistic, materialist attitudes of American society. And by teaching that Christ would return to rule the earth, it shared in the hope of a coming millennial kingdom.

Mormonism was less an outgrowth of evangelicalism, however, than of the primitive gospel movement, which sought to reestablish the ancient church. Indeed, having seen the consequences of excessive emotion in the revivals of his youth, Smith soon curbed enthusiasm among his followers and downplayed the experience of conversion. In restoring what Smith called "the ancient order of things," he drew on both the Old and New Testaments. Thus Mormons created a theocracy uniting church and state, reestablished biblical priesthoods and titles, and adopted temple rituals. With its claims of continuing divine revelation, Mormonism attracted weary seekers of spiritual certainty and the true church.

Movement to restore the ancient church

After a revelation told Smith to gather the saints in the city of Zion in preparation for Christ's return to earth, he undertook to create a spiritual community first in Ohio and then in Missouri. But his unorthodox teachings provoked bitter persecution wherever he went, and mob violence finally hounded him and his followers out of Missouri in 1839. In response, Smith established a new holy city, which he named Nauvoo, located on the Mississippi River in Illinois.

Reinforced by a steady stream of converts from Britain, Nauvoo became the largest and fastest-growing city in Illinois, with a population of 10,000 by the mid-1840s. There, Smith introduced the most distinctive features of Mormon theology, including baptism for the dead, eternal marriage, and polygamy, or plural marriage. He also established the secret ceremonies of the Mormon temple, which rituals bore some resemblance to those of the Masonic order. As a result, Mormonism increasingly diverged from traditional Christianity and became a distinct new religion. Nauvoo's political organization was unorthodox too. To bolster his authority as a prophet, Smith established a theocratic government, under which church leaders controlled political offices and governed the community, with Smith as mayor.

City of Zion: Nauvoo

Discarding his earlier ideas of community property, Smith embraced private enterprise at Nauvoo. But speculation in land soon overran the city, rival neighborhoods vied to become the main commercial district, and dissident groups in the city challenged Smith's power. Neighboring residents, alarmed by the Mormons' growing political power and reports that church leaders were practicing polygamy, demanded that Nauvoo's charter be revoked and the church suppressed. In 1844, while in jail for destroying his opponents' press in Nauvoo, Smith was murdered by an anti-Mormon mob. In 1846 the Mormons abandoned Nauvoo, and the following year Brigham Young, Smith's successor, led them westward to Utah.

Socialist Communities

Not all utopian experiments were based on religious teachings. The hardship and poverty that accompanied the growth of industrial factories also inspired utopian communities based on science and reason. Robert Owen, a Scottish industrialist, came to the United States in 1824 committed to creating a society that balanced agriculture and manufacturing. Owen believed that the character of individuals was shaped by their surroundings and that by changing those surroundings, one could change human character.

Robert Owen and New Harmony

Unfortunately, most of the 900 or so volunteers who flocked to Owen's community in New Harmony, Indiana, lacked the skills and commitment needed to make it a success. Bitter factions soon split the settlement. Having lost most of his own fortune, Owen dissolved the community in 1827. More than 20 other American communities were founded on Owen's theories, but none were particularly successful.

Brook Farm

In 1841 Emerson's friend George Ripley organized Brook Farm, a Transcendentalist community and socialist experiment near Boston where members could live "a more wholesome and simple life than can be led amidst the pressure of our competitive institutions." Brook Farm attracted a number of prominent New England intellectuals, who remained for varying lengths of time. Its most important achievements were a magazine, *The Dial,* edited by Margaret Fuller, and its innovative school, whose curriculum included modern subjects such as history, art, and literature. The school's success, however, was overshadowed by the economic failure of the farm, and in 1847 the community disbanded.

The experiences of Brook Farm, New Harmony, and similar communities demonstrated that the United States was poor soil for socialistic experiments. Wages were too high and land too cheap to interest most Americans. And individualism was too strong to create a commitment to cooperative action.

The Temperance Movement

The most significant reform movements of the period sought not to withdraw from society but to change it directly. One of the most determined of these was the temperance movement.

Attack on drinking

The origins of the campaign against alcohol lay in the era's heavy drinking. Alcohol consumption soared after the Revolution, so that by 1830 the average American consumed four gallons of absolute alcohol a year, the highest level in American history and nearly triple present-day levels. Anne Royale, whose travels took her cross-country by stage, reported, "When I was in Virginia, it was too much whiskey—in Ohio, too much whiskey—in Tennessee, it is too, too much whiskey!" The social costs for such habits were high: broken families, abused and neglected wives and children, sickness and disability, poverty, and crime. The temperance movement undertook to eliminate these problems by curbing drinking.

Led largely by clergy, the movement at first focused on drunkenness and did not oppose moderate drinking. But in 1826 the American Temperance Society was founded, taking voluntary abstinence as its goal. During the next decade approximately 5000 local temperance societies were founded. As the movement gained momentum, annual per capita consumption of alcohol dropped sharply. By 1845 it had fallen below two gallons a year.

The temperance movement lasted longer and attracted many more supporters than other reforms did. It appealed to young and old, to urban and rural residents, to workers and businesspeople. Moreover, it was one of the few reform movements with significant support in the South. Its success came partly for

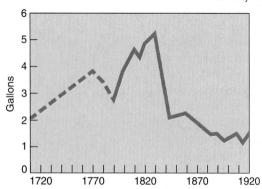

Annual Consumption of Distilled Spirits, per Capita, 1710–1920
Beginning in 1790, per capita levels of drinking steadily rose, until 1830, when the temperance movement produced a sharp decline over the next two decades.

social reasons. Democracy necessitated sober voters; factories required sober workers. In addition, temperance attracted the upwardly mobile—professionals, small businesspeople, and skilled artisans anxious to improve their social standing. Finally, temperance advocates stressed the suffering that men inflicted on women and children, and thus the movement appealed to women as a means to defend the home and carry out their domestic mission.

Educational Reform

In 1800 Massachusetts was the only state that required free public schools supported by community funds. The call for tax-supported education arose first among workers, as a way to restore their deteriorating position in society. But middle-class reformers quickly took control of the movement, looking to uplift the masses, make them responsible citizens, and preserve equal opportunity. Horace Mann, the leading proponent of common schools, hailed education as "the great equalizer of the conditions of men" and contended that it would eliminate poverty. Reformers appealed to business leaders by arguing that the new economic order needed educated workers.

Common school movement

Mann convinced Massachusetts to create a state board of education, which he oversaw from 1837 to 1848. Under his leadership, the state adopted a minimum-length school year, provided for training of teachers, and expanded the curriculum to include subjects such as history, geography, and various applied skills. Massachusetts also took the lead in requiring every town with a population of 500 or more to establish a high school. This innovation was slow to catch on elsewhere; by 1860 the nation could count only about 300 high schools, fully a third of them in Massachusetts. Moreover, compulsory attendance was rarely instated. Many poor parents out of necessity sent their children to work instead of school. Still, by the 1850s the number of schools, attendance figures, and school budgets had all increased sharply. School reformers enjoyed their greatest success in the Northeast and the least in the South, where planters opposed paying taxes to educate poorer white children.

Educational opportunities for women also expanded. Teachers like Catharine Beecher and Emma Hunt Willard established a number of private girls' schools, putting to rest the objection of many male educators that fragile female minds could not absorb large doses of mathematics, physics, or geography. In 1833 Oberlin became the nation's first coeducational college. Four years later Mary Lyon founded Mount Holyoke, the first American college for women.

Female education

The Asylum Movement

After 1820 there was also a dramatic increase in the number of asylums of every sort—orphanages, jails, and hospitals. Advocates of asylums called for isolating and separating the criminal, the insane, the ill, and the dependent from outside society. The goal of care in asylums, which had earlier focused on confinement, shifted to the reform of personal character.

American efforts to rehabilitate prisoners attracted international attention. Pennsylvania and New York developed systems to isolate prisoners, introducing the measures of solitary confinement and absolute silence to give inmates time to reflect on their past errors. The reformers assumed that environment produced criminal behavior and that the new prison routines would rehabilitate criminals. The new measures were not very effective, however, and under the strain of isolation some inmates went insane or committed suicide.

Prison reformers believed that rigid discipline, extensive rules, and (in some programs) solitary confinement were necessary to rehabilitate criminals. Prisoners often had to march lockstep under strict supervision and wear uniforms such as those seen in this photograph from the 1870s.

Dorothea Dix and the insane

Dorothea Dix, a Boston schoolteacher, took the lead in advocating state-supported asylums for the mentally ill. She attracted much attention to the movement by her report detailing the horrors to which the mentally ill were subjected, including being chained, kept in cages and closets, and beaten with rods. In response to her efforts, 28 states maintained mental institutions by 1860.

Like other reform movements, the push for new asylums and better educational facilities reflected overtones of both liberation and control. Asylums freed prisoners and the mentally ill from the harsh punishments and abuses of the past, but the new techniques of "rehabilitation" forced prisoners to march in lockstep. Education brought with it the freedom to question and to acquire knowledge, but some enthusiastic reformers hoped that schools would become as orderly as prisons. Louis Dwight, who advocated solitary confinement for prisoners at night and total silence by day, suggested eagerly that such methods "would greatly promote order, seriousness, and purity in large families, male and female boarding schools, and colleges."

Abolitionism

Late in the fall of 1834, Lyman Beecher was in the midst of his continuing efforts to "overturn and overturn" on behalf of the kingdom of God. As planned, he had gone to Cincinnati to assume leadership of Lane Seminary. The school had everything that an institution for training ministers to convert the West needed—everything, that is, except students. In October 1834 all but 8 of Lane's 100 scholars had departed after months of bitter fighting with Beecher and the trustees over the issue of abolition.

Beecher knew the source of his troubles: a scruffy yet magnetic student named Theodore Dwight Weld. Weld had been firing up his classmates over the need to immediately free the slaves. Beecher was not surprised, for Weld had been

William Lloyd Garrison (shown, left, at age 30) and Theodore Dwight Weld (right) represented different wings of the abolitionist movement. Garrison's growing radicalism led him to repudiate organized religion in the struggle against slavery. Weld, on the other hand, preferred to work through the evangelical churches and cooperate with the clergy.

converted by that firebrand Finney. He knew, too, that Weld had been influenced by the arguments of William Lloyd Garrison, whose abolitionist writings had sent shock waves across the entire nation. Indeed, Beecher's troubles at Lane Seminary provided only one example of how the flames of reform, when fanned, could spread along paths not anticipated by those who first kindled them.

The Beginnings of the Abolitionist Movement

William Lloyd Garrison symbolized the transition from a moderate antislavery movement to the more militant abolitionism of the 1830s. A sober, religious youngster deeply influenced by his Baptist mother, Garrison in the 1820s edited a newspaper sympathetic to many of the new reforms. In 1829 he was enlisted in the antislavery cause by Benjamin Lundy, a Quaker who edited a Baltimore antislavery newspaper, *The Genius of Universal Emancipation*. Calling for a gradual end to slavery, Lundy supported colonization, a strategy for overcoming southern fears of emancipation by transporting free black Americans to Africa.

Embracing colonization, Garrison went to Baltimore to help edit Lundy's paper. It was there that Garrison first encountered the opinions of free African Americans, who played a major role in the genesis of the abolitionist movement. To his surprise, Garrison discovered that most of them strongly opposed the colonization movement as proslavery and antiblack. "This is our home, and this is our country," a free black convention proclaimed in 1831. "Beneath its sod lie the bones of our fathers; for it some of them fought, bled, and died. Here we were born, and here we will die." Under their influence, Garrison soon developed views far more radical than Lundy's, and within a year of moving to Baltimore, the young firebrand was convicted of libel and imprisoned. Upon his release Garrison hurried back to Boston, determined to publish a new kind of antislavery journal.

On January 1, 1831, the first issue of *The Liberator* appeared, and abolitionism was born. In appearance, the bespectacled Garrison seemed frail, almost mousy. In print, however, he was abrasive, withering, and uncompromising. "On this subject,

Free blacks oppose colonization

I do not wish to think, or speak, or write with moderation," he proclaimed. "I am in earnest—I will not equivocate—I will not excuse—I will not retreat a single inch—AND I WILL BE HEARD." Repudiating gradual emancipation and embracing "immediatism," Garrison insisted that slavery end at once. He denounced colonization as a racist, antiblack movement and upheld the principle of racial equality. To those who suggested that slaveowners should be compensated for freeing their slaves, Garrison was firm. Southerners ought to be convinced by "moral suasion" to renounce slavery as a sin. Virtue was its own reward.

Garrison attracted the most attention, but other abolitionists spoke with equal conviction. Wendell Phillips, from a socially prominent Boston family, held listeners spellbound with his speeches. Lewis Tappan and his brother Arthur, two New York City silk merchants, boldly placed their wealth behind a number of humanitarian causes, including abolitionism. James G. Birney, an Alabama slaveholder, converted to abolitionism after wrestling with his conscience, and Angelina and Sarah Grimké, the daughters of a South Carolina planter, left their native state to speak against the institution. And there was Angelina's future husband, Theodore Weld, the restless student at Lane Seminary who had fallen so dramatically under Garrison's influence.

To abolitionists, slavery was a moral, not an economic, question. The institution seemed a contradiction of the principle of the American Revolution that all human beings had been created with natural rights. Then, too, it went against the Romantic spirit of the age, which celebrated the individual's freedom and self-reliance. Abolitionists condemned slavery because of the breakup of marriages and families by sale, the harsh punishment of the lash, slaves' lack of access to education, and the sexual abuse of black women. Most of all, they denounced slavery as outrageously contrary to Christian teaching. As one Ohio antislavery paper declared, "We believe slavery to be a sin, always, everywhere, and only, sin—sin, in itself." So persistent were abolitionists in their religious objections that they forced the churches to face the question of slavery head-on. In the 1840s the Methodist and Baptist churches each split into northern and southern organizations over the issue.

The Spread of Abolitionism

After helping organize the New England Anti-Slavery Society in 1832, Garrison joined with Lewis Tappan and Theodore Weld the following year to establish a national organization, the American Anti-Slavery Society. It coordinated a loosely affiliated network of state and local societies. During the years before the Civil War, perhaps 200,000 northerners belonged to an abolitionist society.

Abolitionists were concentrated in the East, especially New England, and in areas that had been settled by New Englanders, such as western New York and northern Ohio. The movement was not strong in cities or among businesspeople and workers. Most abolitionists were young, being generally in their twenties and thirties when the movement began, and had grown up in rural areas and small towns in middle-class families. Intensely religious, many had been profoundly affected by the revivals of the Second Great Awakening. Whatever their background, they shared a deep alienation from American society—its crass materialism, its shallow politics, and its lack of religion. More and more they came to feel that slavery was the fundamental cause of the Republic's degraded condition.

Certainly Theodore Weld was cut from this mold. After enrolling in Lane Seminary in 1833, he promoted immediate abolitionism among his fellow students.

When Lyman Beecher assumed the Lane presidency a year later, he confronted a student body dominated by committed abolitionists, impatient of any position that stopped short of Garrison's immediatism.

The radicalism of Lane students was also made clear in their commitment to racial equality. Unlike some abolitionists, who opposed slavery but disdained blacks as inferior, Lane students mingled freely with Cincinnati's free black community. Alarmed by rumors in the summer of 1834 that the town's residents intended to demolish the school, Beecher and Lane's trustees forbade any discussion of slavery on campus, restricted contact with the black community, and ordered students to return to their studies. "Who that has an opinion and a soul will enter L. Sem now?" one rebel asked. "Who can do it without degrading himself?" All except a few left the school and enrolled at Oberlin College. That debt-ridden institution agreed to their demands for guaranteeing freedom of speech, admitting black students, and hiring Charles Finney as professor of theology.

But Finney fared no better than Beecher with the Lane rebels. In the end, he too concluded that reform generated discord, distracting Christians from the greater good of promoting revivals. Both men conceived of sin in terms of individual immorality, not unjust social institutions. To the abolitionists, however, America could never become a godly nation until slavery was abolished. "Revivals, moral Reform, etc. will remain stationary until the temple is cleansed," Weld bluntly concluded.

Free African Americans, who made up the majority of subscribers to Garrison's *Liberator,* provided important support and leadership for the movement. Frederick Douglass assumed the greatest prominence. Having escaped from slavery in Maryland, he became an eloquent critic of its evils. Initially a follower of Garrison, Douglass eventually broke with him and started his own newspaper in Rochester. Other important black abolitionists included Martin Delany, William Wells Brown, William Still, and Sojourner Truth. Most black Americans endorsed peaceful means to end slavery, but David Walker in his *Appeal to the Colored Citizens of the World* (1829) urged slaves

Lane Seminary rebellion

Black abolitionists

Black abolitionist Frederick Douglass (second from left at the podium) was only one of nearly 50 runaway slaves who appeared at an abolitionist convention held in August 1850 in Cazenovia, New York. Other runaways included Emily and Mary Edmonson (both in plaid dresses). When the Edmonsons' attempt at escape failed, Henry Ward Beecher (Lyman Beecher's son) rallied his congregation in Brooklyn to raise the money to purchase the girls' freedom.

to use violence to end bondage. Aided by many other African Americans, these men and women battled against racial discrimination in the North as well as slavery in the South.

A network of antislavery sympathizers also developed in the North to convey runaway slaves to Canada and freedom. While not as extensive or as tightly organized as contemporaries claimed, the Underground Railroad hid fugitives and transported them northward from one station to the next. Free African Americans, who were more readily trusted by wary slaves, played a leading role in the Underground Railroad. One of its most famous conductors was Harriet Tubman, an escaped slave who repeatedly returned to the South and eventually escorted to freedom more than 200 slaves.

Opponents and Divisions

The drive for immediate abolition faced massive obstacles within American society. With slavery increasingly important to the South's economy, Southerners forced opponents of slavery to flee the region. In the North, where racism was equally entrenched, abolitionism provoked bitter resistance. Even abolitionists such as Garrison treated blacks paternalistically, contending that they should occupy a subordinate place in the antislavery movement.

On occasion, northern resistance turned violent. A hostile Boston mob seized Garrison in 1835 and paraded him with a rope around his body before he was finally rescued. Another anti-abolitionist mob burned down the headquarters of the American Anti-Slavery Society in Philadelphia. And in 1837 in Alton, Illinois, Elijah Lovejoy was murdered when he tried to protect his printing press from an angry crowd. The leaders of these mobs were not from the bottom of society but, as one of their victims noted, were "gentlemen of property and standing." Prominent leaders in the community, they reacted vigorously to the threat that abolitionists posed to their power and prosperity and to the established order.

Divisions among abolitionists

But abolitionists were also hindered by divisions among reformers. At Oberlin College Charles Finney preferred revivalism over Theodore Weld's abolitionism. Even more conservative than Finney, Lyman Beecher was shocked to hear that his son Edward had stood guard over Elijah Lovejoy's printing press the evening before the editor was murdered. Within another decade, Beecher would see his daughter Harriet Beecher Stowe write the most successful piece of antislavery literature in the nation's history, *Uncle Tom's Cabin*. Even the abolitionists themselves splintered, shaken by the opposition they encountered and unable to agree on the most effective response. More conservative reformers wanted to work within established institutions, using the churches and political action to end slavery. But for Garrison and his followers, the mob violence demonstrated that slavery was only part of a deeper national disease, whose cure required the overthrow of American institutions and values.

By the end of the decade, Garrison had worked out a program for the total reform of society. He embraced perfectionism and pacifism, denounced the clergy, urged members to leave the churches, and called for an end to all government. Condemning the Constitution as proslavery—"a covenant with death and an agreement with hell"—he publicly burned a copy one July 4th. No person of conscience, he argued, could vote or otherwise participate in the corrupt political system. This platform was radical enough on all counts, but the final straw for Garrison's opponents was his endorsement of women's rights as an inseparable part of abolitionism.

The Women's Rights Movement

Women faced many disadvantages in American society. They were kept out of most jobs, denied political rights, and given only limited access to education beyond the elementary grades. When a woman married, her husband became the legal representative of the marriage and gained complete control of her property. If a marriage ended in divorce, the husband was awarded custody of the children. Any unmarried woman was made the ward of a male relative.

When abolitionists divided over the issue of female participation, women found it easy to identify with the situation of slaves, since both were victims of male tyranny. Sarah and Angelina Grimké took up the cause of women's rights after they were criticized for speaking to audiences that included men as well as women. Sarah responded with *Letters on the Condition of Women and the Equality of the Sexes* (1838), arguing that women deserved the same rights as men. Abby Kelly, another abolitionist, remarked that women "have good cause to be grateful to the slave," for in "striving to strike his irons off, we found most surely, that we were manacled *ourselves*."

Two abolitionists, Elizabeth Cady Stanton and Lucretia Mott, launched the women's rights movement after they were forced to sit behind a curtain at a world antislavery convention in London. In 1848 Stanton and Mott organized a conference in Seneca Falls, New York, that attracted about a hundred supporters. The meeting issued a Declaration of Sentiments, modeled after the Declaration of Independence, that began, "All men and women are created equal."

Seneca Falls convention

The Seneca Falls convention approved resolutions calling for educational and professional opportunities for women, laws giving them control of their property, recognition of legal equality, and repeal of laws awarding the father custody of the children in divorce. The most controversial proposal, and the only resolution that did not pass unanimously, was one demanding the right to vote. The Seneca Falls convention established the arguments and the program for the women's rights movement for the remainder of the century.

The women's rights movement won few victories before 1860. Several states gave women greater control over their property, and a few made divorce easier or granted women the right to sue in courts. But disappointments and defeats outweighed these early victories. Still, many of the important leaders in the crusade for women's rights that emerged after the Civil War had already taken their places at the forefront of the movement. They included Stanton, Susan B. Anthony, Lucy Stone, and—as Lyman Beecher by now must have expected, one of his daughters—Isabella Beecher Hooker.

Elizabeth Cady Stanton, one of the instigators and guiding spirits at the Seneca Falls convention, photographed with two of her children about that time.

The Schism of 1840

It was Garrison's position on women's rights that finally split antislavery ranks already divided over other aspects of his growing radicalism. The showdown came in 1840 at the national meeting of the American Anti-Slavery Society, when delegates debated whether women could hold office in the organization. Some of Garrison's opponents favored women's rights but opposed linking the question to the slavery issue, insisting that it would drive off potential supporters. By packing the convention, Garrison carried the day. His opponents, led by Lewis Tappan, resigned to found the rival American and Foreign Anti-Slavery Society.

The schism of 1840 lessened the influence of abolitionism as a benevolent reform movement in American society. Although abolitionism heightened moral concern about slavery, it failed to convert the North to its program, and its supporters remained a tiny minority. For all the considerable courage they showed, their movement suffered from the lack of a realistic, long-range plan for eliminating so deeply entrenched an institution. Garrison even boasted that "the genius of the abolitionist movement is to have *no* plan." Abolitionism demonstrated the severe limits of moral suasion and individual conversions as a solution to deeply rooted social problems.

Reform Shakes the Party System

"What a fog-bank we are in politically! Do you see any head-land or light—or can you get an observation—or soundings?" The words came from a puzzled Whig politician writing a friend after the Massachusetts state elections of 1853. He was in such a confused state because reformers were increasingly entering the political arena to achieve results.

Reform enters politics

The crusading idealism of revivalists and reformers inevitably collided with the hard reality that society could not be perfected by converting individuals. In America's democratic society, politics and government coercion promised a more effective means to impose a new moral vision on the nation. Several movements, including those to establish public schools and erect asylums, had operated within the political system from the beginning. A growing number of other frustrated reformers abandoned the principle of voluntary persuasion and looked to governmental coercion to achieve their goals.

Politicians did not particularly welcome the new interest. Because the Whig and Democratic parties both drew on evangelical and nonevangelical voters, heated moral debates over the harmful effects of drink or the evils of slavery threatened to detach regular party members from their old loyalties and disrupt each party's unity. The strong opposition of German and Irish immigrants to temperance stimulated antiforeign sentiment among reformers and further divided both party coalitions, particularly the Democrats. "The temperance question is playing havock in the old party lines," commented one Indiana politician. The issue of abolition seemed even more disruptive.

Women and the Right to Vote

As the reform impulse shifted toward the political arena, women in particular lost influence. As major participants in the benevolent organizations of the 1820s and 1830s, they had used their efforts on behalf of "moral suasion." But because women could not vote, they felt excluded when the temperance and abolitionist movements turned to electoral action to accomplish their goals. By the 1840s female reformers increasingly demanded the right to vote as the means to change society. Nor were men blind to what was at stake: one reason they so strongly resisted female suffrage was because it would give women real power.

Previously, many female reformers had accepted the right of petition as their most appropriate political activity. But *The Lily,* a women's rights paper, soon changed its tack. "Why shall [women] be left only the poor resource of petition?" it asked. "For even petitions, when they are from women, without the elective franchise to give them backbone, are of but little consequence."

The Maine Law

The political parties could resist the women's suffrage movement because most of its advocates lacked the right to vote. Less easily put off were temperance reformers. Although drinking had significantly declined in American society by 1840, it had hardly been eliminated. After 1845 the arrival of large numbers of German and Irish immigrants, who were accustomed to consuming alcohol, made voluntary prohibition even more remote. In response, temperance advocates proposed state laws that would outlaw the manufacture and sale of alcoholic beverages. If liquor was unavailable, reformers reasoned, drinkers would be forced to reform whether they wanted to or not.

Struggle over prohibition

Party leaders tried to dodge the question of prohibition, since large numbers of Whigs and Democrats were found on both sides of the question. Temperance advocates countered with a strategy of endorsing the legislative candidates who pledged to support a prohibitory law. To win additional recruits, temperance leaders adopted techniques used in political campaigns, including house-to-house canvasses, parades and processions, bands and singing, banners, picnics, and mass rallies.

The movement's first major triumph came in 1851 in Maine. The Maine Law, as it was known, authorized search and seizure of private property and provided stiff penalties for selling liquor. In the next few years a number of states enacted similar laws, although most were struck down by the courts or later repealed. Prohibition remained a controversial political issue throughout the century.

Although prohibition was temporarily defeated, the issue badly disrupted the Whig and Democratic parties. It detached a number of voters from both coalitions, greatly increased the extent of party switching, and brought to the polls a large number of new voters, including many "wets" who wanted to preserve their right to drink. By dissolving the ties between so many voters and their parties, the temperance issue played a major role in the eventual collapse of the Jacksonian party system in the 1850s.

Abolitionism and the Party System

Abolition was the most divisive issue to come out of the benevolent reform movement. In 1835 abolitionists distributed more than a million pamphlets, mostly in the South, through the post office. A wave of excitement swept the South when the first batches arrived addressed to white southerners. Former senator Robert Hayne led a Charleston mob that burned sacks of U.S. mail containing abolitionist literature, and postmasters in other southern cities refused to deliver the material. The Jackson administration allowed southern states to censor the mail, leading abolitionists to protest that their civil rights had been violated. In reaction, the number of antislavery societies in the North nearly tripled.

Censorship of the mails

With access to the mails impaired, abolitionists began flooding Congress with petitions against slavery. Asserting that Congress had no power over the institution, angry southern representatives demanded action, and the House in response adopted the so-called gag rule in 1836. It automatically tabled without consideration any petition dealing with slavery. But southern leaders had made a tactical blunder. The gag rule allowed abolitionists not only to attack slavery but also to

Gag rule

speak out as defenders of white civil liberties. The appeal of the antislavery movement was broadened, and in 1844 the House finally repealed the controversial rule.

Many abolitionists outside Garrison's extreme circle began to feel that an antislavery third party offered a more effective means of attacking slavery. In 1840 these political abolitionists founded the Liberty party and nominated for president James Birney, a former slaveholder who had converted to abolitionism. Birney received only 7000 votes, but the Liberty party was the seed from which a stronger antislavery political movement would grow. From 1840 onward, abolitionism's importance would be in the political arena rather than as a voluntary reform organization.

After two decades of fiery revivals, benevolent crusades, utopian experiments, and Transcendental philosophizing, the ferment of reform had spread through urban streets, canal town churches, frontier clearings, and the halls of Congress. Abolition, potentially the most dangerous issue, seemed still under control in 1840. Birney's small vote, coupled with the disputes between the two national antislavery societies, encouraged political leaders to believe that the party system had turned back this latest threat of sectionalism. But the growing northern concern about slavery highlighted differences between the two sections. Despite the strength of evangelicalism in the South, the reform impulse spawned by the revivals found little support there, since reform movements were discredited by their association with abolitionism. The party system confronted the difficult challenge of holding together sections that, although sharing much, were also diverging in important ways. To the residents of both sections, the South increasingly appeared to be a unique society with its own distinctive way of life.

chapter summary

The Jacksonian era produced the greatest number of significant reform movements in American history.

- The movements grew out of the revivals of the Second Great Awakening, which emphasized emotion and preached the doctrines of good works and salvation available to all.

  - Evangelical Protestantism also endorsed the ideals of perfectionism and millennialism.

  - The revival theologies helped people adjust to the pressures in their daily lives created by the new market economy.

- Romanticism, which emphasized the unlimited potential of each individual, also strengthened reform.

- Women's role in society was now defined by the ideal of domesticity—that women's lives should center on the home and the family.

- Middle-class women turned to religion and reform as ways to shape society.

- Utopian communities sought to establish a model society for the rest of the world to follow.

- Humanitarian movements combated a variety of social evils.

  - Crusades for temperance, educational reform, and the establishment of asylums all gained significant support.

  - Abolitionism precipitated both strong support and violent opposition, and the movement itself split in 1840.

- Temperance, abolitionism, and women's rights movements each turned to political action to accomplish their goals.

- Although it survived, the party system was seriously weakened by these reform movements.

interactive learning

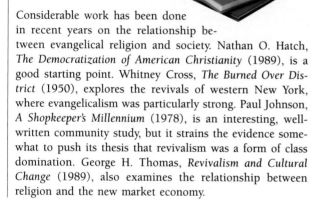

The Primary Source Investigator CD-ROM offers the following materials related to this chapter:

- A collection of primary sources exploring the growing fever for reform in the United States, including Abraham Lincoln's discussion of the Declaration of Independence and the Constitution in regards to slavery and the Declaration of Sentiments, an appeal to Americans for equal treatment of women. Other sources include a certificate of freedom for Harriet Bolling in Petersburg, Virginia; a newspaper produced for a nineteenth century factory; and an image of a homespun stocking.

additional reading

Considerable work has been done in recent years on the relationship between evangelical religion and society. Nathan O. Hatch, *The Democratization of American Christianity* (1989), is a good starting point. Whitney Cross, *The Burned Over District* (1950), explores the revivals of western New York, where evangelicalism was particularly strong. Paul Johnson, *A Shopkeeper's Millennium* (1978), is an interesting, well-written community study, but it strains the evidence somewhat to push its thesis that revivalism was a form of class domination. George H. Thomas, *Revivalism and Cultural Change* (1989), also examines the relationship between religion and the new market economy.

Ronald G. Walters, *American Reformers, 1815–1860* (1978), presents a general history of the reform impulse. A fuller treatment, with more emphasis on evangelical religion, is Alice Felt Tyler, *Freedom's Ferment* (1944), which captures the era's heady optimism. Good discussions of the concept of domesticity and women's lives can be found in Carl Degler, *At Odds* (1977), and Nancy Cott, *The Bonds of Womanhood* (1977). Mary P. Ryan, *The Cradle of the Middle Class* (1981), skillfully traces the connection between economic transformation and family structure. Specific reform movements are analyzed in Carl F. Kaestle, *Pillars of the Republic* (1983), which addresses the common school movement; Ellen C. DuBois, *Feminism and Suffrage* (1978); and James B. Stewart, *Holy Warriors* (1976), which is the best study of abolitionism. Lori D. Ginzberg, *Women and the Work of Benevolence* (1990), and Barbara Epstein, *The Politics of Domesticity* (1981), examine women's participation in reform. For a fuller list of readings, see the Bibliography at www.mhhe.com/davidsonnation5.

significant events

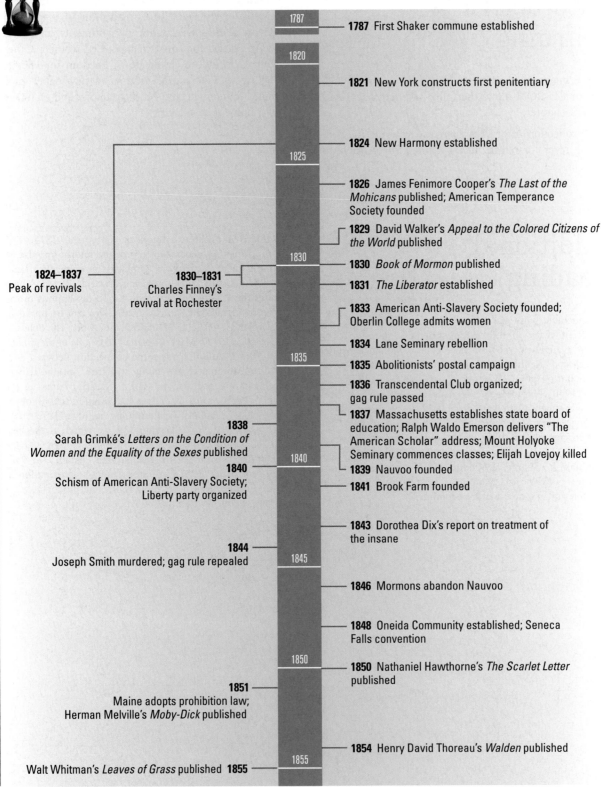

1787 First Shaker commune established

1820

1821 New York constructs first penitentiary

1824 New Harmony established

1825

1826 James Fenimore Cooper's *The Last of the Mohicans* published; American Temperance Society founded

1829 David Walker's *Appeal to the Colored Citizens of the World* published

1830 *Book of Mormon* published

1831 *The Liberator* established

1833 American Anti-Slavery Society founded; Oberlin College admits women

1834 Lane Seminary rebellion

1835 Abolitionists' postal campaign

1836 Transcendental Club organized; gag rule passed

1837 Massachusetts establishes state board of education; Ralph Waldo Emerson delivers "The American Scholar" address; Mount Holyoke Seminary commences classes; Elijah Lovejoy killed

1839 Nauvoo founded

1841 Brook Farm founded

1843 Dorothea Dix's report on treatment of the insane

1846 Mormons abandon Nauvoo

1848 Oneida Community established; Seneca Falls convention

1850 Nathaniel Hawthorne's *The Scarlet Letter* published

1854 Henry David Thoreau's *Walden* published

1824–1837
Peak of revivals

1830–1831
Charles Finney's revival at Rochester

1838
Sarah Grimké's *Letters on the Condition of Women and the Equality of the Sexes* published

1840
Schism of American Anti-Slavery Society; Liberty party organized

1844
Joseph Smith murdered; gag rule repealed

1851
Maine adopts prohibition law; Herman Melville's *Moby-Dick* published

Walt Whitman's *Leaves of Grass* published **1855**

Chapter 13

The impeccably dressed Colonel Daniel Jordan, master of 261 slaves at Laurel Hill, strolls down his oak-lined lawn to the dock along the Waccamaw River, a day's journey north of Charleston, to board the steamship *Nina*. On Fridays, it is Colonel Jordan's custom to visit the exclusive Hot and Hot Fish Club, founded by his fellow low-country planters, to play a game of lawn bowling or billiards and be waited on by black servants in livery as he sips a mint julep in the refined atmosphere that for him is the South.

Several hundred miles to the west another steamboat, the *Fashion*, makes its way along the Alabama River near the village of Claiborne. One of the passengers is upset by the boat's slow pace. He has been away from his plantation in the Red River country of Texas and is eager to get back. "Time's money, time's money!" he mutters to anyone who will listen. "Time's worth more'n money to me now; a hundred percent more, 'cause I left my niggers all alone; not a damn white man within four mile on 'em." When asked what they are doing, since the cotton crop has already been picked, he says, "I set 'em to clairin', but they ain't doin' a damn thing. . . . I know that as well as you do. . . . But I'll make it up, I'll make it up when I get thar, now you'd better believe." For this Red River planter, time is money and cotton is his world—indeed, cotton is what the South is all about. "I am a cotton man, I am, and I don't car who knows it," he proclaims. "I know cotton, I do. I'm dam' if I know anythin' but cotton."

The Old South

1820–1860

preview • In the decades before the Civil War, the rural South depended on the export of staple crops like rice, tobacco, sugar, and cotton—and the slave labor used to produce them. Though most southern whites did not own slaves, those who did reaped prestige, political influence, and wealth. Excluded from white society, enslaved African Americans resisted bondage and developed their own culture, whose religion, songs, and shared experiences helped them survive a cruel and arbitrary regime.

At the other end of the South, the slave Sam Williams works in the intense heat of Buffalo Forge, an iron-making factory nine miles from Lexington, Virginia, in the Shenandoah Valley. As a refiner, Williams has the most important job at the forge, alternately heating pig iron in the white-hot coals, then slinging the ball of glowing metal on an anvil, where he pounds it with huge, water-powered hammers to remove the impurities. Ambitious and hard working, he earns extra money (at the same rate paid to whites) for any iron he produces beyond his weekly quota. In some years his extra income is more than $100. His wife, Nancy, who is in charge of the dairy, earns extra money as well, and their savings accounts at the local bank total more than $150. Additional income allows them to buy extra food and items for themselves and their four daughters, but more important, it helps keep their family intact in an unstable environment. They know that their owner is very unlikely to sell away slaves who work so hard. For Sam and Nancy Williams, family ties, worship at the local Baptist church, and socializing with their fellow slaves are what make life important.

In the bayous of the Deep South, only a few miles from where the Mississippi delta meets the Gulf, Octave Johnson hears the dogs coming. For over a year now Johnson has been a runaway slave. He fled from a Louisiana plantation in St. James

Plantation Burial, painted about 1860 by John Antrobus, portrays the black slave community from a Louisiana plantation burying a loved one. Religion played a central role in the lives of slaves.

Parish when the work bell rang before daybreak and the overseer threatened to whip him for staying in bed. To survive, he hides in the swamps four miles behind the plantation—stealing turkeys, chickens, and pigs and trading with other slaves. As uncertain as this life is, nearly 30 other slaves have joined him over the past year.

The sound of the dogs warns Johnson and his companions that the hound master Eugene Jardeau is out again. This time when the pack bursts upon them, the slaves do not flee but kill as many dogs as possible. Then they plunge into the bayou, and as the hounds follow, alligators make short work of another six. For Octave Johnson the real South is a matter of weighing one's prospects between the uncertainties of alligators and the overseer's whip—and deciding when to say no.

Ferdinand Steel and his family are not forced, by the flick of the lash, to rise at five in the morning. They rise because the land demands it. Steel, in his twenties, owns 170 acres of land in Carroll County, Mississippi. Unmarried, he moved there from Tennessee with his widowed mother, sister, and brother in 1836, only a few years after the Choctaws had been forced to give up the region and march west. His life is one of continuous hard work, caring for the animals and tending the crops. His mother, Eliza, and sister, Julia, have plenty to keep them busy: making soap, fashioning dippers out of gourds, or sewing.

The Steel family grows cotton, too, but not with the single-minded devotion of the planter aboard the *Fashion*. Self-sufficiency and family security always come first, and Steel's total crop amounts to only five or six bales. His profit is never sufficient to consider buying even one slave. In fact, he would have preferred not to raise any cotton—"We are to[o] weak handed," he says—but the five bales mean cash, and cash means that when he goes to market in nearby Grenada, he can buy sugar and coffee, gunpowder and lead, a yard or two of calico, and quinine to treat the malaria that is so common in those parts. Though fiercely independent, Steel and his scattered neighbors help each other raise houses, clear fields, shuck corn, or quilt. They depend on one another and are bound together by blood, religion, obligation, and honor. For small farmers like Ferdinand Steel, these ties constitute the real South.

The portraits could go on: different people, different Souths, all of them real. Such contrasts underscore the difficulty of trying to define a regional identity. Encompassing in 1860 the 15 slave states plus the District of Columbia, the South was a land of great geographic diversity. It extended from the Tidewater coastal plain along the Atlantic seaboard to the prairies of Texas, from the Kentucky bluegrass region to the Gulf coast, from the mountains of western Virginia to the swamps of the Mississippi delta with its semitropical climate. The only geographic feature that separated the North and South was the Ohio River, and it was an avenue of trade rather than a source of division.

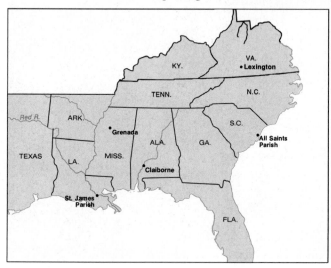

The Diverse South

Yet despite its many differences of people and geography, the South was bonded by ties so strong, they eventually outpulled those of the nation itself. At the heart of this unity was an agricultural system that took advantage of the region's warm climate and long growing season. Cotton required 200 frost-free days, and rice and sugar even more, which meant that in the United States these staples could be grown only in the South. Most important, this rural agricultural economy was based on the institution of slavery, which had far-reaching effects on all aspects of southern society. It shaped not only the culture of the slaves themselves but also the lives of their masters and mistresses, and even of farm families and herders in the hills and backwoods who saw few slaves in their day-to-day existence. To understand the Old South, then, we must understand how the southern agricultural economy and the institution of slavery affected the social class structure of both white and black southerners.

The Social Structure of the Cotton Kingdom

We have already seen (in Chapter 10) that the spread of cotton stimulated the nation's remarkable economic growth after the War of 1812. Demand spurred by the textile industry sent the price of cotton soaring on the international market, and white southerners scrambled into the fresh lands of the Southwest to reap the profits to be made in the cotton sweepstakes.

The Boom Country Economy

Cotton pushes westward

Letters, newspapers, and word of mouth all brought tales of the black belt region of Alabama, where the dark soil was particularly suited to growing cotton, and of the tremendous yields from the soils along the Mississippi River's broad reaches. "The *Alabama Fever* rages here with great violence and has *carried off* vast numbers of our Citizens," a North Carolinian wrote in 1817. "I am apprehensive if it continues to spread as it has done, it will almost depopulate the country." A generation later, as the removal of the southern Indian tribes opened vast tracts of land to white settlement, immigrants were still "pouring in with a ceaseless tide," one observer reported, "including 'Land Sharks' ready to swallow up the home of the redmen, or the white, as oportunity might offer."

By the 1840s planters even began to leave Mississippi and Alabama—virgin territory at the turn of the century—to head for the new cotton frontier along the Red River and up into Texas. A decade later the northern visitor Frederick Law Olmsted came across many abandoned southern homesteads, which he called "Gone to Texas" farms. Amazingly, by the eve of the Civil War nearly a third of the total cotton crop came from *west* of the Mississippi River.

As Senator James Henry Hammond of South Carolina boasted in 1858, cotton was king in the Old South. True, the region devoted more acreage to corn, but cotton was the primary export and the major source of southern wealth. Indeed, by 1860 the United States produced three-fourths of the world's supply of cotton. This boom fueled the southern economy so strongly that following the depression of 1839–1843, the southern economy grew faster than that in the North. Even so, per capita income in the South remained below that of the free states, and wealth was not as evenly distributed in the plantation South as in northern agricultural areas.

Southern prosperity

This prosperity, however, masked basic problems in the economy—problems that would become more apparent after the Civil War. Much of the South's new wealth resulted from migration of its population to more productive western lands. The amount of prime agricultural land was limited, and once it was settled, the South could not sustain forever its rate of expansion. Nor did the shift in population alter the structure of the southern economy, stimulate technological change, improve the way goods were produced and marketed, or generate internal markets.

The single-crop agriculture practiced by southern farmers rapidly wore out the soil. Tobacco was a particularly exhaustive crop, and corn also rapidly drained nutrients. To restore their soils, planters and farmers in the Upper South increasingly shifted to wheat production, but because they now plowed their fields rather than using a hoe, this shift intensified soil erosion. Destruction of the forests, particularly in the Piedmont, where commercial agriculture now took hold, had the same effect, and many streams quickly silted up and were no longer navigable. Row-crop agriculture made floods and droughts more common. In addition, reliance on a single crop increased toxins and parasites in the soil, making southern agriculture more vulnerable to destruction than varied agriculture was.

Environmental impact of single-crop agriculture

Only the South's low population density mitigated the impact on the environment. More remote areas remained heavily forested, wetlands were still common, and as late as 1860 eighty percent of the region was uncultivated (cattle and hogs, however, ranged over much of this acreage). Throughout much of the South, farmers fired the woods in the spring to destroy insects, burn off brush, and increase grass for their browsing stock.

Perhaps the most striking environmental consequence of the expansion of southern society was the increase in disease. The South, especially the Lower South, enjoyed a reputation for unhealthiness. Epidemic diseases such as malaria, yellow fever, and cholera were brought to the area by Europeans. The clearing of land—which increased runoff, precipitated floods, and produced pools of stagnant water—along with the growing white and black population, facilitated the spread of these diseases. In notoriously unhealthy areas, such as the coastal swamps of South Carolina's rice district, wealthy whites fled during the sickly summer months and were only part-time residents.

In this romanticized Currier and Ives print of a cotton plantation, field hands are waist-deep in cotton while other slaves haul the picked cotton to be ginned and then pressed into bales. Mounted on a horse, an overseer rides through the field supervising the work while the owner and his wife look on. Picking began as early as August and continued in some areas until late January. Because the bolls ripened at different times, a field had to be picked several times.

The Upper South's New Orientation

As cotton transformed the boom country of the Deep South, agriculture in the Upper South also adjusted.* Improved varieties and more scientific agricultural practices reversed the decline in tobacco that had begun in the 1790s. More important, however, farmers in the Upper South made wheat and corn their major crops. As early as 1840 the value of wheat grown in Virginia was twice that of tobacco.

Slave trade

Because the new crops required less labor, planters in the Upper South regularly sold their surplus slaves to cotton and sugar planters in the Deep South. Indeed, some planters in the Upper South maintained a profit margin only by these sales. The demand in the Deep South for field hands drove their price steadily up, so that by the late 1850s a prime field hand, who would have sold for $600 in the early 1840s, commanded $1500. Even with increased labor costs, southern agriculture flourished.

---

*The Upper South included the border states (Delaware, Maryland, Kentucky, and Missouri) and Virginia, North Carolina, Tennessee, and Arkansas. The states of the Deep South were South Carolina, Georgia, Florida, Alabama, Mississippi, Louisiana, and Texas.

The Rural South

The Old South, then, was dynamic, expanding, and booming economically. But the region remained overwhelmingly rural, with 84 percent of its labor force engaged in agriculture in 1860, compared with 40 percent in the North. Conversely, the South lagged in manufacturing, producing only 9 percent of the nation's manufactured goods. During the 1850s some southern propagandists urged greater investment in industry to diversify the South's economy. But as long as high profits from cotton continued, these advocates made little headway.

Lack of manufacturing

With so little industry, few cities developed in the South. New Orleans, with a population of 169,000 in 1860, was the only truly southern city of significant size. Only 1 in 10 southerners lived in cities and towns in 1860, compared with 1 out of 3 persons in the North. North Carolina, Alabama, Mississippi, Arkansas, and Texas did not contain a single city with a population of 10,000.

Absence of cities

As a rural society, the South evidenced far less interest in education. Southern colleges were inferior to those in the North, and public secondary schools were virtually nonexistent. Wealthy planters, who hired tutors or sent their children to private academies, generally opposed a state-supported school system. Thus free public schools were rare, especially in the rural districts that made up most of the South. Georgia in 1860 had only one county with a free school system, and Mississippi had

Cotton and Other Crops of the South By 1860, the cotton kingdom extended across the Lower South into the Texas prairie and up the Mississippi River valley. Tobacco and hemp were the staple crops of the Upper South, where they competed with corn and wheat. Rice production was concentrated in the swampy coastal region of South Carolina and Georgia as well as the lower tip of Louisiana. The sugar district was in southern Louisiana.

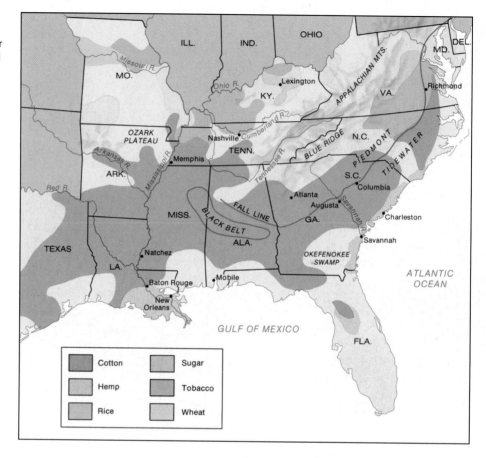

no public schools outside its few cities. On average southern white children spent only one-fifth as much time in school as did their northern counterparts.

The net result was that illiteracy rates were much higher in the South. Among native-born white citizens, the 1850 census showed that 20 percent were unable to read and write. The comparable figure was 3 percent in the middle states and 0.4 percent in New England. In some areas of the South, more than a third of all white residents were illiterate.

Distribution of Slavery

Even more than agrarian ways, slavery set the South apart. Whereas in 1776 slavery had been a national institution, by 1820 slavery was confined to the states south of Pennsylvania and the Ohio River. The South's "peculiar institution" bound white and black southerners together in a multitude of ways.

Slaves were not evenly distributed throughout the region. More than half lived in the Deep South, where African Americans outnumbered white southerners in both South Carolina and Mississippi by the 1850s. Elsewhere in the Deep South, the black population exceeded 40 percent in all states except Texas. In the Upper South, on the other hand, whites greatly outnumbered blacks. Only in Virginia and North Carolina did the slave population top 30 percent.

The distribution of slaves showed striking geographic variations within individual states as well. In areas of fertile soil, flat or rolling countryside, and good transportation, slavery and the plantation system dominated. In the pine barrens, areas isolated by lack of transportation, and hilly and mountainous regions, small family farms and few slaves were the rule.

Almost all enslaved African Americans, male and female, worked in agricultural pursuits, with only about 10 percent living in cities and towns. On large plantations, a few slaves were domestic servants and others were skilled artisans—blacksmiths, carpenters, or bricklayers—but most toiled in the fields. Only about 5 percent of the South's manufacturing employees in the 1850s were slaves like Sam Williams.

Slave occupations

Slavery as a Labor System

Slavery was, first and foremost, a system to manage and control labor. The plantation system, with its extensive estates and large labor forces, could never have developed without slavery, nor could it have met the world demand for cotton and other staples. Slaves represented an enormous capital investment, worth more than all the land in the Old South.

The Spread of Slavery, 1820–1860 Between 1820 and 1860, the slave population of the South shifted southward and westward, concentrating especially heavily in coastal South Carolina and Georgia, in the black belt of central Alabama and Mississippi (so named because of its rich soil), and in the Mississippi valley. Small farms with few slaves predominated in cotton-growing areas that lacked good transportation, such as northern Georgia, and in regions with poor soil, such as the piney woods of southern Mississippi.

Southern Population, 1860

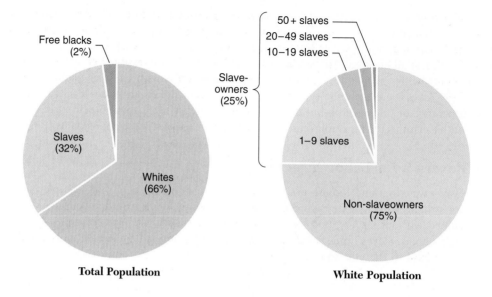

Total Population   White Population

Profitability of slavery

Furthermore, slavery remained a highly profitable investment. The average slaveowner spent perhaps $30 to $35 a year to support an adult slave; some expended as little as half that. Allowing for the cost of land, equipment, and other expenses, a planter could expect one of his slaves to produce more than $78 worth of cotton—which meant that even at the higher cost of support, a slaveowner took about 60 percent of the wealth produced by a slave's labor. For those who pinched pennies and drove slaves harder, the profits were even greater.

Slavery and aristocratic values

By concentrating wealth and power in the hands of the planter class, slavery shaped the tone of southern society. Planters were not aristocrats in the European sense of having special legal privileges or formal titles of rank. Still, the system encouraged southern planters to think of themselves as a landed gentry upholding the aristocratic values of pride, honor, family, and hospitality.

Whereas slavery had existed throughout most of the Americas at the beginning of the century, by the 1850s the United States, Cuba, and Brazil were the only slaveholding nations left in the region. Public opinion in Europe and in the North had grown more and more hostile to the peculiar institution, causing white southerners to feel increasingly like an embattled minority. Yet they clung tenaciously to slavery, for it was the base on which the South's economic growth and way of life rested. As one Georgian observed on the eve of the Civil War, slavery was "so intimately mingled with our social conditions that it would be impossible to eradicate it."

Class Structure of the White South

Once a year around Christmastime, James Henry Hammond gave a dinner for his neighbors at his South Carolina plantation, Silver Bluff. The richest man for miles around as well as an ambitious politician, the aristocratic Hammond used these dinners to put his neighbors under personal obligation to him as well as receive the honor and respect he believed his due. Indeed, Hammond's social and political ambitions caused him to carefully cultivate his neighbors, despite his low opinion of them, by hiring them to perform various tasks and by providing them a variety of services such as ginning their cotton and allowing them to use his grist mill. These services enhanced his ethic of paternalism, but his less affluent neighbors also displayed a strong personal pride. After he ungraciously complained about the inconvenience of these services, only three of his neighbors came to his Christmas dinner in 1837, a snub that enraged him. As Hammond's experience demonstrated, class relations among whites in the Old South were a complex blend of privilege, patronage, and equality.

The Slaveowners

In 1860 the region's 15 states had a population of 12 million, of which roughly two-thirds were white, one-third were black slaves, and about 2 percent were free African Americans. Because of the institution of slavery, the social structure of the antebellum South differed in important ways from that of the North. Even so, southern society was remarkably fluid, and as a result, class lines were not rigid.

Of the 8 million white southerners in 1860, only about 2 million (one-quarter) either owned slaves or were members of slaveowning families. Moreover, most slaveowners owned only a few slaves. If one uses the census definition of a planter as a person who owned 20 or more slaves, only about 1 out of every 30 white southerners belonged to families of the planter class.

A planter of consequence, however, needed to own at least 50 slaves, and there were only about 10,000 such families—less than 1 percent of the white population. This privileged group made up the aristocracy at the top of the southern class structure. Owners of large numbers of slaves were very rare; only about 2000 southerners such as Colonel Daniel Jordan owned 100 or more slaves. Although limited in size, the planter class nevertheless owned more than half of all slaves and controlled more than 90 percent of the region's total wealth.

The typical plantation had 20 to 50 slaves and 800 to 1000 acres of land. On an estate larger than that, slaves would have to walk more than an hour to reach the farthest fields, losing valuable work time. Thus larger slaveowners usually owned several plantations, with an overseer to manage the slaves on each while the owner attended to administrative and business matters. The slaves were divided into field hands, skilled workers, and house servants, with one or more slaves serving as "drivers" to assist the overseer. While planters pioneered the application of capitalistic methods, including specialization and division of labor, to agriculture, plantations remained labor-intensive operations. Only the production of sugar, among the southern staples, was heavily mechanized.

Plantation administration

Tidewater and Frontier

Southern planters shared a commitment to preserve slavery as the source of their wealth and stature. Yet in other ways they were a diverse group. On the one hand, the tobacco and rice planters of the Atlantic Tidewater were part of a settled region and a culture that reached back 150 to 200 years. States such as Mississippi and Arkansas, in contrast, were at or just emerging from the frontier stage, since most residents had arrived after 1815. Consequently, the society of the Southwest was rawer and more volatile.

It was along the Tidewater, especially the bays of the Chesapeake and the South Carolina coast, that the legendary "Old South" was born. Here, masters erected substantial homes, some of them—especially between Charleston and Columbia—the classic white-pillared mansions in the Greek revival style. Here, more than a few planters were urbane and polished.

Tidewater society

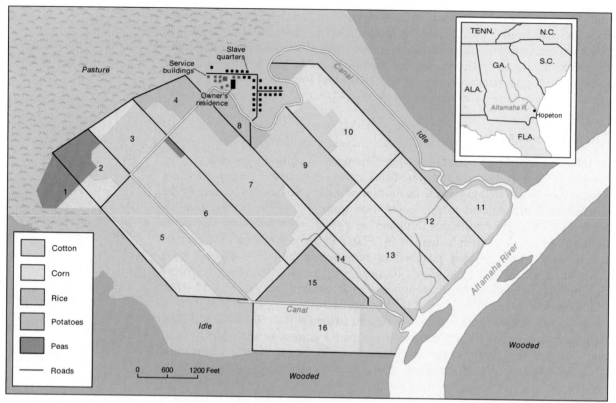

A Plantation Layout, Hopeton, Georgia Often covering a thousand acres or more, a plantation was laid out like a small village and contained several fields and usually extensive uncleared woods. Somewhere near the master's "big house" were the quarters—slave cabins clustered along one or more streets. Service buildings might include a smokehouse, stables, a gin house (for cotton) or a rice mill, and an overseer's dwelling. Like most large plantations, Hopeton produced a considerable amount of foodstuffs, but it grew both rice and cotton as staples. Most plantations concentrated on a single cash crop.

Society in the cotton kingdom

The ideal of the Tidewater South was the country gentleman of the English tradition. An Irish visitor observed that in Maryland and Virginia the great planters lived in "a style which approaches nearer to that of the English country gentleman than what is to be met with anywhere else on the continent." As in England, in the Tidewater South the local gentry often served as justices of the peace, and the Episcopal church remained the socially accepted road to heaven. Here, too, family names continued to be important in politics.

While the newer regions of the South boasted planters with cultivated manners, as a group the cotton lords were a different breed. They were basically entrepreneurs who had moved west for the same reason so many other Americans had: to make their fortunes. Some were planters, such as Thomas Dabney, fleeing the exhausted soils of the Tidewater; others were the sons of planters seeking to improve their lot. Not a few were northerners with an eye for opportunity, such as Henry Watson, who went south as a young tutor, settled in Greensboro, Alabama, and became a leading planter. Overseers sometimes rose into the ranks of slaveowners, as Ephraim Beanland of Mississippi did. Merchants and businessmen such as Maunsel White of New Orleans invested their profits in a plantation; land speculators rode the land grabs of the 1830s into the ranks of the elite. But by and large, the wealthy planters of the cotton gentry were self-made men, who through hard work, aggressive business tactics, and good luck had risen from ordinary backgrounds. For them, the cotton boom and the exploitation of enslaved men and women offered the opportunity to move up in a new society that lacked an entrenched elite.

Slaveholders' values

"Time's money, time's money." For men like the impatient Texan, time was indeed money, slaves were capital, and cotton by the bale signified cash in hand. This business orientation was especially apparent in the cotton kingdom, where planters sought to maximize their profits and constantly reinvested their returns in land and slaves. As one visitor said of Mississippi slaveholders: "To sell cotton in order to buy negroes—to make more cotton to buy more negroes, 'ad infinitum,' is the aim and direct tendency of all the operations of the thorough-going cotton planter: his whole soul is wrapped up in the pursuit." One shocked Virginian who visited Vicksburg claimed that its citizens ran "mad with speculation" and did business "in a kind of phrenzy." And indeed there was money to be made. The combined annual income of the richest thousand families of the cotton kingdom approached $50 million, while the wealth of the remaining 666,000 families amounted to only about $60 million.

This skillful portrait of John Stock, a wealthy South Carolina rice planter, depicts his aristocratic bearing and tastes.

Stately mansions could be found in a few areas of the cotton South. In general, though, most planters lived humbly. Although they ranked among the richest citizens in America, their homes were often simple one- or two-story unpainted wooden frame houses, and some were log cabins. A visitor to one Georgia plantation reported that the house did not have a pane of glass in the windows, a door between the rooms, or a ceiling other than the roof. "If you wish to see people worth millions living as [if] they were not worth hundreds," advised one southwestern planter in 1839, "come to the land of cotton and negroes."

Practical men, few of the new cotton lords had absorbed the culture and learning of the traditional country gentleman. During his extensive journeys in the South, the noted New Yorker Frederick Law Olmsted declared that he "did not see, except perhaps in one or two towns, a thermometer, nor a book of Shakespeare, nor a piano or sheet of music, nor a good reading lamp, nor an engraving or copy of any kind, or a work of art of the slightest merit. A large majority of all these houses were residences of slaveholders, a considerable proportion cotton planters."

The Master at Home

Whether supervising a Tidewater plantation or creating a cotton estate on the Texas frontier, the master had to coordinate a complex agricultural operation. He gave daily instructions concerning the work to be done, settled disputes between slaves and the overseer, and generally handed out rewards and penalties. In addition, the owner made the critical decisions concerning the planting, harvesting, and marketing of the crops. Planters also watched investments and expenditures, and they often sought to expand their production by clearing additional fields, buying more land or slaves, or investing in machinery such as cotton gins. As in any business, these decisions required a sound understanding of the domestic and international market as well as anticipation of future swings.

Paternalism

In performing his duties, the plantation owner was supposed to be the "master" of his crops, his family, and his slaves. Defenders of slavery held up this paternalistic ideal—the care and guidance of dependent "children"—maintaining that slavery promoted a genuine affection between caring master and loyal slaves.

In real life, however, market forces undermined this paternalistic ideal. Even in the Tidewater, planters were concerned with money and profits. Indeed, some of the most brutal forms of slavery existed on rice plantations, where the absenteeism of many owners combined with the sheer numbers of slaves made close personal ties impossible. Except for a few domestic servants, owners of large plantations had little contact with their slaves. Nor could paternalism mask the reality that slavery everywhere rested on violence, racism, and exploitation.

The Plantation Mistress

Upper-class southern white women, like those in the North, grew up with the ideal of domesticity, reinforced by the notion of a paternalistic master who was lord of the plantation. But the plantation mistress soon discovered that, given the demands placed on her, the ideal was hard to fulfill.

Mistress's duties

Growing up, a young genteel lady enjoyed a certain amount of leisure. But once she married and became a plantation mistress, a southern woman was often shocked by the magnitude of her responsibilities. Nursing the sick, making clothing, tending the garden, caring for the poultry, and overseeing every aspect of food preparation were all her domain. She also had to supervise and plan the work of the domestic servants and distribute clothing. After taking care of breakfast, one harried Carolina mistress recounted that she "had the [sewing] work cut out, gave orders about dinner, had the horse feed fixed in hot water, had the box filled with cork: went to see the carpenters working on the negro houses . . . now I have to cut out the flannel jackets." Sarah Williams, the New York bride of a North Carolina planter, admitted that her mother-in-law "works harder than any Northern farmer's wife I know."

Sarah Pierce Vick, the mistress of a plantation near Vicksburg, Mississippi, pauses to speak to one of her slaves, who may be holding feed for her horse. A plantation mistress had many duties and, while enjoying the comforts brought by wealth and status, often found her life more difficult than she had anticipated before marriage.

Unlike female reformers in the North, upper-class southern women did not openly challenge their role, but there is evidence that they found their sphere confining. The greatest unhappiness stemmed from the never-ending task of managing slaves. One southern mistress confessed, "I do not see how I can live my life amid these people! To be always among people whom I do not understand and whom I must guide, and teach and lead on like children. It frightens me." Yet without the labor of slaves, the lifestyle of these women was an impossibility.

Some women drew a parallel between their situation and that of the slaves. Both were subject to male dominance, and independent-minded women found the subordination of marriage difficult. Susan Dabney Smedes, in her recollection of growing up on an Alabama plantation, recalled that "it was a saying that the mistress of a plantation was the most complete slave on it." Some women particularly bristled at their lack of independence and at the necessity of obeying men. "How men can go blustering around, making everybody uncomfortable, simply to show that they are masters and we are only women and children at their mercy!" exclaimed Mary Chesnut, the wife of a South Carolina planter who termed her father-in-law "as absolute a tyrant as the Czar of Russia . . . or the Sultan of Turkey."

Miscegenation

Many women were deeply discontented, too, with the widespread double standard for sexual behavior and with the daily reminders of miscegenation some had to face. A man who fathered illegitimate children by slave women suffered no social or legal penalties, even in the case of rape (southern law did not recognize such a crime against slave women). On the other hand, a white woman guilty of adultery lost all social respectability.

Mary Chesnut, who knew the reality of miscegenation firsthand from her father-in-law's liaisons with slave women and discussed it more frankly than most, sneered in her diary at the assumptions of male superiority. "All the time they seem to think themselves patterns—models of husbands and fathers," she fumed, bitter at the enforced silence among wives. "Like the patriarchs of old, our men live all in one house with their wives and concubines; and the mulattoes one sees in every family partly resemble the white children. Any lady is ready to tell you who is the father of all the mulattoes one sees in everybody's household but her own. Those, she seems to think, drop from the clouds. My disgust sometimes is boiling over." One planter's wife spoke of "violations of the moral law that made mulattoes as common as blackberries," and another recalled, "I saw slavery in its bearing on my sex. I saw that it teemed with injustice and shame to all womankind and I hated it."

Still, only a small minority of women questioned either their place in southern society or the corrosive influence of slavery. Even fewer were willing to forgo the material comforts that slavery made possible. Moreover, racism was so pervasive within American society that the few white southern women who privately criticized the institution displayed little empathy for the plight of slaves themselves, including black women. Whatever the burdens of the plantation mistress, they were hardly akin to the bondage of slavery itself.

Yeoman Farmers

In terms of numbers, yeoman farm families were the backbone of southern society, accounting for more than half the southern white population. They owned no slaves and farmed the traditional 80 to 160 acres, like northern farmers. About 80 percent owned their own land, and the rest were tenant farmers who hoped one day to acquire a homestead. They settled almost everywhere in the South, except in the rice and sugar districts and valuable river bottomlands of the Deep South, which were monopolized by large slaveowners. Like Ferdinand Steel, most were semisubsistence farmers who raised primarily corn and hogs, along with perhaps a few bales of cotton or some tobacco, which they sold to obtain the cash needed to buy items like sugar, coffee, and salt. Some were not so much farmers as herdsmen, who set large herds of scrawny cattle or pigs to forage in the woods until it was time for the annual drive to market. Yeoman farmers lacked the wealth of planters, but they had a pride and dignity that earned them the respect of their richer neighbors.

Farmers and herders

Southern farmers led more isolated lives than their northern counterparts. Yet the social activities of these people were not much different from those of northern farmers. Religion played an important role at camp meetings held in late summer after the crops were laid by and before harvest time. As in the North, neighbors also met to exchange labor and tools, always managing to combine work with fun. The men rolled logs to clear fields of dead trees, turning the activity into a contest. Women met for quilting bees, and adults and children alike would gather to shuck corn. A Tennessee plain farmer recalled that his neighbors "seem to take delight in helping each other sutch as lay[ing] railings, cornshucking and house raising[.] they tried to help each other all they could and dancet all night." Court sessions, militia musters, political rallies—these too were occasions that brought rural folk together.

Because yeoman farmers lacked cheap slave labor, good transportation, and access to credit, they could not compete with planters in the production of staples. When it came to selling their corn and wheat, small farmers conducted only limited

Limits to economic opportunity

A majority of white southerners were members of nonslavehold-ing yeoman farm families. Ruggedly independent, these families depended on their own labor and lived under more primitive conditions than large plantation owners or small farmers in the North. Basil Hall, an Englishman traveling through the South in 1827 and 1828, sketched members of this Geor-gia family with the aid of a cam-era lucida, an optical device that projected an image from real life onto paper, where it could be traced with accuracy.

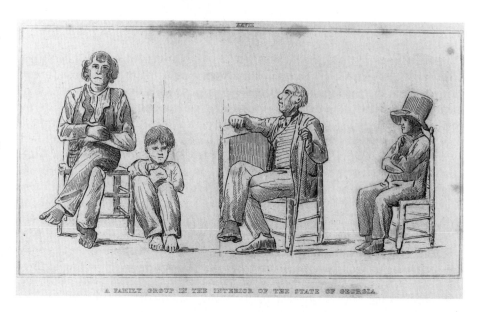

A FAMILY GROUP IN THE INTERIOR OF THE STATE OF GEORGIA.

business with planters, who usually grew as many of their own foodstuffs as pos-sible. In the North urban centers became a market for small farmers, but in the South the lack of towns limited this internal market.

Thus while southern yeoman farmers were not poor, they suffered from a chronic lack of money and the absence of conveniences that northern farm families enjoyed, such as cast-iron stoves, sewing machines, specialized tools, and good furniture. A few chafed at the absence of public schools and greater opportunities. Josiah Hinds, who hacked a farm out of the isolated woods of northern Mississippi, worried that his children were growing up "wild." He complained that "education is but little prized by my neighbours," who were satisfied "if the corn and cotton grows to per-fection . . . [and] brings a fare price, and hog meat is at hand to boil with the greens."

Absence of class conflict

In some ways, then, the worlds of yeoman farmers and upper-class planters were not only different but also in conflict. Still, a hostility between the two classes did not emerge. Yeoman farmers admired planters and hoped that one day they would join the gentry themselves. And even white southerners who owned no slaves accepted slavery as a means of controlling African Americans as members of an inferior social caste based on race. "Now suppose they was free," one poor farmer told Frederick Law Olmsted. "You see they'd all think themselves as good as we." Racism and fear of black people were sufficient to keep nonslaveholders loyal to southern institutions.

Poor Whites

The poorest white southerners were confined to land that no one else wanted: the wiregrass region of southeastern Georgia, the sand hills of central South Carolina, the pine barrens of the coastal plains from Virginia to southeastern Mississippi. In their backgrounds they were similar to other southerners, but they were the least efficient, the least enterprising, and the least lucky of the rural white population. Their num-bers are difficult to estimate. A rough guess would be perhaps half a million, or a lit-tle more than 5 percent of the white population. Poverty-stricken, they lived in rough, unchinked, windowless log cabins located in the remotest areas and were often squat-ters without title to the land they were on. The men spent their time hunting and fishing, while women did the domestic work and what farming they could manage.

Circumstances made their poverty difficult to escape. Largely illiterate, they suffered from malnutrition stemming from a monotonous diet of corn, pork, and whiskey, and they were afflicted with malaria and hookworm, diseases that sapped their energy. Contemporaries repeatedly commented on their sickly cast, liberal use of whiskey and snuff, sexual immorality, and prematurely aged appearance. Encountering one woman of this class in a piney woods cabin, Olmsted described her as "apparently young" but with a face "dry and impassive as a dead man's. . . . Once in about a minute, [she] would suddenly throw up her chin, and spit with perfect precision into the hottest embers of the fire." Other white southerners scornfully referred to poor whites as crackers, white trash, sandhillers, and clay eaters.

Lives of poor whites

Because poor whites traded with slaves, exchanging whiskey for stolen goods, contemptuous planters often bought them out simply to rid the neighborhood of them. For their part, poor whites keenly resented planters, but their hostility toward African Americans was even stronger. Poor whites refused to work alongside slaves or perform any work commonly done by them and vehemently opposed ending slavery. Emancipation would remove one of the few symbols of their status— that they were, at least, free.

Relations with planters

The Peculiar Institution

Slaves were not free. That overwhelming fact must be understood before anything is said about the kindness or the cruelty that individual slaves experienced; before any consideration of healthy or unhealthy living conditions; before any discussion of how slave families coped with hardship, rejoiced in shared pleasures, or worshiped in prayer. The lives of slaves were affected day in and day out, in big ways and small, by the basic reality that slaves were not their own masters. If a slave's workload was reasonable, it remained so only at the master's discretion, not because the slave determined it to be. If slaves married or visited family or friends on a nearby plantation, they did so only with the master's permission. If they raised a family, they could remain together only as long as the master did not separate them by sale. Whatever slaves wanted to do, they had always to consider the response of their masters.

When power was distributed as unequally as it was between masters and slaves, every action on the part of the enslaved involved a certain calculation, conscious or unconscious. The consequences of every act, of every expression or gesture, had to be considered. In that sense, the line between freedom and slavery penetrated every corner of a slave's life, and it was an absolute and overwhelming distinction.

One other stark fact reinforced the sharp line between freedom and slavery: slaves were distinguished on the basis of color. While the peculiar institution was an economic system of labor, it was also a caste system based on race. The color line of slavery made it much easier to brand black people as somehow different. It made it easier to defend the institution and win the support of yeoman farmers and poor white southerners, even though in many ways the system held them back. Hence slavery must be understood on many levels: not only as an economic system but also as a racial and cultural one, not only in terms of its outward conditions of life and labor but also through the inner demands it made on the soul.

Slavery and race

Work and Discipline

The conditions slaves encountered varied widely, depending on the size of the farm or plantation, the crop being grown, the personality of the master, and whether he was an absentee owner. On small farms slaves worked in the fields with the owners and had much closer contact with whites. On plantations, in contrast, most slaves dealt primarily with the overseer, who was paid by the size of the harvest he brought in and was therefore often harsh in his approach. The largest plantations, which raised rice and sugar, also required the longest hours and the most grueling labor.

Organization of slave labor

House servants and the drivers, who supervised the field hands, were accorded the highest status, and skilled artisans such as carpenters and blacksmiths were also given special recognition. The hardest work was done by the field hands, both men and women, who sometimes were divided into plowhands and hoe gangs. In the summer of 1854 Olmsted watched a group of Mississippi slaves return to work in the fields after a thunderstorm. "First came, led by an old driver carrying a whip, forty of the largest and strongest women I ever saw together; . . . they carried themselves loftily, each having a hoe over the shoulder, and walking with a free, powerful swing like [soldiers] on the march." Behind them were the plowhands on the mules, "the cavalry, thirty strong, mostly men, but a few of them women." Bringing up the rear was "a lean and vigilant white overseer, on a brisk pony."

Some planters organized their slaves by the gang system, in which a white overseer or a black driver supervised gangs of 20 to 25 adults. Although this approach extracted long hours of reasonably hard labor, the slaves had to be constantly supervised and shirkers were difficult to detect. Other planters preferred the task system, under which each slave was given a specific daily assignment to complete, after which he or she was finished for the day. This system allowed slaves to work at their own pace, gave them an incentive to do careful work, and freed overseers from having to closely supervise the work. On the other hand, slaves resisted vigorously if masters tried to increase the workload. The task system was most common in the rice fields, whereas the gang system predominated in the cotton districts. Many planters used a combination of the two.

Slaves' workday

Toil began just before sunrise and continued until dusk. During cultivation and harvest, slaves were in the field 15 to 16 hours a day, eating a noonday meal there and resting before resuming labor. Work was uncommon on Sundays, and frequently only a half day was required on Saturdays. Even so, the routine was taxing. "We . . . have everybody at work before day dawns," an Arkansas cotton planter reported. "I am never caught in bed after day light nor is any body else on the place, and we continue in the cotton fields when we can have fair weather till it is so dark we can't see to work."

Often masters gave money, additional food, gifts, and time off to slaves who worked diligently, but the threat of punishment was always present. Slaves could be denied passes; their food allowance could be reduced; and if all else failed, they could be sold. The most common instrument of punishment, however, was the whip. The frequency of its use varied from plantation to plantation, but few slaves escaped the lash entirely. "We have to rely more and more on the power of fear," the planter James Henry Hammond acknowledged. "We are determined to continue masters, and to do so we have to draw the rein tighter and tighter day by day to be assured that we hold them in complete check."

Black slave driver

Slave Maintenance

Clothing and housing.

Planters generally bought rough, cheap cloth for slave clothing and each year gave adults at most only a couple of outfits and a pair of shoes that were worn out by the end of the year. Few had enough clothing or blankets to keep warm when the

The Old South   Chapter 13   409

weather dipped below freezing. Some planters provided well-built housing, but more commonly slaves lived in cramped, poorly built cabins that were leaky in wet weather, drafty in cold, and furnished with only a few crude chairs, benches and a table, perhaps a mattress filled with corn husks or straw, and a few pots and dishes.

Sickness among the hands was a persistent problem. In order to keep medical expenses down, slaveowners treated sick slaves themselves and called in a doctor only for serious cases. Even conscientious masters often employed harmful treatments and dispensed quack patent medicines. Conditions varied widely, but on average, a slaveowner spent less than a dollar a year on medical care for each slave.

Even so, the United States was the only slave society in the Americas where the slave population increased naturally—indeed, at about the same rate as the white population. Nevertheless, a deficient diet, inadequate clothing and shelter, long hours of hard toil, and poor medical care resulted in a lower life expectancy among slaves. Infant mortality was more than double that of the free white population; for every 1000 live births among southern slaves, more than 200 died before the age of 5. As late as 1860, fewer than two-thirds of slave children lived to age 10. For those who survived infancy, enslaved African Americans had a life expectancy about 8 years less than that of white Americans.

Slaves' lower life expectancy

Resistance

Given the wide gulf between freedom and slavery, it was only natural that slaves resisted the bondage imposed on them. The most radical form of resistance was rebellion, which occurred repeatedly in slave societies in the Americas. In Latin America, slave revolts were frequent, involving hundreds and even thousands of slaves and pitched battles in which large numbers were killed. The most successful slave revolt occurred in France's sugar-rich colony Saint Domingue (the western part of the Caribbean island of Hispaniola). There, free blacks who had fought in the American Revolution because of France's alliance with the United States brought back the ideals of freedom and equality. Furthermore, the brutally overworked population of half a million slaves was ready to revolt and received further encouragement from the example of the French Revolution. Under the leadership of Toussaint L'Ouverture, rebellion led to the establishment of Haiti in 1804, the second independent republic in the Western Hemisphere.

Slave revolts in Latin America

Elsewhere, Jamaica averaged one significant slave revolt every year from 1731 to 1823, while in 1823 thousands rose in Guiana. Jamaica too witnessed an uprising, of some 20,000 slaves in 1831. These revolts, and ones in 1823 and 1824 in British-controlled Demarra, were savagely suppressed. And in Brazil, which had the largest number of slaves outside the United States, the government took 50 years to suppress with military force a colony of about 20,000 slaves who had sought refuge in the mountains.

In contrast, slave revolts were rare in the United States. Unlike in Latin America, in the Old South whites outnumbered blacks, the government was much more powerful, most slaves were native-born, and family life was much stronger. Slaves recognized the odds against them, and many potential leaders became fugitives instead. In a sense, what is remarkable is that American slaves revolted at all.

Infrequency of revolts in the United States

Early in the nineteenth century several well-organized uprisings in the United States were barely thwarted. In 1800 Gabriel Prosser, a slave blacksmith, recruited perhaps a couple hundred slaves in a plan to march on Richmond and capture the governor. But a heavy thunderstorm postponed the attack and a few slaves then betrayed the plot. Prosser and other leaders were eventually captured and executed. Denmark Vesey's conspiracy in Charleston in 1822 met a similar fate (page 348).

Nat Turner's rebellion

The most famous slave revolt, led by a literate slave preacher named Nat Turner, was smaller and more spontaneous. Turner, who lived on a farm in southeastern Virginia, enjoyed unusual privileges. His master, whom he described as a kind and trusting man, encouraged him to study the Bible and preach to other slaves on Sundays and gave him great personal freedom. Spurred on by an almost fanatic mysticism, Turner became convinced from visions of white and black angels fighting that God intended to punish white people and that he had been selected "to carry terror and devastation" throughout the countryside. One night in 1831 following an eclipse of the sun, he and six confederates stole out and murdered Turner's master and family. Gaining some 70 recruits as they went, Turner's band eventually killed 57 white men, women, and children. Along the way, the members voiced their grievances against slavery and announced that they intended to confiscate their masters' wealth.

The revolt lasted only 48 hours before being crushed. Turner himself eluded pursuers for more than two months but finally was captured, tried, and executed. While the uprising was quickly put down, it left white southerners throughout the region with a haunting uneasiness. Turner seemed a model slave, yet who could read a slave's true emotions behind the mask of obedience?

Day-to-day resistance

Few slaves followed Turner's violent example. But there were other, more subtle, ways of resisting a master's authority. Most dramatically, they could do as Octave Johnson did and run away. With the odds stacked heavily against them, few runaways escaped safely to freedom except from the border states. More frequently, slaves fled to nearby woods or swamps to avoid punishment or protest their treatment. Some runaways stayed out only a few days; others, like Johnson, held out for months.

Many slaves resisted by abusing their masters' property. They mishandled animals, broke tools and machinery, misplaced items, and worked carelessly in the fields. Olmsted observed one field gang that stopped hoeing every time the overseer turned his back. Slaves also sought to trick the master by feigning illness or injury and by hiding rocks in the cotton they picked. Slaves complained directly to the owner about an overseer's mistreatment, thereby attempting to drive a wedge between the two.

The most common form of resistance, and a persistent annoyance to slaveowners, was theft. Slaves took produce from the garden, raided the master's smokehouse, secretly slaughtered his stock, and killed his poultry. Slaves often distinguished between "stealing" from each other and merely "taking" from white masters. "Dey allus done tell us it am wrong to lie and steal," recalled Josephine Howard, a former slave in Texas, "but why did de white folks steal my mammy and her mammy? Dey lives . . . over in Africy. . . . Dat de sinfulles' stealin' dey is."

Slaves' hidden feelings

Slaves learned to outwit their masters by wearing an "impenetrable mask" around whites, one bondsman recalled. "How much of joy, of sorrow, of misery and anguish have they hidden from their tormentors." Frederick Douglass, the most famous fugitive slave, explained that "as the master studies to keep the slave ignorant, the slave is cunning enough to make the master think he succeeds."

 ## Slave Culture

Trapped in bondage, faced with the futility of revolt, slaves could at least forge a culture of their own. By the nineteenth century, American slaves had been separated from much of their traditional African heritage, but that did not mean they had fully accepted the dominant white culture. Instead, slaves combined strands from their African past with customs that evolved from their life in America. This slave culture was most distinct on big plantations, where the slave population was large and slaves had more opportunity to live apart from white scrutiny.

The Slave Family

Maintaining a sense of family was one of the most remarkable achievements of African Americans in bondage, given the obstacles that faced them. Southern law did not recognize slave marriages as legally binding, nor did it allow slave parents complete authority over their children. Black women faced the possibility of rape by the master or overseer without legal recourse, and husbands, wives, and children had to live with the fear of being sold and separated. From 1820 to 1860 more than 2 million slaves were sold in the interstate slave trade. Perhaps 600,000 husbands and wives were separated by such sales. The chance that a slave family would be broken up—children taken from parents, brothers separated from sisters—was even greater. A slave mother whose three children had all been sold away grieved to Fredrika Bremer: "When they took from me the last little girl . . . I believed I never should have got over it! It almost broke my heart!"

Breakup of families

Despite their vulnerability, family ties remained strong, as slave culture demonstrated. The marriage ceremony among slaves varied from a formal religious service to jumping over a broomstick in front of the slave community to nothing more than the master giving verbal approval. Whatever the ceremony, slaves viewed the ritual as a public affirmation of the couple's commitment to their new duties and responsibilities. Rather than adopting white norms, slaves developed their own moral code concerning sexual relations and marriage. Although young slaves often

Family ties in slavery

An unknown artist (believed to be European) painted this slave auction in the 1850s, at which a young boy (left) is being examined by a prospective buyer as his mother clings to him. A planter and his wife (perhaps the owners?) look on. Once, while walking with a European visitor, Mary Chesnut, an upper-class South Carolinian, passed one such slave sale. "If you can stand that," she acidly remarked, "no other Southern thing need choke you."

engaged in premarital sex, they were expected to choose a partner and become part of a stable family. It has been estimated that at least one in five slave women had one or more children before marriage, but most of these mothers eventually married. "The negroes had their own ideas of morality, and they held them very strictly," the daughter of a Georgia planter recalled. "They did not consider it wrong for a girl to have a child before she married, but afterwards were very strict upon anything like infidelity on her part." Black churches played a leading role in condemning adultery.

Gender roles

The traditional nuclear family of father, mother, and children was the rule, not the exception, among slaves. Within the marriage the father was viewed as the traditional head of the family; wives were to be submissive and obey their husbands. Labor in the quarters was divided according to sex. Women did the indoor work, such as cooking, washing, and sewing, and men performed outdoor chores, such as gathering firewood, hauling water, and tending the animals and garden plots. The men also hunted and fished to supplement the spare weekly rations. "My old daddy . . . caught rabbits, coons an' possums," recalled Louisa Adams of North Carolina. "He would work all day and hunt at night." (See Daily Lives, "A Slave's Daily Bread," pages 414–415.)

Beyond the nuclear family, slaves developed strong kinship networks that promoted a sense of community. Aunts and uncles were expected to look after children who lost their parents through death or sale. When children were sold to a new plantation, a family in the slave quarters took them in. Thus all members of the slave society drew together in an extended network of mutual obligation.

Slave Songs and Stories

Protest and celebration

In the songs they sang, slaves expressed some of their deepest feelings about love and work and the joys and pain of life. "The songs of the slave represent the sorrows of his heart," commented Frederick Douglass. Surely there was bitterness as well as sorrow when slaves sang:

> We raise the wheat
> They give us the corn
> We bake the bread
> They give us the crust
> We sift the meal
> They give us the husk
> We peel the meat
> They give us the skin
> And that's the way
> They take us in

Yet songs were also central to the celebrations held in the slave quarters: for marriages, Christmas revels, and after harvest time. And a slave on the way to the fields might sing:

> Saturday night and Sunday too
> Young gals on my mind.
> Monday morning 'way 'fore day,
> Old master's got me gwine.
> Peggy does you love me now?

Lewis Miller of York, Pennsylvania, painted this picture of Virginia slaves dancing in 1853. Dancing and music were important components of slave culture and provided a welcome respite from work under slavery. Declared one runaway slave, "The sternest . . . master cannot frighten or whip the fun out of us."

Slaves expressed themselves through stories as well as song. Most often these **Folktales** folktales used animals as symbolic models for the predicaments in which slaves found themselves. In the best known of these, the cunning Brer Rabbit was a weak fellow who defeated larger animals like Brer Fox and Brer Bear by using his wits. Sometimes the identity of the trickster was no longer symbolic, but the slave. Because these latter stories contained more overt hostility to white people, slaves usually told them only among themselves. But the message, whether direct or symbolic, was much the same: to laugh at the master's shortcomings and teach the young how to survive in a hostile world.

Steal Away to Jesus

At the center of slave culture was religion. The Second Great Awakening, which had begun on the southern frontier, converted many slaves, most of whom joined the Methodist and Baptist churches. Slaves constituted more than a quarter of the members of both of these southern churches.

Slaveowners encouraged a certain amount of religion among slaves as an effective means of social control. Masters provided slaves with a minister (often white), set the time and place of services, and usually insisted that a white person be present. "Church was what they called it," one former slave protested, "but all that preacher talked about was for us slaves to obey our masters and not to lie and steal. Nothing about Jesus was ever said and the overseer stood there to see that the preacher talked as he wanted him to talk." In response, some slaves rejected all religion, while others continued to believe in conjuring, voodoo, and various practices derived from African religion.

Most slaves, however, sought a Christianity firmly their own, beyond the **Slave religion** control of the master. On many plantations they met secretly at night, in the

Daily Lives

FOOD/DRINK/ DRUGS

A Slave's Daily Bread

Once a week on most plantations, slaves lined up to receive their rations from the master. Although quantities might vary, each adult could expect to receive about a peck of cornmeal, three or four pounds of bacon or salt pork, and some molasses for sweetener. Some masters added vegetables, fruits, or sweet potatoes in season, but only on rare occasions did slaves receive wheat flour, beef, lean meat, poultry, or eggs. Milk, when available at all, was reserved for children and was usually sour.

In terms of simple calories, this ration was ample enough to sustain life. A careful modern study of the slave diet has concluded that on the eve of the Civil War, adult slaves received almost 5400 calories, which exceeds today's recommended levels of consumption. More than 80 percent of the calories, however, came from corn and pork. This monotonous fare of hog-and-hominy lacked several essential nutrients as well as enough protein, afflicting many slaves with diet-related diseases like pellagra and beriberi. The malnutrition was due more to ignorance than miserliness or willful neglect on the part of masters. Although slaveowners and their families enjoyed more variety in their food and better cuts of meat, they too lacked a balanced diet.

On some plantations masters left all cooking to the slaves, who, before going to work in the morning, would eat breakfast and prepare their noon meal to take with them to eat in the fields. At night, they came home to fix a light supper. Other masters established a plantation kitchen where cooks prepared breakfast and dinner, though supper remained the responsibility of the individual slave or family. On these plantations a noon meal was brought to the fields. In general, the quality of food preparation was better under this system because slaves were often too exhausted after work to put much time or care into cooking. Naturally enough, slaves preferred to fix meals according to their own taste and eat as a family in some privacy. Fanny Kemble reported that on her husband's Georgia plantation the slaves sat "on the earth or doorsteps, and ate out of their little cedar tubs or an iron pot, some few with broken iron spoons, more with pieces of wood, and all the children with their fingers." The cooking itself was done in front of a large fireplace.

Wherever their masters permitted it, slaves tended their own vegetable gardens after work or

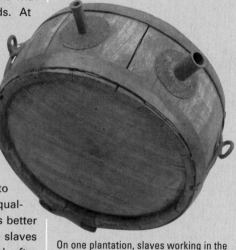

On one plantation, slaves working in the field who became thirsty during the heat of the day drank from this canteen. But so did the overseer or plantation owner, who was provided a separate spout. Which spout was for the slaves?

quarters or at "hush harbors" in the safety of the woods, where they broke into rhythmic singing and dancing, modeled on the ring shout of African religion. Even regular services were characterized by intense enthusiasm. "The way in which we worshiped is almost indescribable," one slave preacher recalled. "The singing was accompanied by a certain ecstasy of motion, clapping of hands, tossing of heads, which would continue without cessation about half an hour. The old house partook of the ecstasy; it rang with their jubilant shouts, and shook in all its joints." In an environment where slaves, for most of the day, were prevented from expressing their deepest feelings, such meetings served as a satisfying emotional release.

Religion also provided slaves with values to guide them through their daily experiences and give them a sense of self-worth. Slaves learned that God would redeem the poor and downtrodden and raise them one day to honor and glory. Rejecting the teaching of some white ministers that slavery was punishment, slave

raised chickens and other animals. Not only did this practice provide eggs and other items not included in the weekly rations, but it also enabled slaves to sell their surplus to the master or in town and use their earnings to buy occasional luxuries such as coffee, sugar, and tobacco. Slaves also raided the master's smokehouse, secretly slaughtered his stock and killed his poultry, and stole from neighboring plantations. Richard Carruthers, a former slave, recalled, "If they didn't provision you 'nough, you just had to slip round and get a chicken."

Slaves who worked all day still had plenty of incentive to stir out at night to fish or to hunt raccoon or opossum. "The flesh of the coon is palatable," admitted Solomon Northup, a northern free black kidnapped into slavery, "but verily there is nothing in all butcherdom so delicious as a roasted 'possum." Possum was parboiled to soften it and then roasted with lard over the fire, along with sweet potatoes. Squirrel meat, though tougher, could be boiled long enough to soften it for squirrel pie served with dumplings. Rabbits, especially young ones, were tender enough to fry.

Along with such meat might come "hoecakes," a popular dish made by slapping cornmeal dough on the blade of a hoe and holding it over the coals. Vegetables were boiled in a pot with a bit of hog jowl, each new vegetable thrown in at the appropriate cooking time: beans first, then cabbage when the beans were half done, then squash, and finally okra. Whenever they could get them, slave cooks used spices to flavor their dishes. Some spices, such as sesame seeds, had come from Africa with the slaves. Red pepper, native to the Americas, added zing to innumerable dishes.

On holidays the master usually provided a banquet for all hands on the plantation. Slaves eagerly filled up on beef, mutton, roast pig, coffee, wheat bread, pies, and other dishes only rarely tasted. Although masters generally tried to keep whiskey away from their slaves, some slaveowners made an exception at Christmas. Feasting was one of the slaves' "princi[pal] sources of comfort," one former slave testified. "Only the slave who has lived all the year on his scanty allowance of meal and bacon, can appreciate such suppers."

preachers assured their congregations that they were the chosen people of God. Just as certainly, on the final Day of Judgment, masters would be punished for their sins. "This is one reason why I believe in hell," a former slave declared. "I don't believe a just God is going to take no such man as my former master into His Kingdom."

Again, song played a central role. Slaves sang religious "spirituals" at work and at play as well as in religious services. Seemingly meek and otherworldly, the songs often contained a hidden element of protest. Frederick Douglass disclosed that when slaves sang longingly of "Canaan, sweet Canaan," they were thinking not only of the Bible's Promised Land but also of the North and freedom. When slaves heard "Steal Away to Jesus" sung in the fields, they knew that a secret devotional meeting was scheduled that evening. Songs became one of the few ways that slaves could openly express, in the approved language of Christianity, their yearning for freedom. While

Slave spirituals

slaves sang lyrics that spoke of an otherworldly freedom from sin in heaven, their hearts were considering a this-worldly escape from physical bondage.

Religion, then, not only served to comfort slaves after days of toil and sorrow; it also strengthened their sense of togetherness and common purpose and held out the promise of eventual freedom in this world and the next. The faith that "some ob dese days my time will come" was one of the most important ways that slaves coped with bondage and resisted its pressure to rob them of their self-esteem.

The Slave Community

Hierarchy

Although slaves managed with remarkable success to preserve a sense of self-worth in a culture of their own, the hard reality of slavery made it impossible to escape fully from white control. Even the social hierarchy within the slave quarters never was entirely free from the white world. Slave preachers, conjurers, and herb doctors held status that no white conferred, but the prestige of a slave driver rested ultimately on the authority of the white master. Similarly, skilled slaves and house servants often felt superior to other slaves, an attitude masters consciously promoted. "We house slaves thought we was better'n the others what worked in the field," one personal servant confessed. Light-skinned slaves sometimes deemed their color a badge of superiority. Fanny Kemble recorded that one woman begged to be relieved of field labor, which she considered degrading, "on *'account of her color.'*"

Lucy Skipworth, who was the daughter of a driver and had been educated by her mistress, was a member of the slave elite on both counts. At Hopewell plantation in Alabama, she was in full charge of the main residence during her master's frequent absences. She ran a plantation school (despite white opposition) and, as a devout Baptist, supervised her fellow slaves' religious life. Eager for her master's approval, Skipworth on several occasions reported slave disobedience, which temporarily estranged her from the slave community. Yet in the end she was always welcomed back. While Skipworth never rebelled or apparently never considered running away, she was far from submissive. She defied white authority, protected her family, and used her influence to get rid of an overseer the slaves disliked. Like many house servants, she lived between two worlds—her master's and the slave quarters—and was never entirely comfortable in either.

But the realities of slavery and white racism inevitably drove black people closer together in a common bond and forced them to depend on one another to survive. New slaves on a plantation were immediately instructed in the mysteries of the quarters, including such vital matters as the best strategies for avoiding punishment. Walled in from the individualistic white society beyond, slaves out of necessity created a community of their own.

Free Black Southerners

Of the 4 million African Americans living in the South in 1860, only 260,000—about 7 percent—were free. More than 85 percent of them lived in the Upper South, with almost 200,000 in Maryland, Virginia, and North Carolina alone. Free black southerners were also much more urban than the southern white and slave populations. In 1860 almost a third of the free African Americans in the Upper South, and more than half in the Lower South, lived in towns and cities. As a rule, free African Americans were more literate than slaves, and they were disproportionately female and much more likely to be of mixed ancestry. Only 10 percent of all slaves were classified as mulattoes, compared to four times as many free African Americans.

Still, most free black southerners lived in rural areas, although usually not near plantations. A majority eked out a living farming or in low-paying unskilled jobs, but some did well enough to own slaves themselves. In 1830 about 3600 free blacks owned slaves, although commonly their "property" was their own wives or children, purchased because they could not be emancipated under state laws. A few free blacks, however, were full-fledged slaveowners.

Following Nat Turner's rebellion of 1831, southern legislatures increased the restrictions on free African Americans. Most states in the Deep South prohibited residents from freeing slaves in their wills, and some required any emancipated slaves to leave the state. All states forbade the entry of free African Americans, and those already living there were subject to ever greater restrictions. They had to carry their free papers, could not assemble when they wished, were subject to a curfew, often had to post a bond and be licensed to work, and could not vote, hold office, or testify in court against white people.

Lighter-skinned black southerners who were free, like their counterparts in the North, tended to set themselves apart from darker-skinned African Americans, free or slave. In such cities as Charleston and New Orleans, they established separate social and cultural organizations and maintained their own exclusive social network. Economically dependent on white customers, they developed close connections with white southerners yet were never accepted in the white world. Free African Americans occupied an uncertain position in southern society, well above black slaves but distinctly beneath even poorer white southerners. They were victims of a society that had no place for them.

This painting shows a free African American market woman in Baltimore. Urban blacks in the South, including slaves, enjoyed greater personal freedom and access to more social activities but had only limited economic opportunity.

From wealthy planters to yeoman farmers, from free black slaveholders to white mountaineers, from cotton field hands to

Southern Society and the Defense of Slavery

urban craftworkers, the South was a remarkably diverse region. Yet it was united by its dependence on staple crops and above all by the institution of slavery. As the South's economy became more and more dependent on slave-produced staples, slavery became more central to the life of the South, to its culture and its identity.

The Virginia Debate of 1832

At the time of the Revolution, the leading critics of slavery had been southerners—Jefferson, Washington, Madison, and Patrick Henry among them. But beginning in the 1820s, in the wake of the controversy over admitting Missouri as a slave state (page 282), southern leaders became less apologetic about slavery and more aggressive in defending it. The turning point occurred in the early 1830s, when the South found itself increasingly under attack. It was in 1831 that William Lloyd Garrison began publishing his abolitionist newspaper, *The Liberator.* In that year too Nat Turner launched the revolt that frightened so many white southerners.

In response to the Turner insurrection, a number of Virginia's western counties, where there were few slaves, petitioned the legislature to adopt a program for gradual emancipation. Between January 16 and 25, 1832, the House of Delegates engaged in a remarkable debate over the merits of slavery. In the end, however, the legislature refused, by a vote of 73 to 58, to consider legislation to end slavery.

Significance of the Virginia debate

The Virginia debate represented the last significant attempt of white southerners to take action against the peculiar institution. In its aftermath, most felt that the subject was no longer open to debate. Instead, during the 1830s and 1840s, southern leaders defended slavery as a positive good, not just for white people but for black people as well. As John C. Calhoun proclaimed in 1837, "I hold that in the present state of civilization, where two races . . . distinguished by color and other physical differences, as well as intellectual, are brought together, the relation now existing in the slaveholding states between the two is, instead of an evil, a good—a positive good."

The Proslavery Argument

Politicians like Calhoun were not alone. White southern leaders justified slavery in a variety of ways. Ministers argued that under the law of Moses, Jews were authorized to enslave heathens and emphasized that none of the Biblical prophets or Christ himself had ever condemned slavery. They traced slavery's origins to the curse of Canaan, in which Canaan (the allegedly black grandson of Noah) was made a servant in punishment for his father's sin.

Religious arguments

Social and racial arguments

Defenders of the institution also pointed out that classical Greece and Rome depended on slavery. They even cited John Locke, that giant of the Enlightenment,

This 1841 proslavery cartoon contrasts the treatment of American slaves, who are allegedly well fed, well clothed, and well cared for, with the plight of English factory workers. Defenders of slavery made the same comparisons to northern laborers.

who had recognized slavery in the constitution he drafted for the colony of Carolina. African Americans belonged to an intellectually and emotionally inferior race, slavery's defenders argued, and therefore lacked the ability to care for themselves and required white guardianship. "Providence has placed [the black man] in our hands for his good, and has paid us from his labor for our guardianship," contended James Henry Hammond, the eminent planter and senator from South Carolina whose "guardianship" of several hundred slaves had netted him a tidy fortune.

Proslavery writers sometimes argued that slaves in the South lived better than factory workers in the North. Masters cared for slaves for life, whereas northern workers had no claim on their employer when they were unemployed, old, or no longer able to work. In advancing this argument, white southerners exaggerated the material comforts of slavery and minimized the average worker's standard of living—to say nothing, of course, about the incalculable psychological value of freedom. Still, to many white southerners, slavery seemed a more humane system of labor relations.

Defenders of slavery did not really expect to influence public opinion in the North. Their target was more often slaveowners themselves. As Duff Green, a southern editor and one of Calhoun's advisers, explained, "We must satisfy the consciences, we must allay the fears of our own people. We must satisfy them that slavery is of itself right—that it is not a sin against God—that it is not an evil, moral or political. In this way only," he went on, "can we prepare our own people to defend their institutions."

Closing Ranks

Not all white southerners could quell their doubts. To take only one example, Robert Scott, an antislavery advocate in the Virginia debate of 1832, was publicly calling slavery "an institution reprobated by the world" as late as 1849. Still, a striking change in southern opinion seems to have occurred in the three decades before the Civil War. Outside the border states, few white southerners after 1840 would admit even in private that slavery was wrong. Those who continued to oppose slavery found themselves harassed, assaulted, and driven into exile. Southern mobs destroyed the presses of antislavery papers and threatened the editors into either keeping silent or leaving the state. Southern mails were forcibly closed to abolitionist propaganda, and defenders of the South's institutions carefully scrutinized textbooks and faculty members in southern schools. Southerners like James Birney and Sarah and Angelina Grimké had to go to the free states to continue their fight against slavery.

Increasingly, too, the debate over slavery spread to the national political arena. Before 1836 Andrew Jackson's enormous popularity in the South blocked the formation of a competitive two-party system there. The rise of the abolitionist movement in the 1830s, however, left many southerners uneasy, and when the Democrats nominated the northerner Martin Van Buren in 1836, southern Whigs seized on the issue of the security of slavery and charged that Van Buren could not be counted on to meet the abolitionist threat. The Whigs made impressive gains in the South in 1836, carrying several states and significantly narrowing the margin between the two parties.

In later presidential elections, both parties in the South attacked the opposing party through its northern supporters as unreliable on slavery. This tactic was less successful in state elections, however, since both parties were led by slaveholders and were committed to protecting slavery. In addition, the depression that began in 1837 focused the attention of southern voters on economic matters. Southern Whigs appealed to the commercially oriented members of society: planters, business leaders and merchants, bankers, professionals, and residents of cities and the plantation black belts. Democrats won their share of slaveowners, but the party's greatest support came from small independent farmers in more isolated regions, where, as in the North, class and occupation were less important than one's economic and moral outlook. Southern voters most comfortable with the market and the changes it brought gravitated toward the Whig party. On the other hand, those farmers who feared the loss of personal independence that banks and commercial development brought with them tended to support the Democratic party.

During the Jacksonian era, most southern political battles did not revolve around slavery. Even so, southern politicians in both parties had to be careful to avoid the stigma of antislavery, since they were under mounting pressure from John Calhoun and his followers. Frustrated in his presidential hopes by the nullification crisis in 1832–1833 (page 348), Calhoun sought to unite the South behind his leadership by agitating the slavery issue, introducing inflammatory resolutions in Congress upholding slavery, seizing on the abolitionist mailing campaign to demand censorship of the mails, and leaping to his feet to insist on a gag rule to block antislavery petitions. During the 1830s and early 1840s, few southern politicians followed his lead, but they did become extremely careful about being in the least critical of slavery or southern institutions. They knew quite well that even if their constituents were not as fanatical as Calhoun, southern voters overwhelmingly supported slavery.

Sections and the Nation

Viewing the events of the 1830s and 1840s with the benefit of hindsight, one cannot help but concentrate on the Civil War looming in the distance and focus on the differences dividing the North and the South. Yet free white northerners and southerners had much in common as Americans.

The largest group in both sections was composed of independent farmers who cultivated their own land with their own labor and were devoted to the principles of personal independence and social egalitarianism. Although southern society was more aristocratic in tone, both sections were driven forcefully by the quest for material wealth. The Texas Red River planter for whom time was money did not take a backseat to the Yankee clockmaker Chauncey Jerome in the scramble for success and status. White Americans in both sections aspired to rise in society, and they looked to the expanding opportunities of the market to help them do so. Moreover, both northerners and southerners linked geographic mobility to opportunity, and both pushed westward in search of better land and a new start.

Many Americans, North and South, also adhered to the teachings of evangelical Protestantism. Southern churches were less open to social reform, primarily because of its association with abolitionism, and southern churches, unlike most in the North, defended slavery as a Christian institution. Eventually both the Methodist and the Baptist churches split into separate northern and southern organizations over this issue, but their attitudes on other matters often coincided.

Finally, white northerners and southerners shared a belief in democracy and white equality. To be sure, the existence of the planter class created greater tensions in southern society between democracy and aristocracy. But southern as

Economics and party affiliation

Forces of national unity

well as northern states embraced the democratic reforms of the 1820s and 1830s, and the electorate in both sections favored giving all white males the vote and making public officeholders responsible to the people. Southerners insisted that the equality proclaimed in the Declaration of Independence applied only to white Americans (and really only to white males), but the vast majority of northerners in practice took no exception to this attitude. Both sections agreed on the necessity of safeguarding equality of opportunity rather than promoting equality of wealth.

With so much in common, it was not inevitable that the two sections would come to blows. Certainly, before 1840 few politicians believed that the differences between the two sections were decisive. It was only in the mid-1840s, when the United States embarked on a new program of westward expansion, that the slavery issue began to loom ominously in American life and Americans began to question whether the Union could permanently endure, half slave and half free.

chapter summary

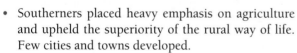

The Old South was a complex, biracial society that increasingly diverged from the rest of the United States in the years before 1860.

- Southerners placed heavy emphasis on agriculture and upheld the superiority of the rural way of life. Few cities and towns developed.
    - Southern commercial agriculture produced staple crops for sale in northern and European markets: tobacco, sugar, rice, and, above all, cotton.
    - As southern agriculture expanded into the fresh lands of the Deep South, the slave population moved steadily westward and southward, and the Upper South became more diversified agriculturally.
- Slavery played a major role in shaping the class structure of the Old South.
    - Ownership of slaves brought privilege and status, and the largest slaveowners were extraordinarily wealthy.
    - Planters on the older eastern seaboard enjoyed a more refined lifestyle than those on the new cotton frontier.
- Most slaveowners, however, owned only a few slaves, and the majority of southern whites were nonslaveowning yeoman farmers.

- At the bottom of the white class structure were the poor whites.
- Slavery hurt nonslaveholding whites economically, but class tensions were muted in the Old South because of racial fears.
- The institution of slavery was both a labor system and a social system, regulating relations between the races.
    - Slaves resisted bondage in many ways, ranging from the subtle to the overt. Slave revolts, however, were rare.
    - Slaves developed their own culture in which the family, religion, and songs played key roles in helping slaves cope with the pressures of bondage.
    - Slaves' shared experiences created a community based on a common identity and mutual values.
- As slavery came under mounting attack, white southerners rallied to protect their peculiar institution.
    - They developed a set of arguments defending slavery as a positive good.
    - Both political parties in the South strongly defended the institution and southern rights.
- Many Americans, both North and South, shared the same values: personal independence, social egalitarianism, evangelical Protestantism. But beginning in the mid-1840s, with renewed westward expansion, the slavery issue increased sectional tensions.

interactive learning

The Primary Source Investigator CD-ROM offers the following materials related to this chapter:

• Interactive map: **Slavery and the Cotton Kingdom** (M11)

• A collection of primary sources exploring the meaning and effects of slavery in the United States. Sources include a Seaman's Protection certificate, which guaranteed freedom for a Black sailor; a sketch of Africans crowded on the slave ship *Wildfire;* and a variety of documents relating to John Brown.

additional reading

Few topics have received more historical attention than slavery and the Old South. The economics of slavery, the values of slaveowners, the nature of the region's social structure, and the content of slave culture are all matters of great controversy. The reports of Frederick Law Olmsted, conveniently available in Lawrence Powell, ed., *The Cotton Kingdom* (1984), provide a fascinating introduction to antebellum southern society. James Oakes, *Slavery and Freedom* (1990), is a good synthesis of the contradictions between slavery and freedom in southern life.

William W. Freehling, *The Road to Disunion* (1990), is a wide-ranging examination of the South to 1854 that emphasizes the diversity and divisions in southern society. James Oakes, *The Ruling Race* (1982), is a controversial study of slaveowners that emphasizes their capitalist orientation.

While old, Frank Owsley's *Plain Folk of the Old South* (1949) has not been superseded on southern yeoman farmers. The lives of upper-class southern white women and their servants are analyzed in Elizabeth Fox-Genovese, *Within the Plantation Household* (1988), while Victoria E. Bynum, *Unruly Women* (1992), deals with white and black women of lower status. The impact of geographic mobility on southern society can be studied in Joan E. Cashin, *A Family Venture* (1991). The best exploration of slavery as a labor system still remains Kenneth M. Stampp, *The Peculiar Institution* (1956), but the most perceptive treatment of slave culture is Eugene D. Genovese, *Roll, Jordan, Roll* (1974). Charles Joyner, *Down by the Riverside* (1984), is a very sensitive recreation of slave culture in the rice districts. Ira Berlin, *Slaves without Masters* (1974), is an excellent account of southern free blacks. Drew Faust, *A Sacred Circle* (1977), is a stimulating discussion of proslavery thought, while William J. Cooper Jr., *The Politics of Slavery* (1978), stresses the role of the slavery issue in southern politics. For a fuller list of readings, see the Bibliography at www.mhhe.com/davidsonnation5.

significant events

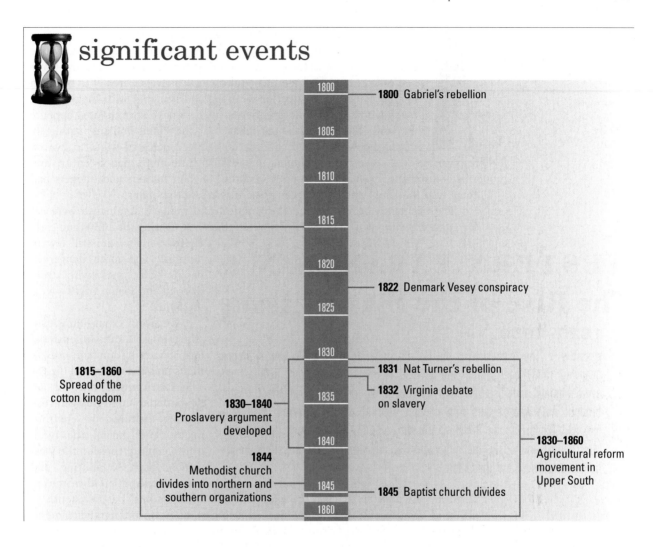

1800 Gabriel's rebellion

1822 Denmark Vesey conspiracy

1815–1860
Spread of the
cotton kingdom

1830–1840
Proslavery argument
developed

1831 Nat Turner's rebellion

1832 Virginia debate
on slavery

1830–1860
Agricultural reform
movement in
Upper South

1844
Methodist church
divides into northern and
southern organizations

1845 Baptist church divides

Chapter 14

A t first the Crows, Arapahos, and other Indians of the Great Plains paid little attention to the new people moving out from the forests far to the east. After all, for as long as they could remember, nations like the Crow had called the plains their own. But the new arrivals were not to be taken lightly. Armed with superior weapons and bringing with them a great many women and children, they seemed to have an unlimited appetite for land. They attacked the villages of the Plains Indians, ruthlessly massacred women and children, and forced defeated tribes to live on reservations and serve their economic interests. In little more than a century and a half—from the first days when only a handful of their hunters and trappers had come into the land—they had become the masters of the plains.

The invaders who established this political and military dominance were *not* the strange "white men," who also came from the forest. During the 1830s and early 1840s, whites were still few in number. The more dangerous people—the ones who truly worried the Plains tribes—were the Sioux.

WESTERN EXPANSION & The Rise of the Slavery Issue

1820–1850

preview • The expansion of the United States to the Pacific was a process involving many overlapping and diverse frontiers–of cultures, peoples, and even animals and disease. From the east, the ideology of Manifest Destiny brought American settlers into conflict with Mexicans in Texas, New Mexico, and California, the British in Oregon, and Native Americans west of the Mississippi. Ominously, the acquisition of new lands also reopened the debate over slavery and the Union.

Westward expansion is usually told as a one-dimensional tale, centering on the wagon trains pressing on toward the Pacific. But frontiers, after all, are the boundary lines between contrasting cultures or environments, and during the nineteenth century, those in the West were constantly shifting and adapting. Frontier lines moved not only east to west, as with the white and Sioux migrations, but also south to north, as Spanish culture diffused, and west to east, as Asian immigrants came to California. Furthermore, frontiers marked not only human but also animal boundaries. Horses, cattle, and pigs, all of which had been imported from Europe, moved across the continent, usually in advance of European settlers. Often they transformed the way Indian peoples lived. Frontiers could also be technological, as in the case of trade goods and firearms. Moreover, as we have already seen, disease moved across the continent with disastrous consequences for natives who had not acquired immunity to European microorganisms.

Three frontiers altered the lives of the Sioux: those of the horse, the gun, and disease. The horse frontier spread ahead of white settlement from the southwest, where horses had first been imported by the Spanish. On the other hand, the Spanish, unlike English and French traders, refused to sell firearms to Indians, so the gun frontier moved in the opposite direction, from northeast to southwest. The two waves met and crossed along the upper Missouri during the first half of the eighteenth century. For the tribes that possessed them, horses provided greater mobility, both for hunting bison and for fighting. Guns, too, conferred obvious advantages, and the arrival of these new elements inaugurated an extremely unsettled era for Plains Indian cultures.

The Sioux were first lured from the forest onto the Minnesota prairie during the early 1700s to hunt beaver, whose pelts could be exchanged with white traders for manufactured goods. Having obtained guns in exchange for furs, the Sioux

Cultural interaction

The cultures of the Plains Indians depended on the large buffalo herds that roamed the plains. Here, two Plains Indians mounted on horses hunt buffalo with bows and arrows.

drove the Omahas, Otos, Cheyennes, and Missouris (who had not yet acquired guns) south and west. But by the 1770s their advantage in guns had disappeared, and any farther advance was blocked by powerful tribes like the Mandans and Arikaras. These peoples were primarily horticultural, raising corn, beans, and squash and living in well-fortified towns. They also owned more horses than the Sioux, which made it easier for them to resist attacks.

But the third frontier, disease, threw the balance of power toward the Sioux after 1779. European traders brought smallpox with them onto the prairie. The horticultural tribes were hit especially hard because they lived in densely populated villages, where the epidemic spread more easily. The Sioux embarked on a second wave of westward expansion in the late eighteenth century, so that by the time Lewis and Clark came through in 1804, they firmly controlled the upper Missouri as far as the Yellowstone River.

The Sioux's nomadic life, centered on the buffalo hunt, enabled them to avoid the worst ravages of disease, especially the smallpox epidemic of 1837, which reduced the plains population by as much as half. Indeed, the Sioux became the largest tribe on the plains and were the only one whose high birthrate approximated that of whites. From an estimated 5000 in 1804, they grew to 25,000 in the 1850s. Their numbers increased Sioux military power as well as the need for new hunting grounds, and during the first half of the nineteenth century, they pushed even farther up

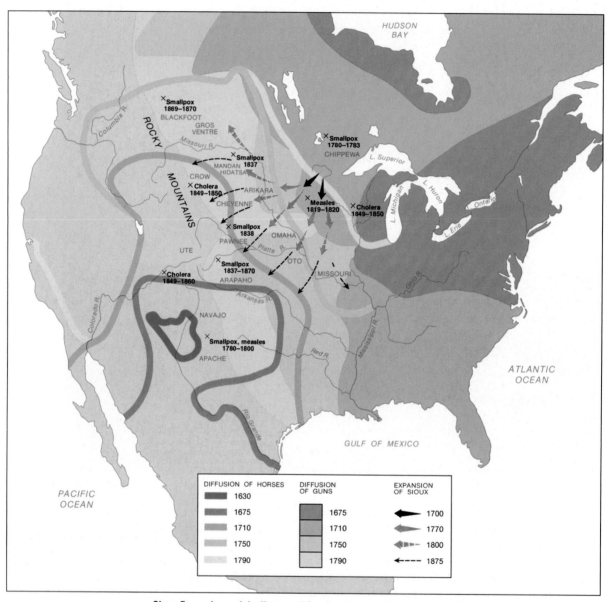

Sioux Expansion and the Horse and Gun Frontiers In 1710 the horse and gun frontiers had not yet crossed, but by 1750 the two waves began to overlap. The Sioux pushed west during the early eighteenth century thanks to firearms; they were checked from further expansion until the 1770s, when smallpox epidemics again turned the balance in their favor.

the Missouri, conquered the plains west of the Black Hills, and won control of the hunting grounds on the Platte River.

These shifting frontiers of animals, disease, firearms, and trade goods disrupted the political and cultural life of the Great Plains. And as white Americans moved westward, their own frontier lines produced similar disruptions, not only between white settlers and Indians but also between Anglo-American and Hispanic cultures.

Ironically, perhaps the greatest instability created by the moving frontiers occurred in established American society. As the political system of the United States struggled to incorporate territories, the North and South engaged in a fierce

debate over whether the new lands should become slave or free. Just as the Sioux's cultural identity was brought into question by the moving frontier, so too was the identity of the American Republic.

"Make way . . . for the young American Buffalo—he has not yet got land enough," roared one American politician

Manifest (and Not So Manifest) Destiny

in 1844. In the space of a few years, the United States acquired Texas, California, the lower half of the Oregon Territory, and the lands between the Rockies and California: nearly 1.5 million square miles in all. John L. O'Sullivan, a prominent Democratic editor in New York, struck a responsive chord when he declared that it had become the United States' "manifest destiny to overspread the continent allotted by Providence for the free development of our yearly multiplying millions." The cry of "Manifest Destiny" soon echoed in other editorial pages and in the halls of Congress.

Manifest Destiny

The Roots of the Doctrine

Many Americans had long believed that their country had a special, even divine, mission, which could be traced back to the Puritans' attempt to build a "city on a hill." Manifest Destiny also contained a political component, inherited from the ideology of the Revolution. In the mid–nineteenth century, Americans spoke of extending democracy, with widespread suffrage among white males, no king or aristocracy, and no established church, "over the whole North American continent."

Americans believed that their social and economic system, too, should spread around the globe. They pointed to its broad ownership of land, individualism, and free play of economic opportunity as superior features of American life. Of course,

With the Star of Empire blazing from her forehead, the Spirit of Progress dominates John Gast's painting *Manifest Destiny*. Indians and wild animals retreat in the face of advancing progress, illustrated by white settlers and farmers, railroads and other forms of transportation, telegraph lines, schools symbolized by a book, and, in the distance, cities. In reality, the movement of the frontier was hardly one-dimensional, as Hispanic, Indian, Asian, and white cultures clashed.

Manifest Destiny also had its self-interested side. American business interests recognized the value of the fine harbors along the Pacific Coast, which promised a lucrative trade with Asia, and they hoped to make those harbors American.

Finally, underlying the doctrine of Manifest Destiny was a widespread racism. The same belief in racial superiority that was used to justify Indian removal under Jackson, to uphold slavery in the South, and to excuse segregation in the North also proved handy to defend expansion westward. The United States had a duty to regenerate the backward peoples of America, declared politicians and propagandists. Their reference was not so much to Indians—who refused to assimilate into American society—but to Mexicans, whose Christian nation had its roots in European culture. The Mexican race "must amalgamate and be lost, in the superior vigor of the Anglo-Saxon race," proclaimed O'Sullivan's *Democratic Review,* "or they must utterly perish."

Before 1845 most Americans assumed that expansion would be achieved peacefully. American settlement would spread westward, and when the time was right, neighboring provinces, like ripe fruit, would fall naturally into American hands. Texas, New Mexico, Oregon, and California—areas that were sparsely populated and weakly defended—dominated the American expansionist imagination. With time, Americans became less willing to wait patiently for the fruit to fall.

The Mexican Borderlands

The heart of Spain's American empire was Mexico City, where spacious boulevards spread out through the center of the city and the University of Mexico, the oldest university in North America, had been accepting students since 1553, a full 85 years longer than Harvard. From the Mexican point of view, the frontier was 1000 miles to the north, a four-week journey to Texas, another two weeks to New Mexico, and three months by land and sea to the missions of California. Being so isolated, these provinces developed largely free from supervision.

California society

California's settlements were anchored by four coastal *presidios,* or forts, at San Diego, Santa Barbara, Monterey, and San Francisco. Between them lay 21 Catholic missions run by a handful of Franciscans (there were only 36 in 1821). The

Although Indians in California worked on both Spanish missions and *ranchos* in conditions of near slavery, Indians were encouraged to adopt Spanish religion and customs. Here an Indian woman, dressed in Spanish fashion, grinds corn for tortillas using a stone roller and a slab.

missions controlled enormous tracts of land on which grazed gigantic herds of cattle, sheep, and horses. The animals and irrigated fields were tended by about 20,000 Indians, who worked for all practical purposes as slaves.

When Mexico won its independence from Spain in 1821, California at first was little affected. But in 1833 the Mexican Congress freed the Indians of California and stripped the Catholic church of its lands. These lands were turned over to Mexican cattle ranchers, usually in massive grants of 50,000 acres or more. The new *rancheros* ruled their estates much like great planters of the Old South. Labor was provided by Indians, who once again were forced to work for little more than room and board. Indeed, the mortality rate of Indian workers was twice that of southern slaves and four times that of the Mexican Californians. At this time the Mexican population of California was approximately 4000. During the 1820s and 1830s Yankee traders set up shop in California in order to buy cattle hides for the growing shoe industry at Lynn and elsewhere. Still, in 1845 the American population in California amounted to only 700.

Spanish settlement of New Mexico was more dense: the province had about 44,000 inhabitants in 1827. But like that of California, its society was dominated by *ranchero* families who grazed large herds of sheep along the upper Rio Grande valley between El Paso and Taos. A few individuals controlled most of the wealth, while their workers eked out a meager living. Mining of copper and gold was also important, and here too the profits enriched a small upper class. Spain had long outlawed any commerce with Americans, but after Mexico declared its independence in 1821, yearly caravans from the United States began making the long journey along the Santa Fe Trail. Although this trade flourished over the next two decades, developments in the third Mexican borderland, neighboring Texas, worsened relations between Mexico and the United States.

New Mexico

The Texas Revolution

At first, the new government in Mexico encouraged American immigration to Texas, where only about 3000 Mexicans, mostly ranchers, lived. In 1821 Moses Austin, an American, received a grant from the Spanish government to establish a colony. After his death, his son Stephen took over the project, laying out the little town of San Felipe de Austin along the Brazos River and offering large grants of land at almost no cost. By 1824 the colony's population exceeded 2000. Stephen Austin was only the first of a new wave of American land agents, or *empresarios,* who obtained permission from Mexican authorities to settle families in Texas. Ninety percent of the new arrivals came from the South. Some, intending to grow cotton, brought slaves.

American immigration to Texas

Tensions between Mexicans and American immigrants grew with the Texas economy. Most settlers from the States were Protestant. Although the Mexican government did not enforce its law that all citizens become Catholic, it barred Protestant churches. In 1829 Mexico abolished slavery, then looked the other way when Texas slaveholders evaded the law. In the 1830s the Mexican government began to have second thoughts about American settlement and passed laws prohibiting any new immigration. But Texans were most disturbed because they had little say in their government, whose legislature lay about 700 miles to the south.

Cultural conflict

For a time the Mexican authorities enforced these policies only erratically and in 1833 allowed American immigration to resume. But the flood of new settlers only made the situation worse. By mid-decade the American white population of 30,000 was nearly 10 times the number of Mexicans in the territory. Mexico also seemed determined to enforce the abolition of slavery. Even more disturbing to the

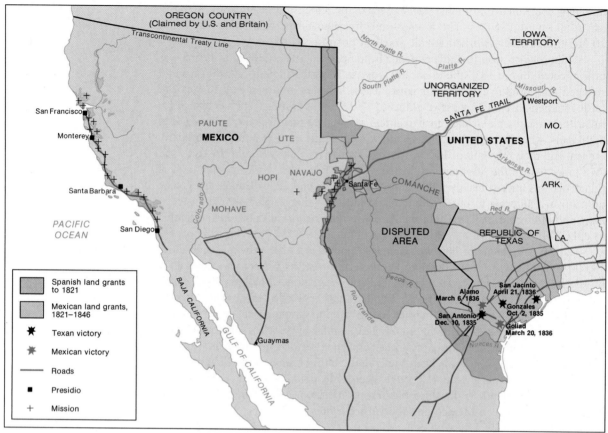

The Mexican Borderlands

American newcomers, in 1834 General Antonio Lopez de Santa Anna dissolved the Mexican Congress and proclaimed himself dictator. When Santa Anna led a military expedition north to enforce his new regime, a ragtag Texas army drove back the advance party and then captured Mexican troops in nearby San Antonio. A full-scale revolution was under way.

The Texas Republic

As Santa Anna massed his forces, a provisional government on March 2, 1836, proclaimed Texan independence. The constitution of the new Republic of Texas borrowed heavily from the U.S. Constitution, except that it explicitly prohibited the new Texas Congress from interfering with slavery. Meanwhile, Santa Anna's troops overran a Texan garrison at an old mission in San Antonio, known as the Alamo, and killed all of its 187 defenders. The Mexicans, however, paid dearly for the victory, losing more than 1500 men. The massacre of another force at Goliad after it surrendered further inflamed American resistance.

But anger was one thing; organized resistance was another. The commander of the Texas forces was Sam Houston, a former governor of Tennessee. Of striking physique and something of an eccentric, Houston had a flair for wearing colorful clothing to attract attention. His political career in Tennessee might have continued, except that the failure of his marriage led him to resign abruptly as governor and go live with the Indians. Eventually he made his way to Texas, where his intellectual ability and unexcelled talent as a stump speaker propelled him to the forefront of the independence movement. Steadily retreating eastward, Houston adeptly forged his ragged army into a disciplined fighting force.

By late April Houston was ready to fight. Reinforced by eager volunteers from the United States, Houston's army surprised the Mexican army camped along the San Jacinto River. With the first Mexican volley rattling overhead, the Texans charged, shouting "Remember the Alamo!" In only 15 minutes they overwhelmed the Mexicans (who had been enjoying an afternoon siesta) and captured Santa Anna.

Sam Houston, the first president of the Texas Republic, once set tongues wagging by appearing at a ball in a suit of black velvet lined with white satin and sporting a large hat trailing plumes of feathers. This daguerreotype, taken about 1850, shows the aging lion's firm determination.

Threatened with execution, the Mexican commander signed treaties recognizing Texan independence and establishing the Rio Grande as the southern boundary of the Texas Republic. The Mexican Congress (which had been reestablished in 1835) repudiated this agreement and launched several unsuccessful invasions into Texas. In the meantime, Houston assumed office in October 1836 as the first president of the new republic, determined to bring Texas into the Union as quickly as possible.

As an old Tennessee crony of Andrew Jackson's, Houston assumed that the United States would quickly annex such a rich and inviting territory. But Jackson worried that any such move would revive sectional tensions and hurt Martin Van Buren's chances in the 1836 presidential election. Only on his last day in office did he extend formal diplomatic recognition to the Texas Republic. Van Buren, distracted by the economic panic that broke out shortly after he entered office, took no action during his term.

Rebuffed, Texans decided to go their own way. In the 10 years following independence, the Lone Star Republic attracted more than 100,000 immigrants by offering free land to settlers. Mexico, however, refused to recognize Texan independence, and the vast majority of its citizens still wished to join the United States, where most of them, after all, had been born. There matters stood when the Whigs and William Henry Harrison won the presidency in 1840.

Texan independence

The Trek West

As thousands of Americans were moving into Texas, a much smaller trickle headed toward the Oregon country. Since 1818 the United States and Great Britain had occupied that territory jointly, as far north as latitude 54°40′. Although white settlement remained sparse, by 1836 American settlers outnumbered the British in the Willamette valley.

Pushed by the Panic of 1837 and six years of depression and pulled by tales of Oregon's lush, fertile valleys and the healthy, frost-free climate along California's Sacramento River, many American farmers struck out for the West Coast. Missouri was "cleaned" out of money, worried farmer Daniel Waldo, and his wife was even more adamant about heading west: "If you want to stay here another summer and shake your liver out with the fever and ague, you can do it," she announced to her husband, "but in the spring I am going to take the children and go to Oregon, Indians or no Indians." The wagon trains began rolling west.

The Overland Trail

Only a few hundred emigrants reached the West in 1841 and 1842, but in 1843 more than 800 followed the Overland Trail across the mountains to Oregon. From

Migration west

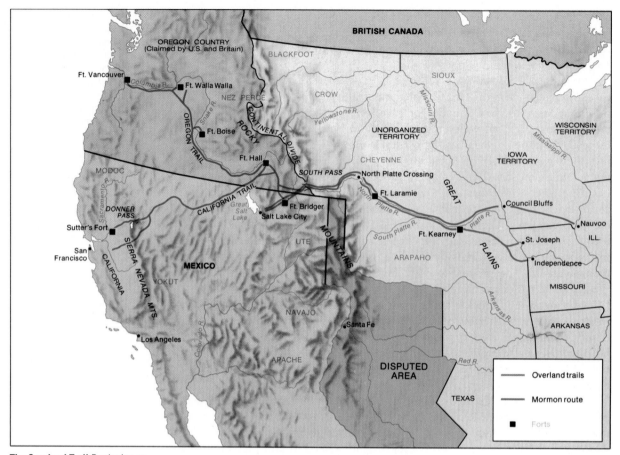

The Overland Trail Beginning at several different points, the Overland Trail followed the Platte and Sweetwater rivers across the plains to South Pass, where it crossed the Continental Divide. The trail split again near Fort Hall. Between 1840 and 1860 more than a quarter of a million emigrants made the trek. Following news of the gold strikes in 1848, the flow of westward emigrants increased and shifted toward California.

then on, they came by the thousands. Every spring brought a new rush of families to Independence or later to St. Joseph, Missouri, or to Council Bluffs, Iowa, where they waited for the spring rains to end and the trails to become passable. The migration was primarily a family enterprise, and many couples had only recently married. Most adults were between 20 and 50, since the hard journey discouraged the elderly. Furthermore, a family of four needed about $600 to outfit its journey, an amount that excluded the poor.

Caravans of 20 to 30 wagons were not uncommon the first few years, but after 1845 parties traveled in smaller trains of 8 to 10 wagons. Large companies used up the grass quickly, disagreements were more likely, and breakdowns (and hence halts) were more frequent. The trip itself lasted about 6 months, since the wagons normally covered only 15 miles a day, and the weather, repairs, deaths, and other eventualities necessitated occasional halts.

Women on the Overland Trail

The journey west placed a special strain on women, for the rugged life along the trail disrupted their traditional sense of the home. Few wives were as eager as Dan Waldo's to undertake the journey. "Poor Ma said only this morning, 'Oh I wish we never had started,'" one daughter reported, "and she looks so sorrowful and dejected." In one study of Oregon-bound parties, three-fourths of the women did not want to make the move.

At first, parties divided work by gender, as had been done back home. Women cooked, washed, sewed, and took care of the children, while men drove the wagons, cared for the stock, stood guard, and did the heavy labor. Necessity placed new demands on women, however, and eventually altered their roles. Within a few weeks, they found themselves helping to repair wagons and construct bridges. When men became exhausted, sick, or injured, women stood guard and drove the oxen. The change in work assignments proceeded only in one direction, however, for few men undertook "women's work."

The extra labor did not bring women new authority or power within the family. Nor, by and large, did they seek it. Women resisted efforts to blur the division between male and female work and struggled to preserve their traditional role and image. Quarrels over work assignments often brought into the open long-simmering family tensions. One woman reported that there was "not a little fighting" in their company, which was "invariably the outcome of disputes over divisions of labor." The conflicting pressures a woman might feel were well illustrated by Mary Ellen Todd, a teenaged daughter who spent hours practicing how to crack the bullwhip. "How my heart bounded," she recalled, "when I chanced to hear father say to mother, 'Do you know that Mary Ellen is beginning to crack the whip.' Then how it fell again when mother replied, 'I am afraid it isn't a very lady-like thing for a girl to do.' After this, while I felt a secret joy in being able to have a power that set things going, there was also a sense of shame over this new accomplishment."

As women strove to maintain a semblance of home on the trail, they often experienced a profound sense of loss. Trains often worked or traveled on the Sabbath, which had been ladies' day back home and an emblem of women's moral authority. Women also felt the lack of close companions to whom they could turn for comfort. One woman, whose husband separated their wagon from the train after a dispute, sadly watched the other wagons pull away: "I felt that indeed I had left all my friends to journey over the dreaded plains without one female acquaintance even for a companion—of course I wept and grieved about it but to no purpose."

Women's sense of loss

Often fatigued, their sense of moral authority eroded, and their ultimate home uncertain, women complained, as one put it, that "we had left all civilization behind us." Civilization to women meant more than law, government, and schools; it also meant their homes and domestic mission. Once settled in the West, they strove to reestablish that order.

Indians and the Trail Experience

The nations whose lands were crossed by white wagon trains reacted in a number of ways to the westward tide. The Sioux, who had long been trading with whites, were among the tribes who regularly visited overlanders to trade for blankets, clothes, cows, rifles, and knives. On the other hand, white migrants took a heavy toll on the Plains Indians' way of life: the emigrant parties scared off game and reduced buffalo herds, overgrazed the grass, and depleted the supply of wood. Having petitioned unsuccessfully in 1846 for government compensation, the Sioux decided to demand payment from the wagon trains crossing their lands. Whether parties paid or not depended on the relative strength of the two groups, but whites complained bitterly of what seemed to them naked robbery.

Pressures on the Plains Indians

Daily Lives

TIME AND TRAVEL

Seeing the Elephant on the Overland Trail

In an era when traveling circuses proved a welcome though rare attraction, Americans used the expression "I have seen the elephant" to indicate they had gotten all—or considerably more than—they had bargained for. To the quarter of a million men and women who migrated overland to the Pacific coast, "seeing the elephant" meant ceasing to be a greenhorn by overcoming hardship and succeeding. The greeting "Have you seen the elephant?" became the unofficial password of the Overland Trail.

Some walked, rode horseback, or accompanied mule pack trains, but the overwhelming majority of emigrants traveled in wagons. Wagons could haul more pounds per animal, did not have to be packed each day, could carry the sick and injured, and could be arranged in a defensive circle at night. Most often, emigrants modified a common farm wagon, about 10 feet long. The wooden wagon bed, made of seasoned hardwood to withstand extreme heat, cold, and moisture, was arched over by cloth or water-proofed canvas that could be closed at each end. Many owners adorned their wagon covers with personal information and slogans or decorated them with paintings and pictures of animals (the elephant was a popular choice) so they would stand out in the crowd.

Pulled usually by four to six oxen, one wagon could carry provisions and gear for a family of four. Most farm families were larger, however, and took at least one additional wagon. Packed within was a supply of bacon, breadstuffs (mostly flour), and coffee. For sleeping, families brought blankets and frequently a tent; a well-equipped wagon might have

Joseph Goldsborough Bruff, who traveled the Overland Trail to California, drew this picture of a Platte River crossing.

Their fears aroused by sensational stories, overland parties were wary of Indians, but this menace was greatly exaggerated, especially on the plains. Few wagon trains were attacked by Indians, and less than 4 percent of deaths on the trail were caused by Indians. In truth, emigrants killed more Indians than Indians killed emigrants. For overlanders the most aggravating problem posed by Indians was theft of stock. Many companies received valuable assistance from Indians, who acted as guides, directed them to grass and water, and transported stock and wagons across rivers.

As trail congestion and conflict increased, the government constructed a string of protective forts and in 1851 summoned the Plains Indians to a conference at Fort Laramie. The U.S. government agreed to make an annual payment as compensation for the damages caused by the wagon trains but also required tribes to confine themselves to areas north or south of a corridor through which the Overland Trail ran. Some tribes were unwilling to surrender their freedom of movement and refused to agree. The Sioux, the most powerful tribe on the plains, signed and then ignored the terms.

a feather bed laid over the packed possessions in the wagon. Parents normally slept there for privacy while children used the tent.

Before starting, the adult male members of a company elected their leaders. In the first years, when trains often ran to 30 wagons or more, a complex set of rules and procedures was adopted. With experience these were simplified. Still, disputes inevitably arose, and leaders were sometimes deposed midjourney. Samuel Tetherow recalled that his father, the captain of an 1845 train, "was capable as well as popular." "But," he continued, if you think it's any snap to run a wagon train of 66 wagons with every man in the train having a different idea of what is the best thing to do, all I can say is that some day you ought to try it."

At first, overlanders were gripped by a spirit of adventure; this feeling soon passed, however, as the monotonous daily routine set in. Women rose before daybreak to cook breakfast and food for lunch; the men followed at around five to care for the animals; the train was off at seven with the call of a bugle. Men and older sons walked alongside the team or herded stock in the rear. Women and children could ride in the wagon as it jolted along, but before long they walked as much as possible to conserve the animals' strength. After a noonday stop for a cold lunch, the journey resumed; by midafternoon the men seemed almost asleep as they plodded under the baking sun beside their teams. At evening camp the men attended to the animals while the women and children collected buffalo dung for fuel and hauled water. Women cooked the evening meal and afterward washed the dishes, took care of the bedding, cleaned the wagons, aired provisions, and mended clothes. After a guard was posted, the exhausted emigrants turned in for the night.

Once the Great Plains were crossed and the Rockies loomed, mutual assistance was critical. The final third of the route lay across deserts, along twisting rivers with difficult crossings, on paths barely wide enough for a wagon. Wagons had to be double- and triple-teamed up steep grades and hoisted over canyon walls with ropes, chains, and winches. Because most wagons lacked brakes, drivers locked the wheels when going down steep slopes, dragged a weight behind, or lowered the wagon by a rope attached to a tree. At some desert crossings, a tradition developed: travelers used supplies left by earlier groups, then hauled water and grass back, after they had safely crossed, for the next party.

Improvements in the 1850s shortened the trip and reduced the hardships. Still, it required considerable courage to embark on the journey and great fortitude to complete it. "To enjoy such a trip," an anonymous overlander testified, "a man must be able to endure heat like a Salamander, . . . dust like a toad, and labor like a jackass. He must learn to eat with his unwashed fingers, drink out of the same vessel with his mules, sleep on the ground when it rains, and share his blanket with vermin. . . . It is a hardship without glory." When they reached their new homes, those who traveled the Overland Trail could boast that they had, indeed, seen the elephant.

The Political Origins of Expansion

President William Henry Harrison made the gravest mistake of his brief presidential career when he ventured out one raw spring day, bareheaded and without an overcoat, to buy groceries at the Washington markets. He caught pneumonia and died only one month after his inauguration.

For the first time in the nation's history, a vice president succeeded to the nation's highest office upon the death of the president. John Tyler of Virginia had been a Democrat who supported states' rights so strongly that, during the nullification crisis, he was the only senator to vote against the Force Bill (page 350). After that, Jackson and the Democrats would have nothing to do with him, so Tyler joined the Whigs despite his strict constructionist principles. In 1840 the Whigs put him on the ticket with Old Tip in order to balance the ticket sectionally. In the rollicking 1840 campaign, the Whigs sang all too accurately: "And we'll vote for Tyler, therefore, / Without a why or wherefore."

Tyler becomes president

Tyler's Texas Ploy

Tyler breaks with the Whigs

Tyler's courteous manner and personal warmth masked a rigid mind. Repeatedly, when Henry Clay and the Whigs in Congress passed a major bill, Tyler opposed it. After Tyler twice vetoed bills to charter a new national bank, disgusted congressional Whigs formally expelled their president from the party. Most Democrats, too, avoided him as an untrustworthy "renegade."

Tyler, in short, was a man without a party. Surrounded by a group of flatterers, the president could claim almost no support except among federal officeholders, who could be fired if they did not endorse him. Still, Tyler's ambition led him to believe that he might win another four years in the White House if only he latched onto the right popular issue. Nursing their own personal and political dreams, his advisers began to whisper in his ear that that issue was the annexation of Texas.

The Texas movement

That advice came mostly from Democrats disgruntled with Martin Van Buren. Jackson's successor was, in their eyes, an ineffective leader who had stumbled through a depression and in 1840 gone down in ignominious defeat. "They mean to throw Van overboard," reported one delighted Whig, who caught wind of the plans. Meanwhile, Tyler's allies launched rumors designed to frighten southerners into pushing for annexation. Britain was ready to offer economic aid if Texas would abolish slavery, they claimed. (The rumor was false.) In April 1844 Tyler sent to the Senate for ratification a treaty he had secretly negotiated to bring Texas into the Union.

Van Overboard

The front runners for the Whig and Democratic presidential nominations were Clay and Van Buren. Although rivals, they were both moderates who feared the slavery issue. Apparently by prearrangement, both men issued letters opposing annexation on the grounds that it threatened the Union and would provoke war with Mexico.

Polk's nomination

As expected, the Whigs unanimously nominated Clay on a platform that ignored the expansion issue entirely. The Democrats, however, had a more difficult time. Those who opposed Van Buren persuaded the Democratic convention to adopt a rule requiring a two-thirds vote to nominate a candidate. That blocked Van Buren's nomination. On the ninth ballot the delegates finally turned to James K. Polk of Tennessee, who was pro-Texas. The 1844 Democratic platform called for the "reannexation" of Texas (under the claim it had been part of the Louisiana Purchase) and the "reoccupation" of Oregon, all the way to its northernmost boundary at 54°40′.

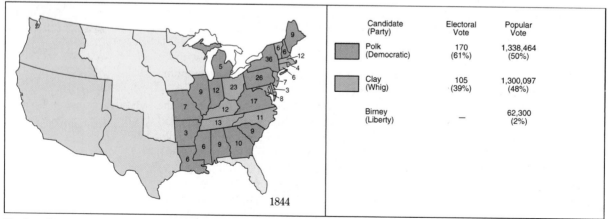

Candidate (Party)	Electoral Vote	Popular Vote
Polk (Democratic)	170 (61%)	1,338,464 (50%)
Clay (Whig)	105 (39%)	1,300,097 (48%)
Birney (Liberty)	—	62,300 (2%)

Election of 1844

Angered by the convention's outcome, Van Buren's supporters in the Senate joined the Whigs in decisively defeating Tyler's treaty of annexation. Tyler eventually withdrew from the race as an independent candidate, but the Texas issue would not go away. Henry Clay found many southerners slipping out of his camp because he opposed annexation; backtracking, he announced that he would be glad to see Texas annexed if it could be done without war or dishonor and without threatening the Union. And in the North, a few antislavery Whigs turned to James G. Birney, running on the Liberty party ticket.

In the end, Polk squeaked through by 38,000 votes out of nearly 3 million cast. If just half of Birney's 15,000 ballots in New York had gone to Clay, he would have carried the state and been narrowly elected president. Indignant Whigs charged that by refusing to support Clay, political abolitionists had made the annexation of Texas, and hence the addition of slave territory to the Union, inevitable. And indeed, Tyler again asked Congress to annex Texas—this time by a joint resolution, which required only a majority in both houses rather than a two-thirds vote for a treaty in the Senate. In the new atmosphere following Polk's victory, the resolution passed, and on March 3, 1845, his last day in office, Tyler invited Texas to enter the Union.

Polk's narrow victory

To the Pacific

Polk pursued his objectives as president with a dogged determination. Humorless, calculating, and often deceitful, he was not particularly brilliant in his maneuvering. But the life of politics consumed him, he knew his mind, and he could take the political pounding. Embracing a continental vision of the United States, Polk not only endorsed Tyler's offer of annexation but also looked beyond, hoping to gain the three best harbors on the Pacific: San Diego, San Francisco, and Puget Sound. That meant wresting Oregon from Britain and California from Mexico.

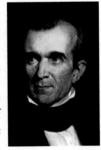

James K. Polk, continentalist (detail from an 1846 portrait by George Healy)

Claiming that the American title was "clear and unquestionable," the new president brushed aside any notion of continuing joint occupation of Oregon with Britain. To pressure the British, he induced Congress to give the required one-year notice terminating the joint occupation of Oregon. His blustering was reinforced by the knowledge that American settlers in Oregon outnumbered the British 5000 to 750. On the other hand, Polk hardly wanted war with a nation as powerful as Great Britain. So when the British offered, in June 1846, to divide the Oregon Territory along the 49th parallel, he readily agreed (see map, page 451). Britain retained Vancouver Island, where the Hudson's Bay Company's headquarters was located. But the arrangement gave the United States Puget Sound, which had been the president's objective all along.

The Mexican War

The Oregon settlement left Polk free to deal with Mexico. In 1845 Congress admitted Texas to the Union as a slave state, but Mexico had never formally recognized Texas's independence. It insisted, moreover, that Texas's southern boundary was the Nueces River, not the Rio Grande, 130 miles to the south, as claimed by Texas. In reality, Texas had never controlled the disputed region; the Nueces had always been Texas's boundary when it was a Mexican province; and if taken literally, the Rio Grande border incorporated New Mexican territory all the way to Santa Fe—lands still controlled by Mexico. Polk, already looking toward the Pacific, supported the Rio Grande boundary.

Disputed boundary of Texas

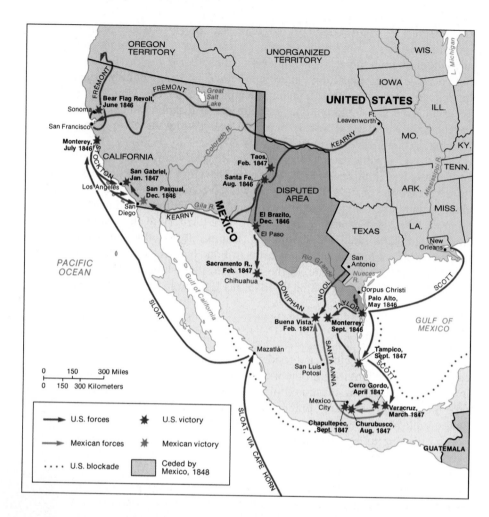

When Mexico broke off diplomatic relations after Texas came into the Union, Polk countered by sending American troops under General Zachary Taylor across the Nueces. At the same time, knowing that the unstable Mexican government desperately needed money, he attempted to buy territory to the Pacific. Sending John Slidell of Louisiana to Mexico as his special minister, Polk was prepared to offer $2 million in return for clear title to the Rio Grande boundary, $5 million for the remaining part of New Mexico, and up to $25 million for California. But the Mexican public overwhelmingly opposed ceding any more territory to the land-hungry Yankees, and the government refused to receive Slidell. "Depend upon it," reported Slidell, as he departed from Mexico in March 1846, "we can never get along well with them, until we have given them a good drubbing."

Blocked on the diplomatic front, Polk ordered Taylor, who had already crossed the Nueces with 4000 troops, to proceed south to the Rio Grande. From the Mexican standpoint, the Americans had invaded their country and occupied their territory. For his part, Polk wanted to be in position to defend the disputed region if the two countries went to war. He also hoped that the Mexican army might attack Taylor's force and make war inevitable.

On May 9 Polk had already begun work on a declaration of war, when word arrived that on April 25 Mexican forces had crossed the Rio Grande and attacked some of Taylor's troops, killing 11 Americans. The president quickly revised his war message, placing the entire blame for the war on Mexico. "Mexico has passed the boundary of the United States, has invaded our territory, and shed American blood upon American soil," he told Congress on May 11. "War exists, and notwithstanding all our efforts to avoid it, exists by the act of Mexico herself." The administration sent a bill to Congress calling for volunteers and requesting money to supply American troops.

Opposition to the War

The war with Mexico posed a dilemma for Whigs. They were convinced (correctly) that Polk had provoked the conflict in order to acquire more territory from Mexico, and many northern Whigs accused the president of seeking to extend slavery. But they remembered, too, that the Federalist party had doomed itself to extinction by opposing the War of 1812. Throughout the conflict, they therefore voted in favor of bills supplying American troops. At the same time they strenuously attacked the conduct of "Mr. Polk's War."

Sentiment for the war was strongest in the Old Southwest and most of the Old Northwest. It was much weaker in the East, where antislavery "Conscience Whigs" were prominent. "If I were a Mexican," Senator Thomas Corwin of Ohio affirmed in the Senate, "I would tell you, . . . 'we will greet you with bloody hands and welcome you to hospitable graves.'" With their party deeply divided over the issue of the expansion of slavery, Whigs opposed the acquisition of any territory from Mexico.

The Price of Victory

Even before any word of hostilities arrived in California, a group of impetuous American settlers around Sacramento launched the "Bear Flag Revolt." In June 1846 they proclaimed California an independent republic. American forces in the area

The fortified heights of Chapultepec fell in 1847 to Winfield Scott's invading forces, but not without fierce resistance by young Mexican cadets. Like the partisans of the Alamo, who gained fame in Texas lore, the defenders of Chapultepec won an honored place in Mexican history.

soon put down any Mexican resistance, and by the following January California was safely in American hands.

Conquest of Mexico

Meanwhile, Taylor moved south from the Rio Grande and won several battles, culminating in the decisive victory at Buena Vista that ended the war in Mexico's northern provinces. Polk had gained the territory he sought to reach the Pacific; now he wanted only peace. But the Mexican people refused to support any government that sued for peace, so Polk ordered an invasion into the heart of Mexico. After an American army commanded by General Winfield Scott captured Mexico City on September 14, 1847, Mexico surrendered.

The war had cost $97 million and 13,000 American lives, mostly as a result of disease. Yet the real cost was even higher. By bringing vast new territories into the Union, the war forced the explosive slavery issue to the center of national politics and threatened to upset the balance of power between North and South. Ralph Waldo Emerson had been prophetic: "The United States will conquer Mexico," he wrote when the Mexican War began, "but it will be as the man who swallows the arsenic which brings him down in turn. Mexico will poison us."

The Rise of the Slavery Issue

When the second party system emerged during the 1820s, Martin Van Buren had championed political parties as one way to forge links between North and South that would strengthen the Union. But the Texas movement increased sectional suspicions, and President Polk did nothing to ease this problem.

Northern discontent

Polk was a politician to his bones: constantly maneuvering, promising one thing, doing another, making a pledge, taking it back—using any means to accomplish his ends. As his term wore on, the pro-southern bent of this Tennessee slaveholder embittered Democrats from the North and West. Western Democrats were furious when Polk vetoed a bill to improve rivers and harbors. Northerners complained that Polk had compromised with the British on Oregon, which was suitable for northern agriculture, at the same time that he had used military force to defend Texas's absurd boundary claims.

Wilmot Proviso

This festering discontent finally erupted in August 1846 when Polk requested $2 million from Congress, as he vaguely explained, to "facilitate negotiations" with Mexico. It was widely understood that the money was to be used to bribe the Mexican government to cede territory to the United States. On August 8 David Wilmot, an obscure Pennsylvania congressman, startled Democratic leaders by introducing an amendment to the bill that barred slavery from any territory acquired from Mexico. The Wilmot Proviso, as the amendment became known, passed the northern-controlled House of Representatives several times, only to be rejected in the Senate, where the South had more power. As such, it revealed mounting sectional tensions.

Wilmot himself was hardly an abolitionist. Indeed, he hoped to keep not only slaves but all black people out of the territories. Denying any "morbid sympathy for the slave," he declared, "I would preserve for white free labor a fair country . . . where the sons of toil, of my own race and color, can live without the disgrace which association with negro slavery brings upon free labor." The Wilmot Proviso aimed not to destroy slavery in the South but to confine the institution to those states where it already existed. Still, abolitionists had long contended that southern slaveholders—the "Slave Power"—were plotting to extend their sway over the rest of the country. The political maneuverings of slaveholders like Tyler, and especially Polk, convinced growing numbers of northerners that the Slave Power did indeed exist and that it was aggressively looking to expand its influence.

The status of slavery in the territories became more than an abstract question when the Senate in 1848 ratified the Treaty of Guadalupe Hidalgo. Under its terms the United States acquired Mexico's provinces of New Mexico and Upper California in return for approximately $18 million. That translated into a half million square miles of territory along with about 75,000 Spanish-speaking inhabitants. With the United States in control of the Pacific Coast from San Diego to Puget Sound, Polk's continental vision had become a reality.

Peace treaty with Mexico

New Societies in the West

As Hispanic, Indian, Asian, and Anglo-American cultures mixed, the patterns of settlement along the frontier varied widely. Some settlers recreated the farm economies and small towns of the Anglo-American East; others continued the cattle-ranching life of the Hispanic West. In California the new settlements were over-whelmingly shaped by the rush for gold after 1848. And in the Great Basin around Salt Lake, the Mormons established a society whose sense of religious mission was as strong as that of the Puritans.

Farming in the West

The overlanders expected to replicate the societies they had left behind. When a wagon train arrived at its destination, members had usually exhausted their resources and thus quickly scattered in search of employment or a good farm site. "Friday, October 27.—Arrived at Oregon City at the falls of the Willamette," read one pioneer diary. "Saturday, October 28.—Went to work."

In a process repeated over and over, settlers in a new area set up the machinery of government. Although violence was common on the frontier, farming communities tended to resolve problems by traditional means. Churches took longer to establish, for ministers were hard to recruit and congregations were often not large enough to support a church. As the population grew, however, a more conventional society evolved. Towns and a middle class developed, the proportion of women increased, schools were established, and the residents became less mobile.

Evolution of western society

Although opportunity was greater on the frontier and early arrivals had a special advantage, more and more the agricultural frontier of the West resembled the older society of the East. With the development of markets and transportation, wealth became concentrated, some families fell to the lower rungs of society, and those who were less successful left, seeking yet another fresh start.

The Gold Rush

In January 1848, while constructing a sawmill along the American River, James Marshall noticed gold flecks in the millrace. More discoveries followed, and when the news reached the East, it spread like wildfire. The following spring the Overland Trail was jammed with eager "forty-niners." Some 80,000 emigrants journeyed to California that year, about 55,000 of whom took the overland route. In only two years, from 1848 to the end of 1849, California's population jumped from 14,000 to 100,000. By 1860 it stood at 380,000.

Among those who went to California was William Swain, a 27-year-old farmer in western New York. Deciding that he had had enough of the hard work of farming, he bid good-bye to his wife and daughter in 1849 and set off for the gold fields to make his fortune. Upon his arrival in November, he entered a partnership and staked a claim along the Feather River, but after several months of back-breaking work in icy waters, he and his partners discovered that their claim was "worth nothing." He sold out and joined another company, but early rains soon forced them to stop work. In October 1850, after less than a year in the diggings, Swain decided to return home. With only a few hundred dollars to show for his labor, he counted himself one of the vast majority of miners who had seen "their bright daydreams of golden wealth vanish like the dreams of night." He arrived home the following February and resumed farming.

Life in the mining camps

Those like Swain intent on making a fortune and returning home gave no thought to putting down roots. Most agreements were made by the month. Mining camps literally appeared and died overnight, as word of a new strike sent miners racing off to another canyon, valley, or streambed. Most settlements were hardly more than a single street, littered with debris and lined with stores, buildings, and miners' shacks—often no more than blankets or cloth tacked to a wooden frame. A saloon and gambling hall, which might double as a hotel and sometimes a brothel, was usually the most prominent building in town. More than 80 percent of the prospectors who poured into the gold country were Americans, including free blacks. Mexicans, Australians, Hawaiians, Chinese, French, English, and Irish also came. Whatever their nationality, the new arrivals were overwhelmingly unmarried men in their twenties and thirties.

The constant movement, the hard labor of mining, the ready cash, and the rootlessness all made camp society unstable. "There is an excitement connected with the pursuit of gold which renders one restless and uneasy—ever hoping to do something better," explained one forty-niner. Removed from the traditional forms of social control, miners engaged in gambling, swearing, drinking, and fighting. One startled minister reported from the California gold fields that unlike back home, immorality "is in the open, unmasked, makes no apologies and asks none." Indeed, he said, "It unfurls its flag in the most public and conspicuous places."

Women in the camps

Only about 5 percent of gold rush emigrants were women or children; given this relative scarcity, men were willing to pay top dollar for women's domestic skills.

With their distinctive clothing and bamboo hats, Chinese miners could be seen throughout the diggings. Chinese immigration reached a peak in 1852, when 20,000 arrived in California. In the heyday of the mining camps, perhaps 20 percent of the miners were Chinese. Confronted with intense hostility from other miners, they worked abandoned claims and unpromising sites with primitive and less expensive equipment.

Women supported themselves by cooking, sewing, and washing, as well as by running hotels and boardinghouses. "A smart woman can do very well in this country," one woman informed a friend in the East. "It is the only country I ever was in where a woman received anything like a just compensation for work." Likewise, they suffered no shortage of suitors. "I had men come forty miles over the mountains, just to look at me," Eliza Wilson recalled, "and I never was called a handsome woman, in my best days, even by my most ardent admirers." Women went to the mining frontier to be with their husbands, to make money, or to find adventure. But the class most frequently seen in the diggings was prostitutes, who numbered perhaps 20 percent of female Californians in 1850.

Predictably, mining the miners offered one of the more reliable roads to prosperity.

Perhaps half the inhabitants of a mining town were shopkeepers, businesspeople, and professionals who provided services for prospectors. Also conspicuous were gamblers, card sharks, and other outcasts, all bent on separating the miner from his riches. In such an atmosphere, violence was prevalent, so when a new camp opened, miners adopted a set of rules and regulations. Justice was dispensed promptly, either by a vote of all the miners or by an elected jury. While effective when administered fairly, the system at times degenerated into lynch law.

Observers praised the diggings' democratic spirit. Yet such assertions overlooked strongly held nativist prejudices: when frustrated by a lack of success, American miners directed their hostility toward foreigners. The miners ruthlessly exterminated the Indians in the area, mob violence drove Mexicans out of nearly every camp, and the Chinese were confined to claims abandoned by Americans as unprofitable. The state eventually enacted a foreign miners' tax that fell largely on the Chinese. Free African Americans felt the sting of discrimination as well, both in the camps and in state law. White American miners proclaimed that "colored men were not privileged to work in a country intended only for American citizens."

Nativist and racial prejudices

Before long, the most easily worked claims had been played out, and competition steadily drove down the average earnings from $20 a day in 1848 to $6 in 1852. That was still higher than eastern wages, but goods and services cost significantly more too. As gold became increasingly difficult to extract, larger corporations using heavy equipment and employing miners working for wages came to dominate the industry. Men who had come to California filled with visions of wealth usually found only shovels of mud. As the era of the individual miner passed, so too did mining camps and the unique society they spawned.

The damage mining did to the land endured longer. Abandoned prospect holes and diggings pockmarked the gold fields and created piles of debris that heavy rains would wash down the valley, choking streams and ruining lands below. Excavation of hillsides, construction of dams to divert rivers, and the destruction of the forest cover to meet the heavy demand for lumber and firewood caused serious erosion of the soil and spring floods. The attitude of the individual miners differed little from that of the capitalists who succeeded them: both sought to exploit the environment as rapidly as possible with little thought to long-term consequences. Untempered by any sense of restraint, the quest for rapid wealth left long-lasting scars on the landscape of the gold country.

Environmental impact of mining

Instant City: San Francisco

When the United States assumed control of California, San Francisco had a population of perhaps 200. But thousands of emigrants took the water route west, passing through San Francisco's harbor on their way to the diggings. By 1856 the city's population had jumped to an astonishing 50,000. In a mere 8 years the city had attained the size New York had taken 190 years to reach.

The product of economic self-interest, San Francisco developed in helter-skelter fashion. Land prices soared, speculation was rampant, and commercial forces became paramount. Residents lived in tents or poorly constructed, half-finished buildings. To enlarge the commercial district, hills began to be leveled, with the dirt used to fill in the bay (thereby creating more usable land). Since the city government took virtually no role in directing development, almost no land was reserved for public use. Property owners defeated a proposal to widen the streets, prompting the city's leading newspaper to complain, "To sell a few more feet of lots, the streets were compressed like a cheese, into half their width."

San Francisco's chaotic growth

San Francisco in 1852

 # The Migration from China

The gold rush that swelled San Francisco's streets was a global phenomenon. Americans predominated in the mining population, but Latin Americans, Europeans, Australians, and Chinese swarmed into California. An amazing assortment of languages could be heard on the city's streets: indeed, in 1860 San Francisco was 50 percent foreign-born.

The most distinctive of the ethnic groups was the Chinese. They had come to Gum San, the land of the golden mountain. Those who arrived in California overwhelmingly hailed from the area of southern China around Canton—and not by accident. Although other provinces of China also suffered from economic distress, population pressures, social unrest, and political upheaval, Canton had a large European presence, since it was the only port open to outsiders. That situation changed after the first Opium War (1839–1842), when Britain forced China to open other ports to trade. For Cantonese, the sudden loss of their trade monopoly produced widespread economic hardship. At the same time, a series of religious and political revolts in the region led to severe fighting that devastated the countryside. A growing number of residents concluded that emigration was the only way to survive, and the presence of western ships in the harbors of Canton and nearby Hong Kong (a British possession since 1842) made it easier to migrate to California rather than southeast Asia.

Between 1849 and 1854, some 45,000 Chinese flocked to California. Among those who went was 16-year-old Lee Chew, who left for California after a man from his village returned with great wealth from the "country of the American wizards." Like the other gold seekers, these Chinese immigrants were overwhelmingly young and male, and they wanted only to accumulate savings and return home to their families. (Indeed, only 16 Chinese women arrived before 1854.) Generally poor, Chinese immigrants arrived already in debt, having borrowed the price of their steamship ticket; they fell further into debt to Chinese merchants in San Francisco, who loaned them money to purchase needed supplies.

When the Chinese were harassed in the mines, many opened laundries in San Francisco and elsewhere, since little capital was required—soap, scrub board, iron, and ironing board. The going rate at the time for washing, ironing, and starching shirts was an exorbitant $8 per dozen. Many early San Franciscans actually found it cheaper to send their dirty laundry to Canton or Honolulu, to be returned several months later. Other Chinese around San Francisco set up restaurants or worked in the fishing industry. In these early years they found Americans less hostile, as long as they stayed away from the gold fields. As immigration and the competition for jobs increased, however, anti-Chinese sentiment intensified.

Gradually, San Francisco took on the trappings of a more orderly community. The city government established a public school system, erected streetlights, created a municipal water system, and halted further filling in of the bay. Industry was confined to the area south of the city; several new working-class neighborhoods grew up near the downtown section. Fashionable neighborhoods sprouted on several hills, as high rents drove many residents from the developing commercial center, and churches and families became more common. By 1856, the city of the gold rush had been replaced by a new city whose stone and brick buildings gave it a new sense of permanence.

The Mormons in Utah

The makeshift, often chaotic society spawned by the gold rush was a product of largely uncontrolled economic forces. In contrast, the society evolving in the Great Basin of Utah exhibited an entirely different but equally remarkable growth. Salt Lake City became the center of a religious kingdom established by the Church of Jesus Christ of Latter-day Saints.

After Joseph Smith's death in 1844 (page 377), the Mormon church was led by Brigham Young, who lacked Smith's religious mysticism but was a brilliant organizer. Young decided to move his followers to the Great Basin, an isolated area a thousand miles from the settled parts of the United States. In 1847 the first thousand settlers arrived, the vanguard of thousands more who extended Mormon settlement throughout the valley of the Great Salt Lake and the West. Church officials also held the government positions, and Young had supreme power in legislative, executive, and judicial matters as well as religious affairs. In 1849 the state of Deseret was officially established, with Brigham Young as governor. It applied for admission to the Union.

State of Deseret

The most controversial church teaching was the doctrine of polygamy, or plural marriage, which Young finally sanctioned publicly in 1852. Visitors reported with surprise that few Mormon wives seemed to rebel against the practice. Some plural wives developed close friendships; indeed, in one sample almost a third of plural marriages included at least two sisters. If the wives lived together, the system allowed them to share domestic work. When the husband established separate households, wives enjoyed greater freedom, since the husband was not constantly present. Moreover, because polygamy distinguished Mormonism from other religions, plural wives saw it as an expression of their religious faith. "I want to be assured of *position in God's estimation*," one such wife explained. "If polygamy is the Lord's order, we must carry it out."

Polygamy

The Mormons connected control of water to their sense of mission and respect for hierarchy. The Salt Lake valley, where the Mormons established their holy community, lacked significant rivers or abundant sources of water. Thus success

Irrigation and community

depended on irrigating the region, something never before attempted. When the first Mormons arrived from the East, they had no experience with irrigation and little capital. But they made up for that lack with a strong sense of unity bolstered by a religious commission to exploit the environment and make it fruitful. By constructing a coordinated series of dams, aqueducts, and ditches, they brought life-giving water to the valleys of the region. Fanning out from their original settlement, they founded a series of colonies throughout the West, all tied to Salt Lake City and joined by ribbons of water. Mormon farmers grew corn, wheat, hay, and an assortment of fruits and vegetables. By 1850, there were more than 16,000 irrigated acres in what would eventually become the state of Utah. The Mormons were the first Anglos to extensively use irrigation in North America.

Manipulation of water reinforced the Mormons' sense of hierarchy and group discipline. Centralization of authority in the hands of church officials made possible an overall plan of development, allowed for maximum exploitation of resources, and freed communities from the disputes over water rights that plagued many settlements in the arid West. In a radical departure from American ideals, church leaders insisted that water belonged to the community, not individuals, and vested this authority in the hands of the local bishop. Control of water resources, which were vital for survival in the desert, reinforced the power of the church hierarchy over not just the faithful but dissidents as well. Community needs, as interpreted by church leaders, took precedence over individual rights. Thus irrigation did more than make the desert bloom. By checking the Jeffersonian ideal of an independent, self-sufficient farmer, it also made possible a centralized, well-regulated society under the firm control of the church.

Temple City: Salt Lake City

In laying out the Mormons' "temple city" of Salt Lake, Young was also determined to avoid the commercial worldliness and competitive individualism that had plagued the Mormons at Nauvoo. City lots, which were distributed by lottery, could not be subdivided for sale, and real estate speculation was forbidden.

Salt Lake City's orderly growth

The city itself was laid out in a checkerboard grid well suited to the level terrain. Streets were 132 feet wide (compared with 60 feet in San Francisco), and each square block contained eight home lots of 1.25 acres each. Unlike in early San

Francisco, the family was the basic social unit in Salt Lake City, and almost from the beginning the city had an equal balance of men and women. The planners also provided for four public squares in various parts of the city. The city lacked any traditional secular authority: it was divided into 18 wards, each under the supervision of a bishop, who held civil as well as religious power.

As the city expanded, the original plan had to be modified to accommodate the developing commercial district by dividing lots into sizes more suitable for stores. Experience and growth also eventually dictated smaller blocks and narrower streets, but the city still retained its spacious appearance and regular design. Through religious and economic discipline church leaders succeeded in preserving a sense of common purpose.

Shadows on the Moving Frontier

Transformations like Salt Lake City and San Francisco were truly remarkable. But it is important to remember that Americans were not coming into a trackless, unsettled wilderness. As frontier lines crossed, 75,000 Mexicans had to adapt to American rule.

The Treaty of Guadalupe Hidalgo guaranteed Mexicans in the ceded territory "the free enjoyment of their liberty and property." As long as Mexicans continued to be a sizable majority in a given area, their influence was strong. But wherever Anglos became more numerous, they demanded conformity to American customs. When Mexicans remained faithful to their heritage, language, and religion, these cultural differences worked to reinforce Hispanic powerlessness, social isolation, and economic exploitation.

New Mexico had the largest Hispanic population as well as the fewest Anglos in the Mexican cession. As a result, the upper-class Mexicans who owned the land and employed large numbers of mixed-blood workers on their ranches managed to maintain their position. This class had cultivated American allies during the Santa Fe trade, and their connections grew stronger as American businesspeople slowly entered the territory in the 1850s. Neither group had much interest in the lower-class Hispanics, whom both exploited.

The rush of American emigrants quickly overwhelmed Hispanic settlers in California. Even in 1848, before the discovery of gold, Americans in California

Hispanic-Anglo conflict

Town plazas, such as this one in San Antonio, were commercial centers in the Mexican Southwest. Traders from outlying *ranchos* enjoy refreshments while their goods, loaded on oxcarts, await sale.

outnumbered Mexicans two to one, and by 1860 Hispanics amounted to only 2 percent of the population. At the time of the American conquest, the 200 or so *ranchero* families owned about 14 million acres, but changes in California land law required verification of their original land grants by a federal commission. Since the average claim took 17 years to complete and imposed complex procedures and hefty legal fees, many *rancheros* lost large tracts of land to Americans.

Lower-class Mexicans scratched out a bare existence on ranches and farms or in the growing cities and towns. Scorned by the dominant Anglo majority and without skills and resources, they were often reduced to extreme poverty. As the Hispanic population in California became primarily urban, women assumed a larger role in the family. Many men were seasonal workers who were absent part of the year, and thus women played a greater role in sustaining the family economically.

Mexicans in Texas were also greatly outnumbered: they totaled only 6 percent of the population in 1860. Stigmatized as inferior, they were the poorest group in free society. One response to this dislocation, an option commonly taken by persecuted minorities, was social banditry. An example was the folk hero Juan Cortina. A member of a displaced landed family in southern Texas, Cortina was driven into resistance in the 1850s by American harassment. He began stealing from wealthy Anglos to aid poor Mexicans, proclaiming, "To me is entrusted the breaking of the chains of your slavery." Cortina continued to raid Texas border settlements until finally imprisoned by Mexican authorities. While failing to produce any lasting change, Cortina demonstrated the depth of frustration and resentment among Hispanics over their abuse at the hands of the new Anglo majority.

Escape from Crisis

Issue of slavery's extension

With the return of peace, Congress confronted the problem of whether to allow slavery in the newly acquired territories. David Wilmot, in his controversial proviso, had already proposed to outlaw slavery throughout the Mexican cession. John C. Calhoun, representing the extreme southern position, countered that slavery was legal in all territories. The federal government had acted as the agent of all the states in acquiring the land, he argued, and southerners had a right to take their property there, including slaves. Only when the residents of a territory drafted a state constitution could they decide the question of slavery.

Between these extremes were two moderate positions. One proposed extending the Missouri Compromise line of 36°30′ to the Pacific, which would have continued the earlier policy of dividing the national domain between the North and the South. The other proposal, championed by Senator Lewis Cass of Michigan and Senator Stephen A. Douglas of Illinois, was to allow the people of the territory rather than Congress to decide the status of slavery. This solution, which became known as popular sovereignty, was deliberately ambiguous, since its supporters refused to specify whether the residents could make this decision at any time or only when drafting a state constitution, as Calhoun insisted.

When Congress organized the Oregon Territory in 1848, it prohibited slavery there, since even southerners admitted that the region was too far north to grow the South's staple crops. But this seemingly straightforward decision made it impossible to apply the Missouri Compromise line to the other territories. Without Oregon as a part of the package, the bulk of the remaining land would be open to slavery, something at which the North balked. Almost inadvertently, one of the two moderate solutions had been discarded by the summer of 1848.

A Two-Faced Campaign

In the election of 1848 both major parties tried to avoid the slavery issue. The Democrats nominated Lewis Cass, a supporter of popular sovereignty, while the Whigs bypassed all their prominent leaders and selected General Zachary Taylor, who had taken no position on any public issue and who remained silent throughout the campaign. The Whigs adopted no platform and planned instead to emphasize the general's war record.

But the slavery issue would not quietly go away. Instead, a new antislavery coalition, the Free Soil party, came together. Alienated by Polk's policies and still angry over the 1844 convention, northern Democrats loyal to Van Buren spearheaded its creation. They were joined by "Conscience Whigs," who disavowed Taylor's nomination because he was a slaveholder. Furthermore, political abolitionists like Salmon P. Chase left the Liberty party in favor of this broader coalition. To widen its appeal, the Free Soil platform focused on the dangers of extending slavery rather than on the evil of slavery itself. Ironically, the party's convention named as its candidate Martin Van Buren—the man who for years had struggled to keep the slavery issue out of politics.

Free Soil party

With the Free Soilers strongly supporting the Wilmot Proviso, the Whigs and Democrats could not ignore the slavery question. The two major parties responded by running different campaigns in the North and the South. To southern audiences, each party promised that it would protect slavery in the territories; to northern voters, each claimed that it would keep the territories free. In this two-faced, sectional campaign, the Whigs won their second national victory. Taylor held on to the core of Whig voters in both sections (Van Buren and Cass, after all, had long been Democrats). But in the South, where the contest pitted a southern slaveholder against two northerners, Taylor won many more votes than Clay had in 1844. As one southern Democrat complained, "We have lost hundreds of votes, solely on the ground that General Cass was a Northerner and General Taylor a Southern man." Furthermore, Van Buren polled five times as many votes as the Liberty party had four years earlier. It seemed that the national system of political parties was being gradually pulled apart.

The Compromise of 1850

Once he became president, Taylor could no longer remain silent. The territories gained from Mexico had to be organized; furthermore, by 1849 California had gained enough residents to be admitted as a state. In the Senate the balance of power between North and South stood at 15 states each. California's admission would break the sectional balance.

Taylor's plan

Called "Old Rough and Ready" by his troops, Taylor was a forthright man of action, but he was politically inexperienced and oversimplified complex problems. Since even Calhoun conceded that entering states had the right to ban slavery, Taylor proposed that the way to end the sectional crisis was to skip the territorial stage by combining all the Mexican cession into two very large states, New Mexico and California. So the president sent agents to California and New Mexico with instructions to set the machinery in motion for both territories to draft constitutions and apply for statehood directly. Even more shocking to southern Whigs, he proposed to apply the Wilmot Proviso to the entire area, since he was convinced that slavery would never flourish there. By the time Congress convened in December 1849, California had drafted a constitution and applied for admission as a free state. Taylor reported that New Mexico (which included most of Arizona, Utah, and Colorado) would soon do the same and recommended that both be admitted as free states. The president's plan touched off the most serious sectional crisis the Union had yet confronted.

Into this turmoil stepped Henry Clay, now 73 years old and nearing the end of his career. A savvy card player all his life, Clay loved politics: the bargaining, the wheeling and dealing, the late-night trade-offs eased along by a bottle of bourbon. Thirty years earlier he had engineered the Missouri Compromise, and in 1833 he had helped defuse the nullification crisis. Clay decided that a grand compromise was needed to save the Union. Already, Mississippi had summoned other southern states to meet in a convention at Nashville to discuss the crisis, and southern extremists were pushing for secession. The points of disagreement went beyond the question of the western territories. Many northerners considered it disgraceful that slaves were bought and sold in the nation's capital, where slavery was still permitted. Southerners complained bitterly that northern states ignored the 1793 fugitive slave law and prevented them from reclaiming runaway slaves.

Clay's compromise

Clay's compromise, submitted in January 1850, addressed all these concerns. California, he proposed, should be admitted as a free state, which represented the

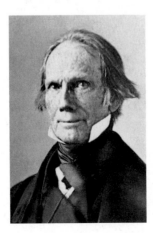

The Great Triumvirate—Clay, Webster, and Calhoun—served together in public life for almost four decades. Clay (left) and Webster (center) supported the Compromise of 1850, whereas in his last speech in the Senate, the dying Calhoun (right) opposed it. By midcentury, power was passing to a new generation of politicians more accustomed to sectional conflict and less amenable to compromise.

clear wishes of most settlers there. The rest of the Mexican cession would be organized as two territories, New Mexico and Utah, under the doctrine of popular sovereignty. Thus slavery would not be prohibited from these regions. Clay also proposed that Congress abolish the slave trade but not slavery itself in the District of Columbia and that a new, more rigorous fugitive slave law be passed to enable southerners to reclaim runaway slaves. To reinforce the idea that both North and South were yielding ground, Clay combined those provisions that dealt with the former Mexican territory and several others adjusting the Texas–New Mexico boundary into a larger package known as the Omnibus Bill.

With the stakes so high, the Senate debated the bill for six months. Daniel Webster of Massachusetts, always deep-voiced, seemed more somber than usual when he

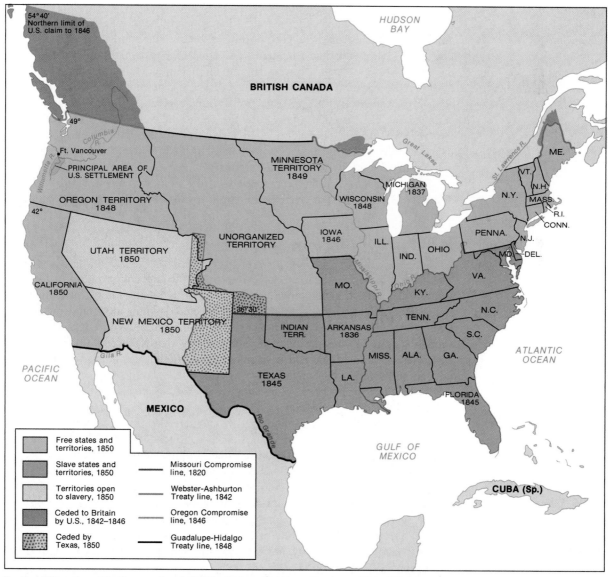

Territorial Growth and the Compromise of 1850 The Webster-Ashburton Treaty established Maine's northern boundary as well as the American-Canadian boundary west of the Great Lakes.

delivered a pro-compromise speech on the seventh of March. "I wish to speak today not as a Massachusetts man, not as a Northern man, but as an American. . . . I speak today for the preservation of the Union. Hear me for my cause." Calhoun, whose aged, crevassed face mirrored the lines that had been drawn so deeply between the two sections, was near death and too ill to deliver his final speech to the Senate, which a colleague read for him as he listened silently. The "cords of Union," he warned—those ties of interest and affection that held the nation together—were snapping one by one. Only equal rights for the South and an end to the agitation against slavery could preserve the Union.

Clay, wracked by a hacking cough, spent long hours trying to line up the needed votes. But for once, the great whist enthusiast had misplayed his hand. The Omnibus Bill required that the components of the compromise be approved as a package. Extremists in Congress from both regions, however, combined against the moderates and rejected the bill.

Passage of the Compromise

With Clay exhausted and his strategy in shambles, Democrat Stephen A. Douglas assumed leadership of the pro-compromise forces. The sudden death in July of President Taylor, who had threatened to veto Clay's plan, aided the compromise movement. One by one, Douglas submitted the individual measures for a vote. Northern representatives provided the necessary votes to admit California and abolish the slave trade in the District of Columbia, while southern representatives supplied the edge needed to organize the Utah and New Mexico territories and pass the new fugitive slave law. On the face of it, everyone had compromised. But in truth, only 61 members of Congress, or 21 percent of the membership, had not voted against some part of the Compromise.

By September 17 all the separate parts of the Compromise of 1850 had passed and been signed into law by the new president, Millard Fillmore. The Union, it seemed, was safe.

Away from the Brink

The general public, both North and South, rallied to the Compromise. At the convention of southern states in Nashville, the fire-eaters—the radical proponents of states' rights and secession—found themselves voted down by more moderate voices.

Rejection of secession

Even in the Deep South, coalitions of pro-Compromise Whigs and Democrats soundly defeated secessionists in the state elections that followed. Still, most southerners felt that a firm line had been drawn. With California's admission, they were now outnumbered in the Senate, so it was critical that slaveholders be granted equal legal access to the territories. They announced that any breach of the Compromise of 1850 would justify secession.

Fugitive slave law

The North, for its part, found the new fugitive slave law the hardest measure of the Compromise of 1850 to swallow. The controversial law denied an accused runaway a trial by jury, and it required that all citizens assist federal marshals in its enforcement. Harriet Beecher Stowe's popular novel *Uncle Tom's Cabin* (1852) presented a powerful moral indictment of the law—and of slavery as an institution. (See Daily Lives, "Uncle Tom by Footlights," pages 478–479.) Despite sentimental characters, a contrived plot, and clumsy dialect, the book profoundly moved its readers. Emphasizing the duty of Christians toward the downtrodden, it reached a greater audience than any previous abolitionist work and heightened moral opposition to the institution.

In reality, however, fewer than 1000 slaves a year ran away to the North, many of whom did not succeed. Despite some cases of well-publicized resistance, the

1850 fugitive slave law was generally enforced in the free states. Many northerners did not like the law, but they were unwilling to tamper with the Compromise. Stephen Douglas spoke accurately enough when he boasted in 1851, "The whole country is acquiescing in the compromise measures—everywhere, North and South. Nobody proposes to repeal or disturb them."

And so calm returned. In the lackluster 1852 presidential campaign, both the Whigs and the Democrats endorsed the Compromise. Franklin Pierce, a little-known New Hampshire Democrat, soundly defeated the Whig candidate, Winfield Scott. Even more significant, the antislavery Free Soil candidate received only about half as many votes as Van Buren had four years before. With the slavery issue seemingly losing political force, it appeared that the Republic had weathered the storm unleashed by the Wilmot Proviso.

But the moving frontier still had changes to work. It had leaped from the Mississippi valley to the Pacific, but in between remained territory still unorganized. And as the North became increasingly industrialized and the South more firmly committed to an economy based on cotton and slavery, the growing conflict between the two sections would shatter the Jacksonian party system, reignite the slavery issue, and shake the Union to its foundation.

chapter summary

In the 1840s the United States expanded to the Pacific, a development that involved the cultural interaction of Americans with other groups and led to the rise of the slavery issue in national politics.

- In the 1840s Americans proclaimed that it was the United States' Manifest Destiny to expand across the North American continent.

- Americans in Texas increasingly clashed with Mexican authorities, and in 1836 Texans revolted and established an independent republic.

- Americans headed for Oregon and California on the Overland Trail.

  - The journey put special pressures on women as the traditional division of labor by gender broke down.

  - White migration also put pressure on Plains Indians' grazing lands, wood supplies, and freedom of movement.

  - The gold rush spawned a unique society that was overwhelmingly male, highly mobile, and strongly nativist and racist.

  - Led by Brigham Young, the Mormons established a tightly organized, centrally controlled society in the Great Salt Lake basin.

  - Throughout the Southwest the Hispanic population suffered at the hands of the new Anglo majority.

- President James K. Polk entered office with a vision of the United States as a continental nation.

  - He upheld President John Tyler's annexation of Texas and agreed to divide the Oregon country with Britain.

  - The United States eventually went to war with Mexico and acquired California and the Southwest.

- The Mexican War reinjected into national politics the issue of slavery's expansion.

  - The Wilmot Proviso sought to prohibit slavery from any territory acquired from Mexico.

  - The struggle over the Proviso eventually disrupted both major parties.

  - Congress momentarily stilled the sectional crisis with the Compromise of 1850.

interactive learning

The Primary Source Investigator CD-ROM offers the following materials related to this chapter:

- Interactive map: **The Mexican War, 1846–1848** (M13)

- A collection of primary sources demonstrating the dramatic impact of slavery on the Union as it expanded westward. Also discover the dynamic and socially disruptive slave trade that emerged to feed the plantations to the west through images of slave pens where humans were held until their sale. Explore the westward expansion with the journal of Maximillian Alexander Philipp. As the nation expanded, conflict with Mexico erupted: view a portrait of Stephen F. Austin, one of the founders of the Republic of Texas, to go along with the interactive map illustrating the Mexican War.

additional reading

In recent years the field of western American history has dramatically expanded to include cultural diversity, environmental problems, racial interaction, and the role of gender, themes that were largely ignored in earlier accounts of western expansion. Good introductions to the "new western history" are Richard White's inelegantly titled *It's Your Misfortune and None of My Own* (1991) and William Cronon et al., *Under an Open Sky* (1992).

David J. Weber, *The Mexican Frontier, 1821–1846* (1982), is a superb study of the Southwest prior to American control. Two excellent accounts from different perspectives of the Overland Trail experience are John D. Unruh Jr., *The Plains Across* (1979), and John Mack Faragher, *Women and Men on the Overland Trail* (1979). Thomas R. Hietala offers a stimulating analysis of the social roots of expansionism in *Manifest Design* (1985). Leonard J. Arrington and Davis Bitton, *The Mormon Experience,* 2nd ed. (1992), is a good survey. Women's experiences in the West are analyzed in Julie R. Jeffrey, *Frontier Women* (1979), while Donald D. Jackson, *Gold Dust* (1980), examines the gold rush. The fullest treatment of politics in this decade is William R. Brock, *Parties and Political Conscience* (1970). The drive to annex Texas is carefully untangled in William W. Freehling, *The Road to Disunion* (1990), and its impact on the Democratic party is the focus of James C. N. Paul's *Rift in the Democracy* (1961). The best discussion of Polk's handling of the Oregon and Texas issues is Charles G. Sellers Jr., *James K. Polk, Continentalist, 1843–1846* (1966). Michael F. Holt presents a magisterial analysis of the Whig party's difficulties in this decade in *The Rise and Fall of the American Whig Party* (1999). Holman Hamilton, *Prologue to Conflict* (1964), is an excellent study of the Compromise of 1850. For a fuller list of readings, see the Bibliography at www.mhhe.com/davidsonnation5.

significant events

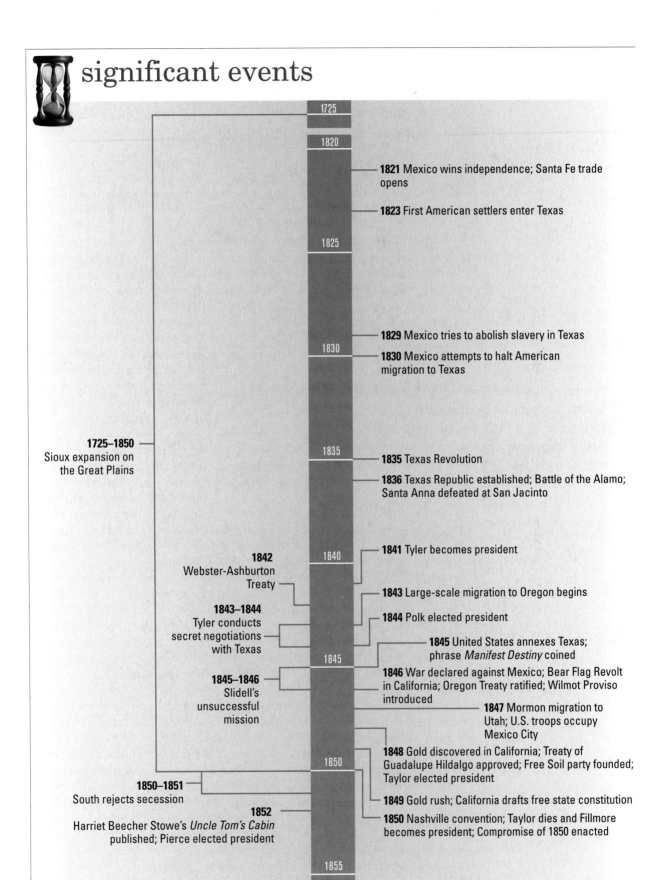

1725–1850
Sioux expansion on the Great Plains

1842
Webster-Ashburton Treaty

1843–1844
Tyler conducts secret negotiations with Texas

1845–1846
Slidell's unsuccessful mission

1850–1851
South rejects secession

1852
Harriet Beecher Stowe's *Uncle Tom's Cabin* published; Pierce elected president

1725

1820

1821 Mexico wins independence; Santa Fe trade opens

1823 First American settlers enter Texas

1825

1829 Mexico tries to abolish slavery in Texas

1830

1830 Mexico attempts to halt American migration to Texas

1835

1835 Texas Revolution

1836 Texas Republic established; Battle of the Alamo; Santa Anna defeated at San Jacinto

1840

1841 Tyler becomes president

1843 Large-scale migration to Oregon begins

1844 Polk elected president

1845

1845 United States annexes Texas; phrase *Manifest Destiny* coined

1846 War declared against Mexico; Bear Flag Revolt in California; Oregon Treaty ratified; Wilmot Proviso introduced

1847 Mormon migration to Utah; U.S. troops occupy Mexico City

1850

1848 Gold discovered in California; Treaty of Guadalupe Hildalgo approved; Free Soil party founded; Taylor elected president

1849 Gold rush; California drafts free state constitution

1850 Nashville convention; Taylor dies and Fillmore becomes president; Compromise of 1850 enacted

1855

455

Chapter 15

Into town they rode, several hundred strong, their faces flushed with excitement. They were unshaven, rough-talking men, "armed . . . to the teeth with rifles and revolvers, cutlasses and bowie-knives." At the head of the procession an American flag flapped softly in the warm May breeze. Alongside it was another with a crouching tiger emblazoned on black and white stripes, followed by banners proclaiming "Southern Rights" and "The Superiority of the White Race." At the rear rolled five artillery pieces, which were quickly dragged into range of the town's main street. Watching intently from a window in his office, Josiah Miller, the editor of the Lawrence *Kansas Free State*, predicted, "Well, boys, we're in for it."

For the residents of Lawrence, Kansas, the worst seemed at hand. The town had been founded by the New England Emigrant Aid Company, a Yankee association that recruited settlers in an effort to keep Kansas Territory from becoming a slave state. Accepting Stephen Douglas's idea that the people should decide the status of slavery, the town's residents intended to see to it that under popular sovereignty Kansas entered the Union as a free state. Emigrants from the neighboring slave state of Missouri were equally determined that no "abolition tyrants" or "negro thieves" would control the territory. There had been conflict in Kansas almost immediately: land disputes, horse thievery, shootings on both sides.

THE UNION BROKEN

1850–1861

preview • During the 1850s the building of a vast railroad network and a rising tide of immigration benefited the North in terms of both economic and political power. As a result, sectional tensions grew. But it was the debate over slavery in the newly acquired territories–especially in Kansas–that brought the crisis to a head. By 1861 the old party system had collapsed, Republican Abraham Lincoln had been elected entirely on the strength of northern votes, and secession was imminent.

In the ensuing turmoil, the federal government seemed to back the proslavery forces. In the spring of 1856, a U.S. district court indicted several of Lawrence's leading citizens for treason, and federal marshal Israel Donaldson called for a posse to help make the arrests. Donaldson's posse, swelled by eager volunteers from across the Missouri border, arrived outside Lawrence on the night of May 20.

Meanwhile, Lawrence's "committee of safety" had agreed on a policy of nonresistance. Most of those indicted had fled, but Donaldson arrested two men without incident. Then he dismissed his posse.

The posse, however, was not ready to go home. Already thoroughly liquored up, it marched into town cheering. Ignoring the pleas of some leaders, its members smashed the presses of two newspapers, the *Herald of Freedom* and the *Kansas Free State*. Then the horde unleashed its wrath on the now-deserted Free State Hotel, which more closely resembled a fort. The invaders unsuccessfully attempted to batter it down with cannon fire and blow it up with gunpowder; finally they put a torch to the building. When the mob finally rode off, it left the residents of Lawrence unharmed but thoroughly terrified.

Retaliation by free state partisans was not long in coming. Hurrying north along a different road to Lawrence, an older man with a grim face and steely eyes heard the news the next morning that the town had been attacked. "Old Man Brown," as everyone called him, was on his way with several of his sons to provide reinforcements. A severe, God-fearing Calvinist, John Brown was also a staunch abolitionist who had once remarked to a friend that he believed "God had raised him up on purpose to break the jaws of the wicked." Brooding over the failure of the free-staters to resist

A torchlight parade staged by the Republican Wide-Awakes, New York City, 1860. In remarkably few years, the new sectional party sensed victory within its reach in the presidential election.

The Free State Hotel was destroyed and burned by the proslavery band that attacked Lawrence, Kansas, on May 21, 1856. News of the so-called Sack of Lawrence greatly agitated northern public opinion and strengthened the struggling Republican party.

Pottawatomie massacre

the "slave hounds" from Missouri, Brown ordered his followers to sharpen their heavy cutlasses. "Caution," he announced, "is nothing but the word of Cowardice."

On the night of May 24, 1856, Brown headed toward Pottawatomie Creek with a half dozen others, including four of his sons. Announcing that they were "the Northern Army" come to serve justice, they burst into the cabin of James Doyle, a proslavery man from Tennessee, with cutlasses drawn. As Brown marched off Doyle and his three sons, Doyle's terrified wife, Mahala, begged him to spare her youngest, and the old man relented. The others were led no more than 100 yards down the road before Owen and Salmon Brown hacked them to death with broadswords. Old Man Brown then walked up to James Doyle's body and put a bullet through his forehead. Before the night was done, two more cabins had been visited and two more proslavery settlers brutally executed. Not one of the five murdered men owned a single slave or had any connection with the raid on Lawrence.

Brown's action precipitated a new wave of fighting in Kansas, and the news of the tumult further angered residents in both sections of the nation. "Everybody here feels as if we are upon a volcano," remarked one congressman in Washington.

The country was indeed atop a smoldering volcano that would finally erupt in the spring of 1861, showering death and destruction across the land. Popular sovereignty, the last remaining moderate solution to the controversy over the expansion of slavery, had failed dismally in Kansas. The violence and disorder in the territory provided a stark reply to Stephen Douglas's proposition: What could be more peaceable, more fair than the notion of popular sovereignty?

Sectional Changes in American Society

The road to war was not a straight or short one. Six years elapsed between the Compromise of 1850 and the crisis in "Bleeding Kansas." Another four would pass before the first shot was fired. And the process of separation involved more than ineffective politicians and an unwillingness to compromise. As we have seen, Americans were bound together by a growing transportation network, by national markets, and by a national political system. These social and political ties—the "cords of Union," Calhoun called them—could not be severed all at once. Increasingly, however, the changes occurring in American society heightened sectional tensions. As the North continued to industrialize, its society came into conflict with that of the South. The Old Northwest, which had long been a political ally of the South, became more closely linked to the East. The coming of civil war, in other words, involved social and economic changes as well as political ones.

The Growth of a Railroad Economy

By the time the Compromise of 1850 produced a lull in the tensions between North and South, the American economy had left behind the depression of the early 1840s and was roaring again. Its basic structure, however, was changing. Cotton remained the nation's major export, but it was no longer the driving force for American economic growth. After 1839 this role was taken over by the construction of a vast railroad network covering the eastern half of the continent. By 1850 the United States possessed more than 9000 miles of track; 10 years later it had over 30,000 miles, more than the rest of the world combined. Much of the new construction during the 1850s occurred west of the Appalachian Mountains—more than 2000 miles in Ohio and Illinois alone.

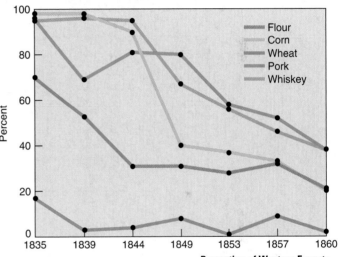

Proportion of Western Exports Shipped via New Orleans, 1835–1860 In 1835 nearly 100 percent of western exports of corn, pork, and whiskey were being shipped via New Orleans. By 1860 only about 40 percent of pork and whiskey and 20 percent of flour and corn were. The change in shipping patterns weakened the political ties between the South and the Old Northwest.

Because western railroads ran through less settled areas, they were especially dependent on public aid. State and local governments made loans to rail companies, invested in their stocks and bonds, backed them with government credit, and sometimes exempted them temporarily from taxes. About a quarter of the cost of railroad construction came from state and local governments, but federal land grants were crucial, too. By mortgaging or selling the land to farmers, the railroad raised construction capital and also stimulated settlement, which increased its business and profits. By 1860 Congress had allotted about 28 million acres of federal land to 40 different companies.

On a national map, the rail network in place by 1860 looked impressive, but these lines were not fully integrated. A few trunk-line roads such as the New York Central had combined a number of smaller lines to facilitate the shipment of freight. But roadbeds had not yet been standardized, so that no fewer than 12 different gauges, or track widths, were in use. Moreover, cities at the end of rail lines jealously strove to maintain their commercial advantages, not wanting to connect with competing port cities for fear freight would pass through to the next city down the line.

The effect of the new lines rippled outward through the economy. Farmers along the tracks began to specialize in cash crops and market them in distant locations. With their profits they purchased manufactured goods that earlier they might have made at home. Before the railroad reached Athens, Tennessee, the surrounding counties produced about 25,000 bushels of wheat, which sold for less than

Railroads' impact on the economy

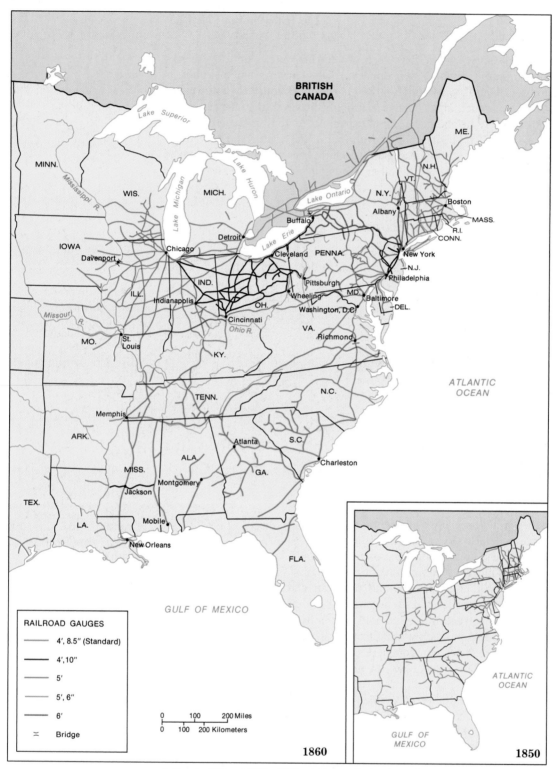

BRITISH CANADA

RAILROAD GAUGES
——— 4', 8.5" (Standard)
——— 4',10"
——— 5'
——— 5', 6"
——— 6'
⋈ Bridge

0   100   200 Miles
0   100   200 Kilometers

1860

1850

Railroads, 1850 and 1860, with Track Gauges During the 1850s a significant amount of railroad track was laid, but total track mileage is misleading, because the United States lacked a fully integrated rail network in 1860. A few trunk-line roads had combined a number of smaller lines into a single system to facilitate shipment. The Pennsylvania Railroad, for example, connected Philadelphia and Pittsburgh. But the existence of five major track gauges as well as minor ones meant that passengers and freight often had to be transferred from one line to the next. And north-south traffic was further disrupted by the lack of bridges over the Ohio River.

50 cents a bushel. Once the railroad came, farmers in these same counties grew 400,000 bushels and sold their crop at a dollar a bushel. Railroads also stimulated other areas of the economy, notably the mining and iron industries.

The new rail networks shifted the direction of western trade. In 1840 most northwestern grain was shipped down the Mississippi River to the bustling port of New Orleans. But low water made steamboat travel risky in summer, and ice shut down traffic in winter. Products such as lard, tallow, and cheese quickly spoiled if stored in New Orleans' sweltering warehouses. Increasingly, traffic from the Midwest flowed west to east, over the new rail lines. Chicago became the region's hub, linking the farms of the upper Midwest to New York and other eastern cities by more than 2000 miles of track in 1855. Thus while the value of goods shipped by river to New Orleans continued to increase, the South's overall share of western trade dropped dramatically.

Reorientation of western trade

A sharp rise in demand for grain abroad also encouraged farmers in the Northeast and Midwest to become more commercially oriented. Wheat, which in 1845 commanded $1.08 a bushel in New York City, fetched $2.46 in 1855; in similar fashion the price of corn nearly doubled. Farmers responded by specializing in cash crops, borrowing to purchase more land, and investing in equipment to increase productivity. These new patterns of commerce and agriculture weakened the traditional political alliance between the South and the West, which had been based on shared economic interests. "The power of cotton over the financial affairs of the Union has in the last few years rapidly diminished," the *Democratic Review* remarked in 1849, "and bread stuffs will now become the governing power."

The new commercial agriculture

Railroads and the Prairie Environment

As railroad lines fanned out from Chicago, farmers began to acquire open prairie land in Illinois and then Iowa, putting its deep black soil into production. Commercial agriculture transformed this remarkable treeless environment.

To settlers accustomed to woodlands, the thousands of square miles of tall grass were an awesome sight. Indian grass, Canadian wild rye, and native big bluestem all grew higher than a person. In 1838 Edmund Flagg gazed upon "the tall grasstops waving in . . . billowy beauty in the breeze; the narrow pathway winding off like a serpent over the rolling surface, disappearing and reappearing till lost in the luxuriant herbage." Long-grass prairies had their perils too: summer or winter storms sent travelers searching for the shelter of trees along river valleys. Dewitt Smith recalled the fierce green-headed flies awaiting the unsuspecting. "A journey across the big praries was, in the summer time, undertaken only at night," he recalled, "because on a hot summer day horses would be literally stung and worried to death."

Because eastern plows could not penetrate the densely tangled roots of prairie grass, the earliest settlers erected farms along the boundary separating the forest from the prairie. In 1837, however, John Deere patented a sharp-cutting steel plow that sliced through the sod without soil sticking to the blade. In addition, Cyrus McCormick refined a mechanical reaper that harvested 14 times more wheat with the same amount of labor. By the 1850s McCormick was selling 1000 reapers a year and could not keep up with demand, while Deere turned out 10,000 plows annually.

Impact of technology

The new commercial farming fundamentally altered the landscape and the environment. Indians had grown corn in the region for years, but never in such large fields as did white farmers, whose surpluses were shipped east. Prairie farmers also introduced new crops that were not part of the earlier ecological system, notably wheat, along with fruits and vegetables. Native grasses were replaced by a small number of plants cultivated as commodities. Corn had the best yields, but

Changes in the landscape

it was primarily used to feed livestock or make whiskey. Because bread played a key role in the American and European diet, wheat became the major cash crop. Tame grasses replaced native grasses in pastures for making hay.

Western farmers altered the landscape by reducing the annual fires, often set by Indians, that had kept the prairie free from trees. In the fires' absence, trees reappeared on land not in cultivation and, if undisturbed, eventually formed woodlots. The earlier unbroken landscape gave way to independent farms, each fenced in the precise checkerboard pattern established by the Northwest Ordinance. It was an artificial ecosystem of animals, woodlots, and crops whose large, uniform layout made western farms more efficient than the irregular farms in the East.

Railroads and the Urban Environment

Railroads transformed the urban environment as well. Communities soon recognized that their economic survival depended on creating adequate rail links to the countryside and to major urban markets. Large cities feared they would be left behind in the struggle to be the dominant city in the region. Smaller communities saw their very survival at stake in the battle for rail connections. When the new railroad line bypassed the prairie village of Auburn, Illinois, its fate was sealed, and residents quickly abandoned it for more promising locations.

Influence on location of towns

Even communities that obtained rail links found the presence of this new technology difficult to adjust to. When a railroad began serving nearby Jacksonville, Illinois, merchants complained about the noise, dirt, and billowing smoke when locomotives hissed through the business district. "The public square was filled with teams [of horses]," one resident recalled, "and whenever the engine steamed into the square making all the noise possible, there was such a stampede. . . . Many of the people were as much scared as the horses at the steaming monster. . . ." After a few years, the tracks were relocated on the outskirts of town. Jacksonville's experience became the norm: increasingly communities kept railroads away from fashionable neighborhoods and shopping areas. As the tracks became a physical manifestation of social and economic divisions, the notion of living "on the wrong side of the tracks" became crucial to defining the urban landscape.

Rising Industrialization

On the eve of the Civil War, 60 percent of American laborers worked on farms. In 1860, for the first time, that figure dropped below 50 percent in the North. The expansion of commercial agriculture spurred the growth of industry. Out of the 10 leading American industries, 8 processed raw materials produced by agriculture, including flour milling and the manufacture of textiles, shoes, and woolens. (The only exceptions were iron and machinery.) Industrial growth also spurted during the 1850s as water power was increasingly replaced by steam, since there were only a fixed number of water-power sites.

Most important, the factory system of organizing labor and the technology of interchangeable parts spread to other areas of the economy. Many industries during the 1850s adopted interchangeable parts. Isaac Singer began using them in 1851 to mass-produce sewing machines, which made possible the ready-made clothing industry, while workers who assembled farm implements performed a single step in the process over and over again. By 1860 the United States had nearly a billion dollars invested in manufacturing, almost twice as much as in 1849.

Immigration

The surge of industry required a large factory labor force. Natural increase helped swell the population to more than 30 million by 1860, but only in part, since the birthrate had begun to decline. On the eve of the Civil War the average white mother bore five children, compared to seven at the turn of the century. It was the beginning of mass immigration to America during the mid-1840s that kept population growth soaring.

In the 20 years from 1820 to 1840, about 700,000 newcomers had entered the United States. That figure jumped to 1.7 million in the 1840s, then to 2.6 million in the 1850s. Though even greater numbers arrived after the Civil War, as a percentage of the nation's total population, the wave from 1845 to 1854 was the largest influx of immigrants in American history. Most newcomers were young people in the prime of life: out of 224,000 arrivals in 1856, only 31,000 were under 10 and only 20,000 were over 40.

Influx of immigrants

Certainly the booming economy and the lure of freedom drew immigrants, but they were also pushed by deteriorating conditions in Europe. In Ireland, a potato blight in 1846 produced widespread famine. Out of a population of 9 million, as many as a million perished, while a million and a half more emigrated, two-thirds to the United States.

The Irish tended to be poorer than other immigrant groups of the day. Although the Protestant Scots-Irish continued as before to emigrate, the decided majority of the Irish who came after 1845 were Catholic. The newcomers were generally mostly

New sources of immigration

Conditions of famine across Ireland led many to buy passage on ships like this one, departing for the United States. New York was the major port of entry for immigrants who surged into the United States during the 1840s and 1850s.

unmarried younger sons and daughters of hard-pressed rural families. Because they were poor and unskilled, the Irish congregated in the cities, where the women performed domestic service and took factory jobs and the men did manual labor.

Germans and Scandinavians also had economic reasons for leaving Europe. They included small farmers whose lands had become marginal or who had been displaced by landlords, and skilled workers thrown out of work by industrialization. Others fled religious persecution. Some, particularly among the Germans, left after the liberal revolutions of 1848 failed, in order to live under the free institutions of the United States. Since coming to America, wrote a Swede who settled in Iowa in 1850, "I have not been compelled to pay a penny for the privilege of living. Neither is my cap worn out from lifting it in the presence of gentlemen."

The revolutions of 1848

Unprecedented unrest and upheaval prevailed in Europe in 1848, the so-called year of revolutions. The famine that had driven so many Irish out of their country was part of a larger food shortage caused by a series of poor harvests. Mounting unemployment and overburdened relief programs increased suffering. In this situation middle-class reformers, who wanted civil liberty and a more representative government, joined forces with lower-class workers to overthrow several regimes, sometimes by also appealing to nationalist feelings. France, Austria, Hungary, Italy, and Prussia all witnessed major popular uprisings. Yet though these revolts gained temporary success, they were all quashed by the forces of the old order. Liberal hopes for a more open, democratic society suffered a severe setback.

In the aftermath of this failure, a number of hard-pressed German workers and farmers, as well as disillusioned radicals and reformers, emigrated to the United States, the symbol of democratic liberalism in the world. They were joined by the first significant migration from Asia, as thousands of Chinese headed to the gold rush in California and other strikes (page 444). This migration was simply part of a century-long phenomenon, as approximately 50 million Europeans, largely from rural areas, would migrate to the Western Hemisphere.

Although many Germans and Scandinavians arrived in modest straits, few were truly impoverished, and many could afford to buy a farm or start a business. Unlike the Irish, Germans tended to emigrate as families, and wherever they settled, they formed social, religious, and cultural organizations to maintain their language and customs. Whereas the Scandinavians, Dutch, and English immigrants were Protestant, half or more of the Germans were Catholics.

Immigrants and industrialization

Factories came more and more to depend on immigrant labor, including children, since newcomers would work for lower wages and were less prone to protest harsh working conditions. The shift to an immigrant workforce could be seen most clearly in the textile industry, where by 1860 more than half the workers in New England mills were foreign-born. Tensions between native- and foreign-born workers, as well as among immigrants of various nationalities, made it difficult for workers to unite.

Urban resources strained

The sizable foreign-born population in many American cities severely strained urban resources. Immigrants who could barely make ends meet were forced to live in overcrowded, unheated tenement houses, damp cellars, and even shacks—"the hall was dark and reeking with the worst filth," reported one New York journalist; the house was "filled with little narrow rooms, each one having five or six occupants; all very filthy." Urban slums became notorious for crime and drinking, which took a heavy toll on families and the poor. In the eyes of many native-born Americans, immigrants were to blame for driving down factory wages and pushing American workers out of jobs. Overshadowing these complaints was a fear that America might not be able to assimilate the new groups, with their unfamiliar social customs, strange languages, and national pride. These fears sparked an outburst of political nativism in the mid-1850s.

Southern Complaints

With British and northern factories buying cotton in unprecedented quantities, southern planters prospered in the 1850s. Their operations, like those of northern commercial farmers, became more highly capitalized to keep up with the demand. But instead of machinery, white southerners invested in slaves. During the 1850s, the price of prime field hands reached record levels.

Nonetheless, a number of southern nationalists, who advocated that the South should become a separate nation, pressed for greater industrialization to make the region more independent. "At present, the North fattens and grows rich upon the South," one Alabama newspaper complained in 1851, noting that "we purchase all our luxuries and necessities from the North," including clothing, shoes, implements and machinery, saddles and carriages, and even books. But most southerners ignored such pleas. As long as investments in cotton and slaves absorbed most of the South's capital, efforts to promote southern industry made little headway.

Despite southern prosperity, the section's leaders complained that the North used its power over banking and commerce to convert the South into a colony. In the absence of any significant southern shipping, northern intermediaries controlled the South's commodities through a complex series of transfers from planter to manufacturer. Storage and shipping charges, insurance, port fees, and commissions together added an estimated 20 percent to the cost of cotton and other commodities. These revenues went into the pockets of northern merchants, shippers, and bankers. The idea that the South was a colony of the North was inaccurate, but southern whites found it a convincing explanation of the North's growing wealth. More important, it reinforced their resistance to federal aid for economic development, which they were convinced would inevitably enrich the North at southern expense. This attitude further weakened the South's political alliance with the West, which needed federal aid for transportation.

White southerners also feared that the new tide of immigration would shift the sectional balance of power. Some immigrants did settle in the South's few cities,

Southern economic dependence

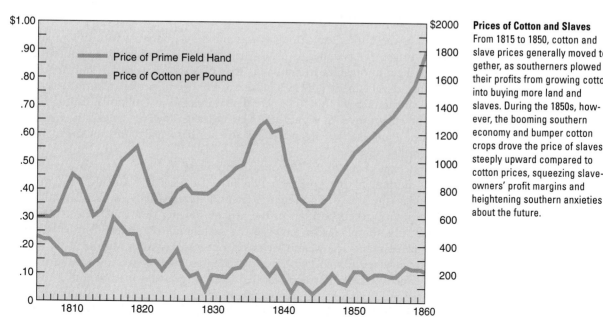

Prices of Cotton and Slaves
From 1815 to 1850, cotton and slave prices generally moved together, as southerners plowed their profits from growing cotton into buying more land and slaves. During the 1850s, however, the booming southern economy and bumper cotton crops drove the price of slaves steeply upward compared to cotton prices, squeezing slave-owners' profit margins and heightening southern anxieties about the future.

but most shunned the South because they did not want to compete with cheap slave labor. The lack of industry and the limited demand for skilled labor also shunted immigrants northward. As a result, the North surged even further ahead of the South in population, thereby strengthening its control of the House of Representatives and heightening southern concern that the North would rapidly settle the western territories.

The Political Realignment of the 1850s

When Franklin Pierce (he pronounced it "Purse") assumed the presidency in 1853, he was only 48 years old, the youngest man yet to be elected president. He was also a supporter of the "Young America" movement of the Democratic party, which eagerly looked to spread democracy across the globe by annexing additional territory to the United States.

The believers in Young America felt it idle to argue about slavery when the nation could be developing new resources. But they failed to appreciate how each new plan for expansion would stir up the slavery issue. In 1853 Pierce did manage to conclude the Gadsden Purchase, thereby gaining control of about 45,000 square miles of Mexican desert that contained the most practical southern route for a transcontinental railroad (see map, page 467).

Gadsden Purchase

Pierce had no success, however, with his major goal, the acquisition of Cuba, a rich sugar-producing region in which slavery had once been strong and still existed. For years many Americans had assumed the United States would eventually acquire Cuba, but Spain rebuffed all efforts to purchase it. Then, in 1854, three American ministers meeting at Ostend in Belgium confidentially recommended that if Spain would not sell Cuba, the island should be seized. The contents of this "Ostend Manifesto" soon leaked, and Pierce was forced to repudiate the notion of acquiring Cuba through naked aggression. In any case, he soon had his hands full with the proposals of another Democrat of the Young America stamp, Senator Stephen A. Douglas of Illinois.

Ostend Manifesto

The Kansas-Nebraska Act

Known as the Little Giant, Douglas was ambitious, bursting with energy, and impatient to get things done. As chairman of the Senate's Committee on Territories, he was eager to organize federal lands west of Missouri as part of his program for economic development. And as a citizen of Illinois, he wanted Chicago selected as the eastern terminus of the transcontinental railroad to California. Chicago would never be chosen over St. Louis and New Orleans, however, unless the rest of the Louisiana Purchase was organized, for any northern rail route would have to run through that region.

Repeal of the Missouri Compromise

Under the terms of the Missouri Compromise of 1820, slavery was prohibited in this portion of the Louisiana Purchase. Douglas had already tried in 1853 to organize the area while keeping a ban on slavery—only to have his bill voted down by southern opposition in the Senate. Bowing to a good deal of southern pressure, the Illinois leader removed the prohibition on slavery that had been in effect for 34 years. The Kansas-Nebraska Act was passed in May 1854.

Popular sovereignty

The new act created two territories: Kansas, directly west of Missouri, and a much larger Nebraska Territory, located west of Iowa and the Minnesota Territory. The Missouri Compromise was explicitly repealed. Instead, popular sovereignty was to determine the status of slavery in both territories, though it was left unclear

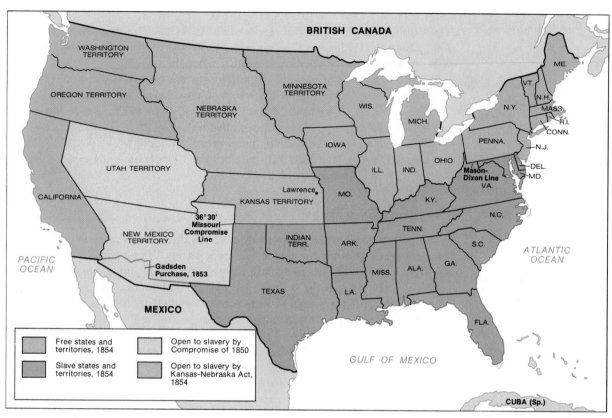

The Kansas-Nebraska Act

Free states and territories, 1854	Open to slavery by Compromise of 1850
Slave states and territories, 1854	Open to slavery by Kansas-Nebraska Act, 1854

The Kansas-Nebraska Act
When the Kansas-Nebraska Act of 1854 opened the remaining portion of the Louisiana Purchase to slavery under the doctrine of popular sovereignty, conflict between the two sections focused on control of Kansas, directly west of the slave state of Missouri.

whether residents of Kansas and Nebraska could prohibit slavery at any time or only at the time of statehood, as southerners insisted. Still, most members of Congress assumed that Douglas had split the region into two territories so that each section could claim another state: Kansas would be slave and Nebraska free.

The Kansas-Nebraska Act outraged northern Democrats, Whigs, and Free Soilers alike. Critics rejected Douglas's contention that popular sovereignty would keep the territories free. As always, most northerners spoke little of the moral evils of slavery; it was the chance that the Slave Power might gain new territory that concerned them. So great was the northern outcry that Douglas joked he could "travel from Boston to Chicago by the light of my own [burning] effigy."

The Collapse of the Second American Party System

The furor over the Kansas-Nebraska Act laid bare the underlying social and economic tensions that had developed between the North and the South. These tensions put mounting pressure on the political parties, and in the 1850s the Jacksonian party system collapsed. Voters who had been loyal to one party for years, even decades, began switching allegiances, while new voters were mobilized. By the time the process of realignment was completed, a new party system had emerged, divided this time along clearly sectional lines.

Political realignment

In part, the old party system decayed because new problems had replaced the traditional economic issues of both Whigs and Democrats. The Whigs alienated many of their traditional Protestant supporters by openly seeking the support of

Disillusionment with the parties

Catholics and recent immigrants. Then, too, the growing agitation by Protestant reformers for the prohibition of alcohol divided both parties, especially the Whigs. Finally, both the Whigs and the Democrats were targets of popular disillusionment, with the existing parties perceived as little more than corrupt engines of plunder designed "to keep a lot of [Old Fogies] in office." Observed one Ohio Whig in 1853, "There is prevailing generally a sort of 'don't care a damn' spirit."

Thus the party system was already weakened when the Kansas-Nebraska Act divided the two major parties along sectional lines. Northern congressional Whigs, who unanimously opposed the bill, found themselves deserted by virtually all their southern colleagues. And fully half the northern Democratic representatives in the House voted against Douglas's bill.

The Know-Nothings

In such an unstable atmosphere, with party loyalties declining, independent parties flourished. The most dramatic challenge to the Whigs and Democrats came first from a movement worried about the recent flood of immigrants.

New York City was the primary gateway for immigrants, and it was here that the American party, a secret nativist society, first organized. Its members were sworn to secrecy and instructed to answer inquiries by replying "I know nothing." In 1853 the Know-Nothings, as they were quickly dubbed, began organizing in several other states; after only a year they had become the fastest-growing party in the nation. Not coincidentally, 1854 also marked the peak of the new wave of immigration.

Nativist impulse

Taking as its slogan "Americans should rule America," the American party advocated that immigrants be forced to wait not 5 but 21 years before becoming naturalized citizens. It also called on voters to oust from office corrupt politicians who openly bid for foreign and Catholic votes. Know-Nothings denounced illegal voting by immigrants, the rising crime and disorder in urban areas, and immigrants' heavy drinking. They were also strongly anti-Catholic, convinced that the "undemocratic" hierarchy of priests, bishops, and archbishops controlled by the pope in Rome was conspiring to undermine American democracy.

To young native-born American workers, the Know-Nothing message was particularly appealing. It was they who bore the brunt of the economic dislocations caused by industrialization and who had to compete with immigrants for jobs. In the 1854 elections, the Know-Nothings won a series of remarkable victories.

Their showing spelled doom for the Whigs, already weakened by the Kansas-Nebraska Act, as the rank and file deserted in droves to the Know-Nothings. Fueled by its success, the American party turned its attention south, and in a few months it had organized in every state of the Union. With perhaps a million voters enrolled in its lodges in 1855, Know-Nothing leaders confidently predicted that they would elect the next president.

Know-Nothings' decline

Yet only a year later—by the end of 1856—the party had collapsed as quickly as it had risen. Many Know-Nothing officeholders proved woefully incompetent. Voters deserted them when the party failed to enact its program. But the death knell of the party was rising sectional tensions. In 1856 a majority of northern delegates walked out of the American party's national convention when it adopted a proslavery platform. Significantly, they deserted to the other new party, the Republicans. This party, unlike the Know-Nothings, had no base in the South. It intended to elect a president by sweeping the free states, which controlled a majority of the electoral votes.

In this nativist print, an eagle guards a schoolhouse while a group of Catholic laborers try to undermine its foundation. Directing the work is a priest, who receives instructions from the pope sitting on a throne. Nativist propaganda extolled the importance of public schools in safeguarding democracy and portrayed Catholics as hostile to American institutions.

The Republicans and Bleeding Kansas

Initially, the Republican party made little headway in the North. Although it attracted in 1854 a variety of Whigs, anti-Nebraska Democrats, and Free Soilers, many moderate Whigs and Democrats viewed the party as too radical. Again in 1855 Republican candidates met defeat almost everywhere they ran. A Democratic newspaper expressed the prevailing view when it declared, "Nobody believes that this Republican movement can prove the basis of a permanent party."

Such predictions, however, did not take into account the emotions stirred up by developments in Kansas. Most early settlers migrated to Kansas for the same reasons other white Americans headed west—the chance to prosper in a new land. But Douglas's idea of popular sovereignty transformed the process of settlement into a referendum on slavery in the territories. A race soon developed between northerners and southerners to settle Kansas first. To the proslavery residents of neighboring Missouri, free-state communities like Lawrence seemed ominous threats. "We are playing for a mighty stake," former senator David Rice Atchison insisted. "If we win, we carry slavery to the Pacific Ocean; if we fail we lose Missouri, Arkansas and Texas and all the territories; the game must be played boldly."

When the first Kansas elections were held in 1854 and 1855, Missourians poured over the border, seized the polls, and stuffed the ballot boxes. A later congressional investigation concluded that more than 60 percent of the votes were cast illegally. This massive fraud tarnished popular sovereignty at the outset and greatly aroused public opinion in the North. It also provided proslavery forces with a commanding majority in the Kansas legislature, where they promptly expelled the legally elected free-state members and enacted a strict legal code designed to intimidate antislavery settlers. This Kansas Code limited such time-honored rights as freedom of speech, impartial juries, and fair elections. Mobilized into action, the free-staters in the fall of 1855 organized a separate government, drafted a state constitution prohibiting slavery, and asked Congress to admit Kansas as a free state. In such a polarized situation, violence quickly broke out between the two factions.

Turmoil in Kansas

Proslavery and antislavery settlers clash in 1856 at the town of Hickory Point in the Kansas Territory. Full-scale battles with artillery were rare in Kansas, but a number of skirmishes took place between the two factions in the territory, which gave credence to the image of "Bleeding Kansas."

The Caning of Charles Sumner

In May 1856, only a few days before the proslavery attack on Lawrence, Republican senator Charles Sumner of Massachusetts delivered a scathing speech, "The Crime against Kansas." Sumner was passionate in his condemnation of slavery, and his speech included remarks that deliberately insulted the state of South Carolina and one of its senators, Andrew Butler. Preston S. Brooks, a South Carolina congressman who was related to Butler, was outraged that Sumner had insulted his relative and mocked his state.

Several days later, on May 22, Brooks strode into the Senate after it had adjourned, went up to Sumner, who was seated at his desk, and proceeded to beat the Massachusetts leader over the head with his cane. The cane shattered into three pieces from the violence of the attack, but Brooks, swept up in the emotion of the moment, furiously continued hitting Sumner until the senator collapsed to the floor, drenched in blood.

Significance of the caning

Northerners were electrified to learn that a senator of the United States had been beaten unconscious in the Senate chamber. But what caused them even greater consternation was southern reaction to Sumner's caning—for in his own region, Preston Brooks was promptly lionized as a hero. Instantly, the Sumner caning breathed life into the fledgling Republican party. Its claims about "Bleeding Kansas" and the Slave Power now seemed credible. Sumner, reelected in 1857 by the Massachusetts legislature, was unable to return to the Senate until 1860, his chair left vacant as a symbol of southern brutality.

The Election of 1856

Given the storm that had arisen over Kansas, Democrats concluded that no candidate associated with the repeal of the Missouri Compromise had a chance to win. So the Democrats turned to James Buchanan of Pennsylvania as their presidential nominee. Buchanan's supreme qualification was having the good fortune to have been out of the country when the Kansas-Nebraska Act was passed. The American party, split badly by the Kansas issue, nominated former president Millard Fillmore.

SOUTHERN CHIVALRY — ARGUMENT versus CLUB'S.

The caning of Senator Charles Sumner of Massachusetts by Representative Preston S. Brooks of South Carolina inflamed public opinion. In this northern drawing, the fallen Sumner, a martyr to free speech, raises his pen against Brooks's club. In the background, several prominent Democrats look on in amusement. Printmakers, rushing to capitalize on the furor, did not know what the obscure Brooks looked like and thus had to devise ingenious ways of portraying the incident. In this print, Brooks's face is hidden by his raised arm.

The Republicans chose John C. Frémont, a western explorer who had helped liberate California during the Mexican War. The party's platform denounced slavery as a "relic of barbarism" and demanded that Kansas be admitted as a free state. Throughout the summer the party hammered away on Bleeding Sumner and Bleeding Kansas. "A constantly increasing excitement is kept up by the intelligence coming every day from Kansas," wrote one observer. "I have never known political excitement—I ought rather to say exasperation—approach that which now rages."

A number of basic principles guided the Republican party, including the ideal of free labor. Slavery degraded labor, Republicans argued, and would inevitably drive free labor out of the territories. Condemning the South as a stagnant, hierarchical, and economically backward region, Republicans praised the North as a fluid society of widespread opportunity where enterprising individuals could improve their lot through hard work and self-discipline. Stopping the expansion of slavery, in Republican eyes, would preserve this heritage of opportunity and economic independence for white Americans. Republicans by and large remained blind to ways in which industrialization was closing off avenues of social mobility for poor workers.

Ideology of the Republican party

Also important was the moral opposition to slavery, which works like Harriet Beecher Stowe's *Uncle Tom's Cabin* had strengthened. Republican speakers and editors stressed that slavery was a moral wrong, that it was incompatible with the ideals of the Republic and Christianity. "Never forget," Republican leader Abraham Lincoln declared on one occasion, "that we have before us this whole matter of the right and wrong of slavery in this Union, though the immediate question is as to its spreading out into new Territories and States."

More negatively, Republicans gained support by shifting their attacks from slavery itself to the Slave Power, or the political influence of the planter class. Pointing to the Sumner assault and the incidents in Kansas, Republicans contended that the Slave Power had set out to destroy the liberties of northern whites. "The question has passed on from that of slavery for negro servants, to that of tyranny over free white men," one Republican insisted in the 1856 campaign.

Concept of the Slave Power

**Heritage of
republicanism**

All these fears played on a strong northern attachment to the heritage of the American Revolution. Just as the nation's founders had battled against slavery, tyranny, aristocracy, and minority rule, so the North faced the unrepublican Slave Power. "The liberties of our country are in tenfold the danger that they were at the commencement of the American Revolution," warned one Republican paper. "We then had a distant foe to contend with. Now the enemy is within our borders."

In the election, Buchanan all but swept the South (losing only Maryland to Fillmore) and won enough free states to push him over the top, with 174 electoral votes to Frémont's 114 and Fillmore's 8. Still, the violence in Kansas and Sumner's caning nearly carried Frémont into the presidency. He ran ahead of both Buchanan and Fillmore in the North and won 11 free states out of 16. Had he carried Pennsylvania plus one more, he would have been elected. For the first time in American history, an antislavery party based entirely in the North threatened to elect a president and snap the bonds of union.

The Worsening Crisis

James Buchanan had spent much of his life in public service: more than 20 years in the House and the Senate, secretary of state under Polk, and minister to Russia and to Great Britain. A tall, heavyset man with flowing white hair, Buchanan struck White House visitors as exceptionally courteous: an eye defect caused him to tilt his head slightly forward and to one side, which reinforced the impression of deference and attentiveness. A dutiful party member, he had over the years carefully cultivated wide personal support, yet he was a cautious and uninspiring leader who had a strong stubborn streak, deeply resented opposition, and overrated his ability to enforce party discipline on those who disagreed with his policies.

Buchanan's character

Moderates in both sections hoped that the new president would thwart Republican radicals and secessionists of the Deep South, popularly known as "fire-eaters." Throughout his career, however, Buchanan had taken the southern position on sectional matters, and he proved remarkably insensitive to the concerns of northern Democrats. Moreover, on March 6, 1857, only two days after Buchanan's inauguration, the Supreme Court gave the new administration an unintended jolt with one of the most controversial decisions in its history.

The *Dred Scott* Decision

Dred Scott

Protection of slavery

The owner of a Missouri slave named Dred Scott had taken him to live for several years in Illinois, a free state, and in the Wisconsin Territory, in what is now Minnesota, where slavery had been banned by the Missouri Compromise. Scott had returned to Missouri with his owner, only to sue eventually for his freedom on the grounds that his residence in a free state and a free territory had made him free. His case ultimately went to the Supreme Court. Two northern justices joined all five southern members of the Court in ruling 7 to 2 that Scott remained a slave. The majority opinion was written by Chief Justice Roger Taney of Maryland, who argued that under Missouri law, which took precedence, Scott was still a slave.

Had the Court stopped there, the public outcry would have been minimal. But the Court majority believed that they had a responsibility to deal with the larger controversy between the two sections. In particular, Chief Justice Taney wanted to strengthen the judicial protection of slavery. Taney, a former Maryland slaveowner who had freed his slaves, ruled that African Americans could not be and never had been citizens of the United States. Instead, he insisted that at the time the Constitution was adopted, they were "regarded as beings of an inferior order, so far inferior that they had no rights which the white man was bound to respect." In addition, the Court ruled that the Missouri Compromise was unconstitutional. Congress, it declared, had no power to ban slavery from *any* territory of the United States.

While southerners rejoiced at this outcome, Republicans denounced the Court. Their platform declared, after all, that Congress ought to prohibit slavery in all territories. "We know the court . . . has often over-ruled its own decisions," Abraham Lincoln observed, "and we shall do what we can to have it over-rule this." But the decision was sobering. If all territories were now open to slavery, how long would it be before a move was made to reintroduce slavery in the free states? For Republicans, the Court's decision foreshadowed the spread of slavery throughout the West and even throughout the nation.

But the decision also was a blow to Douglas's more moderate solution of popular sovereignty. If Congress had no power to prohibit slavery in a territory, how could it authorize a territorial legislature to do so? Although the Court did not rule on this point, the clear implication of the *Dred Scott* decision was that popular sovereignty was also unconstitutional. The Court, in effect, had endorsed John C. Calhoun's radical view that slavery was legal in all the territories. In so doing, the Court, which had intended to settle the question of slavery in the territories once and for all, instead succeeded only in strengthening the forces of extremism in American politics.

Reaction to the decision

Chief Justice Roger Taney

The Panic of 1857

As the nation grappled with the *Dred Scott* decision, an economic depression aggravated sectional conflict. Once again, boom gave way to bust as falling wheat prices and contracted credit hurt commercial farmers and overextended railroad investors. The Panic of 1857 was nowhere near as severe as the depression of 1837–1843. But the psychological results were far-reaching, for the South remained relatively untouched. With the price of cotton and other southern commodities still high, southern secessionists hailed the panic as proof that an independent southern nation was economically workable. Insisting that cotton sustained the international economy, James Henry Hammond, a senator from South Carolina, boasted: "What would happen if no cotton was furnished for three years? England would topple headlong and carry the whole civilized world with her save the South. No, you dare not make war on cotton. No power on earth dares to make war on it. Cotton is king."

For their part, northerners urged federal action to spur the economy. Southerners defeated an attempt to increase the tariff duties, at their lowest level since 1815, and Buchanan, under southern pressure, vetoed bills to improve navigation on the Great Lakes and to give free farms to western settlers. Many businesspeople and conservative ex-Whigs condemned these southern actions and now endorsed the Republican party.

Economic issues increase sectional tensions

The Lecompton Constitution

Although the *Dred Scott* decision and economic depression weakened the bonds of the Union, Kansas remained at the center of the political stage. In June 1857, when the territory elected delegates to draft a state constitution, free-state voters

Attempt to make Kansas a slave state

boycotted the election, thereby giving proslavery forces control of the convention that met in Lecompton. The delegates drafted a constitution that made slavery legal. Even more boldly, they scheduled a referendum in which voters could choose only whether to admit additional slaves into the territory. They could not vote against the constitution, and they could not vote to get rid of slavery entirely. Once again, free-staters boycotted the election, and the Lecompton constitution was approved.

As a supporter of popular sovereignty, President Buchanan had pledged a free and fair vote on the Lecompton constitution. But the outcome offered him the unexpected opportunity to satisfy his southern supporters by pushing the Lecompton constitution through Congress. This action was too much for Douglas, who broke party ranks and denounced the Lecompton constitution as a fraud. Nevertheless, the administration prevailed in the Senate. Buchanan now pulled out all the stops to gain the necessary votes in the House to admit Kansas as a slave state. But the House, where northern representation was much stronger, rejected the constitution. In a compromise, Congress, using indirect language, returned the constitution to Kansas for another vote.

Defeat of the Lecompton constitution

This time it was decisively defeated, 11,300 to 1788. No doubt remained that as soon as Kansas had sufficient population, it would come into the Union as a free state.

The attempt to force slavery on the people of Kansas drove many conservative northerners into the Republican party. And Douglas, once the Democrats' strongest potential candidate in 1860, now found himself assailed by the southern wing of his party. On top of that, in the summer of 1858, Douglas faced a desperate fight in his race for reelection to the Senate against Republican Abraham Lincoln.

The Lincoln-Douglas Debates

"He is the strong man of his party . . . and the best stump speaker, with his droll ways and dry jokes, in the West," Douglas commented when he learned of Lincoln's nomination to oppose him. "He is as honest as he is shrewd, and if I beat him my victory will be hardly won." Tall (6 feet, 4 inches) and gangly, Lincoln had a gaunt face, high cheekbones, deep-socketed gray eyes, and a shock of unruly hair. He appeared awkward as he spoke, never knowing quite what to do with his large, muscular hands. Yet his finely honed logic, his simple, eloquent language, and his sincerity carried the audience with him. His sentences, as spare as the man himself, had none of the oratorical flourishes common in that day. "If we could first know *where* we are, and *whither* we are tending, we could then better judge *what* to do, and *how* to do it," Lincoln began, in accepting his party's nomination for

Lincoln's view of the crisis

senator from Illinois in 1858. He quoted a proverb from the Bible:

> A house divided against itself cannot stand.
>
> I believe this government cannot endure, permanently half *slave* and half *free*.
>
> I do not expect the Union to be *dissolved*—I do not expect the house to *fall*—but I *do* expect it will cease to be divided.
>
> It will become *all* one thing, or *all* the other.
>
> Either the *opponents* of slavery, will arrest the further spread of it, and place it where the public mind shall rest in the belief that it is in course of ultimate extinction; or its *advocates* will push it forward, till it shall become alike lawful in all the States, *old* as well as new—*North* as well as *South*.

The message echoed through the hall and across the pages of the national press.

Lincoln's character

Born in the slave state of Kentucky, Lincoln had grown up mostly in southern Indiana and central Illinois. He could split rails with the best frontier farmer, loved

Superb debaters, Douglas and Lincoln nevertheless had very different speaking styles. The deep-voiced Douglas was constantly on the attack, drawing on his remarkable memory and showering points like buckshot in all directions. Employing sarcasm and ridicule rather than humor, he never tried to crack a joke. Lincoln, who had a high-pitched voice and a rather awkward platform manner, developed his arguments more carefully and methodically, and he relied on his sense of humor and unmatched ability as a storyteller to drive his points home to the audience.

telling stories, and was at home mixing with ordinary folk. Yet his intense ambition had lifted him above the backwoods from which he came. He compensated for a lack of formal schooling through disciplined self-education, and he became a shrewd courtroom lawyer of respectable social standing. Known for his sense of humor, he was nonetheless subject to fits of acute depression, and his eyes often mirrored a deep melancholy.

Lincoln's first love was always politics. A fervent admirer of Henry Clay and his economic program, Lincoln entered the state legislature when he was only 25 and soon became an important Whig manager. After the party's decline, he joined the Republicans and became one of their key leaders in Illinois. In a series of seven joint debates, Lincoln challenged Douglas to discuss the issues of slavery and the sectional controversy.

In the campaign, Douglas sought to portray Lincoln as a radical whose "House Divided" speech preached sectional warfare. The nation *could* endure half slave and half free, Douglas declared, as long as states and territories were left alone to regulate their own affairs. Accusing Lincoln of believing that blacks were his equal, Douglas countered that the American government had been "made by the white man, for the white man, to be administered by the white man."

Lincoln responded by denying any intention to interfere with slavery in the South, but he insisted that the spread of slavery to the territories was a blight on the Republic. Douglas could not be counted on to oppose slavery's expansion, Lincoln warned, for he had already admitted that he didn't care whether slavery

Douglas and Lincoln on the slavery issue

was voted "down or up." For his part, Lincoln denied any "perfect equality between the negroes and white people" and opposed allowing blacks to vote, hold office, or intermarry with whites. But, he concluded,

> notwithstanding all this, there is no reason in the world why the negro is not entitled to all the natural rights enumerated in the Declaration of Independence, the right to life, liberty and the pursuit of happiness. . . . I agree with Judge Douglas [that the negro] is not my equal in many respects—certainly not in color, perhaps not in moral or intellectual endowment. But in the right to eat the bread, without leave of anybody else, which his own hand earns, *he is my equal and the equal of Judge Douglas, and the equal of every living man.*

Freeport Doctrine

At the debate held at Freeport, Illinois, Lincoln asked Douglas how under the *Dred Scott* decision the people of a territory could lawfully exclude slavery before statehood. Douglas answered, with what became known as the Freeport Doctrine, that slavery could exist only with the protection of law and that slaveowners would never bring their slaves into an area that did not have a slave code. Therefore, Douglas explained, if the people of a territory refused to pass a slave code, slavery would never be established there.

In a close race, the legislature elected Douglas to another term in the Senate.* But on the national scene, southern Democrats angrily repudiated him and condemned the Freeport Doctrine. And although Lincoln lost, Republicans thought his impressive performance marked him as a possible presidential contender for 1860.

The Beleaguered South

While northerners increasingly feared that the Slave Power was conspiring to extend slavery into the free states, southerners worried that the "Black Republicans" would hem them in and undermine their political power.

South's internal crisis

The very factors that brought prosperity during the 1850s stimulated the South's sense of crisis. As the price of slaves rose sharply, the proportion of southerners who owned slaves had dropped almost a third since 1830. Land also was being consolidated into larger holdings, evidence of declining opportunity for ordinary white southerners. Between 1850 and 1860 the average farm size rose in the South by 20 percent. Furthermore, California and Kansas had been closed to southern slaveholders—unfairly, in their eyes. Finally, Douglas's clever claim that a territory could effectively outlaw slavery using the Freeport Doctrine seemed to negate the *Dred Scott* decision that slavery was legal in all the territories.

Several possible solutions to the South's internal crisis had failed. Agricultural reform to restore worn-out lands had made significant headway in Virginia and Maryland, but elsewhere the rewards of a single-crop economy were just too great. Like most Americans, southerners preferred to exploit the soil and then move west. Another alternative—industrialization—had also failed. Indeed, the gap between the North and the South steadily widened in the 1850s. A few militant southerners launched their own private military expeditions during the 1850s, hoping to add Cuba, Mexico, or Nicaragua to the United States as slave territories. But all these "filibustering" expeditions came to naught.

---

*State legislatures elected senators until 1913, when the Seventeenth Amendment was adopted. While Lincoln and Douglas both campaigned for the office, Illinois voters actually voted for candidates for the legislature who were pledged to one of the senatorial candidates.

The South's growing sense of moral and political isolation made this crisis more acute. By the 1850s slavery had been abolished throughout most of the Americas, and in the United States the South's political power was steadily shrinking. Only the expansion of slavery held out any promise of new slave states needed to preserve the South's political power and protect its way of life. "The truth is," fumed one Alabama politician, ". . . the South is excluded from the common territories of the Union. The right of expansion claimed to be a necessity of her continued existence, is practically and effectively denied the South."

Failed solutions

The Road to War

In 1857 John Brown—the abolitionist firebrand—had returned to the East from Kansas, consumed with the idea of attacking slavery in the South itself. With financing from a number of prominent northern reformers, Brown gathered 21 followers, including 5 free blacks, in hope of fomenting a slave insurrection. On the night of October 16, 1859, the group seized the unguarded federal armory at Harpers Ferry in Virginia. But no slaves rallied to Brown's standard: few even lived in the area to begin with. Before long the raiders found themselves holed up in the armory's engine house with hostile townspeople taking potshots at them. Charging with bayonets fixed, federal troops commanded by Colonel Robert E. Lee soon captured Brown and his band.

John Brown's raid

John Brown

Brown's raid at Harpers Ferry was yet another blow weakening the forces of compromise and moderation at the nation's political center. The invasion itself was a dismal failure, as were most of the enterprises Brown undertook in his troubled life. But the old man knew well how to bear himself with a martyr's dignity. "Had I so interfered in behalf of the rich, the powerful, the intelligent, the so-called great," he declared at his trial, ". . . it would have been all right. Every man in this court would have deemed it an act worthy of reward rather than punishment. . . . I believe that to have interfered as I have done in behalf of [God's] despised poor, is no wrong, but a right." On December 2, 1859, the state of Virginia hanged Brown for treason.

Reaction to the raid

John Brown's enduring legacy sprang not from his ill-fated raid but from the popular reaction to his cause. Republicans made haste to denounce Brown's raid, lest they be tarred as radicals, but other northerners were less cautious. Ralph Waldo Emerson described Brown as a "saint, whose martyrdom will make the gallows as glorious as the cross," and on the day of his execution, church bells tolled in many northern cities. Only a minority of northerners endorsed Brown, but southerners were shocked by such public displays of sympathy. And they were firmly convinced that the Republican party was secretly connected to the raid. "I have always been a fervid Union man," one North Carolina resident wrote, "but I confess the endorsement of the Harpers Ferry outrage has shaken my fidelity and I am willing to take the chances of every probable evil that may arise from disunion, sooner than submit any longer to Northern insolence and Northern outrage."

A Sectional Election

When Congress convened in December, there were ominous signs everywhere of the growing sectional rift. Intent on destroying Douglas's Freeport Doctrine, southern radicals demanded a congressional slave code to protect slavery in the territories. To northern Democrats, such a platform spelled political death. As one Indiana Democrat put it, "We cannot carry a single congressional district on that doctrine in the state."

Daily Lives

POPULAR ENTERTAINMENT
Uncle Tom by Footlights

In 1850 theaters remained a controversial if popular form of public entertainment. The Puritans had roundly condemned plays of any sort, and many religious critics still frowned on theatergoing as sinful. Nevertheless, with the rise of cities the stage became a medium for mass entertainment and increasingly attracted the urban middle class.

In 1852 George C. Howard, the head of the Museum Theater in Troy, New York, was looking for new material. He was attracted to the issue of slavery by a controversial new novel, *Uncle Tom's Cabin*. Written by Harriet Beecher Stowe, one of the Reverend Lyman Beecher's energetic daughters, the book was a runaway bestseller, with more than 300,000 copies printed in the first year.

The book's plot followed a host of characters to a multitude of locales. George and Eliza Harris, a mulatto slave couple, learn that their young son is to be sold. Eliza flees with her child across the ice-choked Ohio River to freedom, while George escapes separately. At the same time, Tom, an older slave and a devout Christian, is sold and taken to Louisiana. He is bought by the father of Evangeline St. Clare, an innocent, golden-haired child who treats Tom kindly, but after both Evangeline and her father die, Tom is sold to Simon Legree, a hard-drinking, blasphemous Yankee. When Tom refuses to whip other slaves on the plantation, Legree beats him to death; Tom is a martyr to his faith in God and his love for his fellow man.

In this playbill advertising a dramatic production of *Uncle Tom's Cabin,* vicious bloodhounds pursue the light-skinned Eliza, who clutches her child as she frantically leaps to safety across the ice-choked Ohio River.

Disruption of the Democratic party

At the Democratic convention in April in Charleston, South Carolina, southern radicals boldly pressed their demand for a federal slave code. After a heated debate, however, the convention adopted the Douglas platform upholding popular sovereignty, whereupon the delegations from eight southern states walked out. Unable to agree on a candidate, the convention finally reassembled two months later in Baltimore and nominated Douglas. At this point most of the remaining southern Democrats left in disgust. Joining with the Charleston seceders, they nominated their own candidate, Vice President John C. Breckinridge of Kentucky, on a platform supporting a federal slave code. The last major national party had shattered.

In May the Republicans met in Chicago, where they turned to Abraham Lincoln, a moderate on the slavery issue who was strong in Illinois and the other northern states the party had lost in 1856. Republicans also sought to broaden their appeal by supporting economic proposals for a moderately protective tariff, a homestead bill, and a northern transcontinental railroad.

The election that followed was really two contests in one. In the North, which had a majority of the electoral votes, only Lincoln and Douglas had any chance of carrying a state. In the South, the race pitted Breckinridge against John Bell of

Compressing this complex story was not easy. Then, too, no American play on the subject of slavery had been produced before, and many theater managers believed that the public would not accept a black hero. But Howard wanted to cast his four-year-old daughter, Cordelia (already an experienced trouper), as young Eva, and so George Aiken, a member of the repertory company, wrote an adaptation that focused on Tom's experiences in the St. Clare household.

The play's success prompted Aiken to write a sequel based on the Legree section of the novel; finally he combined the two plays into a 6-act, 30-scene epic that took an entire evening to perform. To make the plot coherent would have required almost twice as many scenes, but Aiken's adaptation became the classic stage version. From Troy the production moved to New York City, where it ran for an unprecedented 325 performances and then achieved similar triumphs in other northern cities. No play had ever attracted such large audiences.

Aiken had a good eye for the dramatic: a slave auction, Eva's death after a long illness, and Tom's defiance of Legree when threatened with a whipping. ("My soul a'nt yours, mas'r; you haven't bought it—ye can't buy it.") Eliza's flight across the icy Ohio River—described in two paragraphs in the book—became one of the major scenes, with a pack of bloodhounds added for good measure. As in minstrel shows, blacks were played by whites wearing lampblack.

Aiken added more humor to the plot, but the play remained faithful to the book's antislavery message. Howard worked hard to attract a new middle-class audience. He banned the prostitutes who frequented theaters and in the lobby displayed the endorsements of prominent religious leaders and reformers on posters. A further innovation, matinee performances, attracted women and children. As one reporter for the New York *Atlas* commented, instead of newsboys and apprentices, he saw "many people who have been taught to look on the stage with horror and contempt." Blacks, who normally were barred from New York theaters, were seated in a segregated section.

The play moved audiences of all backgrounds. After wrestling with his religious scruples, John Kirk, a salesman, finally went to see a Chicago production. "The appeals of the dying little Eva to her father, for Uncle Tom's freedom, were overwhelmingly affecting," he testified. "I never saw so many white pocket handkerchiefs in use at the same time, and, for the same purpose before. I was not the only one in that large audience to shed tears I assure you." Equally striking, the play affected the workers and apprentices who made up the theater's normal clientele. Traditionally hostile to abolitionism, these groups cheered wildly over Eliza's escape and shouted approval of her antislavery speeches. By providing vivid images of the cruelty of slavery, theatrical presentations of *Uncle Tom's Cabin*, even more than the book, heightened the sectional tensions that divided the nation in the 1850s.

Tennessee, the candidate of the new conservative Constitutional Union party. Although Lincoln received less than 40 percent of the popular vote and had virtually no support in the South, he won 180 electoral votes, 27 more than needed for election. For the first time, the nation had elected a president who headed a completely sectional party and who was committed to stopping the expansion of slavery.

Secession

Although the Republicans had not won control of either house of Congress, Lincoln's election struck many southerners as a blow of terrible finality. Lincoln had been lifted into office on the strength of the free states alone. With Republicans opposed to slavery's expansion, the South's power base could only diminish. It was not unrealistic, many fire-eaters argued, to believe that Lincoln would use federal aid to induce the border states to voluntarily free their slaves. Once slavery disappeared there, and new states were added, the necessary three-fourths majority would exist to approve a constitutional amendment abolishing slavery. Or perhaps Lincoln might send other John

Southern fears

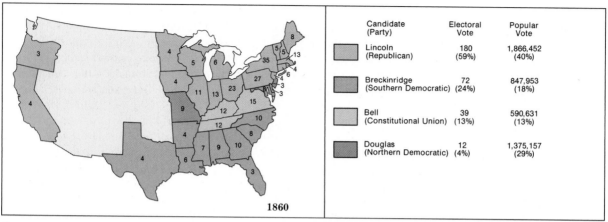

Candidate (Party)	Electoral Vote	Popular Vote
Lincoln (Republican)	180 (59%)	1,866,452 (40%)
Breckinridge (Southern Democratic)	72 (24%)	847,953 (18%)
Bell (Constitutional Union)	39 (13%)	590,631 (13%)
Douglas (Northern Democratic)	12 (4%)	1,375,157 (29%)

1860

Election of 1860 Although Lincoln did not win a majority of the popular vote, he still would have been elected even if the votes for all three of his opponents had been combined, because he won a clear majority in every state he carried except California, Oregon, and New Jersey (whose electoral votes he split with Douglas).

Confederate States of America

Crittenden Compromise fails

Lincoln's approach to the crisis

Browns into the South to stir up more slave insurrections. The Montgomery (Alabama) *Mail* accused Republicans of intending "to free the negroes and force amalgamation between them and the children of the poor men of the South."

Secession seemed the only alternative left to protect southern equality and liberty. South Carolina, which had challenged federal authority in the nullification crisis, was determined to force the other southern states to act. On December 20, 1860, a popular convention unanimously passed a resolution seceding from the Union. The rest of the Deep South followed, and on February 7, 1861, the states stretching from South Carolina to Texas organized the Confederate States of America and elected Jefferson Davis president.

But the Upper South and the border states declined to secede, hoping that once again Congress could patch together a settlement. Senator John Crittenden of Kentucky proposed a constitutional amendment extending to California the old Missouri Compromise line of 36°30′. Slavery would be prohibited north of this line and given federal protection south of it in all territories, including any acquired in the future. Furthermore, Crittenden proposed an "unamendable amendment" to the Constitution, forever preserving slavery in states where it already existed.

But the Crittenden Compromise was doomed for the simple reason that the two groups who were required to make concessions—Republicans and secessionists— had no interest in doing so. "The argument is exhausted," representatives from the Deep South announced, even before Crittenden had introduced his package. "We have just carried an election on principles fairly stated to the people," Lincoln wrote in opposing compromise. "Now we are told in advance, the government shall be broken up, unless we surrender to those we have beaten, before we take the offices. If we surrender, it is the end of us, and of the government." Only the unamendable amendment passed, but war ended any possibility that it would be ratified.

The Outbreak of War

As he prepared to take office, Lincoln pondered what to do about secession. In his inaugural address on March 4, he sought to reassure southerners that he had no intention, "directly or indirectly, to interfere with the institution of slavery in the States where it exists." But he maintained that "the Union of these states is perpetual," echoing Andrew Jackson's Proclamation on Nullification, and that no state could leave the Union by its own action. He also announced that he intended to "hold, occupy and possess" federal property and collect customs duties under the

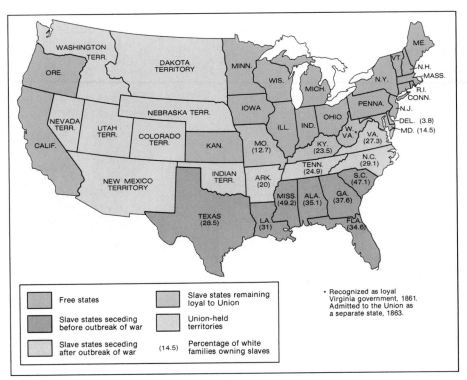

The Pattern of Secession Led by South Carolina, the Deep South seceded between Lincoln's election in November and his inauguration in March. The Upper South did not secede until after the firing on Fort Sumter. The four border slave states never seceded and remained in the Union throughout the war. As the map indicates, secession sentiment was strongest in states where the highest percentage of white families owned slaves.

tariff. He closed by calling for a restoration of the "bonds of affection" that united all Americans.

The new president hoped for time to work out a solution, but on his first day in office he was handed a dispatch from Major Robert Anderson, commander of the federal garrison at Fort Sumter in Charleston harbor. Sumter was one of the few remaining federal outposts in the South. Anderson informed the government that he was almost out of food and that, unless resupplied, he would have to surrender in six weeks. For a month Lincoln looked for a way out, but he finally sent a relief expedition. As a conciliatory gesture, he notified the governor of South Carolina that supplies were being sent and that if the fleet were allowed to pass, only food, and not men, arms, or ammunition, would be landed.

The burden of decision now shifted to Jefferson Davis. From his point of view, secession was a constitutional right and the Confederacy was not a bogus but a legitimate government. To allow the United States to hold property and maintain military forces within the Confederacy would destroy its claim of independence. Davis therefore instructed the Confederate commander at Charleston to demand the immediate surrender of Fort Sumter and, if refused, to open fire. When Anderson declined the ultimatum, Confederate batteries began shelling the fort on April 12 at 4:30 A.M. Some 33 hours later Anderson surrendered. When in response Lincoln called for 75,000 volunteers to put down the rebellion, four states in the Upper South, led by Virginia, also seceded. Matters had passed beyond compromise.

Fort Sumter

Upper South secedes

The Roots of a Divided Society

And so the Union was broken. After 70 years, the forces of sectionalism and separatism had finally outpulled the ties binding "these United States." Why did affairs come to such a pass?

AN EMINENT SOUTHERN CLERGYMAN,
During an eloquent discourse, is wonderfully assisted in finding scriptural authority for Secession and Treason, and the divine ordination of Slavery.

When news of secession spread, many southern white women wore decorative cockades made of woven palmetto leaves and silk (right). "In every direction could be seen Palmetto cockades, fastened with a blue ribbon; there were hundreds of them," reported one observer. Northerners reacted differently. Envelopes like the one shown here (left) portrayed a secessionist southern preacher inspired by the devil to give "an eloquent discourse" on "Treason" and God's approval of slavery.

Diverging economies

In some ways, as we have seen, the revolution in markets that transformed the nation during these years served to link together northerners and southerners. The cotton planter who rode the steamship *Fashion* along the Alabama River ("Time's money! Time's money!") was wearing ready-made clothes manufactured in New York from southern cotton. Chauncey Jerome's clocks from Connecticut were keeping time not only for commercial planters but also for Lowell mill workers like Mary Paul, who learned to measure her lunch break in minutes. Farmers in both Tennessee and Iowa were interested in the price of wheat in New York, for it affected the profits that could be made shipping their grain by the new railroad lines. American society had become far more specialized, and therefore far more interdependent, since the days of Crèvecoeur's self-sufficient farmer of the 1780s.

But a specialized economy had not brought unity. For the North, specialization meant more factories, a higher percentage of urban workers, and a greater number of cities and towns. Industry affected midwestern farmers as well, for their steel plows and McCormick reapers allowed them to farm larger holdings and required greater capital investment in the new machinery. For its part, the South was transformed by the industrial revolution too, as textile factories made cotton the booming mainstay of its economy. But for all its growth, the region remained largely a rural society. Its prosperity stemmed from expansion westward into new areas of cotton production, not new forms of production or technology. The dominant planter class reinforced its traditional concepts of honor, hierarchy, and deference.

Above all, the intensive labor required to produce cotton, rice, and sugar made slavery an inseparable part of the southern way of life—"so intimately mingled with our social conditions," as one Georgian admitted, "that it would be impossible to eradicate it." An increasing number of northerners viewed slavery as evil, not so much out of high-minded sympathy toward slaves but as a labor system that threatened the republican ideals of white American society.

If the United States had not grown so dynamically—if its frontier had not swept so quickly toward the Pacific—the nation might have been able to postpone the day of reckoning on slavery until some form of gradual emancipation could be adopted. But the luxury of time was not available. The new territories became the battlegrounds for two contrasting ways of life, with slavery at the center of the debate. Nor did those Americans, North and South, black and white, who saw the issue in moral terms think the question should be postponed.

It fell to the political system to try to resolve sectional conflict through a system of national parties that represented various interest groups and promoted democratic debate. But the political system had critical weaknesses. The American process of electing a president gave the winning candidate a state's entire electoral vote, regardless of the margin of victory. That procedure made a northern sectional party possible, since the Republicans could never have carried an election on the basis of a popular vote alone. In addition, the four-year fixed presidential term allowed Presidents Pierce and Buchanan to remain in office, pursuing disruptive policies on Kansas even after the voters had rejected those policies in the midterm congressional elections in 1854 and 1858. Finally, since 1844 the Democratic party had required a two-thirds vote to nominate its presidential candidate. Unintentionally, this requirement made it difficult to pick any truly forceful leader and gave the South a veto over the party's candidate. Yet the South, by itself, could not elect a president.

The nation's republican heritage also contributed to the political system's vulnerability. Ever since the Revolution, when Americans accused the king and Parliament of deliberately plotting to deprive them of their liberties, Americans were on the watch for political conspiracies. Such an outlook often stimulated exaggerated fears, unreasonable conclusions, and excessive reactions. For their part, Republicans emphasized the existence of the Slave Power bent on eradicating northern rights. Southerners, on the other hand, accused the Black Republicans of conspiring to destroy southern equality. Each side viewed itself as defending the country's republican tradition from an internal threat.

In 1850 southerners might have been satisfied if their section had been left alone and the agitation against slavery had ended. But a decade later, many Americans both North and South had come to accept the idea of an irrepressible conflict between two societies, one based on freedom, the other on slavery, in which only one side could ultimately prevail. At stake, it seemed, was control of the nation's future. Four years later, as a weary Abraham Lincoln looked back to the beginning of the conflict, he noted, "Both parties deprecated war, but one of them would *make* war rather than let the nation survive, and the other would *accept* war rather than let it perish, and the war came."

Weaknesses of the political system

Belief in conspiracies against liberty

chapter summary

In the 1850s, the slavery issue reemerged in national politics and increasingly disrupted the party system, leading to the outbreak of war in 1861.

- Fundamental economic changes heightened sectional tensions in the 1850s.

  — The construction of a vast railroad network reoriented western trade from the South to the East.

  — A tide of new immigrants swelled the North's population (and hence its political power) at the expense of the South, thereby stimulating southern fears.

- The old Jacksonian party system was shattered by the nativist movement and by a renewed controversy of the expansion of slavery.

  — In the Kansas-Nebraska Act, Senator Stephen A. Douglas tried to defuse the slavery debate by incorporating popular sovereignty (the idea that the people of a territory should decide the status of slavery there). This act effectively repealed the Missouri Compromise.

- Popular sovereignty failed in the Kansas Territory, where fighting broke out between proslavery and antislavery partisans.

- Sectional violence reached a climax in May 1856 with the attack on Lawrence, Kansas, and the caning of Senator Charles Sumner of Massachusetts by Representative Preston S. Brooks of South Carolina.

• Sectional tensions sparked the formation of a new antislavery Republican party, and the party system realigned along sectional lines.

- The Supreme Court's *Dred Scott* decision, the Panic of 1857, the congressional struggle over the proslavery Lecompton constitution, and John Brown's attack on Harpers Ferry in 1859 strengthened the two sectional extremes.

• In 1860 Abraham Lincoln became the first Republican to be elected president.

- Following Lincoln's triumph, the seven states of the Deep South seceded.

- When Lincoln sent supplies to the Union garrison in Fort Sumter in Charleston harbor, Confederate batteries bombarded the fort into submission.

- The North rallied to Lincoln's decision to use force to restore the Union, and in response the four states of the Upper South seceded.

interactive learning

The Primary Source Investigator CD-ROM offers the following materials related to this chapter:

• Interactive maps: **Election of 1860** (M7) and **The Transportation Revolution, 1830–1890** (M12)

• A collection of primary sources illuminating the political and social strife of the 1850s, including "Free At Last!", a document about the role of African Americans in their emancipation, and the First and Second Confiscation Acts. Other sources capture the anxiety of the age, such as a letter written by John Boston proclaiming his freedom and a letter regarding how to handle contraband slaves.

additional reading

The problem of the coming of the Civil War has attracted considerable historical attention over the years. David M. Potter, *The Impending Crisis, 1848–1861* (1976), is a superior political treatment of the period, shrewd in its judgments and penetrating in its analysis. Fuller in its coverage but more melodramatic is Allan Nevins, *Ordeal of the Union* (2 vols., 1947) and *The Emergence of Lincoln* (2 vols., 1950). A stimulating work that, unlike these, focuses on the problem and complexities of the antebellum political realignment is Michael F. Holt, *The Political Crisis of the 1850s* (1978).

The heavy immigration during these years is described in Philip D. Taylor, *The Distant Magnet* (1971). Holt's book, noted in the previous paragraph, presents the most astute discussion of the Know-Nothing party. John McCardell's *The Idea of a Southern Nation* (1979) is a solid, well-written treatment of southern nationalism in this period. The most thorough examination of the blend of factors that produced the Republican party is William E. Gienapp, *The Origins of the Republican Party, 1852–1856* (1987). Eric Foner, in *Free Soil, Free Labor, Free Men* (1970), focuses on the ideas of Republican party leaders. For the turbulent history of Kansas in this period, see James A. Rawley, *Race and Politics* (1969). The critical events of 1857 are the focal point of Kenneth M. Stampp's *America in 1857* (1990). The secession movement has largely been investigated in specific southern states. A particularly good example of this approach is Stephen A. Channing's account of secession in South Carolina, *Crisis of Fear* (1974). Kenneth M. Stampp, *And the War Came* (1950), is the best study of northern public opinion during the secession crisis. An excellent examination of the war's origins, sophisticated in its analysis and up-to-date in its scholarship, is Gabor S. Boritt, ed., *Why the War Came* (1996). For a fuller list of readings, see the Bibliography at www.mhhe.com/davidsonnation5.

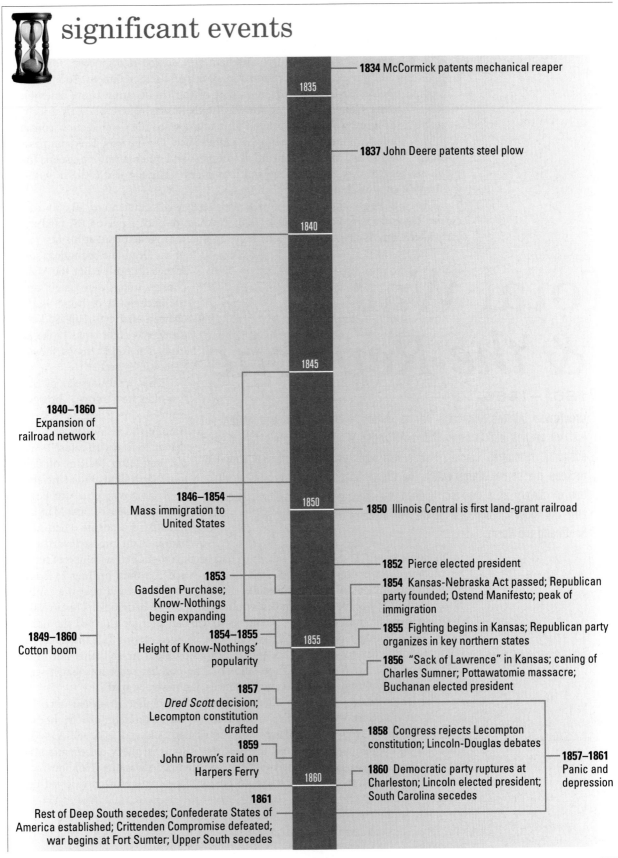

significant events

1834 McCormick patents mechanical reaper

1835

1837 John Deere patents steel plow

1840

1840–1860
Expansion of
railroad network

1845

1846–1854
Mass immigration to
United States

1850

1850 Illinois Central is first land-grant railroad

1852 Pierce elected president

1853
Gadsden Purchase;
Know-Nothings
begin expanding

1854 Kansas-Nebraska Act passed; Republican party founded; Ostend Manifesto; peak of immigration

1849–1860
Cotton boom

1854–1855
Height of Know-Nothings'
popularity

1855

1855 Fighting begins in Kansas; Republican party organizes in key northern states

1856 "Sack of Lawrence" in Kansas; caning of Charles Sumner; Pottawatomie massacre; Buchanan elected president

1857
Dred Scott decision;
Lecompton constitution
drafted

1858 Congress rejects Lecompton constitution; Lincoln-Douglas debates

1859
John Brown's raid on
Harpers Ferry

1860

1860 Democratic party ruptures at Charleston; Lincoln elected president; South Carolina secedes

1857–1861
Panic and
depression

1861
Rest of Deep South secedes; Confederate States of America established; Crittenden Compromise defeated; war begins at Fort Sumter; Upper South secedes

Chapter 16

T he war won't last sixty days!" Of that Jim Tinkham was confident. With dreams of a hero's return, Tinkham quit his job as a grocery store clerk and enlisted for three months in a Massachusetts regiment. Soon he was transferred to Washington as part of the Union army being assembled under General Irvin McDowell. Tinkham was elated when in mid-July the army was finally ordered to march toward the Confederates concentrated at Manassas Junction, 25 miles away. On the way, Tinkham passed carriages carrying members of Congress and other jaunty sightseers, their picnic baskets filled with provisions and fine wines. They too had come to witness the battle that would crush the rebellion.*

The battle began at dawn on July 21, with McDowell commanding 30,000 troops against General Pierre Beauregard's 22,000. Tinkham did not arrive on the field until early afternoon. As his regiment pushed toward the front, he felt faint at his first sight of the dead and wounded, some mangled horribly. But the Massachusetts troops were caught up in the excitement of battle as they charged up Henry Hill. Suddenly the Confederate ranks broke and exuberant Union troops shouted, "The war is over!"

Total War & *the Republic*

1861–1865

preview • As the first total war in history, the Civil War was fought not just by armies but through the mobilization of each society's human and economic resources. Lincoln's leadership was key. He moved slowly at first, to keep the border states within the Union, but later accepted the destruction of slavery as a war aim. Indeed, the freeing of four million slaves was only the most monumental of the war's many transformations, in both the South and the North.

The timely arrival of fresh Confederate troops, however, enabled the rebels to regroup. Among the reinforcements who rushed to Henry Hill was 19-year-old Randolph McKim of Baltimore. A student at the University of Virginia when the war began, McKim joined the First Maryland Infantry as a private when Abraham Lincoln imposed martial law in his home state. "The cause of the South had become identified with liberty itself," he explained. After only a week of drill, McKim boarded a train on July 21 bound for Manassas. When he and his comrades disembarked, they could hear the cannon firing in the distance, so they marched double-quick to the battlefield. The arrival of the First Maryland and other reinforcements in the late afternoon turned the tide of battle. The faltering Confederate line held, then charged, giving full throat for the first time to the famous "rebel yell." "There is nothing like [the yell] this side of the infernal region," explained one Union soldier. "The peculiar sensation that it sends down your backbone under these circumstances can never be told."

The Union troops gave way slowly at first, but discipline dissolved once McDowell ordered a retreat, and the army quickly degenerated into a frightened, stampeding mob. Troops threw away their equipment, shoved aside officers who tried to stop them, and raced frantically past the wagons, artillery pieces, and civilian carriages that clogged the road. Joining the stampede was Jim Tinkham, who confessed he would have continued on to Boston if he had not been stopped by a

---

*The Union and Confederacy often gave different names to a battle. The Confederates called the first battle Manassas; the Union, Bull Run.

Reveille rouses drowsy Union soldiers on a wintry morning as a drummer boy warms his hands. Instead of the glory they expected, reveille, roll call, and drill constituted Civil War soldiers' usual camp routine. A hired black laborer is already at work as the troops awaken.

guard after crossing the Long Bridge into Washington. All the next day in a drizzling rain, mud-spattered troops straggled into the capital in complete disorder. One dispirited officer, conceding that they were "pretty well whipped," declared that he'd had "enough of fighting to last my lifetime" and announced that he was going home.

The rout at Bull Run sobered the North. Gone were dreams of ending the war with one glorious battle. Gone was the illusion that 75,000 volunteers serving three months could crush the rebellion. As one perceptive observer noted, "We have undertaken to make war without in the least knowing how." Having cast off his earlier illusions, a newly determined Jim Tinkham reenlisted for a three-year hitch.

Still, it was not surprising that both sides underestimated the magnitude of the conflict. Previous warfare as it had evolved in Europe consisted largely of maneuverings that took relatively few lives, respected private property, and left civilians largely unharmed. The Civil War, on the other hand, was the first war whose major battles routinely involved more than 100,000 troops. So many combatants could be equipped only through the use of factory-produced weaponry, they could be

Meaning of total war

moved and supplied only with the help of railroads, and they could be sustained only through the concerted efforts of civilian society as a whole. The morale of the population, the quality of political leadership, and the utilization of industrial and economic might were all critical to the outcome. Quite simply, the Civil War was the first total war in history.

The Demands of Total War

When the war began, the North had an enormous advantage in manpower and industrial capacity. The Union's population was 2.5 times larger, and its advantage in white men of military age even greater. The North had a much larger merchant marine; produced more iron, firearms, and textiles; contained more railroad track and rolling stock; and possessed more than ten times the industrial capacity.

Southern advantages

From a modern perspective, the South's attempt to defend its independence against such odds seems a hopeless cause. Yet this view indicates how much the conception of war has changed. European observers, who knew the strength and resources of the two sides, believed that the Confederacy, with its large area, poor roads, and rugged terrain, could never be conquered. Indeed, the South enjoyed definite strategic advantages. To be victorious, it did not need to invade the North—only to defend its own land and prevent the North from destroying its armies. Southern soldiers knew the topography of their home country better, and a friendly population regularly supplied them with intelligence about Union troop movements.

Resources of the Union and the Confederacy, 1861

	Union	Confederacy	Union Advantage
Total population	23,300,000	9,100,000*	2.5 to 1
White male population (18–45 years)	4,600,000	1,100,000	4.2 to 1
Bank deposits	$207,000,000	$47,000,000	4.4 to 1
Value of manufactured goods	$1,730,000,000	$156,000,000	11 to 1
Railroad mileage	22,000	9,000	2.4 to 1
Shipping tonnage	4,600,000	290,000	16 to 1
Value of textiles produced	$181,000,000	$10,000,000	18 to 1
Value of firearms produced	$2,290,000	$73,000	31 to 1
Pig iron production (tons)	951,000	37,000	26 to 1
Coal production (tons)	13,680,000	650,000	21 to 1
Corn and wheat production (bushels)	698,000,000	314,000,000	2.2 to 1
Draft animals	5,800,000	2,900,000	2 to 1
Cotton production (bales)	43,000	5,344,000	1 to 124

*Slaves accounted for 3,500,000, or 40 percent.

Sources: U.S. Census 1860; E. B. Long, *The Civil War Day by Day* (New York: Doubleday, 1971), p. 723.

The North, in contrast, had to invade and conquer the Confederacy and destroy the southern will to resist. To do so, it would have to deploy thousands of soldiers to defend long supply lines in enemy territory, a situation that significantly reduced the northern advantage in manpower. Yet in the end, the Confederacy was not only invaded and conquered but also utterly destroyed. By 1865 the Union forces had penetrated virtually every part of the 500,000 square miles of the Confederacy and were able to move almost at will. The Civil War demonstrated the capacity of a modern society to overcome the problems of distance and terrain with technology.

Political Leadership

To sustain a commitment to total war required effective political leadership. This task fell on Abraham Lincoln and Jefferson Davis, presidents of the rival governments.

Jefferson Davis

Jefferson Davis grew up in Mississippi accustomed to life's advantages. Educated at West Point, he fought in the Mexican War, served as Franklin Pierce's secretary of war, and became one of the South's leading advocates in the Senate. Although he was hardworking and committed to the cause he led, his temperament was not well suited to his new post. He quarreled tactlessly with generals and politicians and refused to work with those he disliked. "He cannot brook opposition or criticism," one member of the Confederate Congress testified, "and those who do not bow down before him have no chance of success with him." His narrow, legalistic approach to problems hampered his efforts to rouse the southern people.

Yet for all Davis's personal handicaps, he faced an institutional one even more daunting. The Confederacy had been founded on the ideology of states' rights. Yet to meet the demands of total war, Davis would need to increase the authority of the central government beyond anything the South had ever experienced.

Lincoln's leadership

When Lincoln took the oath of office, his national experience consisted of one term in the House of Representatives. But Lincoln was a shrewd judge of character and a superb politician. To achieve a common goal, he willingly overlooked withering criticism and personal slights. (The commander of the Union army, General George McClellan, for one, continually snubbed the president and referred to him as "the original Gorilla.") He was not easily humbugged, overawed, or flattered and never allowed personal feelings to blind him to his larger objectives.

Lincoln at the time of the Gettysburg Address

"This is essentially a People's contest," Lincoln asserted at the start of the war, and few presidents have been better able to communicate with the average citizen. He regularly visited Union troops in camp, in the field, and in army hospitals. "The boys liked him," wrote Joseph Twichell, from a Connecticut regiment. "[I]n fact his popularity with the army is and has been universal." Always Lincoln reminded the public that the war was being fought for the ideals of the Revolution and the Republic. It was a test, he remarked in his famous address at Gettysburg, of whether a nation "conceived in Liberty, and dedicated to the proposition that all men are created equal" could "long endure."

Lincoln also proved the more effective military leader. Jefferson Davis took his title of commander in chief literally, interfering with his generals even on the smallest matters. But he failed to formulate an effective overarching strategy. In contrast, Lincoln had a clear grasp of the challenge confronting the Union. He accepted General Winfield Scott's proposal to blockade and surround the Confederacy, cut off its supplies, and slowly strangle it into submission, just as the anaconda snake squeezes its prey. But unlike Scott, he realized that an "anaconda plan" was not enough. The South would also have to be invaded and defeated, not only on an eastern front in Virginia but also in the West, where Union control of the Mississippi would divide the Confederacy fatally. Lincoln understood that the Union's superior manpower and matériel would become decisive only when the Confederacy was simultaneously threatened along a broad front. The Union forces could then break through at the weak points. It took time before the president found generals able to execute this novel strategy.

The Border States

When the war began, only Delaware of the border slave states was certain to remain in the Union. Lincoln's immediate political challenge was to retain the loyalty of Maryland, Kentucky, and Missouri. Maryland especially was crucial, for if it was lost, Washington itself would have to be abandoned.

Suppression in Maryland

The danger became immediately apparent when pro-Confederate forces destroyed the railroad bridges near Baltimore and isolated Washington. Only with difficulty was the administration able to move troops to the city. Once the capital was safe, Lincoln moved vigorously—even ruthlessly—to secure Maryland. He suspended the writ of habeas corpus, the right under the Constitution of an arrested person either to be charged with a specific crime or to be released. That done, he held without trial prominent Confederate sympathizers and suppressed pro-Confederate newspapers. Intervention by the army ensured that Unionists won a complete victory in the fall state election. The election ended any possibility that Maryland would join the Confederacy.

Kentucky's neutrality

At the beginning of the conflict, Kentucky officially declared its neutrality. "I think to lose Kentucky is nearly to lose the whole game," Lincoln wrote with obvious concern. "Kentucky gone, we can not hold Missouri, nor, as I think, Maryland. These all against us, and the job on our hands is too large for us." Union generals requested permission to occupy the state, but the president refused, preferring to act cautiously and wait for Unionist sentiment to assert itself. After Unionists won control of the legislature in the summer election, a Confederate army entered the state, giving Lincoln the opening he needed. He quickly sent in troops, and Kentucky stayed in the Union.

In Missouri, skirmishing broke out between Union and Confederate sympathizers. Only after the Union victory at the Battle of Pea Ridge in March 1862 was Missouri secure from any Confederate threat. Even so, guerrilla warfare continued in the state throughout the remainder of the war.

In Virginia, internal divisions led to the creation of a new border state, as the hilly western counties, where slavery was not strong, refused to support the Confederacy. After adopting a congressionally mandated program of gradual emancipation, West Virginia was formally admitted to the Union in June 1863.

Importance of the border states

The Union scored an important triumph in holding the border states. The population of all five equaled that of the four states of the Upper South that had joined the Confederacy, and their production of military supplies—food, animals, and minerals—was greater. Furthermore, Maryland and West Virginia contained key railroad lines and were critical to the defense of Washington, while

Kentucky and Missouri gave the Union army access to the major river systems of the western theater, down which it launched the first successful invasions of the Confederacy.

As with so many Civil War battles, **Opening Moves**
the Confederate victory at Bull Run
achieved no decisive military results. But a sobered Congress authorized the enlistment of half a million volunteers to serve for three years. Lincoln named 34-year-old George McClellan, a West Point graduate, to be the new commander of the Union army. Energetic and ambitious, McClellan had been working as a railroad executive when the war began. For the next eight months he appeared the very model of businesslike efficiency as he settled into the much-needed task of organizing and drilling the Army of the Potomac.

Blockade and Isolate

The U.S. Navy began the war with only 42 ships available to blockade 3550 miles of Confederate coastline. By the spring of 1862, it had secured several key bases for the blockading squadrons, and the navy also began building powerful gunboats to operate on the rivers. In April 1862 Flag Officer David G. Farragut ran a gauntlet of Confederate shore batteries to capture New Orleans, the Confederacy's largest city and most important port. Memphis, another important river city, fell to Union forces in June.

The blockade was hardly leakproof, and Confederates slipped through it using small, fast ships. Still, southern trade suffered badly. In hopes of lifting the blockade, the Confederacy converted the wooden U.S.S. *Merrimack*, which was rechristened the *Virginia*, into an ironclad gunboat. In March 1862 a Union ironclad, the *Monitor*, battled it to a standoff, and the Confederates were forced to scuttle the *Virginia* when they evacuated Norfolk in May. After that, the Union's naval supremacy was secure.

Ironclads

The South looked to diplomacy as another means to lift the blockade. With cotton so vital to European economies, especially Great Britain's, southerners believed that Europe would formally recognize the Confederacy and come to its aid. The North, for its part, claimed that it was merely putting down a domestic insurrection, and Secretary of State William Seward warned European nations against intervening in America's internal affairs. Nevertheless, European countries extended belligerent status to the government at Richmond, which allowed the Confederacy to purchase supplies abroad.

King Cotton diplomacy

By 1862 cotton supplies were dwindling, and France was ready to recognize the Confederacy, but only if Britain would follow suit. The British government favored the South, but it hesitated to act until Confederate armies demonstrated that they could win the war. Meanwhile, new supplies of cotton from Egypt and India enabled the British textile industry to recover. In the end, Britain and the rest of Europe refused to recognize the Confederacy, and the South was left to stand or fall on its own resources.

Grant in the West

In the western war theater, the first decisive Union victory was won by a short, shabbily dressed, cigar-chomping general named Ulysses S. Grant. An undistinguished student at West Point, Grant eventually resigned his commission. He failed

The War in the West, 1861–1862
Grant's push southward stalled after his costly victory at Shiloh; nevertheless, by the end of 1862 the Union had secured Kentucky and Missouri, as well as most of Confederate Tennessee and the upper and lower stretches of the Mississippi River.

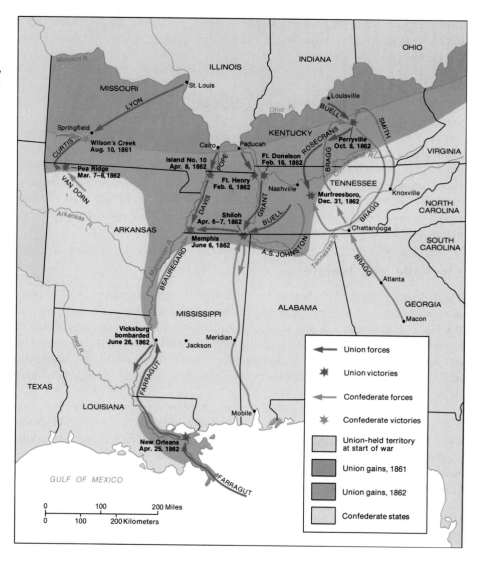

Grant's character

at everything he tried in civilian life, and when the war broke out he was a store clerk in Galena, Illinois. Almost 39, he promptly volunteered, and two months later became a brigadier general.

Grant's quiet, self-effacing manner gave little indication of his military ability or iron determination. Alert to seize any opening, he remained extraordinarily calm and clear-headed in battle. He absorbed details on a map almost photographically, and in battles that spread out over miles, he was superb at coordinating an attack. He would "try all sorts of cross-cuts," recalled one staff officer, "ford streams and jump any number of fences to reach another road rather than go back and take a fresh start." Grant also took full advantage of the telegraph to track troop movements, stringing new lines as he advanced. (Some of his Union telegraphers were so adept that they could receive messages before a station was set up by touching the end of the wire to their tongues to pick up Morse code.) Most important, Grant grasped that hard fighting, not fancy maneuvering, would bring victory. "The art of war is simple," he once explained. "Find out where your enemy is, get at him as soon as you can and strike him as hard as you can, and keep moving on."

Grant realized that rivers were avenues into the interior of the Confederacy. In February 1862, supported by Union gunboats, he captured Fort Henry on the Tennessee River and Fort Donelson on the Cumberland. These victories forced the Confederates to withdraw from Kentucky and middle Tennessee. Grant continued south with 40,000 men, but he was surprised on April 6 by General Albert Sidney Johnston at Shiloh, just north of the Tennessee-Mississippi border. Johnston was killed in the day's fierce fighting, but by nightfall his army had driven the Union troops back to the Tennessee River, where they huddled numbly as a cold rain fell. William Tecumseh Sherman, one of Grant's subordinates, found the general standing under a dripping tree, his coat collar drawn up against the damp, puffing on a cigar. Sherman was about to suggest retreat, but something in Grant's eyes, lighted by the glow of his stogie, made him hesitate. So he said only, "Well, Grant, we've had the devil's own day, haven't we?" "Yes," the Union commander quietly replied. "Lick 'em tomorrow, though." And he did. With the aid of reinforcements, which he methodically ferried across the river all night, Grant counterattacked the next morning and drove the Confederates from the field.

Shiloh

But victory came at a high price, for Shiloh inflicted more than 23,000 casualties. "The scenes on this field would have cured anyone of war," Sherman testified. Grant, who before had doubted the commitment of Confederate troops, came away deeply impressed by their determination. "At Shiloh," he wrote afterward, "I gave up all idea of saving the Union except by complete conquest."

Eastern Stalemate

Grant's victories did not silence his critics, who charged he drank too much. But Lincoln was unmoved. "I can't spare this man. He fights." That was a quality in short supply in the East, where General McClellan directed operations.

The short, handsome McClellan looked like a general, but beneath his arrogance and bravado lay a self-doubt that rendered him excessively cautious. As the months dragged on and McClellan did nothing but train and plan, Lincoln's frustration grew. "If General McClellan does not want to use the army I would like to *borrow* it," he remarked sarcastically. In the spring of 1862 the general finally transported his 130,000 troops to the Virginia coast and began inching toward Richmond, the Confederate capital. In May, when McClellan was within five miles of Richmond, General Joseph Johnston suddenly attacked him near Fair Oaks, from which he barely escaped.* Worse for McClellan, when Johnston was badly wounded the formidable Robert E. Lee took command of the Army of Northern Virginia.

Lincoln fears "McClellan has the slows"

Where McClellan was cautious and defensive, the aristocratic Lee was daring and ever alert to assume the offensive. His first name, one of his colleagues commented, should have been Audacity: "He will take more chances, and take them quicker than any other general in this country." Joining Lee was Thomas "Stonewall" Jackson, a deeply religious Calvinist whose rigorous discipline honed his troops to a hard edge. In the Seven Days' battles, McClellan maneuvered brilliantly to parry the attacks of Lee and Jackson; still, he always stayed on the defensive,

Lee's generalship

---

*Not to be confused with Albert Sidney Johnston, the Confederate general in the western theater killed at Shiloh.

With almost 23,000 casualties, Antietam was the bloodiest single day of the war. A group of Confederate soldiers are shown where they fell along the Hagerstown Pike, the scene of some of the heaviest fighting. Said one Union officer of the fighting there: "Men, I cannot say fell; they were knocked out of the ranks by dozens."

finally retreating until he was under the protection of the Union gunboats. Frustrated, Lincoln ordered the Peninsula campaign abandoned and formed a new army under John Pope. After Lee badly mauled Pope at the second Battle of Bull Run, Lincoln restored McClellan to command.

Lee's invasion fails

Realizing that the Confederacy needed a decisive victory, Lee convinced Davis to allow him to invade the North, hoping to detach Maryland and isolate Washington. But as the army crossed into Maryland, Union soldiers discovered a copy of Lee's orders, accidentally left behind at a campsite by a Confederate officer. From this document McClellan learned that his forces vastly outnumbered Lee's—yet still he hesitated before launching a series of badly coordinated assaults near Antietam Creek on September 17 that Lee barely repulsed. The bloody exchanges horrified both sides for their sheer carnage. Within the space of seven hours, nearly 5000 soldiers were killed and another 18,000 wounded, making it the bloodiest single day in American history. When McClellan allowed the Confederate army to escape back into Virginia, the president permanently relieved him of command in November.

The winter of 1862 was the North's Valley Forge, as morale sank to an all-time low. It took General Ambrose Burnside, who assumed McClellan's place, little more than a month to demonstrate his utter incompetence. In December, at the Battle of Fredericksburg, he suffered a disastrous defeat, which prompted Lincoln to put "Fighting Joe" Hooker in charge. In the West, Grant had emerged as the dominant

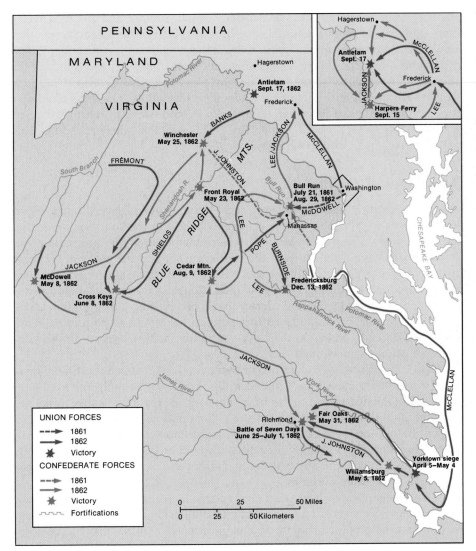

PENNSYLVANIA

MARYLAND

VIRGINIA

The War in the East, 1861–1862
McClellan's campaign against Richmond failed when Joseph Johnston surprised him at Fair Oaks. Taking command of the Army of Northern Virginia, Lee drove back McClellan in the Seven Days' battles and then won a resounding victory in the second Battle of Bull Run. He followed this up by invading Maryland, dividing his forces to take advantage of McClellan's caution, and capturing Harpers Ferry. McClellan checked his advance at Antietam. The Army of the Potomac's devastating defeat at Fredericksburg ended a year of frustration and failure for the Union in the eastern theater.

figure, but the Army of the Potomac still lacked a capable commander, the deaths kept mounting, and no end to the war was in sight.

Emancipation

In 1858 Lincoln had proclaimed that an American "house divided" could not stand and that the United States would eventually become either all slave or all free. When the house divided, however, Lincoln hesitated to strike at slavery. He perceived, accurately, that most white northerners were not deeply committed to emancipation. He feared the social upheaval that such a revolutionary step would cause, and he did not want to alarm the wavering border states. Thus when Congress met in special session in July 1861, Lincoln fully supported a resolution offered by John J. Crittenden of Kentucky, which declared that the war was being fought solely "to defend and maintain the supremacy of the Constitution and to preserve the Union." The Crittenden Resolution passed the House by 117 to 2 and the Senate by 30 to 5.

Crittenden Resolution

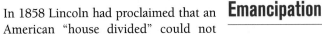

Lincoln gives priority to
the Union

Still, Republican radicals like Senator Charles Sumner and Horace Greeley pressed Lincoln to adopt a policy of emancipation. Slavery had caused the war, they argued; its destruction would hasten the war's end. Lincoln, however, placed first priority on saving the Union. "My paramount object in this struggle *is* to save the Union, and is *not* either to save or to destroy slavery," he told Greeley in 1862. "If I could save the Union without freeing *any* slave I would do it, and if I could save it by freeing *all* the slaves I would do it, and if I could save it by freeing some and leaving others alone, I would also do that." This statement summarized Lincoln's policy during the first year of the war.

The Logic of Events

Congressional attack on
slavery

As the Union army began to occupy Confederate territory, slaves flocked to the Union camps. Octave Johnson, the runaway who hid in the Louisiana bayous for more than a year (page 392), was only one of many slaves who presented themselves to occupying forces. In May 1861 the army adopted the policy of declaring runaway slaves "contraband" of war and refused to return them to their rebel owners. In the Confiscation Act of August 1861, Congress provided that slaves used for military purposes by the Confederacy would become free if they fell into Union hands. For a year Lincoln accepted that position but would go no further. When two of his generals, acting on their own authority, abolished slavery in their districts, he countermanded their orders.

By the time Congress reconvened in December 1861, opinion was beginning to shift. When reintroduced, the Crittenden Resolution was soundly defeated. Congress also prohibited federal troops from capturing or returning fugitive slaves and freed the 2000 slaves living in the District of Columbia with compensation to their owners. In July 1862 it passed the Second Confiscation Act, which declared that the slaves of anyone who supported the rebellion would be freed if they came into federal custody. Unlike with the first act, it did not matter whether the slaves had been used for military purposes.

Process of emancipation during
the Civil War

Lincoln's decision for
emancipation

Lincoln signed this bill and then proceeded to ignore it. Instead, he emphasized state action, since slavery was a domestic institution. In his first annual message to Congress, he proposed that the federal government provide grants to compensate slaveowners in any state-sponsored program of gradual emancipation. Twice the president summoned white representatives from the border states and prodded them to act before the war destroyed slavery of its own momentum. Both times they rejected his plea.

Following the failure of his second meeting with the border state leaders, Lincoln on July 22, 1862, presented to his cabinet a proposed proclamation freeing the slaves in the Confederacy. He was increasingly confident that the border states would remain in the Union, and he wanted to strike a blow that would weaken the Confederacy militarily. By making the struggle one of freedom versus slavery, such a proclamation would also undermine Confederate efforts to obtain diplomatic recognition. But Lincoln decided to wait for a Union military victory so that the act would not appear one of desperation.

The Emancipation Proclamation

Terms of the
Proclamation

On September 22, following the victory at Antietam, Lincoln announced that all slaves within rebel lines would be freed unless the seceded states returned to their allegiance by January 1, 1863. When that day came, the Emancipation Proclamation went formally into effect. Excluded from its terms were the Union slave states, all of Tennessee, and the other areas of the Confederacy that were under Union control. In all, about 830,000 of the nation's 4 million slaves were not covered by its provisions. Because Lincoln justified his actions on strictly military grounds, he believed that there was no legal right to apply the Proclamation to areas not in rebellion.

Following initial criticism of the Proclamation, European public opinion swung toward the Union. In the North, Republicans generally favored Lincoln's decision, while the Democrats made it a major issue in the 1862 elections. "Every white man in the North, who does not want to be swapped off for a free Nigger, should vote the Democratic ticket," urged one party orator. Although the Democrats improved their showing in the elections that fall, the results offered no clear verdict on the Proclamation.

Reaction to the Proclamation

Despite the mixed reaction, the Emancipation Proclamation had immense symbolic importance, for it redefined the nature of the war. The North was fighting not to save the old Union but to create a new nation. The war had become, in Lincoln's words, "remorseless revolution."

African Americans' Civil War

Contrary to white southerners' fears that a race war would erupt behind the lines, the institution of slavery did not explode: it simply disintegrated. Well before federal troops entered an area, slaves took the lead in undermining the institution by openly challenging white authority and claiming greater personal freedom. One experienced overseer reported in frustration that now the "slaves will do only what pleases them, go out in the morning when it suits them, come in when they please, etc." The wife of a Texas planter away at war wrote that she had discontinued whipping, for it only made matters worse. Throughout the Confederacy the vital psychological relationship between master and slave was strained, and sometimes it snapped.

Black men, including runaway slaves, joined the Union army and navy beginning in 1863. These photographs show Hubbard Pryor before (left) and after (right) enlistment. As soldiers, former slaves developed a new sense of pride and confidence. "I felt like a man with a uniform on and a gun in my hand," declared one ex-slave, and Elijah Marrs recalled that at his first roll call, "I felt freedom in my bones."

Early in the conflict slaves concluded that emancipation would be one consequence of a Union victory. Perhaps as many as half a million—one-seventh of the total slave population of the Confederacy—fled to Union lines, where they faced an uncertain reception since northern troops mani-

Slaves within Union lines

fested a deep-seated racism and were often hostile. The ex-slaves, called freedmen, ended up living in refugee or contraband camps that were overcrowded and disease-ridden and provided only rudimentary shelter and food. "The poor Negroes die as fast as ever," one northern missionary reported. "The children are all emaciated to the last degree and have such violent coughs and dysenteries that few survive."

Convinced that freed slaves would not work on their own initiative, the U.S. government put some contrabands to work assisting the army as cooks, teamsters, woodchoppers, and other unskilled laborers. Their wages were well below those paid white citizens for the same work. In the Mississippi valley, where two-thirds of the freedpeople under Union control were located, most were forced to work on plantations leased or owned by loyal planters. This policy was officially adopted in the summer of 1863 as a way to free the army from the cost of supporting former slaves and strengthen Unionism in the South. Freedpeople had no say in the contracts negotiated between military authorities and planters, found themselves strictly disciplined, and had so many deductions taken from their wages that in the end most received only room and board. In short, the conditions often approximated slavery.

Black Soldiers

Blacks in combat

In adopting the policy of emancipation, Lincoln also announced that African Americans would be accepted in the navy and, more controversially, the army. (Throughout its history, the navy had been hard-pressed to get enough recruits, and as a result that service had always included some black sailors.) Resistance to accepting black volunteers in the army remained especially strong in the Midwest. Black northerners themselves were divided over whether to enlist, but Frederick Douglass spoke for the vast majority when he argued that once a black man had served in the army, there was "no power on earth which can deny that he has earned the right of citizenship in the United States."

In the end, nearly 200,000 African Americans served in the Union forces, constituting about 10 percent of the Union's total military manpower. Some, including two of Douglass's sons, were free, but most were former slaves who enlisted after escaping to the Union lines. As a concession to the racism of white troops, blacks served in segregated units under white officers. They were paid only $10 a month, with $3 deducted for clothing. White soldiers, in contrast, received $13 a month plus a $3.50 clothing allowance. Not until June 1864 did Congress finally grant equal pay to black soldiers.

At first given undesirable duties such as heavy labor and burial details, black soldiers successfully lobbied for the chance to fight. They impressed white troops with their courage under fire. "I have been one of those men, who never had much confidence in colored troops fighting," one Union officer admitted, "but these doubts are now all removed, for they fought as bravely as any troops in the Fort." In the end 37,000 African American servicemen gave their lives, a rate of loss about 40 percent higher than among white soldiers. Black recruits had good reason to fight fiercely. They knew that the freedom of their race hung in the balance, they hoped to win civil rights at home by their performance on the battlefield, they resented racist sneers about their loyalty and ability, and they knew that capture might mean death. The effect on African American pride was also apparent. Slaves admired the confidence of the black troops as they marched through the South. One soldier, who discovered his former master among the prisoners he was guarding, summed up the situation succinctly. "Hello, massa," he called cheerfully, "bottom rail on top dis time!"

The Confederate Home Front

"How shall we subsist this winter?" John Jones wondered in the fall of 1862. A clerk in the War Department in Richmond, Jones found it increasingly difficult to make ends meet on his salary. Prices kept going up, essential items were in short supply, and the signs of hardship were everywhere: in the darned and patched clothing, the absence of meat from the market, the desperation on people's faces. Some of the residents of Richmond "look like vagabonds," Jones noted in his diary. "We see men and women and children in the streets in dingy and dilapidated clothes; and some seem gaunt and pale with hunger. . . ." Coffee was a luxury Jones could no longer afford, he sold his watch to buy fuel, and he worried incessantly about being able to feed his family. "I cannot afford to have more than an ounce of meat daily for each member of my family of six," he recorded in 1864. "The old cat goes staggering about from debility, though Fannie [a daughter] often gives him her share. We see neither rats nor mice about the premises now." By the end of the year a month's supply of food and fuel was costing him $762, a sum sufficient to have supported his family for a year in peacetime. "This is war, terrible war!"

Nowhere were the profound effects of war more complete than within the Confederacy. These changes were especially ironic because the southern states had seceded in order to preserve their traditional ways. Not only did the war send hundreds of thousands of "Johnny Rebs" off to the front; it also put extreme burdens on the women and families at home. It fundamentally transformed the southern economy and forced the Confederate government to become more centralized. And, of course, it ended by destroying the institution of slavery, which the South had gone to war to preserve.

The New Economy

With the Union blockade tightening, the production of foodstuffs became crucial to the South's economy. Many men who normally worked in the fields had gone into the army, and with the lessening of discipline, slaves became increasingly assertive and independent. More and more plantations switched from growing cotton to raising grain and livestock. As a result, cotton production dropped from 4.5 million bales in 1861 to 300,000 in 1864. Even so, food production declined. By the last two years of the war, the shortage was serious.

The Union blockade also made it impossible to rely on European manufactured goods. So the Confederate War Department built and ran factories, took over the region's mines, and regulated private manufacturers so as to increase the production of war goods. Although the Confederacy never became industrially self-sufficient, its accomplishments were impressive. As Josiah Gorgas, head of the Confederate Ordnance Department, noted:

Attempts to industrialize

> We began in April, 1861, without an arsenal, laboratory or powder mill of any capacity, and with no foundry or rolling mill except at Richmond, and before the close of 1863, . . . we had built up foundries and rolling mills, smelting works, chemical works, a powder mill far superior to any in the United States, and a chain of arsenals, armories and laboratories equal in their capacity and their improved appointments to the best of those in the United States.

In fact, the Confederacy sustained itself far better in industrial goods than it did in agricultural produce. It was symbolic that when Lee surrendered, his troops had sufficient guns and ammunition to continue, but they had not eaten in two days.

New Opportunities for Southern Women

Southern white women took an active role in the war. Some gained notoriety as spies; others smuggled military supplies into the South. Women also spent a good deal of time knitting and sewing clothes for soldiers. "We never went out to pay a

New responsibilities and opportunities

"Nannie" McKenzie Semple was one of many southern white women who worked for the Confederate government. Semple's salary, from working as a "Treasury Girl," netted her more than what the average soldier received.

visit without taking our knitting along," recalled a South Carolina woman. Perhaps most important, with so many men fighting, women took charge of agricultural production. On plantations the mistress often supervised the slaves as well as the wrenching shift from cotton to foodstuffs. "All this attention to farming is uphill work with me," one South Carolina woman confessed to her army husband.

One such woman was 33-year-old Emily Lyles Harris, the wife of a small slaveowner and farmer in upcountry South Carolina. When her husband joined the army in 1862, she was left to care for her seven children as well as supervise the slaves and manage the farm. Despite the disruptions of wartime, she succeeded remarkably, one year producing the largest crop of oats in the neighborhood and always making enough money for her family to live decently. She took little pride, however, in her achievements. "I shall never get used to being left as the head of affairs at home," she wrote on one occasion. "The burden is very heavy, and there is no one to smile on me as I trudge wearily along in the dark with it. . . . I am not an independent woman nor ever shall be." And on another occasion, realizing that the work was behind schedule, she complained, "I'm tired to death with urging children and negroes to work." Self-doubt, lack of privacy, and the burdens of responsibility left her depressed, and while she persevered, by 1865 she openly hoped for defeat.

The war also opened up new jobs for women off the farm. Given the manpower shortage, "government girls" became essential to fill the growing Confederate bureaucracy; and with economic conditions so desperate, the secretary of the treasury found he had 100 applications for every vacancy. At first women were paid half the wages of male coworkers, but by the end of the war they had won equal pay. White women also staffed the new factories springing up in southern cities and towns, undertaking even dangerous work that normally would have been considered off-limits. A majority of the workers in the South's munitions factories were women, some of whom lost their lives in accidental explosions. "Of all the principles developed by the late war," wrote one Alabama planter, "I think the capability of our Southern women to take care of themselves was by no means the least important."

Confederate Finance and Government

The most serious domestic problem the Confederate government faced was finance, for which officials at Richmond never developed a satisfactory program. The South had few banks and only $27 million in specie when the war began. European governments refused to float major loans, which left taxation as the unappealing alternative. Only in 1863 did the government begin levying a graduated income tax (from 1 to 15 percent) and a series of excise taxes. Most controversial, the government resorted to a tax-in-kind on farmers that, after exempting a certain portion, took one-tenth of their agricultural crops. Even more unpopular was the policy of impressment, which allowed the army to seize private property for its own use, often with little or no compensation.

Above all, the Confederacy financed the war effort simply by printing paper money not backed by specie, some $1.5 billion, which amounted to three times more than the federal government issued. The result was runaway inflation, so that by 1865 a Confederate dollar was worth only 1.7 cents in gold and prices had soared to 92 times their prewar base. Prices were highest in Richmond, where flour sold for $275 a barrel by early 1864 and coats for $350. By the end of the war, flour had reached an astronomical $1000 a barrel. Inflation that ate away at their standard of living was one of the great wartime hardships borne by the southern people.

In politics even more than in finance, the Confederacy exercised far greater powers than those of the federal government before 1861. Indeed, Jefferson Davis strove to meet the demands of total war by transforming the South into a centralized, national state. He sought to limit state authority over military units, and in April 1862 the Confederacy passed the first national conscription law in American history, drafting all white males between 18 and 35 unless exempted. As conditions worsened, those age limits widened to 17 and 50, mobilizing virtually the entire military-age white population. Civilians, too, felt the effects of government control, for in 1862 the Congress authorized Davis to invoke martial law and suspend the writ of habeas corpus.

Critics protested that Davis was destroying states' rights, the cardinal principle of the Confederacy. Concerned foremost about their states' safety, governors wanted to be able to recall troops if their own territory was threatened. When President Davis suspended the writ of habeas corpus, his own vice president, Alexander H. Stephens, accused him of aiming at a dictatorship. Davis, however, used those powers for a limited time and only with the permission of Congress, yet in practice it made little difference whether the writ was suspended or not. With disloyalty a greater problem than in the Union, Confederate authorities more stringently regulated civil liberties, and the army arrested thousands of civilians.

But the Confederate draft, more than any other measure, produced an outcry. The law allowed the rich to provide substitutes, at a cost that eventually rose, on the open market, to as much as $6000. The Confederacy eventually abolished this privilege, but as one Georgia leader complained, "It's a notorious fact if a man has influential friends—or a little money to spare he will never be enrolled." Most controversially, the draft exempted from service one white man on every plantation with 20 or more slaves (later reduced to 15). This law was designed to preserve control of the slave population, but more and more nonslaveholders complained that it was a rich man's war and a poor man's fight. Denouncing the war as a slaveholders' plot, one Alabama yeoman claimed that "all they want is to git you pumped up and go to fight for their infernal negroes and after you do their fighting you may kiss their hind parts for all they care." In some counties where the draft was unenforceable, conscription officers ventured only at risk to their own safety.

Hardship and Suffering

By the last year of the conflict, food shortages had become so severe that ingenious southerners concocted various substitutes: parched corn in place of coffee, strained blackberries in place of vinegar. One scarce item for which there was no substitute was salt, which was essential for curing meat. Scarcity bred speculation, hoarding, and spiraling prices. The high prices and food shortages led to riots in several cities, most seriously in Richmond early in April 1863. There, about 300 women and children chanting "Bread!" wrecked a number of stores and helped themselves to bread, food, and other items. Nor were rural areas immune from these outbreaks. Country women attacked wagon trains carrying supplies and on several occasions even invaded towns and looted stores.

As always, war corroded the discipline and order of society. With the value of paper money dropping and the future uncertain, many southerners spent money in frenzied haste. Gambling halls were crowded with revelers seeking relief, while soldiers on furlough drank heavily, aware of their increasingly poor chances of survival at the front. Even in the army, theft became common, and in Richmond, the House of Representatives was robbed and Jefferson Davis's favorite horse stolen.

The search for escape from the grim reality of the war led to a forced gaiety for those who could afford it. "The cities are gayer than before the war," one refugee reported, "—parties every night in Richmond, suppers costing ten and twenty thousand dollars." Walking home at night after spending several hours at the bedside of a dying soldier, Judith McGuire passed a house gay with laughter, music, and dancing. "The revulsion . . . was sickening," she wrote afterward in her diary. "I thought of the gayety of Paris during the French Revolution, . . . the ball at Brussels the night before the battle of Waterloo, and felt shocked that our own Virginians, at such a time, should remind me of scenes which we were wont to think only belonged to . . . foreign society." The war was a cancer that ate away not only at southern society but at the southern soul itself.

The Union Home Front

Because the war was fought mostly on southern soil, northern civilians rarely felt its effects directly. Yet to be effective, the North's economic resources had to be organized and mobilized.

Government Finances and the Economy

Measures to raise money

To begin with, the North required a comprehensive system to finance its massive campaign. Taxing the populace was an obvious means, and taxes paid for 21 percent of Union war expenses, compared with only 1 percent of the Confederacy's. In August 1861 Congress passed the first federal income tax, 3 percent on all incomes over $800 a year. When that, along with increased tariff duties, proved insufficient, Congress enacted a comprehensive tax law in 1862 that for the first time brought the tax collector into every northern household. Excise fees taxed virtually every occupation, commodity, or service; income and inheritances were taxed, as were corporations and consumers. A new bureaucracy, the Internal Revenue Bureau, oversaw the collection process.

The government also borrowed heavily, through the sale of some $2.2 billion in bonds, and financed the rest of the war's cost by issuing paper money. In all, the Union printed $431 million in greenbacks (so named because of their color on one side). Although legal for the payment of debts, they could not be redeemed in specie, and therefore their value fluctuated. Congress also instituted a national banking system, allowing nationally chartered banks to issue notes backed by U.S. bonds. By taxing state banknotes out of circulation, Congress for the first time created a uniform national currency.

The superiority of northern industry was an important factor in the war's eventual outcome. Here molten ore is cast into cannons at a foundry in West Point, New York. This factory produced 3000 cannons during the war.

During the war, the Republican-controlled Congress encouraged economic development. Tariffs to protect industry from foreign competition rose to an average rate of 47 percent, compared to 19 percent in 1860. To encourage development of the West, the Homestead Act of 1862 granted 160 acres of public land—the size of the traditional American family farm—to anyone (including women) who settled and improved the land for five years. Over a million acres were distributed during the war years alone. In addition, the Land Grant College Act of 1862 donated the proceeds from certain land sales to finance public colleges and universities. Eventually 69 institutions of higher learning were created under its provisions, many in the West.

Western development

A Rich Man's War

Over the course of the war the government purchased more than $1 billion worth of goods and services. In response to this heavy demand, the economy boomed and business and agriculture prospered. Wages increased 42 percent between 1860 and 1864, but because prices rose faster than wages, workers' real income dropped almost 30 percent, from $363 in 1860 to $261 in 1865. That meant the working class paid a disproportionate share of the war's costs.

Corruption and fraud

The Republican belief that government should play a major role in the economy also fostered a cozy relationship between business and politics. In the rush to profit from government contracts, some suppliers sold inferior goods at inflated prices. Uniforms made of "shoddy"—bits of unused thread and recycled cloth—were fobbed off in such numbers that the word became an adjective describing inferior quality. Unscrupulous dealers sold clothing that dissolved in the rain, shoes that fell apart, spoiled meat, broken-down horses, and guns that would not fire. A War Department investigation later revealed that at least 20 percent of government expenditures involved fraud.

Stocks and dividends rose with the economy as investors scrambled after profitable new opportunities. An illegal cotton trade flourished in the Mississippi valley, where northern agents bribed military authorities for passes to go through the lines in order to purchase cotton bales from southern planters. The Confederate government quietly traded cotton for contraband such as food, medicine, and enough arms and equipment to maintain an army of 50,000 men. One War Department investigator asserted in 1863, "Every colonel, captain or quartermaster is in secret partnership with some operator in cotton."

Moral decline

Speculation during the last two years of the war became particularly feverish, and the fortunes made went toward the purchase of ostentatious luxuries. The Chicago *Tribune* admitted: "We are clothed in purple and fine linen, wear the richest laces and jewels and fare sumptuously every day." Like Richmond, Washington became the symbol of this moral decay. Prostitution, drinking, and corruption reached epidemic proportions in the capital, and social festivities became the means to shut out the numbing horror of the casualty lists.

Women and the Workforce

Even more than in the South, the war opened new opportunities for northern women. Countless wives ran farms while their husbands were away at war. One traveler in Iowa reported, "I met more women driving teams on the road and saw more at work in the fields than men." The war also stimulated the shift to mechanization, which made the northern labor shortage less severe. By 1865 three times as many reapers and harvesters were in use as in 1861.

Beyond the farm, women increasingly found work in industry, filling approximately 100,000 new jobs during the war. Like women in the South, they worked as clerks in the expanding government bureaucracy. The work was tedious and the workload heavy, but the new jobs offered good wages, a sense of economic independence, and a pride in having aided the war effort.

Women and medicine

The war also allowed women to enter and eventually dominate the profession of nursing. "Our women appear to have become almost wild on the subject of hospital nursing," protested one army physician, who like many others opposed the presence of women in military hospitals. Led by Drs. Emily and Elizabeth Blackwell, Dorothea Dix, and Mary Ann Bickerdyke, women fought the bureaucratic

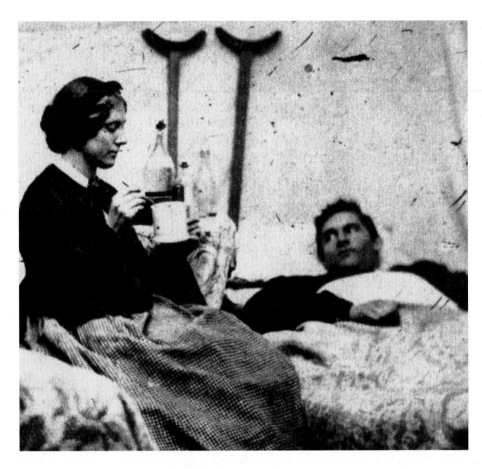

A nurse tends a wounded Union soldier in a military hospital in Nashville, Tennessee. Despite the opposition of army doctors, hundreds of female volunteers worked in army hospitals for each side. Nursing became a female profession after the war.

inefficiency of the army medical corps. Their service in the wards of the maimed and dying reduced the hostility to women in medicine.

Clara Barton, like so many other nurses, often found herself in battlefield hospitals, amidst massive death and suffering. During the battle of Fredericksburg, she wiped the brows of the wounded and dying, bandaged wounds, and applied tourniquets to stop the flow of blood. She later recalled that as she rose from the side of one soldier, "I wrung the blood from the bottom of my clothing, before I could step, for the weight about my feet." She steeled herself at the sight of amputated arms and legs casually tossed in piles outside the front door as the surgeons cut away, yet she found the extent of suffering overwhelming. She was jolted by the occasional familiar face among the tangled mass of bodies: the sexton of the church in her hometown, his face caked in blood; a wayward boy she had befriended years ago; an officer who had kindly assisted her on the way to the front, already dead when she discovered him. Sleeping in a tent nearby, she drove herself to the brink of exhaustion until the last patients were transferred to permanent hospitals. She then returned to her home in Washington, where she broke down and wept.

Before 1861 teaching, too, had been dominated by males, but the shortage of men forced school boards in both sections to turn to women, who were paid half to two-thirds of what men received. After the war teaching increasingly became a female profession, as many women came to see teaching as a career and not just a temporary occupation. Women also contributed to the war effort through volunteer work. The United States Sanitary Commission was established in 1861 to provide

Women and teaching

medical supplies and care. Much of its work was performed by women, who raised funds, collected supplies, and worked in hospitals alongside paid nurses.

Civil Liberties and Dissent

Suspension of the writ of habeas corpus

In order to mobilize northern society, Lincoln did not hesitate to curb dissenters. Shortly after the firing on Fort Sumter, he suspended the writ of habeas corpus in specified areas, which allowed the indefinite detention of anyone suspected of disloyalty or activity against the war. Although the Constitution permitted such suspension in time of rebellion or invasion, Lincoln did so without consulting Congress (unlike President Davis), and he used his power far more broadly, expanding it in 1862 to cover the entire North for cases involving antiwar activities. The president also decreed that those arrested under its provisions could be tried under the stricter rules of martial law by a military court. Eventually more than 20,000 individuals were arrested, most of whom were never charged with a specific crime or brought to trial.

Democrats attacked Lincoln as a tyrant bent on destroying the Constitution. Among those arrested was Clement Vallandigham, an Ohio Democratic congressman who in a speech delivered in May 1863 called for an armistice. He was convicted by a military commission and banished to the Confederacy (in 1864 he returned to the North). The Supreme Court refused to review the case, but once the war was over, in *Ex parte Milligan* (1866) it struck down the military conviction of another civilian, accused of plotting to free Confederate prisoners of war. The Court ruled that as long as the regular courts were open, civilians could not be tried by military tribunals.

The Copperheads

Republicans labeled those who opposed the war Copperheads, conjuring up the image of a venomous snake waiting to strike the Union. Copperheads constituted the extreme peace wing of the Democratic party. Often they had been hurt by the economic changes of the war, but more crucial was their bitter opposition

In this 1862 painting, Lincoln battles the Copperhead dragon to preserve the Union. He is held back by an Irish Democrat from Tammany Hall, who invokes the Constitution and democracy to oppose the war effort. The heavy-handed caricature of the Irish was common in Republican propaganda during the war.

to emancipation and also the draft, which they reviled as a violation of individual freedom and an instrument of special privilege. According to the provisions enacted in 1863, a person would be exempt from the present (but not any future) draft by paying a commutation fee of $300, about a year's wages for a worker or an ordinary farmer. Or those drafted could hire a substitute, the cost of which was beyond the reach of all but the wealthy. Despite this criticism, in reality poor men also bought their way out of the draft, often by pooling their resources; in addition, the government of some communities paid the commutation fee for any resident who was drafted. In all, approximately 118,000 men provided substitutes, and another 87,000 paid the commutation fee. Perhaps another 160,000 northerners illegally evaded the draft. Only 46,000 men were actually drafted into the Union army, out of more than 2 million who served.

In July 1863, when the first draftees' names were drawn in New York, workers in the Irish quarter rose in anger. Rampaging through the streets, the mob attacked draft officials and prominent Republicans, ransacked African American neighborhoods, and lynched black residents who fell into its hands. By the time order was restored four days later, at least 105 people had been killed, the worst loss of life from any riot in American history. (See pages 525–528.)

New York City draft riot

Gone to Be a Soldier

Marcus Spiegel came to the United States after the revolution of 1848 failed in Germany. The son of a rabbi, Spiegel married an American woman, became a naturalized citizen, and was trying to make it in the warehouse business in Ohio when the war began. As an immigrant, he considered it his duty to preserve the Union for his children, and the regular pay of an officer was also enticing, so he enlisted in November 1861 as a lieutenant and eventually became one the few Jewish colonels in the army. A loyal Democrat, Spiegel did not go to war to end slavery and flatly proclaimed that black people were not "worth fighting for." By early 1864, however, his views had changed as a result of his service. He had "learned and seen more of what the horrors of Slavery was than I ever knew before," and though he still doubted African Americans' capabilities, he now was "in favor of doing away with the institution of Slavery." He assured his wife that "this is no hasty conclusion but a deep conviction." A few weeks later, Marcus Spiegel died of wounds he received while fighting in Louisiana.

Fervently committed or not, by war's end about 2 million men had served the Union cause and another million, the Confederate. They were mostly young; almost 40 percent of entering soldiers were age 21 or younger. They were not drawn disproportionately from the poor, and in both the North and the South, farmers and farm laborers accounted for the largest group of soldiers. Unskilled workers, who were poorer than other groups, were actually underrepresented in the ranks. It is also a myth that the North hired an army of foreign-born mercenaries. The overwhelming majority of those who wore the blue and the gray were native-born, and the proportion of immigrants in both armies was roughly the same as in the eligible military population.

Most soldiers, like Marcus Spiegel, took patriotism seriously, and although officers tended to be more ideological, enlisted men were not ignorant of the issues of the war. Chiefly volunteers, they usually expressed their motivation for fighting in general terms, either to defend the Union or protect the South. Only with time did the majority of Union soldiers, like Spiegel, come to endorse the destruction of slavery as a war aim.

Daily Lives

FOOD/DRINK/ DRUGS

Hardtack, Salt Horse, and Coffee

"If a person wants to know how to appreciate the value of good vi[c]tuals he had better enlist," a Vermont soldier declared. "I have seen the time when I would have been glad to [have] picked the crusts of bread that mother gives to the hogs." Whether in the field or in quarters, food was generally Johnny Reb's and Billy Yank's first concern.

At the beginning of the war, the prescribed daily allowance for each soldier included 12 ounces of pork or 20 ounces of beef, a pound or more of bread or flour, and ample quantities of rice, beans, sugar, and coffee. Although both armies experienced shortages from time to time, in general northern soldiers had more food and in greater variety than their opponents. As the war ground on, the Confederacy was forced to reduce sharply the daily ration because of shortages, bureaucratic inefficiency, and the lack of adequate transportation.

Meat, bread, and coffee: these were the soldier's mainstays. The meat was either pork or beef and was usually salted to preserve it. Soldiers, who called salt pork "sowbelly" and pickled beef "salt horse," preferred the former, since the beef was so briny that it was inedible unless thoroughly soaked in water. Many soldiers left salted beef in a creek overnight before they tried to eat it.

Union soldiers normally were given wheat bread or flour, but for Confederates cornbread was the standby. This monotonous fare prompted a Louisiana soldier near the end of the war to grumble, "If any person offers me cornbread after this war comes to a close I shall *probably* tell him to—go to hell." Both armies often replaced bread with hardtack, crackers half an inch thick that were so hard, soldiers dubbed them "teeth-dullers." Cynics claimed that they were more suitable for building breastworks, and some Yanks insisted that the "B.C." (for Brigade Commissary) stamped on the boxes they came in referred to their date of manufacture. The crackers became moldy and worm-infested with age, and hence veterans preferred to eat them in the dark.

Coffee was the other main staple, eagerly consumed. Because of the Union blockade, the Confederacy could not get enough, and Rebel troops resorted to various unappealing substitutes. Despite official opposition, troops often fraternized during lulls in the fighting, swapping tobacco, which was in short supply on the Union side, for coffee and sugar, which Confederates desired most. When the two armies spent the winter of 1862 camped on opposite sides of the Rappahannock River, enlisted

An infantry private from New York eats a meal in camp.

Discipline

The near-holiday atmosphere of the war's early months soon gave way to dull routine. Men from rural areas, accustomed to the freedom of the farm, complained about the endless recurrence of reveille, roll call, and drill. "When this war is over," one Rebel promised, "I will whip the man that says 'fall in' to me." Troops in neither army cared for the spit and polish of regular army men. "They keep us very strict here," noted one Illinois soldier. "It is the most like a prison of any place I ever saw."

By modern standards training was minimal and discipline lax in both armies. Troops from rural families found it harder to adjust to army routine than did urban

men ferried cargoes of sugar and coffee to one bank and tobacco to the other, using makeshift toy boats.

In an effort to create portable rations, the Union War Department produced an experimental "essence of coffee," a forerunner of the modern instant variety. But the beverage was so vile that men would not drink it, and it was eventually abandoned. More long-lasting was the use of dehydrated potatoes, which few men ever developed a taste for, and desiccated mixed vegetables, which were issued in hard, dry cakes that troops dubbed "baled hay."

Members of both armies supplemented their diet by foraging (the army's polite term for stealing), although Union soldiers, being most often in enemy territory, relied more heavily on this tactic. Hungry troops regularly raided pigpens, poultry houses, orchards, gardens, cornfields, and smokehouses. "When we started the colonel tried to prevent our foraging," one Massachusetts soldier reported, "but . . . [soon] we were as expert at it as any of the old hands."

During training and in winter quarters, cooks normally prepared food for an entire company. Neither army, however, established a cooks' or bakers' school, and troops contended that officers regularly selected the poorest soldiers to be cooks. "A company cook is a most peculiar being," one soldier recalled after the war. "He generally knows less about cooking than any other man in the company. Not being able to learn the drill, and too dirty to appear on inspection, he is sent to the cook house to get him out of the ranks." Once the army went on the march, men usually cooked for themselves or formed a mess of four to eight soldiers, taking turns cooking. Either way, food was rarely prepared with any skill.

By war's end, soldiers on both sides had developed a new appreciation for food. One hungry Texan promised that when he got home he was going "to take a hundred biscuit and two large hams, call it three days rations, then . . . eat it all at *one* meal." A poetic Yankee summed up the situation succinctly:

The soldiers' fare is very rough,
The bread is hard, the beef is tough;
If they can stand it, it will be,
Through love of God, a mystery.

soldiers, especially factory workers, who were more familiar with impersonal organizations and used to greater social control. Many southerners were "not used to control of any sort," one Rebel noted, "and were not disposed to obey anyone except for good and sufficient reason given." Manifesting strong feelings of equality that clashed with military hierarchy, Yanks and Rebs alike complained about officers' privileges and had no special respect for rank. "We had enlisted to put down the rebellion," an Indiana private explained, "and had no patience with the red-tape tomfoolery" of the regular army. "The boys recognized no superiors, except in the line of legitimate duty." The Union discontinued the election of lower officers, but this tradition was retained in the Confederate army, which further undermined discipline, since those known as strict disciplinarians were eventually defeated.

Camp Life

Disease and medical care

On average, soldiers spent 50 days in camp for every day in battle. Camp life was often unhealthy as well as unpleasant. Poor sanitation, miserable food, exposure to the elements, and primitive medical care contributed to widespread sickness and disease. Officers and men alike regarded army doctors as nothing more than quacks and tried to avoid them. It was a common belief that if a fellow went to the hospital, "you might as well say good bye." Conditions were even worse in the Confederate hospitals, for the Union blockade produced a shortage of medical supplies. Twice as many soldiers died from dysentery, typhoid, and other diseases as from wounds.

Treatment at field hospitals was a chilling experience. More than anything else, ignorance was responsible for the existing conditions and practices, because nothing was known about germs or how wounds became infected. Years later an appalled federal surgeon recounted:

> We operated in old blood-stained and often pus-stained coats. . . . We used undisinfected instruments . . . and still worse, used marine sponges which had been used in prior pus cases and had been only washed in tap water. . . . Our silk to tie blood vessels was undisinfected. . . . We dressed the wounds with clean but undisinfected sheets, shirts, tablecloths, or other old soft linen rescued from the family ragbag. . . . We knew nothing about antiseptics and therefore used none.

Decline of morality

The boredom of camp life, the horrors of battle, and the influence of an all-male society all corrupted morals. Swearing and heavy drinking were common, and one Mississippian reported that after payday games of chance were "running night and day, with eager and excited crowds standing around with their hands full of money." Prostitutes flooded the camps of both armies, and an Illinois private stationed in Pulaski, Tennessee, wrote home that the price schedule in each of the brothels in town was quite reasonable. "You may think I am a hard case," he conceded, "but I am as pious as you can find in the army." As in the gold fields of

Soldiers leaving for war often had their pictures taken with their loved ones. The Confederate soldier on the left posed with his two sisters. On the right, a member of the Union forces sits with his family for a farewell portrait. Such photographs are reminders of how much the war and its mounting death toll touched civilians as well as soldiers on both sides.

California, the absence of women stimulated behavior that would have been checked back home by the frowns of family and society.

With death so near, some soldiers sought solace in religion. Religious fervor was greater in the Confederate camps, and a wave of revivals swept the ranks during the last two winters of the war, producing between 100,000 and 200,000 conversions. Significantly, the first major revivals occurred after the South's twin defeats at Vicksburg and Gettysburg. Then, too, as battle after battle thinned Confederate ranks, the prospect of death became increasingly large.

The Changing Face of Battle

As in all modern wars, technology revolutionized the conditions under which Civil War soldiers fought. Smoothbore muskets, which at first served as the basic infantry weapon, gave way to the rifle, so named because of the grooves etched into the barrel to give a bullet spin. A new bullet, the minié ball, allowed the rifle to be easily loaded, and the invention of the percussion cap rendered it serviceable in wet weather. More important, the new weapon had an effective range of 400 yards— five times greater than that of the old musket. As a result, soldiers fought each other from greater distances, and battles took much longer to fight and produced many more casualties.

Impact of technology

Under such conditions, the defense became a good deal stronger than the offense. The larger artillery pieces also adopted rifled barrels, but they lacked good fuses and accurate sighting devices and could not effectively support attacking troops. They were a deadly defensive weapon, however, that decimated advancing infantry at close range. Confederate general D. H. Hill described the devastating barrage as his men charged the Union line at Malvern Hill: "As each brigade emerged from the woods, from 50 to 100 guns opened upon it, tearing great gaps in its ranks. Most of them had an open field half a mile wide to cross, under the fire of field artillery and heavy ordnance. It was not war—it was murder." More than 100 regiments on both sides suffered in excess of 50 percent casualties in a single battle.

Strength of the defense

As the haze of gunfire covered the land and the constant spray of bullets mimicked rain pattering through the treetops, soldiers discovered that their romantic notions about war had no place on the battlefield. Men witnessed horrors they had never envisioned as civilians and choked from the stench of decaying flesh and mortal slaughter. They realized that their efforts to convey to those back home the gruesome truth of combat were inadequate. "No tongue can tell, no mind can conceive, no pen portray the horrible sights I witnessed this morning," a Union soldier wrote after Antietam. And still they tried.

Soldiers' hardening outlook

An Indiana soldier at Perryville (7600 casualties): "It was an awful sight to see there men torn all to pieces with cannon balls and bom shells[.] the dead and wounded lay thick in all directions." An Ohio soldier at Antietam (23,000 casualties), two days after the fighting: "The smell was offul . . . there was about 5 or 6,000 dead bodes decaying over the field . . . I could have walked on the boddees all most from one end too the other." A Georgian, the day after Chancellorsville (30,000 casualties): "It looked more like a slaughter pen than anything else. . . . The shrieks and groans of the wounded . . . was heart rending beyond all description." A Maine soldier who fought at Gettysburg (50,000 casualties): "I have Seen . . . men rolling in their own blood, Some Shot in one place, Some another . . . our dead lay in the road and the Rebels in their hast to leave dragged both their baggage wagons and artillery over them and they lay mangled and torn to pieces so that Even friends could not tell them. You can form no idea of a battle field."

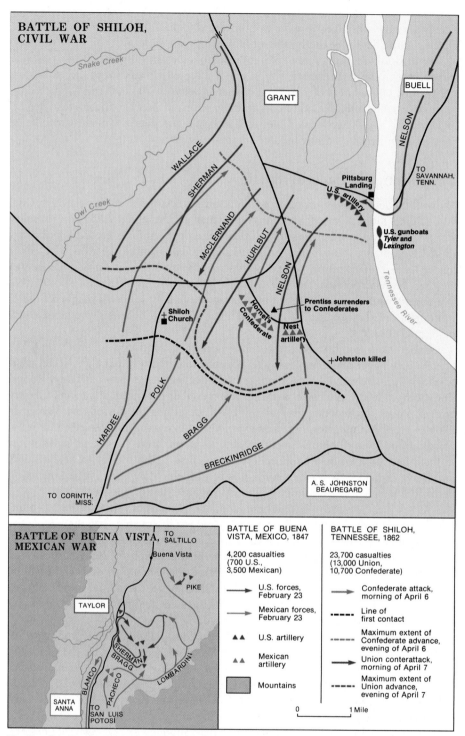

BATTLE OF SHILOH, CIVIL WAR

Snake Creek

GRANT

BUELL

WALLACE

SHERMAN

Owl Creek

McCLERNAND

HURLBUT

NELSON

TO SAVANNAH, TENN.

Pittsburg Landing

U.S. artillery

U.S. gunboats *Tyler* and *Lexington*

Tennessee River

Shiloh Church

Hornet's Nest

Confederate

Prentiss surrenders to Confederates

Confederate

Nest artillery

+Johnston killed

HARDEE

POLK

BRAGG

BRECKINRIDGE

A. S. JOHNSTON BEAUREGARD

TO CORINTH, MISS.

BATTLE OF BUENA VISTA, MEXICAN WAR

TO SALTILLO

Buena Vista

PIKE

TAYLOR

SHERMAN

BRAGG

BLANCO

PACHECO

LOMBARDINI

SANTA ANNA

TO SAN LUIS POTOSÍ

BATTLE OF BUENA VISTA, MEXICO, 1847

4,200 casualties
(700 U.S.,
3,500 Mexican)

→ U.S. forces, February 23

→ Mexican forces, February 23

▲▲ U.S. artillery

▲▲ Mexican artillery

Mountains

BATTLE OF SHILOH, TENNESSEE, 1862

23,700 casualties
(13,000 Union,
10,700 Confederate)

→ Confederate attack, morning of April 6

--- Line of first contact

--- Maximum extent of Confederate advance, evening of April 6

→ Union conterattack, morning of April 7

--- Maximum extent of Union advance, evening of April 7

0 — 1 Mile

The Changing Magnitude of Battle During the Mexican War at Buena Vista, the American army of 4800 men was overextended trying to defend a two-mile line against 15,000 Mexicans. At Shiloh, in contrast, battle lines stretched almost six miles. (The maps are drawn to the same scale.) Against 40,000 Confederates, Grant galloped back and forth, rallying some 35,000 troops organized under five subordinates and coordinating the overnight reinforcement of 25,000 troops. The size of the armies, the complexity of their organization, the length of battle lines, and the number of casualties all demonstrate the extent to which the magnitude of battle had changed.

Hardening Attitudes

Throughout the Civil War, soldiers continued to speak in terms of the traditional ideals of duty, honor, and patriotism. Nevertheless, military service profoundly changed them. For the volunteers of 1861, the war was a test of courage and manhood, and thus they believed the winning side would display superior valor. Expecting a restrained war that would uphold this moral code, they admired the courage of the foe and considered it pointless to kill an isolated soldier.

But the reality of combat did not fit such expectations, and by 1864 the nature of war had been transformed. Soldiers discovered the futility of mass frontal assaults, and under the rain of fire on the battlefield sought cover wherever they could find it. As the fighting intensified, they sought to kill enemy soldiers any way they could in order to hasten the war's end. At the same time, they became indifferent to death and suffering. "The daily sight of blood and mangled bodies," observed a Rhode Island soldier, "so blunted their finer sensibilities as almost to blot out all love, all sympathy from the heart." This hardening of attitudes produced a steady erosion of moral standards. Combatants began taking personal property from the dead and wounded and even prisoners after a battle.

Eroding moral values

As they repudiated their earlier moral assumptions, the soldiers in both armies felt increasingly alienated from civilians back home. In reaction, they developed a stronger sense of comradeship with enemy soldiers, based on their belief that only other soldiers could understand what they had gone through and why they acted the way they did. They felt less an actor in the war than an impersonal object caught in a relentless process of destruction.

In the face of what Charles Francis Adams Jr. termed "the carnival of death," soldiers braced themselves with a grim determination to see the war through to the end. Not glorious exploits but endurance became the true measure of heroism. Exclaimed one chastened Georgia soldier, "What a scourge is war."

The Union's Triumph

While talking to a neighbor, Dolly Lunt suddenly saw the bluecoats coming down the road. Thinking to herself, "Oh God, the time of trial has come!" she ran home as fast as she could. Lunt had left Maine as a young woman and gone to teach school in Covington, Georgia, where she married a local planter. After his death, she took charge of the plantation and its slaves and was still managing it when the Civil War began. Now William Tecumseh Sherman's dreaded army had arrived at her gate. As the Union troops swarmed over the yard, they cleaned out the smokehouse and dairy, stripped the kitchen and cellar of their contents, and killed her fowl and hogs. They broke open locks, smashed down doors, seized items of no military value such as kitchen utensils and even a doll, wantonly destroyed furnishings and personal items, and marched off some of the male slaves. Not content with plundering the main house, the troops entered the slave cabins and rifled them of every valuable, even the money some of the slaves had made by doing extra work. Overcome with anxiety, Lunt spent a supperless night huddled in the house with her remaining slaves, who were clutching their meager possessions. As darkness descended, she reported, "the heavens from every point were lit up with flames from burning buildings." Total war had come to Dolly Lunt's doorstep.

Confederate High Tide

In the spring of 1863 matters still looked promising for Lee. At the battle of Chancellorsville, he brilliantly defeated Lincoln's latest commander, Joseph Hooker. But during the fighting Stonewall Jackson was accidentally shot by his own men, and he died a few days later—a grievous setback for the Confederacy. Determined to take the offensive, Lee invaded Pennsylvania in June with an army of 75,000. Lincoln's newest general, George Gordon Meade, warily shadowed the Confederates. On the first of July, advance parties from the two armies accidentally collided at the town of Gettysburg, and the war's greatest battle ensued.

Gettysburg

For once it was Lee who had the extended supply lines and was forced to fight on ground chosen by his opponent. After two days of assaults failed to break the Union left or right, Lee made the greatest mistake of his career, sending 14,000 men under General George Pickett in a charge at the center of the Union line on Cemetery Ridge. "Pickett's division just seemed to melt away in the blue musketry smoke which now covered the hill," one Confederate officer wrote. "Nothing but stragglers came back." The Union casualties of more than 23,000 represented a quarter of Meade's effective strength, but Lee lost between 25,000 and 28,000—more than a third of his troops. Never again was he able to assume the offensive.

Lincoln Finds His General

Capture of Vicksburg

To the west, Grant had been trying for months to capture Vicksburg, a Rebel stronghold on the Mississippi. In a daring maneuver, he left behind his supply lines and marched inland, calculating that he could feed his army from the produce of Confederate farms, weakening southern resistance in the process. These actions were the tactics of total war, and seldom had they been tried before Grant used them. His troops drove the defenders of Vicksburg back into the city and starved them into submission. On July 4, the city surrendered. With the fall of Port Hudson, Louisiana, four days later, the Mississippi was completely in Union hands. Grant had divided the Confederacy and isolated Arkansas, Texas, and part of Louisiana from the rest of the South.

He followed up this victory by rescuing Union forces holed up in Chattanooga. His performance confirmed Lincoln's earlier judgment that "Grant is my man, and I am his the rest of the war." Congress now revived the rank of lieutenant general, held before only by George Washington, which Lincoln bestowed on Grant. In March 1864 Lincoln brought him east and put him in command of all the Union armies.

Grant in command

Grant recognized that the Union possessed the resources to wear down the Confederacy but that its larger armies had "acted independently and without concert, like a balky team, no two ever pulling together." He intended to change that. While he launched a major offensive against Lee in Virginia, William Tecumseh Sherman, who replaced Grant as commander of the western army, would drive a diagonal wedge through the Confederacy from Tennessee across Georgia. Grant's orders to Sherman were as blunt as his response had been that rainy night when the two had conferred at Shiloh: "Get into the interior of the enemy's country so far as you can, inflicting all the damage you can against their war resources."

Union's summer offensive

In May and June 1864 Grant tried to maneuver Lee out of the trenches and into an open battle. But Lee was too weak to win head-on, so he opted for a strategy of attrition, hoping to inflict such heavy losses that the northern will to continue would break. It was a strategy that nearly worked, for Union casualties were staggering. In a month of fierce fighting, the Army of the Potomac lost 60,000 men—the size of Lee's entire army at the beginning of the campaign. Yet at the

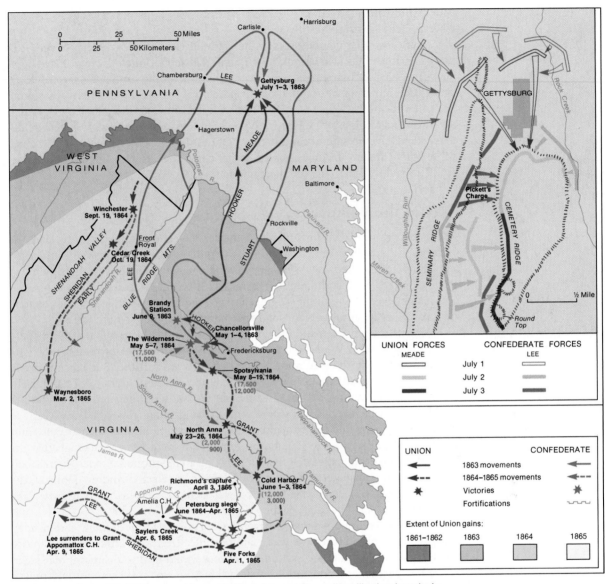

The War in the East, 1863–1865 Lee won his most brilliant victory at Chancellorsville, then launched a second invasion of the North, hoping to score a decisive victory. When the two armies accidentally collided at Gettysburg on July 1, 1863, the Union's Army of the Potomac was driven back through the town until it took up a strong defensive position, shaped like a fishhook and anchored by a hill at each end. On July 2 the Confederate attack drove back the Union's left flank but failed to dislodge the right. Lee's assault on the center of the Union line on July 3 ended in a shattering defeat, and the Army of Northern Virginia retreated back to Virginia. In 1864 Grant delivered a series of heavy blows against Lee's outnumbered forces in Virginia. Despite staggering losses, Grant relentlessly pressed on in a ruthless demonstration of total war. (Note the casualties listed for the spring and summer of 1864; from mid-May to mid-June Grant lost nearly 60,000 men, equal to Lee's strength.) Sheridan's devastating raids against the civilian farms of the Shenandoah Valley helped deprive Lee of desperately needed supplies. In April 1865, too weak to defend Richmond any longer, Lee surrendered at Appomattox Courthouse.

end of the campaign Grant's reinforced army was larger than when it started, whereas Lee's was significantly weaker.

After especially bloody losses at the battle of Cold Harbor, Grant changed tactics. He marched his army around Richmond and settled into a siege of Petersburg, which guarded Richmond's last remaining rail link to the south. A siege would be agonizingly slow, but he counted on his numerical superiority to eventually stretch Lee's line to the breaking point. In the west, meanwhile, the gaunt and grizzled Sherman fought his way by July to the outskirts of Atlanta, which was heavily defended and gave no sign of capitulating. "Our all depends on that army at Atlanta," wrote Mary Chesnut in August, based on her conversations with Confederate leaders in Richmond. "If that fails us, the game is up."

War in the Balance

The game was nearly up for Lincoln as the 1864 election approached. In 1863 the victories at Gettysburg and Vicksburg sparked Republican victories, indicating that public opinion seemed to be swinging toward emancipation. But as the Union war machine swept more and more northerners south to their deaths and as Grant and Sherman bogged down on the Virginia and Georgia fronts, even leaders in Lincoln's own party began to mutter out loud that he was not equal to the task.

1864 election

Perhaps the most remarkable thing about the 1864 election is that it was held at all. Indeed, before World War II, the United States was the only democratic government in history to carry out a general election in wartime. But Lincoln firmly believed that to postpone it would be to lose the priceless heritage of republicanism itself: "We cannot have free government without elections, and if the rebellion could force us to forego or postpone a national election, it might fairly claim to have already conquered and ruined us." Exploiting his control of the party machinery, Lincoln easily won the Republican nomination, and he made certain that the Republican platform called for the adoption of a constitutional amendment abolishing slavery. To balance the ticket, the convention selected Andrew Johnson, the military governor of Tennessee and a prowar Democrat, as his running mate. The two men ran under the label of the "Union" party.

The Democrats nominated George McClellan, the former Union commander. Their platform pronounced the war a failure and called for an armistice and a peace conference. Warned that a cessation of fighting would lead to disunion, McClellan partially repudiated this position, insisting that "the Union is the one condition of peace—we ask no more." In private he made it clear that if elected he intended to restore slavery. Late in August, Lincoln was still gloomy about his prospects as well as those of the Union itself. But Admiral David Farragut won a dramatic victory at Mobile Bay, and a few weeks later, in early September, Sherman finally captured Atlanta. As Secretary of State Seward gleefully noted, "Sherman and Farragut have knocked the bottom out of the Chicago [Democratic] nominations."

Significance of Lincoln's reelection

Polling an impressive 55 percent of the popular vote, Lincoln won 212 electoral votes to McClellan's 21. Eighteen states allowed soldiers to vote in the field, and Lincoln received nearly 80 percent of their ballots. One lifelong Democrat described the sentiment in the army: "We all want peace, but none any but an honorable one. I had rather stay out here a lifetime (much as I dislike it) than consent to a division of our country." Jefferson Davis remained defiant, but the last hope of a Confederate victory was gone.

Equally important, the election of 1864 ended any doubt that slavery would be abolished in the reconstructed Union. The Emancipation Proclamation had not put an end to the question, for its legal status remained unclear. Lincoln argued that as a war measure, it would have no standing once peace returned; and in any case, it had not freed slaves in the border states or those parts of the Confederacy already under Union control. Thus Lincoln and the Republicans believed that a constitutional amendment was necessary to secure emancipation.

Thirteenth Amendment

In 1864 the Senate had approved an amendment that freed all slaves without compensating their owners, but the measure did not receive the necessary two-thirds vote in the House. After the election, Lincoln threw all his influence behind the drive to round up the necessary votes, and it passed the House on January 31, 1865. By December, enough states had ratified the Thirteenth Amendment to make it part of the Constitution.

Abolition as a global movement

The abolition of slavery in the United States was part of a worldwide drive against slavery. The antislavery movement was spearheaded in Britain, where Parliament abolished slavery in the empire in 1833. The other colonial powers were much slower to act. Portugal did not end slavery in its New World colonies until 1836, Sweden in 1847, Denmark and France in 1848, Holland in 1863, and Spain not until 1886. Most of the Latin American republics had ended slavery when they threw off Spanish or Portuguese control, but the institution remained important in Cuba and Brazil; Spain abolished slavery in Cuba in 1886, and Brazil ended the institution in 1888. European reformers also crusaded against slavery in Africa and Asia, and indeed the antislavery movement increased European presence in Africa. At the same time, European nations ended the medieval institution of serfdom. In Russia, where serfdom had most closely approximated slavery, Czar Alexander II emancipated the serfs in 1861, an act that led him to strongly favor the Union in the American Civil War.

The Twilight of the Confederacy

Confederacy's abandonment of slavery

For the Confederacy, the outcome of the 1864 election had a terrible finality. At the beginning of the war, Vice President Stephens had proclaimed slavery the cornerstone of the Confederacy, but now both Lee and Davis endorsed enlisting slaves in the army. In March 1865 the Confederate Congress authorized recruiting 300,000 slaves for military service. When signing the bill, Davis announced that freedom would be given to those who volunteered and to their families. That same month he offered through a special envoy to abolish slavery in exchange for British diplomatic recognition. A Mississippi paper denounced this proposal as "a total abandonment of the chief object of this war" and added that "if the institution [of slavery] is already irretrievably undermined the rights of the States are buried with it." The British rejected the offer, and the war ended before any slaves were mustered into the Confederate army, but the abandonment of slavery surely completed the Confederacy's internal revolution. The demands of total war had forced Confederate leaders to forsake the Old South's most important values and institutions.

In the wake of Lincoln's reelection, the Confederate will to resist rapidly disintegrated. White southerners had never fully united behind the war effort, but the large majority had endured great suffering to uphold it. As Sherman pushed deeper into the Confederacy and General Philip Sheridan mounted his devastating raid on the Shenandoah Valley, the war came home to southern civilians as never before. "We haven't got nothing in the house to eat but a little bit o meal," wrote the wife of one Alabama soldier in December 1864. "Try to get off and come home and fix us all up some and then you can go back. . . . If you put off a-coming, 'twont be no use to come, for we'll all . . . [be] in the grave yard." He deserted. In the last months of the fighting, more than half the Confederacy's soldiers were absent without leave.

U.S. Gunboat Cimerone

Steamers Landing Troops from Harrison

U.S TROOPS BURNING "The COLE HOUSE" and PLANTATION. OPPOSITE HARRISON'S

LANDING JAMES RIVER on the night of 1st August 1862

General William Sherman demonstrated the tactics of total war in the autumn of 1864. "Destroyed all we could not eat . . . burned their cotton and gins . . . burned and twisted their railroads . . . ," wrote one of Sherman's soldiers. This drawing, done by a Union private, depicts a similar destructive raid on a plantation along Virginia's James River in 1862, but by the spring of 1865, Confederate armies were increasingly unable to resist the Union might.

March to the sea

After the fall of Atlanta, Sherman gave a frightening demonstration of the meaning of total war. Detaching a portion of his forces to engage General John Hood's army, which moved back into Tennessee, Sherman imitated Grant's strategy by abandoning his supply lines for an audacious 300-mile march to the sea. He intended to deprive Lee's army of the supplies it desperately needed to continue and to break the southern will to resist. Or as he bluntly put it, "to whip the Rebels, to humble their pride, to follow them to their recesses, and make them fear and dread us."

Moving in four columns, Sherman's army covered about 10 miles a day, cutting a path of destruction 50 miles wide. "We had a gay old campaign," one of his soldiers wrote. "Destroyed all we could not eat, stole their niggers, burned their cotton and gins, spilled their sorghum, burned and twisted their railroads and raised Hell generally." Sherman estimated that his men did $100 million in damage, of which $20 million was necessary to supply his army and the rest was wanton destruction. After he captured Savannah in late December, he turned north and wreaked even greater havoc in South Carolina, which Union troops considered the seedbed of the rebellion.

Meanwhile, General George H. Thomas defeated Hood's forces in December at Nashville, leaving the interior of the Confederacy essentially conquered. Only Lee's army remained, entrenched around Petersburg, Virginia, as Grant relentlessly extended his lines, stretching the Confederates thinner and thinner. On April 2 Confederate forces evacuated Richmond.

Grant doggedly pursued the Army of Northern Virginia westward for another hundred miles. After Union forces captured supplies waiting for Lee at Appomattox

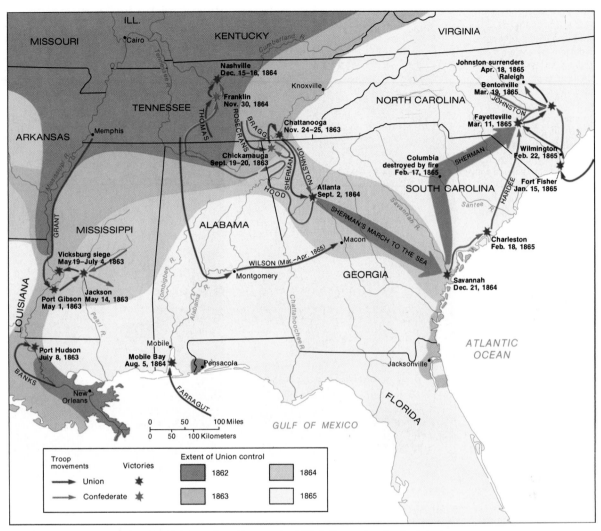

The War in the West, 1863–1865 The Union continued its war of mobility in the western theater, bringing more Confederate territory under its control. After Grant captured Vicksburg, the entire Mississippi lay in Union hands. His victories at Lookout Mountain and Missionary Ridge, near Chattanooga, ended the Confederate threat to Tennessee. In 1864 Sherman divided the Confederacy by seizing Atlanta and marching across Georgia; then he turned north. When Joseph Johnston surrendered several weeks after Lee's capitulation at Appomattox, the war was effectively over.

Courthouse, the weary gentleman from Virginia asked to see Grant. Lee surrendered on April 9, 1865. As the vanquished foe mounted his horse, Grant saluted by raising his hat; Lee raised his respectfully and rode off at a slow trot. "On our part," one federal officer wrote, there was "not a sound of trumpet . . . nor roll of drum; not a cheer . . . but an awed stillness rather." The guns were quiet.

With Lee's army gone, remaining resistance throughout the Confederacy collapsed within a matter of weeks. Visiting the captured city of Richmond on April 4, Lincoln was enthusiastically greeted by the black population. He looked "pale, haggard, utterly worn out," noted one observer. The lines in his face showed how much the war had aged him in only four years. Often his friends had counseled rest, but Lincoln had observed that "the tired part of me is *inside* and out of reach." Day after day, the grim telegrams had arrived at the War Department, or

Lee's surrender

The war's greatest generals, Ulysses S. Grant (left) and Robert E. Lee (right), confronted each other in the eastern theater during the last year of the war. A member of a distinguished Virginia family, the tall, impeccably dressed Lee was every inch the aristocratic gentleman. Grant, a short, slouched figure with a stubby beard, dressed indifferently, often wearing a private's uniform with only the stars on his shoulders to indicate his rank. But his determination is readily apparent in this picture, taken at his field headquarters in 1864.

mothers had come to see him, begging him to spare their youngest son because the other two had died in battle. The burden, he confessed, was almost too much to bear.

Back in Washington the president received news of Lee's surrender with relief. The evening of April 14, Lincoln, seeking a welcome escape, went to see a comedy at Ford's Theater. In the midst of the performance John Wilkes Booth, an unstable actor and Confederate sympathizer, slipped into the presidential box and shot him. Lincoln died the next morning. As he had called upon his fellow Americans to do in his Gettysburg Address, the sixteenth president had given his "last full measure of devotion" to the Republic.

Lincoln's assassination

The Impact of War

Cost of war

The assassination, which capped four years of bloody war, left a tiredness in the nation's bones—a tiredness "inside" and not easily within reach. In every way the conflict had produced fundamental, often devastating changes. There was, of course, the carnage. Approximately 620,000 men on both sides lost their lives, almost as many as in all the other wars the nation has fought from the Revolution through Vietnam combined. In material terms, the conflict cost an estimated $20 billion, or about 10 times the value of all slaves in the country in 1860 and more

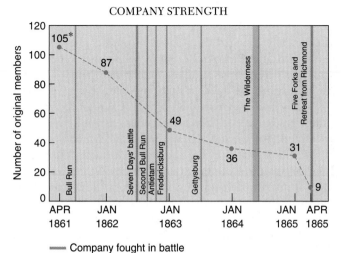

COMPANY STRENGTH

Original members — 122
Killed in battle and died of wounds* — 17
Died of disease — 14
Discharged for various causes — 29
Transferred to other commands — 6
Prisoners of war at war's end — 27
On leave, hospitalized, or at home — 8
Deserted — 12
Surrendered at Appomattox — 9

*Fifty-three members were wounded
one or more times and survived.

■ Company fought in battle
■ Company absent from battle

*Note: 17 members left the company at an
unknown time and are excluded from the graph.

The Attrition of War: Company D, 7th Virginia Infantry, Army of Northern Virginia Organized on April 25, 1861, Company D declined dramatically from its original strength over the course of the war. Combat, disease, and desertion took their toll, but the most important causes of the drop were discharges (often because of wounds) and being captured. As the graph shows, the sharpest declines occurred in 1862 and in 1865, when the company saw heavier military action. The losses also illustrate the relative impact of offensive versus defensive warfare. The sustained, largely offensive campaigning in 1862 reduced the company to half its initial members. In contrast, it missed the brunt of the fighting during Grant's 1864 offensive. The company experienced another sharp falloff in 1865, when most of the remaining original members were captured on the hasty retreat from Richmond. Of those who had volunteered at the beginning of the war, only nine were still in the ranks when the Army of Northern Virginia surrendered at Appomattox Courthouse.

than 11 times the total amount spent by the federal government from 1789 to 1861. Even without adding the market value of freed slaves, southern wealth declined 43 percent, transforming what had been the richest section in the nation (on a white per capita basis) into the poorest.

The effects of total war, however, went well beyond upheaval and destruction. The Civil War rearranged and reordered not only the national economy but also economic relations worldwide. In the nation, demand for the machines of war stimulated industrialization, especially in the heavy industries of iron and coal, machinery, and agricultural implements. Manufacturers were forced to supply the army on an unprecedented scale over great distances. One consequence was the creation of truly national industries in flour milling, meat packing, clothing and shoe manufacture, and machinery making.

People across the globe felt the effects of the war, particularly due to changes in the cotton trade. By 1860 the South was supplying more than three-quarters of all cotton imported by Britain, France, Germany, and Russia. When the war cut off that supply, manufacturers scrambled to find new sources. India, Egypt, and Brazil all improved their railroad facilities and ports in order to encourage planters to open new cotton fields. The Indian city of Bombay experienced explosive growth handling the flood of new cotton. The effect of the trade on Egypt was so great, historians of that nation rank the American Civil War along with the construction of the Suez Canal as the most crucial events in its nineteenth-century history. In the end, the efforts of cotton merchants, textile operators, and European governments

The war's effects on the cotton trade worldwide

marked the first steps by European powers toward a more aggressive imperialism that flourished in the late nineteenth century.

Politically, the war dramatically changed the balance of power. The South lost its substantial influence, as did the Democratic party, while the Republicans emerged in a dominant position. The Union's military victory also signaled the triumph of nationalism. The war destroyed the idea that the Union was a voluntary confederacy of sovereign states, which theorists like John C. Calhoun had argued, and that the states had the right to secede. It was perpetual, as Andrew Jackson had first suggested—truly an indivisible nation. In an important symbolic change, Americans now spoke of the United States in the singular rather than the plural.

Spiritual toll of war

In the short run, the price was disillusionment and bitterness. The South had to live with the humiliation of military defeat and occupation, while former slaves anxiously waited to see what their situation would be in freedom. The war's corrosive effect on morals corrupted American life and politics, destroyed idealism, and severely crippled humanitarian reform. Millennialism and perfectionism were victims of the war's appalling slaughter, forsaken for a new emphasis on practicality, order, materialism, and science. As the war unfolded, the New York *Herald* recognized the deep changes: "All sorts of old fogy ideas, manners, and customs have gone under, and all sorts of new ideas, modes, and practices have risen to the surface and become popular."

George Ticknor, a prominent author and critic who was sensitive to shifting intellectual and social currents, reflected on the changes that had shaken the nation in only a few short years. The war, it seemed to him, had left "a great gulf between what happened before it in our century and what has happened since. . . . It does not seem to me as if I were living in the country in which I was born."

chapter summary

For the first total war in history, the Civil War's outcome depended not just on armies but also on the mobilization of each society's human, economic, and intellectual resources.

- Confederate president Jefferson Davis's policy of concentrating power in the government at Richmond, along with the resort to a draft and impressment of private property, provoked strong protests from many southerners.

- Abraham Lincoln's policies, especially his suspension of the writ of habeas corpus and his interference with civil liberties, were equally controversial.

- But Lincoln skillfully handled the delicate situation of the border states in the first year of the war, keeping them in the Union.

- Lincoln at first resisted pressure to make emancipation a Union war aim, but he eventually issued the Emancipation Proclamation, which transformed the meaning of the war.

- African Americans helped undermine slavery in the Confederacy and made a vital contribution to the Union's military victory.

- The war had a powerful impact on the home front.

  - Women confronted new responsibilities and enjoyed new occupational opportunities.

  - In the Confederacy, hardship and suffering became a fact of life.

  - The Confederate government's financial and tax policies and the tightening Union blockade increased this suffering.

- Both societies also experienced the ravages of moral decay.

- The Civil War changed the nature of warfare.

  - Technology, particularly the use of rifles and rifled artillery, revolutionized tactics and strategy.

– The Union eventually adopted the strategy of attacking the civilian population of the South.

– Soldiers in both armies suffered from disease and inadequate medical care, poor food, moral corruption, and the mounting death toll.

– Union soldiers were more accustomed to order and control and adjusted more effectively to the war's demands.

• The war altered the nation's political institutions, its economy, and its values.

interactive learning

The Primary Source Investigator CD-ROM offers the following materials related to this chapter:

• Interactive maps: **Slavery and the Cotton Kingdom** (M11) and **Civil War, 1861–1864** (M15)

• A short documentary movie on the process of emancipation during the Civil War (D9)

• A collection of primary sources exploring the course of America's first "total war." Several documents reveal African Americans' role in the war: a photograph of contrabands crossing a river, a map of the distribution of slaves, and an image of the 6th Colored Regiment's flag. Other documents explore how the international community reacted to America's Civil War: a political cartoon illustrating England's concerns over its cotton supply, an English cartoon depicting Lincoln asking slaves for help in the war, and a cartoon showing Britannia sympathizing with the Union over Lincoln's assassination.

additional reading

Histories of the Civil War tend to concentrate on either the home front or the military, and on either the Confederacy or the Union. A good single-volume history of the war, up-to-date in its scholarship and balanced in its judgments, covering all these topics is James M. McPherson, *Battle Cry of Freedom* (1988). In recent years military historians have devoted more attention to the relationship between society and the military. An interesting example that traces the evolution of the Union's strategy toward southern civilians is Mark Grimsley, *The Hard Hand of War* (1995).

The best biography of Lincoln, based on extensive research, is David Donald, *Lincoln* (1995). William E. Gienapp, *Abraham Lincoln and Civil War America* (2002), is a concise biography that focuses on the presidential years. Mark E. Neely has written two innovative studies of civil liberties in wartime: *The Fate of Liberty* (1991) examines the Union and *Southern Rights* (1999) deals with the Confederacy. For the South's bid for independence, Emory M. Thomas, *The Confederate Nation, 1861–1865* (1979), is the standard account. The fullest discussion of southern politics is George C. Rable, *The Confederate Republic* (1994). After years of relative neglect, historians have turned their attention to the vital home front. Drew Faust, *Mothers of Invention* (1996), is an imaginative study of slaveholding women in the Confederacy; Daniel Sutherland, *Seasons of War* (1995), and William Blair, *Virginia's Private War* (1998), analyze the experiences of several Virginian counties in the war; and Stephen V. Ash, *When the Yankees Came* (1995), examines southerners under Union occupation. For the northern home front, see J. Matthew Gallman, *The North Fights the Civil War* (1994). Leon Litwack, *Been in the Storm So Long* (1979), is a gracefully written account of African Americans' experiences during the war, and James L. Roark's *Masters without Slaves* (1977) discusses the collapse of the southern slaveholders' world. Gerald F. Linderman, *Embattled Courage* (1987), presents an interesting assessment of soldiers in both armies. Two excellent collections of essays that evaluate the war's outcome from various angles are David H. Donald, ed., *Why the North Won the Civil War* (1961), and Gabor S. Boritt, ed., *Why the Confederacy Lost* (1992). For a fuller list of readings, see the Bibliography at www.mhhe.com/davidsonnation5.

significant events

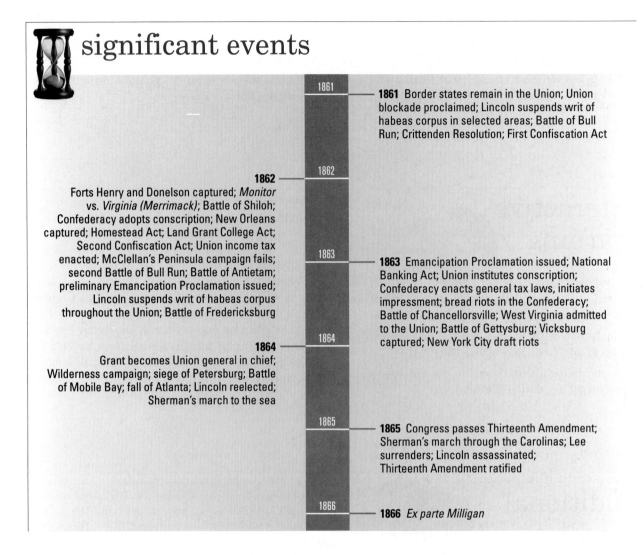

1861 Border states remain in the Union; Union blockade proclaimed; Lincoln suspends writ of habeas corpus in selected areas; Battle of Bull Run; Crittenden Resolution; First Confiscation Act

1862
Forts Henry and Donelson captured; *Monitor* vs. *Virginia (Merrimack)*; Battle of Shiloh; Confederacy adopts conscription; New Orleans captured; Homestead Act; Land Grant College Act; Second Confiscation Act; Union income tax enacted; McClellan's Peninsula campaign fails; second Battle of Bull Run; Battle of Antietam; preliminary Emancipation Proclamation issued; Lincoln suspends writ of habeas corpus throughout the Union; Battle of Fredericksburg

1863 Emancipation Proclamation issued; National Banking Act; Union institutes conscription; Confederacy enacts general tax laws, initiates impressment; bread riots in the Confederacy; Battle of Chancellorsville; West Virginia admitted to the Union; Battle of Gettysburg; Vicksburg captured; New York City draft riots

1864
Grant becomes Union general in chief; Wilderness campaign; siege of Petersburg; Battle of Mobile Bay; fall of Atlanta; Lincoln reelected; Sherman's march to the sea

1865 Congress passes Thirteenth Amendment; Sherman's march through the Carolinas; Lee surrenders; Lincoln assassinated; Thirteenth Amendment ratified

1866 *Ex parte Milligan*

AFTER THE FACT
Historians Reconstruct the Past

What Caused the
New York Draft Riots?

Atop a platform, with a small crowd looking on, a blindfolded man stood beside a cylinder as an attendant cranked it around. When the cylinder stopped, the blindfolded man reached in and pulled out a rolled-up slip of paper with a name on it. The day was Saturday, July 11, 1863, and in New York City the Union draft had begun. The day's selections were completed without incident.

Monday, however, was another story. Bright and early, hundreds of laborers streamed up Eighth and Ninth avenues. Waving "No Draft" placards, they rousted other workers from the stores and factories that they passed, stopping at last outside the draft office. Someone fired a pistol. Then members of the mob burst in, destroyed the selection cylinder, and set the building afire. Firefighters tried to stop the blaze from spreading, but another angry mob arrived in time to prevent them. All over the city the chaos spread. "Men left their various pursuits," wrote one reporter; store owners "put up their shutters; factories were emptied, conductors or drivers left their cars" until a "concourse of over twelve thousand" men, women, and children were roaming the streets.

CHARGE OF THE POLICE ON THE RIOTERS AT THE "TRIBUNE" OFFICE.

Over the next several days, the riots became even more violent. Fires burned out of control, telegraph wires were cut, railroad tracks were torn up, and crowds staged pitched battles with police and troops. Targets of the mob's wrath included both high officials and lowly citizens. Homes of the wealthy were looted and set afire, but so was the Colored Orphan Asylum. Policemen caught by the rioters were stripped of their clothes, and their faces were beaten to bloody pulps. Abraham Franklin, a crippled black coachman, was dragged from his rooms and hung while onlookers cheered for Jefferson Davis. By Friday order was at last restored by troops that had been rushed back from their recent victory at Gettysburg. At least 105 people, mostly rioters, lost their lives, and more than a million dollars in property had been destroyed. It was the highest loss of life in any civil disturbance in American history. A month later, the draft resumed in New York City.

What was the cause of such an immense tumult? "Absolute disloyalty," huffed the Republican New York *Tribune*. "It is absurd . . . to attribute this ruffianism to anything else than sympathy with the Rebels." The Democratic New York *World*, which had condemned the draft beforehand, offered an equally straightforward answer. The riot was a spontaneous protest against Lincoln's "wanton exercise of arbitrary powers." Having perverted the war into a struggle to destroy slavery, the paper complained, the administration was now determined to enforce an unconstitutional conscription law that allowed the rich to escape while sweeping the poor into the army's ranks.

At first glance, the *World's* emphasis on the draft seems sufficient. Rioters, after all, carried "No Draft" placards. They attacked draft officials and, by direct intimidation, forced the government to suspend the draft. Eyewitnesses agreed, moreover, that the rioters were overwhelmingly workers and mostly immigrants. These men certainly could not afford to pay the $300 commutation fee to avoid the draft. For them, $300 represented a year's wages or more.

Still, a closer look at the evidence suggests that there was more to these riots than a simple protest of the Union draft. For one thing, the draft did not apply to immigrants unless they were naturalized citizens or had declared their intention to be naturalized. Thus many foreign-born rioters were not even eligible. In addition, observers noted that rioters, including some of the most violent, were remarkably young. Dismissing talk of an oppressive conscription law, the New York *Times* asserted that "three-fourths of those who have been actively engaged in violence have been boys and young men under twenty years of age and not at all subject to Conscription." And if the $300 clause was what most angered the mobs, why did they attack free blacks, who were also subject to the draft and almost all of whom were too poor to pay the fee?

Historians who have examined Union conscription records cast further doubt on this explanation. Despite complaints by Democrats that the $300 fee was an instrument of class privilege, in reality poor men as well as wealthy ones bought their way out of the draft. In New York City, the rate of commutation was as high in poorer wards as in wealthy ones. In fact, over the course of the war 98 percent of the men drafted in the Irish districts of the city either paid the fee or provided substitutes. For as little as $10, workers could buy the equivalent of draft insurance by joining commutation clubs, in which members pooled their money to pay the fee for any contributor who was drafted.

SACKING A DRUG STORE IN SECOND AVENUE:
Observers noted that many rioters were boys.

If the draft was not the sole cause of the riots, what else was behind the mob's anger? For historians, evidence is not easy to come by. Members of rioting crowds rarely leave written records. More often, descriptions are the work of unsympathetic observers. Still, for historians actions can speak as loudly as words. Look closely at what the mobs did. Whom did they choose as the targets of their violence? Did different mobs express their anger in different ways? By examining the riots as they evolved over several days, it is possible to discover vital evidence concerning motivation. In the New York City disturbances, the makeup of the crowds changed dramatically from one day to the next, and the targets the rioters attacked also varied.

On Monday morning, industrial laborers and skilled workers, especially from the building trades, took a leading role. They were joined by some of the city's fire companies. Although some native-born workers participated, the protesters were largely immigrants, Germans as well as Irish. As they marched to the draft office, they announced a one-day strike in protest against the draft. By noon this throng of workers had halted the selection process.

Other rioters, however, began to attack the police and free blacks. As the mayhem escalated, some members of the morning demonstration, including those from several fire companies, now aided the authorities in trying to restore order. For those who switched sides, opposition to the draft had been paramount, and they were unwilling to sanction looting or murder.

When the riots continued on Tuesday and Wednesday, the crowds became much more heavily Irish. German Americans, some of whom were Republicans, no longer joined in. In fact, on several occasions they stepped in to protect free blacks. Skilled workers such as bricklayers, painters, and stonecutters for the most part also held back. Instead, rioters were largely industrial workers and common laborers and included many women and children. Their anger was directed no longer against the draft but against the Republican government and all its policies, including emancipation. Thus they vandalized homes of prominent Republicans, chanted pro-Confederate slogans, and fought pitched battles with the police and soldiers. The offices of Horace Greeley's pro-Republican New York

Common laborers in particular vented their anger on African Americans. As with colonial mob actions, such protests exhibited ritualistic overtones. The victim here not only is being hanged and burned but is being shot as well.

Tribune were attacked several times, and Greeley was forced to hide in a nearby restaurant to escape a beating.

For common laborers—longshoremen, street pavers, cartmen—African Americans increasingly became the target of vengeance. Mobs assaulted blacks and lynched at least twelve, ransacked businesses that catered to black customers, and destroyed tenements in which African Americans lived. These attacks were designed to purge neighborhoods of any black presence, especially in areas where black workers had been used to break strikes. These common laborers sought to restore the traditional racial order threatened by Republican policies, most notably emancipation.

In contrast, attacks on blacks and black residences were not common in wards where large numbers of industrial workers lived. While heavily Irish, industrial laborers in iron foundries and railroad shops did not work alongside African Americans. Although hostile to blacks, they aimed their anger more directly at the Republican party. Rather than roaming throughout the city as many common laborers did, industrial workers concentrated on their own neighborhoods, from which they tried to remove all reminders of Republican authority, particularly draft officials, policemen, and soldiers.

Although many policemen were not Republicans, the Metropolitan Police had been created by the Republican party in 1857, and its members had been particularly zealous in arresting individuals suspected of disloyalty.

In the end, no single grievance can explain New York's draft riots. Hostility to Republican employers, Protestant reformers, and authorities merged with antiblack racism, fears of job competition, and economic marginality. By itself, opposition to the draft did not produce the escalating violence and extraordinary destruction. But when that inflammatory issue sparked an avalanche of protest, it provided an outlet for more deeply rooted grievances. The result was the most serious civil disturbance of the war.

BIBLIOGRAPHY Iver Bernstein, *The New York City Draft Riots* (1990), does an admirable job of placing the riots within the context of changing class relations and work patterns. Adrian Cook, *The Armies of the Streets* (1974), presents a fuller, more straightforward narrative. For the Union draft, including a discussion of the impact of commutation, see James W. Geary, *We Need Men: The Union Draft in the Civil War* (1991). James M. McPherson, *The Negro's Civil War* (1965), contains primary sources detailing black New Yorkers' experiences during the riots.

Chapter 17

Joseph Davis had had enough. Well on in years and financially ruined by the war, he decided to quit farming. In November 1866, he sold his Mississippi plantations Hurricane and Brierfield to Benjamin Montgomery and his sons. The sale of southern plantations was common enough after the war, but this transaction was bound to attract attention, since Joseph Davis was the elder brother of Jefferson Davis. Indeed, before the war the Confederate president had operated Brierfield as his own plantation, although his brother retained legal title to it. In truth, the sale was so unusual that the parties involved agreed to keep it secret, since the Montgomerys were black, and Mississippi law prohibited African Americans from owning land.

Though a slave, Montgomery had been the business manager of the two Davis plantations before the war. He had also operated a store on Hurricane Plantation for white as well as black customers with his own line of credit in New Orleans. In 1863 Montgomery fled to the North, but when the war was over, he returned to Davis Bend, where the federal government was leasing plots of the land on confiscated plantations, including Hurricane and Brierfield, to black farmers. Montgomery quickly emerged as the leader of the African American community at the Bend.

Reconstructing the UNION

1865–1877

preview • Reconstruction became the battleground of attempts to define the new shape of the Union. Congress rejected Andrew Johnson's lenient terms for the South's reentry and enacted a program that included the principle of black suffrage. African Americans asserted their freedom by uniting divided families, establishing churches, and seeking education and land. But when northern whites became disillusioned with reform, the ideology of white supremacy brought Reconstruction to an end.

Then, in 1866, President Andrew Johnson pardoned Joseph Davis and restored his lands. By then Davis was over 80 years old and lacked the will and stamina to rebuild, yet unlike many ex-slaveholders, he still felt bound by obligations to his former slaves. Convinced that with proper encouragement African Americans could succeed economically in freedom, he sold his land secretly to Benjamin Montgomery. Only when the law prohibiting African Americans from owning land was overturned in 1867 did Davis publicly confirm the sale to his former slave.

For his part, Montgomery undertook to create a model society at Davis Bend based on mutual cooperation. He rented land to black farmers, hired others to work his own fields, sold supplies on credit, and ginned and marketed the crops. To the growing African American community, he preached the gospel of hard work, self-reliance, and education.

Various difficulties dogged these black farmers, including the destruction caused by the war, several disastrous floods, insects, droughts, and declining cotton prices. Yet before long, cotton production exceeded that of the prewar years, and in 1870 the black families at Davis Bend produced 2500 bales. The Montgomerys eventually acquired another plantation and owned 5500 acres, which made them reputedly the third largest planters in the state. They won national and international awards for the quality of their cotton. Their success demonstrated what African Americans, given a fair chance, might accomplish.

The experiences of Benjamin Montgomery during the years after 1865 were not those of most black southerners, who did not own land or have a powerful white

A Visit from the Old Mistress, by Winslow Homer, captures the conflicting, often awkward, emotions felt by both races after the war.

benefactor. Yet Montgomery's dream of economic independence was shared by all African Americans. As one black veteran noted, "Every colored man will be a slave, and feel himself a slave until he can raise him own bale of cotton and put him own mark upon it and say dis is mine!" Blacks could not gain effective freedom simply through a proclamation of emancipation. They needed economic power, including their own land that no one could unfairly take away.

For nearly two centuries the laws had prevented slaves from possessing such economic power. If those conditions were to be overturned, black Americans needed political power too. Thus the Republic would have to be reconstructed to give African Americans political power that they had been previously denied.

War, in its blunt way, had roughed out the contours of a solution, but only in broad terms. Clearly, African Americans would no longer be enslaved. The North, with its industrial might, would be the driving force in the nation's economy and retain the dominant political voice. But beyond that, the outlines of a reconstructed Republic remained vague. Would African Americans receive effective power? How would the North and the South readjust their economic and political relations? These questions lay at the heart of the problem of Reconstruction.

Presidential Reconstruction

Throughout the war Abraham Lincoln had considered Reconstruction his responsibility. Elected with less than 40 percent of the popular vote in 1860, he was acutely aware that once the states of the Confederacy were restored to the Union, the Republicans would be weakened unless they ceased to be a sectional party.

By a generous peace, Lincoln hoped to attract former Whigs in the South, who supported many of the Republicans' economic policies, and build up a southern wing of the party.

Lincoln's 10 Percent Plan

Lincoln outlined his program in a Proclamation of Amnesty and Reconstruction issued in December 1863. When a minimum of 10 percent of the qualified voters from 1860 took a loyalty oath to the Union, they could organize a state government. The new state constitution had to be republican in form, abolish slavery, and provide for black education, but Lincoln did not insist that high-ranking Confederate leaders be barred from public life. Once these requirements had been met, the president would recognize the new civilian state government.

Disavowing any thought of trying prominent Confederate leaders, Lincoln indicated that he would be generous in granting pardons and did not rule out compensation for slave property. Moreover, while he privately suggested permitting some black men to vote in the disloyal states, "as for instance, the very intelligent and especially those who have fought gallantly in our ranks," he did not demand social or political equality for black Americans, and he recognized pro-Union governments in Louisiana, Arkansas, and Tennessee that allowed only white men to vote.

Radical Republicans

The Radical Republicans found Lincoln's approach much too lenient. Strongly antislavery, Radical members of Congress had led the struggle to make emancipation a war aim. Now they were in the forefront in advocating rights for the freedpeople. They were also disturbed that Lincoln had not enlisted Congress in devising Reconstruction policy. Lincoln argued that the executive branch should bear the responsibility for restoring proper relations with the former Confederate states. The Radicals, on the other hand, believed that it was the duty of Congress to set the terms under which states would regain their rights in the Union. Though the Radicals often disagreed on other matters, they were united in a determination to readmit southern states only after slavery had been ended, black rights protected, and the power of the planter class destroyed.

Wade-Davis bill

Under the direction of Senator Benjamin Wade of Ohio and Representative Henry Winter Davis of Maryland, Congress formulated a much stricter plan of Reconstruction. It proposed that Confederate states be ruled temporarily by a military governor, required half the white adult males to take an oath of allegiance before drafting a new state constitution, and restricted political power to the hard-core Unionists in each state. When the Wade-Davis bill passed on the final day of the 1864 congressional session, Lincoln exercised his right of a pocket veto.* Still, his own program could not succeed without the assistance of Congress, which refused to seat Unionist representatives who had been elected from Louisiana or Arkansas. As the war drew to a close, Lincoln appeared ready to make concessions to the Radicals. He suggested that he might favor different—and conceivably more rigorous—Reconstruction plans for different states. At his final cabinet meeting, he approved placing the defeated

---

*If a president does not sign a bill after Congress has adjourned, it has the same effect as a veto.

South temporarily under military rule. But only a few days later Booth's bullet found its mark, and Lincoln's final approach to Reconstruction would never be known.

The Mood of the South

Northerners worried about the attitude of ex-Confederates at war's end. In the wake of defeat, the immediate reaction among white southerners was one of shock, despair, and hopelessness. Some former Confederates, of course, were openly antagonistic. A North Carolina innkeeper remarked bitterly that Yankees had stolen his slaves, burned his house, and killed all his sons, leaving him only one privilege: "To hate 'em. I git up at half-past four in the morning, and sit up till twelve at night, to hate 'em." Most Confederate soldiers were less defiant, having had their fill of war. Even among hostile civilians the feeling was widespread that the South must accept northern terms. And some, like Captain Samuel Foster, a Confederate soldier from Texas, marveled that "mens minds can change so sudden, from opinions of life long, to new ones a week old." Men "who actually owned and held slaves up to this time,—have now changed in their opinions regarding slavery . . . to see that for a man to have property in man was wrong, and that the 'Declaration of Independence' meant more than they had ever been able to see before."

The mood of white southerners at the end of the war was mixed. Many, like the veteran caricatured here by northern cartoonist Thomas Nast, remained hostile. Others, like Texas captain Samuel Foster, came to believe that the institution of slavery "had been abused, and perhaps for that abuse this terrible war . . . was brought upon us as a punishment."

This psychological moment was critical. To prevent a resurgence of resistance, the president needed to lay out in unmistakable terms what white southerners had to do to regain their old status in the Union. Any confusion in policy, or wavering on the peace terms, could only increase the likelihood of resistance. Perhaps even a clear and firm policy would not have been enough. But with Lincoln's death, the executive power came to rest in far less capable hands.

Johnson's Program of Reconstruction

Andrew Johnson, the new president, had been born in North Carolina and eventually moved to Tennessee, where he worked as a tailor. Barely able to read and write when he married, he rose to political power by portraying himself as the champion of the people against the wealthy planter class. "Some day I will show the stuck-up aristocrats who is running the country," he vowed as he began his political career. He had not opposed slavery before the war—in fact, he hoped to disperse slave ownership more widely in southern society. Although he accepted emancipation as one consequence of the war, Johnson remained a confirmed racist. "Damn the negroes," he said during the war, "I am fighting these traitorous aristocrats, their masters."

Johnson's character and values

Because Johnson disliked the planter class so strongly, Republican Radicals in Congress expected him to uphold their views on Reconstruction. In fact, the

Andrew Johnson's contentious personality masked a deep-seated insecurity.

new president did speak of trying Confederate leaders and breaking up planters' estates. Unlike most Republicans, however, Johnson strongly supported states' rights and opposed government aid to business. Given such differences, conflict between the president and the majority in Congress was inevitable, but Johnson's personality and political shortcomings made the situation worse. Scarred by his humble origins, he remained throughout his life an outsider. When challenged or criticized, he became tactless and inflexible, alienating even those who sought to work with him.

Johnson's program

At first, Johnson seemed to be following Lincoln's policy of quickly restoring the southern states to their rightful place in the Union. He prescribed a loyalty oath ordinary white southerners would have to take to have their property, except for slaves, restored and to regain their civil and political rights. Like Lincoln, Johnson excluded high Confederate officials from this group, but he added those with property worth over $20,000, which included his old foes in the planter class. These groups had to apply to the president for individual pardons.

Loyal state governments could be formed after a provisional governor, appointed by the president, called a convention to draft a new state constitution. Voters and delegates had to qualify under the 1860 state election laws and take the new loyalty oath. Once elections were held to choose a governor, legislature, and members of Congress, Johnson announced, he would recognize the new state government, revoke martial law, and withdraw Union troops. Again, the plan was similar to Lincoln's, though more lenient. Unlike the formula Lincoln adopted, Johnson spoke only informally of requiring southern states to repeal their ordinances of secession, repudiate the Confederate debt, and ratify the proposed Thirteenth Amendment abolishing slavery.

The Failure of Johnson's Program

Southern defiance

The southern delegates who met to construct new governments soon demonstrated that they were in no frame of mind to follow Johnson's recommendations. Several states merely repealed instead of repudiating their ordinances of secession, rejected the Thirteenth Amendment, or refused to repudiate the Confederate debt.

Black codes

Nor did any of the new governments allow African Americans any political rights or make any effective provisions for black education. In addition, each state passed a series of laws, often modeled on its old slave code, that applied only to African Americans. These "black codes" did grant African Americans some rights that had not been enjoyed by slaves. They legalized marriages performed under slavery and allowed black southerners to hold and sell property and to sue and be sued in state courts. Yet their primary purpose was to keep African Americans as propertyless agricultural laborers with inferior legal rights. The new freedpeople could not serve on juries, testify against whites, or work as they pleased. South Carolina forbade blacks to engage in anything other than agricultural labor without a special license; Mississippi prohibited them from buying or renting farmland. Most states ominously provided that black people who were vagrants could be arrested and hired out to landowners. Many northerners were incensed by the restrictive black codes, which violated their conception of freedom.

Southern voters under Johnson's plan also defiantly elected prominent Confederate military and political leaders to office, headed by Alexander Stephens, the vice president of the Confederacy, who was elected senator from Georgia. At this point, Johnson could have called for new elections or admitted that a different program of Reconstruction was needed. Instead he caved in. For all his harsh rhetoric, he shrank from the prospect of social upheaval, and he found it enormously gratifying when upper-class planters praised his conduct and requested pardons. As the lines of ex-Confederates waiting to see him lengthened, he began issuing special pardons almost as fast as they could be printed. In the next two years he pardoned some 13,500 former rebels.

In private, Johnson warned southerners against a reckless course. Publicly he put on a bold face, announcing that Reconstruction had been successfully completed. But many members of Congress were deeply alarmed, and the stage was set for a serious confrontation.

Elections in the South

Johnson's Break with Congress

The new Congress was by no means of one mind. A small number of Democrats and a few conservative Republicans backed the president's program of immediate and unconditional restoration. At the other end of the spectrum, a larger group of Radical Republicans, led by Thaddeus Stevens, Charles Sumner, Benjamin Wade, and others, was bent on remaking southern society in the image of the North. Reconstruction must "revolutionize Southern institutions, habits, and manners," thundered Representative Stevens, ". . . or all our blood and treasure have been spent in vain."

Thaddeus Stevens, Radical leader in the House

As a minority, the Radicals could accomplish nothing without the aid of the moderate Republicans, the largest bloc in Congress. Led by William Pitt Fessenden and Lyman Trumbull, the moderates hoped to avoid a clash with the president, and they had no desire to foster social revolution or promote racial equality in the South. But they wanted to keep Confederate leaders from reassuming power, and they were convinced that the former slaves needed federal protection. Otherwise, Trumbull declared, the freedpeople would "be tyrannized over, abused, and virtually reenslaved."

The central issue dividing Johnson and the Radicals was the place of African Americans in American society. Johnson accused his opponents of seeking "to Africanize the southern half of our country," while the Radicals championed civil and political rights for African Americans. Convinced that southern white Unionists were too small a nucleus to build a party around, Radicals believed that the only way to maintain loyal governments and develop a Republican party in the South was to give black men the ballot. Moderates agreed that the new southern governments were too harsh toward African Americans, but they feared that too great an emphasis on black civil rights would alienate northern voters.

Issue of black rights

In December 1865, when southern representatives to Congress appeared in Washington, a majority in Congress voted to exclude them. Congress also appointed a joint committee, chaired by Senator Fessenden, to look into Reconstruction.

The growing split with the president became clearer when Congress passed a bill extending the life of the Freedmen's Bureau. Created in March 1865, the

Johnson's vetoes

bureau provided emergency food, clothing, and medical care to war refugees (including white southerners) and took charge of settling freedpeople on abandoned lands. The new bill gave the bureau the added responsibilities of supervising special courts to resolve disputes involving freedpeople and establishing schools for black southerners. Although this bill passed with virtually unanimous Republican support, Johnson nevertheless vetoed it, and Congress failed to override his veto.

Johnson also vetoed a civil rights bill designed to overturn the more flagrant provisions of the black codes. The law made African Americans citizens of the United States and granted them the right to own property, make contracts, and have access to courts as parties and witnesses. For most Republicans Johnson's action was the last straw, and in April 1866 Congress overrode his veto, the first major legislation in American history to be enacted over a presidential veto. Congress then approved a slightly revised Freedmen's Bureau bill in July and promptly overrode the president's veto. Johnson's refusal to compromise drove the moderates into the arms of the Radicals.

The Fourteenth Amendment

To prevent unrepentant Confederates from taking over the reconstructed state governments and denying African Americans basic freedoms, the Joint Committee on Reconstruction proposed an amendment to the Constitution, which passed both houses of Congress with the necessary two-thirds vote in June 1866. The amendment, coupled with the Freedmen's Bureau and civil rights bills, represented the moderates' terms for Reconstruction.

Provisions of the amendment

The Fourteenth Amendment put a number of matters beyond the control of the president. The amendment guaranteed repayment of the national war debt and prohibited repayment of the Confederate debt. To counteract the president's wholesale pardons, it disqualified prominent Confederates from holding office and provided that only Congress by a two-thirds vote could remove this penalty. Because moderates, fearful of the reaction of white northerners, balked at giving the vote to African Americans, the amendment merely gave Congress the right to reduce the representation of any state that did not have impartial male suffrage. The practical effect of this provision, which Radicals labeled a "swindle," was to allow northern states to restrict suffrage to whites if they wished, since unlike southern states they had few African Americans and thus would not be penalized.

The amendment's most important provision, Section 1, defined an American citizen as anyone born in the United States or naturalized, thereby automatically making African Americans citizens. Section 1 also prohibited states from abridging "the privileges or immunities" of citizens, depriving "any person of life, liberty, or property, without due process of law," or denying "any person . . . equal protection of the laws." The framers of the amendment probably intended to prohibit laws that applied to one race only, such as the black codes, or that made certain acts felonies when committed by black but not white people, or that decreed different penalties for the same crime when committed by white and black lawbreakers. The framers probably did not intend to prevent African Americans from being excluded from juries or to forbid segregation (the legal separation of the races) in schools and public places.

Nevertheless, Johnson denounced the proposed amendment and urged southern states not to ratify it. Ironically, of the seceded states only the president's own state ratified the amendment, and Congress readmitted Tennessee with no further restrictions. The telegram sent to Congress by a longtime foe of Johnson announcing Tennessee's approval ended, "Give my respects to the dead dog in the White House." The amendment was ratified in 1868.

The Elections of 1866

When Congress blocked his policies, Johnson undertook a speaking tour of the East and Midwest in the fall of 1866 to drum up popular support. But the president found it difficult to convince northern audiences that white southerners were fully repentant. News that summer of major race riots in Memphis and New Orleans heightened northern concern. Forty-six African Americans died when white mobs invaded the black section of Memphis, burning homes, churches, and schoolhouses. About the same number were killed in New Orleans when whites attacked both black and white delegates to a convention supporting black suffrage. "The negroes now know, to their sorrow, that it is best not to arouse the fury of the white man," boasted one Memphis newspaper. When the president encountered hostile audiences during his northern campaign, he only made matters worse by trading insults and ranting that the Radicals were traitors. Even supporters found his performance humiliating.

Antiblack riots

Not to be outdone, the Radicals vilified Johnson as a traitor aiming to turn the country over to rebels and Copperheads. Resorting to the tactic of "waving the bloody shirt," they appealed to voters by reviving bitter memories of the war. In a classic example of such rhetoric, Governor Oliver Morton of Indiana proclaimed that "every bounty jumper, every deserter, every sneak who ran away from the draft" was a Democrat; everyone "who murdered Union prisoners," every "New York rioter in 1863 who burned up little children in colored asylums called himself a Democrat. In short, the Democratic party may be described as a common sewer."

Voters soundly repudiated Johnson, as the Republicans won more than a two-thirds majority in both houses of Congress, every northern gubernatorial contest, and control of every northern legislature. The Radicals had reached the height of their power, propelled by genuine alarm among northerners that Johnson's policies would lose the fruits of the Union's victory. Johnson was a president virtually without a party.

Repudiation of Johnson

Congressional Reconstruction

With a clear mandate in hand, congressional Republicans passed their own program of Reconstruction, beginning with the first Reconstruction Act in March 1867. Like all later pieces of Reconstruction legislation, it was repassed over Johnson's veto.

Placing the 10 unreconstructed states under military commanders, the act provided that in enrolling voters, officials were to include black adult males but not former Confederates who were barred from holding office under the Fourteenth Amendment. Delegates to the state conventions would frame constitutions that provided for black suffrage and that disqualified prominent ex-Confederates from office. The first state legislatures to meet under the new constitution were required to ratify the Fourteenth Amendment. Once these steps were completed and Congress approved the new state constitution, a state could send representatives to Congress.

Resistance of southern whites

White southerners found these requirements so obnoxious that officials took no steps to register voters. Congress then enacted a second Reconstruction Act, also in March, ordering the local military commanders to put the machinery of Reconstruction into motion. Johnson's efforts to limit the power of military commanders produced a third act, passed in July, that upheld their superiority in all matters. When elections were held to ratify the new state constitutions, white southerners boycotted them in large numbers. Undaunted, Congress passed the fourth Reconstruction Act (March 1868), which required ratification of the constitution by only a majority of those voting rather than those who were registered.

By June 1868 Congress had readmitted the representatives of seven states. Georgia's state legislature expelled its black members once it had been readmitted, granting seats to those barred by Congress from holding office. Congress ordered the military commander to reverse these actions, and Georgia was then admitted a second time in July 1870. Texas, Virginia, and Mississippi did not complete the process until 1869.

Post-Emancipation Societies in the Americas

With the exception of Haiti's revolution (1791–1804), the United States was the only society in the Americas in which the destruction of slavery was accomplished by violence. But the United States, uniquely among these societies, enfranchised former slaves almost immediately after the emancipation. Thus in the United States former masters and slaves battled for control of the state in ways that did not occur in other post-emancipation societies. In most of the Caribbean, property requirements for voting left the planters in political control. Jamaica, for example, with a population of 500,000 in the 1860s, had only 3,000 voters.

Moreover, in reaction to political efforts to mobilize disfranchised black peasants, Jamaican planters dissolved the assembly and reverted to being a Crown colony governed from London. Of the sugar islands, all but Barbados adopted the same policy, thereby blocking the potential for any future black peasant democracy. Nor did any of these societies have the counterparts of the Radical Republicans, a group of outsiders with political power that promoted the fundamental transformation of the post-emancipation South. These comparisons highlight the radicalism of Reconstruction in the United States, which alone saw an effort to forge an interracial democracy.

The Land Issue

Blacks' desire for land

While the political process of Reconstruction proceeded, Congress confronted the question of whether land should be given to former slaves to foster economic independence. At a meeting with Secretary of War Edwin Stanton near the end of the war, African American leaders declared, "The way we can best take care of ourselves is to have land, and till it by our own labor." During the war, the Second Confiscation Act of 1862 had authorized the government to seize and sell the property, including land, of supporters of the rebellion. In June 1866, however, President Johnson ruled that confiscation laws applied only to wartime.

Congress debated land confiscation off and on from December 1865 until early 1867. Thaddeus Stevens, a leading Radical in the House, advocated confiscating

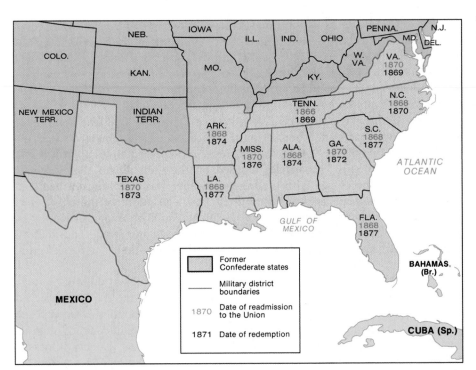

The Southern States during Reconstruction

394 million acres of land from about 70,000 of what he termed the "chief rebels" in the South, who made up less than 5 percent of the South's white families. He proposed to give 40 acres to every adult male freedperson and then sell the remaining land, which would amount to nine-tenths of the total, to pay off the public debt, compensate loyal southerners for losses they suffered during the war, and fund Union veterans' pensions. Land, he insisted, would be far more valuable to African Americans than the right to vote.

But in the end Congress rejected all proposals. Even some Radicals were opposed to land redistribution. Given Americans' strong belief in self-reliance, little sympathy existed for the idea that government should support any group. In addition, land redistribution represented an attack on property rights, another cherished American value. "A division of rich men's lands amongst the landless," argued the *Nation,* a Radical journal, "would give a shock to our whole social and political system from which it would hardly recover without the loss of liberty." By 1867 land reform was dead.

Failure of land redistribution

Few freedpeople acquired land after the war, a development that severely limited African Americans' economic independence and left them vulnerable to white coercion. It is doubtful, however, that this decision was the basic cause of the failure of Reconstruction. In the face of white hostility and institutionalized racism, African Americans probably would have been no more successful in protecting their property than they were in maintaining the right to vote.

Impeachment

Throughout 1867 Congress routinely overrode Johnson's vetoes. Still, the president had other ways of undercutting congressional Reconstruction. He interpreted the

Tenure of Office Act

new laws as narrowly as possible and removed military commanders who vigorously enforced them. Congress responded by restricting Johnson's power to issue orders to military commanders in the South. It also passed the Tenure of Office Act, which forbade Johnson to remove any member of the cabinet without the Senate's consent. The intention of this law was to prevent him from firing Secretary of War Edwin Stanton, the only Radical in the cabinet.

When Johnson tried to dismiss Stanton in February 1868, the determined secretary of war barricaded himself in his office (where he remained night and day for about two months). Angrily, the House of Representatives approved articles of impeachment. The articles focused on the violation of the Tenure of Office Act, but the charge with the most substance was that Johnson had conspired to systematically obstruct Reconstruction legislation. In the trial before the Senate, his lawyers argued that a president could be impeached only for an indictable crime, which Johnson clearly had not committed. The Radicals countered that impeachment applied to political offenses and not merely criminal acts.

Johnson acquitted

In May 1868 the Senate voted 36 to 19 to convict, one vote short of the two-thirds majority needed. The seven Republicans who joined the Democrats in voting for acquittal were uneasy about using impeachment as a political weapon. Their vote against conviction established the precedent that a president could be removed from office only for indictable offenses, which greatly lessened the effectiveness of the threat of impeachment.

Reconstruction in the South

The refusal of Congress to convict Johnson sent a clear signal: the power of the Radicals in Congress was waning. Increasingly the success or failure of Reconstruction hinged on developments not in Congress but in the southern states themselves. Power there rested with the new Republican parties, representing a coalition of black and white southerners and transplanted northerners.

Black Office Holding

Almost from the beginning of Reconstruction, African Americans had lobbied for the right to vote. After they received the franchise, black men constituted as much as 80 percent of the Republican voters in the South. They steadfastly opposed the Democratic party with its appeal to white supremacy. As one Tennessee Republican explained, "The blacks know that many conservatives [Democrats] hope to reduce them again to some form of peonage. Under the impulse of this fear they will roll up their whole strength and will go entirely for the Republican candidate whoever he may be."

Throughout Reconstruction, African Americans never held office in proportion to their voting strength. No African American was ever elected governor, and only in South Carolina, where more than 60 percent of the population was black, did they control even one house of the legislature. During Reconstruction between 15 and 20 percent of the state officers and 6 percent of members of Congress (2 senators and 15 representatives) were black. Only in South Carolina did black officeholders approach their proportion of the population.

Blacks who held office generally came from the top levels of African American society. Among state and federal officeholders, perhaps four-fifths were literate, and more than a quarter had been free before the war, both marks of distinction in the black community. Their occupations also set them apart: two-fifths were professionals (mostly clergy), and of the third who were farmers, nearly all owned land. Among black members of Congress, all but three had a secondary school education, and four had gone to college. In their political and social values, African American leaders were more conservative than the rural black population was, and they showed little interest in land reform.

Hiram Revels, a minister and educator, became the first African American to serve in the U.S. Senate, representing Mississippi. Later he served as president of Alcorn University.

Background of black political leaders

White Republicans in the South

Black citizens were a majority of the voters only in South Carolina, Mississippi, and Louisiana. Thus in most of the South the Republican party had to secure white votes to stay in power. Opponents scornfully labeled white southerners who allied with the Republican party scalawags, yet an estimated quarter of white southerners at one time voted Republican. Although the party appealed to some wealthy planters, they were outnumbered by Unionists from the upland counties and hill areas who were largely yeoman farmers. Such voters were attracted by Republican promises to rebuild the South, restore prosperity, create public schools, and open isolated areas to the market with railroads.

The other group of white Republicans in the South was known as carpetbaggers. Originally from the North, they allegedly had arrived with all their worldly possessions stuffed in a carpetbag, ready to loot and plunder the defeated South. Some did, certainly, but northerners moved south for a variety of reasons. Those in political office were especially well educated. Though carpetbaggers made up only a small percentage of Republican voters, they controlled almost a third of the offices. More than half of all southern Republican governors and nearly half of Republican members of Congress were originally northerners.

The Republican party in the South had difficulty agreeing on a program or maintaining unity. Scalawags were especially susceptible to the race issue and social pressure. "Even my own kinspeople have turned the cold shoulder to me because I hold office under a Republican administration," testified a Mississippi white Republican. As black southerners pressed for greater recognition and a greater share of the offices, white southerners increasingly defected to the Democrats. Carpetbaggers, in contrast, were less sensitive to race, although most felt that their black allies needed guidance and should be content with minor offices. The friction between scalawags and carpetbaggers, which grew out of their rivalry for party honors, was particularly intense.

Divisions among southern Republicans

From the beginning of Reconstruction, African Americans demanded the right to vote as free citizens. The Fifteenth Amendment, ratified in 1870, secured that right for black males. In New York, black citizens paraded in support of Ulysses Grant for president. Parades played a central role in campaigning: this parade exhibits the usual banners, flags, costumes, and a band. Blacks in both the North and the South voted solidly for the Republican party as the party of Lincoln and emancipation, although white violence in the South increasingly reduced black turnout.

The New State Governments

New state constitutions

The new southern state constitutions enacted several significant reforms. They put in place fairer systems of legislative representation, allowed voters to elect many officials who before had been appointed, and abolished property requirements for officeholding. In South Carolina, for the first time, voters were allowed to vote for the president, governor, and other state officers.* The Radical state governments also assumed some responsibility for social welfare and established the first statewide systems of public schools in the South. Although the Fourteenth Amendment prevented high Confederate officials from holding office, only Alabama and Arkansas temporarily forbade some ex-Confederates to vote.

Race and social equality

All the new constitutions proclaimed the principle of equality and granted black adult males the right to vote. On social relations they were much more cautious. No state outlawed segregation, and South Carolina and Louisiana were the only states that required integration in public schools (a mandate that was almost universally ignored). Sensitive to status, mulattoes pushed for prohibition of social discrimination, but white Republicans refused to adopt such a radical policy.

Economic Issues and Corruption

The war left the southern economy in ruins, and problems of economic reconstruction were as difficult as those of politics. The new Republican governments encouraged industrial development by providing subsidies, loans, and even

---

*Previously, presidential electors as well as the governor had been chosen by the South Carolina legislature.

temporary exemptions from taxes. These governments also largely rebuilt the southern railroad system, often offering lavish aid to railroad corporations. These investments in the South's industrial base helped: in the two decades after 1860, the region doubled its manufacturing establishments. Yet the harsh reality was that the South steadily slipped further behind the booming industrial economy of the North. Between 1854 and 1879, 7000 miles of railroad track were laid in the South, but in the same period 45,000 miles were constructed in the rest of the nation.

The expansion of government services offered temptations for corruption. In many southern states, officials regularly received bribes and kickbacks for their award of railroad charters, franchises, and other contracts. By 1872 the debts of the 11 states of the Confederacy had increased by $132 million, largely because of railroad grants and new social services such as schools. The tax rate grew as expenditures went up, so that by the 1870s it was four times the rate of 1860.

Corruption

Corruption, however, was not only a southern problem: the decline in morality affected the entire nation. During these years in New York City alone, the Democratic Tweed Ring stole more money than all the Radical Republican governments in the South combined. Moreover, corruption in the South was hardly limited to Republicans. Many Democrats and white business leaders participated in these corrupt practices both before and after the Radical governments were in power. Louisiana governor Henry Warmoth, a carpetbagger, told a congressional committee that the legislature was as good as the people it represented. "Everybody is demoralizing down here. Corruption is the fashion."

Corruption in Radical governments undeniably existed, but southern whites exaggerated its extent for partisan purposes. Conservatives just as bitterly opposed honest Radical regimes as they did notoriously corrupt ones. In the eyes of most white southerners, the real crime of the Radical governments was that they allowed black citizens to hold some offices and tried to protect the civil rights of African Americans. Race was the conservatives' greatest weapon. And it would prove the most effective means to undermine Republican power in the South.

Emancipation came to slaves in different ways and at different times. For some it

Black Aspirations

arrived during the war when Union soldiers entered an area; for others it came some time after the Confederacy's collapse, when Union troops or officials announced that they were free. Whatever the timing, freedom meant a host of precious blessings to people who had been in bondage all their lives.

Experiencing Freedom

The first impulse was to think of freedom as a contrast to slavery. Emancipation immediately released slaves from the most oppressive aspects of bondage—the whippings, the breakup of families, the sexual exploitation. Freedom also meant movement, the right to travel without a pass or white permission. Above all, freedom meant that African Americans' labor would be for their own benefit. One Arkansas freedman, who earned his first dollar working on a railroad, recalled that when he was paid, "I felt like the richest man in the world."

Freedom included finding a new place to work. Changing jobs was one concrete way to break the psychological ties of slavery. Even planters with

Changing employment

Daily Lives

PUBLIC SPACE/
PRIVATE SPACE

The Black Sharecropper's Cabin

On the plantations of the Old South, slaves had lived in cabins along a central path in the shadow of the white master's "big house." These quarters were the center of their community, where marriages and other festivals were celebrated and family life went on. But with the coming of emancipation, freedpeople looked to leave the old quarters, which stood as a symbol of bondage and of close white supervision. African Americans either built new housing or dismantled their old cabins and hauled them to the plots of land they rented as tenants or sharecroppers. Moving enabled them to live on the land they farmed, just as white farmers and tenants did.

In selecting a cabin site, freedpeople tried to locate within a convenient distance of their fields but close to the woods as well, since cutting wood was a year-round task for boys. To improve drainage, cabins were often built on a knoll or had a floor raised above the ground. A nearby stream, spring, or well provided not only water but also a place to cool butter and other perishable dairy products.

Like slave cabins, most sharecroppers' dwellings were one story high, about 16 feet square, and usually built of logs chinked with mud. The few windows had shutters to protect against the weather; glass was rare. Though the inside walls normally lacked plaster or sheeting, they were given a coat of whitewash annually to brighten the dark interior. To provide a bit of cheer, women often covered the walls with pictures from seed catalogues and magazines. The floor, packed dirt that was as smooth and hard as concrete, was covered with braided rugs made from scraps of cloth and worn-out clothing.

The main room served as kitchen and dining room, parlor, bathing area, and the parents' bedroom. To one side might be a homemade drop-leaf table (essential because of cramped space), which served as a kitchen work counter and a dining table. The other side of the room had a few plain beds, their slats or rope bottoms supporting corn shuck or straw mattresses. (Featherbeds were considered a remarkable luxury.) The social center of the

Chimneys on sharecroppers' cabins were often tilted deliberately so that they could be pushed away from the house quickly if they caught fire.

reputations for kindness sometimes found that most of their former hands had departed. The cook who left a South Carolina family even though they offered her higher wages than her new job explained, "I must go. If I stays here I'll never know I'm free."

Importance of names

Symbolically, freedom meant having a full name, and African Americans now adopted last names. More than a few took the last name of some prominent individual; more common was to take the name of the first master in the family's oral history as far back as it could be recalled. Most, on the other hand, retained their first name, especially if the name had been given to them by their parents (as most

room was the fireplace, the only source of heat and the main source of light after dark. Pots and pans were hung on the wall near the fireplace, and the mother and daughters did the cooking stooped over an open fire. Clothing was hung on pegs in the wall.

The cabin's chimney was made of small logs notched together and covered with several layers of clay to protect it from the heat. It often narrowed toward the top, and sometimes its height was extended by empty flour barrels. A taller chimney drew better, which kept smoke from blowing back down into the house and kept sparks away from the roof. After the evening meal the family gathered around the fireplace, the children to play with homemade dolls and toys, the mother to sew, and the father perhaps to play the fiddle. At bedtime a trapdoor in the ceiling offered access up a ladder to the loft beneath the gabled roof, where older children slept, usually on pallets on the floor, as had been the case in slavery.

In the summer, cooking was done outdoors over an open fire. Women generally preferred to cook under a tree, which offered some protection from rain as well as relief from the sun and the high humidity. Sharecropper families rarely had separate cooking rooms attached to or next to the cabin. Separate kitchens, which were a sign of prosperity, were more common among black landowners and white tenant farmers.

Gradually, as black sharecroppers scraped together some savings, they improved their homes. By the end of the century, frame dwellings were more common, and many older log cabins had been covered with wood siding. The newer homes were generally larger, with wood floors, and often had attached rooms such as a porch or kitchen. In addition, windows had glass panes, roofs were covered with shingles instead of planking, and stone and brick chimneys were less unusual. Ceramic dishes were more frequently seen, and wood-burning stoves made cooking easier for women and provided a more efficient source of heat.

Without question, the cabins of black sharecroppers provided more space than the slave quarters had, and certainly more freedom and privacy. Still, they lacked many of the comforts that most white Americans took for granted. Such housing reflected the continuing status of black sharecroppers as poverty-stricken laborers in a caste system based on race.

often had been the case among slaves). It had been their form of identity in bondage, and for those separated from their family it was the only link with their parents. Whatever name they took, it was important to black Americans that they make the decision themselves without white interference.

The Black Family

African Americans also sought to strengthen the family in freedom. Because slave marriages had not been recognized as legal, thousands of former slaves insisted on

Upholding the family

being married again by proper authorities, even though a ceremony was not required by law. Blacks who had been forcibly separated in slavery and later remarried confronted the dilemma of which spouse to take. Laura Spicer, whose husband had been sold away in slavery, received a series of wrenching letters from him after the war. He had thought her dead, had remarried, and had a new family. "You know it never was our wishes to be separated from each other, and it never was our fault. I had rather anything to had happened to me most than ever have been parted from you and the children," he wrote. "As I am, I do not know which I love best, you or Anna." Declining to return, he closed, "Laura, truly, I have got another wife, and I am very sorry. . . ."

Like white husbands, black husbands deemed themselves the head of the family and acted legally for their wives. They often insisted that their wives would not work in the fields as they had in slavery, a decision that had major economic repercussions for agricultural labor. "The [black] women say they never mean to do any more outdoor work," one planter reported, "that white men support their wives and they mean that their husbands shall support them." In negotiating contracts, a father also demanded the right to control his children and their labor. All these changes were designed to insulate the black family from white control.

The Schoolhouse and the Church

Black education

In freedom, the schoolhouse and the black church became essential institutions in the black community. Next to ownership of land, African Americans saw education as the best hope for advancement. At first, northern churches and missionaries, working with the Freedmen's Bureau, set up black schools in the South. Tuition represented 10 percent or more of a laborer's monthly wages. Yet these schools were full. Many parents sent their children by day and attended classes themselves at night. Eventually, the Bureau schools were replaced by the new public school systems, which by 1876 enrolled 40 percent of African American children.

Black adults had good reasons for seeking literacy. They wanted to be able to read the Bible, to defend their newly gained civil and political rights, and to protect themselves from being cheated. One elderly Louisiana freedman explained that giving children an education was better than giving them a fortune, "because if you left them even $500, some man having more education than they had would come along and cheat them out of it all." Both races saw that education would undermine the old servility that slavery had fostered.

Teachers in black schools

Teachers in the Freedmen's Bureau schools were primarily northern middle-class white women sent south by northern missionary societies. "I feel that it is a precious privilege," Esther Douglass wrote, "to be allowed to do something for these poor people." Many saw themselves as peacetime soldiers, struggling to make emancipation a reality. Indeed, on more than one occasion, hostile white southerners destroyed black schools and threatened and even murdered white teachers. Teachers in urban schools often lived together in comfortable housing, which provided a social network, created a sense of sisterhood, and helped sustain morale. In rural areas, however, teachers often had to live alone or with black families because of white hostility. Then there were the everyday challenges: low pay, dilapidated buildings, lack of sufficient books, classes of 100 or more children, and irregular attendance. Meanwhile, the Freedmen's Bureau undertook to quickly train

After living for years in a society where teaching slaves to read and write was usually illegal, freedpeople viewed literacy as a key to securing their new-found freedom. Blacks were not merely "*anxious* to learn," a school official in Virginia reported, they were "*crazy* to learn."

black teachers, and by 1869 a majority of the approximately 3000 teachers in freed-men's schools were black.

Before the war, most slaves had attended white churches or services supervised by whites. Once free, African Americans quickly established their own congregations led by black preachers. In the first year of freedom, the Methodist Church South lost fully half of its black members. By 1870 the Negro Baptist Church had increased its membership threefold when compared to the membership in 1850, and the African Methodist Episcopal Church expanded at an even greater rate.

Independent black churches

Black churches were so important because they were the only major organizations in the African American community controlled by blacks. A white missionary reported that "the Ebony preacher who promises perfect independence from White control and direction carried the colored heart at once." Black ministers were respected leaders, and many of the black men elected to office during Reconstruction were preachers. As it had in slavery, religion offered African Americans a place of refuge in a hostile white world and provided them with hope, comfort, and a means of self-identification.

New Working Conditions

As a largely propertyless class, blacks in the postwar South had no choice but to work for white landowners. Except for paying wages, whites wanted to retain the old system of labor, including close supervision, gang labor, and physical punishment. Determined to remove all emblems of servitude, African Americans refused to work under these conditions, and they demanded time off to devote to their own interests. Convinced that working at one's own pace was part of freedom, they simply would not work as long or as hard as they had in slavery. Because of shorter

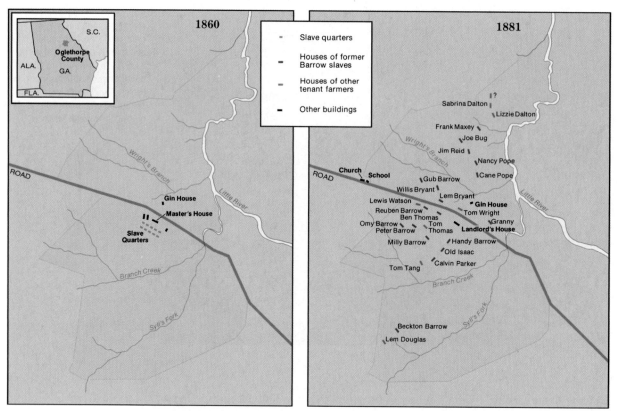

A Georgia Plantation after the War After emancipation, sharecropping became the dominant form of agricultural labor in the South. Black families no longer lived in the old slave quarters but dispersed to separate plots of land that they farmed themselves. At the end of the year each sharecropper turned over part of the crop to the white landowner.

hours and the withdrawal of children and women from the fields, work output declined by an estimated 35 percent in freedom. Blacks also refused to live in the old slave quarters located near the master's house. Instead, they erected cabins on distant parts of the plantation. Wages at first were $5 or $6 a month plus provisions and a cabin; by 1867, they had risen to an average of $10 a month.

Sharecropping

These changes eventually led to the rise of sharecropping. Under this arrangement African American families farmed separate plots of land and then at the end of the year divided the crop, normally on an equal basis, with the white landowner. Sharecropping had higher status and offered greater personal freedom than being a wage laborer. "I am not working for wages," one black farmer declared in defending his right to leave the plantation at will, "but am part owner of the crop and as [such,] I have all the rights that you or any other man has." Although black per capita agricultural income increased 40 percent in freedom, sharecropping was a harshly exploitative system in which black families often sank into perpetual debt.

The Freedmen's Bureau

The task of supervising the transition from slavery to freedom on southern plantations fell to the Freedmen's Bureau, a unique experiment in social policy supported by the federal government. Assigned the task of protecting freedpeople's economic rights, approximately 550 local agents supervised and regulated working conditions in southern agriculture after the war. The racial attitudes of Bureau agents varied widely, as did their commitment and competence. Then, too, they had to depend on the army to enforce their decisions.

Most agents encouraged or required written contracts between white planters and black laborers, specifying not only wages but also the conditions of employment. Although agents sometimes intervened to protect freedpeople from unfair treatment, they also provided important help to planters. They insisted that black laborers not desert at harvest time; they arrested those who violated their contracts or refused to sign new ones at the beginning of the year; and they preached the gospel of work and the need to be orderly and respectful. Given such attitudes, freedpeople increasingly complained that Bureau agents were mere tools of the planter class. "They are, in fact, the planters' guards, and nothing else," claimed the New Orleans *Tribune,* a black newspaper. One observer reported, "Doing justice seems to mean seeing that the blacks don't break contracts and compelling them to submit cheerfully."

Bureau's mixed record

The primary means of enforcing working conditions were the Freedmen's Courts, which Congress created in 1866 in order to avoid the discrimination African Americans received in state courts. These new courts functioned as military tribunals, and often the agent was the entire court. The sympathy black laborers received varied from state to state. In 1867 one agent summarized the Bureau's experience with the labor contract system: "It has succeeded in making the freedman work and in rendering labor secure and stable—but it has failed to secure to the Freedman his just dues or compensation."

In 1869, with the Bureau's work scarcely under way, Congress decided to shut it down, and by 1872 it had gone out of business. Despite its mixed record, it was the most effective agency in protecting blacks' civil and political rights. Its disbanding signaled the beginning of the northern retreat from Reconstruction.

End of the Bureau

Planters and a New Way of Life

Planters and other white southerners faced emancipation with dread. "All the traditions and habits of both races had been suddenly overthrown," a Tennessee planter recalled, "and neither knew just what to do, or how to accommodate themselves to the new situation."

The old ideal of a paternalistic planter, which required a facade of black subservience and affection, gave way to an emphasis on strictly economic relationships. Mary Jones, a Georgia slaveholder before the war who did more for her workers than the law required, lost all patience when two workers accused her of trickery and hauled her before a Freedmen's Bureau agent, with whom she won her case. Upon returning home, she announced to the assembled freedpeople that "I have considered them friends and treated them as such but now they were only laborers under contract, and only the law would rule between us." Only with time did planters develop new norms and standards to judge black behavior. What in 1865 had seemed insolence was viewed by the 1870s as the normal attitude of freedom.

Planters' new values

Slavery had been a complex institution that welded black and white southerners together in intimate relationships. After the war, however, planters increasingly embraced the ideology of segregation. Because emancipation significantly reduced the social distance between the races, white southerners sought

psychological separation and kept dealings with African Americans to a minimum. By the time Reconstruction ended, white planters had developed a new
way of life based on the institutions of sharecropping and segregation and undergirded by a militant white supremacy.

Although most planters kept their land, they did not regain the economic
prosperity of the prewar years. Rice plantations, which were not suitable to tenant farming, largely disappeared after the war. In addition, southern cotton grow-
ers faced increased competition from new areas such as India, Egypt, and Brazil.
Cotton prices began a long decline, and southern per capita income suffered as a
result. By 1880 the value of southern farms had slid 33 percent below the level
of 1860.

The Abandonment of Reconstruction

On Christmas Day 1875, a white acquaintance approached Charles Caldwell
on the streets of Clinton, Mississippi, and invited him into Chilton's store to have
a drink to celebrate the holiday. A former slave, Caldwell was a state senator and
the leader of the Republican party in Hinds County, Mississippi. But the black
leader's fearlessness made him a marked man. Only two months earlier, he had
been forced to flee the county to escape an armed white mob angry about a Republican barbecue he and his fellow Republicans had organized. For four days the
mob hunted down and killed nearly 40 Republican leaders for presuming to hold
a political meeting. Despite that hostility, Caldwell had returned to vote in the
November state election. Even more boldly, he had led a black militia company
through the streets to help quell the disturbances. Now, as Caldwell and his
"friend" raised their glasses in a holiday toast, a gunshot exploded through the
window. Caldwell collapsed, mortally wounded from a bullet to the back of his
head. He was taken outside, where his assassins riddled his body with bullets. He
died in the street.

Charles Caldwell shared the fate of more than a few black Republican leaders
in the South during Reconstruction. Southern whites used violence, terror, and
political assassination to challenge the federal government's commitment to sustaining Reconstruction. If northerners had boldly countered such terrorism, Reconstruction might have ended differently. But in the years following President
Johnson's impeachment trial in 1868, the influence of Radical Republicans steadily
waned. The Republican party was being drained of the crusading idealism that had
stamped its early years.

The Election of Grant

Immensely popular after the war, Ulysses S. Grant was the natural choice of Republicans to run for president in 1868. Although Grant was elected, Republicans were
shocked that despite his great military stature, his popular margin was only
300,000 votes. An estimated 450,000 black Republican votes had been cast in the
South, which meant that a majority of whites casting ballots had voted Democratic.
The 1868 election helped convince Republican leaders that an amendment securing black suffrage throughout the nation was necessary.

Fifteenth Amendment

In February 1869 Congress sent the Fifteenth Amendment to the states for ratification. It forbade any state to deny the right to vote on grounds of race,
color, or previous condition of servitude. Some Radicals had hoped to forbid

literacy or property requirements to protect blacks further. Others wanted a simple declaration that all adult male citizens had the right to vote. But the moderates in the party were aware that many northerners were increasingly worried about the number of immigrants who were again entering the country and wanted to be able to restrict their voting. As a result, the final amendment left loopholes that eventually allowed southern states to disfranchise African Americans. The amendment was ratified in March 1870, aided by the votes of the four southern states that had not completed the process of Reconstruction and thus were also required to endorse this amendment before being readmitted to Congress.

Lucy Stone, a major figure in the women's rights movement.

Proponents of women's suffrage were gravely disappointed when Congress refused to prohibit voting discrimination on the basis of sex as well as race. The

Women's suffrage rejected

Women's Loyal League, led by Elizabeth Cady Stanton and Susan B. Anthony, had pressed for first the Fourteenth and then the Fifteenth Amendment to recognize women's public role. But even most Radicals, contending that black rights had to be ensured first, were unwilling to back women's suffrage. The Fifteenth Amendment ruptured the feminist movement. Although disappointed that women were not included in its provisions, Lucy Stone and the American Woman Suffrage Association urged ratification. Anthony and Stanton, on the other hand, broke with their former allies among the Radicals, denounced the amendment, and organized the National Woman Suffrage Association to work for passage of a new amendment giving women the ballot. The division hampered the women's rights movement for decades to come.

The Grant Administration

Ulysses Grant was ill at ease with the political process. His simple, quiet manner, while superb for commanding armies, did not serve him as well in public life, and his well-known resolution withered when he was uncertain of his goal. Also, he lacked the moral commitment to make Reconstruction succeed.

A series of scandals wracked Grant's presidency. Although Grant did not profit personally, he remained loyal to his friends and displayed little zeal to root out wrongdoing. His relatives were implicated in a scheme to corner the gold market, and his private secretary escaped conviction for stealing federal whiskey revenues only because Grant interceded on his behalf. His secretary of war resigned to avoid impeachment. James W. Grimes, one of the party's founders, denounced the Republican party under Grant as "the most corrupt and debauched political party that has ever existed."

Corruption under Grant

Nor was Congress immune from the lowered tone of public life. In such a climate ruthless state machines, led by men who favored the status quo, came to dominate the party. Office and power became ends in themselves, and party leaders worked in close cooperation with northern industrial interests. The few Radicals still active in public life increasingly repudiated Grant and the Republican governments in the South. Congress in 1872 passed an amnesty act, removing the restrictions of the Fourteenth Amendment on officeholding except for about 200 to 300 ex-Confederate leaders.

Grant swings from a trapeze while supporting a number of associates accused of corruption. Among those holding on are Secretary of the Navy George M. Robeson (top center), who was accused of accepting bribes in the awarding of navy contracts; Secretary of War William W. Belknap (top right), who was forced to resign for selling Indian post traderships; and the president's private secretary, Orville Babcock (bottom right), who was implicated in the Whiskey Ring scandal. Although not personally involved in the scandals during his administration, Grant was reluctant to dismiss from office supporters accused of wrongdoing.

As corruption in both the North and the South worsened, reformers became more interested in cleaning up government than in protecting blacks' rights. These liberal Republicans opposed the continued presence of the army in the South, denounced the corruption of southern governments as well as the national government, and advocated free trade and civil service reform. In 1872 they broke with the Republican party and nominated for president Horace Greeley, the editor of the New York *Tribune*. A onetime Radical, Greeley had become disillusioned with Reconstruction and urged a restoration of home rule in the South as well as adoption of civil service reform. Democrats decided to back the Liberal Republican ticket. The Republicans renominated Grant, who, despite the defection of a number of prominent Radicals, won an easy victory with 56 percent of the popular vote.

Growing Northern Disillusionment

During Grant's second term, Congress passed the Civil Rights Act of 1875, the last major piece of Reconstruction legislation. This law prohibited racial discrimination in all public accommodations, transportation, places of amusement, and juries. At the same time, Congress rejected a ban on segregation in public schools, which was almost universally practiced in the North as well as the South. Although some railroads, streetcars, and public accommodations in both sections were desegregated after the bill passed, the federal government made little attempt to enforce the law, and it was ignored throughout most of the South. In 1883 the Supreme Court struck down its provisions except the one relating to juries.

Civil Rights Act of 1875

Despite passage of the Civil Rights Act, many northerners were growing disillusioned with Reconstruction. They were repelled by the corruption of the southern governments, they were tired of the violence and disorder in the South, and they had little faith in black Americans. William Dodge, a wealthy New York capitalist and an influential Republican, wrote in 1875 that the South could never develop its resources "till confidence in her state governments can be restored, and this will never be done by federal bayonets." It had been a mistake, he went on, to make black southerners feel "that the United States government was their special friend, rather than those . . . among whom they must live and for whom they must work." He concluded, "We have tried this long enough. Now let the South alone."

Waning northern concern

As the agony of the war became more distant, the Panic of 1873 diverted public attention from Reconstruction to economic issues. In the severe depression that followed over the next four years, some 3 million people found themselves out of work. Congress became caught up in the question of whether printing greenbacks would help the economy prosper. Battered by the panic and the corruption issue, the Republicans lost a shocking 77 seats in Congress in the 1874 elections, and along with them control of the House of Representatives for the first time since 1861. "The truth is our people are tired out with the worn out cry of 'Southern outrages'!!" one Republican concluded. "Hard times and heavy taxes make them wish the 'ever lasting nigger' were in hell or Africa." Republicans spoke more and more about cutting loose the unpopular southern governments.

Depression and Democratic resurgence

The Triumph of White Supremacy

As northern commitment to Reconstruction waned, southern Democrats set out to overthrow the remaining Radical governments. Already white Republicans in the South felt heavy pressure to desert their party. In Mississippi one party member justified his decision to leave on the grounds that otherwise he would have "to live a life of social oblivion" and his children would have no future.

Racism

To poor white southerners who lacked social standing, the Democratic appeal to racial solidarity offered great comfort. As one explained, "I may be poor and my manners may be crude, but . . . because I am a white man, I have a right to be treated with respect by Negroes. . . . That I am poor is not as important as that I am a white man; and no Negro is ever going to forget that he is not a white man." The large landowners and other wealthy groups that led southern Democrats objected less to black southerners voting. These well-to-do leaders did not face social and economic competition from African Americans, and in any case, they were confident that if outside influences were removed, they could control the black vote.

This campaign badge from 1868 made the sentiments of white Democrats clear.

OUR TICKET.

For President   Vice President

SEYMOUR.   BLAIR.

OUR MOTTO:

THIS IS A WHITE MAN'S COUNTRY: LET WHITE MEN RULE.

Entered according to Act of Congress, A. D. 1868, by
B. W. Hitchcock, in the Clerk's office of the U. S.
District Court for the Southern Dist. of New York.

Democrats also resorted to economic pressure to undermine Republican power. In heavily black counties, white observers at the polls took down the names of black residents who cast Republican ballots and published them in local newspapers. Planters were urged to discharge black tenants who persisted in voting Republican. But terror and violence provided the most effective means to overthrow the Radical regimes. A number of paramilitary organizations broke up Republican meetings, terrorized white and black Republicans, assassinated Republican leaders, and prevented black citizens from voting. The most famous was the Ku Klux Klan, founded in 1866 in Tennessee. It and similar groups functioned as unofficial arms of the Democratic party.

Congress finally moved to break the power of the Klan with the Force Act of 1870 and the Ku Klux Klan Act of 1871. These laws made it a felony to interfere with the right to vote; they also authorized use of the army and suspension of the writ of habeas corpus. The Grant administration eventually suspended the writ of habeas corpus in nine South Carolina counties and arrested hundreds of suspected Klan members throughout the South. Although these actions weakened the Klan, terrorist organizations continued to operate underground.

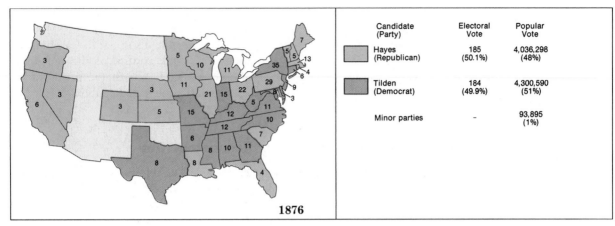

Candidate (Party)	Electoral Vote	Popular Vote
Hayes (Republican)	185 (50.1%)	4,036,298 (48%)
Tilden (Democrat)	184 (49.9%)	4,300,590 (51%)
Minor parties	–	93,895 (1%)

1876

Election of 1876

Then in 1875 Democrats inaugurated what became known as the Mississippi Plan, the decision to use as much violence as necessary to carry the state election. Several local papers trumpeted, "Carry the election peaceably if we can, forcibly if we must." When Republican governor Adelbert Ames requested federal troops to stop the violence, Grant's advisers warned that sending troops to Mississippi would cost the party the Ohio election. In the end the administration told Ames to depend on his own forces. Bolstered by terrorism, the Democrats swept the election in Mississippi. Violence and intimidation prevented as many as 60,000 black and white Republicans from voting, converting the normal Republican majority into a Democratic majority of 30,000. Mississippi had been "redeemed."

Mississippi Plan

The Disputed Election of 1876

With Republicans on the defensive across the nation, the 1876 presidential election was crucial to the final overthrow of Reconstruction. The Republicans nominated Ohio governor Rutherford B. Hayes to oppose Samuel Tilden of New York. Once again, violence prevented many Republican votes, this time an estimated quarter of a million, from being cast in the South. Tilden had a clear majority of 250,000 in the popular vote, but the outcome in the Electoral College was in doubt because both parties claimed South Carolina, Florida, and Louisiana, the only reconstructed states still in Republican hands. Hayes needed all three states to be elected, for even without them, Tilden had amassed 184 electoral votes, one short of a majority. Republican canvassing boards in power disqualified enough Democratic votes to give each state to Hayes.

To arbitrate the disputed returns, Congress established a 15-member electoral commission: 5 members each from the Senate, the House, and the Supreme Court. By a straight party vote of 8–7, the commission awarded the disputed electoral votes—and the presidency—to Hayes.

When angry Democrats threatened a filibuster to prevent the electoral votes from being counted, key Republicans met with southern Democrats on February 26 at the Wormley Hotel in Washington. There they reached an informal understanding, later known as the Compromise of 1877. Hayes's supporters agreed to withdraw federal troops from the South and not oppose the new Democratic state

Compromise of 1877

governments. For their part, southern Democrats dropped their opposition to Hayes's election and pledged to respect African American rights.

Redeemers take control

Without federal support, the Republican governments in South Carolina and Louisiana promptly collapsed, and Democrats took control of the remaining states of the Confederacy. By 1877, the entire South was in the hands of the Redeemers, as they called themselves. Reconstruction and Republican rule had come to an end.

Racism and the Failure of Reconstruction

Reconstruction failed for a multitude of reasons. The reforming impulse that had created the Republican party in the 1850s had been battered and worn down by the war. The new materialism of industrial America inspired in many Americans a jaded cynicism about the corruption of the age and a desire to forget uncomfortable issues. In the South, African American voters and leaders inevitably lacked a certain amount of education and experience; elsewhere, Republicans were divided over policies and options.

Yet beyond these obstacles, the sad fact remains that the ideals of Reconstruction were most clearly defeated by the deep-seated racism that permeated American life. Racism was why the white South so unrelentingly resisted Reconstruction. Racism was why most white northerners had little interest in black rights except as a means to preserve the Union or to safeguard the Republic. Racism was why northerners were willing to write off Reconstruction and with it the welfare of African Americans. While Congress might pass a constitutional amendment abolishing slavery, it could not overturn at a stroke the social habits of two centuries.

Certainly the political equations of power, in the long term, had been changed. The North had fought fiercely during the war to preserve the Union. In doing so, it

Benjamin Montgomery, together with his sons, purchased Jefferson Davis's plantation along the Mississippi River after the war. A former slave, Montgomery pursued the dream of black economic independence by renting land to black farmers at Davis Bend.

had secured the power to dominate the economic and political destiny of the nation. With the overthrow of Reconstruction, the white South had won back some of the power it had lost in 1865. But even with white supremacy triumphant, African Americans did not return to the social position they had occupied before the war. They were no longer slaves, and black southerners who walked dusty roads in search of family members, sent their children to school, or worshiped in churches they controlled knew what a momentous change emancipation was. Even under the exploitative sharecropping system, black income rose significantly in freedom. Then, too, the principles of "equal protection" and "due process of law" had been written into the Constitution. These guarantees would be available for later generations to use in championing once again the Radicals' goal of racial equality.

End of the Davis Bend experiment

But this was a struggle left to future reformers. For the time being, the clear trend was away from change or hope—especially for former slaves like Benjamin Montgomery and his sons, the owners of the old Davis plantations in Mississippi. In the 1870s bad crops, lower cotton prices, and falling land values undermined the Montgomerys' financial position, and in 1875 Jefferson Davis sued to have the sale of Brierfield invalidated.

A lower court ruled against Davis, since he had never received legal title to the plantation. Davis appealed to the state supreme court, which, following the overthrow of Mississippi's Radical government, had a white conservative majority. In a politically motivated decision, the court awarded Brierfield to Davis in 1878, and the Montgomerys lost Hurricane as well. The final outcome was not without bitter irony. In applying for restoration of his property after the war, Joseph Davis had convinced skeptical federal officials that he—and not his younger brother—held legal title to Brierfield. Had they decided instead that the plantation belonged to Jefferson Davis, it would have been confiscated.

But the waning days of Reconstruction were times filled with such ironies: of governments "redeemed" by violence, of Fourteenth Amendment rights designed to protect black people being used by conservative courts to protect giant corporations, of reformers taking up other causes. Disowned by its northern supporters and unmourned by public opinion, Reconstruction was over.

chapter summary

Presidents Abraham Lincoln and Andrew Johnson and the Republican-dominated Congress each developed a program of Reconstruction to quickly restore the Confederate states to the Union.

- Lincoln's 10 percent plan required that 10 percent of qualified voters from 1860 swear an oath of loyalty to begin organizing state government.

- Following Lincoln's assassination, Andrew Johnson changed Lincoln's terms and lessened Reconstruction's requirements.

- The more radical Congress repudiated Johnson's state governments and eventually enacted its own program of Reconstruction, which included the principle of black suffrage.

  - Congress passed the Fourteenth and Fifteenth Amendments and also extended the life of the Freedmen's Bureau, a unique experiment in social welfare.

  - Congress rejected land reform, however, which would have provided the freedpeople with a greater economic stake.

  - The effort to remove Johnson from office through impeachment failed.

- The Radical governments in the South, led by black and white southerners and transplanted northerners, compiled a mixed record on matters such as racial equality, education, economic issues, and corruption.

- Reconstruction was a time of both joy and frustration for former slaves.

  - Former slaves took steps to reunite their families and establish black-controlled churches.

  - They evidenced a widespread desire for land and education.

  - Black resistance to the old system of labor led to the adoption of sharecropping.

  - The Freedmen's Bureau fostered these new working arrangements and also the beginnings of black education in the South.

- Northern public opinion became disillusioned with Reconstruction during the presidency of Ulysses S. Grant.

- Southern whites used violence, economic coercion, and racism to overthrow the Republican state governments.

- In 1877 Republican leaders agreed to end Reconstruction in exchange for Rutherford B. Hayes's election as president.

- Racism played a key role in the eventual failure of Reconstruction.

interactive learning

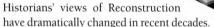

The Primary Source Investigator CD-ROM offers the following materials related to this chapter:

- Interactive maps: **Election of 1876** (M7) and **Barrow Plantation** (M18)

- A collection of primary sources concerning the United States at the close of the Civil War, including an

interview with an ex-slave and an engraving of people celebrating the anniversary of the Emancipation Proclamation. Other sources demonstrate the extent to which African Americans' lives changed after the war and during Reconstruction, such as a picture of a black schoolhouse and a number of firsthand accounts of life after slavery. Several documents reveal increased attempts to restrict and punish newly emancipated slaves during Reconstruction, including examples of the black codes passed by many southern states.

additional reading

Historians' views of Reconstruction have dramatically changed in recent decades. Modern studies offer a more sympathetic assessment of Reconstruction and the experience of African Americans. Indicative of this trend is Eric Foner, *Reconstruction* (1988), the fullest modern treatment. Foner devotes considerable attention to black southerners' experiences but seriously neglects the North. The book is also available in an abridged edition.

Eric L. McKitrick, *Andrew Johnson and Reconstruction* (1966), while very critical of Johnson and his policies, argues that impeachment was unjustified. A different conclusion is reached by Michael Les Benedict in *The Impeachment and Trial of Andrew Johnson* (1973), which is the most thorough treatment of Congress's effort to remove Johnson from office. Political affairs in the South during Reconstruction are examined in Dan T. Carter, *When the War Was Over* (1985), and

Thomas Holt, *Black over White* (1977), an imaginative study of black political leadership in South Carolina. Leon Litwack, *Been in the Storm So Long* (1979), and Willie Lee Rose, *Rehearsal for Reconstruction* (1964), sensitively analyze former slaves' transition to freedom, and James L. Roark, *Masters without Slaves* (1977), discusses former slaveholders' adjustment to the end of slavery. Two excellent studies of changing labor relations in southern agriculture are Julie Saville, *The Work of Reconstruction* (1995), and John Rodrique, *Reconstruction in the Cane Fields* (2001). George R. Bentley, *A History of the Freedmen's Bureau* (1955), is a sympathetic treatment of that unique institution; Donald Nieman, *To Set the Law in Motion: The Freedmen's Bureau and the Legal Rights of Blacks, 1865–1868* (1979), is more critical. Different perspectives on the overthrow of Reconstruction appear in William Gillette, *Retreat from Reconstruction, 1869–1879* (1980), which focuses on national politics and the federal government, and in Michael Perman, *The Road to Redemption* (1984), which looks at developments in the South. For a fuller list of readings, see the Bibliography at www.mhhe.com/davidsonnation5.

significant events

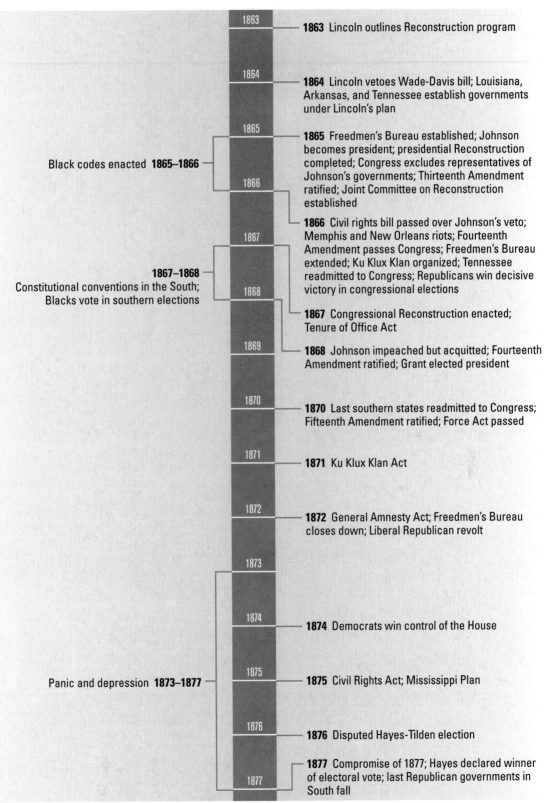

1863 1863 Lincoln outlines Reconstruction program

1864 1864 Lincoln vetoes Wade-Davis bill; Louisiana, Arkansas, and Tennessee establish governments under Lincoln's plan

1865

Black codes enacted **1865–1866**

1866

1865 Freedmen's Bureau established; Johnson becomes president; presidential Reconstruction completed; Congress excludes representatives of Johnson's governments; Thirteenth Amendment ratified; Joint Committee on Reconstruction established

1866 Civil rights bill passed over Johnson's veto; Memphis and New Orleans riots; Fourteenth Amendment passes Congress; Freedmen's Bureau extended; Ku Klux Klan organized; Tennessee readmitted to Congress; Republicans win decisive victory in congressional elections

1867

1867–1868
Constitutional conventions in the South; Blacks vote in southern elections

1868

1867 Congressional Reconstruction enacted; Tenure of Office Act

1869

1868 Johnson impeached but acquitted; Fourteenth Amendment ratified; Grant elected president

1870

1870 Last southern states readmitted to Congress; Fifteenth Amendment ratified; Force Act passed

1871

1871 Ku Klux Klan Act

1872

1872 General Amnesty Act; Freedmen's Bureau closes down; Liberal Republican revolt

1873

1874

1874 Democrats win control of the House

Panic and depression **1873–1877**

1875

1875 Civil Rights Act; Mississippi Plan

1876

1876 Disputed Hayes-Tilden election

1877

1877 Compromise of 1877; Hayes declared winner of electoral vote; last Republican governments in South fall

559

The Declaration of Independence

In Congress, July 4, 1776,

THE UNANIMOUS DECLARATION OF THE THIRTEEN UNITED STATES OF AMERICA

When, in the course of human events, it becomes necessary for one people to dissolve the political bands which have connected them with another, and to assume, among the powers of the earth, the separate and equal station to which the laws of nature and of nature's God entitle them, a decent respect to the opinions of mankind requires that they should declare the causes which impel them to the separation.

We hold these truths to be self-evident, that all men are created equal; that they are endowed by their Creator with certain unalienable rights; that among these, are life, liberty, and the pursuit of happiness. That, to secure these rights, governments are instituted among men, deriving their just powers from the consent of the governed; that, whenever any form of government becomes destructive of these ends, it is the right of the people to alter or to abolish it, and to institute a new government, laying its foundation on such principles, and organizing its powers in such form, as to them shall seem most likely to effect their safety and happiness. Prudence, indeed, will dictate that governments long established, should not be changed for light and transient causes; and, accordingly, all experience hath shown, that mankind are more disposed to suffer, while evils are sufferable, than to right themselves by abolishing the forms to which they are accustomed. But, when a long train of abuses and usurpations, pursuing invariably the same object, evinces a design to reduce them under absolute despotism, it is their right, it is their duty, to throw off such government and to provide new guards for their future security. Such has been the patient sufferance of these colonies, and such is now the necessity which constrains them to alter their former systems of government. The history of the present King of Great Britain is a history of repeated injuries and usurpations, all having, in direct object, the establishment of an absolute tyranny over these States. To prove this, let facts be submitted to a candid world:

He has refused his assent to laws the most wholesome and necessary for the public good.

He has forbidden his governors to pass laws of immediate and pressing importance, unless suspended in their operation till his assent should be obtained; and, when so suspended, he has utterly neglected to attend to them.

He has refused to pass other laws for the accommodation of large districts of people, unless those people would relinquish the right of representation in the legislature; a right inestimable to them, and formidable to tyrants only.

He has called together legislative bodies at places unusual, uncomfortable, and distant from the depository of their public records, for the sole purpose of fatiguing them into compliance with his measures.

He has dissolved representative houses repeatedly for opposing, with manly firmness, his invasions on the rights of the people.

He has refused, for a long time after such dissolutions, to cause others to be elected; whereby the legislative powers, incapable of annihilation, have returned to the people at large for their exercise; the state remaining, in the meantime, exposed to all the danger of invasion from without, and convulsions within.

He has endeavored to prevent the population of these States; for that purpose, obstructing the laws for naturalization of foreigners, refusing to pass others to encourage their migration hither, and raising the conditions of new appropriations of lands.

He had obstructed the administration of justice, by refusing his assent to laws for establishing judiciary powers.

He has made judges dependent on his will alone, for the tenure of their offices, and the amount and payment of their salaries.

He has erected a multitude of new offices, and sent hither swarms of officers to harass our people, and eat out their substance.

He has kept among us, in time of peace, standing armies, without the consent of our legislatures.

He has affected to render the military independent of, and superior to, the civil power.

He has combined, with others, to subject us to a jurisdiction foreign to our Constitution, and unacknowledged by our laws; giving his assent to their acts of pretended legislation:

For quartering large bodies of armed troops among us:

For protecting them by a mock trial, from punishment, for any murders which they should commit on the inhabitants of these States:

For cutting off our trade with all parts of the world:

For imposing taxes on us without our consent:

For depriving us, in many cases, of the benefit of trial by jury:

For transporting us beyond seas to be tried for pretended offences:

For abolishing the free system of English laws in a neighboring province, establishing therein an arbitrary government, and enlarging its boundaries, so as to render it at once an example and fit instrument for introducing the same absolute rule into these colonies:

For taking away our charters, abolishing our most valuable laws, and altering, fundamentally, the powers of our governments:

For suspending our own legislatures, and declaring themselves invested with power to legislate for us in all cases whatsoever.

He has abdicated government here, by declaring us out of his protection, and waging war against us.

He has plundered our seas, ravaged our coasts, burnt our towns, and destroyed the lives of our people.

He is, at this time, transporting large armies of foreign mercenaries to complete the works of death, desolation, and tyranny, already begun, with circumstances of cruelty and perfidy scarcely paralleled in the most barbarous ages, and totally unworthy the head of a civilized nation.

He has constrained our fellow citizens, taken captive on the high seas, to bear arms against their country, to become the executioners of their friends, and brethren, or to fall themselves by their hands.

He has excited domestic insurrections amongst us, and has endeavored to bring on the inhabitants of our frontiers, the merciless Indian savages, whose known rule of warfare is an undistinguished destruction of all ages, sexes, and conditions.

In every stage of these oppressions, we have petitioned for redress, in the most humble terms; our repeated petitions have been answered only by repeated injury. A prince, whose character is thus marked by every act which may define a tyrant, is unfit to be the ruler of a free people.

Nor have we been wanting in attention to our British brethren. We have warned them, from time to time, of attempts made by their legislature to extend an unwarrantable jurisdiction over us. We have reminded them of the circumstances of our emigration and settlement here. We have appealed to their native justice and magnanimity, and we have conjured them, by the ties of our common kindred, to disavow these usurpations, which would inevitably interrupt our connections and correspondence. They, too, have been deaf to the voice of justice and consanguinity. We must, therefore, acquiesce in the necessity which denounces our separation, and hold them as we hold the rest of mankind, enemies in war, in peace, friends.

We, therefore, the representatives of the United States of America, in general Congress assembled, appealing to the Supreme Judge of the world for the rectitude of our intentions, do, in the name, and by the authority of the good people of these colonies, solemnly publish and declare, that these united colonies are, and of right ought to be, free and independent states: that they are absolved from all allegiance to the British Crown, and that all political connection between them and the state of Great Britain is, and ought to be, totally dissolved; and that, as free and independent states, they have full power to levy war, conclude peace, contract alliances, establish commerce, and to do all other acts and things which independent states may of right do. And, for the support of this declaration, with a firm reliance on the protection of Divine Providence, we mutually pledge to each other our lives, our fortunes, and our sacred honor.

The foregoing Declaration was, by order of Congress, engrossed, and signed by the following members:

JOHN HANCOCK

New Hampshire	New York	Delaware	North Carolina
Josiah Bartlett	William Floyd	Caesar Rodney	William Hooper
William Whipple	Philip Livingston	George Read	Joseph Hewes
Matthew Thornton	Francis Lewis	Thomas M'Kean	John Penn
	Lewis Morris		

Massachusetts Bay	New Jersey	Maryland	South Carolina
Samuel Adams	Richard Stockton	Samuel Chase	Edward Rutledge
John Adams	John Witherspoon	William Paca	Thomas Heyward, Jr.
Robert Treat Paine	Francis Hopkinson	Thomas Stone	Thomas Lynch, Jr.
Elbridge Gerry	John Hart	Charles Carroll, of Carrollton	Arthur Middleton
	Abraham Clark		

Rhode Island
Stephen Hopkins
William Ellery

Connecticut
Roger Sherman
Samuel Huntington
William Williams
Oliver Wolcott

Pennsylvania
Robert Morris
Benjamin Rush
Benjamin Franklin
John Morton
George Clymer
James Smith
George Taylor
James Wilson
George Ross

Virginia
George Wythe
Richard Henry Lee
Thomas Jefferson
Benjamin Harrison
Thomas Nelson, Jr.
Francis Lightfoot Lee
Carter Braxton

Georgia
Button Gwinnett
Lyman Hall
George Walton

Resolved, That copies of the Declaration be sent to the several assemblies, conventions, and committees, or councils of safety, and to the several commanding officers of the continental troops; that it be proclaimed in each of the United States, at the head of the army.

The Constitution of the United States of America[1]

We the People of the United States, in Order to form a more perfect Union, establish Justice, insure domestic Tranquility, provide for the common defence, promote the general Welfare, and secure the Blessings of Liberty to ourselves and our Posterity, do ordain and establish this CONSTITUTION for the United States of America.

ARTICLE I

Section 1. All legislative Powers herein granted shall be vested in a Congress of the United States, which shall consist of a Senate and House of Representatives.

Section 2. The House of Representatives shall be composed of Members chosen every second Year by the People of the several States, and the Electors in each State shall have the Qualifications requisite for Electors of the most numerous Branch of the State Legislature.

No Person shall be a Representative who shall not have attained to the Age of twenty-five Years, and been seven Years a Citizen of the United States, and who shall not, when elected, be an Inhabitant of that State in which he shall be chosen.

[Representatives and direct Taxes[2] shall be apportioned among the several States which may be included within this Union, according to their respective Numbers, which shall be determined by adding to the whole Number of free Persons, including those bound to Service for a Term of Years, and excluding Indians not taxed, three fifths of all other Persons.][3] The actual Enumeration shall be made within three Years after the first Meeting of the Congress of the United States, and within every subsequent Term of ten Years, in such Manner as they shall by Law direct. The Number of Representatives shall not exceed one for every thirty Thousand, but each State shall have at Least one Representative; and until such enumeration shall be made, the State of New Hampshire shall be entitled to chuse three, Massachusetts eight, Rhode-Island and Providence Plantations one, Connecticut five, New York six, New Jersey four, Pennsylvania eight, Delaware one, Maryland six, Virginia ten, North Carolina five, South Carolina five, and Georgia three.

When vacancies happen in the Representation from any State, the Executive Authority thereof shall issue Writs of Election to fill such Vacancies.

The House of Representatives shall chuse their Speaker and other Officers; and shall have the sole Power of Impeachment.

Section 3. The Senate of the United States shall be composed of two Senators from each State, chosen by the Legislature thereof, for six Years; and each Senator shall have one Vote.

Immediately after they shall be assembled in Consequence of the first Election, they shall be divided as equally as may be into three Classes. The Seats of the Senators of the first Class shall be vacated at the Expiration of the second Year, of the second Class at the Expiration of the fourth Year, and of the third Class at the Expiration of the sixth Year, so that one-third may be chosen every second Year; and if Vacancies happen by Resignation, or otherwise, during the Recess of the Legislature of any State, the Executive thereof may make temporary Appointments until the next Meeting of the Legislature, which shall then fill such Vacancies.

No Person shall be a Senator who shall not have attained to the Age of thirty Years, and been nine Years a Citizen of the United States, and who shall not, when elected, be an Inhabitant of that State for which he shall be chosen.

The Vice President of the United States shall be President of the Senate, but shall have no vote, unless they be equally divided.

The Senate shall chuse their other Officers, and also a President pro tempore, in the absence of the Vice President, or when he shall exercise the Office of President of the United States.

The Senate shall have the sole Power to try all Impeachments. When sitting for that purpose they shall be on Oath or Affirmation. When the President of the United States is tried, the Chief Justice shall preside: And no person shall be convicted without the Concurrence of two thirds of the Members present.

Judgment in Cases of Impeachment shall not extend further than to removal from Office, and disqualification to hold and enjoy any Office of honor, Trust, or Profit under the United States: but the Party convicted shall nevertheless be liable and subject to Indictment, Trial, Judgment, and Punishment, according to Law.

Section 4. The Times, Places and Manner of holding Elections for Senators and Representatives, shall be prescribed in each State by the Legislature thereof; but the Congress may at any time by Law make or alter such Regulations, except as to the Places of Chusing Senators.

---

[1]This version follows the original Constitution in capitalization and spelling. It is adapted from the text published by the United States Department of the Interior, Office of Education.

[2]Altered by the Sixteenth Amendment.

[3]Negated by the Fourteenth Amendment.

The Congress shall assemble at least once in every Year, and such Meeting shall be on the first Monday in December, unless they shall by Law appoint a different Day.

Section 5. Each House shall be the Judge of the Elections, Returns and Qualifications of its own Members, and a Majority of each shall constitute a Quorum to do Business; but a smaller number may adjourn from day to day, and may be authorized to compel the Attendance of absent Members, in such Manner, and under such Penalties, as each House may provide.

Each House may determine the Rules of its Proceedings, punish its Members for disorderly Behaviour, and, with the Concurrence of two thirds, expel a Member.

Each House shall keep a Journal of its Proceedings, and from time to time publish the same, excepting such Parts as may in their Judgment require Secrecy; and the Yeas and Nays of the Members of either House on any question shall, at the Desire of one fifth of those Present, be entered on the Journal.

Neither House, during the Session of Congress, shall, without the Consent of the other, adjourn for more than three days, nor to any other Place than that in which the two Houses shall be sitting.

Section 6. The Senators and Representatives shall receive a Compensation for their Services, to be ascertained by Law, and paid out of the Treasury of the United States. They shall in all Cases, except Treason, Felony, and Breach of the Peace, be privileged from Arrest during their Attendance at the Session of their respective Houses, and in going to and returning from the same; and for any Speech or Debate in either House, they shall not be questioned in any other Place.

No Senator or Representative shall, during the Time for which he was elected, be appointed to any civil Office under the Authority of the United States, which shall have been created, or the Emoluments whereof shall have been increased, during such time; and no Person holding any Office under the United States shall be a Member of either House during his continuance in Office.

Section 7. All Bills for raising Revenue shall originate in the House of Representatives; but the Senate may propose or concur with Amendments as on other bills.

Every Bill which shall have passed the House of Representatives and the Senate, shall, before it become a Law, be presented to the President of the United States; If he approve he shall sign it, but if not he shall return it, with his Objections, to that House in which it shall have originated, who shall enter the Objections at large on their Journal, and proceed to reconsider it. If after such Reconsideration two thirds of that House shall agree to pass the bill, it shall be sent, together with the objections, to the other House, by which it shall likewise be reconsidered, and if approved by two thirds of that House, it shall become a Law. But in all such Cases the Votes of both Houses shall be determined by Yeas and Nays, and the Names of the Persons voting for and against the Bill shall be entered on the Journal of each House respectively. If any Bill shall not be returned by the President within ten Days (Sundays excepted) after it shall have been presented to him, the Same shall be a Law, in like Manner as if he had signed it, unless the Congress by their Adjournment prevent its Return, in which Case it shall not be a Law.

Every Order, Resolution, or Vote to which the Concurrence of the Senate and House of Representatives may be necessary (except on a question of Adjournment) shall be presented to the President of the United States; and before the Same shall take Effect, shall be approved by him, or being disapproved by him, shall be repassed by two thirds of the Senate and House of Representatives, according to the Rules and Limitations prescribed in the Case of a Bill.

Section 8. The Congress shall have Power To lay and collect Taxes, Duties, Imposts and Excises, to pay the Debts and provide for the common Defence and general Welfare of the United States; but all Duties, Imposts and Excises shall be uniform throughout the United States;

To borrow money on the credit of the United States;

To regulate Commerce with foreign Nations, and among the several States, and with the Indian Tribes;

To establish an uniform rule of Naturalization, and uniform Laws on the subject of Bankruptcies throughout the United States;

To coin Money, regulate the Value thereof, and of foreign Coin, and fix the Standard of Weights and Measures;

To provide for the Punishment of counterfeiting the Securities and current Coin of the United States;

To establish Post Offices and post Roads;

To promote the Progress of Science and useful Arts, by securing for limited Times to Authors and Inventors the exclusive Right to their respective Writings and Discoveries;

To constitute Tribunals inferior to the Supreme Court;

To define and punish Piracies and Felonies committed on the high Seas, and Offenses against the Law of Nations;

To declare War, grant Letters of Marque and Reprisal, and make Rules concerning Captures on Land and Water;

To raise and support Armies, but no Appropriation of Money to that Use shall be for a longer Term than two Years;

To provide and maintain a Navy;

To make Rules for the Government and Regulation of the land and naval forces;

To provide for calling forth the Militia to execute the Laws of the Union, suppress Insurrections and repel Invasions;

To provide for organizing, arming, and disciplining the Militia, and for government such Part of them as may be employed in the Service of the United States, reserving to the States respectively, the Appointment of the Officers, and the Authority of training the Militia according to the discipline prescribed by Congress;

To exercise exclusive Legislation in all Cases whatsoever, over such District (not exceeding ten Miles square) as may, by Cession of particular States, and the acceptance of Congress, become the Seat of the Government of the United States, and to exercise like Authority over all Places purchased by the Consent of the Legislature of the State in which the Same shall be, for the Erection of Forts, Magazines, Arsenals, Dock-yards, and other needful Buildings;—-And

To make all Laws which shall be necessary and proper for carrying into Execution the foregoing Powers, and all other Powers vested by this Constitution in the Government of the United States, or in any Department or Officer thereof.

Section 9. The Migration or Importation of such Persons as any of the States now existing shall think proper to admit, shall not be prohibited by the Congress prior to the Year one thousand eight hundred and eight, but a tax or duty may be imposed on such Importation, not exceeding ten dollars for each Person.

The privilege of the Writ of Habeas Corpus shall not be suspended, unless when in Cases of Rebellion or Invasion the public Safety may require it.

No bill of Attainder or ex post facto Law shall be passed.

No capitation, or other direct, Tax shall be laid unless in Proportion to the Census or Enumeration herein before directed to be taken.

No Tax or Duty shall be laid on Articles exported from any State.

No Preference shall be given by any Regulation of Commerce or Revenue to the Ports of one State over those of another: nor shall Vessels bound to, or from, one State, be obliged to enter, clear, or pay Duties in another.

No Money shall be drawn from the Treasury, but in Consequence of Appropriations made by Law; and a regular Statement and Account of the Receipts and Expenditures of all public Money shall be published from time to time.

No Title of Nobility shall be granted by the United States: And no Person holding any Office of Profit or Trust under them, shall, without the Consent of the Congress, accept of any present, Emolument, Office, or Title, of any kind whatever, from any King, Prince, or foreign State.

Section 10. No State shall enter into any Treaty, Alliance, or Confederation; grant Letters of Marque and Reprisal; coin Money; emit Bills of Credit; make any Thing but gold and silver Coin a Tender in Payment of Debts; pass any Bill of Attainder, ex post facto Law, or Law impairing the Obligation of Contracts, or grant any Title of Nobility.

No State shall, without the Consent of the Congress, lay any Imposts or Duties on Imports or Exports, except what may be absolutely necessary for executing its inspection Laws; and the net Produce of all Duties and Imposts, laid by any State on Imports or Exports, shall be for the use of the Treasury of the United States; and all such Laws shall be subject to the Revision and Control of the Congress.

No state shall, without the Consent of Congress, lay any duty of Tonnage, keep Troops, or Ships of War in time of Peace, enter into any Agreement or Compact with another State, or

with a foreign Power, or engage in War, unless actually invaded, or in such imminent Danger as will not admit of delay.

ARTICLE II

Section 1. The executive Power shall be vested in a President of the United States of America. He shall hold his Office during the Term of four years, and, together with the Vice President, chosen for the same Term, be elected, as follows:

Each State shall appoint, in such Manner as the Legislature thereof may direct, a Number of Electors, equal to the whole Number of Senators and Representatives to which the State may be entitled in the Congress: but no Senator or Representative, or Person holding an Office of Trust or Profit under the United States, shall be appointed an Elector.

[The Electors shall meet in their respective States, and vote by Ballot for two persons, of whom one at least shall not be an Inhabitant of the same State with themselves. And they shall make a List of all the Persons voted for, and of the Number of Votes for each; which List they shall sign and certify, and transmit sealed to the Seat of the Government of the United States, directed to the President of the Senate. The President of the Senate shall, in the Presence of the Senate and House of Representatives, open all the Certificates, and the Votes shall then be counted. The Person having the greatest Number of Votes shall be the President, if such Number be a Majority of the whole Number of Electors appointed; and if there be more than one who have such Majority, and have an equal Number of Votes, then the House of Representatives shall immediately chuse by Ballot one of them for President; and if no Person have a Majority, then from the five highest on the List the said House shall in like Manner chuse the President. But in chusing the President, the Votes shall be taken by States, the Representation from each State having one Vote; a quorum for this Purpose shall consist of a Member or Members from two-thirds of the States, and a Majority of all the States shall be necessary to a Choice. In every Case, after the Choice of the President, the Person having the greatest Number of Votes of the Electors shall be the Vice President. But if there should remain two or more who have equal votes, the Senate shall chuse from them by Ballot the Vice President.][4]

The Congress may determine the Time of chusing the Electors, and the Day on which they shall give their Votes; which Day shall be the same throughout the United States.

No person except a natural-born Citizen, or a Citizen of the United States, at the time of the Adoption of this Constitution, shall be eligible to the Office of President; neither shall any Person be eligible to that Office who shall not have attained to the Age of thirty-five years, and been fourteen Years a Resident within the United States.

In Case of the Removal of the President from Office, or of his Death, Resignation, or Inability to discharge the Powers and

---

[4]Revised by the Twelfth Amendment.

Duties of the said Office, the same shall devolve on the Vice President, and the Congress may by Law provide for the Case of Removal, Death, Resignation, or Inability, both of the President and Vice President, declaring what Officer shall then act as President, and such Officer shall act accordingly, until the disability be removed, or a President shall be elected.

The President shall, at stated Times, receive for his Services a Compensation, which shall neither be increased nor diminished during the Period for which he shall have been elected, and he shall not receive within that Period any other Emolument from the United States, or any of them.

Before he enter on the execution of his Office, he shall take the following Oath or Affirmation:—"I do solemnly swear (or affirm) that I will faithfully execute the Office of President of the United States, and will, to the best of my Ability, preserve, protect, and defend the Constitution of the United States."

Section 2. The President shall be Commander in Chief of the Army and Navy of the United States, and of the Militia of the several States, when called into the actual Service of the United States; he may require the Opinion, in writing, of the principal Officer in each of the executive Departments, upon any subject relating to the Duties of their respective Offices, and he shall have Power to Grant Reprieves and Pardons for Offenses against the United States, except in Cases of Impeachment.

He shall have Power, by and with the Advice and Consent of the Senate, to make Treaties, provided two-thirds of the Senators present concur; and he shall nominate, and by and with the Advice and Consent of the Senate, shall appoint Ambassadors, other public Ministers and Consuls, Judges of the supreme Court, and all other Officers of the United States, whose Appointments are not herein otherwise provided for, and which shall be established by Law: but the Congress may by Law vest the Appointment of such inferior Officers, as they think proper, in the President alone, in the Courts of Law, or in the Heads of Departments.

The President shall have Power to fill up all Vacancies that may happen during the Recess of the Senate, by granting Commissions which shall expire at the End of their next Session.

Section 3. He shall from time to time give to the Congress Information of the State of the Union, and recommend to their Consideration such Measures as he shall judge necessary and expedient; he may, on extraordinary occasions, convene both Houses, or either of them, and in Case of Disagreement between them, with respect to the Time of Adjournment, he may adjourn them to such Time as he shall think proper; he shall receive Ambassadors and other public Ministers; he shall take care that the Laws be faithfully executed, and shall Commission all the Officers of the United States.

Section 4. The President, Vice President and all civil Officers of the United States, shall be removed from Office on Impeachment for, and Conviction of, Treason, Bribery, or other high Crimes and Misdemeanors.

ARTICLE III

Section 1. The judicial Power of the United States, shall be vested in one supreme Court, and in such inferior Courts as the Congress may from time to time ordain and establish. The Judges, both of the supreme and inferior Courts, shall hold their Offices during good Behaviour, and shall, at stated Times, receive for their Services, a Compensation, which shall not be diminished during their Continuance in Office.

Section 2. The judicial Power shall extend to all Cases, in Law and Equity, arising under this Constitution, the Laws of the United States, and Treaties made, or which shall be made, under their Authority;—to all Cases affecting ambassadors, other public ministers and consuls;—to all cases of admiralty and maritime Jurisdiction;—to Controversies to which the United States shall be a Party;—to Controversies between two or more States;—between a State and Citizens of another State;[5]—between Citizens of different States—between Citizens of the same State claiming Lands under Grants of different States, and between a State, or the Citizens thereof, and foreign States, Citizens, or Subjects.

In all Cases affecting Ambassadors, other public Ministers and Consuls, and those in which a State shall be Party, the supreme Court shall have original Jurisdiction. In all the other Cases before mentioned, the supreme Court shall have appellate Jurisdiction, both as to Law and Fact, with such Exceptions, and under such Regulations as the Congress shall make.

The trial of all Crimes, except in Cases of Impeachment, shall be by Jury; and such Trial shall be held in the State where the said Crimes shall have been committed; but when not committed within any State, the Trial shall be at such Place or Places as the Congress may by Law have directed.

Section 3. Treason against the United States, shall consist only in levying War against them, or in adhering to their Enemies, giving them Aid and Comfort. No Person shall be convicted of Treason unless on the Testimony of two Witnesses to the same overt Act, or on Confession in open Court.

The Congress shall have power to declare the Punishment of Treason, but no Attainder of Treason shall work Corruption of Blood, or Forfeiture except during the Life of the Person attainted.

ARTICLE IV

Section 1. Full Faith and Credit shall be given in each State to the public Acts, Records, and judicial Proceedings of every other State. And the Congress may by general Laws prescribe the Manner in which such Acts, Records and Proceedings shall be proved, and the Effect thereof.

---

[5]Qualified by the Eleventh Amendment.

Section 2. The Citizens of each State shall be entitled to all Privileges and Immunities of Citizens in the several States.

A Person charged in any State with Treason, Felony, or other Crime, who shall flee from Justice, and be found in another State, shall on demand of the executive Authority of the State from which he fled, be delivered up, to be removed to the State having Jurisdiction of the crime.

No Person held to Service or Labour in one State, under the Laws thereof, escaping into another, shall, in Consequence of any Law or Regulation therein, be discharged from such Service or Labour, but shall be delivered up on Claim of the Party to whom such Service or Labour may be due.

Section 3. New States may be admitted by the Congress into this Union; but no new State shall be formed or erected within the Jurisdiction of any other State; nor any State be formed by the Junction of two or more States, or parts of States, without the Consent of the Legislatures of the States concerned as well as of the Congress.

The Congress shall have Power to dispose of and make all needful Rules and Regulations respecting the Territory or other Property belonging to the United States; and nothing in this Constitution shall be so construed as to Prejudice any Claims of the United States, or of any particular State.

Section 4. The United States shall guarantee to every State in this Union a Republican Form of Government, and shall protect each of them against Invasion; and on Application of the Legislature, or of the Executive (when the Legislature cannot be convened) against domestic Violence.

ARTICLE V

The Congress, whenever two-thirds of both Houses shall deem it necessary, shall propose Amendments to this Constitution, or, on the Application of the Legislatures of two-thirds of the several States, shall call a Convention for proposing Amendments, which, in either Case, shall be valid to all Intents and Purposes, as part of this Constitution, when ratified by the Legislatures of three-fourths of the several States, or by Conventions in three-fourths thereof, as the one or the other Mode of Ratification may be proposed by the Congress; Provided that no Amendment which may be made prior to the Year One thousand eight hundred and eight shall in any Manner affect the first and fourth Clauses in the Ninth Section of the first Article; and that no State, without its Consent, shall be deprived of its equal Suffrage in the Senate.

ARTICLE VI

All Debts contracted and Engagements entered into, before the Adoption of this Constitution, shall be as valid against the United States under this Constitution, as under the Confederation.

This Constitution, and the Laws of the United States which shall be made in Pursuance thereof; and all Treaties made, or which shall be made, under the Authority of the United States, shall be the supreme Law of the Land; and the Judges in every State shall be bound thereby, any Thing in the Constitution or Laws of any State to the Contrary notwithstanding.

The Senators and Representatives before mentioned, and the Members of the several State Legislatures, and all executive and judicial Officers, both of the United States and of the several States, shall be bound by Oath or Affirmation to support this Constitution; but no religious Tests shall ever be required as a qualification to any Office or public Trust under the United States.

ARTICLE VII

The Ratification of the Conventions of nine States shall be sufficient for the Establishment of this Constitution between the States so ratifying the same.

Done in Convention by the Unanimous Consent of the States present the Seventeenth Day of September in the Year of our Lord one thousand seven hundred and Eighty seven, and of the Independence of the United States of America the Twelfth. In Witness whereof We have hereunto subscribed our Names.[6]

GEORGE WASHINGTON
PRESIDENT AND DEPUTY FROM VIRGINIA

New Hampshire
John Langdon
Nicholas Gilman

New Jersey
William Livingston
David Brearley
William Paterson
Jonathan Dayton

Delaware
George Read
Gunning Bedford, Jr.
John Dickinson
Richard Bassett
Jacob Broom

North Carolina
William Blount
Richard Dobbs Spaight
Hugh Williamson

---

[6]These are the full names of the signers, which in some cases are not the signatures on the document.

Massachusetts	**Pennsylvania**	**Maryland**	**South Carolina**
Nathaniel Gorham	Benjamin Franklin	James McHenry	John Rutledge
Rufus King	Thomas Mifflin	Daniel of St. Thomas Jenifer	Charles Cotesworth Pinckney
	Robert Morris	Daniel Carroll	Charles Pinckney
Connecticut	George Clymer		Pierce Butler
William Samuel Johnson	Thomas FitzSimons	**Virginia**	
Roger Sherman	Jared Ingersoll	John Blair	**Georgia**
	James Wilson	James Madison, Jr.	William Few
New York	Gouverneur Morris		Abraham Baldwin
Alexander Hamilton			

Articles in Addition to, and Amendment of, the Constitution of the United States of America, Proposed by Congress, and Ratified by the Legislatures of the Several States, Pursuant to the Fifth Article of the Original Constitution[7]

[AMENDMENT I]

Congress shall make no law respecting an establishment of religion, or prohibiting the free exercise thereof; or abridging the freedom of speech, or of the press; or the right of the people peaceably to assemble, and to petition the Government for a redress of grievances.

[AMENDMENT II]

A well regulated Militia, being necessary to the security of a free State, the right of the people to keep and bear Arms shall not be infringed.

[AMENDMENT III]

No Soldier shall, in time of peace, be quartered in any house, without the consent of the Owner, nor in time of war, but in a manner to be prescribed by law.

[AMENDMENT IV]

The right of the people to be secure in their persons, houses, papers, and effects, against unreasonable searches and seizures, shall not be violated, and no Warrants shall issue, but upon probable cause, supported by Oath or affirmation, and particularly describing the place to be searched, and the persons or things to be seized.

[AMENDMENT V]

No person shall be held to answer for a capital or otherwise infamous crime, unless on a presentment or indictment of a Grand Jury, except in cases arising in the land or naval forces, or in the Militia, when in actual service in time of War or public danger; nor shall any person be subject for the same offence to be twice put in jeopardy of life or limb; nor shall be compelled in any criminal case to be a witness against himself, nor be deprived of life, liberty, or property, without due process of law; nor shall private property be taken for public use, without just compensation.

[AMENDMENT VI]

In all criminal prosecutions, the accused shall enjoy the right to a speedy and public trial, by an impartial jury of the State and district wherein the crime shall have been committed, which district shall have been previously ascertained by law, and to be informed of the nature and cause of the accusation; to be confronted with the witnesses against him; to have compulsory process for obtaining witnesses in his favour, and to have the Assistance of Counsel for his defence.

[AMENDMENT VII]

In suits at common law, where the value in controversy shall exceed twenty dollars, the right of trial by jury shall be preserved, and no fact tried by a jury, shall be otherwise reexamined in any Court of the United States, than according to the rules of the common law.

[AMENDMENT VIII]

Excessive bail shall not be required, nor excessive fines imposed, nor cruel and unusual punishments inflicted.

[AMENDMENT IX]

The enumeration of the Constitution, of certain rights, shall not be construed to deny or disparage others retained by the people.

[AMENDMENT X]

The powers not delegated to the United States by the Constitution, nor prohibited by it to the States, are reserved to the States respectively, or to the people.
[Amendments I-X, in force 1791.]

[AMENDMENT XI][8]

The Judicial power of the United States shall not be construed to extend to any suit in law or equity, commenced or

---

[7]This heading appears only in the joint resolution submitting the first ten amendments, known as the Bill of Rights.

[8]Adopted in 1798.

prosecuted against one of the United States by Citizens of another State, or by Citizens or Subjects of any Foreign State.

[AMENDMENT XII][9]

The Electors shall meet in their respective States and vote by ballot for President and Vice-President, one of whom, at least, shall not be an inhabitant of the same State with themselves; they shall name in their ballots the person voted for as President, and in distinct ballots the person voted for as Vice-President, and they shall make distinct lists of all persons voted for as President, and of all persons voted for as Vice-President, and of the number of votes for each, which lists they shall sign and certify, and transmit sealed to the seat of the government of the United States, directed to the President of the Senate;—The President of the Senate shall, in the presence of the Senate and House of Representatives, open all the certificates and the votes shall then be counted;—The person having the greatest number of votes for President, shall be the President, if such number be a majority of the whole number of Electors appointed; and if no person have such majority, then from the persons having the highest numbers not exceeding three on the list of those voted for as President, the House of Representatives shall choose immediately, by ballot, the President. But in choosing the President, the votes shall be taken by states, the representation from each state having one vote; a quorum for this purpose shall consist of a member or members from two-thirds of the states, and a majority of all the states shall be necessary to a choice. And if the House of Representatives shall not choose a President whenever the right of choice shall devolve upon them, before the fourth day of March next following, then the Vice-President shall act as President, as in the case of the death or other constitutional disability of the President.—The person having the greatest number of votes as Vice-President, shall be the Vice-President, if such number be a majority of the whole number of Electors appointed, and if no person have a majority, then from the two highest numbers on the list, the Senate shall choose the Vice-President; a quorum for the purpose shall consist of two-thirds of the whole number of Senators, and a majority of the whole number shall be necessary to a choice. But no person constitutionally ineligible to the office of President shall be eligible to that of Vice-President of the United States.

[AMENDMENT XIII][10]

Section 1. Neither slavery nor involuntary servitude, except as a punishment for crime whereof the party shall have been duly convicted, shall exist within the United States, or any place subject to their jurisdiction.

Section 2. Congress shall have power to enforce this article by appropriate legislation.

[AMENDMENT XIV][11]

Section 1. All persons born or naturalized in the United States, and subject to the jurisdiction thereof, are citizens of the United States and of the State wherein they reside. No State shall abridge the privileges or immunities of citizens of the United States; nor shall any State deprive any person of life, liberty, or property, without due process of law; nor deny to any person within its jurisdiction the equal protection of the laws.

Section 2. Representatives shall be apportioned among the several States according to their respective numbers, counting the whole number of persons in each State, excluding Indians not taxed. But when the right to vote at any election for the choice of electors for President and Vice-President of the United States, Representatives in Congress, the Executive and Judicial officers of a State, or the members of the Legislature thereof, is denied to any of the male inhabitants of such State, being twenty-one years of age, and citizens of the United States, or in any way abridged, except for participation in rebellion, or other crime, the basis of representation therein shall be reduced in the proportion which the number of such male citizens shall bear to the whole number of male citizens twenty-one years of age in such State.

Section 3. No person shall be a Senator or Representative in Congress, or elector of President and Vice-President, or hold any office, civil or military, under the United States, or under any State, who, having previously taken an oath, as a member of Congress, or as an officer of the United States, or as a member of any State legislature, or as an executive or judicial officer of any State, to support the Constitution of the United States, shall have engaged in insurrection or rebellion against the same, or given aid or comfort to the enemies thereof. But Congress may by a vote of two-thirds of each House, remove such disability.

Section 4. The validity of the public debt of the United States, authorized by law, including debts incurred for payment of pensions and bounties for services in suppressing insurrection or rebellion, shall not be questioned. But neither the United States nor any State shall assume or pay any debts or obligation incurred in aid of insurrection or rebellion against the United States, or any claim for the loss or emancipation of any slave; but all such debts, obligations, and claims shall be held illegal and void.

Section 5. The Congress shall have the power to enforce, by appropriate legislation, the provisions of this article.

---

[9]Adopted in 1804.

[10]Adopted in 1865.

[11]Adopted in 1868.

[AMENDMENT XV][12]

Section 1. The right of citizens of the United States to vote shall not be denied or abridged by the United States or by any State on account of race, color, or previous condition of servitude—

Section 2. The Congress shall have power to enforce this article by appropriate legislation.

[AMENDMENT XVI][13]

The Congress shall have power to lay and collect taxes on incomes, from whatever source derived, without apportionment among the several States, and without regard to any census or enumeration.

[AMENDMENT XVII][14]

The Senate of the United States shall be composed of two Senators from each State, elected by the people thereof, for six years; and each Senator shall have one vote. The electors in each State shall have the qualifications requisite for electors of the most numerous branch of the State legislatures.

When vacancies happen in the representation of any State in the Senate, the executive authority of such State shall issue writs of election to fill such vacancies: *Provided,* That the legislature of any State may empower the executive thereof to make temporary appointments until the people fill the vacancies by election as the legislature may direct.

This amendment shall not be so construed as to affect the election or term of any Senator chosen before it becomes valid as part of the Constitution.

[AMENDMENT XVIII][15]

Section 1. After one year from the ratification of this article the manufacture, sale, or transportation of intoxicating liquors within, the importation thereof into, or the exportation thereof from the United States and all territory subject to the jurisdiction thereof for beverage purposes is hereby prohibited.

Section 2. The Congress and the several States shall have concurrent power to enforce this article by appropriate legislation.

Section 3. This article shall be inoperative unless it shall have been ratified as an amendment to the Constitution by the legislatures of the several States, as provided in the Con-

---

[12]Adopted in 1870.

[13]Adopted in 1913.

[14]Adopted in 1913.

[15]Adopted in 1918.

stitution, within seven years from the date of the submission hereof to the States by the Congress.

[AMENDMENT XIX][16]

The right of citizens of the United States to vote shall not be denied or abridged by the United States or by any State on account of sex.

Congress shall have power to enforce this article by appropriate legislation.

[AMENDMENT XX][17]

Section 1. The terms of the President and Vice-President shall end at noon on the 20th day of January, and the terms of Senators and Representatives at noon on the 3d day of January, of the years in which such terms would have ended if this article had not been ratified; and the terms of their successors shall then begin.

Section 2. The Congress shall assemble at least once in every year, and such meeting shall begin at noon on the 3d day of January, unless they shall by law appoint a different day.

Section 3. If, at the time fixed for the beginning of the term of the President, the President elect shall have died, the Vice-President elect shall become President. If a President shall not have been chosen before the time fixed for the beginning of his term or if the President elect shall have failed to qualify, then the Vice-President elect shall act as President until a President shall have qualified; and the Congress may by law provide for the case wherein neither a President elect nor a Vice-President elect shall have qualified, declaring who shall then act as President, or the manner in which one who is to act shall be selected, and such person shall act accordingly until a President or Vice-President shall have qualified.

Section 4. The Congress may by law provide for the case of the death of any of the persons from whom the House of Representatives may choose a President whenever the right of choice shall have devolved upon them, and for the case of the death of any of the persons from whom the Senate may choose a Vice-President whenever the right of choice shall have devolved upon them.

Section 5. Sections 1 and 2 shall take effect on the 15th day of October following the ratification of this article.

Section 6. This article shall be inoperative unless it shall have been ratified as an amendment to the Constitution by the legislatures of three-fourths of the several States within seven years from the date of its submission.

---

[16]Adopted in 1920.

[17]Adopted in 1933.

[AMENDMENT XXI][18]

Section 1. The eighteenth article of amendment to the Constitution of the United States is hereby repealed.

Section 2. The transportation or importation into any State, Territory, or possession of the United States for delivery or use therein of intoxicating liquors, in violation of the laws thereof, is hereby prohibited.

Section 3. This article shall be inoperative unless it shall have been ratified as an amendment to the Constitution by conventions in the several States, as provided in the Constitution, within seven years from the date of the submission hereof to the States by the Congress.

[AMENDMENT XXII][19]

No person shall be elected to the office of the President more than twice, and no person who has held the office of President, or acted as President, for more than two years of a term to which some other person was elected President shall be elected to the office of the President more than once.

But this Article shall not apply to any person holding the office of President when this Article was proposed by the Congress, and shall not prevent any person who may be holding the office of President, or acting as President, during the term within which this Article becomes operative from holding the office of President or acting as President during the remainder of such term.

This article shall be inoperative unless it shall have been ratified as an amendment to the Constitution by the legislatures of three-fourths of the several states within seven years from the date of its submission to the states by the Congress.

[AMENDMENT XXIII][20]

Section 1. The District constituting the seat of Government of the United States shall appoint in such manner as the Congress may direct:

A number of electors of President and Vice-President equal to the whole number of Senators and Representatives in Congress to which the District would be entitled if it were a State, but in no event more than the least populous State; they shall be in addition to those appointed by the States, but they shall be considered, for the purpose of the election of President and Vice-President, to be electors appointed by a State; and they shall meet in the District and perform such duties as provided by the twelfth article of amendment.

Section 2. The Congress shall have power to enforce this article by appropriate legislation.

[AMENDMENT XXIV][21]

Section 1. The right of citizens of the United States to vote in any primary or other election for President or Vice-President, for electors for President or Vice-President, or for Senator or Representative in Congress, shall not be denied or abridged by the United States or any state by reason of failure to pay any poll tax or other tax.

Section 2. The Congress shall have the power to enforce this article by appropriate legislation.

[AMENDMENT XXV][22]

Section 1. In case of the removal of the President from office or of his death or resignation, the Vice-President shall become President.

Section 2. Whenever there is a vacancy in the office of the Vice President, the President shall nominate a Vice President who shall take office upon confirmation by a majority vote of both Houses of Congress.

Section 3. Whenever the President transmits to the President Pro Tempore of the Senate and the Speaker of the House of Representatives his written declaration that he is unable to discharge the powers and duties of his office, and until he transmits to them a written declaration to the contrary, such powers and duties shall be discharged by the Vice-President as Acting President.

Section 4. Whenever the Vice-President and a majority of either the principal officers of the executive departments or of such other body as Congress may by law provide, transmit to the President Pro Tempore of the Senate and the Speaker of the House of Representatives their written declaration that the President is unable to discharge the powers and duties of his office, the Vice President shall immediately assume the powers and duties of the office as Acting President.

Thereafter, when the President transmits to the President Pro Tempore of the Senate and the Speaker of the House of Representatives his written declaration that no inability exists, he shall resume the powers and duties of his office unless the Vice President and a majority of either the principal officers of the executive departments or of such other body as Congress may by law provide,

---

[18]Adopted in 1933.

[19]Adopted in 1951.

[20]Adopted in 1961.

---

[21]Adopted in 1964.

[22]Adopted in 1967.

transmit within four days to the President Pro Tempore of the Senate and the Speaker of the House of Representatives their written declaration that the President is unable to discharge the powers and duties of his office. Thereupon Congress shall decide the issue, assembling within forty-eight hours for that purpose if not in session. If the Congress, within twenty-one days after receipt of the latter written declaration, or, if Congress is not in session, within twenty-one days after Congress is required to assemble, determines by two-thirds vote of both Houses that the President is unable to discharge the powers and duties of his office, the Vice President shall continue to discharge the same as Acting President; otherwise, the President shall resume the powers and duties of his office.

[AMENDMENT XXVI][23]

Section 1. The right of citizens of the United States, who are eighteen years of age or older, to vote shall not be denied or abridged by the United States or by any State on account of age.

Section 2. The Congress shall have power to enforce this article by appropriate legislation.

[AMENDMENT XXVII][24]

No law, varying the compensation for the services of the Senators and Representatives, shall take effect, until an election of Representatives shall have intervened.

---

[23]Adopted in 1971.

[24]Adopted in 1992.

Presidential Elections

Year	Candidates	Parties	Popular Vote	% of Popular Vote	Electoral Vote	% Voter Participation
1789	**George Washington**				69	
	John Adams				34	
	Other candidates				35	
1792	**George Washington**				132	
	John Adams				77	
	George Clinton				50	
	Other candidates				5	
1796	**John Adams**	Federalist			71	
	Thomas Jefferson	Dem.-Rep.			68	
	Thomas Pinckney	Federalist			59	
	Aaron Burr	Dem.-Rep.			30	
	Other candidates				48	
1800	**Thomas Jefferson**	Dem.-Rep.			73	
	Aaron Burr	Dem.-Rep.			73	
	John Adams	Federalist			65	
	Charles C. Pinckney	Federalist			64	
	John Jay	Federalist			1	
1804	**Thomas Jefferson**	Dem.-Rep.			162	
	Charles C. Pinckney	Federalist			14	
1808	**James Madison**	Dem.-Rep.			122	
	Charles C. Pinckney	Federalist			47	
	George Clinton	Dem.-Rep.			6	
1812	**James Madison**	Dem.-Rep.			128	
	DeWitt Clinton	Federalist			89	
1816	**James Monroe**	Dem.-Rep.			183	
	Rufus King	Federalist			34	
1820	**James Monroe**	Dem.-Rep.			231	
	John Quincy Adams	Indep.-Rep.			1	
1824	**John Quincy Adams**	Dem.-Rep.	108,740	31.0	84	26.9
	Andrew Jackson	Dem.-Rep.	153,544	43.0	99	
	Henry Clay	Dem.-Rep.	47,136	13.0	37	
	William H. Crawford	Dem.-Rep.	46,618	13.0	41	
1828	**Andrew Jackson**	Democratic	647,286	56.0	178	57.6
	John Quincy Adams	National Republican	508,064	44.0	83	
1832	**Andrew Jackson**	Democratic	688,242	54.5	219	55.4
	Henry Clay	National Republican	473,462	37.5	49	
	William Wirt	Anti-Masonic	101,051	8.0	7	
	John Floyd	Democratic			11	
1836	**Martin Van Buren**	Democratic	765,483	50.9	170	57.8
	William H. Harrison	Whig			73	
	Hugh L. White	Whig	739,795	49.1	26	
	Daniel Webster	Whig			14	
	W. P. Mangum	Whig			11	

Year	Candidates	Parties	Popular Vote	% of Popular Vote	Electoral Vote	% Voter Participation
1840	**William H. Harrison**	Whig	1,275,016	53.0	234	80.2
	Martin Van Buren	Democratic	1,129,102	47.0	60	
1844	**James K. Polk**	Democratic	1,338,464	49.6	170	78.9
	Henry Clay	Whig	1,300,097	48.1	105	
	James G. Birney	Liberty	62,300	2.3		
1848	**Zachary Taylor**	Whig	1,360,967	47.4	163	72.7
	Lewis Cass	Democratic	1,222,342	42.5	127	
	Martin Van Buren	Free Soil	291,263	10.1		
1852	**Franklin Pierce**	Democratic	1,601,117	50.9	254	69.6
	Winfield Scott	Whig	1,385,453	44.1	42	
	John P. Hale	Free Soil	155,825	5.0		
1856	**James Buchanan**	Democratic	1,832,955	45.3	174	78.9
	John C. Fremont	Republican	1,339,932	33.1	114	
	Millard Fillmore	American	871,731	21.6	8	
1860	**Abraham Lincoln**	Republican	1,866,452	39.8	180	81.2
	Stephen A. Douglas	Democratic	1,375,157	29.5	12	
	John C. Breckinridge	Democratic	847,953	18.1	72	
	John Bell	Constitutional Union	590,631	12.6	39	
1864	**Abraham Lincoln**	Republican	2,206,938	55.0	212	73.8
	George B. McClellan	Democratic	1,803,787	45.0	21	
1868	**Ulysses S. Grant**	Republican	3,013,421	52.7	214	78.1
	Horatio Seymour	Democratic	2,706,829	47.3	80	
1872	**Ulysses S. Grant**	Republican	3,596,745	55.6	286	71.3
	Horace Greeley	Democratic	2,843,446	43.9	66	
1876	**Rutherford B. Hayes**	Republican	4,036,298	48.0	185	81.8
	Samuel J. Tilden	Democratic	4,300,590	51.0	184	
1880	**James A. Garfield**	Republican	4,453,295	48.5	214	79.4
	Winfield S. Hancock	Democratic	4,414,082	48.1	155	
	James B. Weaver	Greenback-Labor	308,578	3.4		
1884	**Grover Cleveland**	Democratic	4,879,507	48.5	219	77.5
	James G. Blaine	Republican	4,850,293	48.2	182	
	Benjamin F. Butler	Greenback-Labor	175,370	1.8		
	John P. St. John	Prohibition	150,369	1.5		
1888	**Benjamin Harrison**	Republican	5,477,129	47.9	233	79.3
	Grover Cleveland	Democratic	5,537,857	48.6	168	
	Clinton B. Fisk	Prohibition	249,506	2.2		
	Anson J. Streeter	Union Labor	146,935	1.3		
1892	**Grover Cleveland**	Democratic	5,555,426	46.1	277	74.7
	Benjamin Harrison	Republican	5,182,690	43.0	145	
	James B. Weaver	People's	1,029,846	8.5	22	
	John Bidwell	Prohibition	264,133	2.2		
1896	**William McKinley**	Republican	7,104,779	52.0	271	79.3
	William J. Bryan	Democratic	6,502,925	48.0	176	
1900	**William McKinley**	Republican	7,218,491	51.7	292	73.2
	William J. Bryan	Democratic; Populist	6,356,734	45.5	155	
	John C. Wooley	Prohibition	208,914	1.5		

Year	Candidates	Parties	Popular Vote	% of Popular Vote	Electoral Vote	% Voter Participation
1904	**Theodore Roosevelt**	Republican	7,628,461	57.4	336	65.2
	Alton B. Parker	Democratic	5,084,223	37.6	140	
	Eugene V. Debs	Socialist	402,283	3.0		
	Silas C. Swallow	Prohibition	258,536	1.9		
1908	**William H. Taft**	Republican	7,675,320	51.6	321	65.4
	William J. Bryan	Democratic	6,412,294	43.1	162	
	Eugene V. Debs	Socialist	420,793	2.8		
	Eugene W. Chafin	Prohibition	253,840	1.7		
1912	**Woodrow Wilson**	Democratic	6,293,454	42.0	435	58.8
	Theodore Roosevelt	Progressive	4,119,538	28.0	88	
	William H. Taft	Republican	3,484,980	24.0	8	
	Eugene V. Debs	Socialist	900,672	6.0		
	Eugene W. Chafin	Prohibition	206,275	1.4		
1916	**Woodrow Wilson**	Democratic	9,129,606	49.4	277	61.6
	Charles E. Hughes	Republican	8,538,221	46.2	254	
	A. L. Benson	Socialist	585,113	3.2		
	J. Frank Hanly	Prohibition	220,506	1.2		
1920	**Warren G. Harding**	Republican	16,143,407	60.4	404	49.2
	James M. Cox	Democratic	9,130,328	34.2	127	
	Eugene V. Debs	Socialist	919,799	3.4		
	P. P. Christensen	Farmer-Labor	265,411	1.0		
1924	**Calvin Coolidge**	Republican	15,718,211	54.0	382	48.9
	John W. Davis	Democratic	8,385,283	28.8	136	
	Robert M. La Follette	Progressive	4,831,289	16.6	13	
1928	**Herbert C. Hoover**	Republican	21,391,381	58.2	444	56.9
	Alfred E. Smith	Democratic	15,016,443	40.9	87	
1932	**Franklin D. Roosevelt**	Democratic	22,821,857	57.4	472	56.9
	Herbert C. Hoover	Republican	15,761,841	39.7	59	
	Norman Thomas	Socialist	881,951	2.2		
1936	**Franklin D. Roosevelt**	Democratic	27,751,597	60.8	523	61.0
	Alfred M. Landon	Republican	16,679,583	36.5	8	
	William Lemke	Union	882,479	1.9		
1940	**Franklin D. Roosevelt**	Democratic	27,307,819	54.8	449	62.5
	Wendell L. Wilkie	Republican	22,321,018	44.8	82	
1944	**Franklin D. Roosevelt**	Democratic	25,606,585	53.5	432	55.9
	Thomas E. Dewey	Republican	22,014,745	46.0	99	
1948	**Harry S Truman**	Democratic	24,105,812	50.0	303	53.0
	Thomas E. Dewey	Republican	21,970,065	46.0	189	
	J. Strom Thurmond	States' Rights	1,169,021	2.0	39	
	Henry A. Wallace	Progressive	1,157,172	2.0		
1952	**Dwight D. Eisenhower**	Republican	33,936,234	55.1	442	63.3
	Adlai E. Stevenson	Democratic	27,314,992	44.4	89	
1956	**Dwight D. Eisenhower**	Republican	35,590,472	57.6	457	60.6
	Adlai E. Stevenson	Democratic	26,022,752	42.1	73	
1960	**John F. Kennedy**	Democratic	34,227,096	49.7	303	62.8
	Richard M. Nixon	Republican	34,107,646	49.6	219	
	Harry F. Byrd	Independent	501,643		15	
1964	**Lyndon B. Johnson**	Democratic	43,129,566	61.1	486	61.7
	Barry M. Goldwater	Republican	27,178,188	38.5	52	

Year	Candidates	Parties	Popular Vote	% of Popular Vote	Electoral Vote	% Voter Participation
1968	**Richard M. Nixon**	Republican	31,785,480	44.0	301	60.6
	Hubert H. Humphrey	Democratic	31,275,166	42.7	191	
	George C. Wallace	American Independent	9,906,473	13.5	46	
1972	**Richard M. Nixon**	Republican	47,169,911	60.7	520	55.2
	George S. McGovern	Democratic	29,170,383	37.5	17	
	John G. Schmitz	American	1,099,482	1.4		
1976	**Jimmy Carter**	Democratic	40,830,763	50.1	297	53.5
	Gerald R. Ford	Republican	39,147,793	48.0	240	
1980	**Ronald Reagan**	Republican	43,899,248	51.0	489	52.6
	Jimmy Carter	Democratic	35,481,432	41.0	49	
	John B. Anderson	Independent	5,719,437	7.0	0	
	Ed Clark	Libertarian	920,859	1.0	0	
1984	**Ronald Reagan**	Republican	54,451,521	58.8	525	53.3
	Walter Mondale	Democratic	37,565,334	40.5	13	
1988	**George Bush**	Republican	48,881,221	53.9	426	48.6
	Michael Dukakis	Democratic	41,805,422	46.1	111	
1992	**William J. Clinton**	Democratic	44,908,254	43.0	370	55.9
	George H. Bush	Republican	39,102,343	37.4	168	
	H. Ross Perot	Independent	19,741,065	18.9	0	
1996	**William J. Clinton**	Democratic	47,401,185	49.3	379	49
	Robert Dole	Republican	39,197,469	40.7	159	
	H. Ross Perot	Reform	8,085,294	8.4	0	
2000	**George W. Bush**	Republican	50,455,156	47.9	271	51.2
	Al Gore	Democratic	50,992,335	48.4	266	
	Ralph Nader	Green	2,882,737	2.7	0	

Presidential Administrations

The Washington Administration (1789–1797)

Vice President	John Adams	1789–1797
Secretary of State	Thomas Jefferson	1789–1793
	Edmund Randolph	1794–1795
	Timothy Pickering	1795–1797
Secretary of Treasury	Alexander Hamilton	1789–1795
	Oliver Wolcott	1795–1797
Secretary of War	Henry Knox	1789–1794
	Timothy Pickering	1795–1796
	James McHenry	1796–1797
Attorney General	Edmund Randolph	1789–1793
	William Bradford	1794–1795
	Charles Lee	1795–1797
Postmaster General	Samuel Osgood	1789–1791
	Timothy Pickering	1791–1794
	Joseph Habersham	1795–1797

The John Adams Administration (1797–1801)

Vice President	Thomas Jefferson	1797–1801
Secretary of State	Timothy Pickering	1797–1800
	John Marshall	1800–1801
Secretary of Treasury	Oliver Wolcott	1797–1800
	Samuel Dexter	1800–1801
Secretary of War	James McHenry	1797–1800
	Samuel Dexter	1800–1801
Attorney General	Charles Lee	1797–1801
Postmaster General	Joseph Habersham	1797–1801
Secretary of Navy	Benjamin Stoddert	1798–1801

The Jefferson Administration (1801–1809)

Vice President	Aaron Burr	1801–1805
	George Clinton	1805–1809
Secretary of State	James Madison	1801–1809
Secretary of Treasury	Samuel Dexter	1801
	Albert Gallatin	1801–1809
Secretary of War	Henry Dearborn	1801–1809
Attorney General	Levi Lincoln	1801–1805
	Robert Smith	1805
	John Breckinridge	1805–1806
	Caesar Rodney	1807–1809
Postmaster General	Joseph Habersham	1801
	Gideon Granger	1801–1809
Secretary of Navy	Robert Smith	1801–1809

The Madison Administration (1809–1817)

Vice President	George Clinton	1809–1813
	Elbridge Gerry	1813–1817
Secretary of State	Robert Smith	1809–1811
	James Monroe	1811–1817
Secretary of Treasury	Albert Gallatin	1809–1813
	George Campbell	1814
	Alexander Dallas	1814–1816
	William Crawford	1816–1817
Secretary of War	William Eustis	1809–1812
	John Armstrong	1813–1814
	James Monroe	1814–1815
	William Crawford	1815–1817
Attorney General	Caesar Rodney	1809–1811
	William Pinkney	1811–1814
	Richard Rush	1814–1817
Postmaster General	Gideon Granger	1809–1814
	Return Meigs	1814–1817
Secretary of Navy	Paul Hamilton	1809–1813
	William Jones	1813–1814
	Benjamin Crowninshield	1814–1817

The Monroe Administration (1817–1825)

Vice President	Daniel Tompkins	1817–1825
Secretary of State	John Quincy Adams	1817–1825
Secretary of Treasury	William Crawford	1817–1825
Secretary of War	George Graham	1817
	John C. Calhoun	1817–1825
Attorney General	Richard Rush	1817
	William Wirt	1817–1825
Postmaster General	Return Meigs	1817–1823
	John McLean	1823–1825

Secretary of Navy	Benjamin Crowninshield	1817–1818
	Smith Thompson	1818–1823
	Samuel Southard	1823–1825

The John Quincy Adams Administration (1825–1829)

Vice President	John C. Calhoun	1825–1829
Secretary of State	Henry Clay	1825–1829
Secretary of Treasury	Richard Rush	1825–1829
Secretary of War	James Barbour	1825–1828
	Peter Porter	1828–1829
Attorney General	William Wirt	1825–1829
Postmaster General	John McLean	1825–1829
Secretary of Navy	Samuel Southard	1825–1829

The Jackson Administration (1829–1837)

Vice President	John C. Calhoun	1829–1833
	Martin Van Buren	1833–1837
Secretary of State	Martin Van Buren	1829–1831
	Edward Livingston	1831–1833
	Louis McLane	1833–1834
	John Forsyth	1834–1837
Secretary of Treasury	Samuel Ingham	1829–1831
	Louis McLane	1831–1833
	William Duane	1833
	Roger B. Taney	1833–1834
	Levi Woodbury	1834–1837
Secretary of War	John H. Eaton	1829–1831
	Lewis Cass	1831–1837
	Benjamin Butler	1837
Attorney General	John M. Berrien	1829–1831
	Roger B. Taney	1831–1833
	Benjamin Butler	1833–1837
Postmaster General	William Barry	1829–1835
	Amos Kendall	1835–1837
Secretary of Navy	John Branch	1829–1831
	Levi Woodbury	1831–1834
	Mahlon Dickerson	1834–1837

The Van Buren Administration (1837–1841)

Vice President	Richard M. Johnson	1837–1841
Secretary of State	John Forsyth	1837–1841
Secretary of Treasury	Levi Woodbury	1837–1841

Secretary of War	Joel Poinsett	1837–1841
Attorney General	Benjamin Butler	1837–1838
	Felix Grundy	1838–1840
	Henry D. Gilpin	1840–1841
Postmaster General	Amos Kendall	1837–1840
	John M. Niles	1840–1841
Secretary of Navy	Mahlon Dickerson	1837–1838
	James Paulding	1838–1841

The William Harrison Administration (1841)

Vice President	John Tyler	1841
Secretary of State	Daniel Webster	1841
Secretary of Treasury	Thomas Ewing	1841
Secretary of War	John Bell	1841
Attorney General	John J. Crittenden	1841
Postmaster General	Francis Granger	1841
Secretary of Navy	George Badger	1841

The Tyler Administration (1841–1845)

Vice President	None	
Secretary of State	Daniel Webster	1841–1843
	Hugh S. Legaré	1843
	Abel P. Upshur	1843–1844
	John C. Calhoun	1844–1845
Secretary of Treasury	Thomas Ewing	1841
	Walter Forward	1841–1843
	John C. Spencer	1843–1844
	George Bibb	1844–1845
Secretary of War	John Bell	1841
	John C. Spencer	1841–1843
	James M. Porter	1843–1844
	William Wilkins	1844–1845
Attorney General	John J. Crittenden	1841
	Hugh S. Legaré	1841–1843
	John Nelson	1843–1845
Postmaster General	Francis Granger	1841
	Charles Wickliffe	1841–1845
Secretary of Navy	George Badger	1841
	Abel P. Upshur	1841
	David Henshaw	1843–1844
	Thomas Gilmer	1844
	John Y. Mason	1844–1845

The Polk Administration (1845–1849)

Vice President	George M. Dallas	1845–1849
Secretary of State	James Buchanan	1845–1849
Secretary of Treasury	Robert J. Walker	1845–1849
Secretary of War	William L. Marcy	1845–1849
Attorney General	John Y. Mason Nathan Clifford Isaac Toucey	1845–1846 1846–1848 1848–1849
Postmaster General	Cave Johnson	1845–1849
Secretary of Navy	George Bancroft John Y. Mason	1845–1846 1846–1849

The Taylor Administration (1849–1850)

Vice President	Millard Fillmore	1849–1850
Secretary of State	John M. Clayton	1849–1850
Secretary of Treasury	William Meredith	1849–1850
Secretary of War	George Crawford	1849–1850
Attorney General	Reverdy Johnson	1849–1850
Postmaster General	Jacob Collamer	1849–1850
Secretary of Navy	William Preston	1849–1850
Secretary of Interior	Thomas Ewing	1849–1850

The Fillmore Administration (1850–1853)

Vice President	None	
Secretary of State	Daniel Webster Edward Everett	1850–1852 1852–1853
Secretary of Treasury	Thomas Corwin	1850–1853
Secretary of War	Charles Conrad	1850–1853
Attorney General	John J. Crittenden	1850–1853
Postmaster General	Nathan Hall Sam D. Hubbard	1850–1852 1852–1853
Secretary of Navy	William A. Graham John P. Kennedy	1850–1852 1852–1853
Secretary of Interior	Thomas McKennan Alexander Stuart	1850 1850–1853

The Pierce Administration (1853–1857)

Vice President	William R. King	1853–1857
Secretary of State	William L. Marcy	1853–1857
Secretary of Treasury	James Guthrie	1853–1857
Secretary of War	Jefferson Davis	1853–1857
Attorney General	Caleb Cushing	1853–1857
Postmaster General	James Campbell	1853–1857
Secretary of Navy	James C. Dobbin	1853–1857
Secretary of Interior	Robert McClelland	1853–1857

The Buchanan Administration (1857–1861)

Vice President	John C. Breckinridge	1857–1861
Secretary of State	Lewis Cass Jeremiah S. Black	1857–1860 1860–1861
Secretary of Treasury	Howell Cobb Philip Thomas John A. Dix	1857–1860 1860–1861 1861
Secretary of War	John B. Floyd Joseph Holt	1857–1861 1861
Attorney General	Jeremiah S. Black Edwin M. Stanton	1857–1860 1860–1861
Postmaster General	Aaron V. Brown Joseph Holt Horatio King	1857–1859 1859–1861 1861
Secretary of Navy	Isaac Toucey	1857–1861
Secretary of Interior	Jacob Thompson	1857–1861

The Lincoln Administration (1861–1865)

Vice President	Hannibal Hamlin Andrew Johnson	1861–1865 1865
Secretary of State	William H. Seward	1861–1865
Secretary of Treasury	Samuel P. Chase William P. Fessenden Hugh McCulloch	1861–1864 1864–1865 1865
Secretary of War	Simon Cameron Edwin M. Stanton	1861–1862 1862–1865
Attorney General	Edward Bates James Speed	1861–1864 1864–1865

Postmaster General	Horatio King	1861
	Montgomery Blair	1861–1864
	William Dennison	1864–1865
Secretary of Navy	Gideon Welles	1861–1865
Secretary of Interior	Caleb B. Smith	1861–1863
	John P. Usher	1863–1865

The Andrew Johnson Administration (1865–1869)

Vice President	None	
Secretary of State	William H. Seward	1865–1869
Secretary of Treasury	Hugh McCulloch	1865–1869
Secretary of War	Edwin M. Stanton	1865–1867
	Ulysses S. Grant	1867–1868
	Lorenzo Thomas	1868
	John M. Schofield	1868–1869
Attorney General	James Speed	1865–1866
	Henry Stanbery	1866–1868
	William M. Evarts	1868–1869
Postmaster General	William Dennison	1865–1866
	Alexander Randall	1866–1869
Secretary of Navy	Gideon Welles	1865–1869
Secretary of Interior	John P. Usher	1865
	James Harlan	1865–1866
	Orville H. Browning	1866–1869

The Grant Administration (1869–1877)

Vice President	Schuyler Colfax	1869–1873
	Henry Wilson	1873–1877
Secretary of State	Elihu B. Washburne	1869
	Hamilton Fish	1869–1877
Secretary of Treasury	George S. Boutwell	1869–1873
	William Richardson	1873–1874
	Benjamin Bristow	1874–1876
	Lot M. Morrill	1876–1877
Secretary of War	John A. Rawlins	1869
	William T. Sherman	1869
	William W. Belknap	1869–1876
	Alphonso Taft	1876
	James D. Cameron	1876–1877

Attorney General	Ebenezer Hoar	1869–1870
	Amos T. Ackerman	1870–1871
	G. H. Williams	1871–1875
	Edwards Pierrepont	1875–1876
	Alphonso Taft	1876–1877
Postmaster General	John A. J. Creswell	1869–1874
	James W. Marshall	1874
	Marshall Jewell	1874–1876
	James N. Tyner	1876–1877
Secretary of Navy	Adolph E. Borie	1869
	George M. Robeson	1869–1877
Secretary of Interior	Jacob D. Cox	1869–1870
	Columbus Delano	1870–1875
	Zachariah Chandler	1875–1877

The Hayes Administration (1877–1881)

Vice President	William A. Wheeler	1877–1881
Secretary of State	William M. Evarts	1877–1881
Secretary of Treasury	John Sherman	1877–1881
Secretary of War	George W. McCrary	1877–1879
	Alex Ramsey	1879–1881
Attorney General	Charles Devens	1877–1881
Postmaster General	David M. Key	1877–1880
	Horace Maynard	1880–1881
Secretary of Navy	Richard W. Thompson	1877–1880
	Nathan Goff Jr.	1881
Secretary of Interior	Carl Schurz	1877–1881

The Garfield Administration (1881)

Vice President	Chester A. Arthur	1881
Secretary of State	James G. Blaine	1881
Secretary of Treasury	William Windom	1881
Secretary of War	Robert T. Lincoln	1881
Attorney General	Wayne MacVeagh	1881
Postmaster General	Thomas L. James	1881

Secretary of Navy	William H. Hunt	1881
Secretary of Interior	Samuel J. Kirkwood	1881

The Arthur Administration (1881–1885)

Vice President	None	
Secretary of State	F. T. Frelinghuysen	1881–1885
Secretary of Treasury	Charles J. Folger	1881–1884
	Walter Q. Gresham	1884
	Hugh McCulloch	1884–1885
Secretary of War	Robert T. Lincoln	1881–1885
Attorney General	Benjamin H. Brewster	1881–1885
Postmaster General	Timothy O. Howe	1881–1883
	Walter Q. Gresham	1883–1884
	Frank Hatton	1884–1885
Secretary of Navy	William H. Hunt	1881–1882
	William E. Chandler	1882–1885
Secretary of Interior	Samuel J. Kirkwood	1881–1882
	Henry M. Teller	1882–1885

The Cleveland Administration (1885–1889)

Vice President	Thomas A. Hendricks	1885–1889
Secretary of State	Thomas F. Bayard	1885–1889
Secretary of Treasury	Daniel Manning	1885–1887
	Charles S. Fairchild	1887–1889
Secretary of War	William C. Endicott	1885–1889
Attorney General	Augustus H. Garland	1885–1889
Postmaster General	William F. Vilas	1885–1888
	Don M. Dickinson	1888–1889
Secretary of Navy	William C. Whitney	1885–1889
Secretary of Interior	Lucius Q. C. Lamar	1885–1888
	William F. Vilas	1888–1889
Secretary of Agriculture	Norman J. Colman	1889

The Benjamin Harrison Administration (1889–1893)

Vice President	Levi P. Morton	1889–1893
Secretary of State	James G. Blaine	1889–1892
	John W. Foster	1892–1893
Secretary of Treasury	William Windom	1889–1891
	Charles Foster	1891–1893
Secretary of War	Redfield Proctor	1889–1891
	Stephen B. Elkins	1891–1893
Attorney General	William H. H. Miller	1889–1893
Postmaster General	John Wanamaker	1889–1893
Secretary of Navy	Benjamin F. Tracy	1889–1893
Secretary of Interior	John W. Noble	1889–1893
Secretary of Agriculture	Jeremiah M. Rusk	1889–1893

The Cleveland Administration (1893–1897)

Vice President	Adlai E. Stevenson	1893–1897
Secretary of State	Walter Q. Gresham	1893–1895
	Richard Olney	1895–1897
Secretary of Treasury	John G. Carlisle	1893–1897
Secretary of War	Daniel S. Lamont	1893–1897
Attorney General	Richard Olney	1893–1895
	James Harmon	1895–1897
Postmaster General	Wilson S. Bissell	1893–1895
	William L. Wilson	1895–1897
Secretary of Navy	Hilary A. Herbert	1893–1897
Secretary of Interior	Hoke Smith	1893–1896
	David R. Francis	1896–1897
Secretary of Agriculture	Julius S. Morton	1893–1897

The McKinley Administration (1897–1901)

Vice President	Garret A. Hobart	1897–1901
	Theodore Roosevelt	1901
Secretary of State	John Sherman	1897–1898
	William R. Day	1898
	John Hay	1898–1901
Secretary of Treasury	Lyman J. Gage	1897–1901

Secretary of War	Russell A. Alger	1897–1899
	Elihu Root	1899–1901
Attorney General	Joseph McKenna	1897–1898
	John W. Griggs	1898–1901
	Philander C. Knox	1901
Postmaster General	James A. Gary	1897–1898
	Charles E. Smith	1898–1901
Secretary of Navy	John D. Long	1897–1901
Secretary of Interior	Cornelius N. Bliss	1897–1899
	Ethan A. Hitchcock	1899–1901
Secretary of Agriculture	James Wilson	1897–1901

The Theodore Roosevelt Administration (1901–1909)

Vice President	Charles Fairbanks	1905–1909
Secretary of State	John Hay	1901–1905
	Elihu Root	1905–1909
	Robert Bacon	1909
Secretary of Treasury	Lyman J. Gage	1901–1902
	Leslie M. Shaw	1902–1907
	George B. Cortelyou	1907–1909
Secretary of War	Elihu Root	1901–1904
	William H. Taft	1904–1908
	Luke E. Wright	1908–1909
Attorney General	Philander C. Knox	1901–1904
	William H. Moody	1904–1906
	Charles J. Bonaparte	1906–1909
Postmaster General	Charles E. Smith	1901–1902
	Henry C. Payne	1902–1904
	Robert J. Wynne	1904–1905
	George B. Cortelyou	1905–1907
	George von L. Meyer	1907–1909
Secretary of Navy	John D. Long	1901–1902
	William H. Moody	1902–1904
	Paul Morton	1904–1905
	Charles J. Bonaparte	1905–1906
	Victor H. Metcalf	1906–1908
	Truman H. Newberry	1908–1909
Secretary of Interior	Ethan A. Hitchcock	1901–1907
	James R. Garfield	1907–1909
Secretary of Agriculture	James Wilson	1901–1909

Secretary of Labor and Commerce	George B. Cortelyou	1903–1904
	Victor H. Metcalf	1904–1906
	Oscar S. Straus	1906–1909
	Charles Nagel	1909

The Taft Administration (1909–1913)

Vice President	James S. Sherman	1909–1913
Secretary of State	Philander C. Knox	1909–1913
Secretary of Treasury	Franklin MacVeagh	1909–1913
Secretary of War	Jacob M. Dickinson	1909–1911
	Henry L. Stimson	1911–1913
Attorney General	George W. Wickersham	1909–1913
Postmaster General	Frank H. Hitchcock	1909–1913
Secretary of Navy	George von L. Meyer	1909–1913
Secretary of Interior	Richard A. Ballinger	1909–1911
	Walter L. Fisher	1911–1913
Secretary of Agriculture	James Wilson	1909–1913
Secretary of Labor and Commerce	Charles Nagel	1909–1913

The Wilson Administration (1913–1921)

Vice President	Thomas R. Marshall	1913–1921
Secretary of State	William J. Bryan	1913–1915
	Robert Lansing	1915–1920
	Bainbridge Colby	1920–1921
Secretary of Treasury	William G. McAdoo	1913–1918
	Carter Glass	1918–1920
	David F. Houston	1920–1921
Secretary of War	Lindley M. Garrison	1913–1916
	Newton D. Baker	1916–1921
Attorney General	James C. McReynolds	1913–1914
	Thomas W. Gregory	1914–1919
	A. Mitchell Palmer	1919–1921
Postmaster General	Albert S. Burleson	1913–1921
Secretary of Navy	Josephus Daniels	1913–1921

Secretary of Interior	Franklin K. Lane	1913–1920
	John B. Payne	1920–1921
Secretary of Agriculture	David F. Houston	1913–1920
	Edwin T. Meredith	1920–1921
Secretary of Commerce	William C. Redfield	1913–1919
	Joshua W. Alexander	1919–1921
Secretary of Labor	William B. Wilson	1913–1921

The Harding Administration (1921–1923)

Vice President	Calvin Coolidge	1921–1923
Secretary of State	Charles E. Hughes	1921–1923
Secretary of Treasury	Andrew Mellon	1921–1923
Secretary of War	John W. Weeks	1921–1923
Attorney General	Harry M. Daugherty	1921–1923
Postmaster General	Will H. Hays	1921–1922
	Hubert Work	1922–1923
	Harry S. New	1923
Secretary of Navy	Edwin Denby	1921–1923
Secretary of Interior	Albert B. Fall	1921–1923
	Hubert Work	1923
Secretary of Agriculture	Henry C. Wallace	1921–1923
Secretary of Commerce	Herbert C. Hoover	1921–1923
Secretary of Labor	James J. Davis	1921–1923

The Coolidge Administration (1923–1929)

Vice President	Charles G. Dawes	1925–1929
Secretary of State	Charles E. Hughes	1923–1925
	Frank B. Kellogg	1925–1929
Secretary of Treasury	Andrew Mellon	1923–1929
Secretary of War	John W. Weeks	1923–1925
	Dwight F. Davis	1925–1929
Attorney General	Henry M. Daugherty	1923–1924
	Harlan F. Stone	1924–1925
	John G. Sargent	1925–1929
Postmaster General	Harry S. New	1923–1929
Secretary of Navy	Edwin Derby	1923–1924
	Curtis D. Wilbur	1924–1929

Secretary of Interior	Hubert Work	1923–1928
	Roy O. West	1928–1929
Secretary of Agriculture	Henry C. Wallace	1923–1924
	Howard M. Gore	1924–1925
	William M. Jardine	1925–1929
Secretary of Commerce	Herbert C. Hoover	1923–1928
	William F. Whiting	1928–1929
Secretary of Labor	James J. Davis	1923–1929

The Hoover Administration (1929–1933)

Vice President	Charles Curtis	1929–1933
Secretary of State	Henry L. Stimson	1929–1933
Secretary of Treasury	Andrew Mellon	1929–1932
	Ogden L. Mills	1932–1933
Secretary of War	James W. Good	1929
	Patrick J. Hurley	1929–1933
Attorney General	William D. Mitchell	1929–1933
Postmaster General	Walter F. Brown	1929–1933
Secretary of Navy	Charles F. Adams	1929–1933
Secretary of Interior	Ray L. Wilbur	1929–1933
Secretary of Agriculture	Arthur M. Hyde	1929–1933
Secretary of Commerce	Robert P. Lamont	1929–1932
	Roy D. Chapin	1932–1933
Secretary of Labor	James J. Davis	1929–1930
	William N. Doak	1930–1933

The Franklin D. Roosevelt Administration (1933–1945)

Vice President	John Nance Garner	1933–1941
	Henry A. Wallace	1941–1945
	Harry S Truman	1945
Secretary of State	Cordell Hull	1933–1944
	Edward R. Stettinius Jr.	1944–1945
Secretary of Treasury	William H. Woodin	1933–1934
	Henry Morgenthau Jr.	1934–1945
Secretary of War	George H. Dern	1933–1936
	Henry A. Woodring	1936–1940
	Henry L. Stimson	1940–1945

Attorney General	Homer S. Cummings	1933–1939
	Frank Murphy	1939–1940
	Robert H. Jackson	1940–1941
	Francis Biddle	1941–1945
Postmaster General	James A. Farley	1933–1940
	Frank C. Walker	1940–1945
Secretary of Navy	Claude A. Swanson	1933–1940
	Charles Edison	1940
	Frank Knox	1940–1944
	James V. Forrestal	1944–1945
Secretary of Interior	Harold L. Ickes	1933–1945
Secretary of Agriculture	Henry A. Wallace	1933–1940
	Claude R. Wickard	1940–1945
Secretary of Commerce	Daniel C. Roper	1933–1939
	Harry L. Hopkins	1939–1940
	Jesse Jones	1940–1945
	Henry A. Wallace	1945
Secretary of Labor	Frances Perkins	1933–1945

The Truman Administration (1945–1953)

Vice President	Alben W. Barkley	1949–1953
Secretary of State	Edward R. Stettinius Jr.	1945
	James F. Byrnes	1945–1947
	George C. Marshall	1947–1949
	Dean G. Acheson	1949–1953
Secretary of Treasury	Fred M. Vinson	1945–1946
	John W. Snyder	1946–1953
Secretary of War	Robert P. Patterson	1945–1947
	Kenneth C. Royall	1947
Attorney General	Tom C. Clark	1945–1949
	J. Howard McGrath	1949–1952
	James P. McGranery	1952–1953
Postmaster General	Frank C. Walker	1945
	Robert E. Hannegan	1945–1947
	Jesse M. Donaldson	1947–1953
Secretary of Navy	James V. Forrestal	1945–1947
Secretary of Interior	Harold L. Ickes	1945–1946
	Julius A. Krug	1946–1949
	Oscar L. Chapman	1949–1953

Secretary of Agriculture	Clinton P. Anderson	1945–1948
	Charles F. Brannan	1948–1953
Secretary of Commerce	Henry A. Wallace	1945–1946
	W. Averell Harriman	1946–1948
	Charles W. Sawyer	1948–1953
Secretary of Labor	Lewis B. Schwellenbach	1945–1948
	Maurice J. Tobin	1948–1953
Secretary of Defense	James V. Forrestal	1947–1949
	Louis A. Johnson	1949–1950
	George C. Marshall	1950–1951
	Robert A. Lovett	1951–1953

The Eisenhower Administration (1953–1961)

Vice President	Richard M. Nixon	1953–1961
Secretary of State	John Foster Dulles	1953–1959
	Christian A. Herter	1959–1961
Secretary of Treasury	George M. Humphrey	1953–1957
	Robert B. Anderson	1957–1961
Attorney General	Herbert Brownell Jr.	1953–1958
	William P. Rogers	1958–1961
Postmaster General	Arthur E. Summerfield	1953–1961
Secretary of Interior	Douglas McKay	1953–1956
	Fred A. Seaton	1956–1961
Secretary of Agriculture	Ezra T. Benson	1953–1961
Secretary of Commerce	Sinclair Weeks	1953–1958
	Lewis L. Strauss	1958–1959
	Frederick H. Mueller	1959–1961
Secretary of Labor	Martin P. Durkin	1953
	James P. Mitchell	1953–1961
Secretary of Defense	Charles E. Wilson	1953–1957
	Neil H. McElroy	1957–1959
	Thomas S. Gates Jr.	1959–1961
Secretary of Health, Education, and Welfare	Oveta Culp Hobby	1953–1955
	Marion B. Folsom	1955–1958
	Arthur S. Flemming	1958–1961

The Kennedy Administration (1961–1963)

Vice President	Lyndon B. Johnson	1961–1963
Secretary of State	Dean Rusk	1961–1963
Secretary of Treasury	C. Douglas Dillon	1961–1963
Attorney General	Robert F. Kennedy	1961–1963
Postmaster General	J. Edward Day	1961–1963
	John A. Gronouski	1963
Secretary of Interior	Stewart L. Udall	1961–1963
Secretary of Agriculture	Orville L. Freeman	1961–1963
Secretary of Commerce	Luther H. Hodges	1961–1963
Secretary of Labor	Arthur J. Goldberg	1961–1962
	W. Willard Wirtz	1962–1963
Secretary of Defense	Robert S. McNamara	1961–1963
Secretary of Health, Education, and Welfare	Abraham A. Ribicoff	1961–1962
	Anthony J. Celebrezze	1962–1963

The Lyndon Johnson Administration (1963–1969)

Vice President	Hubert H. Humphrey	1965–1969
Secretary of State	Dean Rusk	1963–1969
Secretary of Treasury	C. Douglas Dillon	1963–1965
	Henry H. Fowler	1965–1969
Attorney General	Robert F. Kennedy	1963–1964
	Nicholas Katzenbach	1965–1966
	Ramsey Clark	1967–1969
Postmaster General	John A. Gronouski	1963–1965
	Lawrence F. O'Brien	1965–1968
	Marvin Watson	1968–1969
Secretary of Interior	Stewart L. Udall	1963–1969
Secretary of Agriculture	Orville L. Freeman	1963–1969
Secretary of Commerce	Luther H. Hodges	1963–1964
	John T. Connor	1964–1967
	Alexander B. Trowbridge	1967–1968
	Cyrus R. Smith	1968–1969

Secretary of Labor	W. Willard Wirtz	1963–1969
Secretary of Defense	Robert F. McNamara	1963–1968
	Clark Clifford	1968–1969
Secretary of Health, Education, and Welfare	Anthony J. Celebrezze	1963–1965
	John W. Gardner	1965–1968
	Wilbur J. Cohen	1968–1969
Secretary of Housing and Urban Development	Robert C. Weaver	1966–1969
	Robert C. Wood	1969
Secretary of Transportation	Alan S. Boyd	1967–1969

The Nixon Administration (1969–1974)

Vice President	Spiro T. Agnew	1969–1973
	Gerald R. Ford	1973–1974
Secretary of State	William P. Rogers	1969–1973
	Henry A. Kissinger	1973–1974
Secretary of Treasury	David M. Kennedy	1969–1970
	John B. Connally	1971–1972
	George P. Shultz	1972–1974
	William E. Simon	1974
Attorney General	John N. Mitchell	1969–1972
	Richard G. Kleindienst	1972–1973
	Elliot L. Richardson	1973
	William B. Saxbe	1973–1974
Postmaster General	Winton M. Blount	1969–1971
Secretary of Interior	Walter J. Hickel	1969–1970
	Rogers Morton	1971–1974
Secretary of Agriculture	Clifford M. Hardin	1969–1971
	Earl L. Butz	1971–1974
Secretary of Commerce	Maurice H. Stans	1969–1972
	Peter G. Peterson	1972–1973
	Frederick B. Dent	1973–1974
Secretary of Labor	George P. Shultz	1969–1970
	James D. Hodgson	1970–1973
	Peter J. Brennan	1973–1974
Secretary of Defense	Melvin R. Laird	1969–1973
	Elliot L. Richardson	1973
	James R. Schlesinger	1973–1974
Secretary of Health, Education, and Welfare	Robert H. Finch	1969–1970
	Elliot L. Richardson	1970–1973
	Caspar W. Weinberger	1973–1974

Secretary of Housing and Urban Development	George Romney James T. Lynn	1969–1973 1973–1974
Secretary of Transportation	John A. Volpe Claude S. Brinegar	1969–1973 1973–1974

The Ford Administration (1974–1977)

Vice President	Nelson A. Rockefeller	1974–1977
Secretary of State	Henry A. Kissinger	1974–1977
Secretary of Treasury	William E. Simon	1974–1977
Attorney General	William Saxbe Edward Levi	1974–1975 1975–1977
Secretary of Interior	Rogers Morton Stanley K. Hathaway Thomas Kleppe	1974–1975 1975 1975–1977
Secretary of Agriculture	Earl L. Butz John A. Knebel	1974–1976 1976–1977
Secretary of Commerce	Frederick B. Dent Rogers Morton Elliot L. Richardson	1975–1976 1975–1976 1976–1977
Secretary of Labor	Peter J. Brennan John T. Dunlop W. J. Usery	1974–1975 1975–1976 1976–1977
Secretary of Defense	James R. Schlesinger Donald Rumsfeld	1974–1975 1975–1977
Secretary of Health, Education, and Welfare	Caspar Weinberger Forrest D. Mathews	1974–1975 1975–1977
Secretary of Housing and Urban Development	James T. Lynn Carla A. Hills	1974–1975 1975–1977
Secretary of Transportation	Claude Brinegar William T. Coleman	1974–1975 1975–1977

The Carter Administration (1977–1981)

Vice President	Walter F. Mondale	1977–1981
Secretary of State	Cyrus R. Vance Edmund Muskie	1977–1980 1980–1981
Secretary of Treasury	W. Michael Blumenthal G. William Miller	1977–1979 1979–1981
Attorney General	Griffin Bell Benjamin R. Civiletti	1977–1979 1979–1981
Secretary of Interior	Cecil D. Andrus	1977–1981
Secretary of Agriculture	Robert Bergland	1977–1981
Secretary of Commerce	Juanita M. Kreps Philip M. Klutznick	1977–1979 1979–1981
Secretary of Labor	F. Ray Marshall	1977–1981
Secretary of Defense	Harold Brown	1977–1981
Secretary of Health, Education, and Welfare	Joseph A. Califano Patricia R. Harris	1977–1979 1979
Secretary of Health and Human Services	Patricia R. Harris	1979–1981
Secretary of Education	Shirley M. Hufstedler	1979–1981
Secretary of Housing and Urban Development	Patricia R. Harris Moon Landrieu	1977–1979 1979–1981
Secretary of Transportation	Brock Adams Neil E. Goldschmidt	1977–1979 1979–1981
Secretary of Energy	James R. Schlesinger Charles W. Duncan	1977–1979 1979–1981

The Reagan Administration (1981–1989)

Vice President	George Bush	1981–1989
Secretary of State	Alexander M. Haig George P. Shultz	1981–1982 1982–1989
Secretary of Treasury	Donald Regan James A. Baker III Nicholas Brady	1981–1985 1985–1988 1988–1989
Attorney General	William F. Smith Edwin A. Meese III Richard Thornburgh	1981–1985 1985–1988 1988–1989
Secretary of Interior	James Watt William P. Clark Jr. Donald P. Hodel	1981–1983 1983–1985 1985–1989
Secretary of Agriculture	John Block Richard E. Lyng	1981–1986 1986–1989

Secretary of Commerce	Malcolm Baldrige	1981–1987
	C. William Verity Jr.	1987–1989
Secretary of Labor	Raymond Donovan	1981–1985
	William E. Brock	1985–1987
	Ann D. McLaughlin	1987–1989
Secretary of Defense	Caspar Weinberger	1981–1987
	Frank Carlucci	1987–1989
Secretary of Health and Human Services	Richard Schweiker	1981–1983
	Margaret Heckler	1983–1985
	Otis R. Bowen	1985–1989
Secretary of Education	Terrel H. Bell	1981–1985
	William J. Bennett	1985–1988
	Lauro F. Cavazos	1988–1989
Secretary of Housing and Urban Development	Samuel Pierce	1981–1989
Secretary of Transportation	Drew Lewis	1981–1983
	Elizabeth Dole	1983–1987
	James H. Burnley	1987–1989
Secretary of Energy	James Edwards	1981–1982
	Donald P. Hodel	1982–1985
	John S. Herrington	1985–1989

The George H. W. Bush Administration (1989–1993)

Vice President	J. Danforth Quayle	1989–1993
Secretary of State	James A. Baker III	1989–1992
Secretary of Treasury	Nicholas Brady	1989–1993
Attorney General	Richard Thornburgh	1989–1991
	William P. Barr	1991–1993
Secretary of Interior	Manuel Lujan	1989–1993
Secretary of Agriculture	Clayton K. Yeutter	1989–1991
	Edward Madigan	1991–1993
Secretary of Commerce	Robert Mosbacher	1989–1992
	Barbara Franklin	1992–1993
Secretary of Labor	Elizabeth Dole	1989–1991
	Lynn Martin	1991–1993
Secretary of Defense	Richard Cheney	1989–1993
Secretary of Health and Human Services	Louis W. Sullivan	1989–1993
Secretary of Education	Lauro F. Cavazos	1989–1991
	Lamar Alexander	1991–1993

Secretary of Housing and Urban Development	Jack F. Kemp	1989–1993
Secretary of Transportation	Samuel K. Skinner	1989–1992
	Andrew H. Card Jr.	1992–1993
Secretary of Energy	James D. Watkins	1989–1993
Secretary of Veterans Affairs	Edward J. Derwinski	1989–1993

The Clinton Administration (1993–2001)

Vice President	Albert Gore	1993–2001
Secretary of State	Warren Christopher	1993–1997
	Madeleine Albright	1997–2001
Secretary of Treasury	Lloyd Bentsen	1993–1995
	Robert E. Rubin	1995–1999
	Lawrence H. Summers	1999–2001
Attorney General	Janet Reno	1993–2001
Secretary of Interior	Bruce Babbitt	1993–2001
Secretary of Agriculture	Michael Espy	1993–1995
	Dan Glickman	1995–2001
Secretary of Commerce	Ronald Brown	1993–1996
	Mickey Kantor	1996
	William Daley	1997
	Norman Mineta	1997–2001
Secretary of Labor	Robert B. Reich	1993–1997
	Alexis Herman	1997–2001
Secretary of Defense	Les Aspin	1993–1994
	William J. Perry	1994–1997
	William Cohen	1997–2001
Secretary of Health and Human Services	Donna Shalala	1993–2001
Secretary of Housing and Urban Development	Henry G. Cisneros	1993–1997
	Andrew Cuomo	1997–2001
Secretary of Education	Richard W. Riley	1993–2001
Secretary of Transportation	Federico Peña	1993–1997
	Rodney Slater	1997–2001
Secretary of Energy	Hazel R. O'Leary	1993–1997
	Federico Peña	1997
	Bill Richardson	1998–2001
Secretary of Veterans Affairs	Jesse Brown	1993–1998
	Togo D. West Jr.	1998–2001

The George W. Bush Administration (2001–   )

Vice President	Richard B. Cheney	2001–
Secretary of State	Colin Powell	2001–
Secretary of Treasury	Paul H. O'Neill John Snow	2001–2002 2003–
Attorney General	John Ashcroft	2001–
Secretary of Interior	Gale Norton	2001–
Secretary of Agriculture	Ann M. Veneman	2001–
Secretary of Commerce	Don Evans	2001–
Secretary of Labor	Elaine Chao	2001–
Secretary of Defense	Donald Rumsfeld	2001–
Secretary of Health and Human Services	Tommy G. Thompson	2001–
Secretary of Housing and Urban Development	Melquiades Rafael Martinez	2001–
Secretary of Education	Rod Paige	2001–
Secretary of Transportation	Norman Mineta	2001–
Secretary of Energy	Spencer Abraham	2001–
Secretary of Veterans Affairs	Anthony Principi	2001–
Secretary of Homeland Security	Tom Ridge	2003–

Justices of the Supreme Court

	Term of Service	Years of Service	Life Span
John Jay	1789–1795	5	1745–1829
John Rutledge	1789–1791	1	1739–1800
William Cushing	1789–1810	20	1732–1810
James Wilson	1789–1798	8	1742–1798
John Blair	1789–1796	6	1732–1800
Robert H. Harrison	1789–1790	—	1745–1790
James Iredell	1790–1799	9	1751–1799
Thomas Johnson	1791–1793	1	1732–1819
William Paterson	1793–1806	13	1745–1806
*John Rutledge**	1795	—	1739–1800
Samuel Chase	1796–1811	15	1741–1811
Oliver Ellsworth	1796–1800	4	1745–1807
Bushrod Washington	1798–1829	31	1762–1829
Alfred Moore	1799–1804	4	1755–1810
John Marshall	1801–1835	34	1755–1835
William Johnson	1804–1834	30	1771–1834
H. Brockholst Livingston	1806–1823	16	1757–1823
Thomas Todd	1807–1826	18	1765–1826
Joseph Story	1811–1845	33	1779–1845
Gabriel Duval	1811–1835	24	1752–1844
Smith Thompson	1823–1843	20	1768–1843
Robert Trimble	1826–1828	2	1777–1828
John McLean	1829–1861	32	1785–1861
Henry Baldwin	1830–1844	14	1780–1844
James M. Wayne	1835–1867	32	1790–1867
Roger B. Taney	1836–1864	28	1777–1864
Philip P. Barbour	1836–1841	4	1783–1841
John Catron	1837–1865	28	1786–1865
John McKinley	1837–1852	15	1780–1852
Peter V. Daniel	1841–1860	19	1784–1860
Samuel Nelson	1845–1872	27	1792–1873
Levi Woodbury	1845–1851	5	1789–1851
Robert C. Grier	1846–1870	23	1794–1870
Benjamin R. Curtis	1851–1857	6	1809–1874
John A. Campbell	1853–1861	8	1811–1889
Nathan Clifford	1858–1881	23	1803–1881
Noah H. Swayne	1862–1881	18	1804–1884
Samuel F. Miller	1862–1890	28	1816–1890
David Davis	1862–1877	14	1815–1886
Stephen J. Field	1863–1897	34	1816–1899
Salmon P. Chase	1864–1873	8	1808–1873
William Strong	1870–1880	10	1808–1895
Joseph P. Bradley	1870–1892	22	1813–1892
Ward Hunt	1873–1882	9	1810–1886
Morrison R. Waite	1874–1888	14	1816–1888
John M. Harlan	1877–1911	34	1833–1911
William B. Woods	1880–1887	7	1824–1887
Stanley Matthews	1881–1889	7	1824–1889
Horace Gray	1882–1902	20	1828–1902
Samuel Blatchford	1882–1893	11	1820–1893
Lucius Q. C. Lamar	1888–1893	5	1825–1893
Melville W. Fuller	1888–1910	21	1833–1910
David J. Brewer	1890–1910	20	1837–1910
Henry B. Brown	1890–1906	16	1836–1913
George Shiras Jr.	1892–1903	10	1832–1924
Howell E. Jackson	1893–1895	2	1832–1895
Edward D. White	1894–1910	16	1845–1921
Rufus W. Peckham	1895–1909	14	1838–1909
Joseph McKenna	1898–1925	26	1843–1926
Oliver W. Holmes	1902–1932	30	1841–1935
William R. Day	1903–1922	19	1849–1923
William H. Moody	1906–1910	3	1853–1917
Horace H. Lurton	1909–1914	4	1844–1914
Charles E. Hughes	1910–1916	5	1862–1948
Edward D. White	1910–1921	11	1845–1921
Willis Van Devanter	1911–1937	26	1859–1941
Joseph R. Lamar	1911–1916	5	1857–1916
Mahlon Pitney	1912–1922	10	1858–1924
James C. McReynolds	1914–1941	26	1862–1946
Louis D. Brandeis	1916–1939	22	1856–1941
John H. Clarke	1916–1922	6	1857–1945
William H. Taft	1921–1930	8	1857–1930
George Sutherland	1922–1938	15	1862–1942
Pierce Butler	1922–1939	16	1866–1939
Edward T. Sanford	1923–1930	7	1865–1930
Harlan F. Stone	1925–1941	16	1872–1946
Charles E. Hughes	1930–1941	11	1862–1948
Owen J. Roberts	1930–1945	15	1875–1955
Benjamin N. Cardozo	1932–1938	6	1870–1938
Hugo L. Black	1937–1971	34	1886–1971
Stanley F. Reed	1938–1957	19	1884–1980
Felix Frankfurter	1939–1962	23	1882–1965
William O. Douglas	1939–1975	36	1898–1980
Frank Murphy	1940–1949	9	1890–1949
Harlan F. Stone	1941–1946	5	1872–1946
James F. Byrnes	1941–1942	1	1879–1972
Robert H. Jackson	1941–1954	13	1892–1954
Wiley B. Rutledge	1943–1949	6	1894–1949
Harold H. Burton	1945–1958	13	1888–1964
Fred M. Vinson	1946–1953	7	1890–1953
Tom C. Clark	1949–1967	18	1899–1977
Sherman Minton	1949–1956	7	1890–1965
Earl Warren	1953–1969	16	1891–1974

*Appointed and served one term, but not confirmed by the Senate.

Note: Chief justices are in italics.

	Term of Service	Years of Service	Life Span
John Marshall Harlan	1955–1971	16	1899–1971
William J. Brennan Jr.	1956–1990	33	1906–1997
Charles E. Whittaker	1957–1962	5	1901–1973
Potter Stewart	1958–1981	23	1915–1985
Bryon R. White	1962–1993	31	1917–2002
Arthur J. Goldberg	1962–1965	3	1908–1990
Abe Fortas	1965–1969	4	1910–1982
Thurgood Marshall	1967–1991	24	1908–1992
Warren C. Burger	1969–1986	17	1907–1995
Harry A. Blackmun	1970–1994	24	1908–1999
Lewis F. Powell Jr.	1972–1987	15	1907–1998

	Term of Service	Years of Service	Life Span
William H. Rehnquist	1972–1986	14	1924–
John P. Stevens III	1975–	—	1920–
Sandra Day O'Connor	1981–	—	1930–
William H. Rehnquist	1986–	—	1924–
Antonin Scalia	1986–	—	1936–
Anthony M. Kennedy	1988–	—	1936–
David H. Souter	1990–	—	1939–
Clarence Thomas	1991–	—	1948–
Ruth Bader Ginsburg	1993–	—	1933–
Stephen Breyer	1994–	—	1938–

A Social Profile of the American Republic

Year	Population	Percent Increase	Population per Square Mile	Population Percent Urban/ Rural	Percent Male/ Female	Percent White/ Nonwhite	Persons per Household	Median Age
1790	3,929,214		4.5	5.1/94.9	NA/NA	80.7/19.3	5.79	NA
1800	5,308,483	35.1	6.1	6.1/93.9	NA/NA	81.1/18.9	NA	NA
1810	7,239,881	36.4	4.3	7.3/92.7	NA/NA	81.0/19.0	NA	NA
1820	9,638,453	33.1	5.5	7.2/92.8	50.8/49.2	81.6/18.4	NA	16.7
1830	12,866,020	33.5	7.4	8.8/91.2	50.8/49.2	81.9/18.1	NA	17.2
1840	17,069,453	32.7	9.8	10.8/89.2	50.9/49.1	83.2/16.8	NA	17.8
1850	23,191,876	35.9	7.9	15.3/84.7	51.0/49.0	84.3/15.7	5.55	18.9
1860	31,443,321	35.6	10.6	19.8/80.2	51.2/48.8	85.6/14.4	5.28	19.4
1870	39,818,449	26.6	13.4	25.7/74.3	50.6/49.4	86.2/13.8	5.09	20.2
1880	50,155,783	26.0	16.9	28.2/71.8	50.9/49.1	86.5/13.5	5.04	20.9
1890	62,947,714	25.5	21.2	35.1/64.9	51.2/48.8	87.5/12.5	4.93	22.0
1900	75,994,575	20.7	25.6	39.6/60.4	51.1/48.9	87.9/12.1	4.76	22.9
1910	91,972,266	21.0	31.0	45.6/54.4	51.5/48.5	88.9/11.1	4.54	24.1
1920	105,710,620	14.9	35.6	51.2/48.8	51.0/49.0	89.7/10.3	4.34	25.3
1930	122,775,046	16.1	41.2	56.1/43.9	50.6/49.4	89.8/10.2	4.11	26.4
1940	131,669,275	7.2	44.2	56.5/43.5	50.2/49.8	89.8/10.2	3.67	29.0
1950	150,697,361	14.5	50.7	64.0/36.0	49.7/50.3	89.5/10.5	3.37	30.2
1960	179,323,175	18.5	50.6	69.9/30.1	49.3/50.7	88.6/11.4	3.33	29.5
1970	203,302,031	13.4	57.4	73.5/26.5	48.7/51.3	87.6/12.4	3.14	28.0
1980	226,545,805	11.4	64.0	73.7/26.3	48.6/51.4	86.0/14.0	2.76	30.0
1990	248,709,873	9.8	70.3	75.2/24.8	48.7/51.3	80.3/19.7	2.63	32.9
2000	281,422,426	13.1	79.6	79.0/21.0	49.0/51.0	81.0/19.0	2.59	35.4

NA = Not available.

Year	Births	Vital Statistics (rates per thousand)				
		Year	Births	Deaths*	Marriages*	Divorces*
1800	55.0	1900	32.3	17.2	NA	NA
1810	54.3	1910	30.1	14.7	NA	NA
1820	55.2	1920	27.7	13.0	12.0	1.6
1830	51.4	1930	21.3	11.3	9.2	1.6
1840	51.8	1940	19.4	10.8	12.1	2.0
1850	43.3	1950	24.1	9.6	11.1	2.6
1860	44.3	1960	23.7	9.5	8.5	2.2
1870	38.3	1970	18.4	9.5	10.6	3.5
1880	39.8	1980	15.9	8.8	10.6	5.2
1890	31.5	1990	16.7	8.6	9.8	4.6
		2000	14.7	8.7	8.5	4.2

NA = Not available.
*Data not available before 1900.

Year	Total Population	Life Expectancy (in years)			
		White Females	Nonwhite Females	White Males	Nonwhite Males
1900	47.3	48.7	33.5	46.6	32.5
1910	50.1	52.0	37.5	48.6	33.8
1920	54.1	55.6	45.2	54.4	45.5
1930	59.7	63.5	49.2	59.7	47.3
1940	62.9	66.6	54.9	62.1	51.5
1950	68.2	72.2	62.9	66.5	59.1
1960	69.7	74.1	66.3	67.4	61.1
1970	70.9	75.6	69.4	68.0	61.3
1980	73.7	78.1	73.6	70.7	65.3
1990	75.4	79.3	76.3	72.6	68.4
2000	76.9	80.0	NA	74.8	NA

The Changing Age Structure

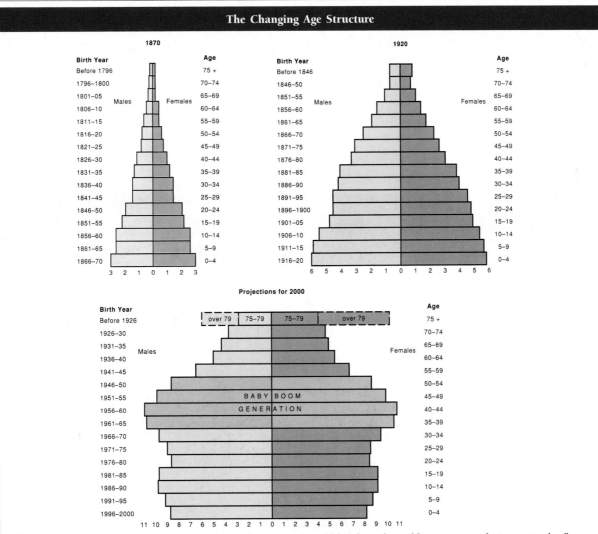

Before the twentieth century, the age distribution of Americans could be charted roughly as a pyramid, as seen in the figures for 1870 and 1920. High birthrates create a broad base at the bottom, while mortality rates winnow the population to a small tip of elderly. But by the year 2000, the pyramid has been transformed more nearly into a cylinder. Over the past two centuries fertility rates have undergone a steady decline, pulling in the base of the pyramid, while higher living standards have allowed Americans to live longer, broadening the top. Only the temporary bulge of the baby boom distorts the shape.

Years	Total Number of Immigrants	Regional Origin of Immigrants (percent) EUROPE				Western Hemisphere	Asia
		Total Europe	North and West	East and Central	South and Other		
1821–1830	143,389	69.2	67.1	—	2.1	8.4	—
1831–1840	599,125	82.8	81.8	—	1.0	5.5	—
1841–1850	1,713,251	93.8	92.9	0.1	0.3	3.6	—
1851–1860	2,598,214	94.4	93.6	0.1	0.8	2.9	1.6
1861–1870	2,314,824	89.2	87.8	0.5	0.9	7.2	2.8
1871–1880	2,812,191	80.8	73.6	4.5	2.7	14.4	4.4
1881–1890	5,246,13	90.3	72.0	11.9	6.3	8.1	1.3
1891–1900	3,687,546	96.5	44.5	32.8	19.1	1.1	1.9
1901–1910	8,795,386	92.5	21.7	44.5	6.3	4.1	2.8
1911–1920	5,735,811	76.3	17.4	33.4	25.5	19.9	3.4
1921–1930	4,107,209	60.3	31.7	14.4	14.3	36.9	2.4
1931–1940	528,431	65.9	38.8	11.0	16.1	30.3	2.8
1941–1950	1,035,039	60.1	47.5	4.6	7.9	34.3	3.1
1951–1960	2,515,479	52.8	17.7	24.3	10.8	39.6	6.0
1961–1970	3,321,677	33.8	11.7	9.4	12.9	51.7	12.9
1971–1980	4,493,300	17.8	4.3	5.6	8.4	44.3	35.2
1981–1990	7,338,000	10.4	5.9	4.8	1.1	49.3	37.3
1991–2000	9,095,417	14.9	4.8	8.6	1.6	49.3	30.7

Dash indicates less than 0.1 percent.

Recent Trends in Immigration (in thousands)					PERCENT		
	1961–1970	1971–1980	1981–1990	1991–2000	1971–1980	1981–1990	1991–2000
All countries	3,321.7	4,493.3	7,338.1	9095.4	100.0	100.0	100.0
Europe	1,123.5	800.4	761.5	1359.7	17.8	10.4	14.9
Austria	20.6	9.5	18.3	15.5	0.2	0.3	0.2
Belgium	9.2	5.3	7.0	7.0	0.1	0.1	0.1
Czechoslovakia	3.3	6.0	7.2	9.8	0.1	0.1	0.1
Denmark	9.2	4.4	5.3	6.0	0.1	0.1	0.1
France	45.2	25.1	22.4	35.8	0.6	1.3	0.4
Germany	190.8	74.4	91.6	92.6	1.7	2.2	1.0
Greece	86.0	92.4	38.3	26.7	2.1	0.4	0.3
Hungary	5.4	6.6	6.5	9.3	0.1	0.1	0.1
Ireland	33.0	11.5	31.9	56.9	0.3	0.9	0.6
Italy	214.1	129.4	67.2	62.7	2.9	0.2	0.7
Netherlands	30.6	10.5	12.2	13.3	0.2	0.1	0.1
Norway	15.5	3.9	4.2	5.1	0.1	1.1	0.5
Poland	53.5	37.2	83.3	163.7	0.8	0.5	1.8
Portugal	76.1	101.7	40.4	22.9	2.3	0.3	0.3
Spain	44.7	39.1	20.4	17.1	0.9	0.2	0.2
Sweden	17.1	6.5	11.0	12.7	0.1	0.1	0.1
Switzerland	18.5	8.2	8.8	11.8	0.2	0.1	0.1
United Kingdom	213.8	137.4	159.2	151.8	3.1	2.2	1.7
USSR	2.5	39.0	57.7	462.8	0.9	0.3	5.1
Yugoslavia	20.4	30.5	18.8	66.5	0.7	0.5	0.7
Other Europe	9.1	18.9	8.2	57.7	0.2	0.0	0.6

Recent Trends in Immigration (in thousands)					PERCENT		
	1961–1970	1971–1980	1981–1990	1991–2000	1971–1980	1981–1990	1991–2000
Asia	427.6	1588.2	2738.1	2795.6	35.2	37.3	30.7
China	34.8	124.3	298.9	419.1	2.8	4.1	4.6
Hong Kong	75.0	113.5	98.2	109.8	2.5	1.3	1.2
India	27.2	164.1	250.7	363.1	3.7	3.4	4.0
Iran	10.3	45.1	116.0	69.0	1.0	1.6	0.8
Israel	29.6	37.7	44.2	39.4	0.8	0.6	0.4
Japan	40.0	49.8	47.0	67.9	1.1	0.6	0.7
Korea	34.5	267.6	333.8	164.2	6.0	4.5	1.8
Philippines	98.4	355.0	548.7	503.9	7.9	7.5	5.5
Turkey	10.1	13.4	23.4	38.2	0.3	0.3	0.4
Vietnam	4.3	172.8	281.0	286.1	3.8	3.8	3.1
Other Asia	36.5	176.1	631.4	735.4	3.8	8.6	8.0
America	1716.4	1982.5	3615.6	4486.8	44.3	49.3	49.3
Argentina	49.7	29.9	27.3	26.6	0.7	0.4	0.3
Canada	413.3	169.9	158.0	192.0	3.8	2.2	2.1
Colombia	72.0	77.3	122.9	128.5	1.7	1.7	1.4
Cuba	208.5	264.9	144.6	169.3	5.9	2.0	1.9
Dominican Rep.	93.3	148.1	252.0	335.3	3.3	3.4	3.7
Ecuador	36.8	50.1	56.2	76.5	1.1	0.8	0.8
El Salvador	15.0	34.4	213.5	215.7	0.8	2.9	2.4
Haiti	34.5	56.3	138.4	179.6	1.3	1.9	2.0
Jamaica	74.9	137.6	208.1	169.2	3.1	2.8	1.9
Mexico	453.9	640.3	1655.7	2249.4	14.3	22.6	24.7
Other America	264.4	373.8	639.3	744.3	8.3	8.7	8.2
Africa	29.0	80.8	176.8	355.0	1.8	2.4	3.9
Oceania	25.1	41.2	45.2	55.8	0.9	0.6	0.6

Figures may not add to total due to rounding.

American Workers and Farmers						
Year	Total Number of Workers (thousands)	Percent of Workers Male/Female	Percent of Female Workers Married	Percent of Workers in Female Population	Percent of Workers in Labor Unions	Farm Population (thousands)	Farm Population as Percent of Total Population
1870	12,506	85/15	NA	NA	NA	NA	NA
1880	17,392	85/15	NA	NA	NA	21,973	43.8
1890	23,318	83/17	13.9	18.9	NA	24,771	42.3
1900	29,073	82/18	15.4	20.6	3	29,875	41.9
1910	38,167	79/21	24.7	25.4	6	32,077	34.9
1920	41,614	79/21	23.0	23.7	12	31,974	30.1
1930	48,830	78/22	28.9	24.8	7	30,529	24.9
1940	53,011	76/24	36.4	27.4	27	30,547	23.2
1950	59,643	72/28	52.1	31.4	25	23,048	15.3
1960	69,877	68/32	59.9	37.7	26	15,635	8.7
1970	82,049	63/37	63.4	43.4	25	9712	4.8
1980	108,544	58/42	59.7	51.5	23	6051	2.7
1990	117,914	55/45	58.4	44.3	16	3871	1.6
2000	135,208	54/46	61.3	45.7	15	3305	1.1

| Year | Gross National Product (GNP) (in billions)* | The Economy and Federal Spending FOREIGN TRADE (in millions) | | | Federal Budget (in billions) | Federal Surplus/Deficit (in billions) | Federal Debt (in billions) |
		Exports	Imports	Balance of Trade			
1790	NA	$20	$23	$−3	$0.004	$+0.00015	$0.076
1800	NA	71	91	−20	0.011	+0.0006	0.083
1810	NA	67	85	−18	0.008	+0.0012	0.053
1820	NA	70	74	−4	0.018	−0.0004	0.091
1830	NA	74	71	+3	0.015	+0.100	0.049
1840	NA	132	107	+25	0.024	−0.005	0.004
1850	NA	152	178	−26	0.040	+0.004	0.064
1860	NA	400	362	−38	0.063	−0.01	0.065
1870	$7.4	451	462	−11	0.310	+0.10	2.4
1880	11.2	853	761	+92	0.268	+0.07	2.1
1890	13.1	910	823	+87	0.318	+0.09	1.2
1900	18.7	1499	930	+569	0.521	+0.05	1.2
1910	35.3	1919	1646	+273	0.694	−0.02	1.1
1920	91.5	8664	5784	+2880	6.357	+0.3	24.3
1930	90.7	4013	3500	+513	3.320	+0.7	16.3
1940	100.0	4030	7433	−3403	9.6	−2.7	43.0
1950	286.5	10,816	9125	+1691	43.1	−2.2	257.4
1960	506.5	19,600	15,046	+4556	92.2	+0.3	286.3
1970	992.7	42,700	40,189	+2511	195.6	−2.8	371.0
1980	2631.7	220,783	244,871	+24,088	590.9	−73.8	907.7
1990	5803.2	394,030	495,042	−101,012	1253.1	−220.5	3206.6
2000	9872.9	1,102,900	1,466,900	−364,000	1788.8	+236.4	5629.0

*For 1990 and after, gross domestic product (GDP) is given.

	U.S. Military Personnel (thousands)	American Wars Personnel as % of Population	U.S. Deaths	U.S. Wounds	Direct Cost 1990 dollars (millions)
American Revolution Apr. 1775–Sept. 1783	184–250	9–12	4004	6004	$100–140
War of 1812 June 1812–Feb. 1815	286	3	1950	4000	87
Mexican War May 1846–Feb. 1848	116	0.5	13,271	4102	82
Civil War: Union	3393	14	360,222	275,175	2302
Civil War: Confederacy Apr. 1861–Apr. 1865	1034	11	258,000	NA	1032
Spanish-American War Apr. 1898–Aug. 1898	307	0.4	2446	1662	270
World War I Apr. 1917–Nov. 1918	4714	5	116,516	204,002	32,740
World War II Dec. 1941–Aug. 1945	16,354	12	405,399	670,846	360,000
Korean War June 1950–June 1953	5764	4	54,246	103,284	50,000
Vietnam War Aug. 1964–June 1973	8400	4	47,704	219,573	140,644
Persian Gulf War Jan. 1991–Feb. 1991	467	0.1	293	467	20,163*

*Amount paid by United States. Total cost of war calculated to be $61.1 billion.

Credits

Page 5 Milwaukee Public Museum; 6 National Anthropological Archives, Smithsonian Institution (#168-B); 7 Cahokia Mounds State Historic Site, painting by Lloyd K. Townsend; 8 Courtesy UBC Museum of Anthropology, Vancouver; 9, 10 The Pierpont Morgan Library/Art Resource, NY; 13 (left and right) Photo Courtesy of The Newberry Library, Chicago; 16 Arizona State Museum, University of Arizona; 17 (bottom) Drawn by Julie Longhill. From Brian Fagan's, *The Great Journey;* 18 Jeff Green/NYT Pictures; 21 Karl Bodmer, *Tåtsicki-Stomíck, Piegan Blackfeet Chief,* Joslyn Art Museum, Omaha, Nebraska; 22 Bulloz; 24 Bibliothèque Nationale de France; 27 By Permission of the British Library (MS. Cott. AUG I i fol 38); 30 © Copyright The British Museum, London; 31 Nicolas Regnier, *The Fortune-teller,* Louvre, Paris. Erich Lessing/Art Resource, NY; 33 (top) The Walters Art Gallery, Baltimore, MD; (bottom left) Pendant: skull, 1600s. Metal, enamel, 1.3 × 1.2 × 3 cm. The Thomson Collection. Courtesy Art Gallery of Ontario; (bottom right) Pendant: skull, 1600s. Enamel on gold, gemstones, 1.4 × 1.2 × 3.4 cm. The Thomson Collection. Courtesy Art Gallery of Ontario; 37 (right) Library of Congress; (left) Document sur l'Aperreamiento, ca. 1540 (ms. mex. 374.). Bibliothèque Nationale, Paris; 41 (top left) Martin Schongauer, *St. Anthony Tormented by Demons* c. 1480–90. Engraving. Metropolitan Museum of Art, New York. Jacob S. Rogers Fund, 1920. (20.5.2); (top right) From Sebastian Münster, *Cosmographia,* Basle, 1550. Rare Books and Manuscripts Division, New York Public Library, Astor, Lenox and Tilden Foundations; (bottom) Culver Pictures, Inc.; 44 Bodleian Library, University of Oxford, England; 46 The Granger Collection, New York; 53 Ashmolean Museum, Oxford, England; 54 National Portrait Gallery, Washington, D.C./Art Resource, NY; 56 Courtesy of the Whitehall-Robins Company. Photo by Don Eiler's Custom Photography; 57 (left) Adrisan Brouwer, *The Smokers,* The Metropolitan Museum of Art, New York, Bequest of Michael Friedsam, 1931 (32.100.21). The Friedsam Collection. Photo © 2000 The Metropolitan Museum of Art, New York; (right) © Fulvio Rolter/CORBIS; 59 Samuel Cooper, *Oliver Cromwell,* By courtesy of the National Portrait Gallery, London; 64 (top left) Benjamin Henry Latrobe, *Blacks Working on the James River,* 1798–99. The Library of Virginia; (bottom left) Musée du Château des ducs de Bretagne. Photo, P. Jean Ville de Nantes; (bottom right) John Gabriel Stedman, *Narrative of a Five Years Expedition,* Plate 53. The Library of Congress; 65 (bottom) *Portrait of Olaudah Equiano,* c. 1789. Royal Albert Memorial Museum, Exeter, Devon, England/Bridgeman Art Library; (top) Foto Marburg/Art Resource, NY; 67 Colonial Williamsburg Foundation, VA; 69 Annenberg Rare Book and Manuscript Library, University of Pennsylvania; 72 The Library Company of Philadelphia; 74 Library of Congress; 76 Philip Georg Friedrich von Reck, *Indian Festival,* 1736. Royal Library, Copenhagen; 78 Arizona State Museum, University of Arizona. Photo by Helga Teiwes; 83 (left) Centre Marguerite-Bourgeoys, Montreal; 86 By permission of the Folger Shakespeare Library, Washington, D.C.; 90 © Copyright British Museum, London; 91 Harold Wickliffe Rose Papers, Manuscripts and Archives, Yale University Library, New Haven; 92 © Copyright British Museum, London; 94 By permission of the Folger Shakespeare Library, Washington, D.C.; 96 CORBIS; 99 Print Division, Phillip Stokes Collection of American Historical Prints, The New York Public Library, Astor, Lenox and Tilden Foundations; 100 George Heriot, *Calumet Dance,* 1799. Collection of the Art Gallery of Windsor, Ontario, Canada; 102 Prints Division, Miriam and Ira D. Wallach Division of Arts, New York Public Library, Astor, Lenox and Tilden Foundations; 104 Bristol Docks and Quay, early 18th century. City of Bristol Museum and Art Gallery, England/Bridgeman Art Library; 111 The Library Company of Philadelphia; 113 Courtesy North Carolina Division of Archives and History; 116 The Library Company of Philadelphia; 120 Courtesy of the Marblehead Historical Society. Marblehead, MA; 121 *Child of the Van Rensselaer Family with Servant* by John Heaton. Collection of Rodman C. Rockefeller; 124 (top) Abby Aldrich Rockefeller Folk Art Museum, Williamsburg, VA; (bottom) The Old Slave Mart Library, Sullivan's Island, SC; 125 Maryland Historical Society, Baltimore, Maryland; 128 © Copyright British Museum, London; 130 Signed A.S., *An Early Coffee House,* c. 1705. British Museum, London, England/Bridgeman Art Library; 131 Courtesy of the Bostonian Society; 132 William L. Clements Library, University of Michigan; 133 Courtesy of the Trustees of Sir John Soane's Museum, London; 139 Courtesy of Caroline Buckler; 140 CORBIS; 142 Detail, *A View of the Town of Concord,* Bequest of Mrs. Stedman Buttrick (Sr. Pi414.). Photograph courtesy Concord Museum, Concord, MA; 145 Paul Revere, detail, *Red Coats Arriving in Boston.* Courtesy The Henry Francis Du Pont Winterthur Museum; 148 With permission of the Royal Ontario Museum, Toronto © ROM; 153 Paul Revere, detail, *A View of the Year of 1765,* 1765. Courtesy of the Massachusetts Historical Society (MHS Neg.#1448); 154 Colonial Williamsburg Foundation, VA; 156 The Victoria & Albert Museum, London; 157 Charles Willson Peale, *John Dickinson,* Atwater Kent Museum/The Historical Society of Pennsylvania (HSP 1926.1); 158 The New-York Historical Society (49494); 160 *British Grenadier,* The Historical Society of Pennsylvania. (HSP 1931.5); 161 Library of Congress; 164 *Samuel Adams,* The New-York Historical Society/Bridgeman Art Library; 166 *A View of the Town of Concord,* Bequest of Mrs. Stedman Buttrick (Sr. Pi414.) Photograph courtesy Concord Museum, Concord, MA; 167 Auguste Milliere, *Thomas Paine.* By courtesy of the National Portrait Gallery, London; 171 (top) The Granger Collection, NY; (bottom) John Lei/Omni Photo Communications, Inc.; 173 Robert Edge Pine and/or Edward Savage, *The Congress Voting Independence,* Atwater Kent Museum/The Historical Society of Pennsylvania (HSP 1904.1); 176 *George Washington,* after a miniature by Charles Willson Peale. Courtesy of Mount Vernon Ladies' Association, VA; 178 Library of Congress; 180 Dietrich American Foundation, Photograph by Will Brown, Philadelphia, PA; 183 Box with medallion top, circular with colored print showing busts of Voltaire, Rousseau, and Franklin, 1883. The Metropolitan Museum of Art, Gift of William H. Huntington (83.2.228). Photograph © 1980 The Metropolitan Museum of Art; 184 Library of

Congress; **187** Charles Willson Peale, *General Nathanael Greene,* 1783. Montclair Art Museum, Montclair, NJ. Museum purchase; Acquisition Fund (1961.12); **189** Library of Congress; **190** The Historical Society of Pennsylvania; **192–193** Detail, Musées Nationaux, Musée de Versailles; **197** (*left*) *Captain Samuel Chandler* by Winthrop Chandler, c. 1780. Canvas, 54-3/4 × 47-7/8 in. Gift of Edgar William and Bernice Chrysler Garbisch, © 2000 Board of Trustees, National Gallery of Art, Washington, D.C.; (*right*) *Mrs. Samuel Chandler* by Winthrop Chandler, c. 1780. Gift of Edgar William and Bernice Chrysler Garbisch, © 2005 Board of Trustees, National Gallery of Art, Washington, D.C.; **198** Prints and Photographs Division, Miriam & Ira D. Wallach Division of Arts, New York Public Library, Astor, Lenox and Tilden Foundations; **199, 201** Collection of the Greenville County Museum of Art; **204** CORBIS; **207** John Lewis Krimmel, *Negro Methodists Holding a Meeting in a Philadelphia Alley,* 1811–1813. Provenance: R.T.H. Halsy, New York. The Metropolitan Museum of Art, Rogers Fund, 1942 (42.95.19). Photo © 2000 The Metropolitan Museum of Art, New York; **209** (*left*) Gilbert Stuart, *The Skater (Portrait of William Grant),* 1782. Andrew W. Mellon Collection, © 2005 Board of Trustees, National Gallery of Art, Washington, D.C.; The New-York Historical Society (1176); **211** (*left*) Tate Gallery, London/Art Resource, NY; (*right*) The Library Company of Philadelphia; **214** The New-York Historical Society; **217** Charles Willson Peale, *James Madison,* The Gilcrease Museum, Tulsa, OK; **218** Independence National Historical Park Collection; **224** Herrnhut, Archiv der Brüder-Unität; **225** Virginia Baptist Historical Society at the University of Richmond; **226** The Print and Picture Collection, The Free Library of Philadelphia. Photograph: Will Brown; **227** Historic New Orleans Collection (1960.46); **229** Culver Pictures, Inc.; **231** *He that by the Plough Would Thrive . . . ,* 1800. Addison Gallery of American Art, Phillips Academy, Andover, MA. Gift of Mrs. Evelyn Roberts; **233** I.N. Phelps Stokes Collection, Miriam and Ira D. Wallach Division of Art, Prints and Photographs, The New York Public Library, Astor, Lenox and Tilden Foundations; **236** John & Lillian Harney Collection; **239** (*right*) John Trumbull, *Alexander Hamilton,* c. 1972. © 2005 Board of Trustees, National Gallery of Art, Washington, D.C. Gift of Avalon Foundation; (*left*) Independence National Historical Park; **243** Bibliothèque Nationale de France; **244** Library of Congress; **248** U.S. Department of the Interior, National Park Service. Adams National Historic Site, Quincy, MA; **250** Charles Willson Peale, *The Artist in His Museum,* 1822. Courtesy of the Pennsylvania Academy of the Fine Arts, Philadelphia. Gift of Mrs. Sarah Harrison, The Joseph Harrison, Jr. Collection (1878.1.2); **253** John Krimmel, detail, *Election Day,* Courtesy The Henry Francis Du Pont Winterthur Museum; **257** Collection of Davenport West, Jr.; **258** Library of Congress; **259** Monticello, The Thomas Jefferson Memorial Foundation, Inc. **261** Chester Harding, detail, *John Marshall,* 1830. Boston Athenaeum (U.R.1830); **267** John Lewis Krimmel, *A Philadelphia Anabaptist Submersion during a Thunderstorm.* The Metropolitan Museum of Art, Rogers Fund, 1942 (42.95.20). Photo © 2000 The Metropolitan Museum of Art, New York; **271** (*right*) Field Museum of Natural History (Neg # A93851C), Chicago; (*left*) George Catlin, *The Open Door, known as The Prophet, Brother of Tecumseh,* 1830; **275** The British Library, London; **279** New Orleans Museum of Art, Gift of Edgar William and Bernice Chrysler Garbisch; **282** John Lewis Krimmel, *Members of the City Troop and other Philadelphia Soldiery,* The Metropolitan Museum of Art, Rogers Fund, 1942 (42.95.21). Photo © 2000 The Metropolitan

Museum of Art, New York; **288, 289** Monticello Foundation, Monticello, The Thomas Jefferson Memorial Foundation, Inc., VA; **290** Thomas Jefferson, *Farm Book,* 1774–1824, page 145. Original manuscript from the Coolidge Collection of Thomas Jefferson manuscripts, Massachusetts Historical Society, Boston, MA; **291** (*bottom*) Abby Aldrich Rockefeller Folk Art Museum, Colonial Williamsburg Foundation, VA; (*top*) Howard University/Moorland-Springarn Research Center; **293** Bibliothèque Nationale de France; **294** theartarchive; **299** American Clock & Watch Museum, Bristol, CT; **302** The New-York Historical Society (1967.6); **306** Adrien Persac, *Princess,* Louisiana State University Museum of Art, Baton Rouge, LA. Gift of Mrs. Mamie Persac Lusk; **309** Beinecke Rare Book and Manuscript Library, Yale University, New Haven; **312** Missouri Historical Society (CT SS831); **315** American Textile History Museum, Lowell, MA; **317** (*bottom right*) University of Massachusetts, Lowell, MA; **321** Library of Congress; **324** Thomas Hicks, *Calculating,* 1844. Gift of Maxim Karolik for the M. and M. Karolik Collection of American Paintings, 1815–1865 (62.273.). © 2005 Museum of Fine Arts, Boston. All Rights Reserved; **331** Tennessee State Museum Collection. Photography by June Dorman; **332** Nicolino Calyo, *The Butcher,* c. 1840–44. Museum of the City of New York, Gift of Mrs. Francis P. Garvan in memory of Francis P. Garvan; **339** George Caleb Bingham, *County Election,* 1851–52. The Saint Louis Art Museum, Gift of Bank of America; **340** The New-York Historical Society (6165); **342** Alabama Department of Archives and History, Montgomery, Alabama; **347** (*left*) Library of Congress; (*right*) Courtesy of the J. Paul Getty Museum, Los Angeles (84.XT.441.3); **349** "Webster's Reply to Hayne" Courtesy of The Boston Art Commision, 2000; **353** The Library Company of Philadelphia; **354** Museum of the City of New York, The J. Clarence Davies Collection; **355** National Museum of American History, Smithsonian Institution; **363** Harriet Beecher Stowe Center, Hartford, CT; **364** Allen Memorial Art Museum, Gift of Lewis Tappan; **365** Library of Congress; **368** Stock Montage, Inc.; **370** W.W. Wilson, *Constructing a Balloon Frame House,* engraving. From Edward Shaw, *The Modern Architect,* 1855. The Metropolitan Museum of Art, Harris Brisbane Dick Fund, 1934. (34.46.9); **372** *The Philosopher's Camp* by William James Stillman. Courtesy Concord Free Public Library, Concord, MA; **374** (*top*) Rare Book Division, New York Public Library, Astor, Lenox and Tilden Foundations; (*bottom*) Culver Pictures, Inc.; **375** Miriam and Ira D. Wallach Division of Art, Prints and Photographs, The New York Public Library, Astor, Lenox and Tilden Foundations; **380** Library of Congress; **381** (*left*) Rare Book and Manuscripts, Boston Public Library. Courtesy of The Trustees; (*right*) CORBIS; **383** Madison County Historical Society, Oneida, NY; **385** Rhoda Jenkins/Coline Jenkins-Sahlin; **393** Historic New Orleans Collection (1960.46); **396–397** Museum of the City of New York, Harry T. Peters Collection; **403** *John Stock,* watercolor portrait on ivory. The Gibbes Museum of Art/Carolina Art Association, Charleston, SC; **404** Historic New Orleans Collection (1975.93.5); **406** Basil Hall, Etching 25, *Forty etchings from sketches made with the camera lucida in North America, in 1827 and 1828.* William L. Clements Library; **411** *Slave Market,* c. 1850–60. Carnegie Museum of Art, Pittsburgh; Gift of Mrs. W. Fitch Ingersoll; **413** Abby Aldrich Rockefeller Folk Art Museum, Williamsburg, VA; **414** Middle Passage Museum's Collection; **417** Thomas Waterman Wood, *Market Woman,* 1858. The Fine Arts Museums of San Francisco, Mildred Anna Williams Collection (1944.8); **418** The Smithsonian Institution. National

Museum of American History (#49747-G); **425** National Museum of American Art, Washington, D.C./Art Resource, NY; **427** Library of Congress; **428** Seaver Center for Western Research, Natural History Museum of Los Angeles County; **431** Courtesy George Eastman House; **434** Joseph Goldsborough Bruff, *Ferriage of the Platte, Above the Mouth of Deer Creek, July 20, 1849.* The Huntington Library, Art Collections, and Botanical Gardens, San Marino, CA/ SuperStock; **437** George P. Healy, detail, *James K. Polk,* 1846. In the Collection of the Corcoran Gallery of Art. Museum purchase, Gallery Fund (79.14); **439** The New-York Historical Society (43120); **442** *The 'Heathen Chinee' with Pick and Rocker,* from *Mining Scenes in California Series,* ca. 1868. Photograph by Eadweard J. Muybrige. Courtesy California Historical Society, San Francisco (FN-138990); **444** Collection of The New-York Historical Society (26280); **446–447** Print Collection, Miriam and Ira D. Wallach Division of Arts, Prints and Photographs. New York Public Library, Astor, Lenox and Tilden Foundations; **448** The Institute of Texan Cultures, San Antonio, Texas; **450** Library of Congress; **457** Culver Pictures, Inc.; **458** Kansas State Historical Society, Topeka, KS; **469** Courtesy American Antiquarian Society; **470** Anne S.K. Brown Military Collection, Brown University Library, Providence, RI; **471** Print Collection, Miriam and Ira D. Wallach Division of Arts, Prints and Photographs. New York Public Library, Astor, Lenox and Tilden Foundations; **472** Missouri Historical Society; **473** Library of Congress; **475** (*left*) Library of Congress; (*right*) Illinois State Historical Library; **477** Whipple & Black, *John Brown,* 1857. Boston Athenaeum (UTB-2 5.4 Bro.j 1857 acc.#1863.1); **478** Library of Congress; **482** (*left*) The New-York Historical Society

(PR-022-3-45-13); (*right*) The Museum of the Confederacy, Richmond, VA. Photography by Katherine Wetzel; **487** Henry Bacon, *Reveille on a Winter Morning,* West Point Museum Collections, United States Military Academy, NY; **489** (*top*) Chicago Historical Society; **489** (*bottom*) Library of Congress; **494, 497** (*left and right*) Library of Congress; **500** The Museum of the Confederacy, Richmond, VA; **503** John Ferguson Weir, *The Gun Foundry.* Putnam County Historical Society, Cold Spring, NY; **505** Department of the Army, U.S. Army Military History Institute Carlisle Barracks, PA; **506** David Gilmour Blythe, *Lincoln Crushing the Dragon of Rebellion,* 1862. Museum of Fine Arts, Boston. Bequest of Martha C. Karolik for the M. and M. Karolik Collection of American Paintings, 1815–1865 (48.5.415.) Reproduced with permission. © 2005 Museum of Fine Arts, Boston. All Rights Reserved; **508** Dale S. Snair Collection, Richmond, VA; **510** (*left and right*) Larry B. Wilford Collection, Civil War Photohistorian; **518** © 1996 Virginia Historical Society; **520** (*left*) Library of Congress; (*right*) The Valentine Museum, Richmond, VA; **525, 526, 527** Culver Pictures, Inc.; **531** Winslow Homer, *A Visit from the Old Mistress,* 1876. National Museum of American Art, Smithsonian Institution, Washington, D.C. Gift of William T. Evans. Art Resource, NY; **533** Culver Pictures, Inc.; **534, 535** Library of Congress; **541** Theodor Kaufmann, *Portrait of Hiram Rhoades Revels,* 1870. Courtesy of the Herbert F. Johnson Museum of Art, Cornell University, Ithaca. NY. Transferred from the Olin (69.170); **542** Library of Congress; **544** The New-York Historical Society (50475); **547** CORBIS; **551** Sophie Smith Collection, Smith College, MA; **552** The Granger Collection, New York; **554** Collection of David J. and Janice L. Frent; **556** Library of Congress

Index